D0984741

PERCY BYSSHE SHELLEY

Shelley as a boy, miniature drawing by the Duc de Montpensier, 1802–?1804, Shelley Relics 7, courtesy of the Bodleian Library.

PERCY BYSSHE SHELLEY
A Biography

Youth's Unextinguished Fire, 1792–1816

James Bieri

Newark: University of Delaware Press

Associated University Presses
2010 Eastpark Boulevard
Cranbury, NJ 08512

The paper used in this publication meets the requirements of the American National Standard for Permanence of Paper for Printed Library Materials Z39.48-1984.

Library of Congress Cataloging-in-Publication Data

Bieri, James.
    Percy Bysshe Shelley : youth's unextinguished fire, 1792–1816 / James Bieri.
        p.   cm.
    Includes index.
    ISBN 0-87413-870-1 (alk. paper)
    1. Shelley, Percy Bysshe, 1792–1822—Childhood and youth.   2. Poets, English—19th century—Biography.   I. Title.
PR5432.B54 2004

821′.7—dc22

                                                                    2004002966

PRINTED IN THE UNITED STATES OF AMERICA

To Sandra Joseph Bieri
"Thy wisdom speaks in me"

Contents

Illustrations

Preface

At the dawn of the twenty-first century, no poet speaks more eloquently and forcefully against the continuing tyrannies of human oppression, social injustice, and political violence than Percy Bysshe Shelley. Controversy has always dogged Shelley, whose political, religious, and social dissent cost him dearly during his lifetime. His radical, humanitarian voice was often attacked, censored, or ignored by the reactionary forces of the day: government, religion, and publishing. However, Shelley's social message never vanished. His *Queen Mab,* pirated during his lifetime, helped rally the radical Chartist movement after his death. During the Victorian era, his radical persona was masked when he was given the less controversial visage of the lyric poet. Later in the nineteenth century, the socialist George Bernard Shaw praised his work, especially the sexually charged drama, *The Cenci,* which was deemed unfit for public audiences. As the human catastrophes of twentieth-century warfare played out, Shelley's incisive poetic voice took its rightful place alongside his beautiful lyric gift. His human vision began to be recognized in all its intellectual, metaphysical, and social dimensions. His philosophical skepticism was tempered with a belief in human betterment and a need to question received forms of social institutions, including the relationships between the sexes.

Edward Dowden, author of the first scholarly Shelley biography (1886), pointed out that all of Shelley's poetical works "are fragments of a great confession." This view was reiterated by the eminent mid-twentieth-century Shelley biographer, Newman Ivey White: "Of few writers more than Shelley can it be said that his works are the man himself." The late distinguished Shelley scholar and biographer, Kenneth Neill Cameron, observed that Shelley was "a great revolutionary poet and thinker, a scholar of wide culture and deep philosophical and political understanding, a writer

11

of versatility almost unmatched in the history of English literature, a man of broad humanitarian understanding." Cameron wrote this in *An Examination of the Shelley Legend,* co-authored with White and Frederick L. Jones as a rebuttal of Robert Metcalf Smith's 1945 polemic, *The Shelley Legend.* The personal, political, and literary controversies that surrounded Shelley in his lifetime have never abated.

Biographers' subtle relationships with their subjects influence the narratives they tell. This influence was magnified in the first two Shelley biographies, those of Thomas Medwin (1847) and Thomas Jefferson Hogg (1858), both of whom had close, complicated personal relationships with Shelley and his wife Mary. These two biographies did much to promulgate some of the controversies, legends, and misinformation that became assimilated into Shelley's life story. Still, the biographies by Medwin and Hogg are valuable in part because of their personal knowledge of Shelley. Hogg's projected four-volume work was cut short after two volumes by Shelley's son, Sir Percy Florence Shelley, and his wife, Lady Shelley, who were incensed by Hogg's depiction of Shelley. Hogg's biography resembles Shelley's description of Hogg, "a pearl within an oyster shell," its value hidden by an often fraudulent shell of base letter-tampering amid a belittling portrait. Shelley's friend Thomas Love Peacock wrote his own short memoirs of Shelley after taking exception to Hogg's biography and to Lady Shelley's subsequent shabby treatment of Harriet Shelley in her *Shelley Memorials.* Sir Percy and Lady Shelley years later turned to Professor Dowden to advance their biographical agenda for Shelley. Despite its family sponsorship, Dowden's biography has continuing value, in part because he was the last Shelley biographer to have personal contact with those who had some link to Shelley or his family.

Many years of research and travel have gone into my writing and re-writing of this biography. Hopefully, I have eliminated errors of fact in previous accounts so as to provide as reliable a narrative as possible. Perhaps my own background in clinical psychology and my long-term interest in literature have brought some new understanding to the unending process of interpreting both Shelley's life and his poetry.

Shelley compressed into less than thirty years a life that yielded a rich legacy of poetry, prose, and correspondence. He had close relationships with important literary figures of his day, including

Mary Wollstonecraft Shelley, William Godwin, Lord Byron, John Keats, Leigh Hunt, Thomas Love Peacock, and Robert Southey. Shelley never met William Wordsworth or Samuel Taylor Coleridge, but their lives and works exerted important influences on his poetry. Nor did Shelley ever meet William Blake; he apparently did not know Blake's work. Both shared a similar vision of humanity, including a psychological understanding that anticipated the age of Freud.

Despite periods of great psychic turmoil, Shelley remained remarkably resilient until his premature death while composing his last great poetic achievement, *The Triumph of Life*. This poem and his life are unfinished fragments. However, both have a richness that will provide future generations continuing sources of wonderment and inspiration to probe the depths of his fertile imagination and of the human condition.

Acknowledgments

THE GREAT REWARD FROM WRITING A LIFE AS PRODIGIOUS AS SHEL-
ley's has come from the many graciously helpful and knowledgeable persons whose contributions to my effort have earned them
my deep gratitude. I hope this resulting work will repay in part the
assistance and support of these contributors.

When I first visited Field Place, its owners, Mr. and Mrs. H. A.
Chisenhale-Marsh, were most cordial. This reception continued
with the current owners, Kenneth Prichard Jones and his wife
Dagmar, to whom I express my heartfelt thanks for the years of
warm friendship and acceptance into their home and family. The
Joneses have restored Field Place with exacting skill to what it
was when the poet lived there as a boy. Numerous persons associated with Shelley's family and friends have been most kind. Elizabeth Esdaile Warmington, descendent of Shelley's daughter
Ianthe, provided invaluable family information. The many contributions of Rodney M. Bennett include providing the portrait of his
ancestor, Sophia Stacey. Timothy Heneage provided the portrait of
his ancestor, Harriet Grove. Desmond Hawkins, biographer of the
Grove family, has been generous with his aid over the years.

Among the many scholars to whom I am indebted, I would like
to express my heartfelt appreciation to Donald H. Reiman, who
characteristically gave unstintingly of his unique knowledge about
Shelley and encouraged my efforts for many years. Also deeply
supportive and giving has been Marion K. Stocking, the last Shelley scholar to have known personally someone who knew Claire
Clairmont. The late Kenneth Neill Cameron provided both astute
observations and inspiration. Other Shelley scholars to whom I am
personally indebted include G. Kim Blank, Judith Chernaik, Nora
Crook, Doucet Devin Fischer, Neil Fraistat, Patrick Story, and
Emily W. Sunstein. Bruce Barker-Benfield, Senior Assistant Librarian, Department of Special Collections and Western Manu-

scripts, Bodleian Library, University of Oxford, has provided indispensable aid since the inception of my work. The Keeper of Special Collections and Western Manuscripts, Richard Ovenden, has kindly given permission to quote materials held by the Bodleian Library. I wish to thank the late Lord Abinger and his son, the 9th Baron Abinger, for permission, granted through the Bodleian Library, to quote from items in the Abinger collection. For access to materials in The Carl H. Pforzheimer Collection, Shelley and His Circle, The New York Public Library, I wish to thank Stephen Wagner and the late Mihai H. Handrea. Wayne Furman, Office of Special Collections, The New York Public Library, facilitated permissions from The Pforzheimer Collection, Shelley and His Circle, and the Berg Collection of English and American Literature, Astor, Lenox and Tilden Foundations.

I especially wish to recognize the many years of invaluable assistance of Jeremy Knight, Curator of the Horsham Museum. His outstanding work in organizing and making available the rich holdings of the Museum's archives has brought to light significant new information about Shelley and his family. The expertise of his colleague, Susan Cabell Djabri, has been of great value. A knowledgeable Horsham resident, Audrey M. Robinson, provided her fine historical records. Elsewhere in England, I wish to acknowledge the help of C. R. Davey, Archivist, East Sussex Record Office; Richard Childs, Archivist, West Sussex Record Office; and David R. Rymill, Archivist, Hampshire Record Office. Michael Meredith, Librarian, Eton College, provided valuable material concerning Shelley's stay there. Nick Baker, Collections Administrator of the Eton College Library, on behalf of The Provost and Fellows of Eton College, gave permission to reproduce the picture of Shelley's boat and final residence. Angus Graham-Campbell assisted in this endeavor.

Among the many who showed me places associated with Shelley, I particularly wish to thank the late Captain "Sandy" Livingston-Learmouth of Tanyrallt, Wales; Mr. and Mrs. Snell, owners of Shelley's cottage at Bishopsgate; Mr. James Nixon, of Chestnut Hill Cottage, Keswick; and Father David Hart, St. Giles, Camberwell. A fond memory from Livorno will always be the enthusiastic help of a poet, Sandro Sandini, who located for me Shelley's Villa Valsovano. I wish to thank Thomas Day and subsequent Curators and their assistants at the Keats-Shelley House, Rome, for aid on numerous visits. On my first visit to Villa Magni, the late Margaret

Brown gave me a fine tour of Shelley's last home. Haidee Jackson, Curator of Newstead Abbey, has been most helpful. I have received expert psychological and medical information from Dr. Mary Sue Moore and Frederick L. Hildebrand, Sr., M.D. Essential classical knowledge was provided by Charles Dominey. W. Thomas Taylor was the force in the development of my Shelley library.

The scholarship of the last quarter century that has greatly facilitated my research includes the Garland facsimiles and analyses of Shelley's notebooks under the general editorship of Donald H. Reiman. Added to this burgeoning Shelley scholarship has been the invaluable editing of Mary Shelley's letters by Betty T. Bennett. Marion K. Stocking's fine editing of the correspondence of Claire Clairmont is an important addition to her earlier editing of Claire Clairmont's journal. Dr. Stocking alerted me to the important Silsbee Family Papers (MSS 74) at the Peabody Essex Museum in Salem, Massachusetts. That museum kindly provided permission for use of these unusual documents. For permission to quote materials from the Pforzheimer Collection in the first ten volumes of *Shelley and His Circle*, I wish thank Carl F. Pforzheimer III, President, The Carl and Lilly Pforzheimer Foundation. I also want to acknowledge material reprinted by permission of the publishers from *Byron's Letters and Journals*, vols. 5–10, edited by Leslie A. Marchand, Cambridge, Mass.: The Belknap Press of Harvard University Press, Copyright © Editorial, Leslie A. Marchand 1976–1980, © Byron copyright material, John Murray 1976–1980. The John Murray Archive of John Murray (Publishers) Ltd. also granted permission for use of these and other letters in the Murray Collection. Oxford University Press gave permission to use material from *The Letters of Percy Bysshe Shelley*, edited by F. L. Jones, and from *The Journals of Mary Shelley*, edited by Paula R. Feldman and Diana Scott-Kilvert.

I wish to thank the staffs of the following libraries and institutions for their assistance and for permission to use materials in their holdings: The Huntington Library, San Marino, California; Harry Ransom Humanities Research Center, The University of Texas at Austin; The Bancroft Library, University of California at Berkeley; Mary Couts Burnett Library, Texas Christian University; University of Oklahoma Press; The Pierpont Morgan Library, New York; The British Library; National Portrait Gallery, London; Newstead Abbey, City of Nottingham Museums; and the Keats-Shelley House, Rome. I also extend my appreciation to the staffs of the following institutions for providing access to their holdings: City of London Library; Guildhall Library, London; Greater London Record Office; National Library of Ireland; Trinity College Library Dublin; University College London Library; The Beinecke Library, Yale University; Wordsworth Museum, Grasmere; The Library of Congress; and Georgetown University Library.

I am grateful for the help of many others over the years. Among those who reviewed my manuscript, I wish to particularly thank Stephen C. Behrendt, Donald H. Reiman, and Charles E. Robinson. I hope my scholarship will not fall unduly short of their excellent standards. Dr. Donald C. Mell, Chair of the Board of Editors, The University of Delaware Press, has been most kind. My appreciation also extends to the Director of Associated University Presses, Julien Yoseloff, and to his exceptional Managing Editor, Christine Retz, whose understanding and skill were blessings at the end of a long publishing experience. Throughout the years devoted to writing Shelley's life, I have received the warm support and assistance of all my family, including my daughter Ann Bieri, who provided expert editorial aid. I have dedicated this biography to my wife, Sandra Joseph Bieri, whose countless contributions and sustained encouragement made everything possible.

Abbreviations

ALH James Henry Leigh Hunt, *The Autobiography of Leigh Hunt: With Reminiscences of Friends and Contemporaries*, 2 vols. (New York: Harpers, 1850).

AM [Thornton L. Hunt], "Shelley. By One Who Knew Him," *Atlantic Monthly*, February 1863, 184–204.

Angeli Helen Rossetti Angeli, *Shelley and His Friends in Italy* (London: Methuen, 1911).

Bancroft The Bancroft Library, University of California, Berkeley.

BL The British Library.

BLJ Leslie A. Marchand, ed., *Byron's Letters and Journals*, 12 vols. (Cambridge: Harvard University Press, Belknap Press, 1972–1982).

BLLJ Thomas Moore, *Life, Letters, and Journals of Lord Byron: Complete in One Volume with Notes* (London, 1839).

Blunden Edmund Blunden, *Shelley: A Life Story* (London: Collins, 1946).

Bodleian Bodleian Library, University of Oxford.

Brown Nathaniel Brown, *Sexuality and Feminism in Shelley* (Cambridge: Harvard University Press, 1979).

BS Bysshe Shelley (poet's grandfather).

BSM Donald H. Reiman, gen. ed., *The Bodleian Shelley Manuscripts*, 23 vols. (New York: Garland, 1986–2001).

Butler Marilyn Butler, *Peacock Displayed: A Satirist in his Context* (London: Routledge & Kegan Paul, 1979).

Byron Leslie A. Marchand, *Byron: A Biography*, 3 vols. (New York: Knopf, 1957).

CC Claire Clairmont.

CC Marion Kingston Stocking, ed., *The Clairmont Correspondence*, 2 vols. (Baltimore: Johns Hopkins University Press, 1995).

CG Nora Crook and Derek Guiton, *Shelley's Venomed Melody* (Cambridge: Cambridge University Press, 1986).

Chernaik Judith Chernaik, *The Lyrics of Shelley* (Cleveland: Case Western Reserve Press, 1972).

Cline C. L. Cline, *Byron, Shelley, and their Pisan Circle* (New York: Russell & Russell, 1952).

Conversations   Thomas Medwin, *Conversations of Lord Byron with Thomas Medwin, Esq.* (London, 1832).

CPPBS   Donald H. Reiman and Neil Fraistat, eds., *The Complete Poetry of Percy Bysshe Shelley,* vol. 1 (Baltimore: Johns Hopkins University Press, 1999).

Crompton   Louis Crompton, *Byron and Greek Love: Homophobia in Nineteenth-Century England* (Berkeley and Los Angeles: University of California Press, 1985).

Curran   Stuart Curran, *Shelley's Annus Mirabilis: The Maturing of an Epic Vision* (San Marino: Huntington Library, 1975).

CW   Roger Ingpen and Walter E. Peck, eds., *The Complete Works of Percy Bysshe Shelley,* 10 vols. (London: Ernest Benn, 1926–1930).

Dawson   P. M. S. Dawson, *The Unacknowledged Legislator: Shelley and Politics* (Oxford: Clarendon Press, 1980).

Deane   Seamus Deane, *The French Revolution and Enlightenment in England 1789–1832* (Cambridge: Harvard University Press, 1988).

DK (1995)   Susan Cabell Djabri and Jeremy Knight, *Horsham's Forgotten Son: Thomas Medwin Friend of Shelley and Byron* (Horsham: Horsham Museum, 1995).

DK (1999)   Susan Cabell Djabri and Jeremy Knight, eds., *The Letters of Bysshe and Timothy Shelley and other documents* (Horsham: Horsham Museum Society, 1999).

DNB   *The Dictionary of National Biography.*

Dowden   Edward Dowden, *The Life of Percy Bysshe Shelley,* 2 vols. (London, 1886).

EH   Elizabeth Hitchener.

EJT   Edward John Trelawny.

EL   Mrs. Shelley, ed., *Essays, Letters from Abroad, Translations and Fragments, By Percy Bysshe Shelley,* 2 vols. (London, 1840).

Esdaile   Kenneth Neill Cameron, ed., *The Esdaile Notebook: A Volume of Early Poems by Percy Bysshe Shelley* (New York: Knopf, 1964).

Everest   Kelvin Everest, ed., *Shelley Revalued: Essays from the Gregynog Conference* (Totowa, N.J.: Barnes & Noble, 1983).

FG   Fanny Godwin.

First Love   Desmond Hawkins, *Shelley's First Love* (London: Kyle Cathie, 1992).

Gelpi   Barbara Charlesworth Gelpi, *Shelley's Goddess: Maternity, Language, Subjectivity* (New York: Oxford University Press, 1992).

Grove Diaries   Desmond Hawkins, ed., *The Grove Diaries: The Rise and Fall of an English Family 1809–1925* (Stanbridge, U.K.: Dovecote Press, 1995).

Grylls	R. Glynn Grylls, *Mary Shelley: A Biography* (London: Oxford University Press, 1938).
GWJL	Frederick L. Jones, ed., *Maria Gisborne & Edward E. Williams: Shelley's Friends Their Journals and Letters* (Norman: University of Oklahoma Press, 1951).
GY	Kenneth Neill Cameron, *Shelley: The Golden Years* (Cambridge: Harvard University Press, 1974).
H6WT	[Percy Bysshe Shelley and Mary Wollstonecraft Shelley], *History of a Six Weeks' Tour through a Part of France, Switzerland, Germany, and Holland: with Letters Descriptive of a Sail Round the Lake of Geneva, and of the Glaciers of Chamouni* (London, 1817).
HM	Horsham Museum
Hoagwood	Terence Allen Hoagwood, *Skepticism and Ideology: Shelley's Political Prose and Its Philosophical Context from Bacon to Marx* (Iowa City: University of Iowa Press, 1988).
Hogg	Thomas Jefferson Hogg, *The Life of Percy Bysshe Shelley*, 2 vols. (London, 1858).
Hogle	Jerrold E. Hogle, *Shelley's Process: Radical Transference and the Development of His Major Works* (New York: Oxford University Press, 1988).
Holmes	Richard Holmes, *Shelley: The Pursuit* (New York: Dutton, 1975).
HRC	Harry Ransom Humanities Research Center, The University of Texas at Austin.
HS	Harriet Shelley.
Hunt	James Henry Leigh Hunt, *Lord Byron and Some of His Contemporaries; with Recollections of the Author's Life, and of His Visit to Italy* (London, 1828).
Huntington	The Huntington Library, San Marino, California.
Ingpen	Roger Ingpen, *Shelley in England: New Facts and Letters from the Shelley–Whitton Papers* (London: Kegan Paul, Trench, Trubner, 1917).
JCC	Marion Kingston Stocking, ed., *The Journals of Claire Clairmont* (Cambridge: Harvard University Press, 1968).
JMS	Paula R. Feldman and Diana Scott-Kilvert, eds., *The Journals of Mary Shelley*, 2 vols. (Oxford: Clarendon Press, 1987).
JW	Jane Williams.
KSJ	*Keats–Shelley Journal.*
KSMB	*Keats–Shelley Memorial Bulletin.*
KSR	*Keats–Shelley Review.*
L	Frederick L. Jones, ed., *The Letters of Percy Bysshe Shelley*, 2 vols. (Oxford: Clarendon Press, 1964).
LA	Iris Origo, *The Last Attachment* (London: Jonathan Cape, 1949).
LAS	Richard S. Garnett, ed., *Letters about Shelley Interchanged by Three Friends—Edward Dowden, Richard Garnett and Wm. Michael Rossetti* (London: Hodder & Stoughton, 1917).

LB   Lord Byron.
LEJT   H. Buxton Forman, ed., *The Letters of Edward John Trelawny*
                (London: Milford, 1910).
LH   Leigh Hunt.
LJK   Hyder Edward Rollins, ed., *The Letters of John Keats*, 2 vols.
                (Cambridge, Mass.: Harvard University Press, 1958).
LMWS   Betty B. Bennett, ed., *The Letters of Mary Wollstonecraft Shelley*,
                3 vols. (Baltimore: Johns Hopkins University Press, 1980–1988).
Locke   Don Locke, *A Fantasy of Reason: The Life and Thought of
                William Godwin* (London: Routledge & Kegan Paul, 1980).
Lovell   Ernest J. Lovell, Jr., *Captain Medwin: Friend of Byron and
                Shelley* (Austin: University of Texas Press, 1962).
Mac-Carthy   D. F. Mac-Carthy, *Shelley's Early Life* (London, 1872).
Medwin   Thomas Medwin, *The Life of Percy Bysshe Shelley: a new edi-
                tion printed from a copy copiously amended and extended
                by the author and left unpublished at his death*, ed. H. Bux-
                ton Forman (London: Oxford University Press, 1913).
Mellor   Anne K. Mellor, *Mary Shelley: Her Life Her Fiction Her Mon-
                sters* (New York: Methuen, 1988).
Moore   Doris Langley Moore, *Lord Byron: Accounts Rendered* (Lon-
                don: John Murray, 1974).
MSR   Betty T. Bennett and Charles E. Robinson, eds., *The Mary Shel-
                ley Reader* (New York: Oxford University Press, 1990).
MWG; MWS   Mary Wollstonecraft Godwin; Mary Wollstonecraft Shelley.
Murray   E. B. Murray, ed., *The Prose Works of Percy Bysshe Shelley*, vol.
                1 (Oxford: Clarendon Press, 1993).
MYR   Donald H. Reiman, gen. ed., *The Manuscripts of the Younger
                Romantics*, 9 vols. (New York: Garland, 1985–1996).
NLRS   Kenneth Curry, ed., *New Letters of Robert Southey*, 2 vols.
                (New York: Columbia University Press, 1965).
Norman   Sylva Norman, *The Flight of the Skylark: The Development of
                Shelley's Reputation* (London: Max Reinhardt, 1954).
PBS   Percy Bysshe Shelley.
Peacock   Howard Mills, ed., *Thomas Love Peacock: Memoirs of Shelley
                and other Essays and Reviews* (New York: New York Uni-
                versity Press, 1970).
Peck   Walter Edwin Peck, *Shelley: His Life and Work*, 2 vols. (Boston:
                Houghton Mifflin, 1927).
Polidori   William Michael Rossetti, ed., *The Diary of Dr. John William
                Polidori, 1816, Relating to Byron, Shelley, etc.* (London:
                Elkin Matthew, 1911).
Prose   David Lee Clark, ed., *Shelley's Prose: or The Trumpet of a
                Prophecy* (Albuquerque: University of New Mexico Press,
                1954).
PS   Geoffrey Matthews and Kelvin Everest, eds., *The Poems of
                Shelley*, vol. 1 (London: Longman, 1989).

PW	Thomas Hutchinson and G. M. Matthews, eds., *Shelley: Poetical Works* (London: Oxford University Press, 1970).
Recollections	Edward John Trelawny, *Recollections of the Last Days of Shelley and Byron,* (London, 1858).
Records	Edward John Trelawny, *Records of Shelley, Byron, and the Author,* ed. David Wright (1878; reprint, Harmondsworth: Penguin Books, 1982).
Rees	Joan Rees, *Shelley's Jane Williams* (London: William Kimber, 1985).
Reiman	Donald H. Reiman, *Percy Bysshe Shelley,* Updated ed. (Boston: Twayne, 1990).
Rieger	James Rieger, *The Mutiny Within* (New York: George Braziller, 1967).
Robinson	Charles E. Robinson, ed., *The Frankenstein Notebooks,* vol. 9, *MYR* (New York: Garland, 1996).
Roe	Ivan Roe, *Shelley: The Last Phase* (London: Hutchison, 1953).
Rogers	Neville Rogers, *Shelley at Work,* 2d ed. (Oxford: Clarendon Press, 1967).
RC	*Romantic Circles,* a website devoted to the study of Romantic-period literature and culture, published by the University of Maryland, http://www.rc.umd.edu.
RR	Donald H. Reiman, ed., *The Romantics Reviewed: Contemporary Reviews of British Romantic Writers. Part C: Shelley, Keats, and London Radical Writers.* 2 vols. (New York: Garland, 1972).
SC	Kenneth Neill Cameron, Donald H. Reiman, and Doucet Devin Fischer, eds., *Shelley and His Circle,* 10 vols. (Cambridge: Harvard University Press, 1961–2002).
Scott	Winifred Scott, *Jefferson Hogg* (London: Jonathan Cape, 1951).
Scrivener	Michael Henry Scrivener, *Radical Shelley: The Philosophical Anarchism and Utopian Thought of Percy Bysshe Shelley* (Princeton: Princeton University Press, 1982).
SE	James Strachey, trans. and ed., *The Standard Edition of the Complete Psychological Works of Sigmund Freud,* 23 vols. (London: Hogarth Press, 1957).
SG	B. C. Barker-Benfield, ed., *Shelley's Guitar: A Bicentenary Exhibition of Manuscripts, First Editions and Relics of Percy Bysshe Shelley* (Oxford: Bodleian Library, 1992).
Shelley and Byron	Charles E. Robinson, *Shelley and Byron: The Snake and the Eagle Wreathed in Fight* (Baltimore: Johns Hopkins University Press, 1976).
Shelley Memorials	Lady Shelley, ed., *Shelley Memorials: From Authentic Sources* (Boston, 1859).
Shelley Papers	T. Medwin, Esq., *The Shelley Papers: Memoir of Percy Bysshe Shelley and Original Poems and Papers of Percy Bysshe Shelley* (London, 1833).

Shelley's Cenci	Stuart Curran, *Shelley's Cenci: Scorpions Ringed with Fire* (Princeton: Princeton University Press, 1970).
Shelley's Satire	Steven E. Jones, *Shelley's Satire* (DeKalb: Northern Illinois University Press, 1994).
Silsbee	Silsbee Family Papers (MSS 74), Peabody Essex Museum, Salem, Massachusetts.
SM	[Lady Shelley, ed.], *Shelley and Mary,* 3 or 4 vols. (N.p.: Privately printed, 1882).
SN	H. Buxton Forman, ed., *Note Books of Percy Bysshe Shelley,* 3 vols. (Boston: Bibliophile Society, 1911). Originals in Huntington.
Sperry	Stuart M. Sperry, *Shelley's Major Verse* (Cambridge: Harvard University Press, 1988).
SPP	Donald H. Reiman and Neil Fraistat, eds., *Shelley's Poetry and Prose,* 2d. ed. (New York: Norton, 2002).
StC	William St Clair, *The Godwins and the Shelleys: The Biography of a Family* (London: Faber and Faber, 1989).
Sunstein	Emily W. Sunstein, *Mary Shelley: Romance and Reality* (Boston: Little Brown, 1989).
Thompson	E. P. Thompson, *The Making of the English Working Class* (New York: Vintage, 1966).
TLP	Thomas Love Peacock.
TLS	*Times Literary Supplement.*
Trelawny	William St Clair, *Trelawny: The Incurable Romancer* (New York: Vanguard Press, 1977).
TS	Timothy Shelley.
UH	Newman Ivey White, *The Unextinguished Hearth: Shelley and His Contemporary Critics* (Durham, N.C.: Duke University Press, 1938).
Wasserman	Earl Wasserman, *Shelley: A Critical Reading* (Baltimore: Johns Hopkins University Press, 1971).
WG	William Godwin.
White	Newman Ivey White, *Shelley,* 2 vols. (New York: Knopf, 1940).
YS	Kenneth Neill Cameron, *The Young Shelley: Genesis of a Radical* (New York: Macmillan, 1950).
Z&SI	Stephen C. Behrendt, ed., *Percy Bysshe Shelley: Zastrozzi and St Irvyne* (Oxford: Oxford University Press, 1986).

PERCY BYSSHE SHELLEY

1

The Politics of Paternity

Two infants named Bysshe born in August 1792 were fathered by two men of the wealthy Shelley family. This doubling had several remarkable features, including the fact that the fathers were father and son. Bysshe Shelley, sixty-one and twice a widower, had fathered ten legitimate offspring before beginning a third family by a woman to whom he was not married. His eldest son and heir, Timothy Shelley, at thirty-eight was fathering his first child by his wife, Elizabeth Pilfold Shelley. Their son was born on Saturday, August 4, at Field Place, the Sussex ancestral Shelley home. Although he was given his paternal grandfather's full name, Percy Bysshe Shelley, his family called him Bysshe.[1] Conceived shortly after his parents' marriage, Bysshe was Elizabeth's first child but her husband's second. Timothy's illegitimate, older son—neither the birth date nor the mother is known—may have lived in or visited Field Place. Although little Bysshe was Timothy's legal heir, he soon felt his older half-brother was his father's favorite.[2]

Nine days after the future poet's birth, his grandfather's illegitimate son Bysshe was born in London. He was old Bysshe's fourth child by "Nell," Mrs. Eleanor Nicholls, who became Bysshe Shelley's mistress shortly after his second wife died in 1781. Mrs. Nicholls lived in the Lambeth house he provided for her, which he called "Nelly's Hotel." The two August-born Bysshes probably never met, but they would share a common passion, sailing the seas.

Bysshe Shelley's presence at Timothy's wedding the previous October apparently aroused his sexual rivalry with his son. Writing a friend, he "Swore" when he arrived home "full of Tim's Wedding" he would "do for Nell on My Return." Bragging in stud talk, Bysshe wrote to his Horsham lawyer friend, Robert Hurst, in late spring 1792, "the time of year is com, and I Cover [have intercourse] as well as ever." Noting the successful outcome of his mat-

27

ing with Nell, he said, "And an Angel recorded the <u>Oath</u>." Comparing his sexual rivalry with his son to a horserace, he had "Run Tim Damned hard Age Considered," having begun trying to get Nell pregnant "only 8 days" after his son's wedding. Comparing their respective sons, Bysshe wrote, "I'l Back Nell's Stoned [testicled] Colt Ag[ains]t F.P. [Field Place] for £1,000."[3]

Upon learning he and his son were expecting offspring about the same time, Bysshe wrote to his friend using a political metaphor, "It will be Another Election Business betwix my Nell and Tim's Bessy." Bysshe Shelley was allied with the politically powerful Duke of Norfolk and his son Timothy's 1790 election to Parliament as the Duke's man from nearby Horsham was being contested.

Legitimate Percy Bysshe, born at ten o'clock at night, was privately baptized an hour later. By accident of gender, he was the entailed heir of his grandsire, one of the wealthiest landowners in Sussex. Little Bysshe's mother proudly lavished the huge sum of £193 on his layette.[4] The infant's gift from his grandfather Bysshe was "a Haunch" of venison.

Field Place lies in the West Sussex parish of Warnham, adjacent to the town of Horsham. The windows in the southwest upstairs room where little Bysshe was born afford panoramic views of the domain of Field Place with its meadows, gardens, farmland, trees, and three ponds. Field Place, a blend of several structures, began as a Medieval Hall, built in 1251 but enlarged in 1325 and 1375. Barns built in 1470 still stand. The Michell family assumed Field Place, probably moated, in 1484. The huge Tudor fireplace and chimney added to the Medieval Hall in 1520 still dominates the kitchen. It was the first of many fireplaces that Percy Bysshe loved to lie close to with his head perilously near the flames. John Michell, about 1678, constructed onto the old house the present commodious east section, attaching his family crest and roofing it with heavy Horsham slate. Later, next to the house, in what became the American garden, two sequoias were planted, a reminder that grandfather Bysshe had been born in New Jersey.

The Shelley family acquired Field Place in 1729 when Edward Shelley, barrister at London's Middle Temple, bought the home from John Michell's descendents. When Edward Shelley died in 1747, his nephew Timothy Shelley inherited Field Place, leasing it to the older of his two sons, John, who moved in with his new bride in 1752. This same year John's younger brother, the poet's grandfather Bysshe, secretly married and built a mansion near Horsham, later torn down when he decided not to live in it. John, a childless widower when he inherited Field Place after his father's death in 1770, never remarried before his death in 1790. Field Place, now the property of John's brother Bysshe, again beckoned newlyweds. Timothy Shelley, in related events, became engaged to Elizabeth Pilfold, received Field Place in a 1791 resettlement with his father, and welcomed his bride to Field Place after their marriage on October 11, 1791.[5]

Probably feeling relief upon providing a legitimate male heir to his father's fortune, Timothy would have five daughters before another son was born. Little Bysshe also inherited a family scenario. He was expected to follow in Timothy's footsteps by becoming a member of the landed gentry, graduating from his father's college at Oxford, dutifully husbanding the family wealth, marrying a woman of respectable social connections, and becoming a Whig Member of Parliament under the political aegis of the Duke of Norfolk. This life script would be severely rewritten in all its particulars.

Profound political, economic, and social changes were affecting Sussex and all of England. The government, reacting to the bloody repercussions of the revolution in France and growing civil unrest at home, instigated repressive measures against human rights. England, shifting from a rural agrarian to an urban economy as the Industrial Revolution gained momentum, was at war with France six months after Shelley's birth. The war and political repression spanned his first nineteen years.

In 1792, Timothy Shelley gained a son and heir but faltered as a politician. Five months before little Bysshe's birth, Timothy was ejected from his Horsham seat in the House of Commons because of falsified election returns. Timothy, at the bidding of the Duke of Norfolk, stood for Parliament in 1788. This was part of Norfolk's attempts to wrest control of Horsham's two seats from the competing local faction of the powerful Lady Irwin. By literally buying the town away, Norfolk was the peer in the all-powerful House of Lords who owned the largest number of seats in Commons. The Horsham solicitor Thomas Charles Medwin, Norfolk's local steward, bought, bribed, and otherwise got the votes of the majority of the eighty-six town burgesses, the male landowners. The illegal recording of votes by Timothy and Medwin, whose wives were first cousins, was discovered when the House of Commons investigated Lady Irwin's routine election challenge. Only ten votes for Timothy Shelley being legitimate, he was unseated in March 1792. Such paternal political corruption was not to be lost later on young Percy Bysshe. Timothy did not regain his political footing until his 1802 election to Parliament to represent the Duke's interest in New Shoreham.[6]

Before Bysshe was two months old, the French Republic was proclaimed. The guillotine, instrument of the September massacre, soon would behead Louis XVI. In England, the second part of Thomas Paine's *Rights of Man* appeared in popular cheap editions available to the masses.[7] William Pitt the younger, the Tory Prime Minister, unable to ignore Paine's threat, instituted an era of authoritarian political repression. Paine, forced to flee England to France, was tried in absentia for treason and officially banished in December 1792. Other major radical literary works included Mary Wollstonecraft's 1792 *A Vindication of the Rights of Woman* and William Godwin's *Enquiry Concerning Political Justice*, published in early 1793.

The Shelley ancestral history included Edward Shelley, of Warminghurst Park and the Manor of Sullington, a Master in the Royal Household of Henry VIII.[8] John Shelley married into the Michelgrove estates of Sussex, forming the more prestigious of the two family branches. His son, Sir William Shelley, had a nephew, Henry Shelley, who became the subject in 1577 of the celebrated "Shelley Case," a legal inheritance rights landmark that reverberated over two centuries later in Sir Bysshe Shelley's attempts to preserve his estate from the inroads of his heir, Percy Bysshe. The more modest family branch of Henry Shelley evolved into the Fen Place Shelleys, the poet's immediate forebears. For eight generations, no member of this very old branch of the Shelley family, heavily represented in the legal profession, attained any particular distinction. It was Shelley's grandfather Bysshe who, becoming a baronet, brought his well-established branch of the Shelley family into a position of greater wealth and aristocratic standing.

Grandfather Bysshe's rise owed little to his mundane father, Timothy Shelley (b. 1700), the third of five sons of John and Hellen Shelley of Fen Place, Sussex. Hellen had inherited Fen Place from her father, Roger Bysshe. Young Timothy, having two older brothers and little prospect of succeeding to the family holdings, in the late 1720s took the rather degrading step of emigrating to America. Settling in Newark, New Jersey, he married Joanna Plum, four years his elder. Most likely the daughter of a prominent Newark family, Joanna was not the New York widow reported in the Shelley Pedigree. Her tomb in Warnham Church records her birth in Newark.[9] Timothy, who would have a stormy relationship with both his sons, perhaps went to America because of his own conflicts with his father. If so, the poet's was the fifth generation of father-son conflict.

Timothy, self-proclaimed in 1735 as "Merchant of Newark," probably was not a "Quack doctor," as the poet's first biographer claimed.[10] He operated a lumber-turning mill but the Essex County court records suggest Timothy's abrasiveness gave him more talent for litigation than for business success. Two surviving sons were born in Newark to Timothy and Joanna, John (b. 1729) and Piercey [sic] Bysshe (b. 1731), the poet's grandfather.[11] Timothy's inheritance prospects brightened when his oldest brother Bysshe died in 1733. Adding to Timothy's expectations was the condition of his remaining older brother, John, a "Lunatic." With this change in his fortunes, in 1735 Timothy sent four-year-old Bysshe—but not his older son John—to England to live with his Fen Place grandparents.[12] This significant fact, previously unknown to Shelley biographers, proved most momentous for Bysshe and his heirs.

It was almost eight years before Bysshe's brother and parents joined him in England. Perhaps the grandparents sent for young Bysshe to replace their recently deceased son Bysshe. One certainty is that Bysshe became his grandparents' favorite. If either parent accompanied the young boy to England, both were back in New Jersey by 1739. A prosperous English-born New York mariner-merchant, Captain William Bryant, possibly accompanied Bysshe to England. In December 1735, Timothy borrowed money from Bryant against his father's estate, possibly to finance the boy's voyage.[13] The Fen Place patriarch, John Shelley, died in early 1739, a year in which his son Timothy, in New Jersey, was involved in several lawsuits. In May 1742, three months after Timothy's mother died, Joanna signed an affidavit certifying the date and place of birth of her two sons. Another record of that date signed by the Reverend Aaron Burr also certified her sons' births.[14] When their fourteen-year-old son John returned to England in 1743, Timothy and his wife probably accompanied him. Upon arrival, Timothy obtained the family inheritance by having his remaining older brother John certified legally insane.[15]

Plucked from his American roots, four-year-old Bysshe had two doting grandparents to himself during his childhood as they tried to impart more genteel English manners. Any rejection he felt from being separated from his parents was more than balanced by the favoritism shown Bysshe by his more affluent grandparents. This special treatment probably contributed to Bysshe's active, narcissistic pursuit of women and wealth in the years ahead. As the chosen grandchild, he became more enterprising than his sedate brother, John.

Bysshe was seven when, having lived at Fen Place three years, his grandfather died. His burial vault was inscribed, "He was very remarkable for that exalted Part of Humanity, Forgiving injuries." John Shelley had formed a strong attachment to his grandson and in his deathbed codicil to his will he left young Bysshe "certain copyholds held of the Manor of Streathem . . . a sum of 2000 pounds and all his jewels, rings, plate, linen, books and things lately belonging to his son Bysshe." Young Bysshe was well on his way toward building his fortune.

The death of Bysshe's grandmother three years later, in 1742, added to his fortune. Perhaps at her insistence, he had dropped his first name P(i)ercy in favor of Bysshe. Hellen Bysshe Shelley left most of her personal possessions to eleven-year-old Bysshe, not to his older brother John, the entail heir she never met. In addition to showering on Bysshe her furniture and "all her ready money, mortgages, bonds, bills, notes, Plate, diamonds, rings, Pearl necklace and half her best linen," she left him "her freehold land near Willetts Bridge in East Grinstead." Brother John received £100. Bysshe probably embarked on adolescence with a strong sense of his success with women.

In her will, Bysshe's grandmother provided that her executor educate him "in a handsome manner . . . to be bred up or put up to the Law or some other gentlemanlike science or employment."[16] No educative program was mentioned for John. Further, to keep Bysshe in England, she did "fully direct" her trustees to "take special care" that he "not be sent or put to sea on any account or pretence whatsoever." As a youth, Bysshe obtained some legal knowledge working at the Six Clerks' Office. His letters show a facility for metaphor that skipped his son to find root in his poet grandson. In a letter written a month before his grandson's birth, Bysshe quoted five of Prospero's lines from The Tempest (4.1).[17] Acquiring a patina of the refined, polished gentleman, he retained his more rough-hewn, egalitarian, and independent American spirit. His letters are pithy and to the point. Anticipating seeing his Nell after an absence, he wrote that he approached "the Citadel, like an Old Veteran Who pants for the signal of Attack," having ordered as an aphrodisiac, "two barrells of the Strongest Oysters to carry on the siege."[18] The eccentric Bysshe was not to be cast in any mold. Eschewing a profession, he devoted his energies to accumulating a new family wealth through marriages, inheritance, fortuitous family deaths, political acumen, moneylending, and adroit real estate transactions.

Bysshe, when twenty-one, aided by his impressive six-foot frame, handsome countenance, and sexual assuredness, married in 1752 his first wife, Mary Catherine Michell of Horsham. The members of the esteemed Michell family, who owned Field Place from 1482 to 1729, for generations were key players in the intermarriages among the neighboring Shelleys, Pilfolds, Whites, and Tredcrofts. Bysshe's bride was either seventeen or eighteen when she married. Her father, the Reverend Theobold Michell, and her mother, Mary Tredcroft, had both died when she was about five. Mary Catherine's uncle and guardian, Edward Tredcroft, adamantly opposed the marriage.

The rebellious Bysshe not only eloped but defied the provision in his great-uncle Edward Shelley's will that if either he or his brother John married before age twenty-three the offending brother would not inherit his estates.[19] John, more conforming, married when he was twenty-three. Bysshe further insulted his wife's guardian by having his runaway marriage performed by the incarcerated Parson Keith of Mayfair in London's notorious debtors' Fleet Prison.[20] Soon, the Marriage Act of 1753 banned such marriages. Fleet Prison had also been the scene, two decades earlier, of the marriage of the poet's maternal great-grandmother.

Bysshe and Mary Catherine extended their honeymoon in Paris due to his father's angry intent to not support him and leave all his estate to his dutiful older son, John.[21] After his first child, Timothy, was born in London on September 7, 1753, Bysshe lost no time securing the estates Mary Catherine was to inherit from her deceased parents. He signed an agreement with her two years after their marriage assuring the estates would be settled on him and his male heirs when she became twenty-one.[22] The sole male heir, Timothy, was seven when his mother Mary Catherine Shelley died at age twenty-six giving birth to her second daughter.

Waiting nine years, Bysshe was thirty-eight before marrying Elizabeth Jane Sidney Perry in 1769. Ten years younger than

Bysshe, she was a more illustrious heiress than his first wife. Her father, William Perry of Turville Park, Buckinghamshire, had died twelve years earlier. However, Elizabeth Jane's mother, Elizabeth Sidney Perry, had inherited the fourteenth-century Sidney estate, Penshurst Place, in Kent. Her father, Thomas Sidney, sixth Earl of Leicester, was the great-great-grandson of Robert Sidney, brother of the poet Sir Philip Sidney. Bysshe, with designs on the inheritance from this socially prominent and aristocratic lineage, had to reckon with his wily mother-in-law. Cherishing her Sidney lineage as the only surviving child of her father, she husbanded the impoverished estate of Penshurst left to her by her late uncle, seventh and last Earl of Leicester. Needing a male heir for the Sidney family line, she eschewed any reservations about the widower Shelley from Sussex. Her hand was very much involved in the marriage of her near-spinster daughter to this proven producer of children. Contrary to what has been reported, Bysshe's second marriage was not an elopement and had none of the odor of a Fleet Prison union. They were married under license from the Bishop of London at St. James, Westminster. Bysshe's brother John, of Field Place, and the bride's mother, were witnesses at the wedding. Further, a settlement at the time of their marriage stipulated that on Mrs. Perry's death the extensive Sidney estates would go to her daughter, with Bysshe having use of them for his lifetime.[23] Bysshe again proved his ability to procreate. In twelve years of marriage to Elizabeth Jane Perry, he fathered five sons and two daughters. The tragic ending of his first marriage was repeated when his second wife died May 1781 giving birth to her last child, Algernon Bysshe Shelley, who died a few months later.

Bysshe's second wife was dead but her mother was very much alive. Before she died in 1783, Mrs. Perry, who preferred her maiden name Sidney, specified in her will that Penshurst Place be passed to her daughter's oldest son, John Shelley. Twelve when his grandmother died, John also came to have a higher regard for the Sidney name. Coming of age in December 1792, John, in order to inherit Penshurst, forsook the name Shelley and, adopting the Sidney arms, became John Sidney. In 1818, John became a baronet, adopting the name Sir John Shelley-Sidney. Not only had old Bysshe spawned two titled lines, but John's son Philip Charles Sidney in 1835 became the first Baron de L'Isle and Dudley.

John's name change may have been influenced by the fact that his prolific father had begun his third family, with Mrs. Eleanor

Nicholls in London, shortly after his mother's death. In 1784, Bysshe Shelley and his Nelly had the first of four illegitimate children, another John Shelley. The insult was compounded when the second bastard son was given his father's name, Bysshe. There were two daughters, Eleanor and Cordelia. Bysshe's third family lived near William Blake, who was producing illustrations for Mary Wollstonecraft's writing.

Bysshe and Nell's son John, apprenticed to a surgeon, later became a Surgeon in the Army.[24] Their younger son, Bysshe, born the same month as the poet, was supported by his father on at least two voyages to the East Indies. In addition to providing for their mother, Bysshe's 1805 will provided for his four illegitimate children as well as "such as I may hereafter have by the said Eleanor Nicholls." At age seventy-four, Bysshe was making it plain that his mistress was considerably younger than himself and that he was still active sexually. After his death in Horsham, his best clothes were still in his London house with Mrs. Nicholls. Legitimate son Timothy Shelley, sensitive to social opinion, did not deign to have anything to do with Mrs. Nicholls.[25]

When his grandson Percy Bysshe was born, old Bysshe had acquired holdings from the Perry estate as far away as Hereford, Worcestershire, and Radnorshire, Wales, where he was High Sheriff in 1784.[26] This wealth neither softened his eccentricities nor diminished his influence over his son Timothy. One form of this influence was political. Drawn into the orbit of the eleventh Duke of Norfolk, Bysshe became involved in Whig political life. His value to the Norfolk interests was recognized in 1786. That year, Charles Howard became the eleventh Duke and had his friend Bysshe Shelley make out the patent for the baronetcy that had to wait for a Whig government twenty years later.[27]

The Duke, the "Jockey of Norfolk," was forty-six in 1792 and was known locally as "the Lord of Horsham." The father of five illegitimate children, he was so obese that, after falling asleep at his club from drinking, four men were needed to carry him to his bed on a specially constructed sling. He had the courage to cut his hair short and renounce the hair powder and queue common at the time. Owning estates ranging from Greystoke in the north to Arundel Castle in the south, he was one of the seven or eight most politically powerful peers in the House of Lords who controlled among them fifty-one members of the House of Commons.[28] A leading borough monger, he controlled eleven MPs, more than any other single political patron. After renouncing his Catholicism in order to start his political life, Norfolk remained a staunch supporter of Catholic emancipation, opposed the war with the American colonies, and early on allied himself with the reform movement led by Charles James Fox.[29]

Norfolk's influence on the elder Bysshe was embodied in Castle Goring. In 1793, using money from the sale of his second wife's estates,[30] Bysshe began building his own castle near the Duke's Arundel Castle. Bysshe's future title was Baronet of Castle Goring and he intended the castle to be a family ancestral home. This grandiose mansion located on 138 acres with a view toward the English Channel became a Janus-like structure, half Palladian villa and half imitation of the Duke's Gothic castle. Despite the common story that Bysshe squandered £80,000 on its construction, records indicate only £2,500 were allocated for the project.[31] Bysshe apparently lived in Castle Goring from about 1795 to 1807 but none of his offspring ever lived there.

Sir Bysshe ended his years living in Horsham's Arun House, inherited from his first wife. Timothy, waiting to inherit his aged father's title and estate, reportedly received daily bulletins of his health.[32] A visitor in 1811 reported that old Bysshe:

> according to the current gossip . . . had in his youth either been "crossed in love," or had in a fit of passion committed some act of violence which had left a strong and a melancholy impression upon his mind. He had become what some people would call eccentric; but he always struck me as having a dash of insanity. Sir Bysshe, although a man of large property, rarely mingled with persons of his own rank in society. . . . The baronet lived in a small house near the town-hall of Horsham, almost without attendance. Sir Bysshe was as indifferent to his personal appearance as he was to his style of living. He wore a round frock, and spent a portion of his time in the tap-room of the Swann Inn in Horsham,—not drinking, indeed, with its frequenters, but arguing with them in politics.[33]

Timothy Shelley, unlike his father, "kept up the style of the country gentleman." Shelley reportedly said his grandfather gave financial aid to the health faddist, Dr. James Graham.[34] Bysshe apparently took enough interest in his grandson's early literary ventures to underwrite their publication, but his fundamental values were acquisitive and materialistic. By the time he inherited the family property in 1790, Bysshe's two earlier marriages to women of property and his strong financial instincts had increased considerably the family holdings into a respectable family fortune. When he died, he had accumulated through inheritance, marriages, and entrepreneurship an estate of over £220,000, not counting £12,816 in bank notes squirreled away in his house. Scheming to the end, Bysshe drew up a long will with codicils, designed to preserve the total estate for future generations of male heirs and prevent his twenty-two-year-old namesake grandson from giving away the family wealth.

The Shelley family lawyer who drew up the elder Bysshe's will, London solicitor William Whitton, would play a vital role in Shelley's life. Just as Norfolk was the Shelleys' political godfather, linking grandfather, father, and son, so Whitton became the family legal force binding these three generations of Shelley men. Whitton knew the family secrets. Overseeing the legal and financial responsibility for old Bysshe's illegitimate offspring, Whitton may have become the father-in-law of Timothy's bastard son. Timothy leaned on and confided in Whitton, seeking his help in his anxious dealings with his explosive father and his rebellious son. Timothy, subject to his father's wrath, wrote Whitton he was surprised his father "was extremely pleasant" when signing "with great gravity" the codicils, Bysshe's pen being "Mrs. Clarke's leg that is sold in Ivory as a Toy at Worthing."[35]

Timothy, having experienced his father's explosive anger, followed suit with his son. Shelley's older cousin, Tom Medwin, wrote: "Sir Timothy was a man entertaining high notions of genitorial rights, but of a very capricious temper; at one moment too indulgent, at another tyrannically severe to his children. He was subject to gout, and during its paroxysms, it was almost dangerous to approach him, and he would often throw the first thing that came to hand at their heads."[36] Timothy probably resented that his son Shelley could express anger towards him, but that he, Timothy, could not express his anger toward his father, Bysshe.

Anger helped link old Bysshe, Timothy, and Shelley. Reportedly, as a schoolboy, Shelley could "curse his father" with great passion and choice epithets, having learned this skill from the verbal broadsides his grandfather directed at his father. When young Bysshe and his father visited old Bysshe, the patriarch "always received him [Timothy] with a tremendous oath, and continued to heap curses upon his head so long as he remained in the room." Timothy, suppressing his anger toward his father, adopted an out-

ward stance of mildness and conformity. However, Shelley reportedly said that if anything went wrong at Field Place his father did
"nothing but swear all day long afterwards."[37]

Timothy, seven when he lost his mother, later acquired a stepmother who soon was occupied taking care of her own seven children before her early death. Young Timothy, for years dependent
on his one parent, his volatile father, had to please him at all costs.
Unable to risk adolescent rebellion, Timothy became dutiful and
conforming. When his son assumed this rebellious role, an uncomprehending Timothy was adrift.

Lacking his father's romantic daring, Timothy avoided a sexual
and emotional commitment to a woman until his marriage at age
thirty-eight. Marrying the mother of his illegitimate child would
have offended his father, who chose wives from socially prominent
families. The woman Timothy married, more assertive than he,
took care not to threaten his passivity, allowing him the role of a
traditional family patriarch. Timothy's late marriage was part of
his developmental lag in reaching a number of life's milestones.
His cautious, methodical life of ninety years contrasted with the
more restless, accelerated pace of his father and of his son.

Timothy's early education reportedly was "much neglected."[38]
He was twenty upon entering Oxford in 1774, having received the
Leicester Exhibition to University College, Oxford, a grant controlled by his stepmother's family. Shelley would be nominated for
the same award by his uncle, John Shelley-Sidney. Timothy's sedate, four-year sojourn at University College in Oxford's lax intellectual climate yielded modest attainments, probably typical for
the time. Students, able to name their examiners and memorize
answers to time-honored examination questions, seldom failed.
This easygoing, unchallenging atmosphere appealed to "steady,
punctilious" Timothy, attributes he carried through life.[39]

Receiving his B.A. in 1778, Timothy likely stayed another term
or two at Oxford pondering his future. That Christmas, he saw
more of Elizabeth Pilfold[40] but marriage was still distant. Sam-
pling the law like his father, he spent part of 1779 at court at Lincoln's Inn Fields before buying an army commission late that year
as a cornet in the 22nd Regiment, Corps of Light Dragoons. He began a four-year stint as a recruiting officer.

In 1780, Timothy was proposed to stand for Parliament from New
Shoreham, a reformed borough partially controlled by the tenth
Duke of Norfolk. Timothy declined to run, preferring the security

offered by the army. Enjoying the privileges of his rank, he disregarded hunting laws. Stationed in Halifax, Yorkshire, he wrote his solicitor friend Thomas Medwin that, having been reviewed by his general for some "trouble," he was ordered to Manchester. Timothy regretted leaving Halifax as "I do as I please."[41]

Single and twenty-seven, he was far less advanced in accomplishment at that age than his father or his future poet son. Returning to Oxford in February 1781, Timothy signed personally for and obtained his M.A. degree, his military service exempting him from five of the required seven terms.[42] A grateful Timothy, having presented University College a pair of silver candlesticks, attained the rank of lieutenant in June 1781, only months before Cornwallis surrendered at Yorktown. When his unit was disbanded in 1783, he went on the half-pay list for the rest of his life. While in the army, Timothy had his miniature portrait painted in red coat and powdered hair.[43] Needing authority, orderliness, and structure, Timothy retained his attraction for the army and became involved in the Horsham volunteers.

At age thirty, Timothy was still searching for an identity as his tireless father launched his third "marriage." Probably about this time Timothy's illegitimate son was born and his widowed uncle John provided him bachelor quarters in the old medieval section of Field Place.[44] Timothy's role model for sedate country squire was his stolid, subdued uncle. Both Timothy and his uncle gave finely bound altar books to Warnham Church. When John died in October 1790, his younger brother Bysshe turned Field Place over to his son Timothy.

His uncle's death gave Timothy a jump-start in life. Soon to begin his aborted Parliament term, Timothy perhaps took his Grand Tour on the Continent at this time. His only trip abroad has been characterized as benefiting him little beyond the acquisition of a bad painting of Vesuvius, hung in Field Place, and a poor command of French. One biographer commented, "he really knew no more of Europe than the luggage that accompanied him."[45]

Both Timothy and his father had their portraits painted by society artists. Timothy, in 1791, chose George Romney, an older, once fashionable artist now noticeably losing his powers. Bysshe chose William Beechey, a new, younger painter of society. Bysshe's imposing portrait, with a distinguished bearing, strong brown eyes, heavy eyebrows, and a firm mouth with a definite smile, resembles Tom Medwin's description of him in old age as "a remarkably handsome man, fully six feet in height, and with a noble and aristocratic bearing."[46] Timothy's portrait has a resigned, almost depressive air. Tall like his father, but with a slighter frame and a fairer complexion, Timothy had soulful blue eyes, modest eyebrows, and Cupid's bow mouth. Romney also painted Shelley's mother's portrait in 1795 while she expected her third child. With some independence, she paid the artist herself, even if it was her husband's money.[47]

Timothy's penchant for self-medication—passed on to his poet son—appeared before his marriage in a letter about a projected trip to London to visit his father. Feeling "very weak & nervous," he postponed his trip but followed his friend Medwin's example "by throwing" his medicine "into the Pot de Chambre." Becoming his ailing Vicar friend's "apothecary," he advised that a daily remedy for "anxity [sic] & Bile" included "An Emetic on Monday—Water Gruel with Brandy, Suggar on Tuesday," culminating in "Duty as to yr Holy Function on Sunday." He ended this letter to the Reverend Marshall, "Believe me in the oddity of expressing myself."[48]

Timothy's election to Parliament in 1802 began an undistinguished sixteen-year political career. The *Times* reported that he added "another member to the great Parliamentary interest of the Duke of Norfolk."[49] Timothy's class act was being a country gentleman who lived continuously in the same house almost sixty years. His restless son and heir would rent quarters for a few weeks or months. Shelley's unconventional lifestyle was as vexatious to the methodical Timothy as the latter's conventionality was "despised" by his father, Bysshe.[50]

Growing up, young Bysshe observed the corrupt practices permeating his father's political life. Horsham, with a reputation for justice only from an outside magistrate, was then one of the most rotten boroughs. When the two ducal candidates, including Timothy Shelley, were thrown out in 1792, Lady Irwin's faction held the seats until 1806. Norfolk bought the Horsham seats when Lady Irwin died in 1807. Timothy, the Duke's member from New Shoreham, controlled almost five hundred votes in the Rape of Bramber. The Duke had consolidated his hold in 1811, buying Lady Irwin's family interests, including her Tudor mansion, Hills Place, also known as St. Irvyne.

Timothy took his son several times to visit Parliament but Shelley found in the politicians the same hypocrisy he experienced in his father. He called the members "wretched beings," and was quoted as saying: "Good God! what men did we meet about the House—in the lobbies and passages! and my father was so civil to all of them—to animals that I regarded with unmitigated disgust."[51] Timothy's political inconsistencies were matched by his religious behavior. Despite an external display of the conventional Christianity of his day, including his parliamentary votes against Catholic relief and for Christian missions to India, he fancied himself somewhat of a religious liberal. Calling himself "A friend to religious liberty," he subscribed to sermons by a Unitarian minister named Sadler, whom he reportedly wanted to replace the local vicar.

Timothy emerges as a dutifully rigid, controlled, low-keyed, hypocritical, and often well-intentioned man. When his sensitive feelings overcame him, tears welled in his eyes. He capably grasped financial matters, but his few pretensions toward intellectual life were blunted, in part, by an underlying sense of inadequacy. His prosaic, kindly, mild-mannered facade easily gave way to his more irascible, angry, and authoritarian behavior. Overly diplomatic on petty matters, he burst with rage when his need to control was challenged. Having appeased his father, he learned that appeasement was alien to his son. This mismatch between Timothy and his son was apparent to a family acquaintance: "Both Sir Timothy and his wife—excellent persons both—were, of all imaginable parents, the very last from whose union a looker-on would suppose it possible that a 'child of fancy' such as the youthful author of 'Queen Mab,' would be likely to spring. The former, clad in his yeoman-like garb and his tanned leather gaiters, was, like the rest of his family (with the exception of Percy) thoroughly practical and prosaic; all were endowed with a fair amount of good sense."[52]

This anecdote, by someone who knew the family a dozen years after Shelley's death, accords with Timothy's obituary in *Gentleman's Magazine*, commending him as an agricultural improver. This same acquaintance reported that Shelley's sister Hellen told her that when her father discovered "Bysshe was trying to inoculate me with his peculiar tenets and opinions," Timothy ejected his son from the house and forbade Bysshe's name from being mentioned again. Hellen warned her friend not to mention her brother's name within hearing of Timothy.[53] Several family stories were handed down about Timothy warning his youngest son John, apparently with success, "Never read a book, Johnnie, and you will be a rich man." He further admonished him, "Don't be like your

brother. Take care you don't learn too much." This last report, by
Shelley's biased cousin and biographer, Tom Medwin, included his
dubious claims that Timothy opposed education for the children of
the poor and would not hire a steward who could read or write.[54]
Commenting on Timothy's sexual hypocrisy, Medwin was suggesting he knew about Timothy's illegitimate child: "He . . . re-
duc[ed] all politeness to forms, and moral virtue to expediency . . .
he once told his son, Percy Bysshe, in my presence, that he would
provide for as many natural children as he chose to get, but that he
would never forgive his making a *mésalliance;* a sentiment which
excited in Shelley anything but respect for his sire."[55]

2

"An Infancy Outlasting Manhood": Mother

SHELLEY'S PATERNAL ISSUES WERE CRUCIAL IN THE DEVELOPMENT of his radical social and political thought, but his mother holds pride of place for influencing his poetic genius. Elizabeth Pilfold Shelley's importance upon her son's life and work, first broached by Cameron, is increasingly recognized.[1] Helping to mask this maternal influence was the obvious conflict between Shelley and his father, preserved in their correspondence. The present biography is the first to present the few extant letters written by Shelley's mother along with details of her early life. Even with these additions, her personality and influence upon her son remain elusive and enigmatic, in part because only two of his letters to her survive and that he barely mentioned her in his correspondence. Elizabeth Shelley acquiesced in her husband's imposition of a curtain of silence and non-recognition during the last ten years of her son's life and for many years after his death. Both parents far outlived their illustrious son; neither ever wrote a memoir or recollection about him and probably destroyed his early papers. This deletion of their son from public view continued after his death, when Timothy forbade Mary Shelley from publishing a biography of her husband.

Elizabeth Pilfold was the oldest of seven children whose parents were from long-established families of Horsham and Warnham. Her father, Charles Pilfold, born in Horsham, was a younger son of John Pilfold and Mary Michell. Apprenticed as a butcher at age seventeen, Charles's station improved nineteen years later by marrying Bethia White of Horsham, whose family owned Effingham Manor in neighboring Surrey.

Elizabeth Pilfold's maternal grandmother, Bethia Waller, daughter of a Horsham inn-holder, eloped in 1730 with William White to be married in London's Fleet Prison. Before she died in 1764, Bethia White had ten children, including a daughter born in 1739 named Bethia, later Elizabeth Pilfold's mother. This young Bethia, called Theyer, twice ran away from home when nineteen. A neighbor recorded in her diary, "hear that Theyer White is eloped, strange inhuman girl to leave her mother already involved in so much trouble." The next day, she "was found at a little alehouse," but two months later she ran away again before being "brought home."[2] Settling down, in May 1762, Bethia married Charles Pilfold in Horsham where, in early 1763, she gave birth to Shelley's mother, Elizabeth.[3]

The oldest child in a large family, Elizabeth probably became the mother substitute at age sixteen when, in 1779, her mother died. Her youngest sibling, Ferdinand, was only four.[4] Her father, overseeing his wife's family manor in Effingham, listed himself at that address as well as Horsham. His upward social mobility through marriage from being a butcher was not lost on his daughters. One early sign of his aspirations was naming his youngest son after his wife's sister's husband, Sir Ferdinando Poole. As the oldest daughter, Elizabeth Pilfold may have felt an obligation to her father, as she did not marry until the year after he died, her two younger sisters already having married.

A miniature of Bethia Pilfold in her maturity bears a remarkable likeness to her grandson Percy Bysshe as a boy. After her death, Elizabeth Pilfold lived the next twelve years with her mother's two surviving sisters. First, she lived with the younger aunt, Charlotte, who became Lady Poole in 1772 at age twenty-three by marrying a baronet, Sir Ferdinando Poole, nineteen years her senior. Elizabeth later lived in West Grinstead, near Horsham, with her namesake aunt Elizabeth Woodward and her rector husband.

As early as 1776 either Elizabeth or her sister Charlotte was living or spending time with the childless Pooles at their home, the Friars, in Lewes.[5] The statement that Shelley's mother was "brought up by her aunt, Lady Ferdinand Pool [sic]," could suggest that Elizabeth lived with the Pooles before her mother's death.[6] Both Elizabeth and her sister Charlotte lived with the Pooles after their mother died, possibly joined by their young brother, Ferdinand.

Sir Ferdinando's numerous ties to the Shelley family prepared the way for his adolescent charge, Elizabeth Pilfold, to eventually marry Timothy Shelley. A neighbor and political colleague in Lewes was Sir John Shelley, MP, a distant relative who, years later, was unsympathetic toward the poet. Elizabeth Pilfold, eventually to become Lady Shelley and the wife of an MP, obviously absorbed many of the values of the privileged upper-class life of her Poole aunt and uncle, including the political machinations of the landed wealthy. Sir Ferdinando had two other Shelley clan friends about his age who shared his interest in cricket, the brothers Bysshe and John Shelley. As early as 1771, unmarried Sir Ferdinando met at a ball in Lewes one of Bysshe's daughters, described as "Miss Shelley . . . a girl with blackish hair, not tall, who danced country dances most incomparably indeed." This would have been either Hellen or Mary Catherine Shelley, younger sisters of Timothy Shelley, who was seventeen.[7]

Sir Ferdinando, his marriage to young Charlotte White having improved his financial position,[8] pursued a more independent political agenda with the support of Sir John Shelley, his brother-in-law Viscount Palmerston, and the politically powerful cabinet member, the Duke of Grafton. Sir Ferdinando's sister, married to the second Viscount Palmerston, died before Elizabeth Pilfold joined the Poole household but Ferdinando was becoming the most "munificent, flamboyant and well-connected" citizen in Lewes. During the local racing season his friend the Prince Regent, and other grandees, dined at the Poole home after attending the races in Lewes. A passionate horse breeder, Sir Ferdinando owned "Waxy," winner of the 1793 Derby. The Pooles' dining room overlooked their paddock and Elizabeth passed along to her poet son a fondness for horseback riding. However, he would reject the political jockeying that Sir Ferdinando and his friend Bysshe Shelley used so successfully in their climbs up the economic ladder.

Both Elizabeth and Charlotte Pilfold had opportunities in the Pooles' social milieu to meet eligible young men, but Charlotte married first. In 1782, at age eighteen, Charlotte Pilfold married Thomas Grove, age twenty-three, of Wiltshire, in the Pooles' family church in Lewes. Elizabeth would not marry for another nine years, by which time her sister had borne seven of her eleven children. By the time of her sister's marriage, Elizabeth certainly knew Timothy Shelley and, if not engaged, they may have had an understanding about a future marriage.[9] Thomas and Charlotte Grove were described as the "handsomest couple in the county" of Wiltshire. Romney's portrait of Charlotte suggests a greater beauty than is evident in his later portrait of her sister Elizabeth.[10] In 1791, just before Elizabeth and Timothy Shelley married, Charlotte and Thomas Grove had a daughter, Harriet.

Thomas Grove and his older brother-in-law, Timothy Shelley, both heirs to large fortunes, were never close friends, due in part to differing personalities. Thomas had entered Oxford's University College at age eighteen in 1777, where he knew Timothy, then twenty-four and in his third year. Unlike staid Timothy, a restless Thomas, with a busy agenda elsewhere, did not stay to graduate. He was from a wealthy established "county" family, and by the time he married Charlotte Pilfold in 1782 he had long since inherited from his deceased father not only the family rural estate Ferne in Wiltshire, but lands in Dorset, Wales, East Anglia, and the Midlands.[11] In contrast to Thomas Grove, Timothy played a waiting game. Still a bachelor in the army in 1782, Timothy was heir to the Shelley estates owned by his uncle John and his father, Bysshe. In 1782, Timothy's father, who would live another thirty-three years,[12] was launching his illegitimate family with Eleanor Nicholls following his second wife's death the year before.

In 1786, Elizabeth Pilfold's aunt, Lady Charlotte, died at age thirty-seven. How long Elizabeth, now twenty-three, continued to live with the childless, mid-fifties Sir Ferdinando is not clear. He visited Elizabeth and Timothy at Field Place a week after their marriage in October 1791, and died in 1804.[13]

Elizabeth next lived with her other maternal aunt, Elizabeth Woodward, in the rectory next to the ancient parish church in the village of West Grinstead.[14] In this church, she was married to Timothy Shelley by her aunt's husband, the Reverend John Woodward, who would christen Percy Bysshe the night he was born. Elizabeth's move about 1786 to West Grinstead brought her just eight miles south of Field Place, where Timothy Shelley often resided with his uncle John.

When living in West Grinstead, Elizabeth Shelley wrote the first of her six surviving letters. These letters confirm some observations about her personality contained in the fullest description of her that has survived. It is a quote of unknown authorship in Shelley's first biography, written by his cousin, Tom Medwin, whose mother and Shelley's mother were Pilfold first cousins.[15] Medwin's veracity is sometimes questionable but he had a long firsthand knowledge of Elizabeth Pilfold Shelley. His quote, from "a popular writer," possibly Medwin himself, has the ring of accuracy:

His mother was . . . "if not a literary, an intellectual woman, that is, in a certain sense a clever woman, and though of all persons most unpoetical, was possessed of a strong masculine sense, a keen observation of character, which if it had had a wider field, might have made her a Madame de Sévigné or a Lady Wortley Montague, for she wrote admirable letters; but judging of men and things by the narrow circle in which she moved, she took a narrow and cramped view of both, and was as little capable of understanding Shelley, as a peasant would be of comprehending Berkeley."[16]

The comment on Elizabeth Shelley's letter-writing ability was echoed by her brother-in-law, the Reverend Jackson, who recalled her letters were in "splendid English & most interesting."[17] Elizabeth Shelley's letters reveal that, without benefit of her husband's Oxford education, she was a more literate, outspoken, and expressive letter writer than he. Indeed, her letters have a spontaneous, conversational, and feisty quality lacking in the more deliberately polite letters of her son, who reserved his warmest profusions of feelings for his poetry. Elizabeth's first extant letter, probably written about 1787–1788, was to her Horsham cousin Mary Pilfold Medwin who, six years her senior, had been married about ten years to Thomas Charles Medwin. Elizabeth wrote from her aunt and uncle's rectory in West Grinstead:

My Dear Mrs. Medwin,
    My Aunt will take it as a great favor if Mr. Medwin will buy half a dozen coffee cups like the tea cups if he can conveniently get them. She begs ten thousand pardons for being so troublesome but you know ladies in general are very fickle.
    The next time I come to Horsham I shall most undoubtedly call upon you to <u>abuse</u> you for not coming to the Assembly. I hope Mr. M. is not the worse for his Dancing for he dances a great deal. Oh I had almost forgot to ask you how you like your hoop if it does not quite meet your approbation I will get it returned and have an other made. if it is a very fine day to morrow my Aunt talks of driving over in the whisky if so I will call upon you. Uncle & Aunt desire their Comp. Pray give my love to Mr. Medwin & Kitty, Believe me ever your
        Affectionate Cousin
        Eliza. Pilfold
Friday night 11 o'clock[18]

Elizabeth Pilfold's barbs include a reference to "very fickle" women, her intention to "<u>abuse</u>" her cousin for not attending the dance, and her implication that Mr. Medwin was having the time of his life with the other ladies in his wife's absence. She undid this hostile undertone by a generous offer to replace the hoop made for her cousin. The complicated relationship Elizabeth and Timothy had with the Medwins was compounded of kinship and the Shelleys' higher class standing. Thomas Medwin, although a leading Horsham solicitor, was the son of a Berkshire draper, an outsider whose home in Horsham's town center was not baronial Field Place. A family man the same age as bachelor Timothy, Medwin probably resented that, doing the Duke of Norfolk's bidding, it was his duty by hook or crook to get the country gentleman Timothy elected to Parliament. The surface friendliness between the two families always had the class edge of the Shelleys, who frequently demanded favors from their subservient cousins. About the time Elizabeth was asking her cousin to buy coffee cups, Timothy wrote from Field Place to ask Thomas Medwin to buy him "six pairs of silk stockings." On another occasion, Timothy, as if pulling his army rank, wrote him: "Mr. Shelley, if he does not hear further from Mr. Medwin, will expect the chaise at Field Place a Quarter of an hour before Six O Clock on Monday morning—which Mr. Medwin will be so good as to order."[19] Some years later, Elizabeth Shelley asked Medwin to deliver a parcel to one of her daughters at school.[20] The senior Medwin's underlying resentment became an overt break with Timothy and Elizabeth Shelley in 1811.

Elizabeth Shelley, writing her lawyer from Field Place after her husband's death in 1844, was confused and grasping about money she erroneously believed the Medwins owed her. She wrote, "I think it is time I should come to an understanding with Mr. [Pilfold] Medwin about the Fields for which he is now indebted to me for many years now." In actuality, her dying cousin, Mary Pilfold Medwin, had the clear use of the property from Timothy Shelley; it reverted to Lady Shelley when Timothy died.[21] Writing about the same time, Mary Wollstonecraft Shelley acidly commented upon her mother-in-law's tightfisted way with money and stripping Field Place when she vacated it.[22]

Elizabeth Shelley's most important letter concerns Percy Bysshe when he was a few years old. It was written to Shelley's great-Aunt Woodward, who attended his birth and watched as her rector husband then baptized the babe, a ceremony publicly repeated at Warnham Church a month later.[23] This letter, written between 1794 and 1796, provides the only behavioral description of Shelley in his first years, as well as glimpses of his infant sister Elizabeth and of his mother's personality. Young Bysshe, called

"Happy P.," was his Aunt Woodward's "dear little boy." Apparently childless, she died in 1797 just before little Bysshe's fifth birthday:

My dear Aunt,

I do not know what excuse to make for not having written to you for so long a time. Idleness and the hopes and expectations of seeing you every day at Field Place, must be my excuse.

Happy P. is as well as can be and the little girl grows every day. We have expected you over every morning this week past as I thought my uncle was engaged every day with Partridges. I thought you would have given one morning up to Happy P. Mrs. Wyatt and Mrs. Barne paid me a visit yesterday. Your note they did not take the trouble of delivering themselves but Mrs. Barne said she believed her servant had got a letter for me, which upon enquiring I found was true. I could not write by them as I could not leave them to entertain themselves. Barne came in just as they were going, he looks shockingly. I believe he intended staying to Dinner but I should not ask him as I told him it was very uncertain when Mr. Shelley would return home, which happened to be true, as I make it a custom not to wait longer than four o'clock for him as it does not agree with little Elizabeth. He did not stay long but asked as many impertinent questions as he used to do. Bysshe picked his pocket and shook hands with him, he opened his fine toothpick case and watch to please him. Your dear little boy behaved very well and asked how Aunt Woodward did. What sport has my Uncle had? Mr. Shelley had pretty good the first days but his shoulder is very indifferent. We shall, I believe, begin to innoculate the servants next week, they will be out of the house when Ann returns. The children will have it at home. What charming rains we have had, just the thing for Innoculation.

Bysshe eats a partridge every other day, you never saw a fellow enjoy anything more than he does boiled partridge and bread sauce.

What sport has my uncle had? I trust good and that he does not over walk himself. The Barnes told me they saw you Sunday and that you were both well. I hope you will spare one day from shooting and that we may see you.

Bysshe desires his duty.

Mr. Shelley joins with me love and affectionate duty.

    Yours affectionately,
        Elizabeth Shelley
Field Place,
    Sept. 10th[24]

This letter possibly was written in 1794 when Bysshe had just turned two and his infant sister was four months old, but the impatience of "little Elizabeth" for her dinner suggests 1795 or 1796 as a more probable date.[25] Elizabeth Shelley displays frankness, biting criticism, and humor that later characterized her daughter Hellen.[26] Her pique at Barne's "impertinent questions" makes one curious about the family matters he was probing. Little Bysshe's early zest for partridge yielded to his later vegetarianism and, although behaving "very well," his lifelong playful proclivities were evident when he picked the visitor's pocket. The "affectionate duty" his mother sent echoed later in Shelley's complaint that as a child love was a duty. Inoculations, probably for smallpox, had been practiced for fifty years.[27] To the "strong masculine sense" Medwin quoted about Elizabeth Shelley can be added the report "there is testimony to show that her temper was violent and domineering."[28]

Shelley's predilection for taking socially unpopular stands probably came in part from his mother. She apparently accepted her husband's illegitimate son, perhaps even including him into the family at Field Place when she married. Shelley once indicated that she was still taking "abuse" for having placed his father's happiness above social opinion.[29]

The "masculine" side of Elizabeth's personality meshed with Timothy's more passive tendencies. Elizabeth's tolerant facade seemingly covered an underlying anger toward Timothy expressed not only in outbursts but, more subtly, in feelings of disdain and disparagement that her son would have sensed. Timothy's tyrannical rages could have reinforced young Bysshe's feelings about his father as a rather weak and ineffectual person. Such parental attributes likely contributed to Shelley's feminine traits and affected his sisters' personalities as well. Only one of Shelley's four sisters married but all three adult daughters of Elizabeth Shelley's sister, Charlotte Grove, married.

A schoolmate's reminiscence about the Shelley sisters suggests the parental problems they encountered. It was recalled "that when first the daughters came to school, their costume, though handsome, was so antique that they could not go out in it, and until some other clothes were provided they had to wear their morning print dresses on Sunday as more modern in appearance." Also vividly described was ex-army officer Timothy commanding his platoon of daughters when visiting them at their London boarding school: "Their father came in great stateliness and waited until his daughters were full dressed as for dancing to receive him. They were then required to enter and even to speak to him in rigid succession of ages, and if they went with him to proceed in the same routine to the post chaise."[30] However, Shelley's parents had a tradition of giving gifts, including food and clothes, to the poorer townsfolk on holidays such as Gooding Day, December 26, and May Day. Their behavior perhaps influenced Shelley's generous nature. As a boy, he rode on horseback accompanied by Lucas, his father's steward, giving money lavishly to the poor and asking Lucas for more when he ran out.[31]

The sole description of Shelley as an infant was of "a pretty fledgling, already distinguished by his delicate hands and feet, his bright down of baby hair (afterwards curling in ringlets), and his great blue, luminous eyes."[32] This account matches the descriptions of Shelley's boyhood appearance given by his sister Hellen, younger by seven years, in a series of letters written thirty-five years after his death: "as I remember Bysshe, his figure was slight and beautiful,—his hands were models ... his eyes ... [had a] wild, fixed beauty. ... As a child, I have heard that his skin was like snow, and bright ringlets covered his head. He was, I have heard, a beautiful boy. ... His forehead was white, the eyes deep blue."[33] These descriptions are consistent with one of two portraits of Shelley as a boy. However, all these images probably reflect some idealization of his appearance. Later physical descriptions that Shelley and others provided included a receding chin, a small, turned-back nose, and somewhat irregular facial features, evident in the only surviving completed portrait from life in his mature years.[34]

Newborn Bysshe, in addition to Aunt Woodward, soon had another surrogate mother figure. Like privileged children of his day, he had his own nurse, most likely in her twenties. She may have been a wet nurse, a common practice even if less in favor than earlier.[35] He was called her "nurse-child," suggesting she was his wet nurse, as does the fact that a possibly non-lactating Elizabeth became pregnant with her second child twelve months after Shelley's birth.[36]

Mother and nurse, dual maternal attachment figures for little Bysshe, perhaps influenced his lifelong pattern of needing simultaneously two or more close nurturing and loving females. Shelley's nurse, included in the family gatherings long after his death, was still alive a few years before Hellen Shelley wrote in 1856 or 1857: "His old nurse lived, within the last two or three years, at Horsham. One of the curates there—a Mr. Du Barry—was a great admirer of my brother's poetry, and we were able, through him, to remind her of those years, when she used to come regularly every Christmas to Field Place, to receive a substantial proof that she was not to be forgotten, though her nurse-child was gone from earth, for ever."[37]

It is often mentioned that Shelley's personality was strongly influenced by the female environment—his mother and four younger sisters—in which he grew up. However, what he experienced specifically in his most formative early years was multiple mothering, including his mother, his nurse, his Aunt Woodward, and probably his mother's cousin, Ann Wood, not to mention female servants, and his mother's Horsham cousin, "Miss Kate." Any problematic, anxious aspects of his early maternal attachment may have been heightened at the vulnerable age of twenty-one months[38] when his sister Elizabeth was born. She was his only sister until he was almost five (the second daughter died at four months).

Whatever the influence of his maternal nurturing, Shelley's poetry abounds with oral imagery, leading one critic to observe, "*Thirst* is a key term for Shelley, present whenever he seeks to formulate his love psychology."[39] He would write discourses on the vegetable diet, avoided alcohol, and used various drugs as a form of self-medication. Preferring a simple diet, he was often so disinterested in meals as to be oblivious to food placed before him.

Shelley, fascinated with personality development and change, often injected his interest in early experience into his poetry. In a letter poem to one of his mother figures, he wrote of making a paper boat, "the impulse of an infancy, / Outliving manhood."[40] It has been argued that Shelley's nuclear poetic universe can be understood, in part, by the experience of *symbiosis* in early infancy.[41] Presumably, the infant experiences a *dual unity* with the mothering one(s), a blissful, merged state in which boundaries between itself and other are absent. Many have noted that Shelley's poetry is infused with intimations of merger and a boundary-less state of oneness. Separation from mother figures, it has been posited, may involve anxiety and a split between feelings of idealized love and those of persecutory rage. One Shelley scholar has suggested that such an internal splitting may have contributed to Shelley's marked ambivalence in relationships with women.[42]

Mirroring, closely associated with symbiosis, absorbed Shelley. It is postulated that the formation of the infant's emerging self involves mirroring the mother's face, especially her eyes.[43] Winnicott observed that what the baby sees in the mother's face is "unverbalizable except perhaps in poetry . . . what the baby sees is himself or herself."[44] Shelley wrote of the mirroring activity involved in creativity and he invoked in his poetry a recurrent image of the world reflected in a mirroring pool. Described by those who knew him as extremely "sensitive," Shelley perhaps was more attuned than most infants to sensory stimuli emanating from the mothering one. His poetry's subtle nuances of sensory images include his noted proclivity for synesthetic experience.[45]

Separation from and felt loss of the mother, the infant's prototypical anxiety experience, may be viewed as leading to subsequent "falling in love" experiences, acts of restoring the lost maternal figure.[46] If so, Elizabeth Pilfold Shelley remained her son's inner collaborator in his creative life as well as a crucial influence in his troubled relationships with women.

3

The Young Prometheus

Fᴿᴏᴍ ᴛʜᴇ ᴏᴜᴛsᴇᴛ, ʟɪᴛᴛʟᴇ ʙʏssʜᴇ ʜᴀᴅ ᴛᴡᴏ ꜰᴀᴍɪʟɪᴇs. ʜᴇ ᴡᴀs ᴘᴜʙ-
licly acknowledged and celebrated by his parents as the first-born
son and heir. More unacknowledged was the family in which he
was his father's second-born son. His ambiguous status may have
intensified if his older brother lived for a time in the family during
Bysshe's infancy and early childhood. This blurred birthright possibly helped instigate Shelley's lifelong refusal to be the sole car-
rier of his family's title and wealth. His feeling that his father favored his older brother intensified any sense of rejection and
perhaps helped set the stage for an enduring motif in Shelley's personality, that of the outsider, the exile. Although he would not be
cast out from the family nest until age ten, he had already internalized the feeling of being separate, different, and apart.

The birth of his sister Elizabeth before he turned two introduced
Bysshe's third family constellation. Alongside his uncertain role as
younger half-brother, he forthrightly assumed his new status as
older brother to a sister whom he wished to mirror his identity. Until he was almost five, with one brief interruption, Bysshe had Elizabeth as his sole prized sister, establishing a twin-like brother–sister bond crucial to his development and his poetry. In January 1796
a sister Hellen was born. Her death four months later was his only
experience of a death in the immediate family. His older brother
status was enhanced with the birth of his next three sisters, Mary
(1797), the second Hellen (1799), and Margaret (1801). A younger
brother born in 1806 arrived too late to challenge Bysshe's role as
favored brother to four younger sisters.

The idyllic pastoral beauty of rural Field Place—with its ponds,
meadows, forests, gardens, and working farm—delighted young
Bysshe and provided a basis for his astonishing poetic talent for
portraying nature. However, what was most influential for this
highly sensitive young boy was not his childhood play and physical

surroundings but the troubling internalized feelings stemming from his relationships with his parents and siblings. A feeling of solitude and aloneness was perhaps shared by his sister Elizabeth who—after her brother had been banished from her home— painted the family drawing room in 1816. No person is present in the sumptuously decorated room. Two crystal chandeliers hang above a piano that evoked for Elizabeth her brother Bysshe, who enjoyed playing simple melodies with one hand. At the room's far end, extending almost to the ceiling, were stacks of books that were among the first he avidly devoured and re-devoured.

One constant in Bysshe's shifting family pattern was his favored role as his mother's firstborn son and eldest child. The power of this exclusive oldest-son position with his mother may have heightened feelings of rivalry toward his father. Young Bysshe also experienced power over his younger sisters, becoming the lord, if not tyrant, over them. As one biographer observed, he was "a pretty complete dictator to his sisters."[1] Each new sibling became a competitor for his mother's affection, threatening his favored position with her. The importance Shelley would come to place upon social equality and social justice probably had roots within this web of hostility and rivalry in his sibling relationships. Freud later observed that the demand for "justice" and "social feeling" has roots in reversing a hostile feeling toward the other children into an identification with them.[2]

Bysshe's identification with his sisters fostered, on the one hand, an effeminate cast to his personality and, on the other, a wish that they be like him. His strong demand for social equality and justice, continuing themes in his political thought, included his concern for equal rights for women. For his sisters, this meant their equal right, denied by their gender, to the family inheritance. Not by chance, the titles of the two books that importantly influenced him were *Political Justice* and *A Vindication of the Rights of Woman.* Another manifestation of Bysshe's early bonding with his sisters was his later passion for communal living arrangements, an urge to recreate his family that endured to the time of his death.

Bysshe's stellar infant role with exclusive rights to his mother was short-lived. The birth of his first and favorite sister, Elizabeth, in May 1794 when he was a twenty-one-months-old toddler, was particularly crucial. At that age, the child experiences both an increased anxiety over separation from the mother and a heightened need for attachment to her. Each sister, especially Elizabeth, had the paradoxical role as a replacement for this sense of loss of his mother's love and as a source of fear of further loss of her love. As if to defend against such a fear of loss, Shelley would need in his future love relationships the presence of a second woman. Seemingly confirming his unconscious fear of loss, the presence of this other woman inevitably threatened the primary love relationship.

Shelley's first love—his mother—was only the first of a number of Elizabeths in his love life. The sister he most identified with, Elizabeth, became the center of his shared childhood well into adolescence. His later fascination with the themes of androgyny and brother–sister incest owes much to his strong involvement with sister Elizabeth, a closeness facilitated by their marked physical similarity. A visitor to the family would remark that the resemblance of Shelley and his sister Elizabeth was as if they were twins.[3] She became for him a prototype, the first female close to his age with whom he merged his identity. As his major, if not sole, playmate, she became his overriding companion. As his twin star, she reflected the literary lights of her brother, composing with him letters, plays, and poems. Some of her poetry suggests she had at least "respectable"[4] talent at age sixteen when Bysshe and Elizabeth published their poetry together. She was the first of a succession of female literary companions so important in Shelley's personal and creative world. What sexual experiences the two shared during their years together at Field Place is not known. A spinster like her sisters Hellen and Margaret, Elizabeth remained in her Field Place family until her death while still in her thirties, the first of the family to die after Shelley.

Shelley's mother was almost thirty-eight when her last daughter was born, her sixth child in little more than eight years. Timothy was now forty-seven and the two may have decided to have no more children. Indeed, Elizabeth Shelley did not become pregnant for another four and one-half years, during which time Bysshe was sole heir to the family estate. However, in March 1806, when Elizabeth Shelley was forty-three, she bore a son John, an event with major implications for the family. Bysshe, age thirteen, was away at school and John came too late to serve as his boyhood companion. John did provide Timothy and grandfather Bysshe with a backup heir should the increasingly problematical young Bysshe or his male children not survive.

Bysshe's childhood was not exclusively a sisterhood; there is evidence of other boys at Field Place. Young Bysshe and his sisters apparently had some contact with their illegitimate half-brother, based on a later report that Timothy's bastard son was believed to be the father's favorite and "not the friend" of young Bysshe.[5] This half-brother almost certainly was not the same youth about seven years older than Bysshe, Edward Fergus Graham, whose father had been in the army. A mutual friend said Timothy took young Graham "into his house" where he was "treated as a member of the family." Timothy supported and fostered the education of the musically talented Graham. Just how long Graham may have been in the Shelley household is unclear, but Bysshe and Edward reportedly had a "warm friendship; they were in fact like brothers."[6] Graham's presence at Field Place probably was longer than holiday visits and he possibly was at Field Place until Shelley went to Syon House Academy, when Graham was about fifteen. Later events suggest Shelley's mother was attracted by the young Graham's musical talent, possibly paying for his musical education in London. Shelley's relationship with Graham would end explosively over romantic charges involving him with Shelley's mother and with his sister Elizabeth.

Shelley's predominantly female companionship in his early youth ill-prepared him for his upcoming attendance at all-male schools. Timothy, owner of a large game preserve, exerted some masculine influence by promoting young Bysshe's fondness for hunting and shooting. However, his influence on his son may have been overshadowed by that of Shelley's mother who, reportedly, was the parent who most encouraged Bysshe in field sports such as hunting and fishing. She apparently had a "special grievance" because of his lack of interest in these pastimes.[7] It was said that she watched him while he fished from a boat. On one hunting expedition she promoted, Bysshe occupied himself with a book while the gamekeeper bagged the birds that later were presented as the boy's catch.

Bysshe was a good marksman. His cousin Tom Medwin noted that "during September, [he] often carried a gun in his father's preserves; Sir Timothy being a keen sportsman, and Shelley himself an excellent shot, for I well remember one day in the winter of 1809, when we were out together, his killing at three successive shots, three snipes, to my great astonishment and envy, at the tail of the pond in front of Field Place." However, Shelley wrote an Eton friend that he had "killed only one" of the "thousands of wild Ducks & Geese in our River and Lake."[8]

Shelley later denounced the shooting of animals, but he never gave up his fondness for pistol shooting, always taking with him his brace of pistols on his travels. However, his familiarity with and strong aversion to the military had roots in local Horsham attitudes. When he was four, as part of the military buildup during the war with France, a barracks housing two thousand soldiers was built in Horsham. In a few years an ordnance depot was added that held ten thousand "stands" of arms. Frequent clashes between townspeople and troops were reported before they left about 1815, about the time Horsham sent petitions to Parliament favoring "reform" and opposing the slave trade. By the 1830s, Horsham had earned a reputation as "a hotbed of sedition."[9]

A budding country squire, Bysshe grew up liking horseback riding and, like his father, he rode the extensive family domains of Field Place and its environs. Young Bysshe's roamings probably made him deeply aware of the contrast between his family's comfortable opulence and the abject poverty among the families of the farm workers living adjacent to Field Place. This class awareness, added to his obvious intellectual precocity, contributed to his early sense of being special and of being different and apart from those who surrounded him.

In addition to the parental indulgence and pampering that went with his privileged family position, his sisters formed an admiring female coterie. Not one to brag, he muted his need for self-display by an obvious shyness and modesty, encouraging in his generous way the intellectual and artistic gifts of others, especially those of his sisters. His position and upbringing, as the son of a Member of Parliament and heir to one of the wealthiest landed estates in Sussex, gave him an aristocratic tinge and class-consciousness that never extinguished in the face of his radicalism and egalitarian values. Not immune from some prejudices of his class, he came to abhor aristocratic bias. His empathy was for the less fortunate, resenting those of rank who were imbued with attitudes of superiority and privilege. It has been observed that most of Shelley's closest friends were from a social class below his.[10]

The physical and emotional isolation young Bysshe experienced at Field Place was perhaps influential in his desire, often expressed in his poetry, for "solitary" places. Such isolation fueled his prolific fantasy life. Bysshe's parents recognized their son's intellectual precocity but it is less clear that they understood his unusually active world of fantasy.

The original, inventive quality of his fantasy led to what his sister Hellen called "eccentric amusements" at Field Place. This free expression of fantasy, intended to amuse himself and others, also caused bewilderment and provoked disapproval: "he would frequently come to the nursery and was full of a peculiar kind of pranks. One piece of mischief, for which he was rebuked, was running a stick through the ceiling of a low passage to find some new chamber, which could be made effective for some flights of his active imagination."[11]

His family, if often puzzled by his fantasies, provided an audience for the young boy's recitations that displayed his prodigious memory. His staged performances and literary recitals were lauded by his parents, while his more spontaneous exuberances could lead to rebuke, chastisement, and punishment. Bysshe was called upon to recite for family and friends such poems as Gray's "Ode on the Death of a Young Cat," which he had committed to memory at a young age. His exceptional facility in learning languages first appeared when he began to learn Latin at the age of six. When his father had him recite Latin verse, Hellen reported it was completely unintelligible to his younger sisters but obviously understood by Bysshe, who gesticulated and enacted scenes during his recital.

Shelley never lost his childhood enjoyment of play. As an adult, he delighted in playing with children and his love of play gives his poetic expression some of its most characteristic originality and flavor. What sister Hellen called the "peculiar" and "eccentric flights" of his boyhood imagination, while not necessarily bizarre, had an idiosyncratic quality, suggesting his need to live in a fantasy world was far greater than that of most children. These childhood fantasies, daydreams, and memories, later recalled and elaborated, became important elements in his poetic creativity. Shelley would have agreed with Freud that, in this sense, creative writing is both a substitute for and continuation of childhood play.[12]

Shelley's vivid childhood fantasies, noted by his sister Hellen, reverberate in many themes in his mature poetry. Some of these fantasies were borrowed from local legends, such as the Great Tortoise reputed to live in nearby Warnham Pond where his father kept a boat. Bysshe would often "excite awe and wonder" in his sisters by attributing noises of unknown origin to this beast, who assumed a strange assortment of sizes and shapes in his boyhood imagination. Local legends about Bysshe's favorite haunt, nearby St. Leonard's Forest, included a "famous DRAGON, or serpent . . .

reputed to be nine feet or rather more in length" as well as the "horrible decapitated spectre" of "former squire Paulett." Another reptile of his early fantasy life, the Great Old Snake, he often mentioned in later years.[13] One legend, reportedly three hundred years old, was that this reptile inhabited the gardens of Field Place and, despite its "unusual magnitude," was said to have been killed accidentally by a gardener. Snakes became an important symbol in Shelley's poetry and a source of several nicknames.

His boyhood attraction to role-playing and disguise was another expression of Shelley's ample fantasy life. One incident related by his sister involved Bysshe as a visiting farmer-physician to his only recorded local girlfriend, a year older than he, appropriately named Elizabeth, the daughter of the local curate, Reverend George Marshall:

> As we were sitting in the little breakfast room our eyes were attracted by a countryman passing the window with a truss of hay on a prong over his shoulders; the intruder was wondered at and called after, when it was discovered that Bysshe had put himself in costume to take some hay to a young lady at Horsham, who was advised to use hay-tea for chilblains. When visitors were announced during his visit to the vicar's daughter, he concealed himself under the table, but the concealment did not probably last long.[14]

Shelley's early interest in acting extended beyond his audience at Field Place. Once, in a Horsham lawyer's office, "he asked, in Sussex language, to be hired as a gamekeeper's boy." His ploy was successful, at which point "there was an explosion of laughter."[15] On another occasion:

> he gave the most minute details of a visit he had paid to some ladies, with whom he was acquainted at our village: he described their reception of him, their occupations, and the wandering in their pretty garden, where there was a well-remembered filbert-walk and an undulated turf-bank, the delight of our morning visit. There must have been something peculiar in this little event, for I have often heard it mentioned as a singular fact, and it was ascertained almost immediately, that the boy had never been to the house. It was not considered a falsehood to be punished; but I imagine, his conduct altogether must have been so little understood, and unlike that of the generality of children, that these tales were left unnoticed.[16]

Hellen's are the most poignant and insightful observations about Shelley's boyhood by any member of his family. She made clear that Bysshe's imaginative fantasies occasionally were construed as a "falsehood," often leading to parental chastisement or punishment. As Hellen observed, young Bysshe's parents, lacking understanding of his fantasy life and its importance to him, often ignored it or responded with punishment and criticism.

Bysshe's boyhood penchant for the fantastic and imaginary was such that "any tale of spirits, fiends, &c., seemed congenial to his taste at an early age."[17] One imaginary occupant of Field Place who found an important place in Bysshe's psyche was "an Alchemist, old and grey, with a long beard."[18] The young explorer found a spacious garret under the roof where a lifted floorboard gave access to a deserted room where the alchemist lived. "We were to go see him 'some day'; but we were content to wait and a cave was to be dug in the orchard for the better accomodation of this Cornelius Agrippa." This persona as alchemist was never lost; at Oxford, Shelley was depicted as "the chemist in his laboratory, the alchemist in his study, the wizard in his cave."[19]

Hellen recalled the consuming enthusiasm of the child alchemist of Field Place for playing with fire:

> we dressed ourselves in strange costumes to personate spirits, or fiends, and Bysshe would take a fire-stove and fill it with some inflammable liquid and carry it flaming into the kitchen and to the back-door; but discovery of this dangerous amusement soon put a stop to many repetitions.

> The tranquillity of our house must have frequently been rudely invaded by experiments, for on one occasion, on the morning our Poet and experimentalist left home (for Eton, probably) the washing-room was discovered to have been filled with smoke, by a fire in the grate with the valve closed; the absence of draught had probably prevented mischief, but much was made of this accident, probably to deter any admiring imitators; and there might have been circumstances connected with it relating to chemical preparations, which did not reach us.[20]

This angry, silent message of the fire in the grate, a pyrotechnic "accident," apparently occurred as Bysshe left home for Eton. Shelley's attraction to, if not obsession with, fire, probably contained elements of hostility and rage. His later friends and acquaintances would report his exploding charges or setting fires at school. As a major symbolic image of his mature poetry, fire assumed such forms as the sun, stars, comets, volcanoes, flames, lightning, hearth, and dying embers, not to mention light, created by fire.

Another boyhood fascination, science, especially chemistry and electricity, provided other ways to experience fire. The sparks generated by his electrical apparatus combined with his interest in flying kites. As a boy, he "made an electrical one, an idea borrowed from Franklin, in order to draw lightning from the clouds— fire from heaven, like a new Prometheus."[21]

Combined with his vital fantasy life, Bysshe's mother's continual pregnancies throughout his childhood suggest that, perhaps more than most children, he had a surfeit of birth fantasies. That such procreative imagery infused much of his poetry is not surprising. Emerging from his early years at Field Place as the new century dawned, young Bysshe's complex, fertile psyche was dealing with his two most important Field Place experiences, the personalities of each of his parents. In addition, leaving his sisterhood, he now confronted new, harsher realities beyond the confines of home.

Fig. 1. Field Place, recently restored as it was in Shelley's time by Mr. and Mrs. K. V. Prichard Jones, with medieval house on right. Photograph by author.

Fig. 2. Lady Elizabeth Shelley by George Romney, 1795, courtesy of The Carl F. Pforzheimer Collection of Shelley and His Circle, The New York Public Library, Astor, Lenox and Tilden Foundations.

Fig. 4. Sir Bysshe Shelley, after portrait by Sir William Beechey, R.A.

Fig. 3. Sir Timothy Shelley by George Romney, 1791, courtesy of The Carl F. Pforzheimer Collection of Shelly and His Circle, The New York Public Library, Astor, Lenox and Tilden Foundations.

4

Exiled to Education

WHEN BYSSHE WAS SIX HE BEGAN HIS FORMAL EDUCATION WITH THE Reverend Evan Edwards, the Welsh curate at Warnham Church who ran a small day school in the vicarage. Edwards, possibly Timothy's friend at Oxford, was affectionately called "Taffy" by his new pupil. The reverend was not a deep scholar but his emotional warmth and liberality came at an opportune time.[1]

Bysshe's first teacher, also his first substitute father, found his young pupil highly receptive to his liberal views. Timothy, defending his own disciplinary diligence over his son, later wrote, "I never gave him Liberties . . . from six years of age he has never been kept *one day* from School when he ought to be there, and in his Holydays I read the Classics and other Books with him in the full hope of making him a good and Gentlemanly Scholar."[2] If Timothy's stern conscientiousness contributed to Shelley's intellectual zeal, he lacked fatherly sensitivity to, or understanding of, his son's expansive, free-spirited, and creative intelligence.

Shelley later recalled that Taffy was the only teacher for whom he had "any degree of respect."[3] His continuing influence was evident in 1811 when Shelley said he had no "quarrel" with Taffy, being "much obliged to him for the complex idea 'tyranny.'" As if echoing Taffy's views on tyranny, he concluded, "So much for Obedience, Parents & Children."[4]

Shelley's identification with Taffy not only influenced his social and political values, it fostered his needs to minister to others. Years later, he once confided to a friend as they came upon a pretty country vicarage house, "I feel strongly inclined to enter the church." When challenged because of his ideas about religion, Shelley commented on the good a clergyman could do, "teaching as a scholar and a moralist" and providing "consolation" and "charity among the poor."[5]

Young Bysshe left Taffy's positive clerical influence in 1802, the year Timothy Shelley finally returned to Parliament, elected as Member from New Shoreham. Timothy's political machinations probably did not entirely escape Bysshe's keen young mind. Timothy's July election owed much to the efforts of his political agent, Thomas Charles Medwin, who, after canvassing seven hundred freeholders throughout the Rape of Bramber, produced four hundred votes promised to Timothy Shelley. Large sums were spent entertaining the voters at inns throughout the area, including over £315 at one inn in Shoreham. Timothy perhaps also paid the Duke of Norfolk's usual fee for occupying one of his seats, another £4,000.[6]

Autumn of 1802 also marked young Bysshe's first extended separation from his family. Like other economically advantaged youths, he was sent away to boarding school for the next eight years. His family rejected Horsham schools, including an "academy" for young gentlemen in the former gaol, and chose the largely middle-class Syon House Academy at Isleworth near Brentford on the Thames west of London. His cousin, Tom Medwin, older by four years, was already a student there.[7] Bysshe began two problematic years at Syon House.

Being ejected from the cocoon of Field Place at age ten, the dawning of adolescence, was a crucial milestone in Shelley's emotional development. The anxiety and stress from this abrupt physical and emotional separation from his family would soon be evident. Long accustomed to his special role as the big brother dominating his adoring younger sisters, he now was lorded over by boys, many older than he.

Compounding his anxiety from this wholly unfamiliar and threatening environment of all boys was the shattering replacement of Taffy by Dr. Greenlaw, master of Syon House. Shelley was unprepared for this harsh new life involving forms of aggression and sex he had never experienced. His somewhat effeminate appearance and his lack of normal boyish athletic skills, combined with his obvious intellectual superiority and emotional sensitivity, made him a vulnerable target for the physical and emotional abuse of his peers. Nascent feelings of alienation and persecution at home now had a more obvious cause. It was probably at Syon House that his later conscious, masochistic self-image—as Actaeon transformed into a lonely, hunted, and wounded deer—began to develop.

At the same time, these Syon House assaults upon his personal integrity promoted an outward anger. Perhaps for the first time, after experiencing his own rage and violent behavior, he developed a determined toughness in fighting back against his persecutors. The earlier unconscious hostilities played out with his siblings and parents at Field Place now became the surface hostilities in the halls of Syon House. Shelley the fighter began to emerge.

The emotional cost of Shelley's Syon House experience is evident in a memoir by a fellow student, Sir John Rennie. Two years younger than the poet, Rennie was second to Shelley as Syon House's most famous alumnus, becoming a distinguished engineer. His autobiography has vivid descriptions of Shelley and his first school:

> It was a large house formerly belonging to the Bishop of London [with] excellent gardens and playground . . . open and healthy . . . the total number of boys was about fifty, ranging from eight to sixteen years of age. They were well fed and taken care of by the Doctor's excellent wife, and his sister-in-law, Miss Hodgkins. The Doctor's eldest daughter, Miss Greenlaw, taught the youngest boys their letters; whilst the Doctor and his assistants devoted themselves to the education of the others, which education consisted chiefly of classics, writing, arithmetic, French, and occasionally geography and the elements of astronomy . . . the most remarkable scholar was the celebrated poet, Percy Bysshe Shelley, who was then about twelve or thirteen (as far as I can remember) and even at that early age exhibited considerable poetic talent, accompanied by a violent and extremely excitable temper, which manifested itself in all kinds of eccentricities. His figure was of the middle size, although slight, but well made. His head was well proportioned, and covered with a profusion of brown locks; his features regular, but rather small; his eyes hazel, restless, and brilliant; his complexion was fair and transparent, and his countenance rather effeminate, but exceedingly animated. The least circumstance that thwarted him produced the most violent paroxysms or rage; and when irritated by other boys, which they knowing his infirmity, frequently did by way of teasing him, he would take up anything or even any little boy near him, to throw at his tormentors. His imagination was always roving upon something romantic and extraordinary, such as spirits, fairies, fighting, volcanoes, etc., and he not unfrequently astonished his schoolfellows by blowing up the boundary palings of the playground with gunpowder, also the lid of his desk in the middle of the school time, to the great surprise of Dr. Greenlaw himself and the whole school. In fact, at times he was considered almost upon the borders of insanity; yet with all this, when treated with kindness, he was very amiable, noble, high-spirited, and generous; he used to write verse, English and Latin, with considerable facility, and attained a high position in the school before he left

for Eton, where, I understand, he was equally, if not more, extraordinary and eccentric.[8]

Rennie was one of a number of contemporaries who described Shelley's precarious emotional balance as bordering at times on "insanity." Rennie's memoir of Shelley is one of three by Syon House schoolmates. Undoubtedly distorted by decades of Shelleyan mythology, all have reasonably consistent views of Shelley's behavioral extremes at that time. Another account concerns a schoolmate about Shelley's age named Gellibrand who "had a lively recollection of his famous schoolfellow, whom he used to describe as like a girl in boy's clothes, fighting with open hands and rolling on the floor when flogged, not from pain but 'from a sense of indignity.'"[9] Gellibrand recalled Shelley once volunteered to help him with a difficult Latin verse assignment. Shelley's completion of the verse (in English, "I wrote this, but I did not make it") earned Gellibrand a flogging from Dr. Greenlaw. Gellibrand then "gave [Shelley] a pummelling." Whether Shelley was playing a joke or had been coerced rather than having volunteered as Gellibrand would have us believe, this is the earliest example of Shelley's writing earning him the wrath of his contemporaries.

Tom Medwin recalled easing his younger cousin's entry into the strange milieu of Syon House, which they both left the same year.[10] Shelley, probably sent to Syon House because his cousin was there, sought out Medwin when under stress:

> We did not sleep in the same dormitory, but I shall never forget one moonlight night seeing Shelley walk into my room. He was in a state of somnambulism. His eyes were open, and he advanced with slow steps to the window, which, it being the height of the summer, was open. I got out of bed, seized him with my arm, and waked him. . . . He was excessively agitated, and after leading him back with some difficulty to his couch, I sat by him for some time, a witness to the severe erethism of his nerves, which the sudden shock produced. This was the only occasion, however, to my knowledge, that a similar event occurred at school, but I remember that he was severely punished for this involuntary transgression.[11]

Medwin, noting that Shelley also experienced nightmares, "strange and sometimes frightful dreams," at Syon House, also said he "was given to waking dreams, a sort of lethargy and abstraction that became habitual to him." Medwin recalled that after "the accès was over, his eyes flashed, his lips quivered, his voice was tremulous with emotion, a sort of ecstacy came over him, and he talked more like a spirit or an angel than a human being."[12] These states, his sleepwalking, his withdrawal into fantasy, and the sporadic outbursts of anger and rage, suggest the severe stress Shelley was experiencing. Syon House, not the last place where Shelley had somnambulistic episodes, perhaps was where his deep interest in his own dreams began.

Shelley's earliest known letter—written "Monday, July 18, 1803" at Field Place to Catherine Pilfold (b. 1761), his mother's first cousin living in Horsham with the Medwins—indicates his fondness for his cousin Tom after a year together at Syon House.

> Dear Kate,—We have proposed a day at the pond next Wednesday, and if you will come tomorrow morning I would be much obliged to you, and if you could any how bring Tom over to stay all the night, I would thank you. We are to have a cold dinner over at the pond, and come home to eat a bit of roast chicken and peas at about nine o'clock. Mama depends upon your bringing Tom over to-morrow, and if you don't we shall be very much disappointed. Tell the bearer not to forget to bring me a fairing, which is some gingerbread, sweetmeat, hunting-nuts, and a pocket-book. Now I end.
> I am not
> Your obedient servant,
> P. B. Shelley[13]

Timothy's son parodied his father's parliamentary franking privilege by writing "Free" on the hand-delivered letter that made clear that, at age ten, he was no one's obedient servant. Young Bysshe regularly borrowed from the Medwin family library and the pocket-book he wanted was probably older cousin Tom's reading matter the two youths shared.

Medwin, recalling Syon House as more austere and punitive than did Shelley's other schoolmates, described Greenlaw as "not wanting in good qualities, but very capricious in his temper." Medwin wrote of the boys' reaction to Shelley's feminine demeanor:

> Exchanging caresses of his sisters for an association with boys, mostly the sons of London shopkeepers, of rude habits and coarse manners, who made game of his girlishness, and despised him because he was not "one of them;" not disposed to enter into their sports, to wrangle or fight; confined between four stone walls, in a playground of very limited dimensions—a few hundred yards—(with a single Elm tree in it, and

that the Bell tree, so called from its having suspended in its branches the odious bell whose din, when I think of it, yet jars my ears,) instead of breathing the pure air of his native fields, and rambling about the plantations and flower gardens of his father's country seat—the sufferings he underwent at his first outset in this little world were most acute. Sion House was indeed a perfect hell to him.[14]

Fagging—slavish work of a younger boy for an older boy—was not practiced in its pure form at Syon House, but the older boys' domination and harassment of the younger boys resulted in a "democracy of tyrants." Shelley was one of about sixty youths ranging from eight to the late teen years, an age spread guaranteeing the physical subjugation of the younger boys by the older and promoting sexual exploitation of less mature by more mature students. Medwin described Shelley upon entering Syon House:

Shelley was at this time tall for his age, slightly and delicately built, and rather narrow chested, with a complexion fair and ruddy, a face rather long than oval. His features, not regularly handsome, were set off by a profusion of silky brown hair, that curled naturally. The expression of countenance was one of exceeding sweetness and innocence. His blue eyes were very large and prominent . . . his voice was soft and low, but broken in its tones,—when anything much interested him, harsh and immodulated; and this peculiarity he never lost.

Medwin, describing "Shelley's agony on his first day at Syon House," said he was "tormented" by the boys' "zest for torture" with questions and "mockery" upon discovering that "he was ignorant of pegtop or marbles, or leap-frog, or hopscotch, much more of fives or cricket." Asked to "spar" or run a race, amid shouts of "derision . . . he made no reply, but with a look of disdain written in his countenance, turned his back on his new associates, and when he was alone, found relief in tears."[15]

The older boys forced the younger boys to run errands until exhausted, to take the punishment for senior boys' transgressions, and suffer their verbal and physical abuse. Shelley, "always the martyr," would strike back physically at his adversaries but more often reacted to tyranny by turning to fantasy and imaginative writing to express his feelings.

Shelley's first poetic response to oppression, the five-stanza "A Cat in distress," usually attributed to the Syon House period, probably was written 1809–1811. Likely, it is his earliest extant poem.[16]

His sister Elizabeth, a gifted artist with more legible handwriting than her brother, transcribed the poem and painted a cat on this "very early effusion," as his sister Hellen called it. The poem's sardonic, biting observations anticipate Shelley's later political satires on oppression, tyranny, and the gluttonous powerful feeding off the poor:

> You migh'n[t] easily guess
> All the modes of distress
> Which torture the tenants of the earth,
> And the various evils
> Which like so many devils
> Attend the poor dogs from their birth[17]

Aside from concern for the poor, these lines reflect Shelley's criticism of his father's role as keeper of tenants on the Field Place farms.[18] These were years when increasingly distressed farm laborers experienced growing economic disparity with the landed wealthy. Enclosure of farmland had left impoverished laborers responsible to support "the tenant farmer, the landowner, and the tithes of the Church."[19] Shelley, raised in a locale that shortly led in the agitation for economic justice, probably saw through the veil of *noblesse oblige* of his parents' ritual distribution of goods. The mask of benevolent paternalism could not hide the inequity and brutality of a class system that made the threat of hunger a living reality.

Reflecting these sentiments in the poem, the young non-conformist refers to himself as a "sinner," mentioning "others" who desire "An old fellow out of the way," as if alluding to his father's impatience that old Sir Bysshe refused to die.[20] The poem concludes:

> But this poor little Cat
> Only wanted a rat
> To stuff out its own little maw
> And t'were as good
> Had some people such food
> To make them hold their jaw

This last phrase, to stop lecturing, probably was advice Shelley got in abundance from his father and others. Another poem about this time has the anti-militaristic line, "No votarist I at Glory's shrine."[21] One of two English poems that Shelley translated into

Latin as school exercises was *Epitaphium* from Gray's *Elegy Written in a Country Churchyard*. The other, *In Horologium*, Shelley found in the 1809 *Oxford Herald*. His translation, about a watch hanging enticingly between the breasts of "Leonora," is racier than the original.[22]

If the poem of the cat hinted at his conflicts with his father, years earlier "at school," probably Syon House, Shelley, about "eleven or twelve," made his first known preadolescent affectionate attachment to a youth his age. He later wrote about this first intense relationship with a male friend in a brief essay, *On Friendship*:

> The object of these sentiments was a boy about my own age, of character eminently generous, brave, and gentle; and the elements of human feeling seemed to have been, from his birth, genially compounded within him. There was a delicacy and simplicity in his manners, inexpressibly attractive. It has never been my fortune to meet with him since my school-days; but either I confound my present recollections with the delusions of past feelings, or he is now a source of honor and utility to every one around him. The tones of his voice were so soft and winning, that every word pierced into my heart; and their pathos was so deep, that in listening to him the tears often have involuntarily gushed from my eyes. Such was the being for whom I first experienced the sacred sentiments of friendship. I remember in my simplicity writing to my mother a long account of his admirable qualities and my own devoted attachment. I suppose she thought me out of my wits, for she returned no answer to my letter. I remember we used to walk the whole play-hours up and down some moss-covered palings, pouring out our hearts in youthful talk. We used to speak of the ladies with whom we were in love, and I remember that our usual practice was to confirm each other in the everlasting fidelity, in which we had bound ourselves toward them and towards each other. I recollect thinking my friendship exquisitely beautiful. Every night, when we parted to go to bed, we kissed each other like children, which we still were![23]

Shelley's precise recollection that his mother did not respond to his impassioned effusions may be his most telling anecdote about his childhood relationship with his mother. This loved male friend possibly was from the Tredcroft family of Horsham, distantly related to the Shelleys.[24] This friendship may be the basis of a recurrent dream Shelley discussed in his dream journal:

> I distinctly remember dreaming three several times, between intervals of two or more years, the same precise dream. It was not so much what

is ordinarily called a dream; the single image, unconnected with all other images, of a youth who was educated at the same school with myself, presented itself in sleep. Even now, after the lapse of many years, I can never hear the name of this youth, without the three places where I dreamed of him presenting themselves distinctly to my mind.[25]

Years later, seemingly remembering this relationship, Shelley described a statue of Bacchus and Ampelus. "Just as you may have seen (yet how seldom from their dissevering and tyrannical institutions do you see) a younger and an elder boy at school walking in some remote grassy spot of their playground with that tender friendship towards each other which has so much of love."[26]

Shelley would later write of an experience of sudden awakening and commitment that occurred either late at Syon House or about 1809–1810 at Eton. This emotional experience, basic to his esthetics and his poetic identity, he first described in *Hymn to Intellectual Beauty*, "While yet a boy." This likely was a specific event, a not uncommon preadolescent, sexually tinged epiphany.[27] Later, recognizing its profound influence on his life, he revisited this school experience in eight notebook pages of drafts of *Laon and Cythna*.[28] His added details underscore Shelley's loneliness, alienation, and depression that prompted the experience. Repeating three times, "none did love me," he wrote in one draft "I remember well the day & hour," which became a "May-dawn" on "the glittering grass . . . near . . . [a] schoolroom." He rejected a passage with a self-image, "Like some wild beast that cannot find its mate: A solitary gazelle . . . Secure in its own swiftness." Depression and anger stem from feeling rejected and "all lonely":

> Mine equals shunned a boy so sad and wild;
> And those who ruled me found untameable
> The spirit of a meek and gentle child,
> For with bitter scorn of wrong I smiled.

Feeling a deep rejection and loneliness, he drafted, "I wept, all lonely I was . . . lone, untameable / Like some wild beast that cannot find its mate." He recalled his schoolmates' hostile voices, "The harsh and grating strife of tyrants and foes," recognizing them as "but one echo from a world of woes," suggesting earlier paternal censure. Mentioning physical and emotional abuse, he wrote of suffering when his "equals shunned a boy so sad and wild" and "When hoary men or youths of strength mature / Struck me

with fruitless blows." He hinted of attempted sexual abuse, being
"thus undefiled." Among many lines he crossed out, Shelley wrote,
"In Childhoods / Soothed by beatings . . . I stood alone . . . in happy
solitude . . . a blight came on my being / A clinging darkness that
would not [?end] . . . I wept, all lonely I was . . . in tears, grieving . . .
hate grew within me of the many crimes."

The agonizing feelings of rejection and alienation reflected in
these pained recollections were crucial in the early development
of Shelley's sense of social injustice. Shunned by "mine equals," he
was well-prepared emotionally for Godwin's message in *Political
Justice* later at Eton. In his darker maturity, Shelley wrote in
Julian and Maddalo:

> To do or suffer aught, as when a boy
> I did devote to justice and to love
> My nature, worthless now!
>
> (380–82)

Shelley's early adolescent search for a secular understanding of
love, beauty, and justice flowed from his rejection of his parents' inconsistent, basically traditional, Christian beliefs. Later, writing to
his future father-surrogate, William Godwin, of the scope and zeal
of his search, Shelley said he "was haunted with a passion for the
wildest and most extravagant romances; ancient books of Chemistry and Magic were perused with an enthusiasm of wonder almost amounting to belief."[29]

Shelley's exile to Syon House reinforced his feelings of loneliness and loss. A loner at school, Shelley, according to Medwin, was
often bored with the schoolwork and "passed among his schoolfel-
lows as a strange and unsocial being." He was often found pacing
alone along the schoolyard wall "indulging in various vague and
undefined ideas, the chaotic elements" that Medwin fancied were
found in his later poetry. He "abominated" the dancing lessons,
avoiding them whenever possible. If forced to attend, he "suffered
inexpressibly." The French dancing instructor despairingly called
him "gauche."[30] Later in life, Shelley danced well.

Another humiliation was being physically punished by Dr.
Greenlaw. The schoolmaster, after making one of his off-color jokes
("the imprisonment of the winds in the Cave of Aeolus"), observed
Shelley's disgust. Taking the earliest pretext to show his irritation
at Shelley, Greenlaw criticized a Latin passage he thought was

faulty. Actually, it was a quote from Ovid.[31] A later friend, Thomas Love Peacock, perceptively said of Shelley's experience at Syon House: "At the best . . . it must have been a bad beginning of scholastic education for a sensitive and imaginative boy."[32]

Amid the unchallenging curriculum, two sources of intellectual stimulation at Syon House had lasting influence, his avid reading for pleasure and his introduction to science. Syon House having no library, Shelley frequented Mr. Norbury's circulating library a few minutes away on the High Street.[33] He read the popular sixpence-each "blue books" of the Minerva Press, stories of "haunted castles, bandits, murderers, and other grim personages" with such titles as *The Midnight Groan; or the Spectre of the Chapel: a Gothic Romance.*[34] Shelley's particular favorite was Robert Paltock's *The Life and Adventures of Peter Wilkins, a Cornish Man.* This story seems a parable of Shelley's life. He re-read it before writing *Alastor,* borrowing for his poem Peter's solitary boat trip through sucking whirlpools and rocky cataracts. Without benefit of clergy, Peter marries a woman capable of flight—a precursor of his *Witch of Atlas*—and their androgynous offspring have anatomical features of both parents. Peter was the first Prometheus Shelley knew, one who brought laws and arts to a winged race, cleansed their degenerate religion, and abolished slavery when he found it.[35]

Shelley's sister Hellen wrote that "He had a wish to educate some child and often talked seriously of purchasing a little girl for that purpose." Perhaps during the Syon House years, Shelley tried to implement this idea by expressing his wish to adopt a vagrant child who came to the back door of Field Place to do her tumbling tricks. Riding his pony around Field Place, he talked of his intention and was only frustrated by his not realizing the cost of room and board.[36]

After Shelley depleted the supply of Minerva Press books, his surreptitious library journeys led him to the realistic novels of Richardson, Fielding, and Smollett. Finding them too prosaic, he turned to Gothic novels to sustain his own preoccupations. His apparent favorites included Matthew (Monk) Lewis's *The Monk* and Ann Radcliffe's *The Italian.* These works, considered pornographic and banned at Syon House, featured perverse, incestuous, and murderous priests, particularly in *The Monk.*[37] This work would influence Shelley's two Gothic novels and he would return to its incest-murder theme in *The Cenci. The Monk* also contained the figure of Ahasuerus, the Wandering Jew, a future presence in

Shelley's works. Hellen Shelley recalled that her brother was also fond of Lewis's poetry, which had the imaginative flair of his prose.

Another erotic Gothic novel from Syon House days, Charlotte Dacre's *Zofloya; or, the Moor,* a particular favorite, featured the misfortunes of virtuous Lilla whose body is rendered into palpitating bits by vicious Victoria. Medwin asserted, and apparently Swinburne later agreed, that this novel, which began in the Alps, also influenced the two Gothic novels Shelley was to write a few years later.[38]

The lectures at Syon House on science and astronomy by the itinerant Dr. Adam Walker left an indelible imprint on Shelley. Walker, a science enthusiast and inventor, gave a series of vivid talks and demonstrations covering many scientific topics, as indicated by the title of his eighty-six page pamphlet, "Analysis of a Course of Lectures on Natural and Experimental Philosophy, viz. Magnetism, Mechanics, Chemistry, Pneumatics, Fortification, Optics, Use of Globes, etc. Astronomy." Fascinated with these lectures, Shelley probably heard them again at Eton, another of Walker's stops.

Shelley's lifelong interest in chemistry, electricity, optics, and particularly astronomy infused his poetic imagery. Before leaving Syon House, when he was about twelve, Shelley began "scientific" experiments on his sisters and others at Field Place. Hellen recalled:

> When my brother commenced his studies in chemistry, and practised electricity upon us, I confess my pleasure in it was entirely negatived by terror at its effects. Whenever he came to me with his piece of folded brown packing-paper under his arm, and a bit of wire and a bottle . . . my heart would sink with fear at his approach; but shame kept me silent, and, with as many others as he could collect, we were placed hand-in-hand round the nursery table to be electrified; but when a suggestion was made that chilblains were to be cured by this means, my terror overwhelmed all other feelings, and the expression of it released me from all future annoyance.[39]

Shelley's electrical experiments upon his sisters had hostile and sexual overtones, and Hellen felt shame and annoyance at her brother's experimentation. That the sexual nature of electricity was much discussed in the science of the day probably did not escape Shelley's curiosity. Walker, reacting to Shelley's enthusiasm, helped him obtain an electric generator, part of his scientific armamentarium at Field Place, Eton, and Oxford.

Shelley's astronomy studies, Medwin reported, led him to be "delighted at the idea of the plurality of worlds." Observing Saturn through a telescope, Shelley thought its atmosphere seemed proof that it was inhabited like Earth. Believing "some planets being more favoured" than ours, he "was enchanted with the idea that we should, as spirits, make the grand tour through the heavens."[40] Walker's fantasies and facts concerning meteorology, astronomy, and outer space were infectious for the youthful Shelley. Anticipating his pupil's future poetics of space, Walker wrote: "Let us on wings of imagination then launch into the immensity of space, and behold system beyond system. . . . How inadequate then must be the utmost stretch of the human faculties."[41] Walker would have been pleased that his engrossed pupil would be praised by Alfred North Whitehead, in *Science and the Modern World*, as a potential "Newton among chemists" had he been born one hundred years later. Shelley probably was not suited to be a physical scientist, but one cannot conceive of his poetry without its imagery and allusions to astronomical and atmospheric phenomena. Years later, he frequented Hampstead Heath when his contemporary, John Constable, was painting from the same locale the clouds that fascinated them both. When Shelley reached Oxford, he poured out his thoughts concerning the possible uses of heat and combustion to transform matter, produce food, and eliminate starvation and slavery. Walker helped Shelley obtain a solar microscope, which used sunlight to project an enlarged microscopic image in a darkened room. It became a favorite possession at Oxford and later.[42] As late as 1814, it was observed that "Shelley makes chemical experiments."[43] The ideas of energy introduced by Walker became features of Shelley's poetics of "visionary physics," including chaos theory in contemporary physics.[44]

The location of Syon House near the Thames provided Shelley an opportunity to explore the river he lived near during much of his subsequent English years. Having loved boating on the tranquil ponds of Field Place and nearby Warnham Pond, he now sought excitement by occasional escapes from Syon House in a skiff. According to Medwin, "A wherry was his beau ideal of happiness, and he never lost the fondness with which he regarded the Thames . . . we had more than once played the truant, and rowed to Kew, and once to Richmond, where we saw Mrs. Jordan in *The Country Girl*, at that theatre, the first that Shelley had ever visited."[45] Dora Jordan, unwed mother of ten by the Duke of Clarence, later William IV, played the well-known role in Garrick's racy Restoration play of an innocent rural young woman confronting the sexual life of London, dressing in one act as a boy.[46]

Approaching his twelfth year and entering adolescence, Bysshe would trade his anxieties at Syon House for the greater stresses of Eton. He still had no mentor equal to the task of meeting his emotional and intellectual needs.

5

"Untaught Foresters": Eton Madness

Bysshe was almost twelve when, accompanied by his father, he signed his name in the headmaster's register at Eton College on July 29, 1804. He would be at Eton for the next six years, one-fifth of his life, undergoing a period of profound personal change. These six Eton years were, at times, painful and traumatic. Fortunately, Shelley would find at Eton a catalytic father surrogate, James Lind, M.D., a worthy replacement for the Reverend "Taffy" Edwards.

The English public school experience is an extended puberty rite of passage. Boys entering adolescence are expected to conform to institutionalized rituals, customs, and rules intended to inculcate and perpetuate a manhood of elitist power and class privilege in English society. Eton's conservative ethos became a powerful stimulus for Shelley's increasing resistance against authoritarian institutions and ideologies. At Eton, outsider status seemed assured by his nonconformity, his resistance to fagging, his sensitive, effeminate manner, and his rage in the face of humiliation and frustration. Shelley would develop an attraction to the person of Christ, whom he considered a nonconformist, a rebel, and a martyr.[1] Eton provided rich opportunities to act out these roles.

One such opportunity was the sexual hypocrisy of the public school, a same-sex enclave teeming with boys uprooted from family relationships. Their needs for affection and love, combined with maturing sexual impulses, found ready expression in relationships involving students and school masters. In this fertile milieu, "homosexual practice of one sort or another was in fact rampant . . . with little attempt to control it."[2] Homosexuality, a word not yet in the English lexicon, was dealt with by a curtain of secrecy, censorship, and outright denial. Sidney Smith in 1810 characterized the public school as a "system of premature debauchery that only prevents men from being corrupted by the world by corrupting them before their entry into the world." Thackeray reported that on arrival at Eton in 1817 the first order a schoolmate gave him was "Come & frig me."[3]

The emerging Regency Period had a stringent sexual morality akin to that of the later Victorian era. Dickens, Ruskin, and Elizabeth Barrett experienced Regency, not Victorian, childhood horrors. Shelley's aristocratic upbringing gave him a Regency-like gentlemanly discreetness and overt decorum concerning sexuality. However, his unusual openness and liberality about sexual issues stemmed in part from the sexual hypocrisy he observed, at home and at school.

Eton—and other public schools—had a sado-masochistic master–slave mentality combined with a macho emphasis on physical aggression and violence, expressed in contact sports, games, and fights. Sado-masochism undergirded the fagging system, the indiscriminate, abusive floggings, rampant bullying, and a system in which senior boys often had almost unrestrained rule over younger boys. The other side of this aggressive, often violently hostile institutional coin was sexual. Older, more mature youths turned to peers and young boys for gratification, if not abuse. There was little effort to control homosexual behavior, and it was tolerated with a striking degree of denial.[4] Sodomy was punishable by death in England until 1861, when the sentence became life imprisonment.[5] Given the public vilification, hysteria, and degrading atrocities perpetrated against those who committed "crimes against nature," it is understandable that Byron concealed his male love affairs at Harrow, and later, by ingenious censorship, in his letters and poems.[6] Toleration of the cruelest kinds of treatment of homosexual "offenders" existed side by side with condemnation of slavery, the burning of witches, and prosecution of religious deviants, "a climate like that of the McCarthy era when it was dangerous to appear soft on Communism."[7] A commentator on Oscar Wilde's conviction wrote: "If all the persons guilty of Oscar Wilde's offences were to be clapped into gaol, there would be a surprising exodus from Eton and Harrow ... public schoolboys are allowed to indulge with impunity in practices which, when they leave school, would consign them to hard labor."[8]

Euphemistic phrases—"unnatural love," "sin," and "immorality"—were used for both homosexual and masturbatory behavior. At Eton, boys routinely slept three to a bed. Collegers, supported by Eton, lived in college dormitories, but the more numerous Oppidans, like Shelley, roomed in the houses of various masters close to the school. Collegers were locked up for the night in their dormitories without supervision. The most notorious was Eton's Long Chamber, where fifty Collegers between the ages of nine and nineteen could live for eight or nine years under physical conditions "not so much primitive as decayed."[9] Opportunities for combining sex with aggression were abundant. The fagging system, in which Shelley apparently refused to cooperate, had a strong underlying sexual current that undoubtedly perpetuated its existence.[10] The masochistic submission of the younger fag to his older fagmaster's sadistic control and punishment, often rationalized as a system for protecting younger boys from the abuse of older boys, was a sexual exercise in learning to enjoy pain. The fag's passive experience was turned into an active one when, upon achieving sixth form status, he inflicted the same aggression. The humiliation, physical pain, and emotional degradation demanded of the fag from his older, often affectionate, "protector" contains essential elements for the development of the sado-masochism of the authoritarian–fascistic character. Similar dynamics characterized relationships between school masters and students.

School authorities emphasized manliness as a denial of homosexual issues and as a way of overcoming "sin." It was hoped that hearty, tiring games and sports would leave the boys too depleted for sexual activity. Games were a passion at Eton and contact sports provided a mix of aggression and sublimated sexuality. Shelley, definitely nonconformist in his lack of interest in most games was, as at Syon House, ridiculed for his effeminate manner in sports. Given his lack of interest, it is unlikely he witnessed Byron's feat, despite his foot deformity, of scoring six goals for Harrow in a cricket match at Eton in 1805. Leonard Woolf blamed England's "philistine" attitudes on the public schools, where his late-nineteenth-century experiences were similar to Shelley's: "Anyone seen to be good at lessons or rudimentarily intelligent was suspect both to masters and to boys . . . to take lessons at all seriously, was entirely despicable."[11] Shelley's intellectuality, combined with disinterest in and ineptitude for sports, guaranteed his being the target for persecution.

Flogging—sanctioned child abuse—was the most flagrant form of sexual sado-masochism. Shelley apparently escaped flogging, even though John Keate, one of the most notorious floggers in

English public school history, taught him in the lower form in his first months at Eton and was headmaster at the end of Shelley's Eton career. The sadistic attraction of flogging for many masters, and its corresponding masochistic attraction to students, provided a scene of mutual gratification. Regularly violating school regulations, students fed the masters' appetites for these wholesale whippings. Algernon Swinburne attributed his attraction to flagellation to his Eton flogging experiences.

The bisexual "peculiar costume" worn by short headmaster Keate, an outmoded tricornered hat and a Doctor of Divinity gown covered by his black cassock, was described "as a fancy dress partly resembling the costume of Napoleon, partly that of a widow-woman."[12] In Shelley's time, "Dame" referred to the master of one's house, usually a male. The younger boy in a relationship between two students was "heterosexually cast," a beautiful loved one who needed protection.[13]

Keate, perhaps unfairly, had the most flagrant reputation of all flog-masters. Part of his well-developed sadistic streak was a distrust of students that led to random accusations of lying; one boy, indignant at such a false accusation, challenged Keate to a duel.[14] The students' often vicious attacks and pranks against Keate included one or two apparently apocryphal incidents involving Shelley. Keate was the subject of three major student rebellions before resigning in 1834.

One Eton master of the time, Benjamin Drury, known as a hard-drinking ruffian, was frequently truant from the school. The personality and intellect of Shelley's tutor, Bethell, were considered inadequate and ineffectual. Keate's predecessor, Dr. Goodall, had led a slack regime during most of Shelley's stay, and Eton was known as one of the least regimented of the public schools. But the reaction against Goodall's easygoing discipline could only explain a portion of the amazing flogging fixation of Keate, who, it is estimated, flogged about ten boys a day (except Sunday, his day of rest). Among the many mass floggings that Shelley probably escaped was one in 1810 when one hundred lower fifth boys each received six strokes, a total of six hundred blows from Keate.[15] So entrenched was flogging, now called caning, that it was not abolished by Parliament (by one vote) in state-run schools until 1986. Finally, in 1998, Parliament abolished caning in privately supported schools.

Added to Shelley's physical abuse at Eton was the emotional pain of his prolonged separation from his family. Six years before

Shelley's birth, Mary Wollstonecraft visited Eton and found the school environment intolerable, confirming her preference for day schools that avoided separation from the family.[16] Shelley had more positive experiences later at Eton, but he never accepted the Eton society and "certainly was not happy" there.[17] Peacock reported that Shelley often spoke of Eton "and of the persecutions he had endured from the elder boys, with feelings of abhorrence" only equal to those he had for Lord Chancellor Eldon. As for fagging, "Shelley was a subject totally unfit for the practice in its best form, and he seems to have experienced it in its worst."[18]

Mary Shelley stated that at Eton Shelley "had to undergo aggravated miseries from his systematic and determined resistance to . . . fagging . . . Shelley would never obey. . . . [T]his . . . was the cause of whatever persecutions might attend him, both at school and in his future life."[19] She recalled that in addition to having an electrical machine at Field Place, at Eton Shelley spent his "pocket money" on "chemical apparatus" and books about "magic & witchcraft." Shelley, having had permission at home to sit among the bones in the "charnel house," at Eton tried to "raise a ghost" after stealing away at midnight from his master's house. Taking a proscribed skull, and fearing "the devil" might be following him, "Colossus like," he stood astride a stream repeating "his charm" and "drank thrice from the scull—no ghost appeared."[20]

Recollections of Shelley by his Eton schoolmates several decades after his death picture him having suffered physical and emotional humiliation from his peers. One sympathetic account of the bullying Shelley endured was by Edward C. Hawtrey, three years Shelley's senior at Eton and later headmaster there.[21] Hawtrey, bullied and almost suffocated by an older student,[22] described Shelley as "a stripling pale and lustrous-eyed" whose refusal to fag and indifference to games and the daily regimen made him an object of bullying and of "Shelley-baits," when he would often be chased "up town." Hawtrey felt that "what Shelley had to endure at Eton made him a perfect devil."[23] This abusive, humiliating baiting was recalled by Shelley's Eton friend, W. H. Merle:

> Shelley was a boy never to be forgotten. He stood apart from the whole school. . . . [T]here is not a man of them living who does not remember Shelley for his wild and marked peculiarity. . . . [H]e dwelt in my memory as one of those strange and unearthly compounds which . . . appear in "human form divine," . . . Either from natural delicacy of

frame or from possessing a mind which in boyhood busied itself in grasping at thoughts beyond his age—probably from something of both—he shunned and despised the usual games and exercises of youth. This made him with other boys a byword and a jest. He was known as "Mad Shelley;"—and many a cruel torture was practiced upon him for his moody and singular exclusiveness.

[We] deemed him as one ranging between madness and folly . . . until one who lived in the same house with Shelley . . . told me that in "Mad Shelley" there were seeds to overflowing of meditation deep and of that wild originality which is the attribute of genius. . . . "Mr. Hester" . . . was [a] professor of pothooks and hangers [with whom] Percy Bysshe Shelley was placed . . . if I remember rightly, Shelley made no friends at Eton. He probably sought, but in vain, for a spirit congenial to his own . . . the mass . . . deemed him mad, and he despised them as fools. Singly they dared not insult him . . . but the herd unite against the stricken,— and boys, like men, envy the strongest and trample on the weak.

. . . [on occasion] poor Shelley's anguish and excitement bordered on the sublime. Conscious of his own superiority—of being the reverse of what the many deemed him—stung by the injustice of imputed madness, by the cruelty . . . his rage became boundless. Like Tasso's jailer, his heartless tyrants all but raised up the demon which they said was in him. I have seen him surrounded, hooted, baited like a maddened bull,—and at this distance of time I seem to hear ringing in my ears the cry which Shelley was wont to utter in his paroxysm of revengeful anger.

. . . it was the practice to assemble under the cloisters . . . some wicked wag would introduce a foot-ball . . . and the cloistered square would echo with shouts and laughter as some hapless "dandy" . . . nailed . . . received a blow from the muddy, bounding ball. Poor Shelley, though anything but a fop, was often marked to this trial of temper. But there was another practice infinitely more galling. The particular name of some particular boy would be sounded by one, taken up by another and another, until hundreds echoed and echoed the name . . . The Shelley! Shelley! Shelley! which was thundered in the cloisters was but too often accompanied by practical jokes,—such as knocking his books from under his arm, seizing them as he stooped to recover them, pulling and tearing his clothes, or pointing with the finger, as one Neapolitan maddens another. The result was, as stated, a paroxysm of anger which made his eyes flash like a tiger's, his cheeks grow pale as death, his limbs quiver, and his hair stand on end.[24]

Merle recalled Shelley's fascination with science and that he avidly bought "small electrical machines" from "Old Walker" of Syon House days. Shelley "nearly blew up himself and Mr. Hexter's house into the bargain." Andrew Amos, one of the three lower-forms boys at Hexter's in addition to Shelley, remembered they had the same fagmaster, Henry Mathews. Amos, saying Shelley was "transported with a love of chemical experiments," recalled a more buoyant Shelley in the early Eton years:

> Shelley and I used to amuse ourselves in composing plays, and act-ing them before the other lower boys,—who constituted our sole audi-ence. Shelley entered with great vivacity into this amusement; I think I hear, as if it were yesterday, Shelley singing, with buoyant cheerful-ness in which he indulged, as he might be running nimbly up and down stairs, the Witches' songs in "Macbeth." From this period my intimacy with him slackened . . . we now seldom walked or boated together in the hours between schooltimes. He used to call me Apurist; indicating . . . one who did not appreciate properly the element of fire.[25]

Shelley's fire fascination was captured in a poem composed by a fellow student years later:

> Full oft, beneath the blazing summer noon,
> The sun's convergent rays with dire address,
> He turned on some old tree, and burnt it soon
> To ashes; oft at eve the fire balloon,
> Inflated by his skill, would mount on high;[26]

John Taylor Coleridge, Shelley's contemporary in the fifth form, wrote in 1818, "At Eton, we remember him notorious for setting fire to old trees with burning glasses." By 1875 the story was that the "stump of the willow thus destroyed by Shelley stands in the north-ernmost point of the South Meadow."[27] Medwin's report, that Shel-ley "had blown himself up at Eton," possibly referred to this inci-dent or to chemical experiments in his room.[28]

Despite being constantly goaded "into a rage," Shelley would not pursue his fleeing tormentors and at times generously helped them with their lessons when asked.[29] His intense rage apparently helped deter boys from engaging him in individual combat. He of-ten related to close friends and family an incident in which he stabbed a student at Eton. Peacock recalled Shelley told him "he had been provoked into striking a penknife through the hand of one of his young tyrants, and pinning it to the desk, and that this was the cause of his leaving Eton prematurely: but his imagination often presented past events to him as they might have been, not as they were."[30]

Any early departure from Eton, reported by Leigh Hunt and others, probably was one of two possible expulsions Shelley mentioned in an 1812 letter: "I was expelled twice, but recalled by the interference of my father."[31] One of these "expulsions" may have involved an "illness," considered below, the other may have involved the stabbing, perhaps provoked by a dare stemming from his resistance to oppression.[32] Mary Shelley often heard Shelley "relate the story of stabbing an Upper Boy with a fork. . . . He always described it in my hearing as an almost involuntary act, done on the spur of anguish . . . as the boy was going out of the room."[33] Shelley's anguish at Eton was part of his long-felt childhood sense of alienation, a "rejection pattern with deep roots."[34]

Pugilistic inexperience may not have deterred Shelley from trying his luck in boxing matches. A schoolmate with an unreliable memory recounted that a younger boy (a future baronet) challenged Shelley who, overconfident after the first round, strode around the ring during the break declaiming Homer in Greek. After a stomach blow the next round, Shelley bolted the ring. A more credible report was of a younger student eager to make his mark on the older Shelley. The challenger's Eton record notes: "Son of a tailor in the Strand. He fought Shelley at school and was soundly beaten."[35]

Shelley's few lasting friendships at Eton, a small circle sharing his creative interests, included C. R. Summer, whose novel, *The White Nun,* was published in 1808–1809, and a top classical scholar, named Price, possibly his closest friend.[36] According to Mary Shelley, the older boys and the masters disliked Shelley but he was "adored" by his age-mates.[37] His later friend at Oxford, Thomas Jefferson Hogg, noted that Shelley's Eton acquaintances dropped by his rooms but Shelley did not pursue these relationships.

Repeating his Syon House escapades, Shelley boated on the upper reaches of the Thames and participated in a regatta. He also took part in the Montem processions and ceremonies of 1805 and 1809, traditional Eton events relished by George III in nearby Windsor Castle. In the first, Shelley was a pole-bearer dressed as a midshipman in blue jacket, white trousers, silk stockings, and pumps. For the second Montem, with his own pole-bearers, he dressed as a full corporal.[38] Shelley bought fine clothes and could cut a very dapper figure in his proper attire. Sartorially in step with current gentlemen's fashions, he was usually relaxed if not careless in how he wore his fine attire, appearing with open shirt, undone shoes, and often unruly long hair. Years later, he still carried off this sophisticated "schoolboy's" informality.[39] His passion for chemical experiments at Eton and Oxford, with possible medicinal purposes, left acid stains and burns on his clothing. One Eton associate, Charles Packe, recalled "Shelley was too peculiar in his genius and his habits to be 'the hare with many friends': but the few who knew him loved him, and, if I may judge from myself, remember him with affectionate regret that his schooldays were more adventurous than happy." One schoolmate later derided Shelley at Eton as "wild-looking, slovenly, dirty . . ."[40]

The son of Shelley's schoolmate, Edmund Leslie, supposed his father was:

> Shelley's best and dearest friend: the one who appreciated his genius more than any other boy except Charles Ball [later a well-known dandy]. . . . They were in the same house, as were also Ball and Lord Howe. . . . Shelley and my father were both suspected [probably incorrectly] of having put a bulldog into Dr. Keate's desk. . . . Shelley used to be fond of composing poems and dramas, and the boys often invited him to rehearse these productions with a mock interest, and then, just when he thought the audience were thoroughly enraptured, burst out into fits of laughter. Though the trick had been played on him frequently, he still could always be induced to incur its repetition. . . . My father often tried to console him . . . but Shelley wandered alone, generally with a book, for hours together, day after day, learning verses or composing them.[41]

Another Eton friend, Walter Halliday, was a clergyman in 1857 when he wrote to the poet's idolatrous daughter-in-law, Lady Shelley, perhaps the most endearing description of his classmate. Halliday evoked some of the nascent poet's inner world at about age sixteen:

> Many a long walk have I had with him in the beautiful neighborhood of dear old Eton. We used to wander for hours about Clewer, Frogmore, the Park at Windsor, the Terrace; and I was a delighted and willing listener to his marvelous stories of fairyland, and apparitions, and spirits, and haunted ground; and his speculations were then (for his mind was far more developed than mine) of the world beyond the grave. Another of his favorite rambles was Stoke Park, and the picturesque churchyard, where Gray is said to have written his Elegy, of which he was very fond. . . . I loved Shelley for his kindliness and affectionate ways: he was not made to endure the rough and boisterous pastime at Eton, for

his was a disposition that needed especial personal superintendence, to watch, and cherish, and direct all his noble aspirations, and the remarkable tenderness of his heart. He had great moral courage, and feared nothing, but what was base, and false, and low. He never joined in the usual sports of the boys. . . . [This account] will please you as a sincere, and truthful, and humble tribute to one whose good name was sadly whispered away . . . in the autumn of 1814, in London . . . he was glad to introduce me to his wife. I think he said, he was just come from Ireland.[42]

Despite the reasonable speculation that "his girlish good looks" probably elicited "homosexual overtures,"[43] at Eton Shelley was coping with his growing erotic feelings for the opposite sex. Years later, meeting an Eton schoolmate, Shelley asked him if he remembered "the beautiful Martha, the Hebe of Spires's? She was the loveliest girl I ever saw, and I loved her to distraction."[44]

Shelley's later strong aversion to prostitution perhaps resulted from his probable first experience of sexual intercourse at Eton. Numerous prostitutes around Eton provided sexual initiation for the students, Shelley's "untaught foresters" in *Epipsychidion*. Prostitutes gave a certain notoriety to the College's reputation by the late eighteenth century. A number of observers, including Mary Wollstonecraft in *The Wrongs of Woman,* commented that prostitutes at Eton provided the students' sexual baptism. Eton historians noted published reports in 1798 that the boys "wenched" as part of the sexual immorality of the school.[45] Public schools at that time often had a physician informally on hand to deal with the boys' venereal infections.

The first speculation about the effects of Shelley's earliest sexual contact was in Thornton Hunt's 1863 memoir of the poet. Leigh Hunt's eldest, most gifted child, Thornton, was a favorite of Shelley. He was about seven and twelve, respectively, when he knew Shelley first in England and later in Italy. Thornton, whose parents were intimates of Shelley, believed the reminiscences about Shelley were too full of "delicacy and discretion." Thornton wished that his father, Mary, or others with whom Shelley talked most intimately "had related some of the more extravagant incidents of his early life exactly as they occurred [to] better understand the tenor of his thought." He believed that Shelley at Eton "was a more practical and impracticable mutineer than his friends have allowed," in regard to fagging, for instance. He thought they were too anxious to "soften his 'faults'; and the consequence is, that we miss the force of the boy's logic and the vigour of his Catonian experiments." As a corrective, Thornton wrote this account of the impact of Shelley's earliest heterosexual experimentation in "early youth" during "college life," probably Eton, not Oxford, as often assumed: "accident has made me aware of facts which give me to understand . . . that . . . Shelley did not go scatheless . . . in tampering with the venal pleasures, his health was seriously, and not transiently, injured." The account continues, "The effect was far greater on his mind than on his body . . . principally marked by horror and antagonism . . . he felt bound to denounce the mischief from which he saw others suffer more severely than himself. . . . I have no doubt that he himself would have spoken even plainer language, though to me his language is perfectly transparent." Thornton Hunt believed Shelley was "restrained" in talking more bluntly about his experience because of his "superstitious notion . . . that the true escape from the pestilent and abhorrent brutalities which he detected around him in 'real' life is found in 'the ideal' form of thought and language."[46]

These remarks may well refer to an important, puzzling sexual episode and its aftermath. Shelley's strong feelings about the experience led him to deal with it directly and indirectly in his poetry. A passage in *Epipsychidion* about "One whose voice was venomed melody" (1.256) is usually interpreted as referring to this sexual encounter, possibly with a prostitute, resulting in a venereal infection and "hair grown grey / O'er a young brow."(ll.264–65) Thornton Hunt stated unequivocally that this passage "is a plain and only too intelligible reference to the college experiences to which I have alluded. . . . [She was a] venal, hideous, and fatal simulacram; and he indicates even the material consequences to himself in his injured aspect and hair touched with gray."[47] At that time, venereal disease was thought to cause premature grayness of the hair. Cameron, believing Hunt's deduction about this passage in *Epipsychidion* "clearly justified," pointed out that the youthful poet in *Alastor* had the same premature graying of hair, Shelley's feature mentioned by Medwin and Hunt, and evident in Williams's portrait of the poet.[48] Cameron thought Shelley probably contracted gonorrhea, but Crook and Guiton, in an extensive analysis, considered either gonorrhea or syphilis was possible. In Shelley's day, the two were confused; gonorrhea was often considered a prior manifestation of syphilis.[49]

The sexual overkill in the *Epipsychidion* lines—including "venomed melody," "blue nightshade" (a poisonous plant, bittersweet, then considered an anti-syphilitic),[50] "electric poison," "flames Out of her looks into my vitals came," "killing air," "pierced like honey-dew . . . my green heart," and "ruins of unreasonable time"—are part of the complex venereal disease imagery pervading Shelley's writing.[51] Similar imagery of disease-and-death-producing female sexuality occur in *Laon and Cythna* (VI.xlviii), where "venom" combines with imagery of two of his most vivid symbols, the snake and the scorpion. The former's phallic seductiveness is matched by the scorpion's association with lust and venereal disease, as Shelley knew from reading Pliny at Eton and his familiarity with *Chambers' Cyclopaedia,* in which the scorpion's sting was considered a cause of syphilis.[52] In his first Gothic novel, *Zastrozzi,* written at Eton, the scorpion appeared in an erotic passage. In his early poem, *Queen Mab,* venom is repeatedly mentioned in relation to venereal disease, including "prostitution's venomed bane."

Shelley first began to write of the iniquities of the double standard and prostitution while at Eton. That this sexual episode, and its probable venereal infection aftermath, likely occurred at Eton finds support in an analysis of Shelley's autobiographical unfinished story, *Una Favola.*[53] In this fable, a fifteen-year-old youth loves an enchantress, but "soon perceived that she was more false than any Siren." For a whole year he was "nourished by the fruit of a certain tree . . . a food sweet and bitter at once, which being cold as ice to the lips, appeared fire in the veins."[54] Shelley later wrote that homosexual Greek love was not "more horrible than the usual intercourse endured by almost every youth of England with a diseased and insensible prostitute."[55] Leigh Hunt wrote that England's "unhappy mass of prostitution . . . was always one of the subjects that at a moment's notice would overshadow the liveliest of [Shelley's] moods."[56] This attitude, and his aversion to certain pastimes of his peers, might suggest Shelley's experience was with a "ruined" girl of good family he was attracted to out of sympathy.[57] Leigh Hunt told the anecdote that Shelley, at a ball probably during his Eton years, "with an air of consolation and tenderness," made it a point to dance with a young lady known to have been sexually taken advantage of and who was being ostracized as "the object of all the virtuous scorn" by others in the room.[58]

The date of this relationship in *Una Favola,* the "dawn of the fifteenth spring of his life," either spring 1807 or spring 1808, was before his romantic interest in his cousin Harriet Grove, which probably began in August 1808. The references to the well and fountain also indicate this sexual experience occurred at Eton. A favorite beauty spot for Etonians, including Shelley, was the Chalvey or Queen Anne's Well, in nearby Slough.[59] In *Epipsychidion,* Shelley, alluding to his first sexual effort in "the clear golden prime of my youth's dawn" (l.193), called himself one of "those untaught foresters" who, "stumbling in my weakness and my haste," encountered the one with the "venomed melody"(ll.251–56). Shelley may have responded to this encounter by being sent home sick. His sister Hellen recalled: "I went to school before Margaret, so that she recollects how Bysshe came home in the midst of the half-year to be nursed; and when he was allowed to leave the house, he came to the dining-room window, and kissed her through the pane of glass. She remembers his face there, with nose and lips pressed against the window, and at that time she must have been about five years old."[60]

If Margaret was five, Shelley would have been fourteen or fifteen. It has been suggested that if Shelley had a venereal disease, he kissed his sister through a pane of glass because he was kept in isolation for fear of contaminating his siblings. Among the erroneous notions of the time about the transmission of syphilis was that it was spread by breath.[61] Whatever his illness, his parents' view that he was mentally disturbed was passed on to his sisters. One of Shelley's elderly surviving sisters, evading enquiries about her brother, reportedly responded, "between you and me, our dear brother Bysshe was a little mad."[62]

Among Shelley's inadequate masters and tutors at Eton, the well-meaning Goodall perhaps provided some intellectual impetus. Shelley found the man he needed in Dr. James Lind, a semi-retired Edinburgh-trained physician living in nearby Windsor. Lind mentored those Etonians interested in science. Ironically, the poet who hated monarchy found this personal physician of George III as his important father surrogate. Shelley possibly first met Lind by going to him for treatment of an illness, perhaps a venereal infection.[63]

Lind, sixty-eight and a widower when Shelley entered Eton, like many physicians of the time was a "natural philosopher" with broad scientific, esthetic, and cultural interests. His friend Fanny Burney—later Madame d'Arblay—who had served Queen Charlotte at Windsor Castle, described Lind as tall and slender, "a mere lath."[64] All agreed the extraordinary Dr. Lind had a gentle and sweet disposition. Shelley's fondness for Lind stemmed from the doctor's personality and from his wide-ranging scientific, offbeat interests. According to Fanny Burney, Lind "follows, as much as he can get practice, his profession, but his taste for tricks, conundrums, and queer things, makes people fearful of his trying experiments upon their constitutions, and think him a better conjuror than physician; though I don't know why the same man should not be both."[65] A latter-day Paracelsus, Lind—and his apparatus-filled study—embodied Shelley's childhood fantasies of the attic alchemist of Field Place. Lind constructed an "Earthquake Machine" (seismograph), an anemometer, and a "Thunder House" for studying Franklin's lightning rod. He suggested using electricity to cure insanity and, possibly influencing a key idea in *Frankenstein*, employed electrical stimulation to animate dead frogs.[66] A friend of Captain James Cook, Lind accompanied Sir Joseph Banks on the Royal Society Iceland expedition of 1772. Among his acquaintances and correspondents were Benjamin Franklin, David Hume, William Herschel, and James Watt. There are many parallels between Lind's interests and those Shelley developed, but both already had a fondness for air balloons when they met. The Iceland Banks expedition had conquered the volcano Hecla, and Lind's talk of this feat would have been much more vivid for Shelley than his father's pallid picture of Vesuvius at Field Place. Lind possibly was one precursor of Demogorgon in his volcanic lair in *Prometheus Unbound*.

Lind, a collector of drawings and antiquities, was an accomplished botanist. His keen interests in science and technology undoubtedly deepened Shelley's passion deriving from Adam Walker's lectures. A fellow of the Royal Society from 1777, Lind read and published papers on eclipses of the moon, wind gauges, and the transit of Venus. He found the true latitude of Islay and made a beautiful map of that island. One can imagine the echoes of his talks with Shelley about these diverse interests as the poet in later years infused imagery of plants, wind, moon, stars, clouds, India, volcanoes, and isles into his major poetry. Lind had his own private press at Windsor; some of the books he wrote and printed were described as mysterious little books printed from characters he invented, called "Lindian Ogham." Lind made his library available to Shelley and Lind probably first introduced his young friend to Godwin's works, including the novel *St. Leon* and *Political Justice*, which Shelley read either at Eton or shortly thereafter. Lind's influence may have extended to introducing Shelley to—or encouraging further study of—Plato, Pliny, Lucretius, Paracelsus, Albertus Magnus, and Condorcet. Headmaster Keate possibly also helped promote Shelley's enduring fondness for Lucretius.[67] Medwin noted that Shelley translated a substantial part of Pliny's formidable *Natural History* under Lind's guidance.[68] Perhaps because of Lind, Medwin said Shelley "swore by" Franklin's ideas, including the notion that the mind affects the body and that the decay of the human body could be slowed by mental activity and medical advances. These ideas coincided with the beginning of Shelley's hypochondriacal preoccupations about his psychosomatic illnesses, which began to flourish at Eton.

Mary Shelley's vignette about Shelley's feelings for Lind expresses clearly the paternal void he was called upon to fill:

> He became intimate, also, at Eton with a man whom he never mentioned, except in terms of the tenderest respect. This was Dr. Lind, a name well known among the professors of medical science. "This man," he often said, "is exactly what an old man ought to be. Free, calmspirited, full of benevolence, and even of youthful ardor; tempered, as it had ever been, by his amiable mind. I owe to that man far, ah! far more than I owe to my father; he loved me, and I shall never forget our long talks, where he breathed the spirit of the kindest tolerance and the purest wisdom."[69]

Lind also may have provided his protégé a more caustic form of inspiration, cursing his monarch. Hogg claimed that Lind, believing George III had treated him like a stepson, would recite an oath that his young disciple transformed into a curse upon his father.[70]

Mary, accurately recounting "my Shelley's words," told of how Lind crucially intervened to thwart Timothy's intent to have his son placed in a mental institution:

> Once, when I was very ill during the holidays, as I was recovering from a fever which had attacked my brain, a servant overheard my father consult about sending me to a private madhouse. I was a favourite among all our servants, so this fellow came and told me as I lay sick in bed. My horror was beyond words, and I might soon have been mad in-

deed, if they had proceeded in their iniquitous plan. I was master of three pounds in money, and, with the servant's help, I contrived to send an express to Dr. Lind. He came, and I shall never forget his manner on that occasion. His profession gave him authority; his love for me ardour. He dared my father to execute his purpose, and his menaces had the desired effect.[71]

Shelley's acute disturbance fostered his not unfounded feelings that his father wanted him removed as heir to the family fortune, like Timothy's "lunatic" great-uncle John Shelley. Shelley's illness apparently was one of two emotional crises during the Eton period. Both so profoundly affected Shelley that he dealt with them in a number of his poems, most obviously in Laon and Cythna (Cantos 3 and 4). These two episodes may be behind Shelley's statement that he was "expelled" twice from Eton, or to a later story that he did not complete his stay at Eton.[72] Shelley, possibly away from Eton for an extended period in 1809, that Easter wrote a friend from Field Place that, feeling bored, it was "a most excellent time to go mad for want of better employment."[73]

The first episode alluded to in Laon and Cythna occurred about 1807–1808, the second about 1809–1810. The first disturbance in Laon and Cythna resembled an acute, psychotic-like episode of paranoid, persecutory anxiety, the second a depression. Both follow the separation of the young hero, Laon, from his abducted, twelve-year-old sister, Cythna. Reminiscent of the Eton stabbing incident, Laon stabs "with one impulse" three of Cythna's captors. The therapeutic relief from his madness is provided by an old Hermit, obviously a Lind figure.

Laon's first madness vividly portrays clinical depersonalization, a state often associated with the onset of schizophrenia. Shelley's remarkable description of a depersonalization experience in Laon and Cythna starts with, "My brain began to fail" as "a fearful sleep" of his "riven soul, sent its foul dreams to sweep / With whirlwind swiftness—a fall far and deep" into "A gulf, a void, a sense of senselessness." His hallucinatory vision, "the forms which peopled this terrific trance," is "like a choir of devils" whose "Foul, ceaseless shadows" are "All shapes like mine own self, hideously multiplied." (3:22–23) The third canto's most vivid images reflect cannibalistic, persecutory fantasies. The stabbing scene starkly suggests a homosexual gang rape, perhaps a real or feared sodomy experience at Eton.

The Lind-Hermit's repeated psychotherapeutic power in Laon's second episode of madness (Canto 4) may relate to Shelley's presumed venereal disease. This "milder madness" is a depression "Which darkened nought but time's unquiet flow / With supernatural shades of clinging sadness," resulting from dwelling upon the loss of Cythna. That Shelley described Laon as having two differing episodes of madness strongly suggests their autobiographical character. This depressive reaction may have been in response to the loss of his cousin Harriet Grove, who terminated their engagement against his wishes late in his tenure at Eton. In this second madness, Shelley presents the Lind-Hermit as protopsychoanalyst, replete with Laon on a "sick couch." The "gentle Hermit in my helpless woe," as physician, "healed" Laon and then applied his psychotherapeutic technique, described with remarkable clarity:

> He knew his soothing words to weave with skill
>   From all my madness told; like mine own heart,
> Of Cythna would he question me, until
>   That thrilling name had ceased to make me start, . . .
>
> Thus slowly from my brain the darkness rolled,
>   My thought their due array did re-assume
> Through the enchantments of that Hermit old
>
> (4:6–7)

Lind seemingly appears again as both psychotherapist and medical healer of Shelley's venereal disease as Zonoras, in *Athanase*, Shelley's self-portrait fragment poem.[74] The first, major fragment is an analysis of the depression ("Sorrow deep & shadowy & unknown") of Athanase, a youth "grown quite weak & grey before his time." Phrases linking a "secret crime" with "hope-consuming shame" and "evil joys which fire the vulgar breast" are strikingly similar to lines of another Athanase manuscript fragment[75] that suggest Lind attended to Shelley's venereal problem: "And when the old man saw that [?on] the [ ] green / Leaves of his opening . . . a blight had lighted," lines couched in Shelley's characteristic allusive, metaphorical style.

Shelley's medical experience with Lind may have influenced his use of drugs, probably begun at Eton, and his fondness for self-medication. His later friend Edward Trelawny recorded: "At Eton, after an illness, the doctor [Lind] who attended him took a liking to him, and Shelley borrowed his medical books and was deeply interested in chemistry from that time . . . he experimented with some of the drugs on himself. The power of laudanum to soothe pain and give rest especially delighted him; he was cautioned, and knew it was wrong; the seductive power of that drug retained a hold on him during the rest of his life, used with extreme caution at first and at long intervals."[76]

Trelawny clearly implied that Shelley, from Eton days, habitually used laudanum, the tincture of opium commonly consumed throughout England. Trelawny did not mention arsenic, used then to treat syphilis. Once at Eton, Shelley "inadvertently" swallowed too much arsenic and apparently later used it at Oxford.[77] Trelawny wrote that Shelley, despite warnings, continued to use laudanum on those "rare occasions when in deep dejection." Despite Shelley's initial cautious use, "he so overdosed himself"— once in London and once in Italy—that his life was threatened. He further pointed out that Shelley "was impatient of remonstrance" about using drugs "and so made a mystery of it." Trelawny believed laudanum's effect can be found "in some of Shelley's flights of imagination, and fancies of supernatural appearances." He also believed, as did at least one of Shelley's physicians, that Shelley's painful spasms in his adult years were due to overdoses of this drug. Trelawny's was a fine line between frankness and discretion in discussing Shelley's early drug use at Eton. He would become Shelley's confidant about drugs and poison.

Shelley did not have the drug addiction of Coleridge and De Quincey. It has been reasonably argued that Shelley was sporadically "compulsive and immoderate" in using drugs and that his biographers have underestimated his drug dependency.[78] Shelley, avoiding hard liquor and drinking wine only in moderation, advanced no such strictures against drugs. Medwin, alluding to Shelley's self-destructive trends in slipshod chemical "operations" that "seemed . . . to promise nothing but disaster," may have been implying that Shelley's experience of having "blown himself up" was a suicidal gesture. Medwin repeated Hogg's words that Shelley believed swallowing poison had "seriously injured his health, and from the effects of which he should never recover." His self-medication by chemical experimentation at Eton would intensify at Oxford.[79]

6

Gothic "Wild Boy" and Harriet Grove

Two crucial family events in March 1806 had important consequences for the thirteen-year-old Etonian. His brother John was born and his grandfather became Sir Bysshe, Baronet of Castle Goring. After the Duke of Norfolk nominated old Bysshe for a baronetcy in February 1806, Timothy corresponded with the family's lawyer, William Whitton, about creating the family's pedigree.[1] Always the dutiful son, Timothy wrote Whitton that his father, not wanting to be bothered, placed the baronetcy matter in Whitton's hands. Timothy would do whatever Whitton wished. The contrasting personalities of Timothy and Whitton were in their signatures; the former's soft and rounded, the latter's large with rapier-like strokes.

Timothy wrote a note stating that the patent establishing the baronetcy had been completed in 1786. It could not be advanced until the younger Pitt's death in early 1806 yielded the short-lived Whig "Ministry of All the Talents." Norfolk's ally, Secretary of State Charles James Fox, provided the Duke an opportunity to recognize the Shelleys' political contributions. Fox died that September, leaving a legacy of abolition of the slave trade, supported by Norfolk and strong abolitionist sentiment in Horsham. This Whig background contributed to Shelley's hatred of slavery and to his cautious stand about immediate slave emancipation.[2]

Perhaps it was not accidental that the baronetcy and a new son arrived at the same time. Timothy, troubled with gout and concerned about young Bysshe's behavior at Syon House and Eton, possibly had misgivings about his son's reliability as an heir. It had been almost five years since Elizabeth's last child, and John's arrival probably fulfilled Timothy's wish, however unconscious, for another male heir. Shelley may have sensed this desire in his father. His belief that his father wished to put him away in an asylum would not be his last fear that Timothy wanted him out of the way by committing, in the words of a later commentator, "any other legal crime to secure his end."[3]

Little is known about Shelley's relationship with John. Hellen left an account of a playfully aggressive older brother repeatedly pushing his gleeful little petticoat-clad brother "gently down" on the lawn and, pulling him in a carriage, upsetting him into a strawberry bed. The unhurt child's screams "brought sympathetic aid" and a rebuke for "Bit," as his "culprit" brother was called by John. Bysshe delighted in teaching his brother "schoolboy words," including "Debbee!" for the devil.[4] The censure of the future author of an essay, *On the Devil, and Devils,* for being rough with his new rival was one of several rebukes Hellen recalled. Shelley was exiled from Field Place before John was old enough to become a convert to his brother's radical beliefs.

While at Eton, Bysshe's bonding to his sister Elizabeth perhaps was heightened by the intrusions he felt his father inflicted upon her. One such incident, probably in 1810, involved the Duke's "corporation," a political front that included Timothy Shelley and the Horsham lawyers, Thomas Medwin senior and Robert Hurst. This incident, "An absorbing glimpse into the domestic interior of the Shelley family,"[5] undoubtedly was conveyed to Hogg by Shelley:

> A friend of mine, an Eton man, told me that his father once invited some corporation to dine at his house, and that he was present. When the dinner was over and the gentlemen nearly drunk, they started up, he said, and swore they would all kiss his sisters. His father laughed, and did not forbid them; and the wretches would have done it; but his sisters heard of the infamous proposal, ran upstairs, and locked themselves in their bedrooms. I asked him if he would not have knocked them down if they had attempted such an outrage in his presence. It seems to me that a man of spirit ought to have killed them if they effected their purpose. The sceptical philosopher [Shelley] sat for several minutes in silence, his cheeks glowing with intense indignation.[6]

Shelley would soon attack such patriarchal sexual attitudes in his two Gothic novels.

Bysshe at this time began his lifelong pattern of encouraging women in his life to share his enthusiasm for writing. He and his sister Elizabeth wrote a play together and each composed poems published in 1810 as *Original Poetry by Victor and Cazire.* Hellen recalled her brother gave her lessons in writing poetry and that he had some of her poems printed with her name on the title page.[7]

One person the sibling poets addressed in *Original Poetry* was their cousin, Harriet Grove, to whom Bysshe had become attracted in 1808.[8] His cousin Tom Medwin believed that none surpassed or "could compete with her" beauty. "She was like one of Shakespeare's women—like some Madonna of Raphael."[9] The resemblance of Bysshe and Harriet Grove—her mother and his were sisters—perhaps was echoed years later in Shelley's poem of "two cousins, almost like twins."[10]

Because Ferne, the Wiltshire Grove ancestral estate near Shaftesbury, was one hundred miles from Field Place, family visits were infrequent. However, early in the nineteenth century the Groves stopped once a year to see the Shelleys on the way to visit their sons in London. Harriet's father Thomas Grove's pedigree dated from the fourteenth century. Having inherited the family estates and becoming an officer in the militia, he sired eleven children in fourteen years, of whom eight survived to adulthood. The staunch, traditional Grove family structure proved to be too tough for the developing young radical at Field Place to crack.

Harriet, the sixth Grove child (b. June 26, 1791), was a little more than a year older than her cousin Bysshe. The two cousins perhaps met as young children but their first recorded meeting was in the spring of 1803, when ten-year-old Bysshe was at Syon House. Harriet's younger brother, Charles, recalled:

> The first time I ever saw Bysshe was when I was at Harrow. I was nine years old; my brother George, ten. We took him up to Brentford, where he was at school, at Dr. Greenlaw's; a servant of my father's taking care of us all. He accompanied us to Ferne, and spent the Easter holidays there. The only circumstance I can recollect in connection with the visit was, that Bysshe, who was some years older than we were, thought it would be a good service to play carpenters, and, under his auspices, we got the carpenter's axes, and cut down some of father's young fir trees in the park. My father often used to remind me of that circumstance.[11]

Bysshe's preadolescent acting-out, not a promising introduction to the father of his future beloved, signaled the mischief to be expected from this Shelley trickster. After Bysshe's Easter 1803 visit, the Grove family probably visited Field Place the summer of 1805, a date carefully attached to his later love poem stating that Harriet's and Bysshe's souls would be forever bound together.[12]

This poem, and Harriet's diary, suggest an adolescent romance between the two cousins began in earnest in August 1808 during a

Grove family visit to Field Place en route to their London Lincoln's Inn Fields residence. This summer visit may have been the first time young Bysshe and Harriet walked to the nearby Elizabethan mansion, Hills Place, called St. Irvyne.

As 1808 ended, Harriet began an 1809 diary, a New Year's gift from her mother. Her first entries, before New Year's day, made clear she and Bysshe were corresponding. This diary, and that of 1810, record the two years that her relationship with Bysshe waxed and waned. After her first entry, "I have heard that Aunt Shelley gave a Ball on Friday–30th 1808," Harriet began writing—and later thoroughly crossed out—a reference to something "Bysshe" said in a letter, possibly an expression of his love.[13] Her 1809 New Year's desire to see him again at "delightful" Field Place was thwarted but her brother John, after a week's January visit at Field Place, told Harriet "a great deal about the Shelleys." During January, Harriet received at least one letter from Bysshe every five days. She occasionally noted her less frequent letters, writing, "Bysshe will get my letter today." In the first nine months of 1809, Harriet recorded forty-four letters she received from Bysshe and twenty she wrote him.

The only time she saw Bysshe in 1809 was four days in April, during a well-chaperoned family visit in London. Given that Bysshe had just turned sixteen and Harriet was seventeen when their romance bloomed in 1808, and that their letters (now lost) were the main form of contact, theirs was destined to be a fantasy-laden relationship. Harriet's doubly censored diary gives only fleeting intimations of her feelings. She kept her entries guarded to foil prying family eyes and—after their relationship ended—crossed out and obliterated references to Bysshe. Her diary is aptly described as the provincial life of "a character in Jane Austen's novels."[14]

Harriet's growing attachment to Bysshe in early 1809 was reinforced by the absence or loss of most of her siblings, leaving her and her older sister Charlotte rather lonely at rural Ferne. Harriet's next younger sister, Marianne, died tragically in 1806 when her dress caught fire. Emma, a year older than Harriet, married at sixteen and was no longer at home. Her youngest sister, Louisa, away at school, would die in 1810 of whooping cough and excessive bloodletting.[15] Harriet's five brothers were away from home, three in the navy, including her younger brothers George and Charles, and her older brother, William, who joined the Royal Navy at age nine.[16] Only her oldest brother Thomas was married. He was living on the Grove ten-thousand-acre estate in Cwm Elan, Wales. Harriet's older brother John, living in London, was studying medicine.

Harriet and Charlotte felt the family pressure to marry. Charlotte, age twenty-six and desperately casting about for a husband, elicited Harriet's diary entry, "Charlotte flirted as usual."[17] The senior Groves perhaps were eager for Harriet to form a more lucrative marriage than Emma, and not be left in the lurch like Charlotte. Her education completed, Harriet dutifully met parental matrimonial expectations with two potential mates, both heirs to family wealth. Her backup for the young, impulsive, radical Bysshe was William Helyar, nearly thirty and oldest son of the Groves' neighbors. By the end of 1811, both Bysshe and Harriet would be married, but not to each other.

Both sets of parents initially supported the developing relationship between the cousins, but at Field Place there was concern about the increasingly problematic Bysshe. Timothy and Elizabeth perhaps hoped a romantic alliance might prove beneficial for their son. Rounding out the cousin matchmaking, Harriet's brother John became interested in Bysshe's lively sister Elizabeth, who invited him to Field Place in July 1809.[18] That May, Timothy added encouragement by giving Harriet a frank to facilitate her correspondence with his son.[19]

Bysshe, with interests beyond Harriet, was establishing his lifestyle of multiple pursuits. Like his father, he was adept at concealing things. His correspondence, including precisely periodic letters to Harriet, was a small part of his increasingly prolific writing, including poetry, novels, dramas, and Gothic romances, not to mention his reading. Shelley's 1809 infatuation with Harriet stimulated his creativity, but his emerging radical religious, sexual, and political beliefs contrasted starkly with those of the conventional Groves.

Among the male friendships Shelley developed in his last years at Eton was James Tisdall (also spelled Tisdale). Bysshe's vacation letters to him from Field Place reveal Timothy's efforts to control his son's social life. Bysshe, in January 1809, wrote Tisdall that Timothy's "punctilios" prevented Bysshe from accepting his invitation for dinner in London. Later, when both youths returned to Eton, Timothy invited Tisdall to the safer confines of Field Place for the Easter vacation. Bysshe apologized to Tisdall that he should have to "perform penance in this temple of Solitude in the dullest time of the year. . . . Dissipation & Pleasure are stagnant at Horsham." He had attended a few balls but "to dissipate the stagnation of my spirits" he wrote letters and "read Novels & Romances all day, till in the Evening I fancy myself a Character."[20] Timothy apparently was concerned about his son's entering into Tisdall's enticing social circles. Tisdall was staying at the Grosvenor Square residence of the Duchess of Sussex, probably with her son. The Duchess's secret marriage to a son of George III was dissolved in 1794, but she was still accorded that name in English society.

As Harriet yearned for "delightful" Field Place in January 1809, her Bysshe again wrote Tisdall thanking him for another invitation to London, "where we could have so much pleasure . . . a thing I have long wished for." He reported that his father vetoed the visit, thinking it inconsistent "with propriety . . . entre nous I think two or three days spent together in London would be productive of much pleasure to both of us." He hoped his friend would join him at Field Place over Easter vacation. The two of them, plus "Il Padre," could "eclipse the Beau's & Belles of the Horsham Ball" and help "enliven our Provincial stupidity."[21] Timothy was sorry, according to Bysshe, that Tisdall avoided dull Field Place. He wrote to his friend, "I have no Employment, except writing Novels & Letters."[22] Back at Eton in May, Shelley wrote a publisher about his novel, *Zastrozzi*, "already written in large portion," which he hoped to finish the end of July.[23]

Shelley's *Zastrozzi* and *St. Irvyne* cannot be dismissed as juvenile effusions, mere imitations and borrowings from others. He later wrote that both novels "serve to mark the state of my mind at the period of their composition."[24] The implicit psychological issues in his two romances meshed with the more explicitly autobiographical poetry he was writing. Further, *Zastrozzi* and *St. Irvyne* expressed his developing beliefs about love and sexual relations freed from the patriarchal power exemplified at Field Place and Ferne. Shelley, aware of the connection between his emotional state and his need to write, later spoke of his "intellectual sickliness and lethargy into which I was plunged two years ago, and of which 'St.Irvyne' and 'Zastrozzi' were the distempered altho unoriginal visions."[25]

Writing Tisdall in April 1809 about "an excellent subject for a poem," Shelley announced he would be in London April 16 (where he was to see Harriet and her family): "observe who I am with . . . you will see me quite wild on the 20th."[26] This meeting, and two back-to-back meetings the following April, were his last direct contacts with Harriet. His sister Hellen's recollections indicate how erratic Shelley's behavior was thought to be at this time. Writing *Zastrozzi*, he was giving a vivid picture of the unconscious conflicts underlying this behavior.

The four days the two families spent together in London April of 1809 included a visit to see Shelley's sisters Mary and Hellen at their Clapham school. Her brother's hypomanic behavior impressed nine-year-old Hellen: "Harriet Grove, his early love, was of the party: how fresh and pretty she was! Her assistance was invoked to keep the wild boy quiet, for he was full of pranks, and upset the port wine on the tray cloth . . . then we all walked in the garden, and there was much ado to calm the spirits of the wild boy."[27]

Timothy Shelley appears in Harriet's journal as a person of negative moods. On April 16 she was "very glad" to see "Dear Bysshe" but "Mr Shelley appears cross—for what reason I do not know." After leaving London, Shelley and Harriet reverted to letter writing until September, when Harriet's diary reveals a break in the relationship was imposed. For the next fifteen months she noted only one letter from Bysshe and two she wrote him. In early August 1809, after receiving a letter from Shelley's sister Elizabeth, Harriet wrote in her diary, "I am afraid Mr Shelley wont ask us to Field Place this Summer."

During the period of prohibited communication—early September 1809 to the following April—Shelley's sister Elizabeth acted as intermediary, exchanging letters with her cousin. Harriet's Aunt Shelley was always glad to hear from her and in October Harriet recorded that Shelley's sister sent "some verses of Bysshe's— which I think very good." Shelley's varied writing projects included his two Gothic novels, his first long poem, *The Wandering Jew*, a number of shorter poems about his agonized relationship with Harriet, and *Original Poetry by Victor and Cazire*.[28] As Christmas 1809 approached, Harriet noted that her sister Louisa heard from Bysshe's sister Mary, age twelve, "that I [Harriet] am going to be married." Mary, looking out for her brother's romantic interests, had learned Harriet was seeing William Helyar.[29] Mary's hunch about Harriet's marital future with Helyar was prescient.

Harriet later tore out the first several pages of her 1810 diary, but wrote in the flyleaf that she and her family will soon go to Field Place. However, only brother John went.[30] Shelley began keeping an 1810 pocket diary at Field Place of his accounts, his writing, and his correspondence. In January he paid Laker the servant and purchased a "knife" and "Dancing gloves." On January 15, "30 copies of Zastrozzi to come—not to forget Harriet," followed by two crosses. Harriet was not the only young lady occupying Shelley's interest. The first several months of 1810 he recorded correspondence with "Emily Sidney," John Shelley-Sidney's nine-year-old daughter, and with "Josephine," as well as payments for "Sally" and for "Miss M's [?Marshall's] music." Back at Eton, he noted in early February paying £2 to "Dr G.," perhaps an early treatment for venereal infection.[31] At this time, Harriet recorded in her diary that her favorite brother, William, wrote to Charlotte, "thinks I shall never be married that I do not care whether I ever do or not, He says he thinks I never liked anyone so much as [———] that is a thing no one will <u>ever know</u> but myself." The name Harriet later deleted undoubtedly was Bysshe's. On February 23, she noted Elizabeth sent "part of Bs poem," possibly *The Wandering Jew,* for which he made Biblical notations in late February in his pocket diary.[32]

Shelley probably did not send Harriet his more explosive "Henry and Louisa," first of several long two-part poems Shelley wrote in late 1809. Its anti-war, anti-religious passages would have been anathema to the Groves. Some lines seem to refer to their attempts to break up his relationship with Harriet. Henry, Shelley's poetic persona, dies on the Mediterranean's Egyptian shore seeking "glory" fighting for Britain, survived by Louisa (the name of Harriet's younger sister), the first of his strong poetic heroines.[33] When Shelley sent a parcel to Harriet in early March she was "Most agreeably surprised" by the parcel and a "letter from my Greatest Friend [———]."[34] She replied to Elizabeth, not Bysshe. When Harriet showed Shelley's poetry to her family later that month, she recorded they "think it nonsense." Two days later she "sent B—— Poem away."

Harriet, pleased that her parents finally agreed to visit Field Place "for one day" on the way to London, happily wrote her cousin Elizabeth the news. The same day, March 28, she acknowledged in her diary that she and Charlotte received from Shelley a copy of *Zastrozzi,* just published. Harriet wrote that her "illnatured" brother "does nothing but abuse B—— Romance."

After a year apart, Harriet and Bysshe met at Field Place in April 1810. Their subsequent meeting in London apparently was not in the offing at this time. Unaware of Bysshe's underlying emotional state, Harriet recorded her puzzlement about his behavior at Field Place. After noting that Bysshe and his family "are all very glad to see us" she added, "I can not tell what to make of it very strange."

In her diary the next day, she wrote: "Still more odd, Walked to Horsham saw the Old House St Irvyne had a long conversation but more perplexed than ever walked in the evening to Strood by moonlight." The next day, leaving this "pleasantest party" for Cuckfield, still perplexed, she wrote, "I still know not what is meant."[35] Perhaps Harriet could not decipher Bysshe's feelings for her. Her parents, cool to the idea of a visit, perhaps misled her by saying she should expect him to exhibit disturbed behavior.[36]

Indeed, her fifteen-year-old brother Charles, who had not seen Bysshe for some years, recalled his cousin's behavior on this visit as exuberant and playful: "Bysshe was at that time more attached to my sister Harriet than I can express, and I recollect well the moonlight walks we four had at Strode, and also at St. Irvyne's." Charles was impressed with his cousin's playful antics:

> I remember on the occasion of our going to the Duke of Norfolk's house, Hills, at Horsham, Bysshe's putting on a working man's dress, and coming to my sister as a beggar, and also taking up one of those very little chests of drawers, peculiar to old houses, such as Hills was, and carrying it off part of the way back to Field Place; and Elizabeth's being in a state of consternation lest her father should meet with us. But Bysshe had the power of entering so thoroughly into the spirit of his own humour, that nothing could stop him when once his spirits were up, and he carried you along with him in his hilarious flight, and made you a sharer in his mirth, in a manner quite irresistible. During my intercourse with Bysshe this was his one happy year. I never saw him after that, but with some care on his mind.[37]

Harriet recorded no further bewilderment when the two families met again in London later that April. For ten days, she and Bysshe spent a considerable amount of time together walking in the fields, shopping, and staying "at home." In early May, Tom Medwin dined with them before they attended the opera. A change in Harriet's feelings about Bysshe was evident in her diary; she began referring to him for the first time as Percy, "Dearest P." Dropping the boyhood name, Bysshe, may have meant that her parents had relented, consenting to a sort of informal engagement after the trial visit at Field Place. Harriet, immobilized by a twisted foot, had time alone with Percy while the others went out. She was "very sorry" when, on May 5, 1810, the Shelley women left and Percy returned to finish at Eton. Their London rapprochement came to naught and Shelley probably never again saw Harriet.

He expressed his sadness from losing Harriet in two poems addressed to her and written during this April. In "Come [Harriet]! sweet is the hour," published in *Original Poetry by Victor and Cazire*, he compared himself to the "anemone's night-boding flower" that "Has sunk its pale head on the ground." He complained that "grief has laid low / The heart which is faithful to thee." Perhaps not expecting to go to London, he ended with, "dearest farewell, / You and I love, may ne'er meet again." His other Harriet poem was enclosed with a letter written at Field Place April 22 to his friend Graham. Mentioned in the ten stanzas are St. Irvyne house and the moonlight walk of Harriet's visit. Writing at two in the morning, Shelley assured Graham, who wanted to set his friend's poetry to music, that these lines "are natural" (not imaginary). Graham should not show them to anyone but he could "set them to music if you think them worth it." He wanted to see Graham in London as he was "the only friend to whom I *can* communicate what perhaps I shall wish to consult with you upon." He asked Graham to burn the letter. Shelley published part of this poem in his novel, *St. Irvyne*, deleting the five most autobiographical stanzas with suicidal overtones that spoke of "His long lost love," the "fiends of tortured love," and "the pangs of death." His attack on "prating priests" who gave advice expressed his resentment about the Christian influence Harriet's family was exerting on her. After, "Within me burns a raging Hell," he longed "for stern death's welcome ho[ur]." Only Harriet "Can still the tumult of my brain" and "calm my bosom's frantic pain."[38]

Harriet wrote Percy in late May acknowledging receiving the drawing pencils he sent. In her diary, she lapsed back to calling him "Bysshe" and dropped the "Dear" from "Aunt Shelley." She noted a letter to "Percy" the end of August,[39] the last appearance of his name in her diary. On September 17 she referred to Shelley and Elizabeth in her diary: "Received the Poetry of Victor & Cazire, Charlotte offended & with reason as I think they have done very wrong in publishing what they have of her." Included in this little volume by Shelley (Victor) and Elizabeth (Cazire) was a poem Elizabeth wrote April 30 in London. It satirized Charlotte's efforts to win the attentions of Colonel Sergison, with whom, Harriet noted, her sister was "half in love."[40]

This immediate condemnation of Shelley's first volume of published poetry was a portent of things to come. Soon after receiving *Original Poetry*, Harriet noted her father had a letter from Timothy Shelley "which I am sorry for, as it gives more trouble." Timothy's letter indicated his growing tension with his son and battle lines were being drawn in the Shelley–Grove–Pilfold nexus. Harriet's May 13 London diary entry reflected the animosity between Timothy and his brother-in-law, Captain John Pilfold. Timothy arrived looking "very unwell" and after shaking hands with Pilfold "[they] were friends during the time he staid." As summer 1810 turned to fall, all references to the Shelleys ceased in Harriet's diary as references increased to the neighboring Helyars.

Shelley was seventeen the winter of 1809–1810 when he probably wrote his elegiac poem, "To St Irvyne," a tentative farewell to Harriet expressing grief about his "transient" pleasures with her.[41] "My Harriet is fled like a fast-fading dream" but he is consoled "That my soul to her soul must eternally bind." Anticipating his later elegy to Keats, he devoted the entire last stanza to fantasizing about his own death.

Despite his melancholy romantic turn, Shelley during his final Eton year gained recognition from his peers for his writing and obvious brilliance, as well as for his successful resistance to the school authorities. In Hogg's meliorating view, this resistance earned him the title of "the Eton Atheist," but it probably came from his emerging religious unorthodoxy.[42] *Zastrozzi* had made him a published author and it was known he was translating Pliny's difficult *Natural History*. He stopped at the section on astronomy which, his mentor Dr. Lind informed him, not even the best scholars understood. Medwin was ecstatic about the beauty of his cousin's translation—now lost—perhaps the first of Shelley's fine literary contributions to this genre.[43] His last honor, at the end of July, was to deliver one of Cicero's orations against Catiline, part of the final academic ceremony. Shelley's more upbeat mood later in his Eton stay perhaps contributed to his desire, reported years later, that his son attend a public school.

In this last Eton year, he was writing a tragedy and "a friend," probably his sister Elizabeth, was writing a farce, perhaps with his collaboration. His two Gothic novels combined more serious thought with tongue-in-cheek comic relief. Awaiting publication of *Zastrozzi* by the firm of Wilkie and Robinson, Shelley noted in his diary, March 11, 1810, "Began Wolfstein" (*St. Irvyne*).[44] With the spoof of *Original Poetry by Victor and Cazire* soon to appear, he was riding a high crest of productivity. That year he completed his longest poem to date, *The Wandering Jew*, and with other poetry to appear, Shelley, at seventeen, had one of the most productive periods of writing in his life in terms of sheer output.[45]

Shelley's emotional lability was evident in his April 23 letter to Graham, with additions by his sister Elizabeth. Written the day after he sent Graham his melodramatic ten-stanza poem expressing "the tumult of my brain," Shelley and Elizabeth now wrote in a Gothic camp style. Parodying *Zastrozzi* and *St. Irvyne*, Elizabeth called her brother the *"Fiendmonger."* Shelley, caught in the bizarre spirit and anticipating seeing Harriet and his sisters in a few days in London, asked Graham to present himself at his sisters' school in Clapham as Harriet's brother, William. Abruptly shifting to the price of cucumbers, he requested two copies of *Zastrozzi* be sent to "Sir J. Dashwood in Harly Street." On June 4, the king's birthday, Shelley would escape Eton with his classmates Francis Dashwood and Edmund Leslie to the nearby Dashwood family estate. Shelley's postscript advised Graham to "keep yourself concealed as my mother brings a blood stained stiletto whic[h] she purposes to make you bathe in the life blood of her enemy."[46] Shelley's flight of ideas suggests an exuberant mood swing, something that possibly "perplexed" Harriet after her long conversation with Shelley several days earlier. His mother's "blood stained stiletto" echoed scenes in *Zastrozzi* and *St. Irvyne*. A suggestion of Graham's special relationship with Shelley's mother was in a letter Shelley wrote Graham a month later of her recovery from a "violent bilious fever."[47] Later, writing Graham from Field Place, he hinted about Graham and his mother: "needless to say that should any business lead you to Sussex (you understand) we should always be happy to see you, I believe I may include my father."[48]

Graham was responsible for a new acquaintance at this time, Joseph Gibbons Merle, who had published a poem and later became an editor. Through Graham, Shelley asked Merle, who worked in an art and music store, to obtain art crayons as a gift for Harriet. Shelley sent his thanks to Merle, who sensed a condescending tone in the letter. Surprised, Shelley wrote Graham, if Merle "takes me for any one whose character I have drawn in Zastrozzi he is mistaken quite." Shelley wondered "if every one that writes a romance draws such a train of eccentric events after him." It has been noted that Shelley's denial that he was representing himself in *Zastrozzi* was "an effective disguise for confessional material."[49] Merle, apparently unburdening himself, sent a long letter to Shelley who then complained to Graham that Merle "will not leave me alone." Shelley, becoming suspicious, admitted Merle was a "liberal fellow—but I have seen too much of the world not to suspect his motives."[50] When the two finally met at Graham's Piccadilly rooms, Merle, expecting to be humiliated by Shelley, instead found "The impressive eye of the young poet beamed upon me in all the radiance imparted by his benevolent heart; he grasped my hand with fervour of old acquaintance, and in a second we were friends." They talked for "three hours in free and unrestrained conversation" as Shelley "discoursed much of literature, and urged me to persevere in my poetical wanderings." Merle described Shelley's "highly interesting" appearance: "His countenance was open, and full of intelligence; the blush of health was upon his cheeks; and his limbs, although delicate in form, were well-knit and vigorous. He was not handsome in the common acceptation of the term; but on the whole he was fascinating."[51] Embedded in Shelley's last suspicious letter about Merle were references to the real sources of his anxiety, Harriet and his parents.

Having enrolled at Oxford in April 1810 and completed his studies at Eton, Shelley was in a very expansive mode at Field Place during July, August, and September. A busy writer, he negotiated with printers and publishers, Graham acting as his London connection. One of Graham's tasks—probably unfulfilled—was to have his music teacher, the well-known pianist and composer, Joseph Woelfl (d. 1812), set Shelley's poems to music. A week after turning eighteen, Shelley asked Graham to dispatch several books, including one by Locke, to Harriet, and mentioned *Original Poetry* was to be printed by James Phillips in Horsham.[52]

Threatened by Harriet's disengagement, Shelley clung to a belief she could still be his. Harriet's sister Louisa's death in June may have helped prompt the poem incorporated into *St. Irvyne* and sent to Graham in September. It began, "How stern are the woes of the desolate mourner" and ended as "he starts from his dreaming / And finds torn the soft ties to affection so dear."[53]

Zastrozzi and *St. Irvyne*, more than Shelley's "juvenile attempts at literary eroticism,"[54] were his initial attempts to delineate his radical politics of sex, views that informed his subsequent writings on love.[55] Reacting to the conventional, power-dominated patriarchal sexual mores at Eton and his romance with Harriet, Shelley was articulating a more egalitarian, liberating sexuality, as well as titillating his acquaintances. Aware of the sales potential of sex in Gothic tales, Shelley increased the two seductions in *Zastrozzi* to three in *St. Irvyne*. Borrowing plots and lurid eroticism from Gothic novels, including Lewis's *The Monk* and Charlotte Dacre's *Zofloya*, he injected his own personal issues into the tales, making them among his most important self-revelatory writings.

In *Zastrozzi*, Shelley established that his writing would blend his "natural" experience—biographical, unfeigned, and candid—with his more fanciful, imaginative "ideal" experience. Seemingly appropriating his father's "natural" sexual history in *Zastrozzi*, Shelley tells of the elder Verezzi, who, before marrying and having a legitimate son, previously had an illegitimate son by Olivia Zastrozzi, whom he had seduced, abandoned, and betrayed. Olivia obtains revenge on the Verezzis, father and son, through her illegitimate, atheist son of this seduction, Zastrozzi. Stabbing the father to death, Zastrozzi brings about the younger Verezzi's suicide by arranging his seduction by the wily Matilda.

Zastrozzi's themes of lust, seduction, abandonment, and prostitution became continuing motifs in Shelley's writing.[56] Shelley's mature tragedy, *The Cenci*, like *Zastrozzi*, is the story of the revengeful murder of the seducing, betraying father.[57] Dr. Lind perhaps made his first appearance in Shelley's writing when a "humane" physician assured Verezzi he was "safe" after having convulsive fits.

Zastrozzi involves a series of doubles, including two maternal figures, one more threatening, the other, lovingly, adopts Verezzi. The evil, powerful, and revengeful Zastrozzi is doubled by the more passive, effeminate, and introspective Verezzi who, torn from those "he held dear . . . the victim of secret enemies, and exiled from happiness," is chained, like Prometheus, to a rock by his "persecutors." Zastrozzi, fighting against societal wrongs and challenging established authority and power, dies at the hands of his oppressors.

The love plot's female doubles are Verezzi's idealized, spiritual, and virtuous Julia, and the treacherous, plotting, and sexually aggressive Matilda. Julia's murder by Matilda suggests a sadomasochistic rape fantasy,[58] Matilda stabbing Julia with a dagger "in a thousand places . . . with exulting pleasure." A dagger—Verezzi's suicide instrument—also appears in *St. Irvyne,* which Shelley was writing when he told Graham in "jest" to beware his mother's bloody dagger.[59]

St. Irvyne; or, The Rosicrucian: A Romance, written *"By a Gentleman of The University of Oxford,"*[60] was published December

1810. It contains Shelley's earliest beliefs on free love versus marriage, religion as priestcraft and superstition, and the deleterious effects of religious education. Begun the previous March, most or all of it was completed before he entered Oxford. Disappointed it was not a three-volume work, like William Godwin's 1799 Gothic *St. Leon,* Shelley ruefully wrote his publisher, John Joseph Stockdale, that *St. Irvyne* would appear as "one small volume."[61] He had just returned the quickly scanned proofs to Stockdale, making the few changes he deemed necessary to meet his publisher's confusions about the plot. Stockdale, like many puzzled critics since, was reacting to Shelley's abrupt shift midway through *St. Irvyne* to a second, seemingly unrelated plot, with all new characters. The novel's Eloise, and *Zastrozzi's* Julia, suggest Shelley's familiarity with Rousseau's *Julie, ou La Nouvelle Héloïse.*[62]

Shelley achieved a strong feeling of the uncanny in *St. Irvyne* by merging the identities of his doubles, two of whom, Ginotti and Wolfstein, have a depth of psychological portrayal not found in *Zastrozzi*. Ginotti, a name borrowed from *Zofloya*, possesses the "'Rosicrucian' . . . [the] elixir of eternal life."[63] Ginotti's six-page self-description is an early testament of Shelley's need to present himself in his work:

> From my earliest youth . . . [I had a] *curiosity,* and a desire of unveiling the latent mysteries of nature. . . . Natural philosophy at last became the peculiar science to which I directed my eager inquiries. . . . I then believed that there existed no God . . . priestcraft and superstition were all the religion which man ever practised . . . now about seventeen . . . I had dived into the depths of metaphysical speculations. . . . I convinced myself of the non-existence of a First Cause . . . I had not a friend in the world;—I cared for nothing but *self.*[64]

The guilt, and a guilty secret, pervading the novel may reflect Shelley's disastrous sexual experience at Eton College. Ginotti, at "college," poisoned a "youth who had offended me." Contemplating "self-destruction" by drowning, Ginotti hears a convent's bell and, thinking "no more of suicide . . . burst into a flood of tears . . . the sensation was new to me . . . inexplicably pleasing . . . almost at that instant, [I] allowed the existence of a superior and beneficent Spirit." Later poems[65] would describe this experience of Shelley's boyhood epiphany at Eton. Entering Oxford, Shelley next proclaimed Ginotti's non-belief in God in his most explosive prose work.

7

A Radical Poetic Identity

THE GROVES' UNEASE AT THE RADICAL TURN OF BYSSHE'S IDEAS AND the unease of Timothy and Elizabeth over their son's emotional crises contributed to the efforts in 1809 to terminate the cousins' informal engagement. During Shelley's final year at Eton, Lind was still serving George III when the aging monarch had his acute psychotic episode. Perhaps Shelley displaced part of his anger about the two families' paternalistic power onto the authoritarian political and religious institutions he held ultimately responsible for his plight. Both Shelley's anguish at losing Harriet and his mounting outrage at social injustices pervade the almost fifty poems he composed between 1808 and 1810, unpublished until 1964 as *The Esdaile Notebook*.[1]

As Shelley's poetic identity coalesced, he had increasing disdain for his family prescription of assuming his father's political role. He told Medwin how he hated all the talk about politics,[2] but as the time approached to enter Oxford, he still entertained a future in Parliament. In early 1811, he wrote the politically persecuted editor of the *Examiner*, Leigh Hunt, that on becoming twenty-one he expected to fill his father's Parliament seat.[3] Shelley's personal profile matched that of the typical MP of the time, including ending his career with baronet status, having a male blood relative in the House before him, graduating from Eton and Oxford, possessing wealth that came from the land, and entering the House before age twenty-five.[4] Working against this scenario were two crucial traits, his genius and his growing revolt against authoritarian power, at Field Place and beyond. His famous characterization of the poet as "unacknowledged legislator" accurately expressed his poetic identity born out of his rejection of his father's role.

A major external influence on Shelley's identity as poetic radical was the continuing war with France. His political awareness and radicalism at Eton had roots similar to those of many activist youths of the Vietnam War period, including affluent, politically aware parents who provided a stimulus for their children's more extreme ideology and greater concern about moral issues than many of their age-mates.[5]

Shelley's anti-militarism received a boost at age fifteen in 1807 when five thousand British soldiers were sent to Egypt to attack the Turks. Defeated twice with heavy losses at Rosetta, the British were forced to evacuate. Shelley combined British campaigns in his 1809 poem, "Henry and Louisa," set "on Egypt's strand." The soldier hero Henry was one of the "legal murderers . . . Britannia's hired assassins," "mowed down" to die in his lover's arms in a war that "religion sanctifies."[6] This 1809 Louisa prefigures the loved woman of his later poetry—strong, independent, and liberated— virtues he found wanting in Harriet Grove, with brothers still in the navy.

Shelley's anti-war feelings were fuelled again in 1809 by the grievous losses suffered by the British forces in two operations. In an indecisive, bloody, and costly July "victory" at Talavera, Spain, the starving British troops suffered fifty-three hundred casualties and Wellington saw fit to retreat to Portugal. The next month brought the disastrous and futile Walcheren expedition, planned by the war secretary, Castlereagh. This vain attempt to capture Antwerp from the French had a particularly strong impact on Shelley. Upwards of twenty thousand British soldiers, left garrisoned in the Walcheren marshes after a withdrawal, died of malaria. The Irish journalist, Peter Finnerty, asked to accompany and report on this ill-fated campaign, was summarily sent home by Castlereagh. Finnerty then offended Castlereagh and the British government by protesting and exposing the government bungling, leading to his arrest for libel and imprisonment.[7] Finnerty and Castlereagh had become enemies in 1797 when Castlereagh was chief secretary for Ireland. Finnerty was pilloried and sent to jail in Dublin for seditious libel for journalistic attacks on British atrocities committed against the Irish. What better hero than the radical writer Finnerty to replace Shelley's disillusionment with his Whig father's politics? Finnerty's radical thought, his attacks on oppressive government, and his agitation for Catholic emancipation, the major political issue in English life, would be advocated by Shelley at Oxford.

"The Irishman's Song" in *Original Poetry*, dated October 1809, is Shelley's first political poem with a specific theme, the British oppression of Ireland. It also reflects the influence of the radical MP and baronet, Sir Francis Burdett, by 1809 the leader for reform in Parliament and briefly imprisoned in 1810.[8]

In early September, before leaving for Oxford, Shelley busily read the last page proofs of *Original Poetry by Victor and Cazire*. The printer possibly was James Phillips, whose Horsham printing press was much closer to Field Place than that of his two sons, C. and W. Phillips, in Worthing. The sons' imprint, however, appeared on *Original Poetry*.[9] James Phillips, with old Bysshe's aid, also printed some of Shelley's earlier efforts, now lost. Shelley wrote to the publisher of *Original Poetry*, Stockdale, correcting an error in the advertisement caused by "the illegibility of my hand-writing."[10] This little volume, with the poem that so irritated Harriet and her sister, disappeared from view until 1898.[11] *Original Poetry*, Shelley's first published volume of poetry, was a practical joke from beginning to end. In addition to the authors' borrowed names (from Dacre's *Nun of St. Omer's*), the multiple plagiarisms included one entire poem, "Saint Edmond's Eve."[12] This plagiarism, from a well-marked copy at Field Place of the anonymously edited *Tales of Terror*, reflected Shelley's fascination with the adolescent master plagiarist, Chatterton.[13] Shelley's soon-to-appear next volume of poems, *Margaret Nicholson*, had similar trickster characteristics. Shelley undoubtedly gave a false name to Stockdale concerning the identity of the coauthor of *Original Poetry*: "The author told me that the poems were the joint production of himself and a friend, whose name was forgotten by me as soon as I heard it." Stockdale discovered the plagiarized "Saint Edmond's Eve" shortly after the volume was published and immediately wrote Shelley, who "expressed the warmest resentment at the imposition, practiced upon him, by his co-adjutor [Elizabeth], and intreated me to destroy all the copies."[14] Shelley probably perpetrated this ruse to fill pages. If Elizabeth knew about it, she went along with the joke.[15] Stockdale quickly withdrew the publication which, amazingly, received three reviews. The first had a bemused tone in harmony with the spoof; the others were indignantly dismissive.[16]

Of the seventeen poems in *Original Poetry*, Elizabeth probably wrote two letter poems, including the one that offended the Grove sisters. Elizabeth was responsible for three others, possibly with Shelley's involvement.[17] Other poems in *Original Poetry* include Shelley's "farewell" entreaties of love to Harriet.[18] The poem "Re-

venge," indebted to Lewis's *The Monk*, repeats *Zastrozzi's* theme
of the half-brother taking revenge on his sibling because the father,
having "ruined" the avenger's mother, "despised me his son."
Shelley's persistence with the half-brother theme may suggest he
had some knowledge or belief about his father's mistreatment of
the mother of Timothy's unacknowledged bastard son.

"Ghasta; or, The Avenging Demon!!!", the collection's most
telling poem, dated January 1810, borrows phrases from Chatterton and plot from *The Monk*, itself largely plagiarized from a German romance. This poem's convoluted plot features a stranger
and the ghost of the betrayed Theresa, also succubus to a warrior.
The stranger is an eternal wandering exile, Shelley's first presentation of the Wandering Jew,[19] whose immortality is at the cost of
eternal damnation. The nightmarish visions in "Ghasta" are reminiscent of the nightmare painting by Fuseli, whom Shelley that
summer seemed interested in contacting.[20]

Shelley's identification with the exiled Wandering Jew, proclaimed in the first sentence of *Zastrozzi*, fully emerged in
1809–1810 in his longest poem to date, *The Wandering Jew*. Tom
Medwin, clerking in his father's Horsham law office, later claimed
coauthorship of the poem. He also said that he and Shelley during
the winter of 1809 wrote alternate chapters of a novel, *Nightmare*.[21] Medwin's muddled claim, first refuted in 1887,[22] kept *The
Wandering Jew* from the major collections of Shelley's poetry as
late as 1970. Shelley always treated the poem as his own and now
is considered its sole author.[23]

Ahasuerus, the Wandering Jew, was an ancient legend popular
with many writers and poets of the late eighteenth and early nineteenth centuries, including Schubart and Goethe. Shelley, not yet
proficient in German, in early 1809 apparently read a translation of
Schubart's poem in a London periodical. Later, he wrote four times
of finding in Lincoln's Inn Fields a scrap of a translation of the Wandering Jew from the German.[24] In addition to Ahasuerus as an
anti-Christ, Shelley was attracted by the Wandering Jew's curse of
everlasting longevity.

A poem of four cantos, *The Wandering Jew* is more notable for
the mystery surrounding its composition and eventual publication
than for its poetry. That it was not published during Shelley's lifetime was not because of lack of effort on his part. Having sent Harriet part of the poem in late March, Shelley—as entrepreneurial
author—wrote Graham from Eton on April 1 expecting "a devil of

a price for my Poem and at least £60 for my new romance."²⁵ *The Wandering Jew* and *St. Irvyne,* written about the same time, had overlapping themes and one chapter of his novel begins with a quote from the poem. Unsuccessful in finding a London publisher, in the late summer Shelley sent a possibly revised *Wandering Jew* to the Ballantyne firm in Edinburgh. Ostensibly rejecting it for its religious radicalism, they wrote Shelley it would not go over well with the "bigoted, narrow spirit" of the Scots, adding that even Scott was assailed for "atheistical doctrines" in *Lady of the Lake.*²⁶ After Stockdale rejected the poem, Shelley asked him in December to return his manuscript for revisions. In the summer of 1811, Shelley took a notebook copy of the poem to Edinburgh where it languished for years at Ballantyne's. Shelley's possible attempt to publish the poem in 1811 may have led to his first meeting with Leigh Hunt. Within ten years of Shelley's death, somewhat different versions of *The Wandering Jew,* based on the Edinburgh copy, appeared in two periodicals.²⁷

The late-nineteenth-century editor pointed out, "from a psychological standpoint *The Wandering Jew* deserves attentive study."²⁸ Writing when he was losing Harriet, Shelley seemingly alludes to suicidal thoughts, his sexual episode at Eton, and his venereal anxiety. Shelley presents the failed romantic life among three characters, Paulo, the Wandering Jew, Rosa, his bride, and Victorio, Paulo's friend who also desires Rosa, whom neither will have. Victorio, seduced by a lost-woman Witch, has an ambiguous fate. Paulo must endure a curse of everlasting life for his religious deviancy of mocking Christ. This curse—suggesting that placed on Shelley by the Grove family for his deviant religious views—leads Paulo to attempt suicide twice in vain, by drowning in a raging ocean and by immolation in volcanic "Etna's womb . . . of electric flame." Playing with his readers, Shelley painted the sexual imagery with a heavy brush.

Victorio, filled with "rage" upon losing Rosa to another, has an encounter with the Witch that yields Shelley's first array of venereal disease imagery. The Witch's "sighs" "pollute the midnight air" (l.1187) in "a meteor's glare" (l.1193), all associations, in Shelley's time, with prostitution. The imagery includes the "poisonous" and "deadly" nightshade (ll.1100–1102), a plant remedy for venereal disease and an epithet for prostitute.²⁹ The possible emotional impact of Shelley's Eton encounter is suggested when the Witch induced a "terror" that "unmanned Victorio's mind." Shelley, using "blue" to refer to the dangers of sex, paints the Witch's picture with "false mouth . . . black tumid lips . . . [that] dropped with deadly dew . . . Projecting teeth of mouldy blue." (ll.1331–35)[30] The Witch, eager to finish the seduction, "bade quickly speed" to "unmanned" Victorio.

During the Easter holidays, a week before Harriet recorded the "odd" behavior at Field Place on April 16, Shelley was in Oxford, probably accompanied by his father. Timothy was mentioned in the newspapers as one of the minority MPs voting April 5 in Parliament against committing Sir Francis Burdett to the Tower. On April 10, Shelley registered twice for the Michaelmas Term that started in October. After signing on at venerable University College, he went through a matriculation ceremony for Oxford University in which every freshman had to subscribe to the Thirty-Nine Articles of the tenets of the established Church and swear the Oath of Supremacy, designed to exclude Catholics and Non-Conformists from the University.[31] Shelley's signature gives no hint of his undoubted rejection of these strictures and beliefs. His act of feigned compliance was the opening salvo in the Oxford phase of his war with established religion. After subscribing to and receiving a copy of the tenets from the Vice Chancellor, he possibly next visited Oxford's Bodleian Library to inquire about their holdings on his current anti-Christian preoccupation, *The Wandering Jew*.[32]

At the end of July, Shelley, at Eton, celebrated graduation by treating eight schoolmates to "a most magnificent banquet,"[33] on the presumed £40 proceeds from *Zastrozzi*. Shelley received autographed books as gifts from some of his classmates. In September, *Zastrozzi* was reviewed positively in *Gentleman's Magazine* as "A short, but well-told tale of horror . . . not from an ordinary pen . . . artfully conducted . . . on the principles of moral justice." This praise, from a periodical that attacked Shelley after his death, was reflected in the novel's 1839 reappearance in *The Romancist and Novelist's Library*. A long, attacking review in the November 1810 *Critical Review* called *Zastrozzi* "one of the most savage and improbable demons that ever issued from a diseased brain." The novel's sexuality was the focus of the attack: "Its open and barefaced immorality" was not "fit to meet the eye of a modest young woman" and it was "fit only for the inmates of a brothel." Castigating Shelley's language with its "battling emotions," "frigorific torpidity of despair," and "Lethean torpor," the reviewer concluded saying the author's "stupid jargon" would not "save him from infamy." In early 1811, *St. Irvyne* received an equal lashing, its "licentious" author condemned for "deviation from religious and moral principle."[34]

Shelley had all of August and September to complete his varied artistic labors in the wake of his increasingly tenuous relationship with Harriet. Many years later, Harriet's brother Charles wrote, "their engagement had been dissolved in the summer of 1810."[35] However, Shelley could not accept losing her. Feeling resentful and betrayed that she had shared his letters with her parents, his increasing attacks on Christianity reflected his bitter feelings that religious opinions contributed to Harriet's and her parents' rejection of him. Harriet apparently invoked the religious issue as the reason for the dissolution, but other factors probably played a role, including misgivings about her cousin's emotional stability. Shelley later suspected the Groves thought they could cut as good a financial bargain elsewhere.[36] Hellen Shelley, years later, said the break between Harriet Grove and Shelley was not "by *mutual* consent." Harriet's father "did not think the marriage would be for his daughter's happiness" but "would not have persisted in his objection, if his daughter considered herself bound by a promise to my brother, but this was not the case."[37]

Shelley became increasingly outspoken when writing on sexual, religious, and political issues. Timothy's hypocrisy towards his son's literary endeavors—produce as long as it does not openly offend conventional morality—was the same advice he gave him about his love life: produce illegitimate children but never enter a *mésalliance*.[38]

Timothy reportedly helped his son get settled in his freshly appointed rooms on the first floor of University College. Also on High Street was the bookshop of John Munday and Henry Slatter, where Timothy took Shelley for writing supplies. Timothy roomed with the Slatter family as an undergraduate and introduced his son to Henry and John Slatter, the latter brother a plumber and glazier. Years later, Henry Slatter reported that Timothy told him before leaving his son at Oxford, "My son here has a literary turn; he is already an author, and do pray indulge him in his printing freaks." The quote may be accurate, as Slatter was trying in vain to collect Shelley's unpaid bills from his father.[39] Timothy later claimed he had warned the Slatters against letting his son get into debt.[40]

Shelley soon made an important literary acquaintance, Henry Slatter's partner John Munday, Oxford printer and publisher of the "ultra-liberal" weekly newspaper, *The Oxford University and City Herald*.[41] The paper's many Sussex subscribers probably included Timothy Shelley and his son would have known its pages well. In the controversy at Oxford University in 1809 over the new chancellor's election, Munday's paper supported the Whig Lord Grenville over the Tory Lord Eldon. Shelley and Timothy possibly collaborated on a letter published in late 1809 in *The Morning Chronicle* supporting Grenville and signed "A.M.Oxon."[42] This letter, attributed to Shelley by both Hogg and Medwin, could reflect Timothy's recruitment of his son's literary talent to support his campaign for Grenville who, unlike Timothy, favored Catholic emancipation but otherwise had conservative Whig beliefs.[43] University College supported Eldon, but Timothy's vote helped Grenville win by a narrow margin. It is possible that Shelley may have been looked upon by the Oxford academic establishment with disfavor from the outset because of this political controversy. Whether or not father and son collaborated, Timothy was said to have encouraged Shelley "to acquire knowledge, to read hard, and particularly to distinguish himself at the university." At his father's prompting, Shelley entered a university competition for a prize poem about "ancient ruins." Shelley chose the Parthenon and Timothy found a vicar, a Sussex historian, to advise his son.[44]

Oxford was a lethargic, conservative intellectual community, largely confirmed in the prejudices of the wisdom of "Kingly power" and the dictates of the Church. Examinations were a farce, lectures loose, discipline lax, and expulsions extremely rare. The Masters and Fellows were all clergymen, including the Reverend James Griffith, the "dreamy, seclusive" Master of University College, who spent £2000 to embellish the chapel. The Bodleian Library would have attracted Shelley, but it was closed to undergraduates.

Shelley's Oxford tenure began and ended with publisher Munday, but its course was influenced by his complex, intense relationship with Thomas Jefferson Hogg, the most important male friend in Shelley's life. Two months older than Shelley, Hogg entered Oxford the previous term. With a reputation as a bright loner and a deviant, he seemed prepared for Shelley's arrival. An Oxford contemporary recalled many years later that Hogg's "ability was unquestioned . . . only Milman—the present Dean of St. Paul's—was preferred above him as an intellectual star." However, Hogg's "character was disliked . . . and only Shelley would speak with the object of college hatred." The students compared "Hogg to some strong ungainly Spider who netted some poor fly [Shelley]."[45] The two were immediately attracted to each other from the time of their first meeting in the College dining hall shortly after Shelley's arrival. Hogg recalled:

> I happened one day to sit next to a freshman at dinner. It was his first appearance in hall. His figure was slight, and his aspect remarkably youthful, even at our table, where all were very young. He seemed thoughtful and absent. He ate little, and had no acquaintance with anyone. I know not how it was that we fell into conversation, for such familiarity was unusual. . . . The stranger had expressed an enthusiastic admiration for poetical and imaginative works of the German school; I dissented from his criticisms . . . the appearance of my very extraordinary guest . . . was a sum of many contradictions. His figure was slight and fragile, and yet his bones and joints were large and strong. He was tall, but he stooped so much that he seemed of low stature. His clothes were expensive, and made according to the most approved mode of the day, but they were tumbled, rumpled, unbrushed. His gestures were abrupt, and sometimes violent, occasionally even awkward, yet more frequently gentle and graceful. His complexion was delicate and almost feminine, of the purest red and white; yet he was tanned and freckled by exposure to the sun, having passed the autumn, as he said, in shooting. His features, his whole face, and particularly his head, were, in fact, unusually small; yet the last appeared of a remarkable bulk, for his hair was long and bushy, and in fits of absence, and in agonies (if I may use the word) of anxious thought, he often rubbed it fiercely with his hands, passed his fingers quickly through his locks unconsciously, so that it was singularly wild and rough. In times when . . . the hair was invariably cropped, like that of our soldiers, this eccentricity was very striking. His features were not symmetrical (the mouth, perhaps, excepted) yet was the effect of the whole extremely powerful. They breathed an animation, a fire, an enthusiasm, a vivid and preternatural intelligence, that I never met with in any other countenance. Nor was the moral expression less beautiful than the intellectual; for there was a softness, a delicacy, a gentleness, and especially (though this will surprise many) that air of profound religious veneration. . . . But there was one physical blemish that threatened to neutralise all his excellence. "This is a fine, clever fellow!" I said to myself, "but I shall never be able to endure his voice"; . . . the voice of the stranger was excruciating . . . intolerably shrill, harsh, and discordant; of the most cruel intention. It was perpetual, and without any remission; it excoriated the ears.[46]

Hogg also noted the lad was beardless. De Quincey later saw a sketch of Shelley in academic robes in which he looked "like an elegant and slender flower whose head drooped from being surcharged with rain."[47] Many noted the high-pitched screeching quality of Shelley's voice when he was excited. Peacock, correcting Hogg, said Shelley's voice:

> under excitement . . . was not only dissonant, like a jarring string, but he spoke in sharp fourths, the most unpleasing sequence of sound that can fall on the human ear: but it was scarcely so when he spoke calmly, and not at all so when he read; on the contrary, he seemed then to have his voice under perfect command: it was good both in tune and in tone; it was low and soft, but clear, distinct, and expressive. I have heard him read almost all Shakespeare's tragedies, and some of his more poetical comedies, and it was a pleasure to hear him read them.[48]

After bantering in the dining hall over German and Italian literature, the two went to Hogg's rooms where each admitted knowing little or nothing of what they were discussing. Hogg, impressed by Shelley's enthusiasm, especially for chemistry and electricity, resisted an invitation to visit his rooms to see his galvanic trough and other paraphernalia. When he did get to Shelley's rooms, Hogg said they had "the same contradiction" he observed "in his person." Shelley's "officious scout" tried to keep things orderly in the freshly furnished, papered, and painted rooms, but disorder prevailed. Despite Hogg's bias for making Shelley appear ludicrous, his description rings true:

> Books, boots, papers, shoes, philosophical instruments, clothes, pistols, linen, crockery, ammunition and phials innumerable, with money, stockings, prints, crucibles, bags and boxes were scattered on the floor and in every place, as if the young chemist, in order to analyse the mystery of creation, had endeavoured first to re-construct the primeval chaos. The tables, and especially the carpet, were already stained with large spots of various hues, which frequently proclaimed the agency of fire. An electrical machine, an air-pump, the galvanic trough, a solar microscope and large glass jars and receivers, were conspicuous amidst the mass of matter. . . . There were bottles of soda water, sugar, pieces of lemon, and the traces of an effervescent beverage. Two piles of books supported the tongs, and these upheld a small glass retort above an argand lamp. I had not been seated many minutes before the liquor in the vessel boiled over, adding fresh stains to the table, and rising in fumes with a most disagreeable odour. Shelley snatched the glass quickly, and dashing it in pieces among the ashes under the grate, increased the unpleasant and penetrating effluvium.[49]

Hogg called Shelley "a whole university in himself" and the two quickly became "through sympathy, most intimate and altogether inseparable companions." For the eight weeks until Christmas vacation, they often had long talks in their rooms and took extended walks throughout the Oxford countryside. Anticipating students of the 1960s, they attracted attention with their long hair and offbeat clothing. If Shelley were the fly to Hogg's spider, he often flew from the web, having more acquaintances and contacts at Oxford. Hogg recounted the time several Eton acquaintances called and entreated Shelley "to curse his father" as he had at his former school. Shelley, first refusing, "suddenly broke out, and delivered, with vehemence and animation, a string of execrations, greatly resembling in its absurdity a papal anathema" which led to a "hearty laugh, in which we all joined."[50]

Shelley and Hogg had similarities in their family backgrounds. Both were the oldest child, their fathers graduates from University College. John Hogg, a conservative country lawyer of modest accomplishment, emulated a country squire existence in the northeastern village of Norton, near Durham. Like Timothy Shelley, John managed a family estate amassed by his father, Thomas Hogg. Grandsire Hogg built the family fortune as lawyer and agent for the Dean and Chapter of the Durham Cathedral, whose wealthy See was the religious, political, and financial center of high Tory Anglicanism in northern England. Like old Bysshe, Thomas embellished his social and financial credentials through marriage. His wife, Ann Jefferson, was sole heiress, and her properties included the Norton manor house. Hogg said his family "were all persons whose first toast after dinner was, invariably, 'Church and State!'—warm partisans of William Pitt, of the highest Church, and of the high Tory party."[51]

Jefferson had two younger sisters, followed by three brothers born while he was at preparatory school in Yorkshire.[52] Groomed to assume the family reins by becoming a lawyer, young Hogg was exposed to a more intellectual set of his parents' associates than those provided by Shelley's parents. Unlike Shelley, Jefferson was never called by the name he shared with his grandfather Thomas.

Jefferson's devout mother, Prudentia, a Welsh parson's daughter, had more staunch, fundamentalist religious views than her more easy-going husband. She began a letter to Jefferson admonishing him to answer her "in a rational Manner & with sincerity" and was clearly concerned about his deviant Christian beliefs. Having advised him on how to handle a conflict with his father about his allowance, she ended, "persevere in your Duty, to <u>your God</u> [who] . . . will . . . <u>remove any doubts</u> from <u>your mind</u>."[53] Prudentia Hogg's intimate religious adviser was a local vicar, the sanctimonious Reverend William Terrot.[54] Whether or not Jefferson believed Terrot had a sexual attraction to his mother, he arrived at Oxford simmering with religious issues coming to full boil.

Shelley wasted no time in having Munday print and sell his first literary "freak" at Oxford. By mid-November, *Posthumous Fragments of Margaret Nicholson* was advertised in the *Oxford Herald* as "just published." Nicholson had attempted to assassinate George III in 1786 and, presumed mad, was still an inmate of Bedlam when *Posthumous Fragments* was composed. She outlived Shelley by six years.[55] Shelley wrote Graham shortly after its publication that, having been confined by a fever for two weeks, he had time to compose. The fever's dying embers ignited two of his major passions, sex and political oppression. The volume he dashed off contained a *mélange* of verses including attacks on war and the monarchy, a piece of sexual ribaldry, an Irish ballad replete with spectral horseman and banshee, and laments on his lost love, Harriet. Shelley assured Graham, "I do not now take more than three hours sleep, & feel quite pleased at the idea that I shall soon be able to live without that *morbid suspension of every energy*." Such hyperactive behavior, possibly abetted by drugs or other self-medication, characterized his stay at Oxford. He exuberantly boasted to Graham, "Nothing is talked of at Oxford but Peg Nicholson" and its sexually provocative "Epithalamium" would make it "sell like wildfire." He intended a second edition would be out soon.[56] His enthusiasm about the sales potential was a slight exaggeration, as Slatter reported twenty-five years later that the work was "almost still-born." However, Hogg claimed the bookseller "was so much pleased with the whimsical conceit that he asked to be permitted to publish the book on his own account."[57] Hogg, and some of Shelley's "liberal" Oxford friends, may have urged on the more prurient passages, but the writing undeniably is Shelley's. Slatter provided a keen picture of Shelley's "astonishing" staccato-like pace in composing this "fugitive work." When proof sheets arrived at Shelley's rooms, "he would frequently start off his sofa, exclaiming that that had been his only bed; and on being informed that the men were waiting for more copy, he would sit down and write off a few stanzas, and send them to the press without even revising or reading them."[58]

In one verse, Shelley referred to himself poetically as a maniac: "I met a maniac—like he was to me . . . canst thou not contend with agony." The "whimsical conceit" of *Posthumous Fragments* began with the title and the name of the "editor," John Fitzvictor, presented as Nicholson's nephew. "J.F." claimed to have more verses of this deranged "genius," should readers demand a subsequent publication. The pseudonym continues Shelley's humorous attempts at anonymity, Fitzvictor being the bastard son of Victor, the pseudonymous Shelley of *Original Poetry*. "John" is also his brother's name, and possibly that of his bastard half-brother, as well as his grandfather Bysshe's bastard son John by a woman with a name similar to Nicholson, Nicholls. Shelley, possibly having heard from Dr. Lind of Nicholson's Bedlam incarceration and her disappointments in love, mentioned her attempted regicide in the subtitle: "being poems found amongst the papers of that noted female who attempted the life of the King in 1786."

Arranging the poems in *Posthumous Fragments* for maximum shock value, Shelley placed two incendiary political poems first. The anti-monarchical lead poem, with its chant "thy work, O Monarch, is the work of Hell," attacks George III and his policies in prosecuting the ongoing war with France. When the press, in late October, reported George's incapacitating mental illness, Shelley expressed interest in the health of both George and Timothy in back-to-back sentences in a letter to Graham.[59] Shelley, leaving the harbor of mere Whig reformism, was sailing into the headier waters of a radicalism advocating abolition of the monarchy ("Kings are but dust") and a "level" society for all.[60]

Eradicating tyrants continued in the sexual fire of the next poem, "Fragment: Supposed to be an Epithalamium of Francis Ravaillac and Charlotte Corday." Shelley's attempts to shock were more successful than his efforts at anonymity. Charles Kirkpatrick Sharpe—an M.A. at Oxford when Shelley was there—recognized him as the author, and wrote to his "titled and rakish" friends about the work. A political conservative, Sharpe considered the volume "stuffed full of treason" and "extremely dull," but recognized "the author is a great genius, and if he be not clapped up in Bedlam or hanged, will certainly prove one of the sweetest swans in the tuneful margin of the Cherwell." Sharpe was particularly taken with "Epithalamium," Shelley's real shocker. Sharpe's letter was to

Lady Charlotte Campbell, published poet and now a mid-thirties widowed mother of nine children and lady-in-waiting to Princess Caroline. Lady Charlotte later married someone who was with Shelley at University College and her family had future intriguing associations with Shelley. Sharpe wrote Lady Charlotte: ". . . we have lately had a literary Sun shine forth upon us here, before whom our former luminaries must hide their undiminished heads—a Mr. Shelley, of University College. . . . Frank is a very foul-mouthed fellow, and Charlotte, one of the most impudent brides that I ever met with in a book."[61]

Frank—François Ravaillac—the 1610 assassin of Henry IV, in Shelley's poem is the lover of Charlotte Corday, the 1793 assassin of Marat in his tub. The doubling of French and English tyrannicide themes, combined with the sexually explicit lovemaking of the two assassins, is Shelley's first poetic foray into sexual politics. Sharpe knew his friends beyond the confines of Oxford would enjoy the freshman's ribaldry. Lady Charlotte published an edited version of Sharpe's letter, apparently deleting the scandalous details of Shelley's poem.[62] Sharpe was more open about the sexual lines than most twentieth-century commentators. His characterization of the lines as "foul-mouthed" is a pun on the implied fellatio the "most impudent bride" is performing on Francis. It did not escape Sharpe, and his fellow sophisticates of the time, that impudent, from the same Latin root as pudendum, meant "sexually shameless."[63] In a passage recent editors consider Shelley's first expression of his lyrical voice,[64] Francis implores his assassin-bride:

> Soft, my dearest angel, stay,
> Oh! you suck my soul away;
> Suck on, suck on, I glow, I glow!
> Tides of maddening passion roll,
> And streams of rapture drown my soul.

Shelley wrote Graham admitting composing the lines "in compliance with the desires of a poetical friend" and soon the wildfire took hold. Trying to hide his authorship, he told Graham they were "the production of a friends mistress" and were omitted in "numbers of copies," including one he sent to his mother. Anticipating his father's gout-ridden anger, he added, "Of course to my Father Peg is a profound secret."[65]

Charlotte is aroused to sing, "I will clasp thy form . . . Till I min-
gle into thee . . . [in] A long, long night of bliss." Hogg, whose Oxford notebook is full of his adolescent sexual interests, claimed to
have had a hand in making the verses "burlesque poetry" and attributed them to Margaret Nicholson. He claimed to have lost his
copy of the poem "with a good deal about sucking" and said Shelley printed it over his objections.[66]

How biographers have dealt, or not dealt, with these lines un-
derscores the long-standing refusal to confront squarely the sexual content of Shelley's writing. By the late nineteenth century,
with Shelley's proper daughter-in-law looking over his shoulder,
Edward Dowden discreetly avoided mentioning these lines, including the "sucking" Hogg discussed in his biography thirty years
earlier. Things were much the same in 1927 when Walter Peck, believing the lines "offend against good taste," quoted only one line,
"Soft, my dearest angel stay." Newman White, in 1940, believing the
lines were "certainly excessive for modern taste," did not print any
of what he called "the licentious passage." Several years later,
A. M. D. Hughes considered the verses "peppered with indecency."[67]
Recognizing the fellatio implied by the lines, these biographers
tried their best to avoid quoting or describing it. In 1974, Richard
Holmes referred to the "apparent eroticism" of the "Epithalamium" without quoting lines. That same year, Kenneth Cameron
was the first to state Shelley "had depicted fellatio."[68] Predictably,
five years later such a reading was considered incorrect as "the
idea [of fellatio] would have been repugnant to Shelley and un-
thinkable to his audience."[69] This too-tender interpretation of
Shelley's (and his times') views of sex was subsequently pointed
out, but a form of oral sex short of fellatio apparently was suggested.[70] Sharpe, and his cohorts, recognized Shelley's desire to
implicate the full range of oral sex in his lines, including fellatio.
The most recent editors of Posthumous Poetry point out the ribaldry of the word twat in the typography of these lines.[71] The history of muted interpretations of Shelley's writing indicates the continuing resistance to recognizing what Hogg termed his "certain
sly relish for a practical joke . . . of a literary nature."[72]

Well-prepared by the peccadilloes of his father, grandfather, and
the Duke of Norfolk, Shelley easily absorbed the sexual vernacu-
lar of his peers at Syon House, Eton, and Oxford. Among Shelley's
future male friends with an eye toward sexual versatility were
Lord Byron, Leigh Hunt, and Thomas Love Peacock, described as

a "thesaurus eroticus."[73] Merging the sexual and the political, Shelley ended "Epithalamium," "than love's sweetest blisses 'tis more dear / To drink the floatings of a despot's knell."

One of Sharpe's letters about *Posthumous Fragments* went to the "talented, debauched E. B. Impey,"[74] who considered Shelley a "literary meteor" with a "fiery tail—which he seems to whisk about with such wonderful volubility that I would have Miss Burton beware of the laws of gravitation and vigilantly guard her centre of attraction."[75] Perhaps Impey thought Shelley's poetry diseased, as having one's tail on fire was slang for "either the clap or the pox" and "To guard her centre of attraction" was "to protect her virginity."[76] Shelley, establishing his intellectual and radical credentials, perhaps donated the proceeds from *Posthumous Fragments* to aid the Irish journalist Peter Finnerty.[77]

Shelley's conspicuous role at Oxford was observed by Elizabeth Grant, the young niece of University College's Master. She derided the university's educational laxness, its "ultra-Tory politics," the society's "stupidity and frivolity," and "dissipated" students staying out all night. She believed Shelley was the "ringleader," being "very insubordinate, always infringing some rule." When reproved about his "slovenly" dress, his "extraordinary gestures" in a display of "humility" provoked "the lecturing tutor."[78]

Shelley's specific sexual activities at Oxford are not known. Hogg's Oxford notebook[79] has musings under headings like "Bawdy" and "Maidenhead" as he expounded on defloration, voluptuousness, and women's provocative dress. Discussing Shelley at Oxford, Hogg declined "within the compass of a brief narrative" to expand directly on Shelley's "moral sense." However, in his "delicate task of composing a faithful history of his whole life," Hogg, by indirection, slyly questioned whether Shelley's "conduct, at certain periods, was altogether such as ought to be proposed for imitation," with his "ardent imagination . . . something of hastiness in choice . . . a certain constitutional impatience."[80]

Sharpe believed Shelley's ardent interest in the opposite sex was indulged to the extent of contracting a venereal disease. He wrote Lady Charlotte Campbell that Shelley "lives upon arsenic, aquafortis, half-an-hour's sleep in the night," a claim Sharpe repeated nine years later when sending a friend *The Cenci*.[81] Shelley possibly knew of the aquafortis and arsenic "cure" for syphilis through Lind at Eton and his reading at Oxford. According to its medical proponent, whom Lind knew, this cure could "disarm this cruel hydra of many of its heads." If Shelley read this medical article, he may have recalled this phrase in *Queen Mab* where he referred to the "hydra-headed woes" of venereal disease. At Oxford, Shelley could have read the ideas of the late renowned Orientalist, Sir William Jones—an honored alumnus of University College—on arsenic as a cure of the "Persian fire," syphilis.[82] For the rest of his life, Shelley linked his prematurely graying hair with some debilitating illness, even if it were *Syphilis imaginaria*, described in a book he owned by Erasmus Darwin, who called it "a very common insanity amongst modest young men."[83]

Hogg said Shelley "used to speak with horror of the consequences of having inadvertently swallowed . . . some medicinal poison, I think arsenic, at Eton, which he declared had not only seriously injured his health, but that he feared he should never entirely recover from the shock it had inflicted on his constitution."[84] Medwin's more explicit accounts of Shelley's illnesses at Eton referred to his use of "medical acids." Hogg recalled that, on first visiting his friend's rooms, Shelley "complained of his health," saying he was "very unwell." Hogg observed that "Shelley's health and strength were visibly augmented, if by accident he were obliged to accept a more generous diet than ordinary."[85] Not yet a vegetarian, Shelley's diet at Oxford may have been the "low diet" or "cooling regimen," thought to cure "any sort of illness caused by dissipation."[86]

Another possible cure involved Walker's Syon House message that electricity had healthful effects on blood circulation, including the removal of "both male and female obstructions" as well as curing chilblains.[87] Shelley had inflicted his electrical apparatus on his sisters for chilblains and demonstrated its use to Hogg by turning the handle so rapidly "that the fierce, crackling sparks flew forth; and presently standing upon the stool with glass feet, he begged me to work the machine until he was filled with the fluid, so that his long, wild locks bristled and stood on end."[88]

Hogg called Oxford an academic "chartered laziness . . . destitute of every literary attainment . . . vulgar sons of vulgar fathers." Shelley, thinking them "all very dull people here," diligently pursued his self-generated intellectual activity. Hogg said Shelley read up to sixteen hours a day and was torn from his books only with difficulty. He was astonished at Shelley's facility in composing verses in Latin and stressed Shelley's strenuous effort in learning his poetic art. Reading "assiduously" in Greek, Shelley was well on his way toward a mastery of that language and its literature few could rival in a much longer lifetime. His tutor prescribed *Prometheus Bound* and, despite Shelley's "Must I care about Aristotle?," Hogg reported he "took to the scholastic logic very kindly [and] seized its distinctions with his accustomed quickness." The two read Locke together, and an examination of a chapter of the *Essay Concerning Human Understanding* was enough for Shelley "at any moment, to quit every other pursuit." Hume's *Essays,* Shelley's particular favorite, induced him, either in his notebook or in face-to-face verbal combat, to argue for the Scotsman's skeptical philosophy. According to Hogg, "the soul of Hume passed . . . into the body of that eloquent young man." His wide-ranging intellectual interests included the French materialists.[89] Hogg thought it laughable but true that their knowledge of Plato came either from a French translation or an English version of a French translation. Sections of Plato dealing with homosexuality were censored in students' texts, a defect Shelley helped correct years later. He was particularly fond of the dialogues in *Phaedo* and of Socrates' doctrine that reminiscences from an earlier life were the basis of knowledge. This led him to stop a young mother carrying her infant across the Magdalen Bridge and inquire of the dumbfounded woman, "Will your baby tell us anything about pre-existence, Madam?"[90]

One literary-minded Oxford student that Shelley sought out was James Roe at Sharpe's college, Trinity. Shelley asked Roe to return a "poetical scrap" and invited him for "wine & Poetry in my room," possibly to celebrate publication of *Posthumous Fragments.*[91] Another Oxford acquaintance, George Marshall, was the son of Timothy Shelley's friend, the curate of Horsham, whose daughter Elizabeth received from Shelley a copy of *St. Irvyne.*[92] Young Marshall introduced Shelley to a visiting friend, Thomas Barnes, subsequently editor of *The Times.* Twenty-five years later, Barnes wrote Leigh Hunt about a long evening's conversation at Oxford that left Barnes with an enduring "impression of the frankness and uprightness of Shelley's character," adding that he was "a fine-looking youth . . . with one of those ingenuous countenances which ought never to look old."[93]

Shelley's "dominant passion," according to Hogg, was arguing skeptical philosophy. He had no use for mathematics and jurisprudence, the latter dear to Hogg's heart. However, religion soon propelled both youths prematurely from Oxford. As if preparing for this rupture, and its attendant paternal rejection, Shelley began searching for a new father surrogate. In November he wrote Stockdale for William Godwin's *Political Justice*.[94] In December, home for the Christmas holiday, he wrote Hogg about trying to locate Godwin's address which he knew was not that of another Godwin named "John" living in Holborn.[95]

Had Shelley found Godwin's address on Skinner Street at this time instead of a year later, his life probably would have been much different. He would have found at the literary home of Godwin and Godwin's second wife an exotic array of three young women, including two daughters of Mary Wollstonecraft. Instead, his quest to replace his Field Place sisterhood led to two daughters of the Westbrook family.

Fig. 5. Percy Bysshe Shelley by Alfred Clint, c. 1829, after Amelia Curran, 1819, and
Edward Williams, courtesy of the National Portrait Gallery, London.

Fig. 6. Shelley's sisters, Hellen and Margaret, Shelley Relics 8, courtesy of the Bodleian Library.

Fig. 7. Harriet Grove, pencil sketch attributed to Shelley's sister Elizabeth Shelley, 1809, courtesy of Timothy Heneage.

Fig. 8. Thomas Medwin, photograph by Emery Walker of painting, courtesy of the National Portrait Gallery, London.

Fig. 9. Thomas Jefferson Hogg, ink drawing, 1857, [PR] Shelley Adds. e. 8, courtesy of the Bodleian Library.

8

Icarus at Oxford

SHELLEY STUDIED GODWIN'S *POLITICAL JUSTICE* FOR PERSONAL IN-
sight as well as social philosophy. Trying to understand his personal "mortification," he told Hogg he agreed with Godwin that no
man had "unmixed" motives.[1] Writing Godwin a year later, Shelley
thought the book's effect was heightened because, his "mind jealous of its independence," he had "duties to perform."[2] One of his
"duties" during his first weeks at Oxford was writing letters under
a pseudonym to strangers, with the intent of engaging them in intellectual discourse. Introduced by Lind to this practice, Shelley
enlisted Hogg and Graham in writing letters under assumed
names and identities. The recipients were clergymen Shelley was
baiting into discussions of religion, a topic he and Hogg were actively pursuing. Using Graham's London mailing address, Shelley
sent him letters for posting in the city. One was "a most beautiful
Joke, it is from a french girl to the king of the Methodists."[3] Eager
for responses, Shelley found "the arrival of the postman was always an anxious moment."[4]

Hoping to defray his debt to Stockdale for *St. Irvyne*, Shelley
acted as literary entrepreneur for other writers. In one strange
venture, apparently begun at Eton, he would commit £750 of his
money—and Munday and Slatter's—to publish a book on Swedish
history, politics, and science. Its mysterious author was a Mr. Bird,
actually a former naval officer named John Brown, a presumed
victim of oppression who was forced to leave the service.[5]

On long Oxfordshire countryside walks with Hogg, Shelley was
drawn to places near water, including walks along the Thames. At
the pond below Shotover Hill, Shelley would "linger until dusk, gazing in silence on the water, repeating verses aloud." Indulging his
passion for paper boats, Shelley "anxiously watched the fortunes
of the frail bark [until it] sank," and only with great difficulty could
Hogg entice him from his play. The "remarkable contrast with his

mild aspect and pacific habits" was carrying his favorite pair of dueling pistols and "a good store of powder and ball."[6] Shelley delighted in shooting a hole in one of his father's franks attached to a tree. Hogg, noting Shelley's "inconceivable carelessness" in handling his weapons, sensed the anger involved in his pistol-shooting preoccupation. Shelley became defensive when asked about his anger, growing "exceedingly hostile." On one walk, Shelley threatened to get his pistols and kill a dog after it ripped his new coat. Hogg had never seen his friend so angry. Another situation provoking his "unbounded" anger was an "awkward jest, especially if it were immodest or uncleanly."[7]

Once, coming across a young girl who was lost, cold, and hungry, Shelley fed her some hot milk until her family arrived. Another time, befriending a Gypsy girl and her brother, he commented on their intelligence despite their poor existence. Later, when he and Hogg stumbled into the Gypsy camp, the little girl returned Shelley's wave of recognition.[8]

During the autumn at Oxford, Shelley's anger from Harriet's rejection and betrayal began to be converted into self-destructive guilt. Like Icarus, he was soaring dangerously ever higher in defiance of his cautious father. Hogg reported that Shelley at this time had "a most affectionate regard for his relations, and particularly for the females of his family." A letter from his mother or his sisters made him especially happy. His idealizing of women was evident in Hogg's comment that Shelley sometimes described "with a curious fastidiousness, the qualities which a female must possess to kindle the fire of love in his bosom . . . he was to be moved by the most absolute perfection alone."

We now know that Hogg, like Shelley, had experienced a recent disappointment in love. Letters found in 1990 reveal that before returning to Oxford in October, Hogg was in Hartlepool, near Norton, having clandestine meetings with a Miss Dillon.[9] His father, fearful his son might elope, corresponded with several advisers as to how to break off his son's infatuation with this "artful" young woman whose "history is a kind of romance" and who was "known to have behaved incorrectly with other young men." John Hogg, separating the two, sent his son quickly back to Oxford for the fall term where Hogg soon told Shelley about this lost love, "Mary." In November, Shelley, after "three weeks of entrancement caused by hearing Mary's story," composed "many" poems about her of which five survive.[10] Shelley encouraged Hogg to begin a novel,

Leonora, featuring Mary as a subsidiary heroine. Shelley's poems reflect his consuming identification with Mary, sharing both her rejection in "perjured" and "thwarted" love and her suicidal inclinations. According to the "Advertisement" and notes Shelley appended to the poems, "Mary died three months ~~after~~ before I heard her tale," having "repeatedly attempted suicide" by poison. In his "Advertisement," Shelley claimed he might have prevented her suicide had he rather than "my friend" endured "the trial" on "a summer night" of having her "fold me to her tremulous bosom in extasies of friendship and despair!" In one poem, Shelley converted this Hogg-mediated sexual fantasy into a wish for a mutual Liebestod. In his lost novel, Hogg apparently transformed Miss Dillon into a beatific Mary ruined, in Shelley's words, by a "vile female."[11]

Shelley's poems make clear Mary was accused of being an immoral woman. In "To the Lover of Mary," with characteristic imagery of prostitution and venereal disease, Shelley assured Hogg, "The wounds shall close of Misery's scorpion goad." Shelley, perhaps emerging from a similar sexual experience at Eton, possibly tried treating Hogg's real or imagined venereal symptoms from his extensive chemical "cures."

Sharing a mix of illicit sex, lost love, parental interference, and erotic fantasies, the bond Shelley and Hogg formed had an undeniable homoerotic attraction. Their relationship was a complex mirroring of unconscious maternal, paternal, and incestuous issues played out in the conscious arena of religious protest and literary activity. Shelley soon was writing his own novel, now lost, "constructed to convey metapnysical & political opinion by way of conversation" but gave up hope of publishing it because "it would certainly be prosecuted."[12]

Shelley's thirteen letters to Hogg over the Christmas vacation suggest his increasing confusion, agitated depression, flights of ideas, and preoccupation with suicide and his sanity. One observer has said, "Shelley's connection with reality at this time was at best intermittent."[13] Shelley, evasive with Hogg, did not mention Charles Grove's presence at Field Place over the holidays. References to his sister Elizabeth merged with those to the unnamed Harriet, emotionally distanced as "she" or "the Being." Shelley's letters featured their joint theological investigations, the novels each was writing, Hogg's romantic interest in Shelley's sister Elizabeth, and Timothy Shelley's pervading influence.

Hogg positioned himself in London the first part of the holiday, hoping for an invitation to Field Place and seeking a publisher for his novel *Leonora*. Shelley soon wrote canceling Hogg's visit to Field Place. Shelley, needing "all my art," had to "resort to deception." Timothy, in London, had called on Stockdale who told him that Hogg was "a supporter of Deistical Principles."[14] After Hogg submitted his religiously scandalous novel to Stockdale, the publisher had his wife investigate Hogg. Stockdale told Timothy his inquiries led him to believe Hogg was leading Shelley into dangerous religious terrain. Stockdale, alarmed about what Shelley was writing, said he told Shelley he would be expelled if he went ahead with plans to publish the essay on atheism, but "He, however, was unmoved. . . . I instantly wrote his father." Stockdale later declared, "that if I did not rush forward, and however rudely, pull my candidate for the bays from the precipice, over which he was suspended by a hair, his fate must be inevitable."[15] Timothy immediately wrote to his son who was at Field Place and feeling "beseiged . . . an outcast . . . They attack me for my detestable principles." Shelley told Hogg, "There lowers a terrific tempest, but I stand as it were on a Pharos, & smile exultingly on the vain beating of the billows below." With murderous bravado, he wrote of anonymous authorship: "I will stab the wretch in secret . . . the wound which we inflict tho' the dagger be concealed, will rankle in the heart of our adversary." His next sentence revealed the real recipient of his wrath: "My father wished to withdraw me from College, I would not consent to it." Linking his romantic fate and religion, he wrote, "Oh! I burn with impatience for the moment of Xtianity's dissolution, it has injured me; I swear on the altar of perjured love to revenge myself on the hated cause . . . it is to the benefit of society to destroy the opinions which can annihilate the dearest of its ties." Shelley told Hogg that everyone at Field Place, except a "select few," believed his "assertion . . . that I will publish no more." This faith in deception and anonymity soon was blasted; Timothy's wish that Shelley withdraw from Oxford was an accurate reading of what ensued.

Shelley's sister Elizabeth now became the romantic link between him and Hogg. Shelley was vicariously gratifying his incestuously tinged feelings for his sister through Hogg's passion for her. At the same time, his feelings for Elizabeth blocked a more conscious awareness of his homosexual attachment to Hogg. Fusing his identity with Shelley's, Hogg wrote poetry and novels, col-

laborated in other writing ventures, and joined him in being expelled. Hogg's mirroring continued thirty years after Shelley's
death when he wrote his friend's biography. This two-volume severely flawed fragment was written primarily to protest his own
separateness by retaliating against his friend in the often deni-
grating and deceitful portrait he painted. It was a narcissistic display of Hogg's life as much as biography. Sixty-five years old, having reverted to his family's High Church Toryism, he wrote
concealing his anti-religious beliefs and his infatuation with Elizabeth Shelley. Blatantly censoring and rewriting Shelley's letters,
he turned his problems into those of Shelley.[16] Hogg expressed his
homosexual feelings for Shelley by a lifelong dependence on Shelley for his heterosexual identity.[17] The three women in his life with
whom he did become involved were all loves of Shelley. At Oxford,
Shelley, in lieu of his sister Elizabeth, found a new collaborator in
Hogg, the first of a number of homosexual currents that fostered
Shelley's creativity.

Before the Christmas holiday, Shelley and Hogg were vigorously
pursuing religious questions by comical letters and serious theological inquiry. Hogg's exercise book shows him studying the Old
Testament, praising "Pagan Religion" because it does not produce
"bigotry, persecution, or intolerance," and attacking the power of
the clergy. Shelley wrote Stockdale for a book in Hebrew he hoped
was translated, "demonstrating that the Christian religion is
false."[18] He still wanted Stockdale to publish *The Wandering Jew*
and indicated he would see him in London on his way home for the
Christmas holiday.[19] From Field Place, he wrote Stockdale for
copies of *St. Irvyne*—just being distributed—saying he would send
him for publication the "metaphysical and political" novel he was
writing.[20]

Shelley next advised Hogg to drop Stockdale and try to publish
Leonora with the publisher of Godwin's *Political Justice*. Not
overly impressed with Hogg's literary ability, Shelley correctly
sensed that Hogg's poem, "The Dying Gladiator," would not win
that year's Oxford prize. He told Hogg he was writing a "Satirical
Poem on L'infame" and kept him informed of the fruits of his pseudonymous letter writing on behalf of religious skepticism.[21] In
what he called his "egotising folly," Shelley was promoting Hogg's
interest in Elizabeth by exaggerating her poetic and intellectual
gifts. Hogg, never having seen her, responded eagerly with a well-
developed set of erotic fantasies. Hogg's comedic epistolary pur-

suit of Elizabeth featured Shelley as doer and undoer, pleading Hogg's suit with his sister as he also tried cooling Hogg's ardor by communicating Elizabeth's rebuffs. If Hogg is "so superior," Shelley reported Elizabeth saying, "a correspondence . . . must end in delusive disappointment when he finds out how really inferior I am to the being which his heated imagination had pictured."[22] Shelley, increasingly emotionally dependent upon Elizabeth, protested that Hogg's exaggeration of Elizabeth's "mental attainments" was "that of a brother who loves his sister as I do." Ten days later Shelley wrote Hogg that he could not visit him in London because "my sister wd. not part with me."[23]

After Hogg wrote that Shelley must think he was insane, Shelley responded, "How can you fancy that I can think you mad; am not I the wildest, most delirious of enthusiasm's offspring." Cryptically apologizing for not inviting Hogg to Field Place, he said he would tell him the reason "when we meet." To assuage Hogg's "despair," he assured him there was no "moral wrong" or "selfishness" in communicating with his sister. Trying to analyze his own "self-love," Shelley's text was Aristotle's *Ethics,* which he was translating.[24] In letter after letter, Shelley agonized over whether his love, and Hogg's, could be virtuous if it were "self-love" or "egotism." He was "afraid there is selfishness in the passion of Love."[25]

Hogg, pouring out his guilt over having exceeded the bounds of "delicacy" with Elizabeth, elicited Shelley's, "I must be severe with you, I must irritate the wound which I wish to heal."[26] Saying his "unhappiness is excessive" and he would "no more speak in riddles," Shelley added, "My sorrows are not so undeserved as you believe. . . . I wish you knew Elizabeth, she is a great consolation to me." Two days later, after Elizabeth received a letter from Hogg, Shelley wrote him she was "distracted" because she feared "injuring" Hogg if she told him "the real wishes of her bosom." Still being elusive, Shelley wrote "in the midst of all the uncongenial jollities of Xmass [sic]" of his "concealment of feelings" and asked, "Why do you still continue to despond." He again began backing away from visiting Hogg in London.[27]

On New Year's Day, Tuesday, he started a rambling, confused letter to Hogg saying he had "just returned to Field Place from an inefficient effort," having left Sunday morning. Shelley said, "I have wandered in the snow for I am cold we[t] & mad." Some conjecture that Shelley's "inefficient effort" was a dash to Wiltshire to see Harriet, a long trip barely possible in the time he was gone, assuming it was two days.[28] December 29 was bitter cold, Harriet noting "a most severe frost" in her diary. Neither her diary nor her sister Charlotte's indicate Shelley was there. Some days later, Shelley wrote Hogg: "I have tried the methods you recommend. I followed her, I would have followed her to the ends of the earth." Hiding his correspondence from his father, now in London,[29] Shelley told Hogg to direct his next letter to Horsham. He would write "To-morrow . . . more connectedly."[30]

By his own account, Charles Grove was twice at Field Place over the holidays. Although Charles was two years younger than Shelley, the two cousins were becoming closer, something Shelley kept from Hogg. Many years later Charles wrote: "During the Christmas vacation of that year, and in January 1811, I spent part of it with Bysshe at Field Place" and they "returned to London" together.[31] Charles's first visit probably was before Christmas when he accompanied Shelley—on his way home from Oxford—from London to Field Place. At Field Place, Charles must have told Shelley of Harriet's growing interest in William Helyar. It was not yet a romance and, contrary to what many have thought, Harriet's engagement did not occur until October 1811, after Shelley's marriage.[32]

Charles Grove left Field Place for Wiltshire in time to join his family on December 28,[33] taking with him a copy of *St. Irvyne* Shelley intended for Harriet. Charlotte Grove soon read it and proclaimed it "Great stuff."[34] Charles left his Wiltshire home with his father and brother John for London January 7. Soon returning to Field Place, Charles then went with Shelley to London later in the month.

Shelley's quick trip remains a mystery. The weather may have caused an aborted journey or he possibly went to nearby Cuckfield to see his uncle, Captain John Pilfold.[35] Most likely, he accompanied his Parliament-bound father to London that Sunday with the cover of seeing Hogg, who was expecting him. However, avoiding Hogg, he may well have tried to see his new interest, Harriet Westbrook. Having her wrong house number on Chapel Street, it was perhaps an "inefficient effort."[36]

Shelley's closeness to his sister Elizabeth, which influenced his views about incestuous love,[37] was reflected in her concern about his suicidal ideas. She "narrowly" watched him on his walks with his gun and dog.[38] In early January he wrote Hogg: "Is suicide wrong? I slept with a loaded pistol & some poison last night but did not die." He said he did not come to see Hogg because his sister insisted he stay. Elizabeth "has felt deeply" and were it not "for a sense of what I owed to her, to you, I should have bid you a final farewell some time ago."[39]

According to Hogg, Shelley told him that shortly before going to Oxford "he had taken poison for love of a young lady who refused his hand. He had swallowed a large dose of arsenic, but his stomach rejected it, and he threw it up, or the principal part of it."[40] When Shelley angrily wrote to Hogg that he would "ensanguine" the "breast of my adversary" with the "hearts blood of Xt's hated name,"[41] Harriet was writing in her diary of hearing a "very good" sermon. Elizabeth was now questioning her brother's beliefs and Shelley wrote Hogg, "never will I forgive Christianity! . . . Oh How I wish I were the Antichrist, that it were mine to crush the Demon . . . she [Elizabeth] is no longer mine, she abhors me as a Deist, as what she was before."[42] Shelley was a deist at this point,[43] as this same letter to the more atheistic Hogg makes clear. Wanting "The word 'God' . . . erased from the nomenclature of Philosophy," he said "it does not imply 'the Soul of the Universe the intelligent & necessarily beneficent actuating principle'—This I believe in."

Upon receiving Hogg's latest letter, Elizabeth returned it unopened. Shelley, referring to Elizabeth, wrote Hogg he will never "forsake one whom I have loved . . . she is gone, she is lost to me forever, forever." He added teasingly, "There is a mystery which I dare not to clear up, it is the only point on which I am reserved to you." Shelley wanted to "amuse" Hogg by including a five-stanza elegy depicting Shelley's wintry grave and Harriet's lost love frozen by the "Pride" of her family.[44] He was "very cold this morning . . . as I have been most of the night pacing a church yard: I must now engage in scenes of strong interest." At this point, a letter from Hogg made him switch abruptly to their religious theorizing and the complaint, "My head is rather dizzy to day on account of not taking rest, & a slight attack of Typhus." Timothy, home from London, franked and addressed the letter for his ailing son.

Two letters Shelley wrote on January 11 indicated someone was replacing Harriet Grove. He asked Stockdale to send a copy of St. Irvyne "to Miss Harriet Westbrook, 10, Chapel Square, Grosvenor."[45] The correct number was "23." Shelley, paying to have his novel published, told Stockdale he would see him in London in a fortnight about the printer's bill. Shelley had left Oxford a week early in December, possibly to have his first meeting with

Harriet Westbrook at Clapham Common where she and his younger sisters were students at Mrs. Fenning's boarding school. Mary, thirteen and the first to signal Harriet Grove's defection,[46] was the friend of fifteen-year-old Harriet Westbrook.

Shelley also wrote to Hogg January 11 reiterating that his relationship with Harriet Grove was over: "She is gone, she is lost to me forever—she is married, married to a clod of earth, she will become as insensible herself, all those fine capabilities will moulder." Shelley's hyperbole—Harriet was far from married—was designed to stop further intervention by Hogg, who apparently wrote Elizabeth seeking her influence on Harriet.[47]

Harriet had seen little of conservative "Billy" Helyar during 1810 but her marriage to him in late 1811 fulfilled her own and her family's expectations. Unlike Shelley's father, Harriet's husband's father died in timely fashion, leaving his son his wealth and family home in 1821. Of Harriet's fourteen children, seven survived before her husband's death in 1841. Becoming increasingly religious, she died in 1867 at age seventy-six.[48] Harriet's brother Charles became a rector, her sister Charlotte married a minister, and her nearby Aunt Bathia married the Reverend Jackson. A relation of the Helyars, Dr. Jackson reportedly backed Harriet's father when the latter "squashed the affair between Shelley and Harriet."[49]

A Jackson descendent reported what was probably Shelley's first political conflict with Harriet's father, probably in 1808. (There is no record that Shelley visited the Groves in 1809 or 1810.) Shelley was visiting Ferne during assizes, local circuit court hearings, held in Shaftesbury. During the legal proceedings he "had been very much shocked at a sentence passed on a starving man who had stolen a sheep. Shelley made himself thoroughly awkward at Fern—& declined to go to any of the festivities held in connection with the Assizes week & argued hotly with his uncle or anyone who would listen to him—I think this upset Mr. Grove—who was a magistrate."[50] At the time, death often was meted out for minor offenses.

Shelley garnered more ill favor with the Grove clan when, probably in early 1811, he and a Grove cousin, John Jackson, served as ushers in a family wedding. Both young men, "being shy & gauche . . . performed their duties extremely badly," much to a Grove aunt's annoyance. Young Jackson apparently often visited Field Place when "Shelley was in his fathers bad books & they used to spend hours together in the harness room at Field Place playing Whist." John Jackson and Elizabeth played against Shelley and his partner, Laker the butler, "who was devoted to Master Bysshe" and always asked, "Be oi to play trumps Master Bysshe?"[51]

In January as the vacation was ending, Shelley wrote to Hogg that his attempt to "Deistify" his father was silenced "with an equine argument." He added, "My mother fancies me in the High road to Pandemonium, she fancies I want to make a deistical co-terie of all my little sisters." He enclosed his anti-war verses, telling Hogg they were Elizabeth's and using her seal on the letter. He mentioned that his unfinished political poem, probably sup-porting Peter Finnerty, was at Munday's.[52]

Hogg had taken a solitary five-day walking tour to the Salisbury Plain. Awaiting Shelley's return to Oxford, he sent him some po-etry he wrote designed to impart advice about love.[53] Shelley, re-plying immediately, suggested ending the poem with his rival, Hel-yar, as a pine tree being strangled by Harriet as entwining ivy. Jealous about Helyar and with feelings of "degradation" over los-ing Harriet, Shelley—citing Godwin—said of his own motives, "the worst is commingled with virtue." Shelley felt betrayed both by Harriet and his sister Elizabeth: "My sister will I fear *never* return the attachment which would *once* again bid *me* be happy."[54] Hogg perceptively noted that Shelley's use of "my sister" to refer to Eliz-abeth was the same emotional distancing he used with Harriet.

Shelley now turned his attack against despised Christianity into a tract, *The Necessity of Atheism,* which emerged from the ideas he and Hogg exchanged in their correspondence.[55] Shelley's volu-ble January 12 letter, written while he had a fever, was full of "my mad arguments" which were "none at all, for I am rather con-fused." In disconnected ramblings, he wondered, "do I not deceive myself . . . I am yet a sceptic on these subjects wd. that I cd. Believe . . . (if a God exists)." Uncertain about his deism, he misquoted Spinoza with a "materialist" view—actually more Lucretian—of "An *infinite* number of atoms" as a "*first* cause" in trying to "prove the existence of a Deity." Responding to Hogg's "argument of the necessity of Xtianity," he excoriated Christianity as "Hideous! . . . Xt how I hate thy influence." For the first time he succinctly stated the growing influence of Godwin's *Political Justice:* "would not an extended system of rational & moral unprejudiced education ren-der each individual capable of experiencing that degree of happi-ness to which each ought to aspire, more for other than self." He believed "Superstition [was] decaying . . . except where Faber, Rowland Hill . . . maintain their posts . . . how I despise them."[56]

Faber and Hill, two prominent clerics, were being baited by letters
into arguments about Christianity by means of pseudonyms, false
identities, and the soon-to-be-printed pamphlet on atheism.

From Oxford, Shelley wrote another correspondent, Mr. Wedgwood—possibly the younger Josiah Wedgwood—without using a
pseudonym. He was surprised that Wedgwood not only promised
a long reply but addressed him as "Revd." Believing his amazement would be "extreme," Shelley replied disabusing him of the
idea he was a minister. Receiving Wedgwood's long reply at Field
Place, Shelley sent it to Hogg, encouraging him to continue the de-
bate and mentioning having sent a letter to the Bishop of London.[57]
Hogg urged upon Wedgwood a rational basis of Christianity and by
mid-January, Shelley, receiving letters from Wedgwood and Hogg,
thought Hogg's "excellent" arguments would convince Wedgwood.[58] Staying up "all night," he wrote five pages of his own, sending them and Hogg's arguments to the unknowing Wedgwood.[59]
The arguments Hogg and Shelley developed in this exchange with
Wedgwood likely formed the kernel of *The Necessity of Atheism.*

Several days later, Shelley wrote Hogg, who was basing his ideas
on Locke, "Your systematic cudgel for Xtianity is excellent." Shelley unsuccessfully tried out the arguments on Timothy, who admitted reading Locke thirty years ago at Oxford.[60] Timothy, changing his attitude about Hogg after hearing laudatory reports of the
Hogg family, extended him an invitation to visit Field Place during
Easter vacation.[61]

Charles Grove recalled that before he and Shelley left Field
Place January 22, Mary Shelley gave her brother "a letter of introduction with a present to her schoolfellow, Miss Westbrook."
Charles recollected they called on Harriet "at Mr. Westbrook's
house."[62] It is not known how much Shelley saw his new Harriet
and her older sister Eliza during his several days in London. Back
in Oxford, his most fateful publishing venture preoccupied him.

Integrating Hogg's atheistical arguments with his own anticler-
ical deism, Shelley probably completed *The Necessity* before returning to Oxford.[63] Like *Original Poetry, The Necessity* perhaps
was printed by James Phillips in Horsham despite its imprint of C.
and W. Phillips in Worthing. James Phillips's daughter, Miss
Philadelphia Phillips—who did much of her father's printing—
may have taught Shelley to set the type of his own works.[64] Hogg,
trekking in Salisbury Plain, later intimated that Shelley published
the tract without consulting him. Shelley obviously was the force

behind its publication and distribution. Shelley's practical idea behind the work was spelled out by Hogg: "It was a small pill, but it
worked powerfully. . . He enclosed a copy in a letter, and sent it by
the post, stating with modesty and simplicity, that he had met accidentally with that little tract, which appeared unhappily to be
unanswerable. Unless the fish was too sluggish to take the bait, an
answer of refutation was forwarded to an appointed address in
London, and then a vigorous reply would fall upon the unwary dis-
putant, and break his bones."[65]

The Necessity of Atheism, a transitional document between
Shelley's wavering deistical beliefs and his developing atheism,
was "almost the first [work] in England to champion atheism
openly."[66] The family sources of Shelley's religious questioning included his grandfather Bysshe, whom he called, a year after publishing *The Necessity*, a "complete Atheist."[67] In matters of religion, Shelley was a safer target for Timothy than his feared sire.
Neither of Shelley's parents attempted to instill strong, let alone
rigid, Christian beliefs; he described his mother as "mild and tolerant and yet a Xtian."[68] Medwin remarked that Timothy's "religious opinions were also very lax; although he occasionally went
to the parish church, and made his servants regularly attend divine service, he possessed no true devotion himself, and incul-
cated none to his son and heir, so that much of Percy Bysshe's
scepticism may be traced to early example, if not to precept."
Medwin also recounted that Timothy, in the presence of his son,
addressed a local chaplain as an "old soul-saver."[69] Timothy, although fancying himself a religious liberal, would assume a conforming, superficial religious stance rather than risk social ostracism, a preoccupation with what his son called "reputation . . .
considered . . . as synonymous with virtue . . . *this* is the supporter
of prejudice."[70]

Timothy, trying to sanitize his son's religious outlook, wrote him
after he returned to Oxford. Shelley replied sarcastically that he
was pleased with his father's "very excellent exposition on . . . religion." Having "seldom seen ideas of Orthodoxy so clearly defined," his father had "proved to my complete satisfaction, that
those who do not think at all . . . should follow the religion of their
fathers whatsoever it may be." His own "reasoning" on religion led
him to believe the "the testimony of the twelve Apostles is insuffi-
cient to establish the truth of their doctrine. . . . Supposing twelve
men [testified] before you that they had seen in Africa, a vast snake

three miles long, suppose they swore that this snake eat nothing but Elephants, & that you knew from all the laws of nature, that enough Elephants cd. not exist to sustain the snake—wd. you believe them?"[71]

Making light of his father's statement that Locke and Newton were Christians, Shelley countered that Voltaire, Lord Kames, Hume, Rousseau, Adam Smith, and Benjamin Franklin were all deists whose lives were "characterised by the strictest morality." Hoping his father now had a better understanding of the basis of his "sentiments," he wished to hear further objections from him "if any yet remain."

On February 9, three days after writing this letter, *The Necessity* was advertised in Munday's *Oxford University and City Herald:*[72]

Speedily will be published
To be had of the Booksellers of London and Oxford
The
NECESSITY OF ATHEISM

Five days later, Shelley sent the "book" to Graham, urging him to "Cut out the title page & advertise it in 8 famous papers," and "be particularly quick about it." However, on February 17 he wrote Graham to "not advertise the Atheism as it is not yet published." Indicating Hogg's involvement, he wrote, "We are afraid of the Legislature's power with respect to Heretics" and said he decided against going to London immediately for fear of being "suspected as Author of the tract." He asked Graham to get as many copies of *St. Irvyne* as he could, wanting "the business out of Stockdales hand." Referring to one of his pseudonyms, he added, "any letter addressed to the Revd. Charles Meyton" was his and ended, "All the Bishops have the Atheism."[73]

Writing to Timothy the same day, Shelley dissembled concerning "the Atheism" tract about to explode on the scene. Politely referring to the death of his father's half-brother's wife, Mrs. Sidney, he said he was dressed in black and assured Timothy he was prepared for the examination Oxford required in Divinity. Playing to his father's anti-Catholicism, he wrote he had "very minutely investigated . . . the impudent & inconsistent falsehoods of priestcraft" and realized the universities are "on the principle of Inquisisatorial [*sic*] Orthodoxy." He would "perfectly coincide" with their beliefs although he could "refute [the] errors" of the "learned doctors . . . by the very rules of reasoning which their *own systems* of logic teach me. . . . I shall not therefore publickly come under the act 'De heretico comburendo.'" His firewall of anonymity was a tinder box, and his frequent allusions to being "burned" for atheism seem a mix of recognition of official power and masochistic fantasy.[74] He concluded saying he had not finished his Oxford competition poem on the Parthenon. Several weeks later Timothy would see the sarcasm of his son's closing, "Your very dutiful affec^t Percy B Shelley."

Shelley, rejecting typical Oxford undergraduate squanderings, "wine, or horses, or the prize-ring, or the cock-pit,"[75] concentrated his spending on publishing. Casting about for promising young female poets, he found two more than worthy of replacing Harriet Grove and his sister Elizabeth. A Mr. Strong at Oxford had shown the verses of Janetta Philipps to Shelley, who offered to pay for their publication hoping to "make even some balances" with Slatter and Munday. He tried to hide his identity from Miss Philipps, afraid "his intention might shock the delicacy of a noble female mind." Undaunted when Strong broke off contact with him, Shelley opened a brief correspondence with Janetta in May after being rebuffed by the other gifted young woman he was championing.[76]

She was Felicia Dorothea Browne, later the well-known poet, Felicia Hemans. Tom Medwin told Shelley he had met the fourteen-year-old published poet in 1808 in Northern Wales and was charmed by her beauty and poetry.[77] Medwin claimed that Shelley, using Medwin's name, corresponded at length with Felicia until her mother wrote Medwin senior insisting there be no further letters. Most likely, Shelley used his own name in writing initially to her over the holiday before returning to Oxford, possibly switching later to an impersonation after being rebuffed by Felicia. Reacting to Shelley's atheistic leanings, Felicia's mother cut short this epistolary relationship but not before Shelley had both his parents writing to Mrs. Browne on his behalf.

This stratagem emerged in a significant letter, recently found, from Shelley to Felicia Browne, written mid-March 1811 from the Grove brothers' London abode. It reveals details about Shelley's emotional state immediately before his expulsion and valuable insights about his relationship with his mother.[78] Writing mid-March, Shelley—probably in London distributing copies of *The Necessity*—used John Grove's respectable Lincoln's Inn address to impress Miss Browne. He wrote the letter with a stylus, a new invention that produced multiple copies. Having a joke on this method, he complained that unless "Felicia" was less subservient to her parents she would have "no originality of character . . . we shall be at best servile copies of our parent. . . . I need not express my contempt for Copies." Perhaps assuming a more androgynous persona, he signed himself "her affectionate Philippe Sidney."[79] Shelley's sister Hellen, only eleven, remembered or was told about her brother's having written to Felicia Browne and receiving a disappointing answer "that gave no encouragement to further correspondence."[80] Shelley's letter began, "My Father and Mother have both writ[t]en Mrs. Browne, and I confess I am not a little hurt that she has not even condescended to answer their letters—I must appear very impertinent for again addressing you, perhaps you will hear me before you condemn me." This letter suggests Shelley sent at least two other letters to Felicia, who probably wrote at least two to Shelley. Eleven years later, after receiving poems by Shelley she had ordered, Mrs. Hemans wrote: "I believe I mentioned to you the extraordinary letters with which I was once persecuted by ——; he, with whom 'Queen Mab' hath been. It was rather a singular circumstance that the parcel in which Mr. ——'s work was forward to me, contained, at the same time, an elegy of the death of that deluded character."[81] Shelley had mentioned to Felicia that he detected a "glaring fault" in her verse, "that you approved of fatal sanguinary war." Having received her "plaintive verses" in her "last letter," he tried to overcome her rejecting him because of his "religious sentiments." In addition to his atheism, she objected to his parents' opinions which "are in direct contradiction to those of the rest of the world." At this point, Shelley further offended her sensibilities by an extended humorous metaphor: "Even supposing I am as vile as many have supposed me, I do not see [?] how it would injure my dear Felicia to indulge me in a correspondence—The sun shines on many a dunghill, but its rays are so pure [?], so celestial that they never were contaminated by it."[82]

Tongue-in-cheek, Shelley told Felicia he "once thought that unlimited [?] passive obedience was the duty of a daughter to her Parents . . . but my Mother with some difficulty succeeded in almost convincing me that we ought to judge for ourselves." If Felicia stopped corresponding, it would be a "cruel sentence upon me, upon my Mother, who has incessantly regretted my dissapointment [sic], for she attributes it entirely to what she calls her faults." Continuing his theme of maternal collaboration, Shelley said if Felicia gave valid reasons for not writing, "I will cheerfully acquiesce in them, for, believe me, however great the pleasure might be to my Mother & myself, we would by no means wish to purchase it by any, the slightest transgression of the commands of reason on your part." Shelley then discussed the circumstances of his parents' marriage, imploring Felicia "do not think ill, very ill of me": "let me enumerate my offences—My Mother valued the happiness of my father, more than the opinion of mankind. I need not say how frivolous that is. how often it is opposite to truth . . . for they abused your Poems, they still abuse my Mother."

In this remarkable passage, the heart of Shelley's identification with his mother, he implied his mother married his father despite the "frivolous" denunciation and abuse of social opinion still directed towards her. Shelley seemingly is referring to the social stigma of his father's illegitimate son, born before his parents' marriage, and perhaps an intermittent family member from at least the time of the marriage. The silence veiling this family secret effectively blotted out this bastard son's existence for two hundred years. Shelley not only identified with his mother as the subject of social injustice and abuse, he specifically identified with her act of adopting an "orphan" child, something he often wished to do and finally would do.

Shelley was still helping Bird with his book on Sweden. He paid £150 on Bird's bills and obtained a £200 loan from Munday and Slatter, the book's printers, who compounded their error by co-signing a £400 bond with Shelley to buy the copyright of the manuscript, in Shelley's possession. Thirty-three years later, Henry Slatter was still trying to collect for his support of Shelley's last Oxford printing freak, now grown (with interest) to £1605.[83]

Identifying with liberal writers persecuted by the government, Shelley in early March 1811 wrote to Leigh Hunt, at twenty-six just acquitted after a third prosecution for seditious libel. "Although perfectly unacquainted privately with you," Shelley enclosed for Hunt's consideration an address he had composed proposing a meeting to form a society of "enlightened unprejudiced members of the community." This society was to "resist the coalition of the enemies of liberty which at present renders any expression of opinion on matters of policy dangerous to individuals." He mentioned as exemplars the Illuminati, a radical anarchist secret society in France advocating abolition of religion, private property, and sexual taboos. After mentioning he probably would take his father's seat in Parliament on attaining his majority, Shelley referred to his ongoing quasi-anonymous radical writing by adding, "On account of the responsibility to which my residence at this University subjects me, I of course, dare not publicly avow all that I think."[84] Three weeks later, his public avowals propelled him from both Oxford and Parliament.

Although Shelley expressed his radical literary interests in Munday's *Oxford Herald,* several poems printed in the *Herald* before and during his Oxford stay probably were not Shelley's.[85] On March 2, he and Bird publicly subscribed a guinea each in Munday's newspaper to support Castlereagh's nemesis, Peter Finnerty. A week later, Shelley advertised in the same paper "A Poetical Essay on the Existing State of Things, By a GENTLEMAN of the University of Oxford, For assisting to maintain in Prison Mr. Peter Finnerty, IMPRISONED FOR LIBEL."[86] No copy of this poem, published with his *St. Irvyne* pseudonym, has been found; Shelley may have incorporated some of it later into *Queen Mab.*[87] Finnerty had been vigorously defended in the press by Sir Francis Burdett and Leigh Hunt. Shelley included in the ad a quote about "famine . . . dead and dying . . . dogs fed on human bones" from Robert Southey's 1810 *The Curse of Kehama,* then his "most favourite poem."[88] In addition to *The Necessity,* Shelley's radical political writing may have played an unspoken role in promoting his expulsion.[89]

Shelley by this time was a well-known radical in the Oxford community. In addition to Charles Kirkpatrick Sharpe, other Oxford denizens were aware of his views and what he was publishing. On March 15, soon after Shelley's ad appeared for "Poetical Essay," Sharpe wrote Lady Charlotte Campbell mentioning Shelley's "Poetical Essay" as his "last exhibition . . . on the State of Public Affairs." He also mentioned that, in addition to *St. Irvyne,* "Our Apollo next came out with a prose pamphlet in praise of Atheism, which I have not yet seen."[90]

It was seen by the Reverend George Stanley Faber, a prolific Christian writer, vicar of Redmarshall, alumnus of University College, and friend of the Hogg family. Shelley had characterized Faber as one "of the Armageddon-Heroes . . . with all the obstinacy of cabalistic dogmatism."[91] In late February or early March Faber received a copy of *The Necessity* with the letter from the "Rev. Charles Meyton" mailed from Graham's Vine Street address.

Faber, completely falling for Shelley's elaborate ruse, became furious after the exposé.[92] Shelley's artifice as Charles Meyton in his exchanges with Faber continued after his expulsion. Shelley-Meyton presented himself as a fifty-year-old clergyman whose doubts about Christianity—leading him to contemplate giving up his preferment—were reinforced by the enclosed pamphlet whose author was a mystery to him. Faber believed Meyton was "highly beneficed," "conscientious," and "under distress of mind," but "had unhappily been perverted" by the pamphlet. Replying immediately, Faber pointed out "the palpable fallacies in the pamphlet," admitting "I had once myself been a sceptic in religion," and recommending "earnest prayers to God, on the supposition there might be a God." Faber promised not to divulge Meyton's name. Indicative of Shelley's excited state in the weeks before his expulsion, Faber said Shelley's twenty-page letter of response "rambled somewhat incoherently . . . [and was] written in a spirit by no means good." Faber wrote his lapsed clergyman another immediate reply.

About this time Faber learned Meyton's identity when a friend received a similar letter in the same handwriting from Oxford with *The Necessity.* Another very long letter arrived from Meyton, written just before or after Shelley's expulsion. Faber felt its "style might well have been deemed peculiarly offensive and impertinent, even had the writer been really a clergyman of 50; but it was doubly so, as proceeding from a boy and as addressed to a perfect stranger." Faber's ire at being duped by this "mere stripling" mounted. Responding to Shelley's latest letter, Faber's long nine-page reply enumerated its six "lies."[93] Among the lies were some of Shelley's most humorous inventions. They included his statement that he kept a middle-aged curate who was "remarkably sedulous in the discharge of his functions," that William Stanhope had shown him a letter of the late Lord Chesterfield, and "that his ill-health, produced by a long residence in foreign climates, rendered him unequal to clerical duties." Shelley said he had "travelled through Palestine, which resembled a stone-quarry more than anything else . . ." Faber was further incensed that Shelley-as-clergyman had assured him that he had not written *The Necessity* and had not "the most distant idea" of the author's identity.

The Necessity of Atheism is a curiously ambivalent work whose title was more inflammatory than its content. Only four by six inches and thirteen pages, it was one of Shelley's smallest publications. A Latin quote from Bacon—the mind cannot accept as true that which lacks a clear demonstration—preceded Shelley's advertisement that Graham placed in *The Globe*. It asserted that "love of truth" having motivated the "little tract," the author "earnestly" wants any reader "who may discover any deficiency in his reasoning," or who has "proofs" or "objections," to present them "as briefly, as methodically, as plainly as he has taken the liberty of doing. Thro' deficiency of proof. AN ATHEIST."[94]

The Necessity rests largely on Hume's consideration of three sources from which knowledge of God might derive: the senses, reason, and testimony. The latter two are most important, and Hogg's arguments for the non-existence of a deity were behind the argument on reason while Shelley's concern about belief and disbelief undergirds the argument on testimony. Shelley's letter to his father about the three-mile-long snake restated these same arguments on belief, directly influenced by Hume's *Essay on Miracles*.[95] Shelley concluded:

> From this it is evident that having no proofs from any of the three sources of conviction: the mind *cannot* believe the existence of a God. It is also evident that as belief is a passion of the mind, no degree of criminality can be attached to disbelief; they only are reprehensible who willingly neglect to remove the false medium thro' which their mind views the subject.
>
> It is almost unnecessary to observe, that the general knowledge of the deficiency of such proof, cannot be prejudicial to society: Truth has always been found to promote the best interests of mankind.—Every reflecting mind must allow that there is no proof of the existence of a Deity. Q.E.D.

The final sting, the mathematician's proof, "Q.E.D.," was Hogg's idea. Shelley often wrote it to end a message on a note of certainty and to provoke refutation of the argument. Hogg reported Shelley saying, "if you ask a friend to dinner, and only put Q.E.D. at the end of the invitation, he cannot refuse to come."[96]

Shelley anticipated Feuerbach's philosophical–psychological atheistic arguments and Marx's atheism. His major point, influenced by Hume and repeated in a post-expulsion letter to his father, was that unconscious, "instinctive" motives—"passions of the mind"—underlay religious belief and "no criminality" can be attached to belief or disbelief. However, reason or "rational motives" can uncover these "instinctive" motives. Shelley congratulated Hogg on his "distinction between instinctive & rational motives" and proceeded to elaborate on them.[97]

One of Shelley's irrational motives, his "unusually strong neurotic sense of guilt,"[98] lurked behind *The Necessity* and its self-punishing consequences. Shelley's atheistic message, an attack on God the Father, proved a more than sufficient attack on his own father.

Shelley tried distributing *The Necessity* through booksellers but was thwarted by Munday and Slatter's refusal to sell such a radical book. When they earlier refused to publish Hogg's anti-religious *Leonora,* Shelley sent his friend's novel to an Abingdon publisher who almost completed printing it when the expulsion aborted Hogg's work for good.[99] Munday and Slatter had asked a literary friend, Mr. Hobbes, to refute Shelley's arguments, but Shelley refused to reply to his critique, saying "he would rather meet any or all the dignitaries of the Church than one philosopher."[100] Blocked on the publishing front, Shelley sent the tract to "all the Bishops" and apparently to many professors, heads of colleges (including his own), the Vice-Chancellor, at least one Cambridge professor, and Medwin.[101] Shelley signed the letter included with each pamphlet with the pseudonym, "Jeremiah Stukeley." Frustrated at Munday and Slatter's refusal, Shelley—placing his work in their shop in their absence—"strewed the shop windows and counter" with copies, telling the shopman to sell quickly as many copies as he could for sixpence each. One of the first to enter the shop, a Fellow of New College, Reverend John Walker, after perusing the shocking tract convinced Munday and Slatter to destroy all the copies. They promptly burned not the atheist but his offensive pamphlet in the back kitchen. Summoning Shelley to their house, an attorney tried "first by entreaties and next by threats, to dissuade him from the errors of his ways" but to no avail as "he appeared to glory in the course he had adopted."[102] Alarmed, Munday and Slatter wrote to the Phillips firm warning of a possible prosecution by the government and urging the destruction of the remaining copies, the manuscript, and even the types of *The Necessity.*[103]

Exactly when these events took place is uncertain; Sharpe had written of Shelley's authorship of *The Necessity* ten days before his expulsion. A deceptive calm settled over University College and its Master, the placid Griffith. However, Shelley apparently sent a copy of *The Necessity* to the Reverend Edward Copleston, professor of poetry and Fellow of Oriel College, later a Bishop. Copleston had earlier answered the attack on Oxford's religious rigidity in the *Edinburgh Review* by stating, "the scheme of Revelation is closed, and we expect no new light to break in upon us."[104] Copleston possibly tracked down Shelley's authorship and presented the evidence to Griffith, stirring him to action.[105] Shelley wrote Godwin ten months later:

> Oxonian society was insipid to me, uncongenial with my habits of thinking.—I could not descend to common life. The sublime interest of poetry, lofty and exalted achievements, the proselytism of the world, the equalization of its inhabitants were to me the soul of my soul.—You can probably form some idea of the contrast exhibited by my character by those with whom I was surrounded.—Classical reading and poetical writing employed me during my residence at Oxford.—In the meantime I became in the popular sense of the word 'God' an Atheist. I printed a pamphlet avowing my opinion, and it's occasion. I distributed this anonymously to men of thought and learning wishing that Reason should decide on the case at issue. It was never my intention to deny it. Mr. Coplestone at Oxford among others had the pamphlet; he shewed it to the master and the fellows of University College, and I was sent for: I was informed that in case I denied the publication no more would be said.—I refused, and was expelled.[106]

About the same time, Southey wrote a similar version of the expulsion related to him by Shelley. There are at least nine versions of the expulsion, five by Shelley, who later significantly changed what he said at his hearing. One later account quoted Shelley telling the Master, "I did write the work; I see nothing in it of which I have not reason to be proud." Peacock said Shelley told him he defended himself by delivering a prepared oration published in an Oxford newspaper. Peacock recalled Shelley showing him a copy, but doubted Shelley gave the oration.[107]

On a "fine spring morning," after breakfast on Lady Day, March 25, near the end of Lent Term, Hogg went to Shelley's rooms and found him absent. According to Hogg, Shelley soon rushed in "terribly agitated," exclaiming:

> I am expelled! I was sent for suddenly a few minutes ago; I went to the common room, where I found our master, and two or three of the fellows. The master produced a copy of the little syllabus, and asked me if I were the author of it. He spoke in a rude, abrupt, and insolent tone.

I begged to be informed for what purpose he put the question. No answer was given; but the master loudly and angrily repeated, 'Are you the author of this book?' If I can judge from your manner, I said, you are resolved to punish me, if I should acknowledge that it is my work. If you can prove that it is, produce your evidence; it is neither just nor lawful to interrogate me in such a case and for such a purpose. Such proceedings would become a court of inquisitors, but not free men in a free country.[108]

Shelley "calmly, but firmly," in the face of the Master's "violent and ungentlemanlike deportment," repeatedly refused to answer questions concerning the pamphlet, and Griffith announced "Then you are expelled," producing a document of expulsion. Shelley was to leave the College no later than the next morning. Hogg reported, "Shelley was full of spirit and courage; frank and fearless; but he was likewise shy, unpresuming, and eminently sensitive. . . . I have never seen him so deeply shocked or so cruelly agitated as on this occasion."

Hogg, wanting to assist his dearest and only friend, immediately wrote a note to the Master implicating himself in the matter. Quickly called before the same tribunal, Hogg perceived "as soon as I entered the room, that it was an affair of party; that whatever could conciliate the favour of patrons was to be done without scruple." He surmised this court of justice, and its spokesman, the Master, were puppets for the "pert, meddling tutor" Copleston, the "secret accuser [who] was rapidly enriched with the most splendid benefices, and finally became a dignitary of the church." Hogg perceived Copleston and his agent Griffith as more cautious in handling his case than Shelley's because of Hogg's grandfather's lucrative political–religious tie. The Master, angrily inquiring if Hogg wrote the tract, looked as if "I alone stood between him and the rich see of Durham." Hogg protested the unfair question and became silent. Asked to retire to think about his answer, he was immediately recalled and refused to answer the question. Handed his notice of expulsion, Hogg protested the word "contumaciously" in reference to his refusal to disavow the publication, causing the Master to dash the pamphlet to the table as he gave Hogg the same deadline as Shelley for leaving.[109]

Shelley, recovering from his immediate shock, made the rounds saying goodbye to his friends. He said to Halliday, "I am come to say goodbye to you, if you are not afraid to be seen with me."[110]

Shelley later told Southey that he also saw Mr. Strong to assure publication of Janetta Philipps' poetry. Hearing of the expulsion, Strong fainted. After Shelley got him outdoors, the recovered Strong hoped never to see Shelley again.[111]

Hogg and Shelley departed the next morning for London on top of the eight o'clock stage. Before leaving, Hogg was told that if they asked the Master, they could stay a while longer. Shelley, "indignant at the insult which he had received," adamantly vetoed this idea and off they went. Hogg, looking back on this experience in his biography of Shelley, regretted—through ten pages—that they did not stay and perhaps try to reverse the expulsion.[112] The expulsion, a decisive turning point in the lives of both youths, elicited quite different reactions in each. Hogg gradually assumed the conventional, Tory attitudes of the oppressors. For Shelley, this was only the first of many brushes with conservative power that in the years ahead solidified his radical resolve and fired his poetic ardor.

A junior fellow at Oxford observed that: "I believe no one regretted their departure for there were but few, if any, who were not afraid of Shelley's strange and fantastic pranks, and the still stranger opinions he was known to entertain; but all acknowledged him to have been very good-humored and of a kind disposition. T. J. Hogg had intellectual powers to a great extent, but, unfortunately, misdirected. He was not popular."[113] Sharpe characterized Shelley as "a strange tatterdemalion looking figure, dressed like a scarecrow; he had no credit for talents at Oxford, where he was thought to be insane." However, he remarked that at his expulsion Shelley "behaved like a hero . . . he showed to Fortune's frowns a brow serene," declaring his intention of emigrating to America.[114] The *Antijacobin Review* printed a statement from "The Oxford Collegian" endorsing their attack on the author of *St. Irvyne,* adding that his expulsion for "singularly wicked tenets" should serve as a warning "that a vigilant eye is still kept in this University over improprieties of conduct."[115] In a book published in 1812, a leading medical scientist criticized the "audacity" and "materialism" of *The Necessity* and approved its authors' expulsion. A year later, *Cobbett's Political Register* asked why the publisher of the pamphlet had not been prosecuted.[116]

The view that Shelley could have avoided expulsion simply by stating to the authorities he was the author of *The Necessity* overlooks an essential theme in his moral position, the right not to incriminate oneself by one's own testimony. This right, embodied in the Fifth Amendment to the United States Constitution, had no counterpart either in English constitutional practice or in a society where, without separation of church and state, political and educational institutions embraced the Church. Shelley's refusal to respond to his inquisitors was one of the high-water marks of his life, representing as it did his fundamental position that received forms of oppression, however subtle or flagrant, had to be met with a resolute no.

9

Doubling After the Fall: Harriet Westbrook and Elizabeth Hitchener

THE TWO EX-STUDENTS ARRIVED IN LONDON MARCH 26 WITH TWENTY pounds Shelley recently had borrowed from Slatter.[1] Checking into a Piccadilly coffeehouse near Graham's lodgings, they had tea with John and Charles Grove at Lincoln's Inn Fields. At four in the morning, Tom Medwin—lamely pursuing the law and living near Gray's Inn—heard Shelley rapping on his door, exclaiming, "let me in, I am expelled," followed by a "sort of loud, half-hysterical laugh."[2] The next day lodgings were found at 15 Poland Street, the name intriguing Shelley because of Poland's fight for freedom.

Hogg wrote his father the day of his expulsion that he had informed the College he was "as much the author as the person accused."[3] Shelley waited four days after the event to write his father, knowing Oxford by then had notified him. In a provocative, nonchalant style, Shelley told his father he had "doubtless heard" of his and Hogg's "misfortune" and feared his father "must be greatly excited." He and Hogg had been "induced to disbelieve the scriptures" as they "found to our surprise that . . . the proofs of an existing Deity were . . . defective." Falsely expecting that men who studied "Divinity" might "disprove our reasoning," instead, they were "publickly expelled." However, Shelley assured him, "I am perfectly indifferent to the late tyrannical violent proceedings of Oxford." He asked his father to "present" his "affectionate duty to my mother," "my love to Elizabeth." He extended nothing to Timothy.[4] On the enclosed *The Necessity of Atheism,* Timothy penned "Impious" across the front. He immediately wrote Hogg, revoking his invitation for Easter.[5]

Timothy was angered and shamed by his son's public and provocative display of socially unacceptable ideas. Shelley had exposed his father's duplicitous religious stance, that private beliefs must not become public if they offend. Timothy also was haunted by the fear that his son would be ensnarled in legal action over such a blasphemous publication.

Girding for battle, Timothy went to London in early April. After establishing headquarters at Miller's Hotel, Westminster Bridge, he consulted the family solicitor, William Whitton, soon to emerge as the strongman. It was several days before father and son met. From the House of Commons, Timothy wrote to Hogg's father, obtaining his first name—John—and proximate address from one of the "men of rank and influence" he consulted.[6] Timothy's second letter to John Hogg repeated the need to separate their sons who not only share "monstrous opinions" but also "want to get into professions together." Anticipating "much trouble," Timothy intended to read Paleys *Natural Theology* to his son, believing a father had more influence "than a Stranger." Timothy, never rebellious, thought he could "exhort him to divest himself of all prejudice already imbib'd fm his false reasoning." He ended as "your Obedt & Afflicted fellow sufferer."[7]

John Hogg was having none of Timothy's affliction. His calmer approach to his son's expulsion came from two friends—the lawyer Robert Clarke, and the Reverend John Brewster—who advised avoiding "severe censure" in favor of "soothing and complacent kindness."[8] John Hogg had also contacted his duped friend, the Reverend Faber.

Both Clarke and Whitton entertained the possibility of prosecution for blasphemy. Clarke told John Hogg that in the unlikely event the two young men were prosecuted, the punishment would be imprisonment, not execution or deportation.[9] Clarke assured Hogg's father that the two sons' "strange Conduct" was due to "a desire to be singular." Finding "no striking Impiety in the Pamphlet," he thought its argument "foolish" but well-written. He repeated others' reports that the pair at Oxford did not dine in College and wore different dress. Shelley had "always been odd . . . and suspected of insanity." He and Hogg were "of great acquirements." Believing things would "blow over," Clarke reassured Hogg's father not to be "anxious . . . about any criminal proceedings" and that Jefferson could "be admitted into any of the Inns of Court" but would not be readmitted "to either of the Universities without a disavowal of his opinions. . . . At this time of life that is not to be expected."[10]

Timothy, convening his first meeting with his son, invited Shelley and Hogg to dine at his hotel April 7. Shelley alerted Hogg to expect his father's peculiar behavior, which Hogg described at length in his account recalled forty-five years later.[11] Arriving punctually, they found Edward Graham with Timothy, who began talking "in an odd, unconnected manner; scolding, crying, swearing, and then weeping again." Reacting to his father's behavior, Shelley emitted a "wild, demonical burst of laughter," falling off his chair flat on his back. While Shelley was out of the room, Timothy sought Hogg's advice on how to deal with his "rather wild" son. After Hogg suggested marriage, Timothy and Graham began assembling names of young women they knew.

The "jolly and hospitable" Timothy, well fortified with port, asked Graham to make tea. After more of his crying, laughter, and swearing, Timothy extolled his importance in Parliament and his being beloved in Sussex. Turning to religion and his belief that there is a God, he began reading his arguments from Paley. Shelley, listening "with profound attention," told Hogg he recognized the arguments. When Hogg identified them as Paley's, Timothy said "Yes! I copied them out of Palley's book this morning myself." When Timothy stated he gave these ideas to "Palley"—rhymed like Sally—Shelley and Hogg laughed at his pronunciation. Shelley's early receptiveness to some of Paley's ideas would turn to disdain for his *Natural Theology*.[12]

Failing to make any inroads upon Shelley and Hogg, Timothy, expressing regret Hogg did not help him empty another bottle of port, said, "Tell me the truth, I am not such a bad fellow after all, am I?"

Port and Paley having failed, Timothy continued meeting daily with Whitton.[13] Increasingly deferring to Whitton's Tory control, Timothy hardened his line with his son with a set of proposals—perhaps Whitton's—Shelley must follow. He threatened to cut off his son personally and financially if he did not obey.

Writing to "My Dear Boy," Timothy said "The Disgrace which hangs over you is most Serious." Although sympathizing with what happened to Shelley because of his "Criminal opinions, and improper Acts," he had "Duty to perform" to his "own Character as well as to your Young Brother & Sisters." Shelley's mother's character went unmentioned. Timothy proposed that Shelley go to Field Place and not communicate with Hogg. Further, Timothy would appoint a gentleman under whose "Instructions & directions" Shelley would be placed. If Shelley did not abandon his "Errors" and "wicked Opinions," Timothy would "withdraw myself from you" and leave Shelley "to the Punishment & Misery" for the "Diabolical & wicked opinions . . . you have dar'd declare."[14]

Shelley's prompt rejection of the proposals parodied his father's sense of "duty." It was "my Duty"—despite wounding his father's "Sense of Duty" and "your feelings as a Christian"—to refuse his "assent" to these proposals and any future requests. He was "yr. Affecte Dutyful Son."[15]

Chagrined, Timothy immediately sent Shelley's rejection note to Whitton asking for his "most kind and friendly advice."[16] Clarke, at this time, told Hogg's father that Shelley "was reputed to be very singular if not a little insane, at Eton: and that report had reached Oxford before he came there." His source also implied that Hogg's Oxford involvement with Shelley left no time for sexual dalliance.[17]

Among those who failed to influence Shelley at this time was Robert Hurst, barrister and Duke of Norfolk's man in Horsham. Shelley indignantly protested to his father after being visited by "such a man."[18] Timothy, in a rare protest, told Whitton he had "no Authority" to enlist Hurst. However, Timothy assured Whitton he would act on any "Principle" he had "the goodness to suggest . . ."[19] Whitton then wrote Sir Bysshe to stiffen Timothy's resolve against Shelley whose "impiety and effrontery in the avowal of it exceeds belief." If anything would bring the son "a sense of his duty" it would be "the firm conduct . . . of Mr. Tim Shelley."[20]

Timothy now made his first definitive move to cease further contact with his son. He wrote Whitton he would "now leave this Young Lunatic to your management as I shall go home."[21] John Hogg, believing Shelley was "completely deranged," blamed him for having "duped" his son. Vicar Faber's wife more accurately wrote, "Shelley's letters to Mr. F are not those of a madman; his conduct throughout has been too systematic to admit of this apology for him."[22] Shelley—once Faber knew his real identity—had proposed that his letters and Faber's be published in a "small pamphlet."[23] Faber, outraged, demanded that his letters to Shelley be burned. Shelley refused because they were "too valuable" to be committed to the flames.[24]

Shelley, to counter Timothy's belief that Hogg was responsible for corrupting his son's principles, wrote a polite denial to John Hogg absolving his son and attacking Timothy who "must know less than his son" on this issue. Hogg only learned of Shelley's letter to his father many years later.[25]

Timothy, hearing from his emissary John Grove of his unsuccessful talk with Shelley, dutifully sent Grove's letter to Whitton saying he "plac'd the business in your hands to guard my honour and character against Prosecution in the Courts."[26] Whitton composed an unmailed letter to the Phillipses in Worthing excoriating them for publishing the "blasphemous work . . . of a stripling only 19 years of age" and threatening to prosecute them if they printed more of Shelley's manuscripts.[27]

Robert Parker, whom Timothy considered his "very intelligent" brother-in-law, also called on Shelley. After their unproductive talk, Parker wrote Timothy that Shelley, "a very accute [sic] reasoner," made "an expression of affection towards his mother and sister." Forwarding Parker's letter to Whitton, Timothy underlined the words about affection and inserted "never to me."[28]

Worried about his father's threat to stop his financial support, Shelley wrote Stockdale and learned that St. Irvyne had poor sales.[29] Meeting with Clarke, Shelley and Hogg negotiated an agreement on the proposals from the Hogg camp. Shelley wrote Hogg's father that the "concessions," although "painful," stemmed from "our high sense of filial duty."[30] John Hogg accepted this agreement, conditioned upon Timothy's acceptance. These proposals—which Shelley spelled out in a letter to his father—were that he and Hogg would apologize to Faber, would "not obtrude Atheistical opinions," and "refrain from publishing Atheistical Doctrines or even speculations." They would return immediately to their homes but "demand an unrestrained correspondence." Shelley was to be permitted to "select that situation in life . . . to which he may judge his abilities adequate." Shelley told his father of his "real and sincere wish for coming to an accommodation."[31]

Receiving Shelley's letter, Timothy consulted immediately with his father and both penned strong rejection letters on April 14. Whitton had triumphed. Old Sir Bysshe agreed with Whitton that "P.B.S. etc. are extraordinary characters" and it was unlikely "unconditional Submission" would be effective with the "rebels." His "plain unrefined Opinion is (I never deceive myself) let these two young men run their career with out interruption, this in my opinion will bring them to their senses sooner than any thing." Adding a postscript, he "had something like a proposal again" from his mistress Mrs. Nicholls in Canterbury Place and had to go to London to deal with it.[32]

In his angry rejection letter to Clarke, Timothy said Hogg's father was "deceiv'd" by these "Opinionated Youngsters" who were "Undutyfull & disrespectful . . . [with] such Insolence."[33] Sending the proposals to Whitton, Timothy was still anxious that his son not enter the legal profession. Timothy, always kowtowing to authority, said his father "very much approved of the decision taken by me" to be firm. Shelley and Hogg were "like two commanding armies" ready to "go to Battle again." Appealing to Whitton for further advice, Timothy wrote, "Don't spare my Apostate Son."[34]

Clarke realized that prohibiting correspondence between the two was unenforceable. He wrote Timothy that he had read them law from Blackstone concerning the penalties for writing or publishing profane doctrine and had discouraged Shelley from practicing law. Implicitly criticizing Timothy for his harsh treatment of his son, he said he used "mild reasoning and mild words" with Hogg.[35]

Timothy wrote Whitton that Shelley, now separated from Hogg, was "left . . . in Solitary Confinement." Whitton then accused Timothy of allowing "your son extraordinary liberties," else he would not have "penned such a proposal." He pointed out that Mr. Hogg's son now does as his father directs but Timothy has resigned to his son's "pleasure" about his future life.[36]

Stung by Whitton's criticism, Timothy's response—a confused analysis of his relationship with his son—revealed his well-meaning but limited power of understanding and insight. Denying having given Shelley "Liberties," he found inexplicable how his son "got all this Heterodoxy in a Place fam'd for Piety of Learning." His son's "conduct and opinions . . . are not only extremely singular, but abhorent in a Christian Society." Believing Shelley had "Temporary Insanity," Timothy had offered him a vacation "to the Greek Islands" to "tranquilize his perturb'd imagination" but Shelley "would not leave Hogg." He would not let Shelley stay at Field Place because he, Timothy, had to "occasionally be away." Finally, Shelley "or Hogg has a Box which they call their Poison Box that should be burnt."[37]

Hogg quickly apologized to Faber but Shelley procrastinated a month. Faber took ten pages to accept Hogg's apology, denouncing Shelley, the "seducer" of the "seduced" Hogg. Listing six lies in Shelley's letters, Faber declared that Shelley's "fortune will probably assure him the society of sycophants . . . and strumpets." As an atheist, Shelley would suffer from "drunkenness," "fornication," and "adultery. . . . What a hell upon earth would be the globe of ours be, if it were peopled by Shelleys!" Only "fear of the gallows" could "restrain" this "infidel" from "murder or treason."[38]

Before starting legal training in York, Hogg went to Ellesmere in mid-April with Robert Clarke and visited Lady Eleanor Butler and Miss Ponsonby in Llangollen, Wales. He commented on the "strong mutual attachment" of the well-known lesbian pair.[39]

Shelley was lonely without Hogg. During their three weeks together on Poland Street, he had read with delight to Hogg all of Byron's *English Bards and Scotch Reviewers*. Earlier, some lines from Byron's *Hours of Idleness* had crept into *St. Irvyne*.[40] When the two walked to Clapham Common to see Shelley's sisters at their boarding school, Shelley was "rapturous" upon seeing Hellen, who soon won a prize for skill in French translation.[41] Shelley secreted cakes in his pockets for his sisters, who saved their pennies to ease his financial destitution and who asked Harriet Westbrook convey the money and other small gifts to him.[42]

Medwin provided some company for Shelley, walking with him along the Serpentine as Shelley delighted in skipping rocks across the water and floating paper boats. At Medwin's dinner party, Shelley and John Grove defended a feminist position on women against some male chauvinists. After accompanying Medwin one Sunday to hear the well-known preacher Rowland Hill, Shelley wrote Hill under a pseudonym, vainly offering to preach to his congregation. Shelley located a copy of Lewis's *The Monk* for Medwin,[43] who doubtfully claimed he tried to burn the scandalous book. Medwin's freewheeling social life soon led to his arrest for debt.

Medwin characterized Shelley at this time as being in a "dreamy state." Shelley, keeping a daily dream journal, found "two sorts of dreams, the Phrenic and the Psychic." Some of his dreams proved "the mind and the soul were separate and different entities." Other dreams were "broken off by a dream within a dream—a dream of the soul, to which the mind was not privy," causing a "start of horror" from which he waked. Such night terror dreams continued until the end of Shelley's life. Medwin noted that Shelley's somnambulism had returned, an ominous renewal. Medwin recalled "in Leicester Square one morning at five o'clock, I was attracted by a group of boys collected around a well-dressed person lying near the rails. . . . I descried Shelley, who had unconsciously spent a part of the night *sub dio*. He could give no account of how he got there."[44]

The separation anxiety that helped precipitate Shelley's Syon House somnambulism was being re-experienced. His recent losses included Harriet Grove, his estrangement from Elizabeth, his expulsion, Hogg's departure, and his father's interdiction against returning to his family. Writing about this period some months later, he was a "maniac-sufferer" in a "friendless solitude." Seemingly, his dream states were "The casket of my unknown mind."[45]

John and Charles Grove, busy with medical pursuits, walked regularly with Shelley in St. James's Park where the soldiers evoked Shelley's objection "to a standing army, as being calculated to fetter the minds of the people." Shelley, having rejected his father's attempts to have him join the army, accused Timothy of wanting him murdered in Spain. Shelley and Charles visited the British Forum near Covent Garden where outspoken radicals of the day "abused all existing governments." Shelley, giving his first political speech, was so successful "that when he left the room, there was a rush to find out who he was, and to induce him to attend there again." Expressing disdain for such meetings, he gave a false name and address.[46]

The Duke of Norfolk, desiring to give Shelley the seat from Horsham, arranged for him and his father to dine at Norfolk House to discuss this plan. Charles Grove recalled Shelley's indignation at this "effort to shackle his mind" and become "a mere follower of the duke." The Duke probably repeated his earlier arguments that such an occupation was "most advantageous, because it is a monopoly . . . the number of competitors is limited" both in ability and in quantity, in contrast to the church and the bar. Norfolk disparaged a career in literature, telling Shelley "your chance of success is still worse . . . it is a struggle for glory—the competition is infinite—there are no bounds . . . a sea without shores."[47]

The metaphor probably pleased Shelley, who thought England in 1811 was a political quagmire. The aged George III was in his final illness and the Regency Act of 1811 made his profligate son Regent. The poverty-stricken Irish agitated for Catholic emancipation while, in England, wages paid by manufacturers barely sustained life. As machines replaced workers, mill-burning and frame-breaking would begin. The sheep of destitute farm laborers died in the cold winters and army deserters became marauding gangs. Any journalist protesting the sufferings of people faced prosecution by The Attorney-General.[48]

Amid this suffering, the corpulent Prince Regent's June grand fête at Carlton House for the Bourbon princes and two thousand guests featured a moss-lined stream with live fish running down the center of the two-hundred-foot main table. Reading of this obscene opulence in the *Morning Herald*, Shelley immediately composed and published a satirical poem. In a gesture he repeated in the years ahead, "he amused himself with throwing copies into the carriages of persons going to Carlton House after the fête."[49] Only four of about fifty lines survive of this poetic satire. With jocular outrage, he wrote Graham to "assist me . . . to magnify . . . our Noble Royal Family . . . thou hast an harp of fire, & I a pen of honey . . . the ode is coming." Shelley translated the *Marseillaise* on the reverse side.[50] Expecting a revolution, he said the £120,000 Carlton House "entertainment" would not be "the last bauble which the nation must buy to amuse this overgrown bantling of Regency."[51]

Shelley, loathing the law, became interested in medicine and was "about to enter the profession of physic" where he could "experiment upon morality, uninfluenced by the *possibility* of giving pain to others."[52] There is no evidence his parents supported his interest in medicine. He probably did not pay the twenty guineas for the lectures and surgical tours he attended.[53] Charles Grove recalled that "The thought of anatomy . . . became quite delightful to Bysshe, and he attended a course with me, and sometimes went also to St. Bartholomew's Hospital."[54]

The course was the anatomical lectures of John Abernethy, successor to John Hunter, an authority on venereal disease. Shelley perhaps met his subsequent physician, the radical and atheist William Lawrence, then Abernethy's protégé and assistant.[55] Walking among the diseased and dying at St. Bartholomew's, Shelley told Medwin he expected "to breathe his last" in a similar fate.[56] The venereal disease ward at St. Bartholomew's was known as the Lazarus ward or "Job's ward."[57] During these spring months of 1811 Shelley possibly expected his last breath from the effects he attributed to an earlier venereal infection, even if he were now cured. This fear was understandable, given his hypochondriacal tendencies and the prevalent belief that syphilis could doom one to permanent ill-health. Shelley followed Abernethy's advocacy of careful attention to the diet and knew of Abernethy's belief that the body operated as a whole organism. Writing of the pain of his "withered vitals"[58] at this time, Shelley perhaps believed his gastrointestinal symptoms came from "nervous disease" engendered by an earlier bout with syphilis.

After Hogg's departure, Shelley wrote John Slatter he would repay his £20 loan when he got his "affairs a little settled" and would send Bird's "writings" when his trunk arrived from Oxford.[59] He then wrote Whitton a brief bombshell that outraged Whitton and Timothy. Shelley offered to relinquish "that part of Sir Bysshe Shelley's property [that] is entailed upon me . . . in case my father will divide it equally wth my sisters & My Mother & allow me now £100 per annum." Significantly, the words "& My Mother" were inserted as an afterthought.[60] Shelley's generosity involved that portion of his grandfather's property—certain estates in Sussex—entailed to him. This amount, about £80,000, still left him £120,000 of inheritance.[61] Refusing the entail was the ultimate attack on his father, who became more upset by this act than by his expulsion. Shelley was not only waging war on the patriarchal system of entail, which Godwin condemned in his writings, he had the gall to propose that the estates revert to the family females. Whitton immediately informed Shelley it was a null proposition because he was not legally an adult. Shelley probably knew this and possibly was planning a later challenge to the agreement.

Shelley, incensed at Whitton's "imperious" tone, threatened to return the lawyer's letters unopened. Responding in kind, Whitton would not "receive" any more "insulting" letters from someone "only about 19."[62] Timothy, still groveling, thanked Whitton for his kind friendship, admitting he was "infinitely" more shocked by Shelley's "insulting" entail proposal than "of his expulsion." His son obviously "wishes to become . . . a martyr." Timothy had heard that Shelley "is woefully melancholy" and that he had corresponded with Lucien Bonaparte and perhaps with Finnerty. He needed "to come to some decision" on how "to act toward a son in such dire disobedience."[63] It is not known if Shelley corresponded with Napoleon Bonaparte's rebellious younger brother, then living in England.

Soon after Hogg left, Shelley wrote to him of being "a little solitary," but keeping busy "writing poetry" and sleeping a lot. When he told Hogg he had resigned his claim to the entail, he said he was asking for a £200 allowance. Again excluding his mother, he said his entail was only for his sisters. His mother had sent him some money but "I of course returned it." After mentioning that his uncle "Mr. Pilfold has written a very civil letter," Shelley told Hogg, "Miss Westbrooke has this moment called on me; with her sister. It certainly was very kind of her."[64]

Shelley had initiated a correspondence with Harriet after visiting the Westbrooks in late January with Charles Grove. After his expulsion, he saw her when visiting his three younger sisters at Mrs. Fenning's School, now run by Miss Hawkes. Eliza, nine years older than Harriet and usually the "Miss Westbrook" in his letters, received him at her father's Chapel Street house. Over the Easter holiday, Harriet and Eliza came to Poland Street to deliver pocket money and gifts from Shelley's sisters and to minister to the ailing youth.

Shelley's culpability in the tragic ending of his relationship with Harriet Westbrook would evoke "one of the most violent controversies in English literary biography."[65] The two were young. Harriet—born August 1, 1795—was only fifteen and Shelley eighteen in early 1811. John Westbrook, Esquire, as he was listed in the guide to London society, at sixty was a prosperous retired business man. Reputedly a "vintner" and hotel manager, he owned two taverns or inns, including "The Mount" coffeehouse located on Lower Grosvenor Street, near his Chapel Street residence. His neighbors included Viscountess Sydney, George "Beau" Brummell, and Lord Fitzroy, aide-de-camp to George III. Also living near his respectable coffeehouse was the scion of the Michelgrove branch of Shelley's family, Sir John Shelley.[66]

John Westbrook endured the social bigotry reflected in his nickname, "Jew Westbrook," derived, Harriet reported, from his "thrifty . . . careful habits" and "his Israelitish aspect." Shelley's attraction to Harriet was not lessened by Timothy's disapproval of her family standing. That Westbrook's two daughters would marry rich men reflected his upwardly mobile social aspirations.[67]

Harriet's mother was mostly absent in accounts of the Westbrook family. Hogg never met Mrs. Westbrook and his derogatory account of her came from Shelley or her daughters. Hogg characterized Harriet's mother as a piece of furniture in the home, "as dignified as silk and satin could make her, but utterly incapable of aught besides . . . except possibly of hearing herself addressed occasionally as Mamma."[68] Apparently, three Westbrook children did not survive childhood.[69] Ann Westbrook seemingly was incapable of providing mothering for her youngest daughter Harriet who, from a very young age, became attached to her sister Eliza as surrogate mother. Harriet, who later called Eliza her "more than mother" to whom she owed "Everything,"[70] would name her daughter after Eliza, not her mother. Hogg believed that Harriet "worshipped" Eliza from "a strong sense of paramount duty, and . . . implicit, unreasoning obedience." Further, "Eliza had tended, guided, and ruled Harriet from her earliest infancy."[71] An emotional vacuum between mother and infant perhaps contributed to Harriet's depressive trends and to her need to cling to her controlling, dominant older sister. Harriet's need for succorance enhanced Shelley's attraction to her. He later complained that Harriet was an inadequately nurturing mother.

As if she were the little girl he wished to adopt, Shelley often called Harriet his "little friend." Desiring to direct her transformation, he believed "Harriet will do for one of the crushers" in his crusade against religious bigotry. Soon he enlisted another new sister to help him "mould" Harriet. Sexual passion and strong feelings of romantic love were not primary driving forces in the attraction between Shelley and Harriet. They were bonded by mutual needs for attachment and dependency.

Harriet's underlying depressiveness was combined with obsessive–compulsive behavior that perhaps had a schizoid quality.[72] Not usually spontaneous, Harriet was controlled, perfectionistic, and rigid. Hogg described her as "smart, usually plain in her neatness; without a spot, without a wrinkle, not a hair out of place. The ladies said of her, that she always looked as if she had just that moment stepped out of a glass-case; and so indeed she did."[73] Preferring "morality" themes with "a high ethical tone," she fondly read aloud "for hours and hours" and "fiercely resented" Shelley's falling asleep during her readings. On her honeymoon she began translating a popular French morality romance, *Claire d'Albe*, writing it out "without blot or blemish" in her "small, neat, flowing, and legible feminine hand." Her attraction was to the "inevitable necessity" of the death of the married heroine because she had taken a lover.[74]

Harriet's father earlier had sent her to a Methodist school with "strict morality" and "sexual puritanism." Inveighing against "the vices of high society," he raised Harriet in the rigid middle class sexual conventions, recognizing the value of her sexual chastity in promoting a marriage into the upper classes.[75] According to Hogg, when her beauty attracted others' eyes as she walked down the street, "her cheeks were suffused with the blush of modesty" and she "bashfully pulled down her veil." Her "modest scrupulousness" made her "always most unwilling to show her ankles, or even her feet, hence her reluctance to move in the presence of a rude, indelicate wind."[76]

More serious was Harriet's preoccupation with suicide, which Hogg called a "monomania of self-destruction." From their earliest acquaintance, he claimed that Harriet talked of suicide, asking the surprised Hogg if he ever thought of destroying himself or "of killing any one; of murdering your mother; of setting stack-yards on fire? . . . She often discoursed of her purpose of killing herself some day or other, and at great length, in a calm, resolute manner." She told him, that being "very unhappy" at school, she "had conceived and contrived sundry attempts and purposes of destroying herself. . . . She spoke of self-murder serenely before strangers." She would talk of suicide "with prolix earnestness; and she looked so calm, so tranquil, so blooming, and so handsome, that the astonished guests smiled."[77]

Harriet's intelligence and friendliness helped balance her underlying vulnerability. Shelley, trying to cope with his own conflicts, was attracted to her blend of strengths and weaknesses. The mother and daughter roles of the two sisters were ready-made replacements for his mother and sister Elizabeth. Both Westbrook sisters attracted him, but Harriet's younger age and more compliant personality, along with her beauty, cast her in the role of Shelley's lover.

Harriet—light-haired, short, and slight—was more attractive than the taller Eliza with glossy, jet-black hair. Medwin, partial to Harriet Grove, regarded Harriet Westbrook as a "handsome blond." One schoolmate remembered Harriet as "a very nice looking girl, and beloved throughout the school for her sweet disposition: she had perhaps not much strength of character."[78] Harriet was considered to play Venus in a school production and Hellen Shelley recalled she was "a very handsome girl, with a complexion quite unknown in those days—brilliant in pink and white—with hair quite like a poet's dream, and Bysshe's peculiar admiration."[79]

Grateful that Harriet called on him when he was sick, Shelley reciprocated and called on her when she became ill. She was, he told Hogg, "a most amiable girl, the eldest is really concieted [sic] but very condescending; I took the *sacrament* with her on Sunday."[80] Eliza's recruitment of Shelley to take the sacrament was part of her attempt to detoxify his atheistic poison. He believed Harriet was "very charitable & good" and had "exposed herself to much possible odium." He wondered if he were "scarcely doing her a kindness" and "perhaps inducing positive unhappiness" by pointing "out to her a road which she is inclined so nobly to follow; A road which leads to perfection, the attainment of which perhaps does not repay the difficulties of progress."[81] His ill luck with Harriet Grove and sister Elizabeth gave Shelley doubts about the wisdom of converting his new Harriet to his religious views.

Shelley's feeling of indebtedness for Harriet's ministrations while he was sick loomed large in his later explanations of their marriage. When his "poor little friend" Harriet became ill one night, Eliza—orchestrating the relationship—sent for Shelley. "Pale" Harriet lay on a couch while he and Eliza "began talking about *l'amour;* I philosophised, & the youngest said she had such a headache that she could not bear conversation." Eliza conveniently departed, leaving Shelley with Harriet until after midnight. Increasingly caught in the Westbrook net, Shelley found Mr. Westbrook and Eliza were "strangely" civil to him, the father even inviting him downstairs to a party. In his *Zastrozzi* style, Shelley wrote, "I refused. Yes! the fiend the wretch shall fall." Making a slip, he called Eliza "Emily," who would need "some taming."[82]

Shelley, having trouble rescuing himself, would rescue Harriet, one of the oldest girls at the Clapham Common "prison house." Miss Hawkes, the schoolmistress, seeing Harriet crumpling up a forbidden letter, read it, "sent for their fathers and temporarily dismissed her from the school."[83] Shelley was angered by the school's severe treatment of his sisters and his "ire was greatly excited" when a black mark was hung around Hellen's throat for some minor misdemeanor. Hellen felt that his great disapproval was "more for the system than that one of his sisters should be so punished." Another time, finding Hellen in an iron collar designed to prevent her from poking others, Shelley "declared it would make me grow crooked, and ought to be discontinued immediately."[84] One of the schoolmates recalled that Shelley's sister Mary, thirteen, "was a lovely girl and the pet of her brother." Elizabeth, almost seventeen, "was too steady for him, she was a very clever girl." Hellen and Margaret, eleven and ten, were "very nice little girls."[85]

When Harriet returned to school after her illness, Eliza tried to please Shelley by reading Voltaire. More provocatively, she invited him to dinner one evening when her father was out. Keeping up her initiative, the next day Eliza "called" Shelley to her home. Her attentions having the desired effect, he now considered his unfavorable first impression of Eliza "was too hasty . . . she is a very clever girl" but he couldn't decide if she were "rather affected." By early May he wrote, "I spend most of my time at Miss [Eliza] Westbrooks, I was a great deal too hasty in critisizing her character." She was "amiable," but perhaps not "in the highest degree."[86] His ambivalence about Eliza reappeared in her nephew who recalled she had "a kind manner to children, but of whom we were somewhat afraid."[87] Mulling over the sisters' comparative merits, Shelley repeatedly asked Hogg—who had met neither—which of the two he preferred. Harriet was "more noble, yet not so cultivated as the elder,—a larger diamond, yet not so highly polished. Her indifference to, her contempt of surrounding prejudice, are certainly fine. But perhaps the other wants opportunity."[88]

Shelley was growing fond of Eliza, but Harriet had the name of the cousin he still clung to emotionally and she was becoming a martyr at school to Shelley's cause. Shelley wrote Hogg of the growing ostracism Harriet was experiencing: "they will not speak to her, her school fellows will not even reply to her questions, she is called an *abandoned* wretch, & universally hated which she remunerates with the calmest contempt." His sister Hellen, "the only exception," spoke to Harriet "in spite of the *infamy*." He had "hopes" for "this dear little girl [Hellen], she would be a divine little scion of infidelity if I could get a hold of her."[89]

Writing a year later, Harriet, never mentioning her mother, depicted her isolated childhood and how naïve she was when she befriended the infidel Percy:

My knowledge has been very confined on account of my youth . . . when I lived with my Father I was not likely to gain much knowledge, as our circle of acquaintance was very limited, he not thinking it proper that we should mix much with society . . . twas but seldom I visited my home, school having witnessed the greater part of my life . . . I will tell you my faults . . . when quite a child I admired the Red Coats. . . . I thought the military the best as well as the most fascinating men in the world: though at the same time I used to declare never to marry one . . . if I married any one it should be a Clergyman . . . you may conceive with what horror I first heard that Percy was an Atheist; at least so it was given out at *Clapham;* at first I did not comprehend the meaning of the word; therefore when it was explained I was truly petrified. I wondered how he could live a moment professing such principles and solemnly declared he should never change mine . . . when I wrote to him I used to try to shake them, making sure he was in the wrong & that myself was right; yet I would listen to none of his arguments, so afraid I was that he should shake my belief. . . . I believed in eternal punishment, and was dreadfully afraid of his supreme Majesty the Devil. I thought I should see him if I listened to his arguments. I often dreamed of him & felt such terror when I heard his name mentioned . . . my soul is no longer shackled with such idle fears.[90]

Her confused syntax mixed Shelley, now her husband, and "the Devil." Her childhood attraction to a military uniform would return.

Attending Parliament, Timothy was still angry from Shelley's proposal to forgo part of his inheritance. The two met accidentally at John Grove's home and Shelley, after a low bow, "politely enquired" about his father's health. Timothy, looking "black as a thunder cloud," uttered curtly, "Your most humble Servant!" and passed by. Several days later, Shelley reported Timothy was still "fierce as a lion." Timothy was determined his son not stay at Field Place. Upon learning Shelley would go there anyway, Timothy indicated that if he came, his sister Elizabeth would be removed before his arrival. Shelley then wrote Hogg, "I shall follow her."[91] The rumors seemingly afoot around the environs of Field Place about Shelley's sexual involvement with his sister probably fuelled Timothy's determination to keep the pair apart.

Shelley, in London, was expecting his sympathetic ally, Captain Pilfold. They planned to return to the retired captain's Cuckfield home, a base for their invasion of Field Place, ten miles away. This foray pitted Timothy, a mere ex-army non-combatant lieutenant, against the younger, battle-proven, decorated ex-navy captain uncle. A midshipman in his early teens, Pilfold saw action against privateers and the French before becoming a young first lieutenant on the seventy-four-gun battleship HMS *Ajax*. With Nelson's approval, Pilfold became commander of the ship in the absence of the regular captain just in time to participate in the Battle of Trafalgar. As captain, he received a decoration and a handsome bounty from the captured French ships, money now available to help his nephew. John Pilfold married and now had two daughters. The dislike he and Timothy Shelley had for one another aided Shelley in gaining his uncle's receptive ear for his atheistic views. Timothy was soon furious at this challenge to his paternal authority.[92]

Awaiting his uncle, Shelley in his "horrible" loneliness saw more of Eliza Westbrook, attended medical lectures, visited hospital wards, and assured Graham of his "resolve to study surgery." Leigh Hunt, editor of the *Examiner*, invited him to breakfast May 5 to discuss a poem (probably *The Wandering Jew*) Shelley was trying to publish. Hunt recalled Shelley was "a youth, not come to his full growth; very gentlemanly, earnestly gazing at every object that interested him, and quoting the Greek dramatists."[93] Impressed by Hunt's "cultivated mind," Shelley thought it "curious" that Hunt and his wife converted each other away from Methodism. Thinking Hunt's form of "Deism" to be atheism, he wanted to rescue him from "this damnable heresy from Reason" even though Shelley suspected himself of being one of the "bigots in Atheism."[94]

Shelley wrote Hogg that loneliness attracted him to prostitutes. He was a "strange being . . . inconsistent . . . thinking I could so far overcome Natures law as to exist in complete seclusion. . . ." Feeling like a "bewildered explorer of the cavern," longing to see his sister Elizabeth, he wished that "vile family despotism [and] the viler despotism of religion did not stand between the happiness of the two beings."[95]

Mocking Hogg's address, Coney Street, Shelley said, "I blush when I write the directions to you.—How salacious a street!"[96] *Coney*, slang for female genitals, elicited Hogg's sex-play on Shelley's Cuckfield address, leading to Shelley's punning comment, "these sallies of imagination are not noticed by vulgar postmen."[97] Shelley, concerned that Hogg needed cash, added, "I have nearly drained you, & all delicacy, like sisters stripping before each other is out of the question."[98]

Shelley's money drain was being pursued by John Grove who, "flattering like a courtier," negotiated a £200 annual allowance from Timothy, who then reneged on his offer. The £200 was reinstated when Captain Pilfold negotiated with Timothy. Hogg, saying his own needs required £600 yearly, repeatedly urged Shelley to ask for more.[99]

Tired of Hogg's lament for Elizabeth, Shelley offered to "minister" to Hogg's "diseased" mind and be his "Dr. Willis," Lind's court physician colleague who was treating the mentally ill George III. Shelley prescribed Covent Garden's prostitutes but Hogg, envious that Shelley had a new Harriet, remained fixated on Elizabeth. Shelley was losing hope for his sister: "She is *not* lost for ever! how I hope that may be true, but I fear *I* can never influence an amelioration, as she does not any longer permit an *Athe-*

ist to correspond with her. She talks of Duty to her *Father*. And this is your Religion."[100]

Shelley, sensing his budding marital inclinations, began attacking Hogg's traditional views, saying marriage was "hateful detestable . . . this most despotic most unrequired fetter. . . . For God's sake . . . read the marriage service before you *think* of allowing an amiable beloved female to submit to such degradation." Rejecting Hogg's claim that it was a duty to comply with "established law," Shelley invoked Antigone, his favorite Greek heroine. Defying paternal authority for love of her dead brother, she "acted in direct noble violation of the laws of a prejudiced society." Further, Shelley admired "sublime" Antigone for seeking an incestuous brother–sister union. Shelley then mentioned his sister Elizabeth, whom he anticipated seeing at Field Place. If his parents had removed her, he would follow.[101]

Shelley, leaving London May 10 for Cuckfield, asked the Westbrook sisters to write him at his uncle's. Confident of legally succeeding to the family fortune, he outlined his plans to Hogg: "The estate is *entirely* entailed on me, totally out of the power of the enemy. . . . I will enter his dominions preserving a quaker like carelessness of opposition, I shall manage l'Amerique & seat myself quietly in his mansion turning a deaf ear to any declamatory objections."[102]

Spending three days at Cuckfield, Shelley informed Hogg his uncle was "a very hearty fellow, and has behaved very nobly to me, in return for which I have illuminated him." Shelley's illumination, destined to fail, was apparent one evening in Cuckfield when the captain "attacked" a physician—"a red-hot saint"—with arguments from *The Necessity of Atheism*. The doctor departed "very much shocked."[103]

The two illuminati, uncle and nephew, invaded Field Place May 13; the next day Shelley wrote Hogg, "I have come to terms with my father, *I* call them very good ones." The captain both "settled matters admirably" for his nephew and persuaded Timothy to ease his restrictions on Shelley's contacts with his sister: "He has forbidden my intercourse with my sister, but the Capt brought him to reason, he prevents it however as much as possible, which is very little." Timothy, acquiescing to all of Shelley's proposals, gave him "free agency" to choose his own profession and place of abode, which he hinted to Hogg would be London. Topping off Timothy's capitulation, Shelley not only continued corresponding with Hogg but extended to him his father's franking privilege, no small amount considering their frequent correspondence.

Ever the conformist, Timothy tried on the religious views of the opposing camp. He told the captain, "to tell you the truth *I* am an Atheist. . . . 'Ah Ah' thought the Capt 'old birds are not to be caught with the chaff' 'are you indeed?' was the cold reply & no more was got out of him. . . . I tell you this as the Capt told it." Shelley considered his father's behavior "the most consummate hypocrisy I ever heard of," calling him an "irrational being . . . a disgrace to reason [who] professes no *ism* but superbism & irrationalism." However, "My Mother is quite rational . . . she says, 'I think *prayer* & thanksgiving is of no use. If a man is a good man, atheist or Xtian he will do very well in whatever future state awaits us.' This I call liberality."[104]

The arrival of a strange letter at Field Place shortly after he came to terms with Timothy provided Shelley a moment of amicability with his parents. He wrote Graham, "We had this morning a letter addressed to my Father accusing him & my mother of [ge]tting drunk, & the latter of being [m]ore intimate with *you* than with my father himself. We all laughed heartily & thought it a good opportunity of making up. But he is as inveterate as ever."[105] Timothy's laughter turned to jealous rage, as Shelley revealed in his mocking verse letter to Graham. This letter, and a subsequent verse letter Shelley wrote about three weeks later, provide an intriguing web of inferences concerning his mother's promotion of her daughter Elizabeth's engagement to Graham as a cover for her own possible sexual involvement with that young music master.

These two ribald verse letters reflect Shelley's facility with sexual humor. One letter includes lines written by his mother, making her a participant with her son in sexually ridiculing Timothy. One joke on Timothy was that he franked the letter, making it doubly written at his expense. Having franked this first verse letter and Shelley's accompanying short letter to Graham, Timothy knew to whom Shelley was writing but was oblivious to what his son wrote at his expense. Shelley said his father, "old Killjoy," is

> eaten up with Jealousy
> brows so dark his ears so blue!
> And all this fury is for you [Graham]

Timothy, "hot with envy blue," can't "bear Graeme me or you." Shelley spoke of his father's "mingled . . . fear" and how his "idiots pride" and "Hatred" made "Suspicion . . . on his poisoned vitals prey." Timothy's "poisoned vitals" refer to psychosomatic symptoms, including a hint of impotency. Turning to the accusation of Graham's cuckoldry, Shelley wrote:

> We fairly may acquit your soul
> Tho your life's pulses fiercely roll
> Of having let one wild wish glow
> Of cornuting old Killjoys brow.

Despite his father's "courageous horn" adorning his "frowning brow," he questioned Timothy's phallic adequacy:

> Oh! Not the fiercest antler dare
> To stretch its full luxuriance there
> Safe mayest thou sin.

Because Shelley's mother, forty-eight, offered "none / Of what is called temptation," it is "no mistake / To say you sinned for sinning['s] sake." He concluded, "this place no news affords / But secret damns & glossy words." In a postscript, he versified about having "wonderous sport" entertaining brother John—now five—with a parachute as "The wind beneath its bosom played."[106]

The second verse letter—initially published in 1973—strongly suggests, if not confirming, Shelley's mother's affair with Graham. A note she penned to Shelley's verse was signed for franking next to the address by Timothy Shelley. This unique document—the only known letter in the hand of Shelley, his mother, and his father—was written June 7 when Shelley had just returned to Field Place from a visit with his uncle in Cuckfield.[107] Shelley began his verse chiding Graham's "penitential letter," saying repenting would not reduce Timothy's anger over being cuckolded: "For the more you repent, the more tears he demands / The more you submit the more the commands."

Continuing his phallic punning on his father's cuckold horn, he asked music-master Graham if he has found his "horn" as Timothy's "brow" does not have a "dancing horn." Commenting on his father's sexual lassitude, Shelley relieves Timothy from further sexual "duty":

> . . . for the rest of his age
> That from all further duty he shall be exempted

> I think that our squire, does mainly desire
>> That an horn on his dark frowning brow were implanted
> I've hit it exactly, he'd get one directly
>> But the worst is that things will not come when
>>> there [sic] wanted
> He wishes to drive, from her native hive
>> His wife who so merrily laughs at each odd whim

Shelley's mother as queen bee in the family—where sexless Timothy is a mere drone—emphasizes her "native" sexually active role. It was the role of her own mother, Bethia White, and became that of her daughter, Mary Shelley.

As Timothy continued to assail Graham, Shelley reassured Graham, "I shall not suffer you to be involved in any crimination with my father."[108] His second verse letter concluded on the front sheet—next to unsuspecting Timothy's franking signature—with the words, ". . . this fun / Would look worse on the side of this letter than Godwin." Part of the fun that escaped Timothy was the note added next to the verse by his wife about her son Bysshe: "B. intends seeing Merle do you think there is any harm in the Man, tell me when you next write—let your letter be directed as the last." Mrs. Shelley was in collusion with her son, both carrying on their shared secret correspondence with Graham through a local address—probably in Horsham—unknown to Timothy.[109] Like his mother, Shelley would use such secret addresses for his clandestine correspondence during his marital life.

Whatever Bysshe intended to ask his acquaintance, Joseph Gibbons Merle, his mother's use of the word "harm" suggests it was to determine if Merle wrote the earlier letter accusing his mother of being "intimate" with Graham. Shelley suspected Merle's motives in 1810 but after Shelley's expulsion Merle visited Horsham. Arriving one evening at Field Place, Merle was refused admittance until Timothy was assured of his conservative views. Timothy almost wept telling Merle of his son's beliefs. Returning to his Horsham inn, Merle found Shelley in the noisy taproom writing by the fire with a glass of brandy and water. Taking Shelley to his room, Merle listened to his outpouring of anger, a discourse the future newspaper editor noted down soon after:

> all this misery . . . and despotism . . . are the consequences of your boasted Christianity. . . . [The aristocracy] condemn all but their first-born to starvation, and place in his hands the rod of despotism. . . . I am

one of these aristocrats. In me, although as it were a living outcast from my parents' bosom, the same machinery of oppression is preparing in order that I also in my turn may become an oppressor. But my father deceives himself. My first act, when in possession of my estate, shall be to divide it equally with my family.

At three in the morning, his anger spilling over onto the hapless Merle, Shelley exclaimed, "Have your own way, mad fool!," grabbed his hat and left the room. Merle never saw him again but Shelley wrote some months later apologizing for his behavior.

Shelley also wrote Merle that he was planning a child-rearing experiment on the effects of non-exposure to social and religious mores: "I wish to find two young persons of not more than four or five years of age; and should prefer females, as they are more precocious than males. . . . I will withdraw from the world with my charge, and in some sequestered spot direct their education. They shall know nothing of men or manners until their minds shall have been sufficiently matured to enable me to ascertain, when brought into play, what impressions of the world are upon the mind when it has been veiled from human prejudice." Shocked by the proposal, Merle saw it as a form of child sexual abuse: "The idea of a youth of twenty shutting himself from the world with two females until an age when, without religious instruction, they would have no guarantee for their chastity than the reason of a man who would then be in the summer of his life, with all his passions in full vigour, was more than absurd—it was horrible." He protested to Shelley, "firmly, but kindly," and the plan was dropped, at least for the time being.[110]

Shelley hid from Hogg his feelings for Harriet Westbrook but evasively admitted writing to her "sometimes." He avowed "interest" in a recent novel of India, *The Missionary,* by Miss Sydney Owenson (later Lady Morgan). The figure of "Luxima the Indian"—echoed later in the Arab maiden of *Alastor*—stimulated his sexual fantasies: "What a pity we cannot incorporate [make bodily] these creations of Fancy; the very thought of them thrills the soul. Since I have read this book . . . I have thought strangely." He enclosed parts of three poems, "a strange melange of maddened stuff which I wrote by moonlight last night." Two were written a year earlier.[111]

Shelley, arriving at Field Place, wrote Hogg that Elizabeth "is no more a Xtian than I am, but she regards as a sacred criterion the opinion of the world . . . I have lost her confidence." He detected "a great & important change" in his sister who treated him with "Scorn, the most virulent, neglect & affected pity for my madness." No longer open with him, Elizabeth ridiculed his "Mad friend Hogg," especially since Hogg had never seen her. Goading Hogg with "hopes of resuscitation" about Elizabeth, Shelley did not show her Hogg's latest letter, explaining, "she is not the singular angelic being whom you adored & I loved."

Shelley playfully encouraged Hogg's interest in a young woman in York but resisted his interpretation that Eliza Westbrook's manipulations were ensnaring Shelley romantically.[112] However, Eliza's machinations continued. In June, she expressed pleasure that his "mind has greatly recovered its accustomed cheerfulness," thanking him for his "proposition" regarding Harriet's school situation. However, a new "little misunderstanding" at Clapham made Harriet so "completely uncomfortable" that her father determined to remove her from the school. Eliza would "do all in my power to expedite this plan" and instructed Shelley: "You will not take any notice to your sister Mary, or indeed any of your family, of your intimacy with us; for particular reasons which I will explain to you when next I have the pleasure of seeing you."[113] In promoting Shelley's liaison with her sister, Eliza knew that knowledge of the relationship should be kept from his family. Shelley, depressed and wandering "wildly," writing "madly," and sleepless, told Hogg that it being Sunday he would "take the sacrament—In spite of my melancholy reflexions the idea rather amuses me."[114]

That same Sunday, Shelley's mother prescribed alcohol for her depressed son, lending some credence to Shelley's parents being excessive drinkers. He told Hogg, "I was Mad! You know that very little sets my horrid spirits in motion; I drank a glass or two of wine at my Mothers instigation." To quiet his "raving," his mother "gave me Pens Ink & Paper." Not only was his sister Elizabeth "unworthy" of Hogg, as for her poetry, "Miss Philipps betrayed twice the genius [and] greater amiability."[115]

Casting about for another female talent to encourage, Shelley corresponded with Janetta Philipps, offering to pay for the publication of her poems. When she flatly rejected both his offer and his ideas on religion, he was "extremely surprised" that she rejected "common morality" for a "theological system" or "the belief of a God." He was once "an enthusiastic Deist, but never a Christian."[116] He did subscribe for twelve copies of her poems for himself, his friends, and his relatives.[117]

Shelley found a more responsive young woman nearer at hand in Elizabeth Hitchener. She became his first "soul sister" at a time when—not accidentally—his emotional and sexual involvement with Harriet Westbrook was intensifying. Shelley's repetitive doubling had begun with sister Elizabeth and cousin Harriet Grove, followed by Eliza Westbrook and her sister Harriet. Elizabeth Hitchener now became the idealized, non-sexual soul sister, balancing his sexual lover, Harriet Westbrook.

Shelley met Elizabeth Hitchener in Cuckfield sometime between mid-May and early June while visiting his uncle. She had a school in nearby Hurstpierpoint and one of her pupils was a daughter of Captain Pilfold. Elizabeth Hitchener, when nine, became strongly attached to her school mistress, Miss Adams. More liberal and free-thinking than Elizabeth's mother, Miss Adams treated her young pupil as if she were her own child, evoking the jealousy and disapproval of Elizabeth's rigid, conventional mother. Identifying with Miss Adams—who had been persecuted for her advanced views—Elizabeth Hitchener entered her mentor's profession, hoping to care for her in her old age. Miss Adams knew of the Shelley family and, on becoming familiar with *The Necessity of Atheism,* she exclaimed, "what a Shelley and Atheist!"[118] Elizabeth Hitchener, an object of some derision in her small, narrow-minded community, was considered "romantic, eccentric & conceited" for her "visionary" sentiments. Two years before meeting Shelley, she was rejected by a close female friend, whom she still admired for "the brilliancy of her mind."[119]

Elizabeth's father, reputedly a former smuggler along the Sussex coast, changed his name from Yorke, became an Innkeeper, and now became another tyrannical father with whom Shelley would do battle for his daughter's enlightenment and allegiance. Eliza Westbrook and Elizabeth Hitchener were about ten years older than Shelley. Miss Hitchener—tall, slender, and dark complexioned—looked younger than her age and had Eliza Westbrook's dark eyes and long black hair. Hogg disliked Elizabeth Hitchener, portraying her as masculine with a hint of a mustache. She was probably the most intelligent and talented woman outside his immediate family that Shelley had met, with the added attraction of an uncertain religious commitment. Interested in writing, she would publish two volumes of undistinguished poetry before her death. Lonely and intellectually isolated, she was vulnerable to the flattery and attentions of this non-conforming and gifted young aristocrat.

Shelley unwittingly spelled out for Hogg the basis of his attraction to Elizabeth Hitchener in a letter from Cuckfield in early June. Shelley, interpreting Hogg's persisting romantic illusions about Elizabeth Shelley, was engaging in a nice instance of projection. His wording is remarkably similar to his future preface to *Alastor,* a poem he considered "allegorical of one of the most interesting situations of the human mind." Further, his words to Hogg anticipate his concept of the "epipsyche" that informed his major autobiographical love poem, *Epipsychidion.* He wrote: "You loved a being, an idea in your own mind which had no real existence. You concreted this abstract perfection, you annexed this fictitious quality to the idea presented by a *name,* the being whom that name signified was by no means worthy of this . . . unless you are determinedly blind, unless you are resolved . . . to seek destruction you must see . . . is it not plain? You loved a being. The being whom you loved is not what she was . . . she never existed but in your mind?"[120]

Shelley plainly saw in Hogg what he had difficulty seeing in himself. His idealized "abstract perfection" of his "concreted" image of Elizabeth Hitchener would elicit a steady profusion of Shelley's most ardent and rapturous letters. Not yet nineteen when their correspondence began, his letters to her were the incubation of his later great love poetry and influenced his maturing ideas concerning love, politics, ethics, and religion. Virginia Woolf wrote of these letters, "Shelley's character is always amazing."[121]

At Cuckfield in late May, Shelley encouraged his mother and sister to join him for several days while "killjoy" was in London. Perhaps because of meeting Elizabeth Hitchener, Shelley extended his stay with his uncle. His first letter to her, written soon after returning to Field Place, suggested his anxiety about his ability to influence her. He prophetically observed, "I fear our arguments are too long, & too candidly carried on to make any figure on paper; feelings do not look so well as reasoning on black & white." Jokingly, if she would "attempt my proselytism" he would "be most happy to subject myself to the same danger." "Truth is my God, & say he is Air Water, Earth or Electricity but I think your's is reducible to the same simple Divinityship." His only reason not to engage her in a "polemical correspondence" was that her time as a

teacher was valuable, "mine is totally vacant." However, he prescribed books that she should read, including Locke, Southey's
The Curse of Kehama, and George Ensor's *On National Education,* possibly brought to his attention by Dr. Lind. Shelley considered Ensor "a very clever man" whose ideas on poetry were
preferable to Sir Walter Scott's "aristocratical tone."[122] Shelley absorbed Ensor's words: "Poetry seems to me the most powerful
means of instructing youth, which, as Plato says of Music, pene-
trates the recesses of the soul . . . it was under . . . the power of song
that legislators have used poetry to subdue the savage nature of
people."[123]

Quickly replying, Miss Hitchener teased him with his own con-
cepts: "*Self-love* you see prompts me eagerly to accept the opportunity you offer of improving my mind by a correspondence with
you. . . . I presume not to *argue* I love to *discuss.*" Reading the
Locke he had sent to refute her belief in God, she adroitly used
Locke's arguments to reverse Shelley's intent.[124] Surprised, Shelley replied, "Am I to expect an enemy or an ally in Locke?" Knowing his new pupil was more sophisticated than Harriet Westbrook,
he put on a show of false maturity in commenting on *The Missionary.* Having just told Hogg this book excited him sexually, he told
his new woman friend, "It dwells on ideas which when young I
dwelt on with enthusiasm, now I laugh at the weakness which is
past."[125] Elizabeth Hitchener probably had the last laugh. Defending her views on virtue, Christianity, and reason, she told Shelley,
"You reason almost *too clearly* for me on the subject of the Deity;
the feeling has taken *deep root* . . . if I reject *one side,* I receive on
the other, & you are corresponding with two Miss Hitcheners, & do
allow one sometimes to introduce the other, tho' her presence
serve no other purpose than to exercise *your forbearance.*"[126]
Shelley's forbearance ultimately collapsed when he constructed
the second of the "two Miss Hitcheners."

Shelley, inveighing against Hogg's "tyrannic passion" for his sister, finally agreed he could visit Field Place to test Elizabeth's reaction to his presence. She had no interest in meeting him and refused to enter the rooms he and Shelley would share.[127] With luck,
Hogg might view Elizabeth on the lawn from his window.

At the end of June while Timothy was away, Hogg arrived from
York. Elizabeth's continued refusal to see him was not due to her
mother who—more forthcoming with young men—became interested in Hogg and his cause. He was from a respectable, well-to-

do family, and Mrs. Shelley tolerated the two youths' religious views more than her husband. She was concerned about Hogg's health after his long trip and received two letters from him after he returned to York. Hogg recounted to her the circumstances of the expulsion from Oxford in terms which make clear his views on religion found some sympathy with Shelley's mother.[128]

Mrs. Shelley's activist role at this time in her son's and Hogg's affairs of heart has been unrecognized. As Shelley's verse letters to Graham suggest, Timothy—almost fifty-eight—had dubious sexual prowess and his wife involved herself in her son's correspondence with Felicia Browne. Far from discouraging Hogg's interest in her daughter, she promoted it with her own libidinal attraction to him.

Hogg's only "peep" at young Elizabeth came as she sat in Warnham Church. Noticing him outside peering at her, she complained to Shelley. Hogg later wrote to Mrs. Shelley he was "amused" by "the strange reports" caused by his visit. He believed Elizabeth was "prejudiced," seeing him as an "Atheistical Clergyman . . . looking through the windows of Warnham Church in a treasonable manner." Writing Mrs. Shelley the following month, Hogg indicated his trip had reinforced his resolve to pursue Elizabeth. Trying to rationalize how he could "adore a female without having seen her . . . An idea worthy of a madman," he asked Mrs. Shelley's advice on how to "procure" a brief "interview" with her daughter.[129] Hogg's failure with his friend's sister would not deter him from pursuing the women Shelley loved.

During June, Shelley misled both Hogg and Elizabeth Hitchener about his shifting summer plans. After telling Hogg that "Old Westbrook" had invited Shelley to accompany him and his daughters to their probably fictitious house in Aberystwyth, Wales, he told Hogg he would join him in York after a week-long London visit with the Westbrooks. His story to Elizabeth Hitchener was that he would see her in London on his way to Wales for a summer-long walking tour the "better remarking the manners & dispositions of the peasantry."[130] Neither friend knew that in May he was invited by his cousin Thomas Grove to visit him and his wife in Wales that summer.[131] Leaving Field Place for London with Hogg the end of June, Harriet Westbrook was his immediate concern.

10

Elopement and Betrayal

Bᴀᴄᴋ ɪɴ ʟᴏɴᴅᴏɴ, ᴡʜɪʟᴇ sʜᴇʟʟᴇʏ sᴜʀʀᴇᴘᴛɪᴛɪᴏᴜsʟʏ ᴘᴜʀsᴜᴇᴅ Harriet Westbrook, his suspicious father was keeping an eye on him. Shelley lodged with either Graham or the Grove brothers and probably saw very little of Hogg during the few days both were in the city. Elizabeth Hitchener, also in London, did not get her expected visit from Shelley. His rationalization two weeks later in a letter from Wales was his "several nights of sleeplessness and days of pressing & urgent business." Most urgent was his probable proposal to Harriet that they unite in a free-love relationship, an idea she either rejected or put on hold. Timothy having blocked his trip to York by threatening to cut off his funds, Shelley was short on money. Acting on Thomas Grove's invitation, he left London shortly after July 4 for Wales. Several days later he arrived in Cwm Elan, near Rhayader in Radnorshire, with a brief "violent nervous illness."[1]

Rallying quickly, he wrote Hogg—as if to a jilted lover—that he was still "most sincerely yours" and would shortly explain "why I could not come to York."[2] Shelley, trying to mollify Hogg again with his likely ruse of meeting the Westbrooks in Aberystwyth, probably knew they were not leaving London. He mentioned that because Timothy would terminate his money if he went to York, he could not join Hogg "for a while." He had felt free to tell his father of going to York since Hogg had "made no secret" of these plans, probably in his talks with Mrs. Shelley at Field Place. Timothy had "magically" learned of Hogg's visit to Field Place but Shelley assured Hogg he had thrown "cool water on the rage of the old buck" to forestall Timothy writing to Hogg's father. Shelley would "keep quiet here for a few weeks" in Cwm Elan, avoid "open warfare" with Timothy, but use "Mr. Peyton" as a "nom de guerre . . . [that] will easily swallow up Mr. Shelley."[3]

Shelley's month-long retreat in Cwm Elan afforded time to continue his intense introspection of June.[4] In addition to self-analysis, he occupied himself at Cwm Elan writing poetry, corresponding, reading, taking solitary walks, and changing his diet. Emotionally collapsing, his poetry and letters indicate his "nervous illness" continued during his Cwm Elan stay. The unsettled situation with Harriet Westbrook was especially vexing.

Thomas Grove senior purchased, in 1792, ten thousand acres in Wales. The house he built, Cwm Elan, was now used as a summer home for his son Thomas.[5] The poems Shelley composed in remote Cwm Elan advanced his persona as a solitary poet in exile. Quoting the introspective Hamlet at Elsinore (*Hamlet*, 1.2.133–34), he wrote Hogg that despite "divine scenery . . . all [was] very dull stale flat & unprofitable" and he held more dialogues with himself than with the boring Groves.[6] Writing Elizabeth Hitchener, his frustrating self-analysis was like "attempting to arrest th[e] fleeting Phantom . . . like the chemists aether it evaporates under our observation." Further, it interfered with enjoying the "loveliness and grandeur" of the valley, its surrounding mountains with "Rocks [of] immense height . . . [and] waterfalls midst the umbrage of a thousand shadowy trees." In his "lonely walks," he longed for a "thunderstorm."[7]

His Cwm Elan poems reflect a continuing internal thunderstorm.[8] Depression, isolation, and hint of suicidal preoccupations, later themes in *Alastor*, appeared in "Death-spurning rocks!" A "maniac-sufferer" whose agony was like "A brood of mad and venomed snakes,"[9] he echoed his sister's rejection and his wintry "inefficient effort" as "he fled to the wild moor." Hinting at seeing Harriet Grove or someone he was seeking, "Turned was the way-worn wanderer from the door."[10]

Revisiting this theme in "Zeinab and Kathema," young Kathema searched for his lost "betrothèd," Zeinab, stolen from him by "Christian murderers." On a bitter cold "dark December" moonlit night Kathema, a "lone wanderer" on "a wild heath," comes across the gibbeted, decaying body of his lost love as it "swung slowly in the wind." Hanging "the chain around his neck," he leaps to join her in death. The poem registers the depth of Shelley's depression over the loss of Harriet Grove and justifies Elizabeth's concern in closely watching her suicidal brother.[11]

Harriet Westbrook, filling this depressive void, appears in an epistle poem probably written to her at Cwm Elan. His feeling for her is of loving friendship devoid of erotic passion but thinking of her relieves his "pain . . . and despair" as he hopes "My ever dear Harriet to save." Other lines suggest that he could not talk to her about his deeper pain and "grief."[12] A year later, recalling his feelings at Cwm Elan, he wrote of his "spirit of solitude . . . emphatic gloominess" that evoked a nocturnal vision of a "Dark Spirit."[13]

Apparently cured of what he might have thought were syphilitic symptoms, he seemed convinced he had not long to live. Perhaps he believed his disease either had turned into another illness or that medication had permanently damaged his health. His desire to marry was supported by current medical wisdom that a venereal infection, if arrested early, might impair one's health but posed no threat of infection to a partner.[14]

The fullest expression of his 1811 Cwm Elan depression, "The Retrospect," was written a year later.[15] Seeking solace on solitary nocturnal walks, in the "wild-woods' gloomiest shade" he tried "to quench the ceaseless flame / That on my vitals preyed," a "pain" that "Wrote madness on my withering mien." Harriet Grove's "broken vows" became the "envenomed arrow" that struck him just as their relationship was becoming most intimate.[16]

Apparently believing his secret "unuttered" venereal disease could affect him sexually ("froze my heart"), he wondered if the cure—arsenic, among other chemicals—might have affected his nervous system ("burned my brain"). For the first time, Shelley expressed the idea that the cure of sexual love involves an electric, "magnetic" current passing from one lover to the other. A lover's "glowing cheek" resting on his would "breathe magnetic sweetness thro' the frame" and "knit" his "corporal nature."[17]

Shelley had earlier written to Graham that he still resolved "to study surgery—You will see that I shall."[18] Now, concerned about his own health and reading Erasmus Darwin, he wrote to Hogg that he had begun practicing vegetarianism: "I am what the sailors call banyaning."[19] He assured Hogg of his mother's continuing interest in Hogg's pursuit of Elizabeth, forwarding to Mrs. Shelley the first of Hogg's two long letters seeking her advice on how to proceed. Hearing frequently from his mother, he told Hogg he was "well assured" she would "do nothing prejudicial to our interests." Her hints added to Shelley's suspicions that his father was secretly learning of his activities.[20] According to several accounts, to the end of his life Shelley continued to believe his father carried on a secret vendetta against him.

Becoming more preoccupied with social injustice, he protested to Elizabeth Hitchener, "I am no courtier, aristocrat, or loyalist . . . the peasant has too little," a condition which only "*equality* can annihilate." If he were a "moral legislator" he would propose changing "the present aristocratical system." Reacting to Elizabeth Hitchener's retort that his "Paradise is all visionary!,", he exclaimed, "Why is it visionary, have you tried?"

Reflecting this clash between his aristocratic origins and his egalitarian views was his "only adventure" in Cwm Elan, a beggar's arrival at the kitchen beneath his window. Shelley, running to give him something, "followed him a mile asking a thousand questions" until the exasperated beggar asked him to leave, commenting, "I see by your dress that you are a rich man—they have injured me & mine a million times." He assured Elizabeth Hitchener that religion "intimately connected with politics" created an "empire of terror. . . . Monarchy is it's prototype, Aristocracy . . . symbolising . . . its very essence."[21]

Godwin's *Political Justice* was influencing Shelley's protosocialist lectures to Elizabeth Hitchener and his growing vacillation about marriage. He was still berating Hogg for his devotion to his sister Elizabeth, comparing her poetical talents unfavorably to those of Felicia Hemans, "certainly a tyger."[22] Hogg, trying to convert Shelley from Godwin's anti-matrimonialism, found an ally in Harriet Westbrook. When Shelley discussed Godwin's (earlier) marital theories with Harriet, she skeptically responded by sending him Amelia Opie's novel attacking the evils of unmarried love, *Adeline Mowbray*. If Shelley ever read *Adeline Mowbray*, he learned that the novel's two unmarried lovers, Adeline and Glenmurray—modeled on Mary Wollstonecraft and William Godwin[23] —suffered social condemnation. Glenmurray recanted his beliefs which were "right in theory" but "the mass of society could never at *once* adopt them,"[24] words similar to Shelley's when he later rationalized his marriage to Harriet. Shelley perhaps was swayed by the pro-marriage preface of Godwin's 1805 novel *Fleetwood*, which he possibly read at Cwm Elan.

Irritated at Hogg's jokes about Shelley's attraction to Harriet, he assured Hogg that if he knew "anything about *Love* I am *not* in love. . . . I have heard from the Westbrooks both of whom I highly esteem."[25] In his attempt to reduce Hogg's jealousy about Harriet, Shelley had tried to conceal his pursuit of her.[26] However, Hogg was reading his friend's feelings accurately as Harriet and Shelley moved fitfully toward an eventual union.

The arrival of a desperate letter from Harriet—probably written August 1, her sixteenth birthday—led Shelley to leave for London on August 5. On August 3—one day before his nineteenth birthday—he wrote Hogg of his pending departure, his agitation and excitement bordering on confusion. Reassuring Hogg that his relationship with Harriet would not lessen his affection for him, he would "certainly come to York, but *Harriet Westbrook* will decide whether now or in 3 weeks."

> Her father has persecuted her in a most horrible way, & endeavours to compel her to go to school. . . . She asked my advice: resistance was the answer. . . . I essayed to mollify Old W . . . in vain! . . . I set off for London on Monday . . . she wrote to say that resistance was useless, but that she would fly with me, & threw herself on my protection.—We shall have 200 £ a year, when we find it run short we must live I suppose on love. . . . Gratitude & admiration all demand that I should love her *forever*. . . . We shall see you at York. I will hear your arguments for matrimonialism by which I am now almost convinced.[27]

His agitation suggests Harriet threatened suicide in her letter, something he later told Elizabeth Hitchener.

Shelley's "gratitude" as a "demand" for his enduring love for Harriet was an ominous, repetitive theme in his feelings about her. This letter makes clear Shelley intended—before leaving Cwm Elan—to elope with Harriet, although unsure if marriage was in the offing. Harriet's wanting to be under his "protection" implied they would live together unmarried. Hinting that York would be their destination, he repeated to Hogg his intention to live near him "as Mr Peyton." He correctly told Hogg it would be about three weeks when he and Harriet eloped, when he hoped for his next quarterly allowance from Timothy.

Shelley also wrote of his elopement plan to Charles Grove. Later, Charles recalled his cousin previously had confided to him in person what was in his letter, another indication Shelley had moved far in his decision about Harriet even before going to Cwm Elan. Shelley wrote Charles about "what circumstances had induced Harriet Westbrook to throw himself [*sic*] upon his protection." Shelley said his "happiness was altogether blighted in having lost the hope of being united to my sister . . . he considered the only thing worth living for was some self-sacrifice for the happiness of others." Shelley, after expressing to Charles his "resolution" to join Harriet, revealed his ambivalence with a paraphrase from Macbeth, "Hear it not Percy, for it is a knell / That summons thee to Heaven or to Hell."[28]

Shelley's ambivalence yielded a number of rationalizations whenever he explained the reasons for his first marriage. One partisan friend believed ". . . he never had for her any strong attachment [and] was *married to her when quite a boy,* under circumstances so very peculiar as could never have happened to any one but one of so very strange a turn of mind of [as] himself."[29] Years later, Shelley related his rescue-and-gratitude version. Being out of funds and "residing in obscure lodgings," he "fell so dangerously ill as to feel the near approach of death." Having been "most tenderly and carefully nursed by a very young woman of little or no pretensions . . . the only way" to reward "her disinterested conduct was to marry her on, as he thought, his death-bed, for as his widow she would have certainly been provided for by his family. Shelley however unexpectedly recovered . . ."[30]

This version accords with that of Byron's physician, Dr. Polidori, in 1816: "Gone through much misery, thinking he was dying; married a girl for the mere sake of letting her have the jointure that would accrue to her; recovered."[31] Mary Wollstonecraft Shelley would write that at this time Shelley's "Ill-health made him believe that his race would soon be run."[32] Shelley's preoccupation about an early death also appeared in several early letters to Godwin, including commenting on the cyclical nature of his emotional ill health: "Until my marriage, my life had been a series of illness, as it was of a nervous, or spasmodic nature."[33]

Two months after marrying Harriet, the embarrassed antimatrimonialist wrote to Elizabeth Hitchener of first becoming interested in Harriet at Mrs. Fenning's through his sister Mary. When Harriet's letters became more frequent "in Wales, I answered them; they became interesting." Harriet complained of her family's "irrational conduct" and her "misery of living where she could *love* no one. Suicide was with her a favorite them[e and] her total uselessness was urged as its defence . . . her letters became more & more g[loomy]; at length one assumed such a tone of despair, as induced me to quit Wales precipitately."[34]

Harriet's suicidal thoughts were a cry for help, reflecting a more deep-seated hopelessness than her desire to escape an "irrational" family. On the latter issue, Shelley would rescue her from paternal oppression and fulfill her father's expectation for upward social mobility.

Shortly after arriving in London, Shelley wrote Hogg he had substituted a proposal of marriage for his earlier rejected proposal of free love. However, Harriet, and the Westbrooks, rejected the marriage proposal. He again mentioned "the force of gratitude" motivating his marriage and he remained in London, "embarassed & melancholy." The entire decision "I fear more resembles exerted action than inspired passion."[35] Trying to ease Hogg's jealousy, Shelley also had to deal with Harriet's depression and with negotiating with the Westbrooks the details of their elopement and union.

Harriet's strong attachment need was crucial to her wanting Shelley. Being "shocked" at Harriet's changed "looks" upon returning to London, he wrote Elizabeth Hitchener that Harriet "had become violently attached to *me*, & feared that I should not return her attachment." He "promised to unite my fate with her's," stayed "several days" in London until she was better, but returned when she wrote him her family tried "to compel her to return to school." On returning "to London, I proposed marriage for the reasons I have given you, & she complied."[36]

Several inaccuracies appear in this account. Shelley probably proposed marriage to Harriet upon first arriving from Wales and made not one but at least two trips from London to Field Place before his elopement. Stalled in his efforts to unite with Harriet, initially he remained in London a week before a quick one-day trip to Field Place. Learning from Charles Grove that John Grove was pushing his suit for Elizabeth Shelley's hand, Shelley wanted to talk to his sister. Returning to London, he wrote immediately to Hogg, who now had Harriet as a rival for Shelley's affection and John Grove as a rival for Shelley's sister. Trying to retain Hogg's emotional tie to him, Shelley assured him "you & your interest still is predominant." Although John Grove was Hogg's "rival" for Elizabeth, she was not interested in Grove. As to Harriet, "my father is here wondering possibly at my London business—He will be more surprised soon possibly!" Shelley's "unfortunate friend Harriet is yet undecided—Not with respect to me but herself." Now "a perfect convert to matrimony," he was swayed by Hogg's arguments of "the sacrifice made by the woman." Not having given up fully on his "anti-matrimonialism," it was not "likely that *I* shall directly be called upon to evince my attachment to either theory." To assuage Hogg's feelings of being ousted by Harriet, he feigned uncertainty that she would accept his offer of marriage.[37]

Timothy now began making inquiries. Shelley, returning to Sussex, told Harriet to write him at his uncle's when she was ready to fly with him. About August 17, he had his second meeting with Elizabeth Hitchener. Telling her he planned to become a physician, he would not convince Hitchener that Harriet wasn't his prime interest.[38] Possibly feeling used, Hitchener wrote Shelley after he returned to Field Place from Cuckfield, admonishing him about the propriety of his visit, implying his aristocratic background increased local gossip. He immediately replied of being "disappointed" in her "trivial sacrifizes to custom," flattering her *"real* distinction" of using her "talents & virtue" while he was merely from "a race of rich men." Not willing to "give up" her "friendship & correspondence," he admitted "the impropriety of dining with you, even of calling upon you."[39] Shelley likely received Harriet's letter at Cuckfield affirming the plans for elopement and marriage. His uncle's antipathy for Timothy soon made him a willing actor in Shelley's marital drama. The recent personal and political falling out between Timothy and Thomas Medwin senior also made the latter an unknowing ally, for Shelley next went to Horsham and borrowed £25 from the elder Medwin, unaware his loan was financing an elopement.

Charles Grove probably was the only person in whom Shelley confided his elopement plans. Years later, Charles told Richard Garnett he believed Shelley still had very strong feelings for his sister, Harriet Grove, and that both Harriets having the same first name was a factor in Shelley's marriage. Charles thought Shelley's motives in marrying Harriet Westbrook included a sense of "self-sacrifice" to oblige her wish for protection. Charles believed her "personal attractions . . . had been considerably overrated."[40]

Charles possibly knew that Edinburgh was the pair's destination and that Hogg was considering Scotland for his upcoming vacation. Shelley, according to Charles, went to John Grove's at Lincoln's Inn Fields upon returning to London on August 24. Charles, perhaps without John's knowledge, worked out the elopement plans with Shelley, and the two visited Harriet at her home. That night, Shelley went to a small Mount Street coffeehouse, the rendezvous spot near the Westbrook home, and wrote Harriet the time he would be ready in the morning with a hackney coach. Spending the night at John Grove's, Shelley waited with Charles the next morning at the coffeehouse for Harriet, who apparently was late. Shelley, breakfasting on oysters, stood at the inn's door and "amused himself by flinging shells across the street, saying meanwhile, 'Grove, this is a Shelley business!'" Punning on his namesake grandfather's elopement with a sixteen-year-old, Shelley made no effort to hide his elopement from "old Westbrook." Waiting in broad daylight just around the corner from his Chapel Street home made secrecy difficult. Apparently, the Westbrooks had agreed to an elopement if the couple got married. Any intended secrecy was against the curious Timothy, who had Whitton as detective.[41] In due course, Harriet "was seen tripping around the corner from Chapel Street" and the three took the coach to another inn to await the evening departure of the northern mail to York and Edinburgh.[42] When the coach departed at seven, Charles bade the pair goodbye. While waiting for the coach, Shelley adroitly turned a possible revelation of his secret plans into a minor financial coup. A family friend, Mr. Dunn, recognized Shelley, who told him he was just returning from Wales and was going home as soon as he paid his fare. Dunn promptly loaned him £10.[43]

As the elopement coach left on Sunday August 25, Whitton apparently tried to contact John Grove about Shelley's plans. John, still with hopes for Elizabeth Shelley, perhaps absented himself to conceal any knowledge of Shelley's plans. Whitton wrote Timothy the next day that Grove was out of town and suspected it was "highly probable" that Mr. Westbrook "may be at least passive if not aiding in the intercourse between the young persons." Timothy evidently also considered having Whitton call on Shelley, Mr. Westbrook, and even the Prince of Wales. Whitton, loathe to act without Timothy's authorization, doubted anyone except his father could influence Shelley.

Timothy learned of his son's elopement from Shelley's brief letter written in London August 25 before he and Harriet embarked in the coach. Correcting his opening—"My dear Mother"—to "Father," he would have felt more comfortable relating his news to his mother. Shelley probably told Charles Grove to mail it the next day, as it was postmarked August 26. Shelley, not stating directly he was eloping with Harriet, began: "Doubtless you will be surprised at my sudden departure . . . you will be more surprised at its finish, but it is little worth the while of it's inhabitants to be affected at the occurrences of this world." He asked that his personal property, in-

cluding his "clothes gun papers" be sent to Charles Grove, adding
he has heard his father might refuse and take "pitiful revenge for
the uneasiness I may have occasioned." Trying to throw Timothy
off his scent, he would next write from Holyhead, the departure
point for Ireland.[44]

Timothy was irate. Not only had his son not confided in him
about his plans, this was a *mésalliance*. A tavern-keeper's daughter was not an appropriate wife for a Shelley who was to inherit a
baronetcy. Ironically, Timothy's father was spending his time in
Horsham taverns with lowly townsmen away from his third "wife."
Another irony was that the social class slide in Shelley marriages
began with Timothy, his wife's family having less standing than Sir
Bysshe's two legal wives. Timothy, sensitive on this issue, con-
ferred with Whitton about the possibility of disinheriting his son.
Whitton examined the two family settlements and found "there
was not any power of revocation and new appointment."[45]

Timothy and Whitton called at the Westbrook home and learned
from Harriet's father and Eliza the details of the elopement. The
next day, August 28, Timothy and Whitton, joined by John Grove,
met with Westbrook and his attorney. Timothy wrote Hogg's father
that Shelley had set off for Scotland "with a young female," con-
jecturing he might make York on the way. The two Grove cousins
were split in supporting Shelley, John toadying to Timothy in his
doomed efforts to win Shelley's sister. Timothy, ignorant about
Charles's elopement collaboration, now took two drastic steps. He
cut off Shelley's allowance and refused to answer his son's letters,
sending them on to Whitton. Mr. Westbrook apparently had not
given his daughter any money before she left and may have decided to suspend support to the couple, at least for a while.[46] Timothy again wrote Hogg's father saying he had a letter from a gentleman, probably Graham—who was forwarding Shelley's mail
—informing Timothy his son was in Edinburgh and Hogg had
joined him there.[47]

Harriet and Shelley spent the first three nights and two days of
their elopement in uncomfortable coach travel to Edinburgh. During a brief midnight stop in York, Shelley wrote a note to Hogg saying to write him in Edinburgh under "my own name" and "Harriet
is with me." Being in "slight pecuniary distress," Hogg should send
£10, adding he would have £75 on September 1. Unaware of Timothy's suspension of his allowance, he was expecting to add his
quarterly £50 to what he had extracted from Medwin senior and

Dunn.[48] Receiving Shelley's note August 27, Hogg decided on Edinburgh for his vacation and wrote Shelley he would see him there by the time his letter arrived. A few days earlier, he had drafted his second long letter to Shelley's mother asking her advice on how he might see her daughter Elizabeth.[49]

The tired couple's coach wound through the "mean, narrow streets" of Edinburgh in the early morning of August 28. Shelley found lodgings on the ground floor at 60 George Street, a broad avenue in the newer section of the city. He quickly implemented plans for getting married, but the actual conditions of his marriage are obscured in Shelleyan ambiguity. Possibly, the young lawyer from Edinburgh Shelley later told Hogg he met on the coach informed him how to proceed with a Scottish marriage. Hogg stated Shelley saw this lawyer several times in Edinburgh, but Shelley rebuffed Hogg's appeals to meet him with the excuse "It was impossible; it was vacation, and all the courts were closed."[50]

To be married, it was necessary first to get a proclamation of banns before the actual ceremony by a minister. In lieu of the session clerk's knowledge that they had resided in the parish for the required six weeks, they needed a certificate verifying this signed by two householders and an elder. Perhaps helped by his lawyer acquaintance, on August 28 Shelley procured this falsified certificate:

August 28. Mr. Percy Bysshe Shelley, Farmer, Sussex, and Miss Harreit [sic] Westbrook, St. Andrew's Parish, Daughter of John Westbrook, London. That the parties are free, unmarried, of legal Age, not within the forbidden Degrees, and she has resided in Edinburgh upwards of Six Weeks is certified by Mr. Patrick Murray, Teacher, and Mr. Wm. Cumming, Hostler, both of Edinburgh, and the Bridegroom. Entd. [signed] Percy Bysshe Shelley Willm Cumming Patrick Murray[51]

A one-sentence summary of this certificate dated "August 28, 1811" was then entered in the books of the Edinburgh Register House.[52] Because banns had to be proclaimed on three successive Sundays, the earliest marriage date would have been September 16, but this delay frequently was not observed for such clandestine marriages as Shelley's. The evidence that a marriage ceremony took place August 28 was printed by Ingpen in the form of a marriage certificate of that date signed by Reverend Joseph Robertson.[53] It was not the last clandestine marriage Robertson performed. Shelley had successfully emulated the murky first marriage ceremony of his grandfather Bysshe. Seven years later Robertson was deposed from the Church and banished from Scotland for performing such irregular marriages.[54]

Shelley's marriage to Harriet may have been more problematical than biographers have previously known. His qualms about the legality of his marriage led him to write the senior Medwin in October 1811 from his uncle John Pilfold's that he would soon "take the precaution of being remarried."[55] In January 1813, Shelley's uncle wrote the senior Medwin, "P.B.S. was married, in another name, is it valid."[56] If Shelley, despite using his actual name for the banns, married Harriet using another name, his remarriage to her in 1814 rectified the matter.

Shelley added humor to the improvised marriage when he evidently asked his landlord for a loan to get married, expecting his allowance within days. The accommodating landlord agreed, if Shelley treated him and his friends to a supper in honor of the marriage. Shelley, getting more than he bargained for, later reported that during the evening the landlord knocked at the newlyweds' door, saying, "It is customary here at weddings for the guests to come in, in the middle of the night, and wash the bride with whisky." Shelley, quickly producing his brace of pistols, pointed them at the landlord and caused his quick retreat by threatening to "blow your brains out."[57]

Deprived of her whiskey wash, Harriet soon met Hogg for the first time. He knocked on their door within several days of their marriage and remained with them all of September. Shelley reportedly greeted him with, "we will never part again! You must have a bed in the house!" The landlord obligingly found Hogg a room several floors above the Shelleys. Pleasantly cocooned with Shelley and his lovely young bride, Hogg found Harriet "bright, blooming, radiant with youth, health, and beauty."[58] The few days before Hogg's arrival were almost the only time in their marriage that Harriet and Shelley did not have a friend or relative living with them. Other than his forays alone before breakfast and a visit to the Parliament, Hogg intimated he and Harriet frequently were alone together. When with Shelley, the two made fun of him.

Harriet, "well-read in the sorrowful history" of Mary Queen of Scots, according to Hogg, insisted on seeing Holyrood Palace, finding particular interest in Mary's bedroom and Rizzio's bloodstains. Shelley went home, leaving Hogg to escort Harriet up the summit of Arthur's Seat. Modest about her blowing skirts, Harriet sat on a rock before proceeding with Hogg. Awaiting money, Shelley went alone each morning before breakfast to the post office. He received "prodigious numbers" of letters from Charles Grove, Graham, and his uncle John but none with his father's £50 allowance. At the end of August, Shelley sent a letter to his father trying to disguise its writer. Hogg addressed it and Harriet wrote on it, "if not there to be forwarded immediately." Still not mentioning his marriage and wishing he had been more "frugal," he asked his father to send his quarterly £50, adding hopefully, "I know you are kind to forgive youthful errors." Asking Timothy to direct letters to him through Graham, he sent his love to his mother and sister, but only "great respect" to his father.[59] He wrote five more letters to Timothy in the next six weeks, expressing increasing anger at his father's refusal to support him and refusal to answer his letters.

Finding nurturance elsewhere, Shelley, according to Hogg, delighted in devouring "virgin honey." Shelley was usually "indifferent to food, particularly to all meats and drinks" and Hogg teased him that eating the "beautiful" honeycomb "approaches cannibalism . . . indeed, it is too like eating Harriet! I think you would eat Harriet herself!" Shelley reportedly replied, "So I would if she were as good to eat, and I could replace her as easily!" Other anecdotes suggest Shelley was encouraging Hogg's flirtatious behavior with Harriet.

Shelley brought home "lots of good books," probably borrowed from the library or from his lawyer friend. He read the French philosophers and translated a treatise of the naturalist Georges Buffon, intending to publish it. Its influence later appeared in *Mont Blanc*. Harriet, translating the moralizing romance *Claire d'Albe,* was meeting Shelley's desire for women who pursued literary activity. Hogg said she avoided religious works and often read aloud to the two men. Her voice enthralled Hogg but its soporific effect on Shelley led Harriet and Hogg to encourage the housemaid to speak, knowing her unmusical voice irritated Shelley. Hogg tried to get Shelley to resume their long walks of Oxford days but, out of deference to Harriet, he refused. It was the year of Halley's comet and the crystal-clear nights accommodated Shelley's keen interest in astronomy. From nearby Princes Street they often contemplated the comet and stars as they talked of astrological myths.

Shelley and Hogg, but not Harriet, attended several Sunday church services that succeeded in evoking Shelley's amusement at Scottish dialect. On one Sunday walk, Shelley's raucous laugh brought a reprimand from a passing local for this forbidden breach of Sabbath reserve.

Shelley's most intriguing socializing was a dance he apparently attended with the attorney, Gilbert Hutchinson, and Charles Kirkpatrick Sharpe, his acerbic but admiring Oxford critic living in Edinburgh. Hutchinson may have been Shelley's stagecoach lawyer acquaintance. Shelley's reputation having preceded him to Edinburgh, a lady hostess asked Sharpe to bring him to a dance at her home. Shelley apparently hinted at his secretive entry into Edinburgh society when he wrote his father "a friend" might "lionize me."[60]

Shelley's father was unresponsive but his uncle, Captain Pilfold, sent him money in "cheerful, friendly, hearty letters." The captain wrote of Timothy, "To be confoundedly angry is all very well; but to stop supplies is a great deal too bad!"[61] None of the threesome's fathers sent money. Shelley wrote Thomas Medwin senior for another loan but, hearing of the elopement, he refused. Timothy had rebuked Medwin for aiding his son's elopement, a charge Shelley would rebut. Driven to distraction by his son's latest escapade, Timothy shared his woes with a broad audience. Whitton, hearing this, told him to curtail the family gossip and share his woes "in privacy with Mrs. Shelley."[62]

Shelley, the only one not hearing from Timothy, wrote him a letter seemingly designed to provoke his gout. He admitted having "perhaps acted with impoliteness" by not informing his father of his marriage plans. Playing family therapist, Shelley pointed out the "inutility" of his father's anger for Timothy's mental health and that of his family, not to mention it would "distract your own mind" from his "legislative duties." Shifting to religion, Shelley's sarcasm could not escape Timothy: "the base passion of anger, is certainly as wrong as it is inconsistent with the Christian forbearance & forgiveness with which you are so eminently adorned.—The world too, which considers marriage as so venial a failing would think the punishment of a fathers anger infinitely disproportioned to the offence committed—That two beings who like each other's society should live together by the law of the land, is too comfortable to the opinion of the world for *it's* approbation to justify any resentment on your part."[63]

Shelley had attacked Timothy on two points. One was his familiar volley on his father's hypocritical Christian stance. The second referred to Timothy's unmarried status in a relationship that produced an illegitimate son. He was asking, how can you be angry at me for marrying—in conformity with the opinion of society—when you yourself flouted this Christian institution? Shelley again addressed the letter in a disguised hand, fearing Timothy would not open it.

Eleven days later, getting no response, he wrote a more attacking letter. His father not having "condescended to answer either of my letters," he knew from his correspondents the cause of his father's silence. Raising the volume on his attack on Timothy's hypocrisy, he alluded more explicitly to his father's illegitimate family, lecturing him that having obtained the "legal sanction" of marriage, "I have neither transgressed custom, policy, nor even received notions of religion, my conduct in this respect will bear the severest scrutiny . . . nor however well calculated you may be to judge in other respects, as I suppose you neither aspire to infallibility or intuition." Stating his father's "tastes are diametrically opposed to his," Shelley unleashed his most direct accusations concerning his father's previous behavior:

> Father, are you a Christian? it is perhaps too late to appeal to your love for me. I appeal to your duty to the God whose worship you profess. . . . Father are you a Christian? judge not then lest you be judged . . . if my crime were even deadlier than parricide, forgiveness is your duty.— What! will you not forgive? How then can your boasted professions of Christianity appear to the world, since if you forgive not you can be no Christian—do not rather these hypocritical assumptions of the Christian character lower you in real virtue beneath the *libertine* atheist, for a moral one would practice what you preach. . . . Forgive then! & let me see that at least your professions do not bely your practise . . .[64]

This letter, with allusions to parricidal fantasies, was Shelley's ultimate confrontation with his father and could serve as a preamble to Shelley's tragedy of "unforgivingness," illicit paternal sexuality, and hypocritical Christianity, *The Cenci*. Shelley espoused the virtues of forgiveness, but his "severe" disdain of his father's sexual and religious hypocrisy blunted his forgiveness of him.

Shelley's postscript, requesting his £50 allowance be sent "immediately," was futile. His accusation that his father was worse than a "libertine atheist" was the cruelest stab. Ironically, this appellation became a standard tag for Shelley during his life and beyond.

If Timothy's son married beneath him, John Westbrook made a coup. Hogg said Westbrook feigned anger towards the two by tightening his purse strings,[65] but her father only demanded that Harriet send him "lines" confirming her marriage, which dutifully she did. Shelley would write to Elizabeth Hitchener that without money from his "generous" uncle, "we shd. still be chained to the filth & *commerce* of Edinburgh." Trying to square his desire for money with his emerging social philosophy, he told her, "Money—I covet it." He denied being a "slave" to a crass ambition for money because he knew its "use." "It commands labor" and that "to give leisure to those who will employ it in the forwarding of truth is the noblest present an individual can make to the whole."[66]

September was ending and Hogg had to return to York, where Harriet would be a pleasant addition to Hogg's life with Shelley. With Captain Pilfold's loan, they traveled to York on the less arduous post chaise, stopping overnight at inns. Harriet read aloud Thomas Holcroft's novels during much of the three-day trip, ignoring Shelley's plea that she skip parts. Because Hogg delayed leaving Edinburgh "for the convenience of his friends," his Coney Street lodgings were unavailable and they located "dingy" rooms down the street at the Misses Dancers, two "dingy milliners."[67]

Shelley immediately wrote his father requesting his clothes, papers, and books be sent. He added, even if Timothy were offended by his actions he would not "suppose you so meanly revengeful" as not to send his things. Money was not mentioned.[68] Ten days later, Shelley learned that his belongings were on the way, but his father's silence continued. He again attacked his father, "*If* you are a professor of Christianity, which I am not," then he should not judge his son "lest thou shouldst be judged." After stating that "*Obedience* is in my opinion a word which should have no existence," he gave his sharpest barb, saying he recognized that society made Timothy "the Head of the family; and I confess it is almost natural for minds not of the highest order to value even errors whence they derive their importance."[69]

That day he also wrote to his grandfather asking for money. The emotional distance between grandfather and grandson was in his single-word salutation, "Sir," followed by his acknowledgment that this was the first letter he had ever written to him. He attempted to reawaken some of old Bysshe's past which they had in common. Both had eloped, and Shelley defended himself against Timothy's attack "for having consulted my own taste in marriage." Appealing to his grandfather's earlier outspoken democratic views, Shelley declared "he who fetters [language] is a Bigot & a Tyrant." Probably echoing his grandfather's views he heard in early youth, Shelley appealed to his "liberality & justice" in interpreting what "fools in power would denominate *insolence*." He underlined his signature, using his full name, hoping to forge another sympathetic link to his namesake. It was in vain. Old Bysshe, implacable and alarmed by his grandson's marriage, was about to change his will to keep his accumulated wealth from being dissipated by Shelley. Sir Bysshe, with his cautious lawyer, Mr. Butler, probably was making sure that Timothy did not vacillate in dealing with young Bysshe.[70]

Feelings of betrayal now began to overtake Shelley. By mid-October, he was experiencing persecutory feelings seemingly bordering occasionally on the delusional. The damp, gloomy streets of autumnal York matched his mood. Hogg tried to inspire Shelley with York Minster's beauty, only to hear him remark that churches were "gigantic piles of superstition."[71] Preoccupied by Timothy's persecution, he was unaware of Hogg's growing attraction to his wife and of his role in promoting it. Shifting into action, Shelley decided to go to Sussex for more battle, a trip that served to leave Harriet and Hogg alone.

Before leaving, Shelley wrote two extraordinary letters, one to his father, the other to Elizabeth Hitchener. Both letters reveal the extent to which he felt persecuted by his father. Shelley listed for his father the persecutions he had suffered because of his "defencelessness" to Timothy. He accused him of having "treated me ill, vilely" by turning Hogg's parents against him, of going back on his promise to support him, and of libeling him through his misrepresentations to Stockdale. He said his father wished "I had been killed in Spain" by encouraging him to join the army after his expulsion. As if referring to his own parricidal wishes, he wrote, "The desire of its consummation is very like the crime, perhaps it is well for me that the laws of England punish murder, & that *cowardice* shrinks from their animadversion." He told Timothy, "Think not I am an insect whom injuries destroy—had I money enough I would meet you in London, & hollow in your ears Bysshe, Bysshe, Bysshe—aye Bysshe till you're deaf."[72] This oracular curse upon his father was from Hotspur in *Henry IV, Part One*. In

Prometheus Unbound, Shelley's hero would be persecuted because of his curse upon the father-god, Jupiter. Soon, Shelley's accusatory rage would be turned upon his mother and Hogg.

Reaching out to a largely illusory Elizabeth Hitchener, he wrote her that it was *"you* who understand my motives." Espousing his love for her for the first time, he offered to share with her his inherited wealth: "I will dare to say I *love.* . . . Henceforth will I be your's . . . not a thought shall arise which shall not seek its responsion in your bosom. . . . I love you more than any relation I posess; you are the sister of my soul, its dearest sister." She should not think his love was in the carnal "degrading & contemptible interpretation of this sacred word," adding in his best gauche, intellectual manner, "nor do I risk the supposition that the lump of organised matter which enshrines thy soul excites the love which that soul alone dare claim." Such condescending denial of sexual feelings for her suggests their presence.

Wishing to install Elizabeth Hitchener into his new family, he said that "on my *coming* to the estate . . . Justice demands that it shd. be shared between my real sisters." Hitchener is the "sister of *my soul"* and Hogg his soul "brother." Because he and Hogg considered what they owned as common property, *"we* shall do the same." Timothy's "blind resentment" against him being something from "the regions of dullness comedies & farces," he would visit his father and leave that night for Cuckfield. Ending his lengthy outpouring, he made a significant slip, "Henceforth I shall have no secrets for [*sic*] you." He hoped to see her during his two days in Sussex: "Sister of my soul adieu. With I hope eternal love your Percy Shelley."[73] She quickly declined the offer to share his inheritance.

Leaving Harriet with Hogg, Shelley rode to Cuckfield on the outside of a coach for three nights and two days. He wrote Elizabeth Hitchener that he and the captain were discussing a "plan of attack" on Timothy and looked forward to seeing her at dinner with the Pilfold family. The assault on Field Place was brief, tumultuous, and abortive. His father refused to discuss matters with him, referring him to Whitton concerning his allowance. Shelley, apparently having talked with his mother and his sister Elizabeth, created a furor before he retreated by threatening his father. Timothy wrote Whitton several days later: "had he stay'd in Sussex I would have sworn in Especial Constables around me. He frightened his mother and sister exceedingly, and now if they hear a Dog

Bark they run upstairs. He has nothing to say but the £200 a year
. . . he must be humbl'd, for I never before oppos'd or closely pursued him." He told Whitton: "don't spare him in his absurdities. . . .
He is capable of any mischief, particularly in the Family. He has no
regard to character himself. Father, Mother, Sisters and Brother
all alike."[74] Shelley also talked to his unbending grandfather who
told him being obedient and dutiful was the way to be admitted
again into the family.

Turning to the real power, Shelley wrote Whitton saying he
wanted to know by return post where he could meet him in London concerning the "pecuniary matters which concern me [that]
are entrusted to you." The next day Shelley wrote Medwin senior
indicating his intention to remarry Harriet and asking that a marriage settlement of £700 a year be drawn up for her in case of his
death.[75] The day after Shelley's appearance at Field Place, Timothy wrote his brother-in-law in Cuckfield telling him to keep out of
his son's affairs. Timothy would not "admit" his son to Field Place
and had placed "everything respecting him into the hands of Mr.
Whitton, that no other person may interfere."[76] Ignoring his
brother-in-law, Pilfold accompanied his nephew back to London
several days later to consult with Whitton. Medwin senior, also in
league against Shelley's father, sensed Timothy's hand in his recent dismissal as the Duke of Norfolk's steward. Captain Pilfold in
early October wrote the senor Medwin, "Dukes, my good Sir when
they have their ends to serve, can be as fawning and as mean as *a
Shelley*, their purposes once answered, and they'll cast you off."[77]

Timothy then received a letter from Hogg's father saying he and
his wife were "greatly alarmed . . . at your son's leaving this lady
on my son's hands."[78] Mrs. Hogg wrote Harriet hoping she would
not stay with Hogg and offering to write friends in York who could
assist her. Harriet declined her help with thanks.

Before leaving for London with his uncle, Shelley vented his persecutory rage against his mother. Having heard rumours that his
mother was trying to arrange a marriage between Graham and his
sister Elizabeth, he either wrote his mother sometime before leaving York or talked to her during his visit. According to Timothy, he
told her "that he did not come from York on his own business but
to inform her what was said of her."[79] Shelley enclosed the following letter to his mother inside a brief letter to his father, asking him
to deliver it to her. Acknowledging his father's warning to Captain
Pilfold, he added sarcastically, "*very* much obliged for this morn's

intimation to my uncle."[80] Shelley's mother never saw his letter as Timothy sent it unopened to Whitton, along with one Shelley sent separately at the same time to his sister Elizabeth.

Dear Mother
I had expected before this, to have heard from you on a subject so important as that of my late communication. I now expect to hear from you, unless you desire the publicity of my sister's intended marriage with Graham. You tell me that you care not for the opinion of the world, this contempt for it's consideration is noble if accompanied by consciousness of rectitude; if the contrary, it is the last resort of unveiled misconduct, is the daringness of despair not the calmness of fortitude.—You ask me if I suspect you. I do, my suspicions of your motives are strong & such as I insist upon shd. be either confirmed or refuted. I suspect your motives for *so violently so persecutingly* desiring to unite my sister Elizabeth to the music master Graham, I suspect that it was intended to shield *yourself* from that suspicion which at length has fallen on you. If it is unjust, prove it, I give you fair opportunity, it depends on yourself to avail yourself of it. Write to me at ~~Mr. Westbrooks 23 Chapel St. Grosvenor Square~~ — Your's Son P B Shelley[81]

It is significant and ironic that this accusatory letter is only one of two that Shelley wrote to his mother which survives. It was in Shelley's second verse letter to Graham—June 7, 1811—that she added a note asking Graham to write her about any possible "harm" that might come from Merle. Shelley's suspicions about his mother's sexual involvement with Graham could have had a basis in fact. He could accept that but not her effort to hide such a relationship behind an intended union of the music master and his sister. In his simultaneous letter to his sister Elizabeth, he stated he had written his mother about "Graham's projected union with you," imploring her to "speak truth" if his mother showed that letter to his father.[82] Presumably, Elizabeth had assured her brother on his visit that she had no intention of marrying Graham. A week after writing his accusatory letter to his mother, Shelley wrote to Charles Grove. Still infused with jealousy and paranoia, he told Charles not to show his letters to anyone. He had heard of his beloved Harriet Grove's imminent marriage to her wealthy neighbor, William Helyar; the wedding took place two weeks later, November 14. Revealing his deep jealous and bitter feelings, he told Charles, "a new brother as well as a new cousin must be an invaluable acquisition." If Charles continued to be the "unprejudiced

friend he once was . . . I shall have reason to rejoice." After telling
Charles in a written aside that he knew his brother John was still
angling for Shelley's sister, he added: "Graham's business is at
length made public. I suspected my Mother of such baseness tho'
I knew her intentions & counterac[ted the]m."[83]

Shelley was feeling betrayed by the three family members most
important to him: his mother, his father, and his closest sister. Having felt betrayed by his fiancée, Harriet Grove, he now felt betrayed
by his friend Graham and feared Charles Grove would be his next
friend to fail him. Soon after writing Charles, he would find himself
betrayed by Hogg. This network of felt betrayals seemingly reflected a crisis in trust deeply rooted in Shelley's personality. His
feeling of mistrust erupted in times of personal crisis; under more
benign conditions, it was expressed as skepticism, balanced by a
hopeful outlook.

Graham now faded from Shelley's life. The strength of his suit
for Shelley's sister is unclear, as is the role Shelley's mother played
in any matchmaking. However, Shelley was clear; if he could not
have his sister, neither could John Grove nor Graham. Hogg, an ex-
tension of himself, was the only man Shelley condoned to pursue
his sister, but he orchestrated Hogg's illusory pursuit to assure its
failure.

Shelley made two accusations against his mother in his letter.
Not only was she trying to unite Graham with his sister, the deeper
accusation was her doing this to conceal her sexual involvement
with Graham. This last accusation appeared in the letter about
which he and his parents had joked earlier in May. It gained support from Shelley's two verse letters to Graham and from the note
his mother appended to the last letter to Graham. His mother's affair with Graham cannot be ruled out. Shelley's belief that it happened fed his sense of persecution and betrayal.

Shelley's accusations against his parents involved their sexual
behavior. Timothy's evasion and cover-up of his illegitimate son
evoked Shelley's wrathful "judge not lest ye be judged" and his
blast "Bysshe, Bysshe, Bysshe." He resisted having his father
erase him, make him a non-son, as he had his bastard son. Timothy attempted such an erasure, during and after his son's life. Shelley's mother's presumed sexual behavior hurt him doubly. Unconsciously, she rejected him in favor of his friend. More consciously,
she compounded her rejection by promulgating a union between
his beloved sister and a quasi-brother who was part of the family

over the years. Mrs. Shelley's fondness for young men may have been part of her resentment toward her older husband's past.

Shelley later returned to his accusations against his mother in a letter to Elizabeth Hitchener. Observing that Hitchener was "much shocked" when he told her in Cuckfield about his "mother's depravity," he said his conclusion was not based on "reason" but "*Feeling* here affords sufficient proof."[84] Shelley's doubts about his mother's fidelity and her sincerity in expressing love were reinforced by another experience, perhaps this same year, and conveyed to Tom Medwin:

> during Sir Timothy's absence in London, on his parliamentary duties, Lady Shelley invited Shelley to Field Place, where he was received, to use his own words, with much *show-affection*. Some days after he had been there, his mother produced a parchment-deed, which she asked him to sign, to what purport I know not; but he declined so doing, and which he told me he would have signed, had he not seen through the false varnish of hypocritical caresses. This anecdote is not idle gossip— but comes from Shelley himself.[85]

Shelley's uncle accompanied him to London on October 22, the same day Timothy was dining with Norfolk, the friendly mediator. Shelley wrote Whitton that evening saying he was "in haste to quit Town for a remote part of the kingdom" and asked Whitton to answer immediately concerning his allowance. Whitton's response was that Timothy would not give him money until Shelley's "conduct ... [is] more consonant to your duty to him as your parent."[86] The Duke met with Whitton, who wrote Shelley that Norfolk would like to see him before noon.[87] Shelley was on the coach to York before the letter arrived. It was forwarded to a new York address, indicating Shelley knew Harriet had moved. Having called at the Westbrooks to find Eliza had left for York, he was eager to return there.

Whitton mentioned in his letter that he had opened and read Shelley's accusatory letter to his mother. Well-versed in Shelley family peccadilloes, Whitton—without denying the validity of Shelley's accusations against his mother—deemed the letter "not proper" with "harsh and unfeeling sentiments." He asked Shelley's permission to destroy the letter and the one to his sister. Realizing that his letter to his mother had not been seen by her, Shelley angrily sent Whitton's back with an added note: "Mr. S commends Mr. W when he deals with gentlemen (which opportunity may not often occur) to refrain from opening private letters, or impudence may draw down chastisement upon contemptibility."[88] Whitton wrote to Sir Bysshe about "the most scurrilous letter that a mad viper could dictate."[89] Shelley, writing the elder Medwin a month later, maintained the accuracy of his accusations against his mother and sister: "I find that affair on which those letters spoke is become the general gossip of the idle newsmongers of Horsham. They give *me* credit for having *invented* it.—They do my invention honor:—but greatly discredit their own penetration."[90]

Away from York ten days, Shelley arrived back to find drastic changes. Eliza had arrived earlier, armed with money.[91] She took immediate charge in the more commodious quarters on Blake Street where she, Harriet, and Hogg were living when Shelley arrived. It was four days before Shelley learned the reason for her early arrival. In the charged emotional atmosphere, Shelley was aware of the animosity between Hogg and Eliza, not to mention Harriet's chilly attitude toward Hogg. Besieged by Eliza, Hogg said her pockmarked white complexion was like "a mass of boiled rice" and her black hair resembled "the tail of a horse." Worse, Eliza swarmed over Harriet, fretting about her "nerves." Eliza constantly invoked Miss Warne—another controlling maternal figure from Harriet's past—as one who would disapprove of this or that behavior of the younger sister. Shelley, "overwhelmed" by Eliza's "affectionate invasion," "lay prostrated and helpless, under [her] insupportable pressure." Hogg wanted Shelley to declare, "Either Eliza goes or I go."[92]

Amid these perplexing changes, Shelley ignored Whitton and wrote to his father, repeating his accusations about Timothy's libels. Hogg addressed Shelley's letter, but Timothy knew Hogg's handwriting and Hogg obligingly sealed the letter with his family's coat of arms containing three boar's heads. Timothy sent it unopened to Whitton who decided the contents were not for Timothy's eyes.[93] Timothy was writing Whitton that his son was now "such a Pupil of Godwin" there was scarce hope he would obey "the wishes or directions of his Parents."[94]

Shelley received Elizabeth Hitchener's rejection of his offer to share his inheritance and he replied that they had two years to argue the subject. Hitchener, "sister of my soul," must keep this "the most secret of communications." He explained his marriage to Harriet, saying she could "Blame me if thou wilt dearest friend, for *still* thou art dearest to me." Shelley asked if she had read Godwin's novels, *St. Leon* and *Caleb Williams.*[95]

Acting on Charles Grove's suggestion, Shelley wrote to the Duke of Norfolk to intervene on his behalf with his father. The obliging Duke replied he would be glad to interfere but was not optimistic about changing his father's views. Norfolk was going north and hoped to see Shelley in York. Shelley, thanking Charles Grove, expected "salutary effects" and asked for any "intelligence concerning Field Place affairs."[96]

Intelligence about affairs within his own household soon stunned Shelley. Four days after his return, Harriet told him that Hogg had tried to seduce her after Shelley left for London. Harriet, summoning Eliza from London, rebuffed Hogg and talked to him about his behavior. Remorseful, he wanted to write a confession, but Harriet, fearing the letter's effect on Shelley's mind, forbade him. Shelley, shaken by this news, took a long walk with Hogg. He wrote Elizabeth Hitchener of being aware of Harriet's "greatly altered" attitude toward Hogg and kept pressing her to explain. When she finally did, Shelley told a "terrorstruck, remorseful" Hogg that he "pardoned him, freely, fully." Shelley would remain a friend and hoped "to convince him how lovely virtue was, that his crime not himself was the object of my detestation."[97]

Shelley had no plans to leave Hogg, who said he had instantly fallen in love with Harriet in Edinburgh. Hogg felt that his passion, "far from meeting resistance was . . . purposely encouraged." He had avowed his love for her when they first arrived in York. Forbidding Hogg from further mention of his love, Harriet did not tell Shelley, hoping Hogg would drop the matter. As soon as Shelley departed for Sussex, the attempted seduction took place. In six letters to his "soul-sister" Elizabeth Hitchener, Shelley revealed what we know of what transpired between his "soul-brother" Hogg and Harriet. In Edinburgh, an erotically aroused Hogg had probably experienced Harriet's unknowing seductiveness and Shelley's subtle promotion of a liaison between the two. Hogg's ensnarement was completed when Shelley left Harriet alone with Hogg and when Harriet did not tell Shelley before he left of Hogg's avowal of love. Shelley told Elizabeth Hitchener of his amazement and admiration that Harriet resisted Hogg's "sophistries," with his "pathetic eloquence" and "the illumination of that countenance on which I have sometimes gazed till I fancied the world could be reformed by gazing too."[98] Harriet had withstood Hogg's charms better than Shelley.

This latest betrayal left Shelley in a bind. Ambivalent about deserting his closest friend, he felt obligated to respect Harriet's wishes, which merged with those of Eliza. He told Hogg the three would leave York and wanted him to write. They departed several days later, in early November, without telling Hogg the hour of their departure. They left behind Shelley's trunk, the bill for the lodgings, and a note saying they were going to Richmond. Actually, their destination was Keswick in the Lake District.

11

Seeking New Fathers: Keswick

SHELLEY HAD SEVERAL REASONS FOR GOING TO KESWICK DESPITE telling Elizabeth Hitchener that Harriet and Eliza made the decision to go to the Lake District.[1] He had recently written to the Duke of Norfolk at Greystoke Castle, near Keswick, seeking his help with his father. Keswick also was a hub for the Lake poets Shelley admired. Southey lived in Greta Hall with Coleridge's family. Coleridge, alienated from both his wife and Wordsworth, left Keswick in 1803. He was in London giving his Shakespeare lectures. The poet Charles Lloyd lived nearby and further south at Grasmere were Wordsworth and Thomas De Quincey. Shelley only met Southey.

The three travelers temporarily lodged at Mr. Crosthwaite's, a local artist, and Shelley immediately wrote to Hogg, "You are suprised at our sudden departure." Remarking about Hogg's "disgusting & horrid" behavior, he confessed "I shall perhaps think you a *liar* . . . still I shall be your friend. . . . I can never forget what you once were." He asked Hogg to send his trunk.[2]

After a few days, the newcomers moved to Chestnut Cottage, a mile from town off the Penrith Road. Their cottage, one of four in a row on the rise of Chestnut Hill, afforded a view from their bow window across the garden to the heights of Latrigg and Skiddaw, and the two lakes, Derwentwater and Bassenthwaite.[3] It was the first of Shelley's isolated abodes nestled on a hill and commanding a fine view. The cottage's owner, Mr. Gideon Dare, soon regretted permitting his new guests to use the garden.[4] Shelley said one November evening he was educating Harriet and Eliza about the atmosphere. Shelley ignited in the garden some hydrogen gas he had made and its "vivid flame" was visible for "some distance." Soon Mr. Dare asked him to vacate the premises, saying the "country talks very strangely of your proceedings." Shelley "quieted Mr.

D's fears; he does not however much like us, and I am by no means certain that he will permit us to remain."[5] According to local lore, Shelley was evicted for rocking the neighbors with his chemical explosions and for scaring them by using the garden for pistol practice.[6] Shelley's run-in with his landlord was the prelude to a strange affright, the first of several in the months ahead.

The emotional letters Shelley and Hogg exchanged resembled those between two feuding lovers, professions of love alternating with angry threats. Shelley's second Keswick letter to Hogg was his most effusive epistolary expression of love to either sex: "I will adore you as the first of men, as now I love you as the dearest to me.... I tremble ... love me as I love you.... I was ashamed to tell you how ... I am like a child in weakness."[7]

In mid-November Shelley wrote Hogg he became "ill from the poison of laurel-leaves." Shelley knew they contained prussic acid, a poison he later coveted. He would throw himself off "yon dark rock" into the lake if his placing Harriet's happiness above his love for Hogg were "unworthy."[8] Composing poetry with some diligence, his ingestion of the laurel may have come from reading in Erasmus Darwin that it stimulated poetic creativity and acted as an opium substitute.[9]

Hogg sent several letters to Harriet, the first eliciting Shelley's incensed reply, "You deceive yourself terribly my friend."[10] However, the two continued their agonized "investigations" into the morality of Hogg's behavior. Hogg's attempt to seduce Harriet merely confirmed Shelley's suspicions about his friend's "self-centred, self-devoted, self-interested" ideas. Shelley repeatedly told Hogg the essential point was the consent and desire of both parties to such a free-love arrangement, and Harriet most decidedly was opposed. Shelley would not object to sharing Harriet sexually with him if she so desired, but she obviously refused. Hogg should think of her happiness and cease and desist.[11] He was particularly angered by Hogg's "sophistry" in pressuring Harriet by assuring her "There is no injury to him who knows it not."[12] Shelley admitted being "*perhaps* . . . not quite free" of the common prejudice against free love, but Hogg "*certainly*" had this prejudice and Harriet had it "interwoven with the fibres of her being."[13]

Hogg repeatedly asked Shelley's permission to join them, but Shelley, unsure Harriet could resist Hogg sexually, was adamant he not come.[14] After Hogg invoked Rousseau's *La Nouvelle Héloïse*, Shelley replied that "Harriet is *not* an Heloisa, even were

I a St Preux—but I am not jealous." Denying three times he was jealous, Shelley concluded: "on her opinions of right & wrong alone does the morality of the present case depend." If Harriet "was convinced of its innocence would I be so sottish a slave to opinion as to endeavor to monopolize what if participated w^d give my friend pleasure without diminishing my own." Shelley was paraphrasing Godwin's *Political Justice* about free love and mentioned he was "at times very much inclined to think that the Godwinian plan is best."[15] Hogg, undeterred, incorporated his beliefs several years later into his novel, *Memoirs of Prince Alexy Haimatoff.*

Shelley, lecturing Hogg about the power of the sex drive, said he knew "how tyrannic . . . how resistless its influence . . . presence without fullest satiation will kindle the passions to an inextinguishable flame." He implored Hogg to "be a god" and not let himself become "the sport of a womans whim; the plaything of her inconsistencies, the bauble with which she is angry: the footstool of her exaltation."[16] Shelley was reading Hogg the texts of his feelings about Harriet Grove. About this time Shelley composed a poem, "Passion" ("Fair are thy berries"), about a plant—possibly nightshade—whose "deadly poison," like passion, could unite "good and ill." The beautiful berry hides its "deadly poison," as a "lawyer whose smooth face" promises "good, while hiding so much ill."[17] Hogg, the budding lawyer, had received Shelley's angry letter denying he regarded Hogg as "smooth tongued traitor."[18]

In their heated exchanges about Harriet and love, the largely unspoken issue was their love for each other. Shelley repeatedly called one of Hogg's now-lost letters, "the letter of *your soul* . . . [it] has been my companion: my study since I received it."[19] Shelley's appreciation of Hogg's sacrifice by joining him in being expelled complicated his feelings about Hogg's attempted seduction. Shelley perhaps allowed himself to physically express love for Hogg with occasional embraces. Shelley was revulsed by pederasty and later argued that intense, intimate same-sex relationships could be nonsexual. His defense against his homosexual impulses probably contributed to his attraction and marriage to Harriet. Hogg's seduction effort afforded Shelley the feelings of anger, disappointment, and betrayal, assuring never again would the two friends experience the close intimacy they enjoyed at Oxford. It was not the end of their mutual forays into a *ménage à trois*, but the passion between them was now spent.

Hogg, growing dramatic, would "have Harriet's forgiveness or blow my brains out at her feet." Shelley found the threat "not convincing."[20] Hogg's anger remained years later. In his biography of Shelley he hid his seduction attempt and his friend's reaction to it by disguising Shelley's letter as a "Fragment of a Novel," claiming it was Shelley's attempt to continue Goethe's *The Sorrows of Young Werther.* Among other changes, Harriet became "Charlotte." Hogg criticized Shelley's writing as being more like Godwin than Goethe or Rousseau.[21]

Hogg, hinting of challenging Shelley to a duel, drew Shelley's scorn. Shelley wrote Elizabeth Hitchener, "I shall not fight a duel with him whatever he may say or do." Hogg's life was not "a fair exchange for mine, since I have acted up to my principles, and he has denied his."[22] His last Keswick letter to Hogg was short and blunt; he had chosen Harriet over Hogg. It was *"impossible"* to think of meeting again and Shelley would "resign" his friendship for Hogg for the sake of Harriet's "tranquillity." Hogg was "capable of great things," and "If I were free. I were yours . . . But I am Harriet's."[23] It was a year before he wrote Hogg again.

Shelley tried to fit Elizabeth Hitchener into his marital relationship, writing her that his "terrible headache" was alleviated both by "Harriets love" and by the "pleasure" of his "thoughts" about his spinster correspondent. His "nervous attack" led him "reluctantly" to take laudanum but his "illness" would go away when his "mind is at ease." Several weeks later he hoped he would no longer need laudanum.[24]

Shelley, having written to Norfolk from Keswick, accepted the Duke's late November invitation to visit Greystoke Castle with Harriet and Eliza.[25] Before leaving for Greystoke, Shelley wrote two letters to Medwin senior in Horsham. Finding Keswick a *"manufacturing dissipated* town," Shelley was interested in finding a house in Sussex, perhaps St. Leonards Forest, near Field Place. He then inquired about raising money without the "exorbitant interest" of seventy percent, "until my coming of age." Begging for "a small Sum," Shelley pleaded poverty, being almost "deprived of the necessaries of life." They were using nearly their last guinea to visit the Duke but entertained "very few hopes" for the Greystoke visit.[26]

Expecting to stay only several days, the three traveled twenty miles up the Penrith road to Greystoke in sleet and snow the first of December. The visit proved fruitful and they extended their stay to ten days. The Duke, whose other guests were mostly aristocrats, was pleased with Harriet and Eliza.[27] Shelley—in Byron's words, "as perfect a Gentleman as ever crossed a drawing room"—also must have made a good impression.[28] Although Shelley later complained to Elizabeth Hitchener of being "fatigued with aristocratical insipidity," he admitted indulging his fondness for arguments with the guests and defended the Duke against Hitchener's "unfounded" charge that he believed in Catholicism.[29] The ex-Catholic Norfolk strongly supported Catholic emancipation and talk about it at Greystoke may have stimulated Shelley's nascent plans to go to Ireland to further the cause.

The Duke had wanted Shelley to meet William Calvert, the guest who most intrigued Shelley. He wrote Hitchener the "elderly" Calvert "seemed to know all my concerns" and responded to Shelley's "arguments" with an "expression of his face . . . I shall not readily forget."[30] Calvert, whose brother Raisley had been Wordsworth's patron, lived on a farm close to Chestnut Cottage. Still liberal politically and with scientific interests that matched Shelley's, Calvert and his wife became his closest friends during the Keswick months.

Having arranged Shelley's visit with a view toward reconciling him and his father, Norfolk wrote Timothy upon Shelley's arrival and departure from Greystoke. He had successfully urged Shelley to write a conciliatory letter to his father.

Returning to Chestnut Cottage, Shelley informed Elizabeth Hitchener of his "design . . . to visit Ireland" at some vague future time. After trying to entice her to visit by describing the beautiful scenery, he announced a major event: "I have now my dear friend in contemplation a Poem." It would anticipate "a picture of the manners, simplicity and delights of a perfect state of society; tho still earthly." Intending to "publish" it, he wanted her "hints" as to how he should "draw a picture of *Heaven*."[31] This poem, to be called *Queen Mab*, would bring Shelley his greatest recognition in his lifetime and in the years after his death. By announcing its conception to Elizabeth Hitchener, Shelley recognized her role in fostering his creativity.

Deftly composing his conciliatory letter to his father, Shelley gently chastised him for revoking his allowance and mentioned, "I married a young lady whose personal character is unimpeachable." Broaching the Duke's suggestion of an apology, Shelley desired "a reconciliation" with his father and asked him to "accept my apologies for the uneasiness which I have occasioned." He regarded "family differences as a very great evil" but could not promise "concealing my opinions in political and religious matters." Indirectly stabbing his father, he reminded him, "I have not employed hypocrisy . . . [or] meanness. . . . Such methods would be unworthy of us both."[32] Timothy replied immediately, suggesting the allowance be restored "in due time" but Shelley must follow through on "having promis'd to enter into some Professional line." He reminded his son, "I never can admit within my Family of the Principles that caus'd your expulsion from Oxford."[33]

Shelley, answering his father by playing a trump card recently dealt into his hand, mentioned that Harriet's father was now providing her £200 a year.[34] Timothy matched the ante of the retired wine merchant and restored his previous offer of £200.[35] The couple's annual income was now £400.

In other financial plots, Sir Bysshe, having modified his will to check his grandson's wish to break up his estate, now contemplated a further move. Shelley heard from his uncle Pilfold of a "meditated proposal" of his father and grandfather. Shelley would immediately have an income of £2000, larger than his father's, if he would agree "to entail the estate on my eldest Son, and in default of issue on my brother." Expressing "indignant contempt" of the contemplated offer to Elizabeth Hitchener, Shelley called it a bribe to "forswear my principles." It was an "insultingly hateful" proposal to make "to the face of any *virtuous* man." He would not agree, by entailing "120,000£," to pass this "command over labor" and the "power . . . to *employ* it for beneficent purposes." His grandfather's and father's proposal "put in its genuine light the grandeur of aristocratical distinctions," demonstrating "that contemptible vanity will gratify its *unnatural* passions at the expense of every just humane and philanthropic consideration: 'Tho to a celestial angel linked will sate itself on a celestial bed & prey on garbage.'"[36]

Shelley's quote, the ghost of Hamlet's father speaking to his son, reflected his oedipal outrage which, as he mentioned to Elizabeth Hitchener, "probably confused my language." Censoring Shakespeare for his soul sister, he omitted the quote's two initial words, "So lust."

This proposal apparently was never made to Shelley by his father or grandfather. Shelley began being less open with his uncle,

suspecting he might reveal too much to Field Place. Captain Pilfold told Elizabeth Hitchener he regretted Shelley treated him
"with a half confidence." She reassured Shelley she would be tight-
lipped to his "too open" uncle, who would never learn "the circumstances of Hogg's apostacy." Shelley now told Hitchener "I demand" that she "be my mentor my guide my cou[n]sellor the half
of my soul." Having promoted a correspondence between Harriet
and Hitchener, he said Harriet "sends her love to you—she is quite
what is called *in* love with you." Wary that Elizabeth Hitchener's
idealization of him might turn to disillusionment—she wrote he
was "a living example of my idea of a truly virtuous man"—he
replied prophetically: "Do not praise me so much. My counsellor
will overturn the fabric she is erecting."[37]

When Elizabeth Hitchener confided she recently was rejected
by a woman friend, Shelley replied that she had been stung by "one
of the vipers of the world." Both he and Harriet wrote, urging her
to live with them. After Harriet related to Hitchener a scare she
and Shelley had on a "water excursion," Hitchener wrote to her, "I
cannot *spare* you . . . be not either of you so hazardous again."[38]

Shelley, in a final fanciful attempt to contact twelve-year-old
Hellen, wrote the family's huntsman, Etheridge, asking he give an
enclosed letter to his sister. He told Hellen to "Think for yourself,"
he was not "the Devil," only "her brother who loved her."[39]
Etheridge, against Shelley's wishes, dutifully gave the letters to
Timothy, who sent them to Whitton.

Shortly after first arriving in Keswick, Shelley sought out
Southey, whose *Thalaba* he memorized at Eton and whose *The
Curse of Kehama* was a favorite. Believing Southey was still a radical poet, Shelley located Greta Hall on a small rise on the river
Greta just outside town. Mistakenly believing Southey was out of
town, he told Elizabeth Hitchener he contented himself by "contemplating the outside" of Greta Hall. Southey *was* inside, writing
to a friend in London to record in shorthand the Shakespeare lectures of the unpredictable Coleridge, now addicted to opium. Godwin, who earlier had mentored Coleridge, attended every lecture
and brought his fourteen-year-old daughter Mary to one, where
she first saw Byron.[40]

Calvert, informing Shelley at Greystoke that Southey was in
Keswick, arranged a meeting at the Calvert farm. Shelley, en-
thused, erroneously told Elizabeth Hitchener he would also see
Calvert's two other poet friends there, Wordsworth and Coleridge.

Calvert, knowing Shelley's radical religious and political views before meeting him, now told him of Southey's shift to conservative Tory views. Shelley wrote Hitchener, "Southey has changed. . . . I shall reproach him [for] his tergiversation." Southey had become "the votary" of "Bigotry Tyranny and Law" by supporting the Church of England and the war in Spain, and by having "inflated" the English constitution with "the prostituted exertions of his pen." Shelley believed Wordsworth was a potential mentor, unaware he now shared Southey's conservative views. Shelley mistakenly believed Wordsworth's "poverty is such that he is frequently obliged to beg for a shirt to his back."[41] Only De Quincey, alone with his laudanum in Dove Cottage, had the books and intellectual spark Shelley would have appreciated the most. Even Calvert had qualms about Shelley's openness with his views. Seventy-nine years later, Calvert's daughter vividly recalled Shelley's visits and the workbox he gave her. In perhaps the last personal reminiscence about Shelley, she remembered best the "sort of look" that came over her father's and Southey's faces when Shelley talked, and how she and her brothers were spirited from the room "lest we should hear the conversation."[42]

The meeting with Southey provided some economic relief. Calvert, learning that Shelley's rent was two and one-half guineas a week, had his landlord lower it to one guinea and loaned linen to his new young friend. Shelley and Southey, by Christmas, were "much engaged in talking." Appointed Poet Laureate two years later, Southey was the first major literary and intellectual figure Shelley had met. Struggling to maintain his idealized image of him despite their "total difference" in "sentiments," he thought Southey was "far from being a man of great reasoning powers" but "is a great Man . . . a man of virtue." Shelley was gratified to learn Southey believed mankind was moving toward a more perfect state and advocated "liberty and equality." This despite the fact that "Southey hates the Irish, he speaks against Catholic Emancipation, & Parliamentary reform." Further, Southey "calls himself a Christian" even though Shelley felt he fit the clear "definition of a Deist."[43] Southey soon tried to convince Shelley *he* was the Deist.

The future author of *The Three Bears* warmly opened his home to Shelley, lending him books from his ample library.[44] Shelley's inevitable disillusionment with Southey set in, but the household intrigued him. Southey's wife Edith was one of three Fricker sisters living at Greta Hall with their children. Shelley considered Mrs.

Southey "very stupid," and Coleridge's wife, Sara, "is worse." He approved of the third sister, Mary, former actress and widow of the poet Robert Lovell. Shelley detected "venality" in Southey but commented favorably on his relationship with his children.[45]

As Shelley's esteem for Southey lessened, Southey became enamored of his new young disciple, writing to friends about him and his family problems. Seeing much of his earlier self in Shelley, Southey told him the only difference between them was that Shelley was nineteen and he was thirty-seven.[46] He urged one correspondent to intervene with Timothy on the son's behalf, considering Shelley his "patient" who, coming "to the fittest physician in the world," was at "the Pantheistic stage of philosophy." Within a week he could make him a "Berkeleyan" and "succeed in convincing him that he may be a true philosopher, and do a great deal of good with 6000£ a year."[47] He wrote another friend that Shelley possessed "a great deal of genius, a great deal of enthusiasm, and high notions of sincerity and virtue." Shelley told him he tried prayer at Oxford for two months before giving it up, having followed "the prescription as regularly as if it had been to take three table spoonfuls of julep." Southey hoped Shelley would stay to the summer.[48]

Southey also had been expelled, from Westminster School, for writing a tract denouncing flogging. *Thalaba* reflected Southey's study of Rousseau, later one of Shelley's ideological forebears. Years earlier, Southey and Coleridge abandoned their Godwinian plan for a utopian community, Pantisocracy, on the banks of America's Susquehanna River. Shelley had hopes for a similar scheme. Shelley's physical similarity to Southey was commented upon by those who knew both, including William Hazlitt, who thought each had "fire" in their eyes.[49] Upon Shelley's urging, Southey borrowed from Charles Lloyd a copy of Berkeley in which Lloyd had penciled a thought that Shelley recalled years later: "Mind cannot create; it can only perceive."[50] Shelley's skeptical position, built upon Berkeley and Hume, was also influenced by Sir William Drummond's *Academical Questions.*[51]

Southey wrote a friend that Oxford, expelling Shelley, "sent away more genius and better principles than they kept behind." Southey was perhaps the first to predict Shelley's future greatness: "He will get rid of his eccentricity, and he will retain his morals, his integrity and his genius, and unless I am greatly deceived there is every reason to believe he will become an honour to his name and his country."[52]

Southey read and discussed his own poetry with Shelley, including the early radical *Wat Tyler* and *The Devil's Thoughts*. The poetry Shelley wrote at Keswick reflected Southey's influence in social content and the use of unrhymed stanzas.[53] Shelley sent Elizabeth Hitchener seven stanzas of a poem, "a Tale of Society as it is from facts." The poem's subject, "literally true,"[54] recounts how a crippled veteran, disabled from the "rapine, drunkenness and woe" of war, lives in poverty unable to support his aged mother. Struck by the poverty in Keswick that reduced exploited factory workers to starvation, he told Hitchener the town seemed "more like a suburb of London than a village of Cumberland." Shelley was horrified that "Children are frequently found in the River which the unfortunate women employed at the manufactory destroy."[55]

Rejecting Southey's charge that he was not an atheist, Shelley wrote Hitchener, "I believe that God is another signification for the Universe." Addressing Hitchener's doubts about Christianity, Shelley told her "Jesus Christs divinity . . . is the falsehood of human-kind." Finding Southey "corrupted" and "terribly narrow," Shelley was eager to see Wordsworth, having memorized one of his poems. Urging Hitchener to come "*live* with us," he entreated her, "Have confidence in yourself—dare to believe 'I am great.'"[56]

Planning his Irish expedition, Shelley wrote Elizabeth Hitchener that "*the* Poem" (*Queen Mab*) "is not *now* to my mind" and he was postponing further work on it. He continued writing one hundred fifty pages of his "moral & metaphysical" essays and two hundred pages of his novel, *Herbert Cauvin*, "a tale in which I design to exhibit the cause of the failure of the French Revolution." Both works have disappeared. Decrying the "violence and blood" of the revolution, in his novel he would exclude "sexual passion," believing his silence would be "the keenest satire on its intemperance."[57] Later, recasting the French Revolution in *Laon and Cythna*, sexual passion was audaciously featured.

By year's end, Southey unwittingly replaced himself with Godwin in Shelley's paternal universe. Southey, influenced by *Political Justice* at Oxford, later knew Godwin and Mary Wollstonecraft. He informed Shelley that Godwin was alive and had changed his anti-matrimonialist stance, marrying a second time. Shelley told Elizabeth Hitchener he admired Godwin and, not expecting a reply, would "write him today" and see him in London.[58] The next day, January 3, he wrote Godwin the most fateful letter of his life, incorrectly addressed to "Mr. J. Godwin's Juvenile Library." William, not his wife Jane, promptly replied. Godwin was fifty-five, three years younger than Timothy. Coleridge, visiting Keswick shortly after Shelley left, was too late to challenge his friend Godwin for Shelley's discipleship.

In his worshipful letter, Shelley wrote, "The name of Godwin . . . excite[s] in me feelings of reverence and admiration." Considering Godwin "a luminary too dazzling for the darkness which surrounds him," he had "enrolled your name on the list of the honorable dead" but "It is not so—you still live." This was the pinnacle of Shelley's idealization of Godwin. Mentioning twice being "young," Shelley had "suffered much from human persecution" but was sure Godwin was "a veteran to me in the years of persecution." Hinting of monetary assistance, he concluded saying he would "endeavor to make my desire useful by [a] friendship with William Godwin. . . . I am convinced I could represent myse[lf] to you in such terms as not to be thought wholly unworthy of your friendship."[59]

Godwin's hungry monetary eye widened at the hint; he probably suspected Shelley's letter emulated Casimir's letter of introduction to an older mentor in his novel *Fleetwood*.[60] Godwin, addicted to taking youthful male admirers under his tutelage, currently was assisting an impoverished young man to gain admittance to a university.[61] Replying by return mail, Godwin complained that Shelley's "generalizing" letter "renders it deficient of interest." Shelley answered immediately. To "remedy the fault," a financial statement was the first item in his carefully constructed self-portrayal. Shelley's statement, "I am the Son of a man of fortune in Sussex," sealed the monetary basis of his relationship with Godwin. Further, an incompatibility between "my Father and myself" stemmed from childhood "passive obedience" having been "enforced" as part of his "*duty* to love." Such "external impediments," though "numerous" and "strongly applied," had only "temporary" effects.[62]

Turning to literature, Shelley said he wrote and published *Zastrozzi* and *St. Irvyne* "before the age of seventeen," younger than his actual age when he composed each. In the two years since first reading "your inestimable book on 'Political Justice,'" his mind was opened to "fresh & more extensive views, it materially influenced my character, and I rose from its perusal a wiser and better man." He was "no longer the votary of Romance," having "duties to perform." Because his mind, before reading *Political Justice*, was already "jealous of its independence," he had a "peculiar susceptibility" to its message.[63]

Unknowingly, Shelley was invoking an earlier ghost of his new mentor, as he had with Southey. Godwin, a lapsed third-generation dissenting minister, was raised in a strict family in which his minister father demanded obedience to the stern traditions of Calvinism. Barred by law from Oxford and Cambridge because of his dissenting beliefs, the brilliant Godwin received a more rigorous education in the classics, philosophy, religion, and languages at the dissenting academy that prepared him for the ministry.[64] Like Shelley, he filled his lonely, isolated childhood in rural England by becoming an avid reader. He published soft-porn novels of seduction and heaving bosoms before becoming the illustrious author of *Political Justice*, published when Shelley was seven months old. Godwin had revised *Political Justice* twice, becoming more conservative in some of his views. Shelley recommended the first edition to Elizabeth Hitchener and was now more a believer in Godwin's earlier doctrines than their author. Shelley accurately stated this in his first letter to Godwin, "my feelings and my reasonings correspond with what yours were." Godwin's philosophical anarchism was congenial to Shelley, with its emphasis upon the tyranny of social custom and opinion, not to mention despotical government. He shared Godwin's basic beliefs in human "perfectibility"—mankind's potential for continuing development—and in "necessity," the deterministic causal "chain" linking all phenomena in the universe from inorganic matter to the highest forms of organic life. As for antimatrimonialism, both had violated the precept and Godwin had renounced it.[65]

Shelley asked Godwin to be his "friend" and "adviser. . . . I [am your] pupil . . . I do not feel the least disposition to be Mr. S[outhey]'s proselyte."[66] Godwin's bloom of fame and income from *Political Justice* had long since faded; its once meteoric influence was now barely a dying ember. Shelley's breath might revive its message but his inheritance could materially rekindle the chronically penniless Godwin, who read in Shelley's second letter that he was "heir by entail to an estate of 6000£ per an." Regarding "the law of primogeniture an evil of primary magnitude," Shelley said his "father's notions of family honor" were "incoincident with my knowledge of public good." His father "ever regarded me as a blot and defilement to his honor" and "wished to induce me by poverty to accept of some commission in a distant regiment, and in the interim of my absence to prosecute the pamphlet [*The Necessity*] that a process of outlawry might make the estate on his death devolve to my younger brother."[67] The Shelley "fortune" promised fiscal relief for Godwin in accordance with the tenets of equitable distribution of wealth advocated in *Political Justice* and subscribed to by his new pupil.

The year just ended had been trying for both Shelley and Godwin and each needed the other. Godwin's 1811 crises included trying to support a family of five children in a nearly destitute condition, continuing ill health, and having his shrewish second wife leave him briefly.[68] Godwin replied to Shelley's second letter by expressing a "deep and earnest interest" in the "welfare" of this intellectually gifted and financially blessed disciple. After Godwin criticized him for his animosity towards Timothy, Shelley denied being "angry" with his father. Desiring "a reconciliation," he could not accept the "price" demanded. His father "*acted* for my welfare" only in "certain considerations of birth," not in "feeling for me.—I never loved my father; it was not hardness of heart for I have loved, and I do love warmly."[69] Frustrated by Godwin's tenacity about Shelley's disavowal of love for his father, Shelley said the "sole reason" his father recently renewed his £200 yearly allowance "was to prevent my cheating strangers." He denied feeling "repulsion or hatred towards him" for these words, but his father's "prejudice against me" made him "despair of conciliation."[70]

Indicative of his breach with his father, Shelley, before his allowance was restored, apparently asked a "small sum" from Timothy's bitter political enemy, Horsham attorney William Sandham.[71] Naïvely hoping the intimacy lacking with his father would be found in Godwin, Shelley said he should know "as much of my thoughts and feelings as I know myself." It was a "blessing" that he could be "drinking the streams of your mind at their fountainhead." Godwin, like Timothy, would not accept having his authority challenged. He criticized Shelley for rushing into print instead of being a "scholar." Taking on his new mentor, Shelley conceded he would "not again crudely obtrude the question of atheism on the world." He would willingly "become a scholar, nay a pupil" if he could "perceive" in Godwin "talents & powers . . . undoubtedly superior." Rejecting false modesty and "the deceit of self distrust by which much power has been lost to the world," it was right for him to publish when many others no more talented were "by publications scattering the seeds of prejudice and selfishness."[72]

Shelley next asserted, "If any man would determine sincerely and cautiously at every period of his life to publish books which should contain the real state of his feelings and opinions, I am willing to suppose that this portraiture of his mind would be worth many metaphysical disquisitions."[73] Adopting this credo, Shelley's compositions reflected his psychological development throughout his life.[74] In his letters, Shelley quietly criticized Godwin for emphasizing rationality, making *Political Justice* a metaphysical disquisition rather than a portrayal of the deeper feelings controlling human conduct.

Godwin's contemporaries also criticized his coldly intellectual approach to changing human behavior. Godwin was a virgin at age forty when he began his relationship with Mary Wollstonecraft, who tried to soften his extreme rationality. Southey, who had desired Mary Wollstonecraft, remarked to Coleridge that Godwin was like "a close Stool pan, most often empty, & better empty than when full."[75]

Control of feelings was behind Godwin's admonishment of Shelley about the inflammatory effect of his writing in his pending political Irish expedition. Godwin rejected inciting popular mass political activity and knew something of Ireland. He was hosted in Dublin in 1800 by his esteemed friend and Irish barrister, John Philpot Curran. Godwin's 1786 article, "To the People of Ireland," urged a course of moderation, and his novel *St. Leon*, which Shelley had read, focused on the dangers of religious rivalry. Shelley, now writing *An Address, to the Irish People*, optimistically informed Godwin in late January that his address "to the Catholics of Ireland" was written in simple language that those in "uneducated poverty . . . may clearly comprehend." It would not "excite rebellion" but produce "peace & harmony." Ten days earlier, Elizabeth Hitchener was the first to receive quotes from his address.[76]

Once in Ireland, Shelley returned to his argument with Godwin justifying early publication, analyzing his urge to write and his creativity. Reading this remarkable statement by a nineteen-year-old, Godwin must have been perplexed, if not impressed, by its insight, hubris, and determination. Because of his "physical constitution," Shelley could not "hope" to live as long as Godwin. Although "constitutionally nervous, and affected by slight fatigue," when his "mind is actively engaged in writing or discussion . . . it gains strength." He would publish "nothing that shall not conduce to virtue" and hoped "my publications will present to the moralist and metaphysician a picture of a mind however uncultured and unpruned which had at the dawn of its knowledge taken a singular turn." Leaving out his "early" writing would deprive "the world of right angled originality.—Thus much for egotism." In an after-thought, he added, "Besides you must know that I either *am* or fancy myself something of a Poet."[77] This was Godwin's first knowledge that Shelley wrote anything but prose.

A month before writing to Godwin of being "constitutionally nervous," Shelley experienced an "attack," the first of a series. It occurred on Sunday, January 19, several days after he wrote Elizabeth Hitchener he had lost his "terrible headache" and recovered from a "nervous attack" with the aid of laudanum. The incident was reported in the county paper nine days later:

> Several attempts at robbery have been made within the last fortnight, at Keswick and its neighbourhood. One of the most remarkable was about seven o'clock, on the night of Sunday 19th inst. at Chestnut Cottage near Keswick, the seat of Gideon Dare, Esq.—A part of the house, it seems, is occupied by Mr. Shelley and his family.—Mr. Shelley being alarmed by an unusual noise, (but not knowing, or suspecting the cause) went to the door; was knocked down by some ruffians, and had remained senseless for a time, when Mr. Dare, hearing the disturbance, rushed out of the house. The villains, no doubt perceiving that he was armed, fled immediately. It could not be ascertained how many the gang consisted of; but the attack was of a very formidable nature, and must stimulate the magistrates for the security of the town and of the neighbourhood.[78]

Two days earlier, Southey, alarmed over the presence of two rough men loitering about town, was looking for a watchdog and arming himself.[79] He probably shared his apprehension with Shelley, whose version of the attack, as transmitted to the paper, has the same "ruffians." The day of the attack, Southey wrote another friend, "the panic has reached us" and "Half the people in Keswick sat up on Thursday night last [January 16] because two 'ugly fellows' had been seen in town." Suspecting imported Irish laborers, he loaded his old Spanish fowling piece.[80] Shelley possibly appropriated Southey's story of the community's anxiety to rationalize a nonexistent attack. Some inhabitants questioned whether an actual attack occurred. Mr. Calvert's daughter reported that Keswick residents "supposed that Shelley was laboring under an illusion as to the attack." Writing four days after the incident, Southey accepted Shelley's story.[81]

Harriet, obviously upset, first wrote to Elizabeth Hitchener of the attack. A week passed before Shelley wrote to her about it, minimizing its significance. The "circumstance" that "alarmed" Harriet was a "complete casual occurrence" not "likely" to occur again: "The man evidently wanted to rifle my pockets; my falling within the house defeated his intention. There is nothing in this to alarm you." Shelley indicated "the blow [had not] injured me" and Hitchener should "Dismiss all fears of assassins, and spies and prisons." They were prepared for Ireland pending the arrival from Whitton of Shelley's one hundred pounds.

Harriet asked Elizabeth Hitchener to burn her earlier (now lost) letter if she had not read it as it was too alarmist and she was now "quite angry that I sent it." They expected no more alarms but Harriet was cautious of Shelley's emotional state. He was "much better than he has been for some time and I hope as he gets stronger he will outgrow his nervous complaints." Shelley added a postscript: "I am now as Harriet can tell you quite recovered from the little nervous attack I mentioned. Do not alarm yourself either about murderers, spies, government, prisons, or nerves.—I must as I said have hopes."[82]

The panic and flight from Keswick became a pattern for Shelley. An intruder or someone from the community may have tried to frighten him to leave. He was aware of the hostility of his landlord and his neighbors. Likely, there was no intruder, the attack being a panic reaction, with delusional and hallucinatory features, triggered by additional stress-related events. Whatever the contributory effects of prussic acid from the cherry laurel leaves, and of laudanum, panic attacks in which he lost consciousness would become a periodic occurrence.

The newspaper report makes clear that only Shelley saw the "ruffians," reduced to only one intruder in his account to Hitchener. As he was "knocked down" and "senseless for some time" before Mr. Dare's arrival, any attackers had fled by this time. Countering the newspaper's hyperbole of an attack "of a very formidable nature," Shelley went to great lengths a week later to play down the incident as a "casual occurrence" in which his "falling within the house" foiled any presumed robbery. In Harriet's letter to Elizabeth Hitchener undoing the incident's seriousness, she asserted her earlier alarming account was "true," either believing what Shelley told her or hiding the actual nature of Shelley's attack.

Shelley's January letters to Elizabeth Hitchener indicate his mounting anxiety about external threats. In early January, mentioning his "depression," he feared government persecution: "I shall *not* be poisoned . . . I do not anticipate prison . . . I do not fear it.—But, yes I do." Preoccupied with death, he wrote, "Thomas Paine died a natural death—his writings were far more violent in opposition to government than mine perhaps ever will be."[83]

Soon after writing this letter he had his "nervous attack" for which he took laudanum. By mid-January, just before his "attack" by ruffians, Shelley's concerns about others' intent to harm him had a realistic basis. In addition to chemical experiments, flaming balloons, and garden pistol practice that antagonized the locals, his landlord possibly gave him notice to leave.[84] Preparing to depart on his political Irish expedition, Shelley's persecutory fears were fanned by the hostile attitudes toward his radical ideas in conservative Keswick. In the garrison-state mentality of wartime England, imprisonment for treason and sedition was not unusual. By the summer of 1812, the twelve thousand troops positioned in the northern industrial districts rivaled Wellington's forces in the Peninsular campaign.[85]

Shelley was also stressed by his finances, his emerging marital problems, his break with Hogg, and his approaching trip to Ireland. Having stopped taking laudanum shortly before the "attack," he told Elizabeth Hitchener: "anyone who got hold of this letter would think I was a Bedlamite—well you do not, and my reputation for *madness* is too well established to gain any firmness or addition from this letter."[86]

This long rambling letter suggested increasing marital tensions, complicated by Harriet's possible pregnancy. Shelley asked Hitchener, "Have you any idea of *marrying*," before his answer, "You have not." Harriet was over "the little jealousy" Elizabeth Hitchener had detected, but he admitted Harriet's affection for her did not have "the same intensity" as his. A poem of this time, "To Harriet," suggests her jealousy, Shelley protesting he was not "untrue."[87]

However, he soon implored Hitchener, "do feel, that I may feel with you, that every vibration of your nerves may be assimilated to mine, mine to your's.—Dare all."[88] His daring was to include his incomplete political poem with sexual images, *The Devil's Walk*, commenting, "I was once very fond of the Devil." This political satire, his first poetic attack on Castlereagh, derived from the

Southey / Coleridge ballad, *The Devil's Thoughts*. Shelley's phallic devil "poked his hot nose into corners so small," and "innocents" might be thought to be "settling some dress or arranging some ball / —The Devil saw deeper there."[89]

Having entreated Hitchener to "Come and live with us," Shelley denied at length any thoughts of "infidelity." People would say "What they please, precisely" about this arrangement, just as they would "give credit" to the "scandal" about Sir Francis Burdett's "keeping *five* mistresses," which Shelley read about in the *Morning Post*. A year later, Lady Oxford, mistress of Burdett and Byron, possibly tried to enlist Shelley's help in Burdett's cause.[90] Shelley assured Hitchener that if she joined him it would "excite me to just speculation." He perceived in her "the embryon of a mighty intellect which may one day enlighten thousands."[91]

Shelley had told Elizabeth Hitchener that contrary to what Harriet had implied, his wife was not pregnant. He "could not expect" such "good fortune" but hoped "to have a large family of children" as it would "bind *you* and me closer & Harriet." Harriet's enclosed letter expressed relief she was not pregnant for the pending sea trip to Ireland. Modestly discussing pregnancy, she could now "bear the Journey better than if I were you know what, which I do not expect will be the case for some time, years perhaps—but now adieu to that subject."[92] Several weeks later, Shelley again mentioned "a little stranger," a hope he anticipated "at some distance."[93]

Shelley vacillated on where Elizabeth Hitchener should join them, considering in turn Sussex, Keswick, Ireland, or, lastly, Wales, where they would all live in "some antique feudal castle." He hoped that his uncle Pilfold's family would join them, as well as Hitchener's American pupils, and perhaps Godwin, admitting that his "hopes . . . are always rather visionary."[94]

Shelley, grudgingly evaluating Eliza Westbrook, told Elizabeth Hitchener she was "a woman rather superior to the generality . . . prejudiced" but not "unvanquishable."[95] Harriet, however, assured Hitchener that Eliza has "long loved and admired you my dear . . . she is your Sister and mine."[96] Inevitably, the orbits of the two spinsters began colliding. Shelley soon asked Elizabeth Hitchener, "Pray what are you to be *called*," for they already had one Eliza.[97] She would suffer three nicknames.

Finding names for his grandfather was no problem for Shelley when he heard from his uncle that Sir Bysshe "will soon die." This premature death notice released Shelley's bitter portrait of his grandfather as "a complete Atheist [who] builds all his hopes on annihilation." Having "acted very ill toward three wives," he is a "bad man" for whom Shelley "never had respect. . . . [He is] a curse on society." "I shall not grieve at his death," neither "wear mourning" nor "attend [the] funeral" of such "a hardhearted apostate."[98]

Shelley's relationship with Elizabeth Hitchener was in full flower as he prepared to leave for Ireland. Mrs. Calvert expressed surprise after seeing one of Hitchener's long letters. Shelley felt her letters had "eloquence [that] comes more from the soul" and, in a frank self-assessment, considered her letters "not so legal as mine. . . . I sometimes doubt the source of mine, and suspect the genuineness of my sincerity." She was his "second conscience" who would inspect "each shadow however fleeting."[99] After his break with Hogg, no other letters were so revealing of his self-doubts, so honest in his self-appraisal, and so effusive in his praise of another. As the "sister of my soul" and his "second self," she struck a deeper emotional chord than did Harriet. Her letters were "like angels sent from heaven . . . sacredly dear" and "revive me . . . an exhaustless mine of pleasure."[100]

Before embarking for Ireland, Shelley wrote Elizabeth Hitchener a gloss of the fantasy nature of the Keswick attack: "Assassination either by private or public enemies appear[s] to me to be the phantoms of a mind whose affectionate friendship has outrun the real state of the case. Assure yourself that such things are now superannuated, & infeasible."[101] His reported attack, and his allowance, advanced the timetable for leaving Keswick. Ten days after the event, he wrote Hitchener they would depart for Ireland in four days. Godwin, although opposed to Shelley's political activism, provided him a letter of introduction to John Philpot Curran. Shelley again reassured his mentor that his "benevolent and tolerant" *Address* to the Irish Catholics "cannot excite rebellion."[102] Shelley told Hitchener "Southey regrets our going" and "all the Calverts were much against it," except Mrs. Calvert. He had written much of his "address to the Irish which will be printed as Paine's works were, and pasted on the walls of Dublin." His trip was also a publishing venture; he planned to have printed there "my Poems" (*Esdaile*), his novel *Hubert Cauvin,* and "the Essays." After asserting he would make money in Ireland from his publications, his more sober judgment was, "My Volume of Poetry will be I fear an inferior production" with "some bad versification" and only of interest to those "philosophical and reflecting minds who love to trace the early state of human feelings and opinions."[103]

Shelley, having long since rejected his father's views against Catholic emancipation,[104] told Elizabeth Hitchener the avowed purpose of his *Address* was to "familiarize" the "uneducated" Irish about the "ideas of liberty, benevolence *peace* and toleration." However, "It is *secretly* intended . . . to shake Catholicism at its basis." He wanted "to induce Quakerish and Socinian principle[s] of politics without objecting to the Christian Religion, which would do no good to the vulgar just now."[105] Like Godwin before him, Shelley was infusing religious fervor into his political thought. He wrote Elizabeth Hitchener, "Oh! that I [may] be a successful apostle of this only true religion, the religion of philanthropy."[106]

Before leaving Keswick on February 3, the threesome spent the final week with the Calverts who, in Harriet's words, were their "amiable friends . . . extremely kind and attentive." The stormy weather increased Harriet's concern about seasickness, but she hoped "Percy will escape all prosecutions."[107] Arriving in "miserable" Whitehaven, Shelley wrote Elizabeth Hitchener before boarding the packet that night for Ireland. He had passed Southey's house "without *one* sting," admitting he "*may* be amiable in his *private* character stained and false as is his public one." He would miss Mrs. Calvert "but will preserve her memory as another flower to compose a garland which I intend to present to *you*." Switching from gardener to snake charmer, with some prophetic accuracy he hoped she would not leave if she came to live with them in the summer, for then—paraphrasing Psalms—he would be "the deaf adder that stoppeth her ears, and hearketh not to the voice of the Charmer." Abruptly deciding to "stop the wheels of the former sentence," he denied trying to "allegorize myself by the 'Charmer.'"[108] Sailing at midnight, perhaps he was concerned that his message to the Irish would fall on deaf ears.

12

The Irish Expedition

THE SEAFARERS DISEMBARKED FOR SEVERAL DAYS AT THE ISLE OF Man and Shelley continued writing *An Address, to the Irish People*. Expecting a short passage to Dublin, they boarded a small galiot used for transporting slate only to be caught in a "violent gale" and driven "to the North of Ireland." After "28 hours tossing," the "very much fatigued" voyagers landed, taking a coach south.[1]

Nine days after leaving Keswick, the weary trio arrived in Dublin at night and found rooms in a house owned by Mr. Dunne, a woolen draper, at No. 7, Lower Sackville Street (now O'Connell Street), Dublin's widest avenue. Close by the Liffey, their first-floor balcony afforded views of the river, Trinity College, and the Houses of Parliament. The Parliament building housed the National Bank, soon dubbed by Shelley the "temple of Mammon." Immediately writing to Elizabeth Hitchener, he postdated the letter by a year and forgot to include his new address, provided by Harriet with her message, "Write soon."[2] John Philpot Curran was not at home when Shelley called. His disillusionment with the old radical increased upon learning that Curran, after accepting the office of Master of the Rolls, had accommodated to the prevailing political power. Shelley located a printer for his *Address* and ordered fifteen hundred copies to be printed.

Shelley knew his planned contribution to Irish freedom was admittedly "visionary" but he understood certain forces contributing to the current ferment.[3] Daniel O'Connell had helped wrest control of the Catholic Committee from the aristocrats led by Lord Fingall. O'Connell believed emancipation was less important than repeal of the Union Act, but Shelley believed neither emancipation nor repeal of union with England was a panacea. Even if these two goals were met, he thought Ireland's long history of subjection to the devastating brutalities of war, imperialism, and economic exploitation would continue. What was needed was a fundamental

232

change in the rights and conditions of the poor, the great mass of the Irish population.

This belief of Shelley's harked back to the radical Republicanism of Wolfe Tone's United Irishmen, who held sway in the 1790s. Tone, influenced by Paine's *Rights of Man,* envisioned the same oppression of the poor by Irish aristocrats unless separation from England brought a democratic Parliament representing all classes of Irishmen. Another United Irishmen champion for Shelley was Mary Wollstonecraft's friend, Archibald Hamilton Rowan, tried in 1794 and imprisoned for passing out seditious pamphlets. After another United Irishman, Arthur O'Connor, was arrested and tried in England, the Duke of Norfolk testified on his behalf. The armed rebellion of the United Irishmen was crushed in 1798 with the help of torture chambers and flogging arenas set up by the young English Chief Secretary for Ireland, Lord Castlereagh, destined to be enshrined as "Murder" in Shelley's *The Mask of Anarchy.*[4] After the passage of the 1800 Act of Union between England and Ireland, Robert Emmet, leading another unsuccessful armed uprising, was captured and executed. Shelley's first elegy was apparently written after visiting Emmet's grave in Dublin.[5]

The month Shelley arrived in Dublin, restrictions were removed on the Regent, who then abandoned his former Foxite pro-emancipation sympathies shared with the Duke of Norfolk. Shelley had suspected—probably from talks with Norfolk at Greystoke—that the Regent would revert to the anti-emancipation position of his father, George III. Norfolk, outraged at the Regent's reversal, refused to accept the Order of the Garter in a blistering letter to the future George IV. Still speaking out despite his waning political base, the Duke would die in another three years. Timothy Shelley, an increasingly conservative and absentee MP, presumably yielded his rotten borough to the new Duke of Norfolk.

Shelley, with radical if anachronistic positions, was alert to new revolutionary activity. The day after arriving in Dublin, reading of the Mexican revolution, he wrote Elizabeth Hitchener, enclosing four stanzas of a revolutionary poem containing his first use of volcano imagery.[6] He assured Hitchener the government would not "*dare*" to attack his address which "will soon come out." Telling her not to "fear postmasters" censoring their letters, he was energized by her letters and again hoped she would join them in the summer in Wales. After she mentioned her father's disapproval and her desire not to be dependent upon Shelley financially, he assured her that their £400 a year was enough, plus anything he got from his publications. However, he was finding Dublin expensive. Eliza controlled the purse strings, safely keeping their pooled money "in some hole or corner of her dress." Not only did Hitchener "animate me," her approbation, like Plato's, was "more exhilirating [*sic*] than the applause of thousands."[7]

Around mid-February Shelley dispatched to Hitchener the printed first sheet of his "first address." His magnanimous *An Address, to the Irish People* was not Paine's broadsheet but an unwieldy, thick pamphlet Shelley called his "book." He told Hitchener of writing a second pamphlet about the same length. The *Address* was written for the "lowest comprehension" but the second pamphlet, *Proposals for an Association of Philanthropists,* would be "in my own natural style."[8] As soon as his *Address* was off the press on February 24, copies went to Godwin and Hitchener. The next day, *The Dublin Evening Post* advertised "AN ADDRESS TO THE IRISH PEOPLE by Percy B. Shelley" priced at "Fivepence, to be had of all the Booksellers." This "lowest possible price," Shelley explained in his notice, met his "intention . . . to awaken in the minds of the Irish poor a knowledge of their real state, summarily pointing out the evils of that state, and suggesting rational means of remedy.—Catholic Emancipation and a Repeal of the Union Act (the latter the most successful engine that England ever wielded over the misery of fallen Ireland)."[9] Running an ad several times the next week, Shelley sent a copy with a letter to Hamilton Rowan. Although Rowan did not respond, Shelley's letter and *Address* were later found among Rowan's papers.[10] Writing Elizabeth Hitchener of his ingenious broadcasting methods, Shelley mentioned he had "already sent 400 of my little pamphlets into the world." Sixty of the remaining eleven hundred copies went to "public houses" and "no prosecution is yet attempted."[11] By mid-March, Harriet reported few copies were left, Shelley "having taken great pains to circulate them."[12]

From among Dublin's poor, Shelley hired a servant to help get the pamphlet onto the streets. Shelley termed this fellow, Daniel Healey or Hill,[13] "the blundering honest Irishman" after he mistakenly sent copies of the *Address* to Godwin and Elizabeth Hitchener by post rather than the much cheaper coach. Godwin, angry that the charges exceeded one pound, enough for several weeks' groceries for his family, rebuked Shelley for having to pay this amount for a tract whose contents he found offensive.[14] Godwin's quarrel with Shelley over money had begun. Daniel Healey, devoted to Shelley, spread not only his pamphlet but misinformation about its author's age. Shelley wryly noted that his "youth is much against me here," not helped when Healey "gave out that I was only 15 years of age." Shelley and Harriet tossed his *Address* to passersby from their balcony and "give them to men we pass in the streets." Harriet was "ready to die of laughter" when "Percy," looking "grave," deposited a copy in the hood of an unknowing woman. Harriet had "seen very little" of the Irish but that might change "when Percy is more known."[15]

Neither Shelley nor Harriet mentioned in this February 27 letter the speech he would deliver the next day that helped rectify his unknown status in Dublin. He was pleased that people approved of his principles but found they differed with his ideas about "my enforcing these principles." Infusing the underlying sexual current characteristic of his rhapsodic letters to Hitchener, he wondered, "My friend my dearest friend do you pant to be with us? . . . I desire your presence, and that not merely for the inexpressible gratification of immediate communion." Switching to safer phrasing, he asked her help in "awakening a noble nation from the lethargy of its bondage," needing her "powerful intellect" to "organize" his "immature . . . schemes." More constrained in early March, he wrote to Hitchener, "My brain has scarcely time to consult my heart or my heart to consult my brain," but she was "the *Trinity* of my Essence."[16]

Shelley, disappointed that neither Curran nor Rowan had responded to his overtures, found "Good principles are scarce here," and the press was "either oppositional or ministerial." Furthermore, "*I* of course am hated by both of these parties." He had met "no determined Republicans, but I have found some who are DEMOCRATIFIABLE." Announcing they would leave Ireland the end of April, he was contemplating "a little book" containing "the moral sayings of Jesus Christ" which "might be very useful if selected from the mystery and immorality which surrounds them."[17] Shelley did write *Biblical Extracts,* another early work now lost.[18]

The only record of how well the *Address* was received was Shelley's report to Elizabeth Hitchener that it had "excited a sensation of wonder in Dublin."[19] Perhaps "wonder"—not comprehension—was accurate for its intended audience, the uneducated poor. The hidden agenda, attacking Catholicism, was a strategic mistake as Shelley did not realize Catholicism's importance to Irish nationalistic feeling. Catholics wanted respect for, not criticism of, their religion. Shelley perhaps relied on outdated ideas from the 1807 *Pieces of Irish History,* which he hoped to republish.[20] He appealed for religious toleration, but his discourse on Catholic persecutions, including the Inquisition and the massacre of French Huguenots, probably offended his readers. Despite its shortcomings, the *Address* is a remarkable document by someone not yet halfway through his nineteenth year.

The *Address* shared the prevailing opinion that emancipation was imminent, but it was 1829 before enactment of the ironically titled Roman Catholic Relief Act. Accommodating Godwin, Shelley argued against the use of force, urging the masses to promote change through individual reform and study. Opposed to violent revolution, Shelley was prepared to condone it as a last resort.[21] He advocated "universal emancipation"—a worldwide revolution—where "the lower classes" would not "waste their lives and liberty to furnish means for their oppressors to oppress them yet more terribly."[22] In Shelley's "happy state of society," what the rich "now keep to themselves" would "be distributed among the people. . . . No lover would then be false to his mistress, no mistress would desert her lover."[23]

The zenith of Shelley's Irish mission was his lengthy speech on February 28 at the Aggregate Meeting of O'Connell's Catholic Committee in Dublin's Fishamble Theatre. To circumvent government prosecution, the Aggregate Meetings were open to all, including the press and government agents. Despite these precautions, there was some danger of arrest to those who attended.[24] The famed O'Connell spoke first but years later he did not recall Shelley's speech.[25] After recent government attacks, the Catholic Committee wanted to send a moderate "address" to the Prince Regent and Parliament, seeking relief from laws limiting the rights of Catholics.[26]

Shelley spoke in the afternoon in the brightly lit theater, its boxes filled with well-dressed gentlemen and ladies from the conservative, aristocratic Irish Catholic community. He took a dislike to the meeting's chair, Lord Fingall, one "of the Catholic aristocracy" whose "intolerance . . . equalled . . . the hardy wickedness and falsehood of the prince."[27] How Shelley came to give the speech is unclear. One newspaper report of his speech stated, "Mr. Shelley requested a hearing." Not having mentioned either the speech or the meeting in his long letter to Elizabeth Hitchener the day before, he probably did not ask to speak until just before the meeting.[28] A future ambassador to Greece possibly alluded to Shelley when he concluded, "we shall remember with gratitude the Protestant who stood by us in our struggle and bore our broken standard to the front of the battle."[29]

Very favorable reports of Shelley's speech appeared in six local newspapers and notice of the meeting appeared in the London *Morning Chronicle*.[30] Shelley told Elizabeth Hitchener, "I spoke for more than an hour; the hisses with which they greeted me when I spoke of *religion,* tho' in terms of respect, were mixed with applause when I avowed my mission. The newspapers have only noted that which did not excite approbation."[31] Hogg later disparaged Shelley's Irish views, misleadingly reporting that Shelley told him he received "savage yells" and was "threatened with personal violence."[32] The newspaper accounts, the only record of his speech's content, commented on his effective speaking style and described Shelley as "an English gentleman (very young) . . . received with great kindness. . . . He drew a lively picture of the misery of the country." Another account reported loud applause, some for several minutes, when he spoke of the corrupting effects of arbitrary power and of the "fane of liberty converted into a temple of Mammon." Shelley sent Godwin the very effusive report from the *Dublin Weekly Messenger* containing a personal sketch and the first one hundred forty-nine lines of his *Proposals.* Shelley told Godwin, "I am vain, but not so foolish as not to be rather piqued than gratified at the eulogia of a Journal."[33] His disgust—that the press's superficial praise overlooked his challenging and controversial points—was part of his continuing disillusionment with the moderate reformers. The writer of the notice possibly was John Lawless, future editor of the *Dublin Weekly.* He wrote of learning from a "conversation" with Shelley that his "Father is a Member of the Imperial Parliament" and Shelley was an "immediate heir of one of the first fortunes in England." Further, at Oxford Shelley helped support Finnerty on profits of "nearly one hundred pounds" from "a very beautiful poem." This notice, Shelley's first recognition by name in the press as a poet, preceded by four years the same recognition in the English press.[34]

Shelley made a "highly interesting appearance," according to the *Weekly Messenger,* and the "publications which he has circulated with uncommon industry . . . has set curiosity on the wing to ascertain who he is." Shelley perhaps blushed in frustration upon reading that he "seems devoted to the propagation of those divine and Christian feelings . . . bold and intrepid advocate . . . *missionary of truth* . . . child of Chimera, the creature of fancy, an imaginary legislator. . . . To this gentleman Ireland is much indebted, for selecting *her* as the theatre of his first attempts in this holy work of human regeneration."[35]

Shelley—trying to gain attention for his forthcoming pamphlet of association proposals—possibly wrote two pseudonymous letters to the editor published in March that attacked his speech. The first, from "An Englishman," castigated "a most disgusting harangue from a stripling, with whom I am acquainted." The "invectives of this renegade Englishman against his native country were *hailed* by the assembly. . . . Joy beamed in every countenance . . . the delirium of ecstasy got the better of prudential control; the veil was for a moment withdrawn."

A longer attack on his speech and the *Proposals*—signed "A Dissenter," another possible Shelley pseudonym—appeared later in the same paper. Assailed as "this modern Apollonius who travels but for the improvement of the human race," he was "a poet, and his very prose is full of poetic fire, so vivid, so redundant." His style suggested he might occasionally "compose under the influence of the moon. . . . [His purpose was] the abolition of the aristocracy." Shelley, writing Elizabeth Hitchener of another letter to the editor, said, "Some will call it violent. I have at least made a stir here, and set some minds afloat."[36]

Two government agents in the audience at the Fishamble Theatre floated reports back to the English Home Secretary, opening the first official file on Shelley's subversive activity. One report mentioned Shelley by name, the other said, "a young boy, delivered a speech of considerable length and replete with much elegant language" in which "he lamented that the Regent should abandon Mr. Fox's principles and join in a shameful coalition, or that he had been so far *womanized*—here he was interrupted by a question of order."[37]

Only days after his speech, Shelley's second pamphlet appeared.[38] More tightly reasoned than the *Address,* the *Proposals for an Association of Philanthropists* were more important to Shelley. Aimed at intellectual radicals, it carried his unveiled attack on Catholicism: "I hear the teeth of the palsied beldame Superstition chatter, and I see her descending to the grave!"[39] He told Elizabeth Hitchener that after setting up an association in Dublin, he would do the same in Wales while she assessed the prospects in Sussex. He asked, "Might I not extend them all over England, and *quietly* revolutionize the country?" His group network idea was influenced by Abbé Barruel's *History of Jacobinism,* which excited him at Oxford with discussions of the Illuminati and other secret organizations. He recently wrote to Elizabeth Hitchener that Barruel's *History,* although "half filled with . . . unsupported falsehoods . . . [was] worth reading." Citing Barruel in his *Proposals,* he would reread him in the years ahead.[40]

In his proposed associations, Shelley wanted leaders with the intellectual and moral commitment to avert the violent, regressive aftermath of the French Revolution. Recognizing the metaphysical bent of his political argument, he said his hopes would be thought "visionary and inconsistent with human nature" and inveighed against Malthus's pessimistic view that war and poverty were necessary to control population growth.[41]

In his Dublin correspondence, Shelley directed and advised Elizabeth Hitchener as his protégé. Reversing roles with Godwin, he appealed for direction, criticism, and frankness. Obliging, Godwin acknowledged Shelley's gifts but was critical, demanding, and exhortatory. Shelley, alternatively obsequious and resolutely in disagreement, took some of Godwin's advice but preserved his own independence.

Godwin, in one of his longest letters, said Shelley's "character" —"an extraordinary assemblage of lovely qualities"—had "considerable defects" due to his youth. He excoriated Shelley for ignoring Godwin's injunction in *Political Justice* against forming political associations that might "light again the flames of rebellion and war." Only "Discussion, reading, enquiry, perpetual communication" would improve mankind.[42]

Shelley's initial contrite response would have amazed Timothy and Whitton. He asked Godwin, "guide thou and direct me.—In all the weaknesses of my inconsistencies bear with me." However, sharpening his barbs, he had "impatient scepticism" with humanity's progress since the 1793 publication of *Political Justice.* Men had not "ceased to fight" and "vice and misery" had not "vanished." Many who read Godwin's "inestimable book" were "blinded by prejudice" and returned to the fashionable "arguments of Mr. Malthus."[43]

Godwin's censure, and the futility of a philanthropic association in Ireland, helped terminate Shelley's Dublin visit. He told Godwin,

"The poor of Dublin are assuredly the meanest & most miserable of all . . . one mass of animated filth!" The local antagonistic response to his ideas led Shelley to confide to Elizabeth Hitchener that associations would not be formed: "Prejudices are so violent in contradiction to my principles that more hate me as a free-thinker than love me as a votary of Freedom."[44]

Godwin, unswayed by Shelley's letter, continued attacking his "inconsistencies" and lashed out, "Shelley, you are preparing a scene of blood!" Then Godwin extended himself, "come immediately to London." He added a lure of romantic familial largesse: "You cannot imagine how much all the females of my family, Mrs. G. and three daughters are interested in your letters and your history."[45] The next phase of Shelley's love life had begun.

Shelley replied he had not acquiesced to Godwin's "decisions" but had "withdrawn from circulation the publications wherein I erred & am preparing to quit Dublin." Still believing in associations, he requested, "if I err probe me severely." Godwin was pleased, even if Shelley was still only "half a convert to my arguments."[46] Shelley was hiding from Godwin his continuing political activity. That same day he mailed a box full of his incendiary writings to Elizabeth Hitchener.

Shelley was bringing the most intense political activism of his life to a close. In his last Dublin letter to Godwin, Shelley began articulating a new literary identity that shaped the future course of his life and his major poetry. He would no longer write for "the illiterate" but "look to events in which it will be impossible that I can share, and make myself the cause of an effect which will take place ages after *I* shall have mouldered into dust." This "requires Stoicism," but he could not "return to the heartless bustle of ordinary life." Again criticizing *Political Justice* for its lack of influence, he told Godwin, "if your book had been as general as the Bible human affairs would now have exhi[bi]ted a very different aspect."[47]

Godwin's *Political Justice* and his own Irish pamphlets had been ineffective because of their cold, inert, and rational didacticism. They lacked the expressive power of imagination and poetry, a style more akin to the imaginative writings of Rousseau. Shelley wrote that "Most of the [errors] of philosophers have arisen from considering the human being in a point of view too detailed and circumscribed."[48] Recasting politics into moral terms, Shelley sought a deeper impact through his imaginative poetic writing. He soon resumed writing his first major poem, *Queen Mab,* a poetic fantasy of humanitarian regeneration with extensive, didactic prose notes. It proved to be his most influential poem carrying his political ideology to the English people.

Years later, Shelley wrote, "Doctrines of reform were never carried out to so great a length as by Jesus Christ; the Republic of Plato and the Political Justice of Godwin are probable and practical systems in comparison."[49] His criticism of Godwin's writing reflected his own disappointment in his pamphlets' efficacy. Finding impoverished Dubliners had an intellectual level akin to that of an oyster,[50] his aristocratic sensibilities interfered with sympathizing with those among the literate who, like Godwin's friend Curran, had unsavory humor. After Curran finally called, Shelley dined twice at his house. Unimpressed by the old leader, he pointedly wrote Godwin that Curran was "*your* intimate friend."[51]

Shelley also kept Godwin in the dark about his latest publication, *Declaration of Rights,* and about his ongoing efforts to help Dublin's oppressed. Writing to Elizabeth Hitchener concerning incidents "of unrestricted & licensed tyranny," he exclaimed, "My blood boils to madness to think of it." Shelley had become interested in an Irishman named Redfern who was forced to serve in the Portuguese army and later pursued the matter in England. He also "found" and "rescued" a "poor boy . . . starving with his mother" who was sent to "military servitude" as a soldier by "a magistrate of *Hell*" on "false" charges. Another time, he pleaded in vain with a constable to save "from ultimate ruin and starvation" a "widow woman with three infants" who had stolen "a penny loaf."[52]

Shelley also withheld from Godwin his friendship with John Lawless, who lived close to Shelley's household on Grafton Street, where they had moved in early March.[53] "Honest Jack Lawless," a popular if affected orator, was muting his radicalism by following Daniel O'Connell. Believing Lawless was "a valuable man" and "a republican," Shelley planned to "have command of a newspaper" with Lawless.[54] However, what Lawless wanted was Shelley's money to finish his *History of Ireland,* over two hundred pages having been printed. Shelley turned again to the senior Medwin for advice on raising £250 for a work that would "produce great profits." Medwin, he said, should look in the Lewes paper for evidence that he was "in the midst of overwhelming engagements."[55]

Shelley, commissioning Elizabeth Hitchener to print his Irish works in the Lewes papers, asked her to send the *Dublin Weekly* sketch about him to the Sussex papers.[56] She apparently also submitted the *Address* to the editor of the Lewes *Sussex Weekly Advertiser* who politely cited the "benevolent and humane intentions" of "P.B.S., Esq." but rejected the "address" lest it provoke "the lash of tyranny and oppression against the object of his commiseration."[57]

The editor of the Dublin paper, Frederick Conway, had more insidious ideas. Unknown to Shelley and Lawless, he was sending secret letters about them to the Home Secretary, Lord Sidmouth. Years later Conway wrote that Shelley had been a "pecuniary dupe" of Lawless. It is not known how much money Shelley gave Lawless for his book, but the history, first published in 1814, went through several revisions.[58]

Word of Shelley's Irish activities had reached his family in early March when Whitton wrote Sir Bysshe that his grandson "is in Dublin, publishing some hints for bettering the state of the nation." Whitton had a red-penciled copy of the favorable notice in the *Dublin Weekly Messenger* and a copy of the *Address* corrected in Shelley's hand.[59]

The Shelleys' closest Dubliner friend was Catherine Nugent, an ardent, articulate liberal spinster in her early forties who called herself "Mrs. Nugent." She worked below her capacities as seamstress and shop assistant for a furrier on Grafton Street, near the Shelley lodgings. A friend described her as "a wonderful woman ... very plain, little, and republican looking." Her "great intellect" combined with "depth of charity and love of mankind."[60] She knew many of the leaders of the 1798 revolution and Harriet wrote admiringly of "her notions of Philanthropy and justice." During the Rebellion she visited the prisons exhorting "the people to have courage and hope." Catherine Nugent commented she would have been executed for her involvement had she been a man.[61]

Catherine Nugent called on Shelley after receiving a copy of his *Address* from Daniel Healey. He was out but returned her call and later reminded her it was he, not Harriet, who first befriended her. Mrs. Nugent recalled the Shelleys as "very much attached" to each other, Harriet being "an amiable and unaffected person—very young and very pleasing."[62] Harriet quickly attached herself to this new maternal figure, inviting her to visit in the evenings and on her free day, Sunday. She became Harriet's correspondent for the next four years.

Early in March, Shelley reactivated his vegetarian diet begun fitfully the year before in Wales. Mrs. Nugent, commenting about his dietary regimen, said, "Shelley spoke as a man believing in metempsychosis."[63] Harriet enthusiastically wrote Elizabeth Hitchener, "we have forsworn meat and adopted the Pithagorean system . . . and do not find ourselves any the worse for it."[64] Bending their doctrine for guests, Harriet, inviting Mrs. Nugent to dine, said, "a murdered chicken has been prepared for her repast."[65]

Shelley was overseeing the printing of his third Irish publication, the *Declaration of Rights,* printed as a single sheet for posting among the populace. Its thirty-one brief theses of human rights evolved from the 1789 French Declarations of Rights, from Paine and Godwin, and from Shelley's pamphlets.[66] The ringing first thesis began, "Government has no rights; it is a delegation from several individuals for the purpose of securing their own." Not ready to affirm nonviolent resistance, Shelley espoused Godwin's view that one had no right disturbing "the public peace by personally resisting the execution of the law, however bad." One should "acquiesce, using at the same time the utmost powers of his reason to promote its repeal." The alcoholism of the Dublin masses and his own abstemious asceticism led Shelley to moralize, "Sobriety of body and mind is necessary to those who would be free." His last declaration, "The only use of government is to repress the vices of man," was followed by his ambivalent reference to the "dignity" and "degeneracy" of the Irish who, in the words of Milton's Satan to the fallen angels (*Paradise Lost,* I:330), should "Awake!—arise!—or be forever fallen."[67]

Responding to Shelley's request that she change her name, Elizabeth Hitchener chose to be called "Portia." When Harriet later disliked the name "Portia," Hitchener finally became "Bessy." Harriet's letter to "My dear Portia" soon became the object of more high-level government attention than any letter her husband wrote. Conveniently for the prying authorities, she began her letter saying it was enclosed with "a large Box so full of inflammable matter." The wooden box contained copies of the *Declaration* and the remaining copies of the *Address* and *Proposals.* Harriet also spoke of the starving poor and the authorities' fear of hunger riots. She attacked unjust laws that "condemn a Person to Death for stealing 13 shillings and 4 pence" and bluntly told Portia, "Dispense the Declarations," adding, "Percy says the farmers are very fond of having something posted on their walls." The idea of an Association being "impracticable," they would "leave this noisy town on the 7th of April, unless the Habeas Corpus Act should be suspended, and then we shall be obliged to leave here as soon as possible."[68] Her letter was unsigned.

Habeas corpus was not suspended, possibly sparing those attending the Aggregate Meeting from arrest.[69] When the customs inspector at Holyhead opened Harriet's box, he was duly alarmed by the anonymous remarks about "inflammatory matter" whose radical contents were to be broadcast in Sussex. The inspector and the Holyhead post office agent each sent copies of Harriet's letter and samples of Shelley's work to higher authorities in London. The zealous postal agent wrote to the Secretary of the General Post Office of this "important" find of "an open letter, of a tendency so dangerous to Government." He indicated his colleague had written to the Prime Minister, Mr. Perceval. Actually, the customs officer wrote to the Secretary of State, who expeditiously sent the materials to the Secretary for Ireland in Dublin. They were returned April 8 to the Home Department and added to Shelley's file. The Postmaster General, Lord Chichester, placing Elizabeth Hitchener under surveillance, wrote from his seat in Stanmer, a few miles from her home in Hurstpierpoint, what he knew of Shelley's personal life: "I hear [Mr. Shelley] has married a Servant, or some person of very low birth; he has been in Ireland some time, and I heard of his speaking at the Catholic Convention." He noted Elizabeth Hitchener's father had been a smuggler, had changed his name, and that she "keeps a school . . . is well spoken of." He would "have a watch upon the Daughter, and discover whether there is any connexion between her and Shelley."[70] Beyond any surveillance, no action was taken against Shelley. Surveillance rather than entrapment was the government's modus operandi until several years later. There is no evidence for Medwin's assertion that Shelley fled Ireland on a hint from the police, although the timing of the Irish Secretary's receipt of his file from London was close to April 4, the day the Shelleys left Ireland.[71]

Shelley's seven weeks in Dublin conformed to his original plan for a brief stay. He failed to set up an association, but gained some measure of appreciation and recognition for his efforts. Given his gifts, his energy, and his status as heir to a baronetcy, had he stayed in Ireland within O'Connell's movement, he might have had a significant impact.[72]

In addition to his publishing schemes with Lawless, Shelley was attempting to have his "younger" poems published by the radical Dublin publisher, John Stockdale, who still possessed Shelley's manuscripts when he left Ireland.[73] Beyond that, we know little of Shelley's final several weeks in Dublin. Catherine Nugent observed a surface compatibility between the married pair but Shelley, responding to Godwin's inquiries about his wife, emphasized the role of anxiety and depression in their mutual attraction: "She is a woman whose pursuits hopes fears & sorrows were so similar to my own that we married a few months ago." However, Elizabeth Hitchener was "A woman of extraordinary talents" and Eliza possessed "one thing . . . zeal and sincerity."[74]

Shelley was busy during his Irish venture. In less than two months, he wrote, published, and distributed three political tracts, gave a speech, contacted and met leading political figures, engaged in acts of humanitarian aid to the poor, and considered publishing a newspaper. In England, his father soon cast the first of his five votes in Parliament against Catholic emancipation.[75] Shelley was on the threshold of adulthood and his Irish exile helped solidify his poetic political mission. Summing up his Irish experiences, he wrote, "I am dissatisfied with my success, but not with the attempt."[76]

Fig. 10. Mary
Wollstonecraft by John
Opie, c. 1797, courtesy
of the National Portrait
Gallery, London.

Fig. 11. William Godwin by
James Northcote, 1802,
courtesy of the National
Portrait Gallery, London.

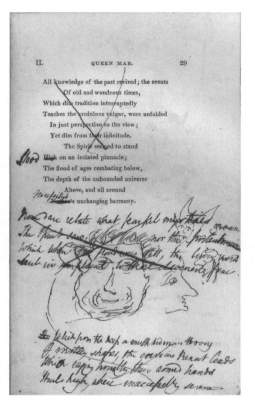

Fig. 12. Page from first edition of *Queen Mab*, showing Shelley's manuscript changes for "The Queen of the Universe" and drawings of four faces, courtesy of The Carl F. Pforzheimer Collection of Shelley and His Circle, The New York Public Library, Astor, Lenox and Tilden Foundations.

Fig. 13. Tanyrallt. Photograph by author.

13

Wandering Reformer

THE STORMY WEATHER ON THEIR RETURN TO ENGLAND WAS AT least as severe as on the trip to Ireland. The expected twelve-hour trip took thirty-six hours. Harriet fared better than Shelley and Eliza, both "weakened by the vegetable system." At Holyhead, where they arrived at two in the morning with Daniel Healey in tow, sailors led them a mile through the stormy night "over rock and stone" to lodgings. Not having eaten since leaving Dublin, they compromised their belief and "immediately began upon meat."[1]

Resting a day, they began a week-long search throughout northern Wales for a place to live. Shelley, becoming the hero of Godwin's novel *Fleetwood,* wrote its author he intended "to settle in Merionethshire, the scene of Fleetwood's early life."[2] Wandering without success, at Barmouth they braved the sea once more, sailing in an open boat thirty miles south to Aberystwyth, due west of Rhayader and Cwm Elan. Shelley took his group briefly to Thomas Grove's Cwm Elan where, one mile away, they quickly located Nantgwillt ("Wild Brook"), a venerable gray mansion on a farm among the firs and birches in the Claerwen River valley.

Shelley wrote Elizabeth Hitchener of the "embosomed" solitude of their new home, which came with a ghost "frequently seen by the servants" and seven bedrooms. If Hitchener's father came, he could help manage the farm.[3] Emulating Southey, Shelley wanted the largest room for a library. Nantgwillt, "an old family house with a farm of 200 acres of meadow land,"[4] had a cataract tumbling down the steep tree-covered hills above. Shelley felt the "mountains & rocks" formed "a barrier around this quiet valley which the tumult of the world cannot overleap."[5] However, Shelley was not told that in winter the house was snowbound, bitterly cold, and damp. It would be torn down years before a 1903 reservoir submerged what was left, the garden walls. Shelley hoped to reduce the annual rent of £98 to £20 by renting out the arable acres, but his

Arcadian fantasies went on hold. The property was caught up in bankruptcy proceedings involving its occupant, Mr. Hooper, and to get a lease, Shelley would have to buy the furniture and livestock. They were allowed to move into the house temporarily while Shelley tried to raise the money.

Harriet now became severely depressed. Shelley wrote that she was "confined by a tedious intermittent fever" brought on by "gloomy feelings" and that her "bilious attack . . . so overpowered her with languor that she could not hold a pen."[6] It took over a week before the nearest physician—forty miles away—arrived. Shelley thought Harriet's "indisposition has begun to wear so serious an appearance." He denied being "alarmed" but was "anxious" that "without any visible cause, any violent fever . . . her weakness has increased so much that she cannot walk across the room without assistance" and was "so languid that she can scarcely speak."[7] As Harriet recovered, Shelley became ill.

Probably contributing to the marital pair's disturbance was the news from Hitchener that rumors once more were circulating that she was soon to become Shelley's mistress. Captain Pilfold, hearing the stories, joined Hitchener's father in disapproving her becoming part of Shelley's "little circle." Hitchener, too, became ill. Reluctant to give up her teaching, she proposed a trial visit in the summer, resolving to return to her students. Shelley grudgingly accepted.[8]

Shelley, initially blaming the rumors on Captain Pilfold's wife, protested to Hitchener, "*I* unfaithful to my Harriet! *You* a female Hogg!" He insisted Harriet would not hear of any change in Hitchener's plans to come live with them.[9] His linking Hitchener with Hogg suggests Harriet's depression was partly a response to Shelley's unconscious wish to avenge her seductiveness toward Hogg. He told Hitchener's father that his daughter's "considerable distress of mind" came from the slurs against her reputation. Asserting, "*my* moral character is unimpeached, & unimpeachable," he added, "My wife loves your daughter." Incensed by the former smuggler's intransigence, Shelley asked, "who made you her governor?" and accused him of having "agitated her mind until her frame is seriously deranged—take care Sir."[10]

Shelley now thought "the bigots to World-Religion" had inspired the rumors and he told Hitchener they should not sacrifice their "attachment" because of the "swinish multitude." Shelley's uncle now "professed to disbelieve the Mistress-business" but believed

Shelley felt love for Hitchener. Shelley, sensing the rumors were being spread by those with influence, asked Hitchener who her agents were and advised her not to let any "priests or aristocrats" see his "Declarations."[11] Shelley's suspicions were probably correct. Lord Chichester likely circulated these rumors to forestall Hitchener joining the young radical in Wales.[12]

After four months' silence, Shelley wrote to his father requesting a £500 advance for the house. Timothy's prompt denial to Whitton[13] led Shelley to ask Medwin senior and his uncle to stand security for him as a minor for "6. or 700£." Medwin rejected Shelley's proposal upon learning that he and Pilfold would have to occupy the premises and that the total amount needed was £1000.[14]

After unsuccessfully appealing to his grandfather and to a Kington solicitor,[15] Shelley became incapacitated for two weeks with an "inflammatory fever . . . & a head disordered with illness."[16] Unable to write to Hitchener, he enlisted Harriet for the task. He wrote to Godwin that his silence was caused by "far from good" health brought on by his being "tormented" and "anxious" over the delay in procuring the house. He told his mentor he was now reading "Locke, Hume, Reid & whatever metaphysics came in my way." Pursuing materialist philosophy, he had read Holbach's *Le Système de la nature,* "a work of uncommon powers."[17]

Not obtaining a lease by the early June deadline, Shelley vacated Nantgwillt for a temporary haven with the Groves at Cwm Elan. He rejected Hitchener's offer to live in her house and did not tell her they were thinking of going to Italy to escape their financial problems until, in Harriet's words, "Percy is of age." She wrote to Mrs. Nugent that Italy's warmer climate was an added inducement as "Percy's health is so extremely delicate." Harriet indicated they occasionally heard from Lawless and that the Dublin printers were "very slow" in getting out Shelley's poems.[18] Sometime during June, Harriet began her Commonplace Book, making entries until late 1813 or early 1814. Among her wide range of reading, the writer most frequently cited was Byron. She copied parts of his poems and was drawn to a vision of early death in "The Tear."[19]

The poetry Shelley composed during this return to Cwm Elan probably included "On Robert Emmet's Tomb." In "The Retrospect," he revisited his depression and anxiety during his first stay, ending with a guarded view of Harriet's "ardent friendship" as a "reviving ray."[20]

When no allowance had arrived, they again changed their plans, deciding to settle on the Devon coast at Ilfracombe. Shelley, with Harriet's endorsement, urged Hitchener to join them there after she spent the night en route at Mr. Westbrook's in London.[21] A week later, their plans changed again after hearing from Godwin of an available house in Chepstow. After Shelley unsuccessfully tried to include Hitchener in their Chepstow trip, he warned her to tell no one of their plans, suspecting that government surveillance "utterly unknown to us" has been "practised" on her. He also suspected the Pilfolds' "conspiracies" and his aunt's "malice."[22]

In June, Shelley gratefully responded to Godwin's much delayed "most affectionate & kind" March 30 letter. After he likened Daniel Isaac Eaton's trial and imprisonment to the treatment of Socrates and Jesus, Shelley mentioned having begun outlining an address. It was to the Chief Justice, Lord Ellenborough, who on May 15 passed down the sentence on Eaton for publishing the third part of Paine's *Age of Reason.* Building on his Irish pamphlets, Shelley wrote *A Letter to Lord Ellenborough* with such fervor that he soon told Hitchener of being so agitated by Eaton's case that "today I have not the coolness to go on."[23]

In addition to his efforts on behalf of Eaton and Redfern, Shelley was agitated by the Luddite and food riots, and the scandals of the Regent.[24] England's manufacturing heartland became the focal point of this social unrest and the Luddite uprisings perhaps were the closest England came to revolution in Shelley's lifetime. His alarm a year earlier suggests that his Irish mission was in part a displaced reaction to the spreading Luddite disturbances.[25] Shelley probably underestimated the deeper social and political forces behind the Luddite movement, but he was incensed by the government's reaction to it, including stationing troops in the Midlands. By May 1812, when Prime Minister Perceval was assassinated in the House of Commons, Shelley correctly was fearful of war with the United States and expressed outrage over the building of barracks throughout England, including his native Horsham.[26]

Shelley, unfamiliar with the provincial English radical movements,[27] had offered to help Elizabeth Hitchener organize an association. He was unaware that Major John Cartwright, pursuing the same goal, formed his Hampden Club in London about this time.[28] Among the Club's notables who figured large in Shelley's life were the Duke of Norfolk, Lord Byron, Sir Francis Burdett, and William Madocks.[29]

Upon arriving in Chepstow from Wales, the Shelleys found the house Godwin had recommended was too small for their family.[30] Continuing south toward Ilfracombe, they traversed the Devonshire cliffs above the Bristol Channel. Reaching the precipitous drop into the lovely little port of Lymouth, now called Lynmouth, they abandoned their carriage for the steep two-mile descent. Captivated by this remote fishing community of about thirty cottages, they forgot Ilfracombe and rented the only available abode, a thatched cottage twined with late-June roses. Their landlady, Mrs. Hooper, immediately took a warm interest in the Shelleys. They planned to stay for the summer months before moving to London for the winter.

Harriet felt Lynmouth's "fairy scene" more beautiful than Nantgwillt because of the sea, which Shelley said "dashes against the rocky & caverned shore." The steep mountains were "broken abruptly into vallies of indescribable fertility & grandeur."[31] Adjoining the village were the gigantic boulders of the Valley of the Rocks, a scene Shelley often mentioned to Hogg.[32] Sketches of its jagged pinnacles towering over the sea soon appeared in his notebooks and in letters he mailed twice a week from Barnstaple, eighteen miles away. The extraordinary volume of Shelley's outgoing mail soon caught the attention of the Barnstaple authorities, and the strange activities of this boyish-looking stranger soon aroused the scrutiny of the locals. He again came under official surveillance.

Shelley, writing to Godwin, suggested that Hitchener bring for the summer the oldest of the five children in the Godwin household, eighteen-year-old Fanny. He explained they rejected the too-cramped Chepstow house for the "poverty & humbleness" of "a small Cottage" with more rooms. Further, if he had used money for the Chepstow house from his "patrimony . . . [it] would interfere with schemes on which it is my fondest delight to speculate."[33]

Godwin, offended by Shelley's refusal to take the house of his friend in Chepstow, lectured him about violating the most "fundamental" principle in *Political Justice,* not to spend money on a "caprice." Only prudence would reconcile him with his father.[34] Godwin was tightening his claim on the purse strings of his pupil, who had no inkling of his mentor's deep financial troubles. Shelley was now positioned between two stubborn fathers. One refused to give, the other refused not to receive.

In words Timothy never heard from him, Shelley bowed down to Godwin's tongue-lashing, asking him to "accept my thanks, con-

sider yourself as yet more beloved by me" for having "reproved my
. . . errors." As Godwin's "proselyte," he would "pursue undeviat-
ingly the path which you first cleared thro' the wilderness of life."[35]

Shelley was unable to convince Godwin of the propriety of
Fanny's visit, but Elizabeth Hitchener, succumbing to Shelley's appeals, gave up her school and left her father to join the Lynmouth
family. She stayed overnight in London with Godwin and his second wife, green-spectacled Mary Jane Clairmont Godwin. At home
were her two children, Charles Clairmont, seventeen, and fourteen-year-old Clara Mary Jane Clairmont, as well as the Godwins'
nine-year-old son William and Fanny Imlay Godwin. Born in
France in 1794, Fanny was the illegitimate child of Mary Wollstonecraft and the American, Gilbert Imlay. Wollstonecraft, after
two suicide attempts, became Godwin's first wife in 1797 only to die
later that year from complications shortly after giving birth to
Mary Wollstonecraft Godwin. Young Mary, almost fifteen, was absent when Hitchener visited, having been sent off a month earlier
to live with a family in Scotland.

Arriving in Lynmouth, Hitchener's troubles began when Harriet, disliking her name "Portia," had her change it to "Bessy." Harriet told Mrs. Nugent, "If you like great talkers she will suit you."
At thirty, "Bessy" looked "only 24" and was "very dark in complexion, with a great quantity of long black hair . . . taller than me or my
sister, and as thin as it is possible to be . . . her spirits are excellent
. . . she is very busy writing for the good of mankind." Bessy's news
about Godwin was not to their liking, as "he lives so much from his
family, only seeing them at stated hours." Thinking himself "such
a very great *man*," Godwin told Hitchener that Fanny could not
join the Shelleys "because he had not seen our faces."[36]

Shelley, completing *A Letter to Lord Ellenborough,* found a
printer and bookseller in Barnstaple named Syle. Arriving at his
shop with a stack of manuscripts, he ordered one thousand copies
of the *Letter* be printed. Syle, who also edited journals, composed
verse, and encouraged young writers, probably printed Shelley's
newly revised satirical poem *The Devil's Walk,* which appeared as
a broadside. Shelley was regularly in Syle's shop reading copy, correcting the press, and possibly setting type for *The Devil's Walk.*

Shortly after arriving in Lynmouth, Shelley wrote to a young liberal publisher and bookseller in London, Thomas Hookham, Jr.
With his brother, Hookham had a business in their father's large
lending library near the Westbrook home. Shelley ordered books

from Hookham and apparently sent him an outline of *A Letter to Lord Ellenborough* for possible publication. Hookham sent a "very flattering letter" but declined to publish the *Letter.* Shelley had the twenty-three-page *Letter* privately printed, sent Hookham twenty-five copies of "the little work," and asked him to show it to "any friends who *are not informers.*" Because of "knowledge I now posess," including fear of government prosecution and of being under surveillance, Shelley dropped his plan to have the *Letter* published.[37]

Among the books Shelley ordered were Milton's prose, Davy's just-published book on chemistry, David Hartley's *Observations on Man,* Wollstonecraft's *Rights of Woman,* and Thornton's *Medical Extracts.* He was particularly interested in essays in the *Extracts* concerning taking opium, reviving drowning victims, and Paracelsus's influence on modern chemistry.[38] Shelley would order nearly seventy books the coming December.[39]

A Letter to Lord Ellenborough, a significant advance over Shelley's Irish pamphlets, should rank among the classic defenses of freedom of speech and freedom of the press.[40] Eaton's trial and sentencing for "blasphemous libel" was a travesty of justice, Lord Chief Justice Ellenborough having repeatedly attacked the defendant from the bench. Shelley, having followed detailed reports of the nine-day trial in March, argued that Eaton was being punished for his deistic opinions:

> The time is rapidly approaching ... when the Mahometan, the Jew, the Christian, the Deist, and the Atheist, will live together in one community, equally sharing ... and united in the bonds of charity and brotherly love.—My Lord, you have condemned an innocent man. ... I raise my solitary voice, to express my disapprobation ... of the cruel and unjust sentence you passed upon Mr. Eaton; to assert ... those rights of humanity, which you have wantonly and unlawfully infringed.[41]

Later in the nineteenth century, the *Letter* was reprinted twice to protest sentences for blasphemy in New York and London.[42] Shelley omitted his name on a pamphlet whose contents could have led to his prosecution. One report stated that when Shelley received copies of the *Letter* and *The Devil's Walk* from his printer, he excised Syle's name, aided by his landlady's twelve-year-old niece (later Mrs. Blackmore). The only surviving copy of *The Devil's Walk* has no printer's name, required by law, suggesting Shelley possibly set the single sheet himself.[43] Years later, Mrs.

Blackmore vividly remembered the "boyish . . . great writer" who "thought the poor people were overtaxed."[44]

To distribute his seditious works, Shelley sent them to sea in corked bottles. Two women lodgers, seeing him launch green wine bottles, notified a lawyer in Barnstaple. Shelley also carried his message aloft in fire balloons and commemorated his methods with two sonnets, including "To a balloon, laden with Knowledge."[45] Another seaborne method involved inserting a broadside within a waterproofed bladder with a lead keel and two stick masts for a sail. In addition to launching his fleet from Lynmouth's rocky shore, Shelley occasionally went offshore in a boat. Two of his bottles containing *A Declaration of Rights* were found by government revenue cutters, one across the Bristol Channel. Their damp but legible contents were duly reported to Lord Sidmouth at the Home Office in London. The reporting naval officer, identifying the Lynmouth author as Shelley, imagined he was heading a group that produced this flotilla of subversive propaganda. With "this novel mode of disseminating their pernicious opinions," they could reach "many hundreds . . . and do incalculable mischief." To aid the local officials, several Lynmouth citizens went out in boats to retrieve message-laden bottles and sailing bladders.[46]

Mrs. Blackmore recalled Shelley was "very kind hearted, and would give to any one who stood in need." She heard Daniel Healey "say repeatedly that he would go through fire and water for him." Shelley, protecting himself from arrest, made Dan a sacrificial lamb for liberty by sending him to Barnstaple to post and distribute his broadsides. Mrs. Blackmore remembered that when Shelley handed the illiterate Dan a broadside, he turned it upside down. When, on August 19, Dan began pasting up the *Declaration of Rights* and *The Devil's Walk* in Barnstaple, he was arrested and put in jail.

Dan, perhaps given a cover story by Shelley, was tight-lipped about his beloved master. The town clerk, Henry Drake, wrote letters to Sidmouth indicating that Dan, giving his last name as Hill, told the authorities a stranger dressed in black paid him five shillings to distribute the papers. Dan identified his master, saying Shelley was the son of an MP and lived principally in London on Sackville Street but currently resided with his wife and "two Sisters" in Lynmouth. Drake confirmed being informed of Shelley's sea launchings and reported that Shelley was "regarded with a suspicious eye" since being in Lynmouth. Drake knew that many of Shelley's letters and packages were addressed to Sir Francis Burdett and learned from the Barnstaple Postmaster that Shelley sent as many as sixteen letters in the same day's post. Confirming this, Mrs. Blackmore recalled posting this number at a time for Shelley, saying his correspondents included Lord Byron and Sir Francis Burdett.[47] Shelley, having dedicated *The Wandering Jew* to Burdett, sent him *A Letter to Lord Ellenborough* and possibly was enlisting his support to free the Irishman Redfern.[48]

The day after Dan's arrest Shelley went to the Barnstaple jail to find Dan had been convicted on ten technical counts at £20 each for "dispersing Printed papers without the Printer's name being on them." Lacking the £200, Shelley arranged to pay fifteen shillings a week so Dan would have "immunities and privileges" not accorded a common prisoner. Drake was suspicious when Shelley failed to reprove his servant's actions. In default of paying his fine, Dan was sentenced to six months in jail. Shelley, amply confirmed in his suspicions of government surveillance, prepared to move his family again.

Actually, two local agents were detailed to watch Shelley and reported on his wading among the rocks to sail his pamphlets. Once again the Earl of Chichester received material on Shelley, this time the Barnstaple Postmaster's report with a copy of the *Declaration*. Chichester replied, "it would have no effect to speak to Mr. Shelley's family, they suffer enough already for his conduct." The local authorities, knowing Shelley's family position and his minority status, were uncertain about how to deal with him until receiving further directives from Sidmouth.

The active interest of Lord Sidmouth's Home Office in Shelley's case reflected the government's concern that political unrest was reaching Cornwall and Devon. In late April, *Cobbett's Political Register* reported Cornwall disturbances had spread to Barnstaple where "some threatening letters of rather a serious style" were circulating. Sidmouth, taking a personal interest in Shelley, replied immediately to Drake's initial letter, approving the actions taken against "Daniel Hill" and asking for the names of Shelley's correspondents and any further information on him as it became available. Chichester also sent his information about Shelley to Sidmouth, whose office assigned the espionage duties on Shelley to the Mayor of Barnstaple.[49]

Drake went to Lynmouth in early September and matched Shelley's seaborne seditions with the broadsides distributed by Dan. He wrote to Sidmouth that Shelley, the author, had a launching assistant who was a "Female Servant (supposed a Foreigner)," probably a reference to Hitchener. Drake's man had slipped through his fingers. Some days earlier, after a Lynmouth sailor refused to take Shelley and his group across the Bristol Channel, they fled westward along the coast to Ilfracombe. Drake reported Shelley took "large chests, which were so heavy that scarcely three men could lift them, which were supposed to contain papers." Arriving in Ilfracombe after the Shelley retinue had embarked for Swansea, Drake wrote Sidmouth, "Mr. Shelley is rather thin, and very young; indeed, his appearance is, I understand, almost that of a boy."

Of the two broadsides uncorked by the worried authorities, the *Declarations* had been seen earlier by Sidmouth but not *The Devil's Walk*, which retained the "brainless King" of Shelley's previous version. New stanzas ridiculed the Prince Regent's "Fat . . . maudlin brain" and "pantaloons . . . like half-moons / Upon each brawny haunch." Shelley's poetic powers reached a new level of sophistication in his thirty-stanza satire, *The Devil's Walk*. Sidmouth, unnamed, was like "A Statesman" unclothed "To show each feature, every limb" by "The Devil," who was "Secure of an unchanging lover" (ll.114–17).

Syle, hearing of Daniel Healey's conviction, destroyed the remaining nine hundred copies of *A Letter to Lord Ellenborough* and tried unsuccessfully to have Shelley return his copies.[50] The day before Dan's arrest, Shelley sent Hookham fifty more copies of *A Letter* and a copy of *Pieces of Irish History*. He told Hookham his plan to complete *Biblical Extracts* was uncertain as all his manuscripts were in Dublin. He sent Hookham "a specimen" of *Queen Mab*, saying he was making good progress with "matter enough for 6 more cantos." He was still translating Holbach's *Le Système de la nature* and, sending Hookham his two Irish pamphlets, wondered if they could be safely published in London with "an explanatory preface." Shelley asked Hookham to deliver a letter he enclosed to "Chevalier [James] Lawrence," author of a novel of free love in a matriarchal society, *The Empire of the Nairs, or the Rights of Woman: An Utopian Romance*.[51]

Shelley had read Lawrence's novel in the spring as well as his narrative poem, "Love: An Allegory." The poem and the novel's introductory essay advocated free love and attacked religion's influence on false notions of chastity. Shelley told Lawrence he admired his poem even if it was unappreciated by "the British public." Having become a "perfect convert" to the "doctrines" in the *Nairs,* he would always "Perfectly & decidedly" subscribe "to the truth" of the novel's "principles." Citing the reasoning of "Mrs. Wollstonecraft," Shelley said he had "no doubts of the evils of marriage," but reading Lawrence made him aware that "the greatest argument against it [was] prostitution both *legal* and *illegal.*"[52]

Shelley rationalized his marriage to Lawrence, saying that an unmarried woman living with a man in "the present state of society" would be "treated worse" than if she were married. This worse treatment, "seduction," was a term that would have "no meaning, in a rational society." However, in today's society, "If there is any enormous and desolating crime, of which I shudder to be accused, it is seduction." Shelley, composing *Queen Mab,* developed the free-love ideas of Lawrence and Wollstonecraft in the essay on marriage appended to the poem, "Even love is sold."

Before leaving Lynmouth, Shelley had written Hookham and first mentioned his future friend, Thomas Love Peacock. Hookham had sent Shelley two volumes of Peacock's poems, seeking his criticism and financial aid for Peacock. Shelley kept the two volumes but regretted his "circumscribed" resources prevented helping *"your friend."* Lavishly praising Peacock's poetry, Shelley added, "I lament the object of their application," criticizing Peacock's support of "Commerce" and the crown.[53] Within a few months, Shelley would meet Peacock.

Harriet, turning seventeen on August 1, was the object of several poems Shelley composed, including "To Harriet" and a sonnet, "To Harriet on her birth day." "Harriet! thy kiss to my soul is dear," probably written in Devon, hints of discord involving his political activity and Eliza's possible thought of leaving.[54] In addition to his considerable progress on *Queen Mab,* Shelley composed another long political poem, "A retrospect of Times of Old." Anticipating his sonnet "Ozymandias," it tells of "some ruined pile" containing "grim effigies of the Gods of old." Shelley's most revealing Devon poem, "The Voyage. A Fragment.," has a dream sequence that recent editors suggest is a "curious rehearsal" of the future "attack" awaiting Shelley in Wales.[55]

Godwin decided to visit Shelley in Lynmouth in early September, unaware he had left. Depressed during August, Godwin was experiencing narcolepsy, *petit mal* type attacks, and his chronic bowel complaints.[56] His trip west provided an escape from bailiffs who served an order to pay one of his debts or face arrest. On a storm-tossed fifty-one-hour voyage from Bristol, Godwin suffered a seizure.[57] Arriving in Lynmouth, Godwin learned from Mrs. Hooper that the Shelleys had departed three weeks earlier "in a great hurry." She had given them twenty-nine shillings plus three pounds she borrowed from a neighbor. Godwin was relieved they had "faithfully returned" the money.[58] The Shelleys left word— probably to mislead the authorities—that they would be in London in two weeks. Godwin walked in the Valley of the Rocks before taking the Barnstaple coach to London to await Shelley.

However, Harriet wrote to Mrs. Nugent, her "most firmly . . . attached friend," that they thought of going to Llangollen in northern Wales.[59] At Ilfracombe, Shelley composed a sonnet while waiting for their packet boat to Swansea,[60] arriving there about the first of September. In Swansea, Shelley met an Eton schoolmate, Captain Gronow, who recalled rendering him "a service." Gronow thought Shelley was "in a state of great distress and difficulty" which he supposed "was some mysterious *affaire du coeur.*" More likely, Shelley was anxious about money and escaping the pursuing authorities, something he wished to hide from Gronow.[61]

Skipping the Vale of Llangollen, the group went west to Carnarvonshire and the coastal town of Tremadoc, due south of Snowdon, arriving the second week of September.[62] Shelley was attracted to the reclamation project of William Alexander Madocks, a reformist Whig MP. Harriet's Commonplace Book suggests that a poem by William Robert Spencer possibly attracted Shelley to the Tremadoc project and to Madocks's home, Tanyrallt.[63]

Madocks, politically liberal, was a practical philanthropist and exuberant entrepreneur.[64] In 1800, he began his development plan to shorten the route to Ireland by constructing a dirt embankment and draining two thousand acres. The name Madocks gave to the planned community on the reclaimed land, Tremadoc, harked back to a legendary warrior featured in Southey's 1805 epic, *Madoc*. Planning to link the counties of Carnarvon and Merioneth, Madocks was now well into his larger project of reclaiming nearly five thousand acres at nearby Traeth Mawr. A huge celebration in 1811 marked the near-completion of the second longer embankment of stone that extended across the estuary to Portmadoc. Madocks was engulfed in financial problems the February before Shelley's arrival when high tides ruptured the dike. Already £30,000 in debt, Madocks needed many thousands more to finance the repairs.[65] With unpaid laborers leaving the project, Madocks, aided by his trusted partner and Tremadoc manager, John Williams, actively tried to raise funds. Williams, in his midthirties, and Madocks's friend for ten years, probably thought his prayers were answered when the enthusiastic heir to a fortune arrived in his midst. Williams soon wrote about his new friend to Madocks, in London attending Parliament, where, in 1809, he proposed that Prime Minister Perceval and Foreign Secretary Castlereagh be impeached for irregularities. Shelley and his family, lodging at the Madocks Arms on Tremadoc's town square, possibly read about Madocks's home, Tanyrallt ("under the wooded cliff"). A June ad in the *North Wales Gazette* listed a "Romantic residence in North Wales to be let for a term of years, and entered upon immediately unfurnished, or the elegant furniture to be taken at valuation." Financially strapped, Madocks was eager to lease his home, whose contents belonged to his London creditor, Girdlestone. There were no takers for Tanyrallt in the locally depressed economy. A disturbing, unusual murder of a servant girl in a local farmhouse about the time of Shelley's arrival might have deterred prospective tenants.[66] If the Shelleys heard this grisly news, their qualms were overcome by Tanyrallt's spaciousness and lofty sea view.

Solitary Tanyrallt nestles on a hill beneath the high rocky cliff paralleling the distant shore. The two-story white stone villa, with roof of local slate and ample windows, commands a view of the embankment and sea to the south. Directly behind the house, Shelley could wind through trees and ascend a steep path to gain a higher magnificent view from the cliff top. Madocks had enlarged his house and updated it with a rare but troublesome water closet. Above the two parlors were three bedrooms; servants' quarters were over the adjacent stables.[67] From the corner master bedroom with vaulted ceiling, Shelley could descend the stairs to a spacious parlor or billiard room, directly below his bedroom. The parlor and its adjacent "office" had tall windows allowing access to the lawn.

Leasing arrangements for Tanyrallt almost came to the same dead end as Nantgwillt. Williams wrote Girdlestone that Shelley, giving Mr. Westbrook as a reference, desired to lease Tanyrallt for a year. Girdlestone called on Westbrook, who refused to back up Shelley financially. Noting Shelley was "under age," Girdlestone doubted he was the "sort of tenant that would be useful to us." Suspecting that Shelley had "married beneath him, and thereby offended his family," Girdlestone correctly predicted Shelley probably would be unable to pay his rent and "would incur debts with the tradesmen in the town which he would be unable to pay." He warned Williams not to let Shelley take "possession of the house or premises for if he gets in we may have great difficulty in getting him out again."[68]

However, Williams, impressed with Shelley's family wealth and his offer to help raise funds, allowed the Shelleys into Tanyrallt. Girdlestone, becoming more disposed toward Shelley's occupation of Tanyrallt, tried to track down proof of his inheritance. Ultimately, it was agreed that the "large" rent would be unpaid until Shelley reached his majority. Settling into Tanyrallt, Shelley thought it "extensive & tasty enough for the villa of an Italian prince."[69]

On September 28, Williams took Shelley north to the town of Beaumaris for a "well-attended" meeting of Madocks's corporation, presided over by Lord Bulkeley and his deputy mayor, Sir Robert Williams, MP. After toasts, Williams introduced Shelley as a "friend" whose "providential interference" enabled him to employ enough men to "fortify the Embankment against any appreciable damage." The local paper reported Shelley gave a speech, saying he was the "proud" friend of Williams and saluting the "honesty, faithfulness, and fortitude" of Mr. Madocks, "even though he had never seen him." Shelley, proclaiming this "glorious" work will employ "three thousand souls," was quoted as saying, "How can anyone look upon that work and hesitate to join me, when I here publicly pledge myself to spend the last shillings of my fortune, and devote the last breath of my life, to this great, this glorious Cause."[70]

Sir Robert Williams rose to thank and toast Shelley for his "honourable and liberal exertions," after which Shelley again spoke, having "through inadvertence" omitted the "generous and praiseworthy support" of Lord Bulkeley and Sir Robert. Shelley's name, with a pledge of £100, was added to the corporation's subscription list.[71] This generous amount, matching that of Lord Bulkeley, was twice Sir Robert's pledge.

Madocks, initially cautious about accepting Shelley's generous proposals, told Medwin after Shelley's death that he "idolised" Shelley for his numerous acts of benevolence in "relieving the distress of the poor, visiting them in their humble abodes, supplying them with food and raiment and fuel during the winter." Shelley "raised a considerable sum," enabling Madocks to "employ hundreds of workmen" and stop "the progress of the waves."[72]

Years later, Williams's wife reported that her husband often said, "Mr. Shelley could make everybody love him if they had the least heart; he was so kind and fascinating with such feeling." Shelley, hearing of a "very indigent" widow living nearby, "sent her five pounds, which she could not accept from a stranger and returned: it was much talked of at the time, and left a lasting favourable impression."[73]

About the time of the Beaumaris meeting, Shelley was arrested in Carnarvon by some unknown creditor for unpaid debts of £70, probably incurred when Shelley passed through the town the previous year on returning from Ireland. John Williams and a Carnarvon surgeon, William Roberts, stood bail for Shelley. Dr. Roberts, who soon would "attend" Shelley's family at Tanyrallt, was still trying to recover his money thirty-two years later.[74] Shelley's precarious finances needed attention. At the end of September, after about two weeks in Tremadoc, the group, accompanied by Williams, left for London. Shelley would meet Madocks and, after ten months of correspondence, meet Godwin.

In early October, after obtaining rooms at Lewis's Hotel in St. James Street, Shelley, Harriet, and Elizabeth Hitchener dined at the Godwins' home. The talk probably was lively and the two men, separated by thirty-seven years, were pleased with each other. Godwin presided over his punctual four o'clock afternoon dinner with his wife, their son William, and Fanny. Mrs. Godwin, about twelve years younger than her husband, married Godwin in late 1801, after becoming pregnant by him. Although English, she spoke fluent French. A Roman Catholic, she took Godwin to Mass at least once. She and Godwin operated the Juvenile Library from their home. The two illegitimate children she brought to the marriage were both away when the Shelleys first visited. Charles Gaulis Clairmont (b. 1795) was apprenticed to a publishing magnate in Edinburgh and Clara Mary Jane Clairmont was becoming proficient in French at a boarding school a few miles away in Walham Green. She and Charles had different fathers but used the same last name, Clairmont, probably invented by their mother, whose veracity was not an outstanding trait.[75] Clara Mary Jane Clairmont, lacking a birth record, gave April 27, 1798, as her birth date. Possibly, she was a year or so older. Her family called her Jane and by 1814 she began to call herself in succession Clara, Clary, Clare, and finally Claire, the name that now will be used for her. The vivacious, dark-eyed Claire dined with the Shelleys on her two weekend visits home.

Initially euphoric about the Godwins, Harriet wrote Mrs. Nugent, "I love them all." Defying "even an enemy to be displeased with" Godwin, they decided "to settle near London." As for Fanny, the "beauty of her mind fully overbalances the plainness of her countenance." Her half-sister, Mary, "in Scotland," was "very much like her mother, whose picture hangs up in his study." Harriet commented that Wollstonecraft "must have been a lovely woman" whose "countenance speaks for a woman who would dare to think and act for herself."[76] Harriet conveyed Shelley's request that Mrs. Nugent go to his Dublin printer and collect his "manuscript poems and other pieces." If necessary, she should "steal them away from him." Shelley owed money to the printer and his encouraging Mrs. Nugent to theft reflected his continuing cavalier attitude about his debts to tradesmen.

Shelley and Godwin met for hours in the succeeding days. Godwin was so impressed with Shelley that for the first time in years he made notes in his diary of each day's conversations. One entry read, "matter and spirit, atheism, utility and truth, Church government or the characteristics of German thought and literature."[77] However, the Shelleys' feelings about the Godwins soon soured. Harriet experienced Mrs. Godwin as scheming, self-centered, and quick-tempered. Charles Lamb called her a "bitch" and "Bad Baby;" another close friend of Godwin considered her "a clever, bustling second-rate woman . . . with a temper undisciplined and uncontrolled."[78] Harriet found Godwin "grown old and unimpassioned" and filled "with prejudices" and expecting "universal homage from all persons younger than himself." She was angry that Godwin wanted Shelley to join the Whig party. Harriet was also displeased with the artist, writer, and musician, Amelia Curran, whom the Shelleys met for the first time at the Godwin home. Amelia had her father's salacious wit that had offended the Shelleys in Dublin. To Harriet, Amelia was "a coquette, the most abominable thing in the world."[79]

The attraction women felt toward Shelley probably upset Harriet. Most susceptible to Shelley's charming manner was shy Fanny Godwin, who saw a great deal of him. For the first time, she became close to a male her own age outside the family. In this unusual family of five children from four fathers, Fanny was the only child who had lost both parents. Harriet's repeated emphasis upon Fanny's plainness suggests she was threatened by her year-older rival. Significantly, Harriet became pregnant in late September or early October, after thirteen months of marriage. She assumed an air of sophistication and, perhaps trying to meet her intellectual competition, resolutely began learning Latin under Shelley's tutelage.[80] Fanny, shortly after Shelley returned to Wales, asked him if it was "proper" that she write to him. He mockingly replied he was just "a Man," "inoffensive," and living "on vegetable food, & never bit since I was born." He defensively took exception to Fanny's characterization and implied criticism of Harriet as a "fine lady," protesting that she had no interest in the "fashionable life . . . & its vulgar & noisy eclat." Harriet's "greatest charms" were her "ease & simplicity" of habits, an "unassuming plainness of her address," and an "uncalculated connexion of her thought & speech."[81]

Also disconcerting to Harriet were Shelley's new friends, the intellectual-bohemian Newton family. John Frank Newton, his wife, and their four children all practiced nudism, or "air bathing." One early November evening, Shelley and young William Godwin, after setting off fireworks, found themselves at the Newton home on Chester Street. Newton, an ardent vegetarian and health faddist, was delighted with Shelley, who had "so much knowledge of numerous authors."[82] Shelley perhaps had read Newton's 1811 book, *The Return to Nature*, mentioned in *Queen Mab* and in the essay he would soon write, *A Vindication of Natural Diet*. In his book, Newton quoted Shelley's Dr. Lind on the evils of impure water. Newton was influenced by the respected Dr. William Lambe's ideas of diet in relation to cancer, insanity, and syphilis. Shelley also cited Lambe's work in *Queen Mab*, having learned from him the deadly effects of using arsenic, perhaps reinforcing his belief that his prior use of arsenic would shorten his longevity.[83]

In London, Shelley, after a year's lapse, renewed his friendship with Hogg, now admitted to study law at the Middle Temple. He perhaps was planning to enlist Hogg's unwitting aid in reshuffling his household. When Hogg came for dinner at their hotel, Harriet and Eliza greeted him. Shelley was out. Hogg found Eliza still fretting about Harriet, "her nerves are in a fearful state; most dreadfully shattered." Harriet's request that Hogg read a report on Robert Emmet's trial evoked his retort, "the sooner all such rascals are hanged the better!" Harriet snapped back, attacking

him for being "horribly narrow-minded" and "terribly unfeeling!"
When Shelley returned, Hogg's derogatory remark about a book
on Irish history only elicited Shelley's quietly removing the book
from Hogg's hands.[84] Shelley talked of Tremadoc and the beauty of
Wales, suggesting some day they all should see Niagara Falls. He
never mentioned Godwin to Hogg.

Before leaving London, Shelley first met Thomas Love Peacock,
probably at the shop of their mutual friend, Thomas Hookham.[85]
Peacock, an autodidact without university training, would stimulate Shelley's interest in the classics. The reserved, cool, ironic,
scholarly bachelor with a wry sense of humor was seven years
older than Shelley. Peacock, whom Shelley would describe as "an
enemy to every shape of tyranny and superstitious imposture," became Shelley's confidant in times of personal distress, received his
longest letters, and served as executor of his estate. Shelley's relationship with Peacock had neither the intensity nor the emotional
volatility of his relationship with Hogg. An only child with an absent
father, Peacock lived with his intelligent and devoted mother.

Several years before meeting Shelley, Peacock was a wandering
recluse in North Wales and lived for fifteen months near Tremadoc,
where he met William Madocks. Shelley would meet a Welsh
woman who described Peacock as "associating with no one, & hiding his head like a murderer," but, she added, "he was *worse than
that*, he was an Atheist."[86] Peacock probably told Shelley of his cyn-
ical attitude towards Madocks and his project, which he conveyed
in his first (1815) satirical novel, *Headlong Hall*.

In mid-October, Shelley met Madocks and Williams at his hotel
when Godwin stopped by. Probably at Madocks's suggestion, Shelley contacted an insurance broker, John Bedwell, who wrote
Madocks's Carnarvon solicitor to settle Shelley's £70 debt.[87] In
early November, Shelley wrote Williams—who was back in
Wales—of his futile efforts raising funds for the embankment. Shelley acknowledged the "honorable perseverance of the men" working on the embankment who periodically went on strike for being
paid little or nothing to support their families. Despite avowing to
Williams his "unabated and unconquerable ardour" for the project,
Shelley was becoming disillusioned. He was pessimistic about having any "effect . . . until the expiration of my minority." Unconsciously revealing how he would escape Tremadoc's troubles, he
told Williams, "my unremitting personal exertions (so far as my

health will allow) are all engaged in that cause which I will desert *but with my life.*" Shelley asked Williams to locate a "trustworthy undermaidservant" as they now needed three.[88]

Dramatically, just before returning to Wales, the Shelley family lost a member. Godwin's brief, guarded diary entry on November 8 announced the dismissal of Elizabeth Hitchener: "Call on E. Westbrook (E.H. *congé*)."[89] According to Hogg, Eliza "would not tolerate" Hitchener's influence on Shelley and had "worked on Harriet's feelings" until "Harriet succeeded in making his former favourite odious to Bysshe."

When Hogg arrived at the Shelleys' hotel, he was delegated to take the mutual enemies, Eliza and Bessy, on a walk. Harriet had a headache and Shelley was off on one of his innumerable errands. Hogg's derogatory description of Elizabeth Hitchener—"tall and thin, bony and masculine, of a dark complexion; the symbol of male wisdom, a beard, was not entirely wanting"—was countered by his mild assessment of her personality. She elicited neither "raptures at meeting her [nor] excessive delight at parting." Hogg walked arm-in-arm with the two dark "jewels," presiding over a verbal duel between the two thirty-year-old women. In the awkward silence after dinner while they waited for the carriage to take Hitchener away, Hogg prompted her on women's rights. She talked "with fluency and animation," and Shelley responded with a final flicker of his idealized admiration. Harriet and Eliza "eyed him with manifest displeasure, as a person holding treasonable communication with a public enemy."[90]

Shelley now gave Elizabeth Hitchener her final name, "The Brown Demon." Recognizing his responsibility for her emotional and financial plight, Shelley agreed to give her £100 a year, although no evidence exists that any payment was ever made. Further, the £100 she loaned the Shelleys had not been repaid at her death.[91] Shelley later wrote Hogg a vivid picture of his idealization of Elizabeth Hitchener having turned to bitter rejection, even as he admitted culpability in her suffering:

The Brown Demon, as we call our late tormentor and schoolmistress, must receive her stipend. I pay it with a heavy heart and an unwilling hand; but it must be so. She was deprived by our misjudging haste of a situation, where she was going on smoothly: and now she says, that her reputation is gone, her health ruined, her peace of mind destroyed by my barbarity; a complete victim to all the woes mental and bodily that heroine ever suffered! This is not all fact; but certainly she is embarrassed and poor, and we being in some degree the cause, we ought to obviate it. She is an artful, superficial, ugly hermaphroditical beast of a woman, and my astonishment at my fatuity, inconsistency, and bad taste was never so great, as after living four months with her as an inmate. What would Hell be, were such a woman in Heaven?[92]

Harriet broached the sexual issues behind the Brown Demon's dismissal in a letter to Mrs. Nugent. They had been "deceived in her character" as "She built all her hopes on being able to separate me from my dearly beloved Percy, and had the artfulness to say that Percy was really in love with her, and [it] was only his being married that could keep her within bounds now."[93] Years later, Medwin recalled that Shelley, tears of laughter running down his cheeks, recited a line of a poem Hitchener had written on the rights of women, "All, all are men—women and all!"[94]

Elizabeth Hitchener returned to Hurstpierpoint, attempting to rebuild her professional life. The townsfolk, believing she had been living in sin with Shelley, ostracized her and refused to enroll their children in her school. When Shelley's former friend, Merle, soon visited her at her father's home, she dejectedly read one of Shelley's works. "Her fine black eye lighted up, her well-formed Roman countenance was full of animation when I spoke of Shelley." However, she did not allude to Shelley.[95] Her anger emerged in a letter forwarded to Shelley by John Williams several months later in which she threatened them both and hinted at exposing Shelley's activities to the government. Shelley's jocular response to these "wiles of a scorned & dissappointed woman" included a suggestion that Williams send his letter on to her: "I am above all secrecy & her threats are surely calculated . . . to amuse than alarm any but little boys & girls." This letter, like many he wrote, was for Harriet's eyes; she wisely added a postscript asking Williams not to send the letter on.[96]

Elizabeth Hitchener did not carry through on her threats. Never marrying, she later ran a successful school with her sister in Edmonton. A former pupil fondly remembered her as a "high principled, clever woman, with a remarkable capacity for teaching."[97] Shelley's apparent final word about Elizabeth Hitchener was in *Epipsychidion* (270), "Others were wise, but honeyed words betray." Elizabeth Hitchener, in a poem published the year both she and Shelley died, recalled:

> Yet once,—a vision waked thy slumbering lyre,
> Which fancy whispered wise and great and fair;[98]

Before leaving London, Shelley wrote to his mother offering to send "anything" she or his sisters needed in town as he had "been rendered by a most disinterested friend to a certain degree *independent*." He asked his mother to send his "Galvanic Machine & Solar Microscope" before returning to Wales. His solar microscope was "essential to a branch of philosophy which I am now pursuing." He recognized that his mother possibly "felt piqued at the deception which I practised on my marriage" but assured her he was now "one of the happiest of men" and would be happier if "the *temporary* estrangement" from his family ended.[99]

If Shelley went to Sussex in early November, this letter indicates he did not go to Field Place. Perhaps having seen either his uncle or the senior Medwin, he wrote Williams that "In Sussex I meet with no encouragement [from the] cold selfish & calculating animals."[100] He had called upon the Duke of Norfolk, who refused to contribute to the Madocks' effort. On November 11, the Shelleys dined with the Godwins. Present was Mary, who returned from Dundee the day before. This probable first meeting between Shelley and Mary went unrecorded. Two days later the Shelleys left for Wales.

It was an abrupt departure. Despite what he wrote his mother, Shelley was none too happy. She wrote on his letter that he had written the Vicar of Warnham, "Taffy" Edwards, for a certificate proving his age. Either this involved his financial machinations or he had discussed with his uncle the idea of remarrying Harriet.[101] Godwin, needing funds to meet a December deadline on the Juvenile Library accounts, undoubtedly hoped that Shelley might provide some financial relief.

Friday, November 13, proved unlucky for Godwin. Arriving at Shelley's hotel to dine with him and John Bedwell, he found that for the third time Shelley had stood him up, having left for Wales that morning without notifying Godwin. Shelley had kept his plans from Godwin, but a week earlier had written Williams he was leaving on November 12.[102] Shelley wanted to avoid the embarrassment of having to refuse Godwin aid. Godwin immediately resumed correspondence with his mercurial potential benefactor and obtained debt deferment from his creditor, Francis Place.[103]

En route to Wales, Harriet wrote to Mrs. Nugent expressing relief over Elizabeth Hitchener's departure and anxiety about Shelley's poems in Dublin.[104] Fanny Godwin wrote to Shelley, possibly trying to discover for her father why he left so suddenly. In reply, Shelley defended himself against her accusations of insincerity concerning "the abruptness of our departure." Admitting previous instances of insincerity, he said his hasty departure was due to the "pain" they were experiencing.[105] Calling Shelley to account for his inconsiderate behavior toward Elizabeth Hitchener, Fanny seemingly was expressing the rejection which she felt from him.

Harriet, beginning her second month of pregnancy, had Shelley to herself with Hitchener's ejection. Eliza was restored to her position of unquestioned control. Shelley, disappointed over failing to raise funds for the embankment, was agitated in London over the British declaration of war on the United States, the burning of Moscow, and the Tories' vilification of the Whigs in a general election. Savoring his bitterness, he composed a poem in Spenserian stanzas, "On Leaving London for Wales," that began "Thou miserable city!" His anger, "the weapon that I burn to wield," now would be directed into renewed efforts to assist the embankment and into helping the destitute laborers: "I am the friend of the unfriended poor; / Let me not madly stain their righteous cause in gore."[106]

Shaken by the "tremendously rough" roads of northern Wales, they changed from the mail coach to a chaise in Capel Curig for the "jumbled" ride past Snowdon to Tremadoc. Descending into the sheltering warmth of Tanyrallt for the harsh Welsh winter, they enjoyed a false sense of security.

14

Phantasmagoria at Tanyrallt

SHELLEY IMMEDIATELY TOOK UP THE PLIGHT OF THE EXPLOITED embankment workers who, he commented in a footnote to *Queen Mab*, "seldom received their wages" and "supported large families by cultivating small spots of sterile ground by moonlight."[1] Tracking down the local gentry who had pledged money, Shelley was in Williams's office "from morning to night."[2] Shelley soon irritated Madocks's Carnarvon solicitor, John Evans, by writing him of the "propriety" of "immediate payment" of his £50 embankment subscription. Often indifferent about his own debts, Shelley went out of his way to antagonize Evans by sending him a second note reiterating the "apathy & backwardness of defaulters."[3]

Shelley's real nemesis, the Hon. Robert Leeson, lived directly across the valley from Tanyrallt in Morfa Lodge. Son of a wealthy Irish peer, Leeson was a hard-line Tory Anglo-Irish aristocrat who managed the quarry that supplied stone for the embankment. Leeson's quarry was a major employer of the area, and Shelley saw that the opposing political allegiances of Leeson and Madocks did not interfere with their cooperation for economic gain.

Through Williams, Leeson obtained a copy of Shelley's *An Address, to the Irish People.* Hearing this radical interloper had "been in the practice of haranguing 500 people at a time when in Ireland," Leeson made no secret of sending the pamphlet to the government authorities.[4] In his pamphlet, Shelley castigated absentee Irish landlords, of whom Leeson was one, as "Protestant aristocracy and gentry" who had "withdrawn" from Ireland, leaving "the very poor people . . . most infamously oppressed." Shelley also attacked Leeson's Protestant religion for its "barbarous" history and "barefaced intoleration."[5]

The Shelleys befriended the more congenial Nanneys, who lived seven miles away. David Ellis Nanney, the Solicitor-General of the county, was active in the embankment project. Settling into Tany-rallt with the Nanneys' help, the Shelleys had some furniture made for their new home. Harriet shared with Mrs. Nanney some Irish melodies from London. After several weeks, Shelley wrote to Dr. Roberts, his Carnarvon bail benefactor, inviting him to stay at Tanyrallt. Roberts, now Shelley's doctor, probably advised Harriet on her diet during her pregnancy. Shelley told Hogg she was "slightly animal" but he continued "vegetable" and credited his "much improved" health to being away from "nerve racking" London.[6]

Eager to resume *Queen Mab*, he wrote Hookham to forward a package from Mrs. Hooper containing the poem.[7] By early December the parcel had not arrived, though Hookham had sent some of Peacock's poetry deriding the ignorance of the Welsh. Shelley wrote Hookham an equally hostile evaluation, saying Wales was "the last stronghold of the most vulgar & common place prejudices of aristocracy . . . the peasants are mere serfs & are fed & lodged worse than pigs, the gentry have all the ferocity & des-potism of the ancient barons."[8]

Calling himself "a determined sceptic," Shelley was becoming increasingly suspicious. He denied Hogg's complaint that in Lon-don he had been unfriendly: "Of such motives I do not accuse you . . . of which you indirectly accuse me, by the very spirit of suspi-cion, which produces the accusation." After mentioning "The Brown Demon . . . our late tormentor," Shelley made a prophecy soon to be played out: "The society in Wales is very stupid . . . they hunt people to death, who are not so likewise."[9] Shelley next ac-cused Williams, who had helped him obtain coal for Tanyrallt. Shel-ley, unable to pay for it, was "undeceived" about his understanding with Williams and blamed him for not letting him know about the arrangement.[10]

The crucial person behind these displaced paranoid feelings, Timothy, was enjoying temporary cordiality from his son. Timothy was "oblig'd" by Shelley's "kind enquiries, & good wishes of the New Year, we all join in returning them tenfold to you & yours, & that you may see many & more happy ones." Regretting "the pres-ent difficulties," he hoped "the mountains of Wales may produce Reflections that you well know would be so congenial to my own sentiments, as well as those of yr. Mother."[11]

Shelley was also cordial with Godwin, who responded to Shel-ley's request for a plan of reading and study by sending a lengthy educational prescription including history, the classics, poetry, and prose. However, Godwin criticized Shelley's "false taste in poetry. . . . You love a perpetual sparkle and glittering."[12] Shelley, composing the lengthy *Queen Mab*, supplemented Godwin's prescription with his own encyclopedic interests and perhaps with suggestions Peacock gave him. Settling in for "some stiff reading," the staggering list of books he requested from Hookham and Thomas "Clio" Rickman, a liberal London bookseller, included philosophy, history, classics, medicine, science, law, language, and poetry, not to mention encyclopedias, works on India, astronomy, and a book on stoves for the Welsh winter. He ordered all in the cheapest editions.

Among the many "metaphysical works to which my heart hankers," Shelley ordered Spinoza, Kant, Hume, Berkeley, and Plato. Not yet fluent in German, he wanted a translation of Kant's *Critique of Pure Reason* and later, "all Kants works." Fluent in Greek, Latin, and French, he confidently ordered works in Spanish and Italian by Vega and Spallanzani.[13] Godwin had prescribed a good dose of history to a reluctant Shelley, who requested Southey's work on the revolution in Brazil as well as English, Scottish, Greek, and Roman histories. In addition to Greek and Latin literature, he wanted Shakespeare and Spenser. Among contemporary poets, he ordered the works of Wordsworth and Coleridge as well as Southey's *Thalaba*. His Godwin collection would include his *Enquirer* essays on education and the novels *Caleb Williams, St. Leon*, and *Fleetwood*.

Perhaps Shelley's most interesting request was for "a work by a French Physician Cabanis." A revolutionist and ideologue, Pierre Cabanis's materialist philosophy figured importantly in Shelley's emerging thought.[14] Cabanis emphasied the importance of sex in moral development, focusing on the nervous system, mental illness, and the relation of physique to temperament. Shelley's continuing deep interest in recent physiological theory was evident in the number of medical works he ordered, including Thomas Trotter's *A View of Nervous Temperament* and *On Drunkenness*. He also ordered *Nicholson's British Encyclopaedia*, from whose numerous medical and obstetrical articles he fortunately learned about applying ice to stop severe uterine hemorrhaging.[15]

Shelley assimilated this reading into his developing revolutionary moral thought in *Queen Mab*. In late January he wrote

Hookham of (accurately) expecting to finish the poem by March. It would have "10 cantos and 2800 lines," an overstatement by one canto and about five hundred lines. He believed its "long & Philosophical" notes would be a "safe" way "of propagating my principles. . . . A poem very didactic is I think very stupid." He planned to publish *Queen Mab* in one volume with his "Minor Poems," about which he also had concern of possible government prosecution. Although "some of the later ones have . . . merit" and all "are faithful pictures of my feelings at the time of writing" he thought them mostly "[abru]pt & obscure." The poems were "breathing hatred to government & religion, but I think not too openly for publication."[16] Having sent Hookham his completed *Biblical Extracts*, he eagerly inquired if Daniel Eaton might publish them. After Mrs. Nugent's intervention, Shelley finally heard from his Dublin publisher, Stockdale.[17]

December's tolerable weather had turned to January's "Russian cold" of twelve degrees below freezing.[18] Shelley's feelings about his Tremadoc situation began to harden. In mid-January, Harriet wrote Mrs. Nugent of their deepening disillusionment with Madocks, his project, and his exploitation of the workers. They were "dreadfully deceived" about Madocks. The embankment project pleased Madocks's "stupid vanity" and replaced "a bold fine sea" with "nothing but a sandy marsh uncultivated and ugly to the view." Madocks's "harm" was "incalculable," and after building Tremadoc he had "almost ruined its shopkeepers by never paying their just debts." Harriet's declaration, "We have been the means of saving the bank from utter destruction,"[19] apparently included Shelley's initiative in filling a dangerous breach in the embankment. Williams reported riding "round the country" with Shelley, whose "eloquence persuaded the people . . . to send men & materials to repair it, first sinking a laden vessel, then adding stones etc. But for his efforts it would soon have been quite destroyed."[20]

By early February Shelley had been "teazed to death for the last fortnight" by "Embankment affairs in which I thoughtlessly engaged, for when I come home to Harriet I am the happiest of the happy. . . . They have teazed me out of all poetry." His "rough sketch" of *Queen Mab* was completed but, dissatisfied with its "innumerable faults invisible to partial eyes," he incorrectly predicted his most politically influential poem would be "very unpopular." He would be consoled, "Like all egotists," if it were appreciated by "the chosen few who can think & feel" and by "friends . . . blind . . . to all defects."[21]

By mid-February, Shelley had completed and transcribed the poetry of *Queen Mab* but not its notes.[22] Subtitled *A Philosophical Poem: With Notes,* the poem had one demon Shelley wished to crush, Christianity. After Voltaire's epigram, "ECRASEZ L'IN-FAME!" [Crush the infamous thing!], Shelley next quoted Lucretius, proclaiming his mission was "to loose men's minds from the tight knots of superstition." Among the radical Enlightenment ideas advanced in *Queen Mab*[23] was Necessity, "an immense and uninterrupted chain of causes and effects" that vitiated the concept of free will and "tends to introduce a great change into established notions of morality, and utterly to destroy religion." Anticipating Nietzsche and Freud, Shelley used Necessity to attack notions of good and evil. Aligning himself with "moral philosophy," the depth psychology of his day, Shelley believed that our inability to explain some aspects of human behavior is due to inadequate knowledge of its causes: "Were the doctrine of Necessity false, the human mind would no longer be a legitimate object of science." Advocating thoroughgoing psychic determinism, his revealing example was that otherwise "we could not predict with any certainty that we might not meet as an enemy of to-morrow with whom we have parted in friendship to-night."[24]

The revolutionary and subversive solutions to social evils the twenty-year-old Shelley proposed in *Queen Mab* reflect his diverse reading and impressive encyclopedic knowledge. The poem's notes—occupying as many pages as the poetry—cite poets, physicians, philosophers, and social critics, including the French intellectuals Rousseau, Laplace, Cabanis, and Holbach. Particularly influential were the works of two revolutionary French thinkers, Condorcet's *Progress of the Human Mind* and Constantin Volney's *The Ruins of Empires.*[25] Shelley's interest in holistic health, expressed in his long note on vegetarianism, was evidenced by separate publication as *A Vindication of Natural Diet,* followed by a second essay on the subject.[26] In other notes, he discussed the evils of marriage, chastity, and prostitution.

The influence and popularity of *Queen Mab* among nineteenth-century political reformers came from its revolutionary message of sociopolitical change and renewal. Its psychological underpinning has led a scholar to find "remarkable how much *Queen Mab* is dominated by imagery of mother, father, and child."[27] The powerful change agent—the maternal figure Mab—works her transforming therapy on the soul of the youthful, feminine Ianthe. Mab's targets are the tyrannical, patriarchal authorities, "grave and hoary-headed hypocrites . . . Kings, priests, and statesmen." Expressive of Shelley's anger toward his father,[28] Mab's fierce monologues blend political outrage with the restorative power of love.

Queen Mab's dedicatory verses, "To Harriet," are a muted "pledge of love." Harriet, "my purer mind," becomes Ianthe's "sinless soul" to be transformed by Mab. As Ianthe's lover Henry gazes upon her sleeping form, the Queen descends in her heavenly chariot to carry the soul of Ianthe into the outer reaches of the universe where she instructs her charge that the ruinous evils of past and present despotic civilizations will be replaced by "Necessity! thou mother of the world!"

Shelley's note on marriage, "Even love is sold," is an attack on the legal sanction of "the despotism of marriage." The sexual attitudes of "The narrow and unenlightened morality of the Christian religion" promote both "Chastity . . . a monkish and evangelical superstition" and "Prostitution . . . the legitimate offspring of marriage." No "system [is] more studiously hostile to human happiness than marriage," whose "abolition" would result in "the fit and natural arrangement of sexual connection." Shelley "by no means" was asserting "that intercourse would be promiscuous."

Shelley never deviated from these views, called "the most incisive free love argument of his time."[29] Arguing against both legalized marriage and sexual relations without love, Shelley knew individual action was futile against the dictates of society. Echoes of his underlying feelings about his ill-considered marriage and limitations he perceived in Harriet are heard in his extended note.

Shelley, always concerned about his longevity, stated his age at death in his note on Time: "the life of a man of virtue and talent, who should die in his thirtieth year, is, with regard to his own feelings, longer than that of a miserable priest-ridden slave, who dreams out a century of dullness."

Longevity also appears in *Queen Mab*'s timeless figure of Ahasuerus. In a dramatic confrontation between Ahasuerus and Christ, Shelley wrote that Christ, "so far from being a God, was only a man like themselves" trying humbly to save mankind from destructive superstition. The "guilt and mutual recrimination" between Ahasuerus and Christ, it has been observed, resembles that between

Shelley and his father.[30] Christ, after being attacked by Ahasuerus, pronounces on the Wandering Jew his curse of eternal wandering "o'er the unquiet earth."[31] Ahasuerus, struck unconscious to the ground from this curse, gave a speech upon awakening that reads like Shelley's own credo for a life of exile:

> Therefore I rose, and dauntlessly began
> My lonely and unending pilgrimage,
> Resolved to wage unweariable war
> With my almighty tyrant, and to hurl
> Defiance at his impotence to harm
> Beyond the curse I bore.
>
> (7:196–201)

Shelley's "unweariable war" was now directed into two national political causes, the trials of the Yorkshire Luddites and of John and Leigh Hunt. In mid-January, seventeen Luddites were hanged and six transported to Botany Bay.[32] Harriet wrote Hookham to initiate and advertise a subscription for the children of those "executed at York." Harriet, Shelley, and Eliza subscribed "for two guineas each."[33]

Shelley, since December, had followed the Hunt brothers' delayed fourth trial for libel. The previous March, they had excoriated the Prince Regent in their weekly *Examiner.* Shelley acutely analyzed how the government's gag rules had hamstrung the liberal defense lawyer, Brougham. Shelley also attacked the "barefaced . . . timeservingness" of the presiding judge, his old enemy Lord Ellenborough,[34] who sentenced each brother to a fine of £500 and two years imprisonment. Incensed, Shelley wrote to Leigh Hunt as he had two years earlier at Oxford after the brothers' third trial. Because of his imprisonment, Hunt said he became "acquainted with my friend of friends, Shelley . . . he wrote to me making me a princely offer, which at the time I stood in no need from." Unaware that Hunt refused any outside aid, Shelley in his mid-February letter to Hookham said he was "boiling with indignation at the horrible injustice & tyranny of the sentence pronounced on Hunt & his brother." Hunt being "a brave, a good, & an enlightened man," Shelley, despite being "rather poor at present," in addition to his "subscription for the widows & children of those poor men hung at York," enclosed £20 for Hunt.[35]

Twelve days later, Shelley's disjointed letter to Hookham, asking him to return the £20, was the first word about one of the strangest and most controversial experiences of Shelley's life: "I have just escaped an atrocious assassination.—Oh send the 20£ if you have it—you will perhaps hear of me no more. friend Percy Shelley." Harriet added a postscript: "Mr Shelley is so dreadfully nervous today from having been up all night that I am afraid what he has written will alarm you very much. We intend to leave this place as soon as possible as our lives are not safe so long as we remain.—it is no common Robber we dread but a person who is actuated by revenge & who threatens my life & my Sisters as well.—if you can send us the money it will greatly add to our comfort."[36] Unmentioned was Dan Healey's arrival from the Barnstaple jail just before the attack.

Shelley wrote only two other brief accounts of what occurred on that last night at Tanyrallt, February 26. The first—to Williams shortly after the event—was from the home of Attorney General Nanney where they stayed from February 27 to about March 6:

> I am surprised that the wretch who attacked me has not been heard of.—Surely the Inquieries have not been sufficiently general or particular?—Mr Nanney request[s] that you will order that some boards shd. be nailed against the broken windows at Tanyralt.
>
> We are in immediate want of money.—Could you borrow 25£ in my name to pay my little debts? I know your brother could lend me that sum. I think you cd. ask him on such an occasion as this.[37]

Shelley's misdating, "Jan. 6 1814," indicated his continuing emotional disorientation. Caught in a cross fire of competing financial obligations, Shelley wrote to Hookham from Bangor a week later thanking him for sending him the £20: "I am now recovering from an illness brought on by watching fatigue & alarm, & we are proceeding to Dublin, ~~whither we proceed~~ to dissipate the unpleasing impressions associated with the scene of our alarm. We expect to be there on the 8th. You shall hear the detail[s] of our distresses. The ball of the assassins pistol (he fired at me twice) penetrated my night gown & pierced the wainscott. He is yet undiscovered tho' not unsuspected as you will learn from my next."[38]

Two weeks after the event, Shelley had Harriet write a fuller version to Hookham. She apparently repeated the lost version she sent several days after the event to Hogg and perhaps others.[39] Harriet was writing the account because she wanted "to spare" Shelley because "of the present state of his health, every thing that can recal [sic] to his mind the horrors of the night." Retiring that

Friday night "between ten and eleven o'clock," Shelley, "about half an hour" later, "heard a noise proceeding from one of the parlours." Shelley "immediately went down stairs with two pistols, which he had loaded that night, expecting to have occasion for them." Entering the billiard room, he heard "footsteps retreating" and "followed into another little room . . . [where he] saw a man in the act of quitting the room through a glass window which opens into the shrubbery."

The man fired at Mr. S., which he avoided. Bysshe then fired, but it flashed in the pan. The man then knocked Bysshe down, and they struggled on the ground. Bysshe then fired his second pistol, which he thought wounded him in the shoulder, as he uttered a shriek and got up, when he said these words: By God I will be revenged! I will murder your wife. I will ravish your sister. By God. I will be revenged. He then fled—as we hoped for the night. Our servants were not gone to bed, but were just going, when this horrible affair happened. This was about eleven o'clock. We all assembled in the parlour, where we remained for two hours. Mr. S. then advised us to retire, thinking it impossible he would make a second attack. We left Bysshe and our manservant, who had only arrived that day, and who knew nothing of the house, to sit up. I had been in bed three hours when I heard a pistol go off. I immediately ran down stairs, when I perceived that Bysshe's flannel gown had been shot through, and the window curtain. Bysshe had sent Daniel to see what hour it was, when he heard a noise at the window. He went there, and a man thrust his arm through the glass and fired at him. Thank Heaven! the ball went through his gown and he remained unhurt, Mr. S. happened to stand sideways; had he stood fronting, the ball must have killed him. Bysshe fired his pistol, but it would not go off. He then aimed a blow at him with an old sword which we found in the house. The assassin attempted to get the sword from him, and just as he was pulling it away Dan rushed into the room, when he made his escape.

This was at four in the morning. It had been a most dreadful night; the wind was as loud as thunder, and the rain descended in torrents. Nothing has been heard of him; and we have every reason to believe it was no stranger, as there is a man of the name of Leeson, who the next morning that it happened went and told the shopkeepers of Tremadoc that it was a tale of Mr. Shelley's to impose upon them, that he might leave the country without paying his bills. This they believed, and none of them attempted to do anything towards his discovery.

. . . This Mr. Leeson had been heard to say that he was determined to drive us out of the country. He once happened to get a hold of a little pamphlet which Mr. S. had printed in Dublin; this he sent up to Government. In fact, he was forever saying something against us, and that because we were determined not to admit him to our house, because we had heard his character and from many acts of his we found that he was malignant and cruel to the greatest degree.[40]

A significantly different version of the evening has come down from Williams, who was summoned to Tanyrallt the next morning. This account suffers both from being recounted long after the event, in 1860, and from being told by Williams's wife, who did not come to the scene until she married Williams in 1820. However, with one possible exception, it is the only account derived from one who was close to Shelley at Tremadoc and who was the first non-family person to be with him immediately after the event.

My husband has often talked to me about "Shelley's ghost," as it used at the time I married in 1820, to be the topic of conversation among strangers who used to visit this place. They were seldom satisfied, as my kind husband never used to talk of Mr. Shelley to people who wished only to gratify their curiosity. His answer was, "He was my friend;" but to me he often said that he believed there was no attempt at burglary, or was there anything like an apparition at Tanyrallt at the time alluded to; it was all produced by heated imagination. The poor gentleman had been in England trying to procure money to go on with, but failed to get what he wanted: he also met with other causes of sorrow to his kind fine feelings. I fancy that his wife and her sister had neither of them much mind, they were not very suitable companions for such a man; and to make up the void he took to his house a Miss Hitchener . . . a very clever, talented person, who used to write for him and help him in his literary study; it was not very likely that peace and harmony would longer reign in such adverse elements, and he found confusion and anarchy in his house, as well as poverty. This for a short time overbalanced his mind. Mr. Williams was sent for, and found Mr. Shelley in a sad state of distress and excitement; he had fancied that he saw a man's face on the drawing room window; he took his pistol and shot the glass to shivers, and then bounced out on the grass, and there he saw leaning against a tree the ghost, or, as he said the Devil; and to shew Mr. Williams what he had seen he took his pen and ink and sketched the figure on the screen, where it is at this moment, showing plainly that his mind was astray. Mr. Williams took him home with him to Ynys y Towyn, and soothed him and procured £100 from his brother as a loan. When I add that Mr. Shelley set fire to the woods (with some trouble were they saved) to burn the apparition you may suppose that all was not right with him. At that time political party feelings ran high, and Mr. Leeson accused Mr. Shelley of having written a very seditious pamphlet against

Government, and that they were going to punish him for it. When Mr. Shelley asked for his informant Mr. Leeson pointed to my husband as the one who told him, but when the three met Mr. Leeson made an apology, and confessed that he had been told by Miss Hitchener. He [Leeson] was, like his countrymen, an envious unfeeling sort of man, and was not very particular what he said of any one; but I have never heard his name coupled with what I have related above.

He was a very unhappy man while here; his poor wife and sister were mere toys in the society of such a man, but they seemed fond of each other. She doted on him. My husband used to say that Mr. Shelley could make everybody love him if they had the least heart; he was kind and fascinating with such feeling . . . I know he was very generous and kind hearted.[41]

Contrary to Dowden's biography, Mrs. Williams clearly wrote that Shelley set fire to "the woods," not "wood," and "*they*" [emphasis added] were saved "with some trouble." The date of this fire-setting is uncertain. It refers not to burning the wooden fire screen but to Shelley's—at some time—setting fire to trees near the house where he saw the apparition. John Williams gave a similar account to Miss Fanny Holland, who told a friend, "the poet once set fire to a plantation in the grounds which was extinguished with some difficulty. She said the Devil had appeared to him there & he wanted to 'burn him out.'"[42] Harriet in her letter did not mention that Williams took Shelley to his home in Ynys y Towyn. His brother, Owen Williams, loaned Shelley £100 from his "hard earnings as a very small farmer," which Shelley secured with a bond paying £200 on the death of Shelley's father and grandfather.[43] Owen Williams's earlier loan to Shelley apparently was repaid before the February 26 incident.[44]

Another version of the attack, reported by Medwin from talks with Madocks after Shelley's death, has elements from the accounts of both Harriet and Mrs. Williams:

At midnight, sitting in his study, he [Shelley] heard a noise at the window, saw one of the shutters gradually unclosed, and a hand advanced into the room, armed with a pistol. The muzzle was directed towards him, the aim taken, and the trigger drawn. The weapon flashed in the pan. Shelley, with that personal courage which particularly distinguished him, rushed out to discover and endeavour to seize the assassin. In his way towards the outer door, at the end of a long passage leading to the garden, he meets the ruffian, whose pistol misses fire a second time. A struggle now ensues.—This opponent he described as a short powerful man. Shelley, though slightly built, was tall, and at that time strong and muscular. They were no unequal match. It was a contest between mind and matter.—After long and painful exertion the victory was fast declaring itself for Shelley, which his antagonist finding, extricated himself from his grasp, rushed into the grounds, and disappeared among the shrubbery. Shelley made a deposition before Maddocks the next day to these facts. An attempt at murder caused a great sensation in the principality, where not even a robbery had taken place for twenty years. No clue could be found to unravel the mystery; and the opinion generally was, that the whole scene was the effect of imagination.[45]

If a deposition were given, it was not to Madocks but probably to Attorney General Nanney. Medwin's account also does not indicate that Madocks believed that an attack occurred. In a business letter to Williams, probably written some months after the event, Madocks commented: "How could Shelly [sic] mind such a contemptible trick as has been played upon him to get him out of the Country on account of his liberal principles? Whoever the hoxters are, it is a transportable offence, if discovered."[46] Although Madocks downgrades the attack to a "contemptible trick" by "hoxters," his belief in its actuality must have reflected Williams's initial belief, which over time changed to the version communicated by his wife. Madocks's question as to why Shelley got "out of the Country" has one obvious answer irrespective of the reality of the attack: Shelley wanted to leave Tremadoc. The conscious reasons for fleeing were political, social, literary, and financial, as well as his disaffection with the embankment project. Three weeks before the event he was "teazed" by the project which he had "thoughtlessly engaged." Shelley needed a face-saving escape from his dilemma, and the events of the night of February 26 provided such an escape.

More unconscious fears probably amplified Shelley's conscious anxieties, including his emerging marital discontent and feelings associated with that "tormentor" and "hermaphroditical beast," the "Brown Demon." All three explanations of the circumstances surrounding this night are consistent with Shelley's need for flight. Whether it was a staged production by Shelley, a panic attack with delusional and hallucinatory aspects, or an actual assault perpetrated by one or more persons eager to have him leave for political or personal reasons, Shelley wished to escape. Irrespective of the triggering events, the question is not "Why did he leave?" but

"How might he leave?" A major reason to doubt an actual attack is that the attack was too convenient given his desire to escape. Dan Healey had just arrived and could accompany Shelley to his planned escape to Dublin. The overriding reason for Shelley staying was to honor his commitment to Madocks and not renege on his pledge to support what had seemed an honorable project. Shelley, who had difficulty admitting defeat, could not admit to Madocks and Williams he had made a mistake.[47]

Thus, one reason for his flight from Tanyrallt was akin to that behind his previous flight from London. Unable to face the humiliation of rejecting Godwin's financial entreaties, fleeing London answered his dilemma. Leaving without notifying Godwin made it appear he could still be a financial supporter at some future date and not risk his mentor's rejection. Godwin's reaction to Shelley's departure indicated Shelley's strategy had its desired effect. Escaping any immediate financial entanglement with Godwin, he preserved their relationship. The same motives operated at Tremadoc. By being hounded out of Tremadoc, he could escape the emotional and financial drain of his commitment but preserve his tie with Madocks and Williams. He apparently accomplished this by experiencing a panic attack in which he became the victim of a murderous persecutory plot. This face-saving means of escape, partly unconscious, was capped by an important conscious stratagem, the belief he imparted to Williams and Madocks that his departure was temporary, and that he would return to Tremadoc.[48] Shelley's unconscious issues expressed in the scenario of his earlier poem, "The Voyage," found similar expression in his account of what happened as conveyed through Harriet.

The inconsistencies of previous explanations of that evening at Tanyrallt begin with Shelley's accounts. After immediately writing Hookham that he had "escaped an atrocious assassination," he wrote him several weeks later and referred only to Harriet having related the "mysterious events" that "caused our departure." Harriet's letter to Hookham is the primary document of Shelley's version of what happened. Given Shelley's varied accounts of his other major life events, including his expulsion from Oxford and his marriage to Harriet, Harriet's letter is best construed as a version probably constructed to conceal or distort both what actually happened and the reasons underlying the events. It reads like a carefully constructed "official" version, a scenario with overtones, not just of "The Voyage," but of Shelley's two Gothic novels. On this moonless, dark, and stormy night, the wind "loud as thunder" did not prevent Shelley, already primed with two loaded pistols, from hearing noises in a room below. Harriet wrote that only Shelley, not herself, heard the noise. Besides Harriet and himself in bed, the five others in the house included the servants, not yet retired. After being fired on by the intruder and wrestling him on the ground, Shelley somehow found his second pistol, perhaps wounded his assailant, who fled into the woods after pronouncing a curse of revenge consisting of threats of murdering his wife and raping her sister. Later that night the intruder or his agent returned to fire upon Shelley who, having conveniently excused Dan, was alone. Miraculously, the ball went through his gown without harming him and lodged in the wooden wainscot. Attacking the intruder with a handy sword necessary to continue the plot, Dan's reentrance caused the attacker to flee once more into the night. Dan would testify to anything Shelley said.

The early chapters of *Zastrozzi* provide a text for this account. The powerful Zastrozzi was seeking revenge upon Verezzi, "the hapless victim of unmerited persecution." Kidnapped by Zastrozzi in his sleep on a dark night, Verezzi "awoke—and overcome by excess of terror, started violently from the ruffians' arms" as they carried him through the woods. After the night's "violence of the storm" with "pealing thunders . . . and lightning," Verezzi is taken to "a cottage . . . remote from other habitation" where a physician declared "that the disorder having attacked his brain, a tranquillity of mind was absolutely necessary for his recovery." Deceived by his captors, Verezzi's "whole thoughts were now bent upon the means for effecting his escape." After a lonely walk to a "woody eminence," Verezzi returned to the cottage "convinced . . . he was at this instant in the power of his bitterest enemy," Zastrozzi. Bent on revenge, Zastrozzi was on the heath with his underling, Ugo.

As "Verezzi leaned against the casement," he saw in the "darkness . . . the towering form of Zastrozzi, and Ugo" speaking "denunciations of anger." Having "advanced from the casement to the door," they called for another henchman, Bernado, who "entered, and Verezzi, lifting his arm high, aimed a knife at the villain's heart." Bernado stepped aside "and the knife was fixed firmly in the door-case." Bernado and Verezzi fought a "violent contest" until Verezzi's "dextorous blow . . . precipitated" Bernado "down the steep stair case." Verezzi escaped through an open door, running in fright across the moonlit heath believing he could see Zastrozzi's eye and hear his voice.[49]

This Tanyrallt-like scenario, and similar stalker themes in *St. Irvyne,* illumine the complicated set of conscious and unconscious motives contributing to Shelley's fleeing Wales. The immediate trigger was Dan Healey's arrival that day after six months' imprisonment. After paying fifteen shillings a week for his support, Shelley borrowed £5 on February 10 from John Williams, sending it to Dan for travel expenses from Barnstaple to Tanyrallt.[50] Dan's arrival meant Shelley now had four servants to support. The Shelleys had wanted to dismiss Dan before arriving in Lynmouth and by the time they let him go six months later they were dissatisfied with his "unprincipled conduct."[51] Dan probably brought stories of the government's surveillance, and Shelley could have been worried that an agent had followed Dan to Tanyrallt. Dan's arrival reinforced Shelley's suspicion and anxiety about Leeson having contacted the Home Office about his radical behavior. In her account, Harriet went out of her way to exonerate Dan because of his unfamiliarity with the house. Shelley had Dan exit the room, clinching his being alone when the supposed assailant's bullet pierced Shelley's nightgown. Dan reentered as the attacker was escaping from Shelley's sword. This is one of the most contrived events in the account, lending credence to Cameron's surmise that Shelley shot the hole in his gown, the ball lodging in the wainscot.[52] Hogg's disbelief in the assassination story was based in part on the "unanimous" opinion of those who had "carefully investigated the matter." Suspecting Dan's possible role in the affair, Hogg had prejudiced, anti-Irish views of Dan, a "short, thickset, hard-featured . . . pure Celtic type . . . a stupid, starved savage."[53] Dan was not too limited to reach remote Tanyrallt expeditiously. After Dan's arrival, Shelley loaded his two pistols before retiring, "expecting to have occasion for them," as Harriet reported. She was silent as to why Shelley expected to need them. Peacock shared Hogg's view of the event after he visited North Wales the summer of 1813 and heard "the matter much talked of." He reported that those who "examined the premises on the following morning" found the grass "appeared to have been much trampled and rolled on, but there were no footmarks on the wet ground, except between the beaten spot and the window; and the impression of the ball on the wainscot showed that the pistol had been fired towards the window, and not from it." Peacock thought this "appeared conclusive" that all the "operations" occurred indoors and believed the "mental phenomena" involving Shelley's "semi-delusion" recurred later in his life.[54]

Any explanation of that night's events must consider the very different versions presented by Harriet and by Mrs. Williams. Most likely, neither account gives a full or reliable account of what happened. Harriet's account, omitting any mention of the devil apparition, accomplished two things for Shelley in his need to escape Tremadoc: it placed the blame on external persecutors and it absolved his behavior and emotional condition for what took place. Conversely, Mrs. Williams's account, absolving anyone in the Tremadoc community or other outside agents, lodged the incident in Shelley's disordered emotional state. This version must be given serious credence as Williams was the person with whom Shelley spent most time outside the Tanyrallt household. Shelley and Harriet acknowledge his emotional disturbance but imply it was the result of the trauma of the two attacks. Did the guerrilla warfare of that night's two engagements produce a post-traumatic stress syndrome in Shelley or was there no intruder, Shelley's behavior being the result of an acute panic attack? Or, as Leeson thought, was this a hoax of Shelley's, designed to extricate himself from Tremadoc?

These three interpretations, or some mix of them, have split Shelley's biographers. Those who knew him personally—Medwin, Hogg, and Peacock—adopted the hallucination theory. Dowden, in 1886, straddled the fence but believed Shelley's mind was "unhinged" with "thick-coming fancies [that] painfully oppressed him." He gave guarded credence to the actuality of the night's events.[55] In 1940, White, concluding "the assault on Shelley almost certainly never happened," presented a detailed and measured case for Shelley's mental state as the reality in the situation.[56]

The major break with these two interpretations came in Cameron's variant of Leeson's belief that Shelley staged the evening's activities while in an emotional state of "trapped desperation" over an urgent need to escape Tremadoc. Cameron argued that Shelley perpetrated a hoax with a "novel-of-terror scene" consistent with his earlier and later behavior.[57] Anxiety about his £400 in debts was preying upon Shelley. As part of his early effort to lease Tanyrallt, Shelley had told Williams of a "deed in Doctors' Common" that proved he would "come into posession of a large property" when he became of age. This belief had no basis, but Shelley could reasonably expect Timothy to give him some kind of settlement to avoid his son depleting the family estate with *post obit* bonds.[58] Shelley was uncertain what his father might do, and his August birthday was not imminent. He had been imprisoned for his local debts, he was burdened by the embankment project, he wanted to rescue his poems in Dublin (with Dan's help), and he was anxious about knowledge of the government's surveillance Dan may have brought. Cameron believed that as Shelley enacted the night's hoax he entered into "the mood" of his fantasies. At some point, ruse and psychological reality became one.

Holmes, following an article by Dowling, believed Shelley actually was attacked.[59] Dowling thought only the first attack was real; Holmes believed both attacks happened but was silent concerning the identity of the intruders. He suggested the first intruder's mission was to "search for incriminating papers." To explain how this benign thief became a would-be murderer and rapist, Holmes believed Shelley "muddled" his account to Harriet, intentionally or otherwise. It was Shelley who fired the first shot, breaking one of the windows that was shattered that night. Holmes, believing the intruder probably sent "a friend or servant" to take his "revenge" on the second attack, accounts for the devil by assuming Shelley was being intentionally frightened "by some deliberately contrived theatrical 'apparition.'" Cameron skeptically responded to Holmes's version: "It must have been a busy night at Tremadoc, what with hit-man servants and mobile stage effects."[60]

The "Devil" apparition, seemingly a hallucination, fits the interpretation of a panic attack with hallucinatory and delusional features. The drawing of the devil is an "exact copy" made from the original drawing Shelley made on the screen for Williams. The drawing's validity was questioned by Holmes as part of a "myth" that Shelley saw an apparition.[61] However, the devil's body and horn-like projections are strikingly similar to nude torsos and fantasy heads, including a two-horned devil, which Shelley drew in the manuscript notebook in which he was composing his essay, *On the Devil, and Devils*.[62] In another notebook, he drew a nude torso similar in stance to the Tanyrallt devil, a walking or running figure holding a sword-like object.[63] An important feature of Shelley's drawing of the Tanyrallt devil, often overlooked, is its two-headed quality. Both heads are drawn to fit the torso. This Doppelgänger fits the probable nature of Shelley's increasingly regressive hallucinatory experience that night. In the Williamses' account, he first "fancied that he saw a man's face on the drawing room window." After shooting this image in the window, which was shattered, he "bounced out on the grass" where "he saw leaning against a tree the ghost, or as he said the Devil." The man's head is a profile peering through a window-like square; the devil's head is a frontal view replete with horns and a Medusa-like snake in his hair. The devil's head in his manuscript notebook is an amalgam of these two heads, having the profile and hooked nose of the man's head. Both devils have teeth in their open mouths, which have a smiling if not leering quality. The human torsos that resemble the Tanyrallt devil's torso are a sexless figure with a dagger pursuing a hermaphrodite in a landscape evocative of Tanyrallt. An earlier appearance of the devil's horns in Shelley's fantasy life was influenced by his accusation about his mother's infidelity with Graham in which he cornuted his father's brow with a pair of horns.[64]

If there were no intruder that night, the reconstruction of the events, including the physical evidence, must be consistent with Shelley as the one actor. Whether there were two episodes, as seems likely, or only one, Shelley was the only observer of each. If Dan appeared on the scene in the second episode, it was in time to hasten the disappearance of the "intruder," but not in time to allow Dan to see him as he escaped. The only physical description of the intruder, in Medwin's first account, was embellished years later. Given Medwin's unreliable memory, little confidence can be placed in this description. If three shots were fired, both shots in the first episode could have come from Shelley's two pistols, which he would have reloaded in the interval before the second episode. It appears two windows were broken, one in each episode, as Shelley asked Williams to cover the "broken windows." One of the balls lodged in the wainscot and apparently came from within the room. Assuming this was the ball that also pierced Shelley's gown and the curtain, it is certainly possible that Shelley fired through his own gown as Cameron suggested. Only Shelley and Harriet report this hole in the gown. If Shelley did fire through his gown it would not rule out a "mental reality" theory of the events.[65] As for the struggle on the ground, assuming it involved neither an intruder nor Dan, Shelley could have been grappling with an illusory persecutor on either the first or second episode.

What was Shelley's emotional state this night? This complex issue bears on our understanding of this night's events and on our understanding of Shelley's personality. The separate accounts

given by Shelley, Harriet, and the Williamses agree that Shelley
was emotionally disturbed at the end of the second episode.
Williams, apparently the first person sent for, found Shelley "in a
sad state of distress and excitement" and after seeing his drawing
of the "Devil" considered "his mind was astray." If the report that
Shelley set fire to the "woods" to burn the apparition is accurate,
it may have been earlier, given the wet, stormy weather. Shelley's
continuing disturbance is evident in his letter to Hookham the next
day, including Harriet's appended note that he was "dreadfully
nervous." A day or two later, writing to Williams, he was coherent
enough to request money and repairs to the windows, but wildly
misdated his letter. As we shall see, his next letter to Williams
about a week later has a clear paranoid tone. About this time he
wrote Hookham he was "now recovering from an illness brought
on by watching fatigue & alarm," and two weeks after the episodes
Harriet wrote Hookham the account of the evening to "spare" the
still "nervous" Shelley from recalling "the horrors of that night."

There has been agreement, first emphasized by Hogg and Peacock and reiterated by subsequent biographers, that Shelley's experience that night was part of a pattern of behavior extending
from a time much earlier than Tanyrallt until the end of his life.[66]
Dramatic as it was, it was not an isolated event. In addition to the
earlier Keswick incident, there were at least two other related incidents, including one several years later in which Shelley tried to
convince an unbelieving Peacock that Williams of Tremadoc had
mysteriously visited him to warn him that his father and uncle
were plotting to have him locked up. Peacock said he had argued
with Shelley on several other occasions against such "semi-delusions," believing Shelley was encouraged to repeat them by the
"credulity" of others. Peacock believed that the "fabric" of these
"semi-delusions . . . vanished under the touch of investigation."[67]

A version of the Tanyrallt incident involving Eliza Westbrook was
provided by a later friend of Shelley's. Henry Reveley believed
Eliza's "persecution of the young couple" was "backed" by "Sir
Timothy, whose rage against his son was unbounded, unrelenting
even after Shelley's death."[68]

The Tanyrallt and Keswick attacks, a year apart, bear remarkable similarities. Each community was concerned by press reports
of robbers or murderers in the vicinity, including accounts of several murders in North Wales.[69] Tremadoc villagers believed that
the murderer of a farm servant girl before the Shelleys arrived was

a madman who would strike again. Caught in nearby Dolgelly, the murderer was hanged in April, after the Shelleys had left the area. Shelley probably was aware of this murder which aroused local alarm while he was there, and one hundred fifty years later was still being written about.[70]

Both the Tanyrallt and Keswick incidents occurred one week before Shelley left the communities, some of whose inhabitants he had antagonized. Both episodes were disbelieved as actual attacks by locals. After each incident, the Shelleys found refuge for a week with a sympathetic family before departing for Ireland, their destination both times. Shelley, the sole witness of both attacks, responded in both cases to a "noise" and then scuffled on the ground with an intruder who fled when another man came onto the scene. Shelley reported no physical harm or pain from his Tanyrallt scuffles, but years later he believed that pressure from his Tanyrallt assailant's knee caused his excruciating recurrent side pain until an Italian doctor convinced him otherwise. Physical harm also accompanied the attack in "The Voyage." Prior to the Keswick and Tanyrallt incidents, Shelley had anxiety symptoms, depression, headaches, and paranoid fears. Harriet was the first to write of the details of each incident, Shelley recovering from continuing fear and anxiety. Several days before the Keswick attack, he sent Elizabeth Hitchener *The Devil's Walk*. Its description of the devil's "grin so wide" with "Iron teeth" fits both the drawing of the Tanyrallt devil and the toothy devil in his manuscript notebook.

Another possible scenario for the Tanyrallt attack, mentioned years later by John Cam Hobhouse, was that Shelley copied his "pretended attack" from "exactly the same trick . . . played by Rousseau."[71] In *The Confessions* (Book 12), which Shelley read as early as 1811, Rousseau's account of being attacked at night by some locals has similarities to Shelley's Tanyrallt attack, including being awakened at midnight upon hearing a noise and having a servant come to his aid. In addition to a predilection for acting out literary scenes, Shelley indulged in acts of fait accompli, precipitously escaping a conflict scene without directly confronting the parties involved.[72]

At crucial times of stress, including Keswick and Tanyrallt, Shelley's acute "attacks" were suggestive of transient psychotic episodes with paranoid overtones. Others have identified Shelley's "clearly defined paranoid pattern," an "obvious persecution complex," or a "delusion of persecution" that at times was on "the verge of insanity."[73] Placing Shelley in any diagnostic category ignores the strengths and weaknesses that formed his unique, complex personality.

Recovering from his Tanyrallt attack, Shelley slowly regained his composure during the week with the Nanneys and implemented his plan to revisit Ireland. He had led Williams to believe he would come back to Tremadoc, but made their continuing friendship contingent on a complete reversal of any suspicions Williams may have had as to his motives. A week after the attack, awaiting the ferry from Bangor to Ireland, Leeson's letter arrived claiming he had received Shelley's Irish pamphlet from Williams. Feeling betrayed, Shelley wrote Williams he knew Leeson's claim "to be perfectly true." Despite Williams's "deciet" [sic], Shelley knew "the unalterable goodness" of his heart. However, Shelley asserted he was able to "trace all the springs of your conduct . . . all the windings of your mind are known to me." Williams knew him "but little, whilst I know you very well." Projecting his suspiciousness, Shelley added, "you suspect & I confide. . . . As I told you when we parted unless you are explicit & unreserved to me I am fighting in the Dark. . . . I shall believe you in the future . . . but never decieve me again."[74] Shelley's "fighting in the Dark" perhaps tipped his hand as to dynamics behind his earlier traumatic evening. This letter and Harriet's subsequent censored letter to Hookham express their "horrible suspicion" that "every one seemed to be plotting against us."[75]

Before embarking for Dublin, the money from Hookham arrived. Shelley gratefully felt "rescued" and Hookham's "confidence made amends to our feelings wounded by the suspicion coldness & villainy of the world." Having recovered from his "illness," they expected to arrive in Dublin in two days, March 8. He assured Hookham, "we are perfectly relieved from all pecuniary difficulties."[76]

Shelley's flight from Tremadoc involved feelings of being under siege, not only from a delusional attacker, suspicious neighbors, untrustworthy friends, and carping creditors, but from his changing relationship with Harriet.

15

Marital Disengagement

THEY WERE ALL "DREADFULLY ILL" DURING THE STORMY FORTY-hour crossing to Dublin. For Harriet, almost six months pregnant, the voyage was particularly difficult.[1] Shelley came to Dublin to obtain his earlier poems, which he planned to publish with *Queen Mab*. He sent *Queen Mab* without the notes to Hookham, asking him to candidly criticize the poem as a "friend." Despite "its various errors, I am determined to give it to the world. . . . If you do not dread the arm of the law, or any exasperation of public opinion against yourself, I wish that it should be printed & published immediately." Not sanguine about its reception, Shelley hoped it would appeal to an influential younger generation, the "sons & daughters" of "aristocrats."[2] *Queen Mab*'s later success came from its appeal to the lower and middle classes ready for the emerging socialist thought of the nineteenth century.

Pleading poverty, Shelley wanted Williams to ask his brother Owen to lend him £25 until an expected London loan arrived. Testing Williams's loyalty, Shelley said his non-compliance would indicate the cooling of Williams's friendship. He enticed Williams with possible future financial support, professing "the greatest zeal for your interests."[3] However, he soon intimated to Williams he might not return to Tremadoc. After Williams objected to Shelley's accusing him of treachery, Shelley denied the charge condescendingly. Shelley said that failure to obtain his £400 London loan to pay his Tremadoc debts would give "Leeson's lies" credence and Shelley would "never return again."[4] His statement confirmed the financial motivation behind his fleeing. Eliza wrote Williams that she and Harriet would never again reside at Tanyrallt and asked him to send their boxes to their father's residence. Downgrading the Tanyrallt attack to "unpleasant scenes," she thought the "neighbourhood is too corrupt for us." Williams eventually sent the

Westbrook boxes but never sent Shelley's, one of which probably contained his lost seditious poem, "God Save the King."[5]

Staying two weeks in Dublin, Shelley used John Lawless's address and wrote Hogg to join them in Dublin before they all returned to London. Upon arriving at Lawless's home, Hogg learned that the Shelleys had just gone to Killarney. He spent a week in Dublin before returning home.

Despite Shelley's desire to re-inject Hogg into Harriet's life, Eliza and Harriet probably wanted to avoid Hogg and they departed for western Ireland. Harriet was subjected to three tiring days—with one brief overnight at Cork—over two hundred forty miles of rough Irish roads to Killarney. Finding a cottage on one of the islands of the lakes of Killarney, Shelley unpacked his traveling library. He later told Hogg that miserable weather made "navigation" of the lakes "perilous" and "vessels were swamped and sunk in a moment" from the "sudden gusts and treacherous whirlwinds."[6]

Receiving a note from Hogg after six days in Killarney, Shelley and Harriet immediately departed, leaving behind Eliza, Dan, and Shelley's library. The two transferred without rest in Cork and arrived in Dublin to find Hogg had left for London the day before. Awaiting Shelley was Williams's letter with Elizabeth Hitchener's final attack on her former soul mate. Shelley's stratagem to get money from Owen Williams evidently succeeded, as he thanked John Williams for his brother's £25 and denied having used the "request as a test of your goodness." Some of Owen Williams's loan may have freed his poems from Stockdale in Dublin.[7] Despite their hard traveling, Harriet got little rest as they departed April 2 for Holyhead.

Shelley and Harriet stayed briefly at Mr. Westbrook's before moving to Cooke's Hotel on Albemarle Street. Hogg, calling on Shelley and Harriet before Eliza arrived, learned that Shelley was "evidently weary" of Eliza. When Shelley made no secret of enjoying her absence, "Harriet smiled in silence." Shelley's freedom from Eliza was short-lived. After sending Shelley's books, Eliza and Dan arrived mid-April in London where she "assumed her sovereign functions."[8]

When Eliza and Dan arrived, Shelley took lodgings at 41 Half Moon Street, retaining one or more rooms at nearby Cooke's Hotel. Hogg said Harriet wanted this more "fashionable situation" on Half Moon Street where Shelley placed his books in rows along the floor, piled on tables and chairs, and tucked into corners of the fireplace. Mrs. Newton pictured Shelley on Half Moon Street perched in "a little projecting window . . . book in hand . . . like some young lady's lark, hanging outside for air and song."[9] Criticized by "some persons" for the expense of maintaining two abodes, Shelley said the hotel was "more convenient for negotiations" than his Half Moon Street lodgings.[10] Living beyond his means, Shelley soon was negotiating with his father. He also met with Williams, in town from Tremadoc, about his Welsh debts.

Hookham's refusal to publish *Queen Mab* possibly hastened Shelley's return. He and Hookham apparently quarreled and their relationship cooled.[11] Hookham became more concerned about prosecution for publishing the poem, as its blasphemous message became clearer with accumulating notes. Hookham possibly helped produce the handsome volume, but his name is absent. Conforming to English law, Shelley's name as printer appeared twice. Harriet wrote to Mrs. Nugent that *Queen Mab* was being printed but "it must not be published under pain of death, because it is too much against every existing establishment." It was "to be privately distributed to his friends, and some copies sent over to America."[12] Two hundred fifty copies with notes probably appeared in late June. Sending out copies, Shelley removed the two pages with his name and the page with the four-stanza poem dedicated to his wife, "Harriet *****."[13]

From that summer of 1813 until the present, *Queen Mab* has never been out of print. Extracts were printed in the *Theological Inquirer* in 1815, but only seventy copies had been distributed in 1822 when the remaining one hundred eighty were offered for sale.[14] Spearheaded by Richard Carlile in 1821, radical publishers were selling four pirated editions. With the flowering of reviews in 1821, *Queen Mab* "became an important weapon in the arsenal of British working-class radicalism."[15] Following the rising trade union movement of the 1820s, the link between Shelley and the emerging socialism of the Owenites was forged in 1831 when Robert Dale Owen and Frances Wright published an American edition of *Queen Mab*. The influential 1832 pocket-sized pirated edition of *Queen Mab* became "the Chartists' Bible."[16] At least fourteen editions of *Queen Mab* had appeared by 1845. Three years later, Engels began translating it.

Queen Mab had legal and political influence. In Shelley's lifetime, the pirate publisher William Clark was imprisoned after being attacked by The Society for the Suppression of Vice. In 1842, the respected publisher Moxon won a moral victory in a court case involving the charge of blasphemous libel for printing *Queen Mab*.[17]

In a triumph of style over budget, Shelley bought a carriage from coachmaker Thomas Charters soon after arriving in London. The handsome vehicle, correctly called a chariot, was intended for in-town use, accomodating two in the cab and a third on a sliding seat. However, it became Shelley's primary mode of long-distance travel on his subsequent trips in Britain and on the Continent. Deeply in debt, Shelley had no cash to pay the carriage's approximately £200 price, not to mention the costs of horses, maintenance, and driver.[18] Hogg called it "Harriet's fine, new carriage," and before long Charters had the bailiffs out for Shelley's arrest for non-payment of his bills. At John Newton's home, Hogg was mistaken for Shelley and pounced upon by the bailiffs.[19]

Harriet optimistically wrote to Mrs. Nugent that "Mr. Shelley's family are very eager to be reconciled to him" and she would not be surprised if they were invited to Field Place "in a week or two.... Their conduct is most surprising, after treating us like dogs."[20] Harriet, who would never see Field Place, had a dinner guest, "Mr. Ryan," apparently an Irish friend of both Lawless and Mrs. Nugent. A month later, just before her baby's birth, Harriet again mentioned Ryan, who was about to leave London.

Shelley, having written to the Duke of Norfolk, was surprised when Norfolk called on him and invited him to meet the next day. Using illness as a pretext to avoid Norfolk, Shelley began a fruitless exchange with his father, desiring "a Restoration to the intercourse with yourself & my Family which I have forfeited by my Follies." Trying to "convince" Timothy that his "most unfavourable traits" had changed, Shelley was willing "to make any concessions" for a family reconciliation.[21]

This hopeful note briefly buoyed Harriet, but Timothy was unmoved. Whitton again instructed Timothy how to reply, apparently telling him his son should "publickly disavow" his atheistic views by writing to the Oxford authorities that he had returned to Christianity. Shelley's angry retort made Timothy "sorry" that no "change had taken place in some of the most unfavourable Traits in your Character [and] avow'd opinions." Timothy declined "all further Communication, or any Personal Interview" until Shelley changed and "you will consider this as my final answer to anything you may have to offer."[22] Shelley then wrote Norfolk regretting taking his valuable time in the "vain and impossible task of reconciling myself and my father," whose letter he enclosed.[23] Responding to Shelley's willingness to "compromise," the Duke brought father and son together at a large party. According to Hogg, the Earl of Oxford pointed to Timothy and asked a pleased Shelley, "Pray who is that very strange old man . . . who talks so much, so loudly, and in so extraordinary a manner, and all about himself?" Shelley identified his father and walked home with the Earl.[24]

Hogg, still Harriet's ardent admirer, visited and noted that Shelley's emotional difficulties were evident. Writing to Harriet, he was "sorry that Bysshe is unwell it is hard that his heart should be so good & his head so bad." Hogg called her "une jolie petite dèesse." Almost eight months pregnant, Harriet frostily spurned being Hogg's goddess by penning her rejection on his letter.[25] Despite Shelley's efforts that she respond to Hogg's attentions, she resisted having him in their lodgings. When Harriet did acquiesce to invite him, Shelley wrote Hogg saying he was "extremely hurt by Harriets conduct towards you." In this marital sparring, Harriet agreed to address the letter.[26]

Shelley poetically implored Harriet ("To Harriet," or "Thy look of love") not to reject Hogg, begging her, "In mercy let him not endure / The misery of a fatal cure." Protesting Eliza's controlling influence over Harriet, he ended, "Oh, trust for once no erring guide! . . . And pity if thou canst not love."[27]

Shelley was trying to avoid his guide—Godwin—and his financial demands until he turned twenty-one. Godwin, after writing eleven letters to Shelley since being stood up the previous November, finally located him in early June. Shelley's informing him of Harriet's aversion to his wife brought Mrs. Godwin's reconciliation call. Godwin then dined with Shelley, along with Peacock and Hookham,[28] whose presence suggested the conflict over publishing *Queen Mab* was past.

Harriet's letter to Mrs. Nugent from Cooke's Hotel June 22 did not mention her imminent child, born the next day. Sorry to hear Lawless was in debtor's prison, she said that Daniel Healey would be returning to Ireland. Only from Shelley's financial correspondence do we hear of Ianthe Eliza Shelley's birth. Her pending birth and his approaching twenty-first birthday made him increasingly anxious about any inheritance changes his father might have made. In mid-June, he sent the first of a series of urgent letters to his Horsham legal adviser, Thomas Medwin, senior. Shelley anxiously inquired if Medwin had "the least doubt" that he was "the

safe heir to a large landed property?" Wishing to consult with Medwin, he was unable to leave town because he was "hourly expecting Mrs. Shelley's confinement."[29]

Medwin agreed to take up Shelley's "professional Business. . . .
Your Father's Conduct has been towards Me in every respect so offensive and Insolent . . . his Gross and malicious Behaviour (totally
Unprovoked). . . . I despise him too much even to Renew any intercourse with him." Medwin contacted a London solicitor, H. Silverlock, whose early July opinion was that Shelley had no immediate way to access money from the estate.[30]

Shelley then wrote Medwin, "Mrs. Shelley has been safely delivered of a little girl & is now rapidly recovering." Shelley hoped to
meet Medwin soon in London. Knowing his father would be furious
if he knew of their correspondence, he assured Medwin of "my secrecy & prudence."[31] Shelley may also have heard rumors about
Timothy's efforts to disinherit him. By the time Medwin dined with
the Shelleys in early July, his further service, after Silverlock's
opinion, was moot.

Harriet's blue-eyed daughter was born June 23, most likely at
their Half Moon Street lodgings. Her name on her birth certificate,
which she possibly never saw, is Eliza Ianthe Shelley. Her first
name was for Harriet's sister, the second for Shelley's *Queen Mab*
heroine. The babe quickly became Ianthe, perhaps due to Eliza's
continuing presence. She was called Ianthe Eliza in her father's
early poems and on her tombstone when she died in 1876.[32]

After Ianthe's birth, Harriet's social circle contracted as Shelley's expanded. He took long walks with Hogg through obscure
London streets, hoping to avoid his creditors. When Shelley took
Hogg to meet the Newtons, the two were greeted by the five naked
Newton children, ranging in age from five to twelve. Expecting
their friend Shelley, but not the stranger, the children quickly ran
upstairs from the eyes of the startled Hogg. Mrs. Newton privately
practiced nude air bathing three hours a day but failed to convert
Hogg, who was more susceptible to her "delightful" vegetarian din-
ners. Hogg temporarily practiced the vegetable diet but Shelley
went further, refusing to wear material made from animals, including wool and leather. Inveighing against "the muffling of our
bodies in superfluous apparel," he preferred going hatless and eschewed a heavy overcoat for a long black coat made of cotton jean.[33]

Generally indifferent to meals, Shelley preferred tea or water
and bread, often eaten with honey or "common pudding raisins."

Following Dr. Lambe's stricture, he installed a distillation apparatus to avoid lead in ordinary water. Rejecting hard liquor, he took an occasional glass or two of wine, preferably white. Hogg believed Shelley's most eccentric taste, indulged on walks among pine forests, was licking "with relish" the resinous turpentine oozings from the bark of fir and larch trees. Hogg claimed that fiddlers at a dance complained that Shelley had "eaten up all our rosin!" Shelley's favorite dish, panada, was water-soaked bread sprinkled with sugar and nutmeg.

Shelley's food preferences and dietary practices came from such sources as John Newton's *Return to Nature* and Trotter's *The Nervous Temperament*. Joseph Ritson, a politically radical scholar quoted by Shelley in *A Vindication of Natural Diet*, stressed the moral benefits of vegetarianism.[34] Another authoritative source, Monboddo's *Origin and Progress of Language*, denounced clothes, liquor, meat, smoky air, excessive wealth, and war, not to mention Monboddo's emphasis on sexual excess and venereal disease.[35] Shelley's food fads were fed by his health fears. He probably read that panada could aid in the recovery from gonorrhea. He enjoyed raisins and bread, prescribed by physicians, including Erasmus Darwin, for such problems as leprosy, syphilis, and gleet. Products of pine trees, including turpentine and resin, were prescribed for urethral discharge and other gonorrheal complications.[36] Shelley's hypochondriacal fears increased in the last months of 1813, paralleling his increasing tension with Harriet and his financial conflict with his father. Soon, he developed his most peculiar hypochondriacal delusion.

While Harriet was recovering from her delivery, Shelley was socializing. A young lady had enticed him to dance at a social given by Mrs. Newton, who also was the hostess at a social evening at Vauxhall Gardens attended by Shelley and Hogg. Shelley and Mrs. Newton, Hogg observed, might strike a "mundane critic" as having "a most desperate flirtation between them." Mrs. Newton was less impressed with Hogg's unpublished novel, *Leonora*, "the production of a very young man."[37]

Shelley now became enamored of another Harriet, Mrs. Newton's startlingly attractive older sister, Harriet Boinville. An added interest was Harriet Boinville's beautiful eighteen-year-old married daughter, Cornelia Turner, who lived with her mother in Pimlico. Cornelia's lawyer husband, Thomas Turner, was content to live near Bracknell, thirty miles west of London. He preceded Shelley as Godwin's protégé, having begged Godwin to save him from "a violent affection" for a male youth who was "dragging me to ignorance and vice."[38] Turner now served Godwin in his tangled legal and financial matters, including those involving Shelley.

Mrs. Boinville—who with her husband had helped free Lafayette from an Austrian prison—was painted wearing the red sash of a French republican.[39] Presiding over a radical salon when she met Shelley, Mrs. Boinville did not know that her husband, serving Napoleon in the Russian campaign, had died on the retreat from Moscow. With prematurely white hair framing her striking face, Shelley called her "Maimuna," the mysterious spinner by a pinewood fire in Southey's *Thalaba*.

Mrs. Boinville soon induced Shelley and Hogg to learn Italian. Shelley outdistanced Hogg's slow pace with Tasso's *Jerusalem Delivered* and quickly absorbed on his own Ariosto's *Orlando Furioso*. Shelley found this tale of madness through love "exciting, stimulating, provoking," re-reading passages with "wild rapture" to Hogg, presumably including its more ribald cantos. Shelley became fond of Petrarch's love sonnets through "a most engaging lady," probably Cornelia Turner.

A week or two after Ianthe's birth, Shelley again uprooted his family, moving to a quiet street in Pimlico closer to Mrs. Boinville and the Newtons. During their month-long stay in Pimlico, Hogg called frequently but was not allowed inside the house. He never saw Ianthe, claiming Harriet did not want him to see the baby's slight blemish in one eye. However, Harriet wrote Mrs. Nugent her baby "is so fair, with such blue eyes, that the more I see her the more beautiful she looks."[40] By early August, as Hogg prepared to leave London for the north, Thomas Love Peacock took his place with the Shelleys.

Just returned from Wales, Peacock was a sympathetic companion for Harriet. He and Harriet made fun of the Boinville–Newton social set and drew the disdain "of the more hot-headed of the party."[41] Newton told his fellow atheist, Peacock, about the upper and lower realms of Oromazes and Ahrimanes in Zoroastrian religion. These ideas influenced Peacock's long poem *Ahrimanes*, begun about this time. Shelley's later allusion to Zoroaster in *Prometheus Unbound* suggests he and Peacock discussed these ideas.[42]

Contradicting Hogg, Peacock considered Shelley was "extremely fond of his children . . . pre-eminently an affectionate father." Shelley tenderly walked up and down the room for a long time with Ianthe in his arms repeating a song of his own making, "Yáhmani, Yáhmani, Yáhmani, Yáhmani." Peacock found the song discordant, but it lulled the fretful babe.[43] Shelley's sonnet, "To Ianthe," played on the meaning of her name, "violet flower," praising her "azure eyes," a "fair and fragile blossom." Another sonnet, "Evening: to Harriet," was composed during a time of intense sunspot activity. Shelley, as Harriet's questioning lover, asks should he "coldly count the spots within thy sphere?" and "Pick flaws in our close-woven happiness."[44]

According to Hogg, Shelley spent the late hours conversing with the young women in the Newton–Boinville circles, who found his conversation so "enchanting." His new fame as the author of the revolutionary *Queen Mab* added to his charm. One young woman thought that Shelley, "so modest," could create "terrible havoc . . . if he were at all rakish." His admirers tried in vain to induce him to match conversational styles with Fanny Burney, now Madame D'Arblay, the old friend of the deceased Dr. Lind. After promising to attend a lecture on women's bodily deformities from wearing stays, Shelley stayed away. The woman lecturer regretted his defection, telling Hogg, the only male attending, that Shelley could have affected a great change in this deplorable custom.

When Mrs. Boinville and her daughter Cornelia moved from Pimlico to outlying Bracknell, Shelley soon followed. A week before turning twenty-one, and shortly before Harriet's eighteenth birthday, he again uprooted his family, moving close to the Boinville mother and daughter and fleeing from the creditors and bailiffs. Owing more than £2000, he had failed to reach a settlement with his father upon attaining his majority.[45] Harriet told Mrs. Nugent they were uncertain how long they would be in their small Bracknell house, High Elms, as they might have to go "a greater distance." Her hopes dashed for a visit to Field Place, Harriet felt "our doom is decided." Shelley was "of age," but "no longer heir to the immense property of his sires," who were "trying to take it away, and will I am afraid succeed." They believed Timothy secretly had put the matter "into Chancery." John Williams asked for payment on Shelley's debts, but Harriet replied they lacked the £10 needed to pay for Daniel Healey's return to Dublin. Hopefully, selling their Tanyrallt furniture might "fetch a great sum" to reimburse Girdlestone. By early September, Shelley saw his father who, receiving him "very kindly," denied the rumors about disinheriting him. One of Shelley's sisters wrote that his father was "doing all in his power" to prevent Shelley from being arrested for debts and that his mother tells Shelley "everything she hears." The Shelleys again thought of returning to Nantgwillt.[46]

Although debt-ridden, Shelley was often in London during August trying to raise money for the Godwins' failing book business. Legally an adult, Shelley could enter into Godwin's machinations by obtaining *post obit* bonds payable upon the death of his grandfather and father at exorbitant rates of interest. Godwin, relying on a baronet's estate to secure his wanted capital,[47] not only took Shelley to obtain the necessary life insurance for a *post obit* bond but sent Mrs. Godwin to Horsham to obtain the necessary family settlement papers. In early October, Shelley sold his first *post obit* bond for £2000 at a four for one rate to a moneylender named Starling. The £500 Shelley received went to Godwin and to Francis Place, Godwin's creditor. Place noted that these *post obit* bonds from Shelley meant that the wily Godwin, free from being sued for the debts he had "wholly transferred" to Shelley, could say he had now paid these debts. It was the opening move in a tortuous Shelley–Godwin interplay of money and love that dogged the poet until he died. Shelley told Hookham, privy to this *post obit* deal, to keep secret everything he told him.[48]

Shelley's early October letter to Hookham from Warwick, said they were "on our way to the Lakes." Barely two months at Bracknell, Shelley again was fleeing. Peacock had joined the three Shelleys and Eliza in their overloaded carriage to Ambleside where they stayed at the Lowood Inn. Shelley again was acting the hero in Godwin's novel *Fleetwood.* The Lowood Inn was where Fleetwood wrote a letter of introduction to his philosopher friend.

Not mentioning the bailiffs they were fleeing, Harriet wrote Mrs. Nugent that their journey was a secret. She hoped Mrs. Nugent would join them, reciting a litany of betrayed Irish friendships, including Lawless and Daniel Healey (who later complained of the Shelleys' mistreatment). They still planned to go to Nantgwillt via Keswick and Shelley would see his father in November. Harriet had no hope the two "would settle anything."[49]

This journey north was a closing out of their marriage. In Keswick, they visited the Calverts, but Southey, recently made the Tory Poet Laureate, was away. Unable to find a suitable house for the winter and disliking the locals they met, they decided against Nantgwillt. Their pilgrimage ended where their marriage had begun, Edinburgh. After finding lodgings at 36 Frederick Street, Harriet wrote Mrs. Nugent that the two years she had been united "with Mr. Shelley . . . have been the happiest and longest years of my life." She felt she had lived "a long time. . . . Tho' my age is but eighteen, yet I feel as if I was much older."[50]

The Edinburgh stay had a medical cast, as John Grove was there pursuing his training. Possibly through him, Shelley befriended a young medical student from Brazil who took a warm interest in the poet and his work. Joachim Baptista Pereira, who "abominated" medicine, was a "frank, warm-hearted, very gentlemanly young man." Eagerly sharing Shelley's beliefs, he became a vegetarian and began translating *Queen Mab* into Portuguese. Years later, Peacock remembered two lines from an ode Pereira planned to append to his translation, "Sublime Shelley, cantor di verdade!" and "Surja *Queen Mab* a restaurar o mundo." Shelley met Pereira again in London and last corresponded with him in 1815 before his untimely death from tuberculosis.[51]

Encouraged by Peacock, Shelley read enthusiastically in the classics, including Tacitus, Cicero, and Homer, who became "Shelley's delight." Hogg pictured Shelley reading *The Iliad* and *The Odyssey* "by firelight . . . straining his sight" so close to the fire that his cheek "assumed the appearance of a roasted apple."[52] Shelley returned to Hume and after reading Laplace, was determined to attain "considerable proficiency in the physical sciences." He translated two essays of Plutarch as part of the second essay on vegetarianism he was writing, *On the Vegetable System of Diet*. Shelley's near-religious devotion to vegetarianism received brief treatment in another essay he was writing, *A Refutation of Deism*. Apparently, even the skeptical Peacock was temporarily converted to the vegetable diet.[53] Shelley had read Hogg's novel *Alexy Haimatoff* and, hearing the Hookhams had published it, warmly encouraged Hogg to write more. As for Hogg's replacement in the Shelley ménage, Peacock "is not very ardent, nor his views very comprehensive" but he is "a very mild agreable man, & good scholar."[54]

Things began unraveling in Edinburgh toward the end of November. Shelley, writing to Hogg that he would see him soon in London, first directly stated his desire to separate from Harriet: "I shall return to London alone. My evenings will often be spent at the Newtons, where I presume you are no infrequent visitor."[55] Hogg later said Shelley "was in a great hurry to quit Edinburgh . . . by himself . . . to get speedily out of the ocean of delights into which he had inconsiderately plunged." However, Shelley returned to London neither "a solitary" nor "free, but in custody."[56]

Peacock, carefully avoiding mentioning having accompanied the Shelleys to and from Edinburgh, resolutely denied any marital disharmony until Shelley met Mary months later.[57] Subsequent events indicate this was untrue. Shelley lived away from Harriet shortly after their return from Edinburgh. Shelley's letter to Hogg about returning alone to join friends and leaving his wife behind indicated obvious marital problems. Peacock possibly helped convince Shelley to abandon his idea of returning to London alone.[58] Before leaving, Shelley incurred a £13 bill for carriage repairs and the coachmaker did not release the vehicle until he received the guarantee of a William Dumbrick. Years later, the coachmaker was trying vainly to collect his money from Shelley's father.[59] To pay his lodgings bill, Shelley drew upon Hookham's account, explaining his "emergency is very pressing."[60]

Still wary of bailiffs, Shelley either deposited his family at Bracknell before proceeding into London or left them at Harriet's father's home. The murky details of the next months reflect an increasingly troubled period marked by frequent separations from Harriet. On December 10, a day or two after arriving in London, Shelley surprised Godwin by calling at Skinner Street. Having written twenty-three mostly unanswered letters to Shelley in the last months of 1813, Godwin eagerly resumed negotiations with his young rescuer.[61] If Shelley were trying to allay his guilt over hostile feelings toward Timothy by playing the good son to Godwin, it was a losing maneuver. Godwin's demands were incessant and all three characters in this economic drama had serious symptoms as the year ended. Timothy suffered another gout attack and Godwin, severely depressed, wrote a critique of *Queen Mab* and composed a self-analytic essay that stated, "But I shall not die."[62] By the end of 1813, Peacock reported, "Shelley was troubled by one of his most extraordinary delusions."[63]

Shelley's elephantiasis episode was recounted by Peacock, Hogg, and the Newtons' daughter, Madame Gatayes. As a young girl, she recalled Shelley was seated talking to her parents when "he suddenly slipped down to the ground, twisting about like an eel." When Mrs. Newton cried out "'What is the matter?' . . . In his most impressive tone, Shelley answered, 'I have the elephantiasis.'"[64] Peacock emphasized that the time of Shelley's elephantiasis episode was not "unimportant," late 1813, not the summer of 1813 assumed by some biographers. Peacock's precise dating was to counteract Hogg's wish to downplay Peacock's closeness to Shelley at this time.[65] Peacock's date also fits Hogg's reference to Shelley's medical reading on the topic. Among Shelley's Edinburgh medical contacts, his friend Pereira was writing his dissertation on a skin disease.

Hogg recounted that Shelley was seated in "a crowded stage-coach . . . opposite an old woman with very thick legs, who, as he imagined, was afflicted with elephantiasis." Shelley having "recently read a formidable description in some medical work" of the disease, it "had taken entire possession of his fanciful and impressible soul." Because the woman had been "dozing quietly" against Shelley, he believed he had caught her "very infectious" disease and "began to discover . . . unequivocal symptoms." Shelley's "female friends tried to laugh him out of his preposterous whim, bantered him and inquired, how he came to find out that his fair neighbour had such thick legs?" Although "a skilful and experienced surgeon" assured him he did not have elephantiasis, Shelley became "more thoroughly convinced than ever, that he was the victim of a cruel and incurable disease" and was "doomed to a miserable and inevitable death." After several weeks, Shelley forgot the disease "as suddenly" as it had begun.[66] Peacock, trying to comfort Shelley, quoted Lucretius's idea that elephantiasis only occurs in Egypt and "the delusion died away" as Shelley observed his legs and skin remained normal.

His friends' accounts suggest the sexual aspect of Shelley's hypochondriacal delusion. According to Peacock, Shelley "would draw the skin of his own hands, arms, and neck very tight" looking for any roughness. Discovering a lack of smoothness, "he would seize the person next to him" looking for such a deviation on their skin. This often included "startled young ladies in an evening party." Hogg's description suggests this occurred at the Newtons'. Shelley, "curiously surveying them," placed "his eyes close to their necks and bosoms, and feeling their breast and bare arms, in order to ascertain whether any of the fair ones had taken the horrible disease." Because of his "gravity and seriousness . . . they did not resist, or resent, the extraordinary liberties, but looked horrified, and as if they were about to undergo some severe surgical operation at his hands." Although the men watched "in silent and angry amazement . . . nobody interrupted his heartbroken han-

dlings." After the "lady of the house" assured Shelley that none of
the young ladies "had been infected," the dancing proceeded
"without further examinations."

Hogg's account, it has been suggested, possibly was infused with
a memory of a visit he and the "rather wild" Shelley had made to a
London brothel after their expulsion. Mrs. Newton was "the lady
of the house," and the "country dance" was one of Hogg's sexual
puns.[67] Hogg's pun-titled novel, *Alexy Haimatoff,* published about
the time of Shelley's elephantiasis delusion, hinted of high-toned
pornography. His Oxford notebook was strewn with sexual themes;
under the caption "Maidenhead," Hogg wrote, "the pleasure of being first to communicate good news."[68]

Hogg was not immune to his friend's probings. Shelley would rub
Hogg's arms, measure his legs and ankles, and "stealthily . . .
opened the bosom" of his shirt, inspecting for signs of the disease.
He repeated this ritual with associates and with strangers. Young
ladies were so impressed by his "solemnity . . . and the profound
melancholy of his fear-stricken and awe-inspiring aspect" that
they would "unquestionably have submitted themselves" to more
"delicate . . . researches."[69]

Peacock, by insisting Shelley's marriage was intact until the
spring of 1814, was trying to avoid connecting Harriet with the late
1813 delusion. Further, Peacock's intact marriage claim diverted
attention from his own amorous interest in Harriet, including
Hogg's dubious charge from "positive information" (Shelley) that
"Peacock was Harriet's lover."[70]

The medical sources influencing Shelley's elephantiasis delusion suggest that fear of sexual disease was involved.[71] He apparently believed he had *Elephantiasis Graecorum,* the "elephantiasis of the ancients" that Peacock quoted to Shelley from Lucretius.
Shelley had read from inconsistent sources that the illness was
contagious and formed his own conception of the disease. One authority, Sir William "Oriental" Jones—whom Shelley possibly read
at Oxford—believed that leprosy was the final stage of venereal
disease, a view also expressed in Shelley's *Chambers' Cyclopedia.*
This common association of leprosy and syphilis reinforces the
possibility that Shelley believed he had latent syphilis that was de-
generating into leprosy or that he believed the old woman in the
coach was a prostitute whose contagious disease could have infected him without sexual contact.[72] In either case, Hogg's and

Peacock's accounts perhaps tried to hide Shelley's belief he had venereal disease.

The delusional quality of Shelley's hypochondriacal belief resulted in the inability of the surgeon he consulted, probably Sir William Lawrence, to convince him of his erroneous ideas. Lawrence, disbelieving elephantiasis was contagious, wrote an article on two cases of "true elephantiasis" admitted to London hospitals early in 1814.[73]

Shelley called his melancholic disengagement from Harriet "the dismaying solitude of myself."[74] He criticized Eliza, his current "Brown Demon," for intruding on raising his daughter and he felt that Harriet was not being a good mother. After returning from Edinburgh, he became upset when Harriet, refusing to nurse Ianthe, hired a wet nurse he did not like. Peacock reported Shelley feared "the nurse's soul would enter the child." Becoming the nurturing mother, Shelley opened his shirt and tried to suckle the infant himself.[75]

Hogg was aware of a change in Harriet's behavior when she returned from Edinburgh.[76] Losing interest in being Shelley's literary and intellectual disciple, she sought Hogg's company when buying bonnets. She was often out when Hogg called on Shelley. He did observe her seeming affectless reaction when she watched, against the surgeon's advice, a tumor being removed from Ianthe. When she showed no sign of emotion, the astonished surgeon told Hogg he had never met such a female who "could have no feeling whatever." The surgeon noted that she could "discourse so calmly, so apathetically of suicide."[77]

As 1813 ended, Shelley finished *On the Vegetable System of Diet*. Becoming less extreme, he no longer claimed meat-eating caused Napoleon's destructiveness. One of his most unusual literary works, the philosophical dialogue, *A Refutation of Deism*, appeared in early 1814.[78] Since writing *The Necessity of Atheism*, Shelley had studied the skeptics, including Cicero, Diogenes Laertius, Hume, and the contemporary, Sir William Drummond.[79] *A Refutation* was his most sophisticated statement on atheism. Careful to avoid being charged with blasphemy, he published it anonymously and its form, including the title, was designed to conceal its blasphemous intent. Although he stated that his "object . . . is to prove that the system of Deism is untenable," he was refuting both Christianity and deism with the skeptics' literary device of a dialogue.[80] In *A Refutation,* the deist Theosophus wittily but systematically demolished Christianity and the skeptical Christian Eusebes destroyed Deism, leaving—by implication—only atheism.

Shelley wrote *A Refutation* when he was entering the major crisis of his personal life. Expressing his matured intellectual powers and buttressed with his incisive humor, it is a work of wit in the full meaning of that word. *A Refutation* is a literary expression of the personal strengths that helped Shelley through his most troubling periods.

Shelley, a lingering deist when he wrote *The Necessity of Atheism,* by May 1811 was an intellectual atheist.[81] Both *Queen Mab* and *A Refutation* were influenced by Holbach's materialist arguments in *Le Système de la nature.* Believing Holbach's book "one of the most eloquent vindications of Atheism," Shelley began translating *Le Système* in Lynmouth in 1812 and apparently was still working on it a year later.[82] In his major poetry from *Queen Mab* onward, Shelley evolved a unique spiritual materialism that retained an uncertain balance between good and evil.

Meeting frequently with Godwin about finances during the several weeks he was in London, Shelley was preparing for his romantic link with Godwin's daughter Mary. Immediately after Godwin's December 27 visit, Shelley moved his family to Windsor, renting a furnished house for several months. He avoided Godwin until February and had distance from his creditors. Most important, the Boinvilles were in Bracknell, only eight miles away. Shelley kept a room at Mrs. Boinville's and probably availed himself of Hookham's lodgings when in London.[83]

About mid-February, a despondent Shelley left Harriet, Eliza, and Ianthe to move in with the Boinvilles. First word of this move, and of Shelley's precarious emotional condition, came in Mrs. Boinville's mid-March letter to Hogg. She wrote that Shelley's "Mind & body want rest" and he would write Hogg when "he is in the humour for writing." Shelley "has deeply interested us" and was "seeking a house close to us." Among his "homespun pleasures" was the nurturing of Mrs. Boinville and her daughter Cornelia.[84]

His depression and marital alienation, alluded to by Mrs. Boinville, were clear several days later in his long letter to Hogg. Living with the Boinvilles the past month, he was "astonished at my own indifference" to his life's events. Feeling "much changed," he lived "here like the insect that sports in a transient sunbeam" wondering at "the excess of madness" that encouraged his hopes in the past. He was "a feeble, wavering, feverish being, who requires support and consolation" and the Boinvilles had "revived in my heart the expiring life of flame." His "heart sickens" at the thought of having to leave this "happy home." Having "sunk into a premature old age of exhaustion, which renders me dead to everything," he had "a terrible susceptibility to objects of disgust and hatred."

If prostitutes, "objects of disgust," tempted Shelley, a desirable alternative was Cornelia Turner, who assisted him in learning Italian. Cornelia was "the reverse of everything bad . . . [and] inherits all the divinity of her mother." Her evil counterpoint, Eliza, "will be with me when the infinite malice of destiny forces me to depart. . . . I certainly hate her with all my heart and soul." The sight of Eliza caressing his "poor little Ianthe . . . awakens an inespressible sensation of disgust and horror . . . she is no more than a blind and loathsome worm, that cannot see to sting."

Despairing of separating Harriet from Eliza, Shelley relinquished hope for his marriage with the wistful wish for Ianthe's sympathy in the future. Too depressed "to write a common letter," he had "sometimes forgotten that I am not an inmate of this delightful home" and he will be "cast . . . again into the boundless ocean of abhorred society." He concluded his letter to Hogg with a stanza "which has no meaning, and that I have only written in thought." On the contrary, his lines reveal his sexual attraction to Cornelia, whose "dewy looks sink in my breast" and whose "gentle words stir poison there." Controlling his feelings for her, he was "Subdued to Duty's hard control" by "chains that bind."[85] Trying to wish away Cornelia's sexual attraction, she was "the vision of a delirious and distempered dream . . . [having] no more reality than the colour of an autumnal sunset."[86] Later events indicate his feelings for Cornelia were not so ephemeral.

Shelley temporarily returned to Harriet shortly after writing this letter. In London several days later—March 22, 1814—Shelley, accompanied by Godwin, obtained a license to marry Harriet in the rites of the Church of England. Despite Peacock's assertion, this remarriage neither indicated the marital relationship was stable nor suggested Shelley was not alienated from Harriet. It was a legal act designed, as stated in the "Allegations" supporting his marriage license application, "to obviate all doubts which have arisen or may arise" concerning his Scotland marriage when he was underage, and may have used an assumed name.

The next day, Mr. Westbrook swore before the same authorities that he was the father of Harriet, a minor, and consented to her marriage. He obviously wished to solidify the legal rights to the Shelley estate of any male heirs his daughter might have. On March 24, Harriet and Shelley were married in St. George's Church, Hanover Square, the scene of Ianthe's earlier baptism. John Westbrook was present, but not Godwin.

In early March, Shelley had dined with Godwin and spent the next day with him before returning to the Boinvilles. The matter at hand was the large *post obit* bond on the Shelley inheritance Godwin was negotiating. Godwin had placed ads in *The Times* for several weeks announcing the auction of a £8000 bond which he expected would fetch £3000 for his failing bookshop. Shelley did not attend the March 3 auction of the bond for £2593 to the Nash brothers, who only paid £519 down pending clarification of the legal status of the Shelley estate, including Godwin's seeking life insurance on Shelley's life should he die before his father.[87]

Shelley obtained a London solicitor, Mr. Amory, who went to Field Place to negotiate with his father. On March 13, Shelley wrote to his father from Bracknell thanking him for giving Amory a "polite reception" but lamenting his grandfather's continuing refusal to "relieve my necessities." Not mentioning the *post obits* he had sold—news Amory probably gave Timothy—he warned his father that Sir Bysshe should know he could no longer delay selling "ruinous" *post obit*s that would result in "dismembering the property should I survive himself & you."[88] Old Bysshe toyed with selling Castle Goring, but Timothy opposed, saying it would reward Shelley for his "unchristian and unfeeling-like spirit." Timothy sent Whitton Shelley's letter, saying if "he would first acknowledge his God, then I might be led to believe his assertions." Timothy missed a saving strategy for his son: pay his debts, give him an allowance, and bond him to keep him within terms.[89] Back in London, Shelley wrote his final known letter to his father, requesting hunting rights on the family estate for a Mr. Shoubridge. This was a ruse to allow Francis Place to appraise the Shelley estate. Unmentioned by Shelley was his remarriage the next day.[90]

Immediately after the marriage ceremony, two crucial events occurred whose impact on Harriet and Shelley would take some weeks to become apparent. On March 30, while Shelley was away from London, sixteen-year-old Mary Godwin returned home from Scotland to her adored father and her detested stepmother. About the same time, Harriet became pregnant. Sometime that spring, the Shelleys apparently moved from Windsor to a house in Bracknell. Shelley retained his room at Mrs. Boinville's and continued to see Cornelia.

Before the remarriage, Hogg went to Bracknell hoping to see Shelley, who was in London. A young Frenchman, probably Mrs. Boinville's son Alfred, showed Hogg Shelley's previous rented house, High Elms, and recounted how Shelley broke the bottoms out of the washtubs he used as boats in navigating the stream in Mrs. Boinville's garden.[91] Presumably on another visit, Hogg observed the disoriented Shelley being served tea by a young lady. Shelley, "trembling with emotion," after spilling the tea on his clothes, was gently wiped by the lady with a handkerchief.[92]

By mid-April, Mrs. Boinville wrote Hogg, "Shelley is again a widower," his "beauteous half" having gone to London with her sister.[93] Months later, Shelley looked back at this idyllic time with Cornelia and her mother:

In the beginning of the spring, I spent two months at Mrs. Boinville's without my wife. If I except the succeeding period these two months were probably the happiest of my life: the calmest the serenest the most free from care. The contemplation of female excellence is the favorite food of my imagination. Here was ample scope for admiration: novelty added a peculiar charm to the intrinsic merit of the objects: I had been unaccustomed to the mildness the intelligence the delicacy of a cultivated female. The presence of Mrs. Boinville & her daughter afforded a strange contrast to my former friendless & deplorable condition. I suddenly perceived that the entire devotion with which I had resigned all prospects of utility or happiness to the single purpose of cultivating Harriet was a gross & despicable superstition . . . I saw the full extent of the calamity which my rash & heartless union with Harriet had produced: an union over whose entrance might justly be inscribed
Lasciate ogni speranza voi ch'entrate![94]

This bitter quote, Dante's inscription over the gate of hell, led Shelley to be frank with Hogg about his marital relationship: "I felt as if a dead & living body had been linked together in loathsome & horrible communion. It was no longer possible to practise self-deception: I believed that one revolting duty yet remained, to continue to deceive my wife.—I wandered in the fields alone."

Shelley's now-dead love for Harriet was never a love of passion. The conscious deadness of Shelley's sexual response to Harriet accords with what his daughter-in-law, Lady Shelley, reported many years later. She believed that Harriet's extreme passion was beyond Shelley's physical ability to satisfy her, particularly since his loving feelings for her were muted from the beginning.[95]

16

Mary Wollstonecraft Godwin

SHELLEY'S PASSION FOR CORNELIA TURNER LED HER MOTHER TO ask him to leave her home. His haunting poem composed at Bracknell, "Stanzas.—April, 1814," expresses his anguish over leaving Mrs. Boinville and the romantic Cornelia to return to Harriet and his "sad and silent home" with its "desolated hearth," buffeted like the "leaves of wasted autumn woods." Not wishing to further arouse Mrs. Boinville's "ungentle mood," he leaves with "remembrance, and repentance, and deep musings" of Cornelia's sweet smile. According to Harriet, Shelley's falling in love with Cornelia led Thomas Turner, her husband, to take his wife to Devon.[1]

Writing in awkward Latin, Shelley apparently recorded his heated passion for Cornelia in five pages of his notebook: "S[he] pressed kisses upon my lips! . . . from a terrible solitude I contemplated love like a wretched and content prisoner . . . I awoke from dreams, denied delicious desire. Why do I drink the filthy cup of life-giving desire? . . . S[he] held me in her arms in bed. I nearly died of madness and delight. Sweet lips again sought mutual kisses of life. S[he] calmed my fears." Someone later tore out a page and burned out words from three of the lines.[2]

In his last verses about Cornelia ("Oh! there are spirits of the air"), Shelley chastised himself for being infatuated with a married woman: "And thou hast sought in starry eyes / Beams that were never meant for thine, Another's wealth." Shelley confided to Cornelia he stayed up late conversing with her because "he dreaded the visions which pursued him when alone at night."[3] Sixty years later, Cornelia recalled reassuring the discouraged Shelley that his faded poetic inspiration after *Queen Mab* would blossom again.[4]

Returning to Skinner Street in early May, Shelley met Mary Wollstonecraft Godwin for the first time since their brief meeting in November 1812. They probably met May 5, when Shelley dined with Godwin. He called again the next day. For Mrs. Godwin, "all our

311

troubles began in May.["5] Godwin, preoccupied with raising money
from Shelley's estate, was seemingly unaware of Shelley's growing attraction to Mary.[6] The renewed spark between Shelley and
Fanny Imlay Godwin, who turned twenty May 14, possibly first
aroused the Godwins' concern. Mrs. Godwin reported Shelley paid
"immense attention" to Fanny while Mary was in Scotland and
Claire was away at school. The Godwins, concerned Fanny might
be falling in love with Shelley, sent her to visit relatives in Wales on
May 23. Mrs. Godwin, believing Shelley was securely married to
Harriet, claimed Shelley's interest in Claire the previous Christmas was "much like a brother to his younger sister." The two had
read Italian and took walks together.[7] Claire, sixteen in April, apparently was at school in May when Shelley's Skinner Street visits
resumed.

Because of her vague paternity, Claire possibly adopted Mary
Wollstonecraft's birthday, April 27, as her birthday.[8] A striking contrast to Mary physically and emotionally, Claire had curls of dark
hair framing her compact, rounded face set off by dark eyes. Claire
was more attractive than plain Fanny, but felt inferior to the
slighter-framed Mary. Mary's oval face had deep-set hazel eyes
below a high forehead, all surrounded by brown hair Claire enviously described as a "burnished brightness like the autumnal
foliage."[9] A later admirer considered Mary's "calm, grey eyes" her
most striking feature.[10]

Though less brilliant than Mary, Claire was highly intelligent.
Her flair for displaying her feelings openly was captured in her
singing, which enthralled Shelley. Mary, less impulsive, had her father's intellectualized control. Perhaps Mary's closeness to her father gave her a deeper sense of herself as a woman, something
foreclosed to Claire.

Godwin was masterminding the large, second *post obit* with the
Nash brothers that involved insurance on Shelley's life for £3000.
Godwin not only wrote to the Duke of Devonshire about the sale of
some of the Shelley property, he asked Shelley to write the Nashes'
lawyer confirming the matter.[11]

In early June, Shelley either sent or delivered a brief letter to Byron's Albany House residence, Piccadilly. He enclosed a poem, possibly Shelley's sonnet, "Feelings of a Republican on the Fall of
Bonaparte."[12] Shelley had also sent Byron *Queen Mab,* but two
years passed before the two poets met. The feelings between Shelley and Mary were deepening as May ended. To be near Skinner

Street, Shelley took lodgings on Hatton Garden. On June 8, accompanied by Hogg, he called on Godwin who paid no rent on his Skinner Street home due to confusion over the wedge-shaped building's ownership. The two walked up the stairs to the family's book-lined living room where Opie's portrait of Mary Wollstonecraft was enshrined over the mantel. Godwin was away but at home was his daughter, Mary Wollstonecraft Godwin.

Shelley was impatiently pacing the floor when a door opened, revealing Mary wearing her tartan frock from Scotland. Her "thrilling voice called 'Shelley!'" and his "thrilling voice answered 'Mary!'", as he darted out of the room to spend a few minutes alone with her. When Hogg later asked Shelley the identity of the "very young female . . . with a piercing look," wearing so unusual a dress for London, Shelley reticently replied, "The daughter of Godwin and Mary."[13] Shelley idealized Mary Wollstonecraft, whose works he had read and quoted. He could never feel as strongly for Fanny and Claire as for Mary, the only daughter of Shelley's idealized parents.

Elizabeth Shelley wrote her son early in June, urging him to visit as his father was away. On his day-long forty-mile walk from Bracknell to Field Place, Shelley had sexual reveries about Mary, later communicated to Hogg. His "approaching change tinged my waking thoughts. . . . I had met the female who was destined to be mine . . . already were the difficulties surmounted that opposed an entire union."[14]

A few miles from Field Place a farmer gave Shelley a ride in his cart. The farmer, unaware of his passenger's identity, amused Shelley by saying the most remarkable thing about Field Place was that its "Young Master Shelley never went to church." This event was recalled by an adolescent youth who had taken Shelley's place in Timothy's affections. Arriving home, in addition to finding his mother, his sisters Elizabeth and Hellen, and Laker the butler, Shelley met John Mackenzie Kennedy, a young army officer, barely seventeen, stationed in Horsham. Kennedy had become a member of the family and considered Timothy his "second father." Shelley deeply impressed Kennedy who, decades later, reminisced about the Shelleys. Elizabeth Shelley spoke often to Kennedy of her son, and "Her heart yearned after him with all the fondness of a Mother's love. She saw the necessity of her husbands decree, and acquiesced in its propriety. Condemning her sons opinions, she comforted herself by assigning them to the most charitable origin." Shelley, winning Kennedy's heart, treated him "as a younger brother whom he had known from childhood." Kennedy was impressed with Shelley's "unmistakable sincerity and simplicity" and remarked that Shelley's resemblance to his sister Elizabeth "was as striking as if they had been twins."

Shelley, exchanging his refurbished "old black coat" for Kennedy's scarlet uniform, enjoyed his new identity, walking about outside as Captain Jones. To fit Shelley's "remarkably small" head, Kennedy's cap had to be stuffed. Hearing that Kennedy was a friend of the philosopher Sir James Mackintosh, Shelley "expressed the highest admiration" for Mackintosh, an "intimate" of Godwin. Shelley discussed his metaphysical and religious views with Kennedy, who felt Shelley treated his arguments "with as much consideration and respect as if I had been his equal in ability & attainments."

Shelley's mother, concerned that her son was indoctrinating the young soldier with "his sentiments," told Shelley she hoped "such had not been the case." Shelley's reply, "Never mind Kennedy, he has mistaken his profession," was remembered by the army officer years later as "one of the highest compliments that has ever been paid me." When Shelley's mother observed her son's "eagerness and delight" in launching a "fleet of paper boats," she remarked "how singular it was that a person, of his age, should enjoy such a childish amusement." Shelley replied, "Why should you be surprised," adding that "Kennedy takes pleasure in shooting . . . I spill no blood—yet I receive pleasure." Kennedy was impressed by Shelley's reading aloud a translation of a poem by Goethe and commented on his "delight" in music. Shelley played several times with one hand on the piano "an exceedingly simple air, which I understood his Earliest love was wont to play to him."

Kennedy adored Timothy Shelley as the personification of an "English gentleman the Squire of Olden time" whose "generous heart" included "noble acts of munificent benevolence" hidden from "the public eye. . . . So far from being austere, he was lively & cheerful—full of quaint fun & amiable and playful wit." Shelley's expulsion "seized upon his mind, & oppressed his spirit, that, often times, his sensibility to external objects was deadened."[15]

At the time of Shelley's brief visit to Field Place he knew of Harriet's pregnancy, now beginning its third month. Aware of Shelley's romance with Cornelia, Harriet had some inkling of his developing infatuation with Mary. In a last futile act to restore past illusions, Shelley wrote from Bracknell on June 12 to the solicitor Davies

about leasing Nantgwillt.[16] However, Shelley probably realized—
as Mary Shelley would write in her novel, *Lodore*—that Harriet's
dependence upon Eliza was a deeper emotional claim than Harriet's love for him.[17] Harriet's replacement by Mary was signaled
in July when Shelley gave his new love a copy of *Queen Mab* inscribed to "Mary Wollstonecraft Godwin." Below the dedication to
Harriet he wrote, "Count Slobendorf was about to marry a
woman, who attracted solely by his fortune, proved her selfishness by deserting him in prison."[18] Wrong about both the Count
and Harriet, Shelley had convinced himself that Harriet had not
loved him, that she was only interested in his rank and money, and
that she had deserted him. His progressively poisoned feelings
about Harriet would include the beliefs that she had been unfaithful and another man had fathered her unborn child. He later
retracted the paternity charge, but his accusation of Harriet's
hardness stuck. Three years later, drafting *Laon and Cythna,* he
spoke sequentially of Harriet Grove and Harriet Shelley: "One
whom I found was dear but false to me / The other's heart was like
a heart of stone."[19]

A week after writing about the Nantgwillt lease, Shelley left Harriet at Bracknell for his Hatton Garden lodgings in London. His
overt agenda was to complete arrangements on the Nashes' *post
obit* bond; Mary was the hidden agenda. Shelley dined almost
every day at Skinner Street from June 19 to June 29. During this
time, although he was closely "watched, & regarded with a suspicious eye, opportunities of frequent intercourse were not wanting." His "almost constant residence" at Godwin's house revealed
to him the "originality and loveliness of Mary's character" with her
"irresistible wildness & sublimity of her feelings." She was "gentle, to be convinced & tender; yet not incapable of ardent indignation & hatred." After a glowing description of the "excellence" of
"her character," he caught himself in a flash of insight, adding that
his description of "her excellencies" were "as if I were an egoist
expatiating upon his own perfections."[20]

Shelley, after later writing to Mary that she was "the intelligence
that governs me," checked his idealizing flattery by disavowing
this "simile" as "unjust . . . false." He denied "that I consider you
much my superior [still] you surpass me in originality & simplicity."[21] His judgment rings true in terms of her future renown as the
author of *Frankenstein,* the best known and perhaps most original
work of English Romanticism.

Mary, born August 30, 1797, was two years younger than her lover's wife. Shelley quickly learned of Mary's early devotion to writing. At age ten, she revised verses for her father's publication of *Mounseer Nongtongpaw,* a poetic version of a comic song.[22] Godwin instilled in his daughter the discipline and love for writing and learning that Shelley desired in his women. Mary's schooling was primarily in her father's house, in one room reserved for the three girls' education by their governess and occasional tutors. Both Fanny and Claire received more formal education than Mary. Fanny was expected to teach in the Dublin school of her Woll- stonecraft aunts, and Mrs. Godwin hoped that Claire would teach French or be a governess. Godwin, Mary's intellectual exemplar, encouraged her to read first thing every day and to read two or three books at a time. Godwin tried out on Mary his latest publica- tions for the Juvenile Library, having joined his wife in writing books for children.[23] In Godwin's pseudonymous 1806 *Pantheon or Ancient History of the Gods of Greece and Rome,* Mary's favorite tale was of Prometheus, the fire-bringing hero who became the subtitle of *Frankenstein.*[24]

Among Godwin's friends that Mary knew were Charles and Mary Lamb, who wrote *Tales from Shakespeare* for the Juvenile Library.[25] An influential favorite was Coleridge, who was missed when he moved to the Lake District in 1800. Just before Mary's ninth birthday, Coleridge came to dine, and she never forgot his recital of *The Rime of the Ancient Mariner.* When Mary was four- teen, her father took her and the family to hear Coleridge's lec- tures on Shakespeare and Milton. There she first saw Lord Byron, whose *Childe Harold* she soon admired. Four years earlier the family had moved to 41 Skinner Street, not far from three jails where public hangings were held. One frequent visitor in late 1811 and early 1812 was the political exile Aaron Burr, whose father of the same name had certified Shelley's grandfather's New Jersey birth. In addition to romancing John Philpot Curran's daughter Amelia, Burr had eyes for Mrs. Godwin and the three early- adolescent girls. Burr was impressed by a lecture he thought probably written by Mary, "The Influence of Governments on the Character of the People," delivered by young William Godwin with aplomb.[26]

Approaching puberty, Mary had increasingly unsettling feelings about her strange family. Frankenstein's monster was motherless and the heroines in Mary's novels and stories were often raised by fathers with whom they were strongly attached. However, Godwin's emotional coldness and stern demandingness crept into her story "The Elder Son." Mary wrote: "He never caressed me.... Yet, strange to say, my father loved me almost to idolatry; and I knew this and repaid his affection with enthusiastic fondness, notwithstanding his reserve and my awe."[27]

After Mary Wollstonecraft's death, Godwin adopted her older daughter, three-year-old Fanny Imlay, who grew up as Fanny Godwin. Believing Godwin was her biological father, his telling her otherwise at about age twelve was one more loss in her depressive history.[28] Godwin, searching for a new wife, was rebuffed by, among others, Maria Reveley, who for a time cared for infant Mary after her birth. In 1801, Godwin met and wedded "Mrs." Clairmont, the unmarried mother of two offspring. Like Mary Wollstonecraft, she married Godwin after becoming pregnant by him. Among Mary's emotional legacies from her troubled parental history were Mary Wollstonecraft's depressive tendency and Godwin's difficulty in expressing intimate feelings. Godwin had Mary's character analyzed by a phrenologist when she was not yet three weeks old and later characterized his only biological daughter as "singularly bold, somewhat imperious, and active of mind," traits that undoubtedly increased her friction with her stepmother.[29]

In early 1811, Mary, antagonistic toward her stepmother and finding her father increasingly remote, developed a skin disorder on her hand and arm that led to surgical intervention and six months of saltwater therapy away from home.[30] When Mary's symptom recurred more severely, Godwin sent her to Dundee to live with the family of William Thomas Baxter, whom Godwin barely knew. In November 1812, soon after returning home for a six-month visit, she met Shelley for the first time.

Mary's closest female friend, the youngest Baxter daughter, Isabella, had married her deceased older sister's husband, David Booth, who was older than her father. Perhaps such incestuous overtones stirred sixteen-year-old Mary when she returned to her family the end of March 1814 just before Shelley once more crossed her threshold.

Mary and Shelley pursued their June romance at two rendezvous sites. Claire, accompanying Mary to the garden of Charterhouse School, walked at a distance as Mary and Shelley sat in the arbor. A more electric meeting place was Mary's mother's grave in the yard of Old St. Pancras Church, where Mary's parents had been married five months before her birth. In childhood, Mary's father brought her to Mary Wollstonecraft's grave marker. Mary knew much about her mother's life, probably having read Godwin's frank biography, written shortly after Mary Wollstonecraft died. The explicit *Memoirs* included startling revelations that shocked, outraged, and alienated many, including some of his friends. Godwin discussed his wife's suicide attempts, her affair and illegitimate child with Gilbert Imlay, her frustrated love for the married Henry Fuseli (whom Godwin disliked), his own relationship with her, and the clinical details of her death.[31]

In late June, Shelley made a last effort to escape his enveloping passion for Mary. Taking his meals at Skinner Street and amidst bond negotiations, he ignored Godwin's plea to stay and visited Harriet overnight in Bracknell. It was on June 26, Shelley wrote Hogg, that Mary declared her love for him at her mother's grave. This overcame his conflict between duty to Harriet and passion for Mary. Unable to conceal his "ardent passion," Shelley implied that "the *manner* in which she dispelled my delusions" involved consummation of their love. It was a "sublime & rapturous moment when she confessed herself mine."[32] Mary's version of "that night" was that Shelley turned "friendship" to "ardour of love . . . [and] opened . . . his whole heart to me."[33]

Shelley's reference in Mary's journal suggests they consummated their passion on June 27, a day when Shelley did not dine at Skinner Street.[34] Godwin stated that on Sunday, June 26, Shelley, Mary, and Claire went "to the tomb of Mary's mother . . . there, it seems, the impious idea first occurred to him of seducing her, play[ing] the traitor to me, & deserting his wife."[35] Many years later, Mary's novel *Falkner* told of a young girl declaring her passion in a cemetery. Her lover responded by shedding tears on her bosom.

Mary inscribed in her copy of *Queen Mab:* "This book is sacred to me . . . by that love we have promised to each other although I may not be your[s] I can never be another's. But I am thine, exclusively thine."[36] She added lines from Byron's love poems, "To Thyrza," unaware they were addressed to a choirboy. She penned Shelley's words, "in the solitude of your chamber I shall be with you—yes you are ever with me sacred vision." Godwin saw nothing sacred in their relationship, calling it "impious."

When Godwin talked to Shelley about his "devoted attentions" to Mary, Mrs. Godwin claimed Shelley replied, "it was only his manner with all women."[37] Harriet, now in Bath, wrote to Hookham July 6 or 7, anxious from not hearing from Shelley in four days: "I always fancy something dreadful has happened if I do not hear from him. . . . I cannot endure this dreadful state of suspense."[38] Not knowing Shelley's whereabouts, she enclosed a letter Hookham should give him. Shelley sent for her to come to London.

Shelley now inflicted two pieces of bad news upon Godwin. The completion of the Nashes' *post obit* bond came July 6 and Godwin expected to receive the full amount, close to £3000. Shelley, dining that day with Godwin, announced he would give his mentor only half a loaf. After expenses, £1120 was for Godwin and the same amount for himself. Stunned, Godwin felt betrayed after his exertions over the months. Rather than rescuing him, Shelley was prolonging his agony.[39] The second thunderbolt came when, as the two walked in Spa Fields, Shelley announced his love for Mary and his intention to live with her and leave Harriet. Perhaps Shelley reminded Godwin he had said in *Political Justice,* "The system of marriage is a system of fraud," and Mary Wollstonecraft called marriage "legalized prostitution." Godwin later wrote that Shelley "had the madness to disclose his plans to me, & to ask my consent." Godwin "expostulated" vigorously with Shelley who "promised to give up his licentious love and return to virtue." Godwin then attempted "to waken up a sense of honour and natural affection in the mind of Mary, and I seemed to have succeeded. They both deceived me."[40]

Mary briefly agreed not to see Shelley, whom Godwin forbade to enter his home or communicate with Mary. Shelley bribed Godwin's shop porter and notes passed between the two lovers.[41] Sending Mary *Queen Mab,* Shelley inscribed it, "You see, Mary, I have not forgotten you." Harriet arrived from Bath in mid-July to hear her husband profess his love for Mary. After their long "interview," Shelley wrote Harriet, addressing her, "My Dearest Friend." Although Harriet felt deceived, shocked, and deeply hurt, Shelley wrote he was "made calmer & happier by your assurances," having intimated he and Mary had considered suicide. He confronted Harriet with his long-term dissatisfaction with their relationship: "Our connection was not one of passion & impulse. Friendship was its basis, & on this basis it has enlarged & strengthened. It is no reproach to me that you have never filled my heart with an all-sufficing passion—perhaps, you are even yourself a stranger to these impulses, which one day may be awakened by some nobler & worthier than me, and may you find a lover as passionate and faithful, as I shall ever be a friend affectionate & sincere!" Bringing Mrs. Boinville into his argument, Shelley said she had "predicted that these struggles would one day arrive; she saw that friendship & not passion was the bond of our attachment."[42]

Months later, Harriet, writing Mrs. Nugent, placed the "blame" on Mary, who "determined to seduce him . . . heated his imagination by talking of her mother, and going to her grave with him every day . . . she told him she was dying in love for him, accompanied with the most violent gestures and vehement expostulations. . . . He thought of me and my sufferings and begged her to get the better of a passion." Harriet said Mary, threatening suicide, asked: "Why could we not all live together? I as his sister, she as his wife? He had the folly to believe this possible." After Harriet's talk with Shelley, she "was laid up" for two weeks, and "could do nothing for myself." Shelley "begged me to live" and the "doctors gave me over [saying] 'twas impossible." However, "owing to the great strength of my constitution I lived."[43]

When Godwin visited an agitated and weeping Harriet, she told him of Shelley's love for Cornelia Turner at Mrs. Boinville's and implored Godwin not to let Shelley into his house or see Mary. Harriet believed that if Shelley did not see Mary, he would forget her.[44] The Godwins spoke to Mary about renouncing Shelley and she apparently told Harriet personally that she would not see him again.[45] Godwin, having talked to Shelley and sent him three long letters,[46] now felt things were under control. The separated lovers agreed to give up their plans, the *post obit* arrangements were retained, and a brief surface calm descended. Godwin's willingness to accept Shelley's bond money would begin rumors he had sold his daughter.

Mrs. Godwin's account, if reliable, had Shelley proposing to Mary a dual suicide pact, he by pistol, she by laudanum. When Godwin was out, Shelley supposedly burst into the house and tried to enter the schoolroom against Mrs. Godwin's protest. Looking "extremely wild," Shelley violently pushed her aside and offered a bottle of laudanum to Mary, saying, "Death shall unite us." Shelley took "a small pistol from his pocket" and said it "shall reunite me to you." Claire was shrieking and a weeping Mary begged him to calm down, refused to take the laudanum, and promised "to be ever faithful" to Shelley.[47] Shelley placed the laudanum vial on the table and left. Late in her life, Claire conveyed this as an actual event to Edward Augustus Silsbee, a forty-eight-year-old retired American sea captain from Salem, Massachusetts.[48] Silsbee was pursuing his avid quest for Shelley's manuscripts and letters in Claire's possession.

Shelley seemingly threatened suicide again.[49] Some days later the Godwins were awakened at midnight with news that Shelley was at "death's door" from an overdose of laudanum. Rushing to Hatton Garden, they found a physician had Shelley walking up and down his room. Mrs. Godwin, watching over him the next day, reported he could speak only "yes" or "no." First a local couple, then Mrs. Boinville, looked after Shelley the next several days. After this event, according to Claire's report, Shelley kept up the pressure on Mary, saying in his smuggled letters he would commit suicide "unless she joined him as Partner of his Life." Mary, agitated by his suicide attempt "a few weeks before," was fearful her father would see Shelley's letters, stop the correspondence, and "Shelley would destroy himself." Mary "wept bitterly" when telling this to Claire.[50] Shelley's mood improved when Mary agreed to elope with him. No definitive scenario exists for these events leading to their elopement. Shelley's overall elopement scenario with Mary was similar to that with Harriet. As he wrote in several early poems, he would free the woman from family tyranny and she would save him from dying.

Divorce was a less viable option for Shelley. Only a few were granted each year after a lengthy process requiring, first, a church court's approval of a separation on grounds of adultery followed by a common-law suit brought against the correspondent for adultery. Finally, the case was heard before the House of Lords for a private Act of Parliament that achieved a complete divorce. Witnesses' verbatim testimony about sexual details became public record.[51] Had Shelley used his family influence to seek a divorce, the Westbrooks undoubtedly would not have agreed. Short of giving up Mary and returning to Harriet, his only other recourse was to remain in his marriage and have Mary become his mistress, a commonly accepted choice of the day.[52]

Distraught, Shelley summoned Peacock, who was shocked by his changed appearance. Shelley, saying his mind was in "insurrection," was relying heavily on laudanum to ease his emotional and physical pain. Peacock claimed Shelley was *not then separated* from Harriet. Holding his laudanum bottle, Shelley said, "I never part from this" and calmly told Peacock, "Every one who knows me must know that the partner of my life should be one who can feel poetry and understand philosophy." Harriet was a "noble animal," but Shelley believed "she could do neither." Peacock's protest that Shelley seemed "very fond of Harriet" brought Shelley's retort, "But you did not know how I hated her sister."[53] He did not tell Peacock his ideas about Harriet having been unfaithful, ideas he possibly used to induce Mary to elope. According to Claire's later account, Mary told her that Shelley "succeeded in persuading" Mary to elope "by declaring that Harriet did not really care for him; that she was in love with a Major Ryan; and that the child she would have was certainly not his . . . this justified his having another attachment." Mrs. Godwin and the Boinvilles knew nothing of Ryan.[54] Harriet mentioned the Irish Ryan in two letters to Catherine Nugent in 1813. If she had been intimate with Ryan or someone else, the affair must have been brief. Ryan, possibly in London the spring of 1814, would reappear in this story.

Shelley's paranoia about Harriet's infidelity was part of his being distraught. Robert Browning reportedly said that Hookham told him Shelley was practically insane at this time.[55] Later, Shelley still spoke of Harriet's infidelity but recognized his paternity of their child. Those who knew Harriet gave no credence to her having been unfaithful. Claire wrote later, "It was no fault of her's [Harriet's] that S—— quitted her."[56] When Harriet first heard from Shelley of his love for Mary, she expected he would return to her once his infatuation with Mary passed.

Later in July, Shelley and Mary made secret plans to elope. A lawyer named Tahourdin prepared for Shelley two deeds and a settlement plan for his separation from Harriet, and Shelley notified her that she could draw on his account from Hookham.[57] On July 25, Godwin wrote a sharply accusatory letter to Shelley: "I could not believe that you wd. sacrifice your own character and usefulness, the happiness of an innocent and meritorious wife, and the fair and spotless fame of my young child to fierce impulse of passion—I could not believe that you wd. enter my house under the name of benefactor, to leave behind an endless poison to corrode my soul."[58] Shelley was ejected scornfully from his final paternal home.

At this time, Shelley's romantic complications possibly were compounded by a mysterious woman's appearance the evening before his departure from London. This episode, usually placed two years later, occurred in 1814, according to Medwin. He reported that Shelley "more than once" made it "a subject of conversation with me during my visit to Pisa" and that Byron "was equally acquainted with the story, as told to us mutually."[59]

Medwin wrote that Shelley was visited that last night by "a married lady, young, handsome, and of noble connections." Medwin did not divulge her name. Having "long known" *Queen Mab*, she came to profess her love for him "after many vain and useless struggles with myself." Shelley was "the *beau ideal* of what I have long sought for in vain," and she had "renounced my husband, my name, my family and friends: and have resolved, after mature deliberation, to follow you through the world, to attach my fortune, which is considerable, to yours, in spite of all obloquy that [may] be cast upon me." Shelley, feeling "deep gratitude—admiration without bounds for that enthusiastic and noble-minded person" and for her avowal of love, explained "his engagement" and tried to "infuse a balm into her wounded soul, to soothe her hurt pride." Disdaining anger, she implored him to "lend me some aid to endure the trial you have brought upon me . . . blighted hopes—a life of loneliness—withered affections." Medwin wrote that Shelley parted, saying, "Cold indeed would have been my heart if I should ever cease to acknowledge with gratitude, the flattering, the undeserved preference you have so nobly confessed to me." After this likely 1814 meeting, the two seemingly met again in 1816 when he told her of his pending trip to Geneva. Apparently meeting again in Italy in 1818, her shadowy presence would form one of the most intriguing mysteries of Shelley's life.

At four in the morning, July 28, 1814, the chaise Shelley ordered was waiting not far from Skinner Street. Watching the lightning and stars, he wondered about their plan's success. After Mary joined him, she apparently returned home to make "some arrangements" before rejoining him.[60] She had left her father a note. Upon awakening at his usual early hour, he wrote in his journal, "Five in the morning." Exactly how Claire was included on the trip is unclear. Shelley reported they had delayed going to the Continent because of "Godwin's distress," and Claire claimed late in her life she had no idea of the plans. Thinking she was accompanying Mary on an early morning walk, she only understood what was afoot when they reached the corner of Hatton Garden. Perhaps the pair pressed her to join them because of her command of French. Claire must have known where she was going; she and Mary were wearing black silk traveling dresses, their only clothing for the trip.[61]

As dawn broke on the Dover road, one of the most outlandish travel fantasies in literary history began unfolding. It was, Mary later said, "acting a novel, being an incarnate romance."[62] A young married father, not yet twenty-two, deserting his pregnant wife and child, was fleeing both the bailiffs and the parents of the two unmarried sixteen-year-old females accompanying him. They had little money and not much more than the clothes they were wearing. Shelley had his usual traveling library, including his four-volume set of Barruel, three volumes of Shakespeare, Tacitus, Mary Wollstonecraft's semi-autobiographical novel *Mary,* and her *Letters from Norway.* Mary had a box containing her childhood writings and family letters, including one from her lover's wife. Claire brought her ability to speak French, which the others could only read. There was one other unplanned addition; about the time they eloped or shortly into the trip, Mary became pregnant.

Fearing being overtaken by the early-rising Godwins, upon arriving in Dartford they added four horses.[63] Shelley anxiously tried to comfort Mary, who became ill on one of the hottest days in years. Not until early afternoon did the shocked Godwins learn that the trio were going to Dover and France. Mrs. Godwin caught the evening mail to Dover in an attempt to retrieve Claire, if not both daughters. After the elopers arrived in Dover that afternoon, Mary bathed in the sea while Shelley bargained with sailors and customhouse officials. Eager to leave before the next day's packet, he engaged a small boat for Calais whose crew promised a two-hour voyage.

After setting sail at six, they were almost becalmed until a fresh breeze soon became a "violent & contrary" wind, tossing the boat wildly and making Mary seasick. Shelley, exhausted, held Mary's head as the anxious sailors considered Boulogne if they could not make Calais. A sudden squall struck the sail, the boat shipped water, and "even the sailors perceived that our situation was perilous." As the sailors struggled to reef the sails, Shelley's knees no longer could support Mary, who closed her eyes and rested against his legs. At dawn, a wind shift blew them into Calais as lightning cleared the red storm clouds. As Mary awoke she heard Shelley say, "Mary look, the sun rises over France."

The three found two rooms at Dessein's Hotel and awaited their luggage on that day's packet boat. Upon its arrival, the captain announced to Shelley that "a fat lady" said he had "run away with her daughter." Claire spent that night with her mother, listening to her arguments about why she should return home. Mrs. Godwin avoided Shelley for fear of his anger. She claimed that Shelley said he was not in love with Claire, "a nice little girl" whose "vulgar" mother was not "a proper person to form the mind of a young girl."[64] Claire, wavering in her resolution, was "counselled" by Shelley to think over her decision a half hour before responding to her mother. After Claire told her mother she would stay, Shelley met Mrs. Godwin, who did not say a word. The Godwins' troubles continued when, soon after, ten-year-old William ran away from home for two nights. That same day, Patrick Patrickson, Godwin's other protégé, committed suicide at Cambridge.[65]

Spending the night of July 30 at Boulogne, they hired a two-wheeled cabriolet for the two-day trip to Paris. Shelley, still role-playing Godwin's Casimir Fleetwood, determined they should follow his route from Paris to Troyes and the Jura Mountains to the Uri area of Switzerland on Lake Lucerne. Uri, the origin of Swiss liberty, was the setting in *Fleetwood* of an idyllic cottage where the sage, Ruffigny, lived among his books.

After a night at Abbeville, they traveled all the next day and night to reach Paris as quickly as possible because of Mary's sickness, arriving August 2. Securing an apartment for a week at the Hotel de Vienne near the Place Vendôme, Shelley and Mary bought a journal book in which they both recorded their journey. He gave his almost empty notebook, with his verses about Cornelia Turner, to Claire for her journal.

Feeling like "prisoners in Paris," much of their week was spent trying to obtain funds to continue their trip. Shelley had practically nothing, apparently having given Harriet most of his £1100 share from the *post obit* bond. A "cold & stupid" letter came from Hookham, who joined Peacock and the Boinvilles in disapproving of Shelley's desertion of Harriet. Hookham, refusing to send money, told Shelley the Boinvilles were in "the utmost misery" because of the £40 Shelley owed them. Through Hookham, Shelley contacted a banker or moneylender named Tavernier, "an idiot" who became their Paris guide. Shelley celebrated his twenty-second birthday by selling his watch and chain. One source of a possible loan was out of town, the liberal writer Helen Maria Williams, known to both Mary Wollstonecraft and Godwin.[66] Disappointed with Notre Dame and the Tuileries Gardens, they were impressed by one painting in the Louvre, apparently Poussin's *The Deluge*. After another "dull & insolent" letter from Hookham and four days of negotiating, Tavernier loaned Shelley £60. To economize, they decided to be real vagabonds and walk to Uri, a choice Mary thought "eccentric" but its "romance was very pleasing to us." She mused that the French would be more blasé about three young gypsies of privilege on the road than the intolerant English. They bought an ass to carry their light portmanteau and the two women by turns, but Mary walked less than Claire. To ease the beast's burden, Mary left her box containing her early manuscripts and family correspondence in Paris. They were never recovered.

The landlady at their hotel warned the naïve three of the dangers of their walking tour. Two young women certainly would be abducted or raped by Napoleon's demoralized soldiers, recently disbanded and hungrily returning to their ravaged villages. Warfare had just ended between France and the Allied forces of England, Russia, Prussia, and Austria. Paris capitulated March 31, the Bourbon dynasty was restored, and Napoleon was banished to Elba in April. Among the first on the Continent after cessation of hostilities, the three seemed unaware that their route would take them through locales where scorched-earth warfare had raged only five months earlier. These atrocious realities of war indelibly imprinted Shelley's poetic visions.

Soon after leaving Paris, Shelley had to carry their weak, underfed animal part of the way to Charenton, five kilometers down the road. The "horrible spasm" Shelley promptly suffered was the first in many painful recurrent attacks. Selling the ass at a loss, Shelley purchased a sturdier mule that could carry Mary, who was well enough to walk eight miles while Claire rode. That night in Guignes, their landlady assured them their bed was the one Napoleon had slept in last February. The suffering and misery of war pressed upon them as they encountered villages that were burned and cows slaughtered, as the locals told them, by the Cossacks. They found appalling the "disgusting" squalor and filth of the inns in which they stayed. After passing through the destroyed towns of Nogent-sur-Seine and St. Aubin, Shelley sprained his ankle stumbling into Ossey-les-Trois-Maisons after dark. Following supper of sour bread and milk, the landlord, proposing to sleep with Claire, was "terrified" by an irate Shelley. Claire joined Mary and Shelley in bed after rats put "their cold paws on her face." With Shelley riding the mule because of his sprain, they passed through more destroyed villages, finding a "dirty . . . nasty" apartment in Troyes. Buying a conveyance to get to Neuchâtel because of Shelley's ankle, they lost fifteen napoleons selling the mule and saddle.

Before leaving Troyes August 13, Shelley wrote Harriet, urging her to come to Switzerland "where you will at least find one firm & constant friend" and asking her to write him at Neuchâtel. He implied that Harriet need not live in his new household as he could find her "some sweet retreat." Knowing that without more money they could not go much further, and angered at Hookham's recalcitrance, Shelley told Harriet he had written Peacock "to superintend money affairs." Peacock was "expensive inconsiderate & cold," but "surely not utterly perfidious & unfriendly and unmindful of our kindness to him." Seemingly believing the pregnant Harriet would come, bringing fourteen-months-old Ianthe and the *post obit* money, he told her, "Do not part with your money." She also should bring the two deeds and copy of the settlement Tahourdin was preparing.[67]

That Shelley misperceived Harriet's emotional state was apparent two weeks later from her woeful letter to Mrs. Nugent written from her father's house.[68] After writing, "Mr. Shelley is in France," she said that for the sake of her infant she hoped "to live for many years" but supposed there is another world "where those that have suffered keenly here will be happy." She again expressed her wish that Mrs. Nugent lived near her in England and wondered, "What I should have done without this dear babe and my sister I know not." Eliza was Harriet's last prop in her fragile, imploding world of loss. Still clinging to the hope Shelley would return to her, it was three months before Harriet mentioned Mary and the elopement to Mrs. Nugent.

Buying a cart and hiring a driver in Troyes, the trio stopped for the night at "exquisitively beautiful" Bar-sur-Aube. His ankle well enough to climb a hill, Shelley exclaimed that the "Sun . . . bequeathed a lingering look to the Heaven, he has left desolate." Claire, writing her first journal entry, considered this "a most beautiful thought."[69]

Moving faster in their mule-drawn carriage, they stopped at Langres, and dined the next day at Champlitte, where Shelley indulged his fantasy of adopting a young girl. Marguerite Pascal was apparently motherless, and Mary had never seen such a lovely child. Her father refused to let her accompany them. That night, at Gray, Shelley bought some meat and induced the surly proprietress to show him how to make soup. She and her husband were won over when Shelley insisted they share the supper he prepared. Claire reported this homey scene; Mary's journal entries featured more judgmental social-class biases. Pushing on to Morre, Mary and Shelley read Wollstonecraft's *Mary*, while Claire read *As You Like It*. Faced with dirty beds and being told their driver would have to share the room with them, the three sat up all night on chairs around the kitchen fire before setting off at four in the morning. As the sun rose at Noè, Shelley again recorded his sensitivity to nuances of light as "a ray of the red light lay on the waves of this fluctuating vapour."

Claire, more earthy, wrote that having washed only their hands and faces since leaving Paris, Shelley asked the driver to stop at a clear shallow stream. Shelley proposed taking off his clothes and bathing, asking Mary to do the same as the bank was sheltered from view. Rejecting his "indecent" idea and saying she had no towel, Shelley's offer of leaves to dry herself evoked Mary's disdainful retort, "how could he think of such a thing." Refusing to stop his carriage, the driver shot "a wondering stare [at Shelley] as if he thought he was rather crazy."[70] Near Nods, they left the driver to seek a secluded shady glen to picnic. Mary and Claire, still protesting the filthy conditions of the French poor, received a two-hour Godwinian dissertation from Shelley on human perfectibility. After his protracted discourse, they found their unenlightened driver had left them stranded. Because Shelley's ankle was again bad, they hired another cart for Pontarlier, where they caught up with their driver. That night, before sleeping in the first clean bed since leaving Paris, Claire reported Shelley asked Mary why she looked so sad. After answering that she was thinking of her father, Shelley asked, "Do you mean to reproach me?"

The next day, August 19, they passed into Switzerland at Les Verrièrs. After obtaining a new driver and carriage at St. Sulpice, on approaching Neuchâtel they had their first view of the Alps. Shelley wrote that the Alps were as "accumulated clouds of dazzling white. . . . Their immensity staggers the imagination, & far surpasses all conception that it requires an effort of understanding to believe that they are indeed mountains."

No letters awaited them at Neuchâtel but Shelley somehow procured £38 from the local bank and staggered back with a large canvas bag filled with coins. An amiable Swiss, taking Shelley and Mary for two lovers running away from their parents, helped them hire a *voiturier* to take them to Lucerne the next day. Claire, asked if she also had run away for love, answered, "Oh! dear No—I came to speak french." Claire became much "vexed" with Shelley for making her translate "one of Rousseau's Reveries" when she wanted to see Neuchâtel.[71] Shelley talked with Claire about her "character," but it was he who was in "a jocosely horrible mood."[72]

For a week, no letters came and Shelley felt that he "alone looks grave on the occasion," fearing their money would be "gone before you can say Jack Robinson." They decided to continue to Uri, but Shelley realized their flight was futile. Growing weary of "wheeled machines," after napping at Zofingen, they gave up crossing Mont St. Gothard to Italy's warmth, which they sought for Shelley's "precarious" health. Still "tired to death," in Sursee they got up at four in the morning for Lucerne, hired a boat and glided on to Brunnen. All three were reading Barruel's *History of Jacobinism*, one stimulus for a story gestating in Shelley's mind.[73]

With some difficulty they found an inn, but they had not reached the cottage Shelley sought from *Fleetwood* and the spot where Wilhelm Tell conspired to overthrow Swiss tyrants.[74] The next day, desperate over being unable to find an available house, they settled for two unfurnished "wretched" rooms in "an ugly big house," paying six guineas for a six-month lease. As if the overheated stove was not discomfort enough, they were irritated when the local priest and doctor visited to pry on the morals of this youth and his two young female companions. After two days in their lodgings, Shelley abruptly abandoned his Fleetwoodian fantasy. They would return to England.

On August 25, before leaving Brunnen, Shelley began dictating to Mary a "romance," *The Assassins,* the first of three prose stories he would write.[75] This story fragment expressed his revolutionary views of society and, seemingly, his wish to recreate a family in isolated exile. Literary influences included Tacitus's siege of Jerusalem and Barruel's account of the secret revolutionary society, the Illuminati, Delisle de Sales's *Le vieux de la montagne* and Gibbon's *Decline and Fall of the Roman Empire*. Shelley continued writing his story on the way home and would read to Hookham what he had written. However, he abandoned the story by April 1815 before completing the fourth chapter.[76]

Shelley's Assassins—not an Ismaili sect of Muslims—were Gnostic-like Christian dissidents who fled from the Roman siege of Jerusalem to the beautiful valley of "Bethzatanai" in Lebanon.[77]

The actual Assassins' strict chief reputedly dispensed hashish and voluptuous sexuality to reward his followers. Shelley, possibly more accurately, wrote of an "obscure" sect "of speculators" who evolved after four hundred years into a "sacred hermitage" of benevolent, egalitarian love. However, the society's long isolation led to committing acts of violence against those "with narrow views and the illiberality of sectarian patriotism." The "perplexed" Assassins, reflecting Shelley's ambivalence about revolutionary violence, justified "the means" of causing "immediate pain . . . for . . . future benefit," and waged "unremitting hostility from principle." Shelley's Assassins attacked not only the "phantasms" of tyrannical power, but those, perhaps like Wordsworth, "who retire to nature and conform to despotic rule," pay "tribute to the God of Nature . . . submissively temporize with vice, and in cold charity become a pander to falsehood and desolation."[78]

In Shelley's narrative, the mangled but alive body of a priestlike healer is found crucified in a tree by a young man, Albedir. In a grisly Gothic passage that Mary excised, the old man was "prey" for a "monstrous snake" as "innumerable worms disputed for the putrid morsel even at his pestilential jaws." The old man, whose matted hair was "a mass of bloody snow," had a gaping wound exposing his "naked heart . . . beating violently against his naked ribs." In a mutual rescue fantasy, Albedir recognized the old man he was saving was his childhood "partner . . . the brother of his soul." In turn, the old man could now minister to Albedir's personal shortcomings, an outcome Shelley did not pursue in his unfinished story.

The threatening, monstrous serpent now became "a small snake," a loving playmate for Albedir's two children. The son, and his two-years-younger sister—like Shelley and his sister Elizabeth—played with the snake by the lake's edge where it leapt into the girl's bosom as "she crossed her fair hands over it, as if to cherish it."[79] Aside from intimations of childhood sibling sexual play, Shelley may have been aware of the snake symbolism of the Ophite Gnostics.[80]

Their laundry still wet from the dampness, the three delayed departing Brunnen until August 27. Leaving in their hired boat, Mary noted "the astonishment" of the townsfolk and Claire thought the people would think them "wild" for leasing a house for six months and leaving after two days due to a faulty stove.

Boat travel was cheaper and easier on Mary, whose pregnancy was kept from Claire. In Lucerne, Mary helped "write a part" of

The Assassins and the three read *Richard III* and *King Lear.* That night, they were "Interrupted by Janes horrors," the first of Claire's occasional night terrors.[81]

Proceeding down the Reuss and Aare Rivers, Mary was repelled by their fellow voyagers' "horrid and slimy faces . . . our only wish was to absolutely anihilate such uncleansable animals." Claire mentioned being subjected to leers, crude laughter, and swearing. Later, in a ruckus with their rude companions over seating, Shelley responded to the leader's verbal attack by knocking him down. The decked fellow "continued his vociferations" but did not return Shelley's blow.[82]

Several days later, at Laufenburg on the Rhine, they engaged a small, crude, flat-bottomed "canoe" so leaky they had to bail constantly. Winding down the rapid river in their "frail boat," they dodged "rocks, which it was death to touch." Switching to land travel, friendly Swiss soldiers carried their box as the three trudged into the next village for the boat to Basel. Upon awakening the next morning, they realized it was August 30, Mary's seventeenth birthday. Embarking on another exciting river trip, their boat "dashed with inconcievable [*sic*] rapidity" as Shelley admired the beautiful whirlpools. For three days he read aloud Wollstonecraft's *Letters from Norway.*[83]

Continuing north past the Rhine castles, they arrived in Cologne September 5. Mary and Claire, repelled by "the lower order of Germans," found disagreeable the public kissing between men. After two days' land travel through Holland, they arrived September 8 in Rotterdam. Out of money, the next morning they arranged passage to England for three guineas each. Sailing only a few leagues, they remained at Marsluys several days because of bad winds. Shelley wrote more of *The Assassins* and Mary began a story she titled *Hate.* Not to be outdone, Claire began a story, *Ideot,* about a woman "who knew no other guide than herself or the impulses arising from herself."[84]

On September 11, their English captain braved the elements as the ship barely cleared the bar leaving the Rhine for the open sea. Everyone became seasick except Claire. Mary, "sick as death," ended her seven-week elopement as it began, on a stormy sea. Anchoring at Gravesend the morning of September 13, Shelley had difficulty persuading the Captain to let them disembark to obtain funds. Accompanied by the boatman who rowed them up the Thames, they took a coach midafternoon for Shelley's banker.

Fig. 14. Mary Wollstonecraft Shelley, posthumous miniature by Reginald Easton, after her death mask and Edward Williams's 1821–1822 pencil sketch, Shelley Relics (d), courtesy of the Bodleian Library.

Fig. 15. Claire Clairmont by Amelia Curran, 1819, courtesy of City of Nottingham Museums; Newstead Abbey.

Fig. 16. Thomas Love Peacock, miniature by Roger Jean, c. 1805, courtesy of the National Portrait Gallery, London.

Fig. 17. Shelley's Bishopsgate cottage. Photograph by author.

Fig. 18. Lord Byron by Thomas Phillips, 1813, courtesy of City of Nottingham Museums; Newstead Abbey.

17
Births and Deaths

S HELLEY, FINDING NO FUNDS IN HIS LONDON BANK ACCOUNT OR AT Thomas Hookham's bookshop, had Mary and Claire wait two hours in the coach in front of the Westbrook house. Inside, Shelley talked to Harriet, now six months pregnant, before finally emerging with enough money to pay the patient boatman. The tired threesome spent the night in a hotel.

After calling on Harriet again the next day, September 14, Shelley wrote her the first of a series of letters with insensitive and cutting remarks. Seemingly uncomprehending of Harriet's need for support in this time of crisis, he complained she "wounded" him with her "reproach & blame." His "violent and lasting passion" for Mary made him "prefer her society to yours." After commenting about being united with Mary in "passion," he told Harriet his remarks were not "cold and unfeeling."[1] After seeing Harriet for the third time, Shelley reconciled with Hookham. Having read aloud to the young publisher *The Assassins*, Shelley wrote further on his story.

Moving to 56 Margaret Street, the three travelers read part of Wordsworth's *The Excursion*, just published by Hookham. They were "much disappointed," Mary judging Wordsworth "a slave."[2] In the next several years, Shelley's sustained poetic challenge to Wordsworth's conservative political and religious views found expression in his sonnet to Wordsworth, *Alastor, Laon and Cythna,* and *Peter Bell the Third.*

During Shelley's absence, Harriet's spirits lifted when people said he would return to her. She even told Godwin personally that she would try to squelch the rumors that he had sold his two daughters to Shelley, Mary for £800 and Claire for £700. These rumors surfaced when Godwin started paying off his debt with Shelley's £1120 *post obit* money.[3]

Feelings between Harriet and Shelley soon hardened after his return. He wanted a private settlement with her but her advisors led her to hope for a formal settlement from the Shelley estate. Working on a new *post obit* bond, Shelley kept his lawyer Amory in the dark about details of his marital situation. Sounding like his father, Shelley asked Harriet how much she desired her life "to be placed within the influence of my superintending mind."[4]

When the bond went to auction September 21, no one offered to buy it. Harriet, briefly away from London, wrote a letter to Shelley that Claire considered "mean & worldly." Harriet, more confrontational about money due her, had found an attorney, "an act of determined hostility" according to Shelley. He had heard a rumor, presumably originating from Eliza Westbrook, that Harriet's father intended to "take legal steps in consequence of my conduct." If Harriet persisted "in appealing to the law," Shelley would consider her "an enemy" who practices "the basest & blackest treachery." Resenting her "contumelious language toward Mary," he added, "You are plainly lost to me."[5] With Peacock in tow, he began making the rounds among insurance agents, bankers, lawyers, and moneylenders.

Godwin soon extended his embargo on communication with Shelley to Mary and Claire, and the two camps settled into a month-long standoff. However, Fanny and Mrs. Godwin came to Margaret Street to talk to Mary and Claire through an open window. Charles Clairmont brought news of Godwin's idea to put Claire into a convent. As Godwin's business dealings disintegrated, his financial backer, Francis Place, washed his hands of Godwin and threatened legal action.[6] The Godwins were on the verge of being thrown out onto the street.

Afraid of bailiffs after the failed bond sale, Shelley did not tell Harriet of his September 27 move to more remote lodgings at 5 Church Terrace, St. Pancras. He did write her offering reassurances about Dr. Sims's skill in delivering her baby and about her having a less painful labor than her first.[7] A temporary civility settled over their correspondence and Shelley assured her he was avoiding lawyers in trying to arrange a monetary settlement with her.[8]

Mary and Claire were receiving their first lessons in Greek from Shelley. Claire continued writing her *Ideot* but Mary's *Hate* was in limbo. All three kept busy with reading, Shelley making sure Claire and Mary read Chevalier Lawrence's *The Empire of the Nairs; or, the Rights of Woman,* with its equation of legal marriage with prostitution. Hookham and Peacock, although regular visitors to Shelley's circle, continued to sympathize with Harriet.

Shelley now entered a period of growing emotional instability, introspective analysis, and creative stalemate. Peacock recalled this fall and winter of 1814 as perhaps "the most solitary period of Shelley's life." Walking with Peacock, Shelley quoted Wordsworth's verses and asked his friend if Wordsworth "could have written such poetry, if he had ever had dealings with money-lenders?"[9]

Together with Mary and Claire, Shelley concocted a scheme at the end of September to collect his two sisters, twenty-year-old Elizabeth and fifteen-year-old Hellen, from their nearby boarding school in Hackney, and carry them off to western Ireland. Shelley also thought Peacock and his woman friend, Marianne de St. Croix, might join them.[10] The scheme collapsed and Shelley pursued his passions for sailing paper fireboats, setting off fireworks, and conducting nighttime chemical experiments.

Mary, starting her third month of pregnancy in early October, began retiring early. Shelley and Claire talked late, after being out together during the day while Mary stayed home. One evening, after Mary retired, Shelley and Claire conversed by the fireside until one o'clock. Shelley said it was "the witching time" and talked of the "horrible" feeling of the night's "silence." Thinking Shelley looked "passing strange," Claire said, "How horribly you look . . . take your eyes off!" and ran upstairs to bed. Shelley went to Mary, kissed her, and began to read when Claire came running down the stairs. She had been frightened when she saw a pillow in the middle of her bed had mysteriously moved to a chair. She sat up "all night" with Shelley, and at dawn the two examined the room to find "every thing" as Claire described.

After Claire flew down the stairs in fright, Shelley recalled that she had "most dreadful convulsions," writhing and shrieking on the floor. After telling Claire that Mary was pregnant, Shelley brought her to Mary where "Her convulsions gradually ceased & she slept."[11] Shelley, discouraging Claire from returning to Skinner Street, continued his late night séances with her. She later crossed out her entries about these talks, observing that Peacock laughed about her "horrors." Shelley was not impressed with Peacock's derisiveness.

Shelley's tranquility was disturbed when his latest effort to obtain money failed and he received a "cold & even sarcastic" letter from Mrs. Boinville. He wrote Harriet that without monetary relief by November 1, "I must go to prison." Ten days later, he appealed to her for funds, saying his money "vexations have induced my antient illness."[12]

Apparently fearing being arrested for debt, Shelley decided to flee London. A letter that arrived on October 12 was burned unopened after they argued over what it might contain. Shelley arranged for Hookham to receive his allowance and Hookham then sent Shelley five pounds. Impulsively, Shelley deferred leaving town, taking Mary and Claire to the Drury Lane Theatre to see Edmund Kean in *Hamlet*. Shelley was critical of Kean's weak performance—as were the critics—and they left after the second act.[13] Returning home, they had an "Alarm" and, frightened of bailiffs, spent the night at a hotel.[14]

Claire quarreled with Shelley, who enlightened her about her shortcomings. He then felt he had been too severe on her because her "unformed" character might change. Writing in the journal Mary would see, he warned himself against erotic entanglements and contented himself "with one great affection . . . never suffer more than one even to approach the hallowed circle." Claire soon refused Godwin's appeal to come home, acquiescing to Shelley's wishes.[15]

Prohibited from seeing Godwin, Shelley sent Peacock to Skinner Street on October 20, but Godwin would only deal with his daughter's seducer through an attorney. Fanny, uncharacteristically defying Godwin, warned Shelley that Hookham planned to reveal their Church Terrace hideout to Shelley's creditors, including Charters the coachmaker. After consulting his lawyer, Shelley came home, argued with Mary and Claire about how to raise £50 for Charters and decided to go into hiding to avoid arrest. On Sunday evening, October 23, he said goodbye to Mary and departed Church Street for a furtive underground existence that lasted until November 9. That night, Claire took Shelley's place in bed next to Mary.

During the next sixteen days, Shelley spent two Saturday nights at Church Terrace, debtors being exempt from arrest from midnight Saturday to midnight Sunday. He moved constantly to foil the bailiffs, who showed up at Church Terrace the day after he left. In addition to Peacock's lodgings, Shelley and Mary met sporadically at St. Paul's Cathedral and at a variety of hotels and coffeehouses, favoring those outside the bailiffs' jurisdiction.

Separated from Mary, Shelley became anxious and quickly wrote her that "the separation is a calamity . . . I cannot support your absence."[16] Trying to arrange another *post obit* loan, Shelley wrote Mary of finding Hookham a "cool villain." As for Mary's "cold and worldly" father, Shelley was "shocked & staggered" by his "cold injustice" and his "cutting cruelty."[17] His money depleted, Shelley would sell his cherished solar microscope to the charitable Hogg for five pounds.[18]

St. Paul's became a favorite meeting place, perhaps because Mary felt she would not be mistaken for a streetwalker. Shelley, encountering prostitutes in Covent Garden, felt "infected" and "loathsome" when they stared at him. He wished for Mary's "redeeming eyes" awaiting their next sexual union. His mind "without yours is dead & cold as the dark midnight river when the moon is down," a first reference to Mary as the moon.[19] Hookham, back in favor, warned Shelley to avoid a certain coffeehouse when having his Saturday night of love with Mary. Dreaming again of a distant, safe nesting place, Shelley wrote to Wales about Nantgwillt where Mary was convinced things would be "much better."[20]

Shelley had declined a "rascally" offer from Ballachey, £300 a year until Timothy died for a £15,000 *post obit*. Had he accepted, and outlived his father, Shelley would have made £9000. Another lawyer, Pike, offered £12,000 for the reversion of Sir Bysshe's Castle Goring. Shelley refused, complaining it was unfairly priced.[21] Thirty years later, Castle Goring sold for less. Shelley, turning to relatives, tried unsuccessfully to raise money from his uncle, Sir John Shelley-Sidney.[22]

In addition to seeking his own financial salvation, Shelley was trying to keep Godwin out of debtor's jail. Mary heard from Fanny and Charles Clairmont of Godwin's threatened arrest for failing to pay a major creditor £150 due November 3. On November 5, Shelley successfully deferred Godwin's debt until November 22. The *post obit* bond that was arranged on the Shelley estate provided Godwin the use of Shelley's good offices without breaking his vow not to see him. Similar *post obit*s were arranged in December to cancel two other Godwin debts. The total liability of these *post obit*s was possibly as high as £5000.[23]

Shelley now hoped to meet his November 6 deadline for coming out of hiding. Hookham helped him pay his £100 bill to Charters, but a much larger bill would come due to the coachmaker in several months.[24] In vain, Shelley wrote Whitton for an increase in his allowance from his father.[25] On November 8, still in hiding, Shelley contemplated moving from Church Terrace. By the time he emerged from hiding November 9, he was assuring Mary in Greek that kissing her fantasized body at night when retiring produced the desired lover's sleep.[26]

Two days earlier, Shelley met Hogg and was disappointed by his old friend's "very cold" joking about Shelley's "*two Wives.*"[27] Mary was disappointed in her closest friend, Isabella Booth, whose husband, David Booth, forbade her from corresponding with Mary.[28] Mary was also unhappy that Claire was again under the same roof. On November 9, the three moved to more desirable quarters, 2 Nelson Square, Blackfriars Road.

An emotional storm apparently broke out crossing Blackfriars Bridge. Claire tore out three pages describing the trip to Nelson Square and did not resume her journal until early 1818. Triumphantly, Mary noted in her journal, "Jane very gloomy—she is sullen with Shelley—Well never mind. my love we are happy." Claire, dropping "Jane," now, adopted her first name, "Clara." Mary, still retiring early, on November 13 was "very unwell," threatening to miscarry.

Godwin threatened Fanny not to see Mary or he would not speak to her again. However, Fanny did visit, trying to bring Claire back to Skinner Street by saying her mother was dying. Claire, "disappointed" in Shelley, went back to the Godwins but stayed only two nights.

Hogg arrived November 14 for a planned visit and met Mary for the first time. The two were pleased with each other and Mary's symptoms temporarily improved. Perhaps, Shelley thought, Hogg "still may be my friend" despite their differences. After Hogg left, Mary again was "very unwell."[29]

Hogg, now a regular visitor, assuaged Mary's loneliness. Shelley and Claire resumed their evening talks and were often away all day. Shelley was reading Charles Brockden Brown's 1799 novel, *Edgar Huntley; or, the Sleep-walker.* Like Shelley, Brown scoffed at the conventions of marriage, religion, and private property. The plot of Brown's *Wieland,* Shelley's favorite, involved night terrors of the sister, Clara, obviously akin to Shelley's Clara. Peacock observed that nothing blended more into the "structure" of Shelley's "interior mind" as Brown's creations, particularly the heroine in Brown's *Ormond,* Constantia Dudley.[30] Constantia become Shelley's poetic name for Claire.

Shelley was "strangely captivated" by the scene in *Edgar Huntley* in which the sleepwalker digs his own grave. He identified with the hunted characters in Brown's novels and in Godwin's *Caleb Williams,* whose hero was pursued by an avenger. About this time, Shelley's paranoia about Leeson apparently resurfaced. Claire later reported that Shelley insisted on her company whenever he went out on the London streets because he feared he could be stabbed by his Tanyrallt enemy.[31] Still controlling Claire, Shelley for a time prohibited her from pursuing her interest in music and singing.[32]

Shelley at this time wrote an anonymous review of Hogg's pseudonymous 1813 novel, *Memoirs of Prince Alexy Haimatoff.*[33] In his review, Shelley expressed "horror and detestation" over Hogg's views on sex, a timely concern considering Hogg's reintroduction into his ménage. Destroying the novel, Shelley found Hogg's ideas "pernicious and disgusting . . . a most impressive and tremendous allegory of the cold-blooded and malignant selfishness of sensuality."[34]

After failing with Shelley's sister and with Harriet, Hogg now became interested in Shelley's latest love. Shelley encouraged "complete reciprocity" in Hogg's developing relationship with Mary, but her pregnancy was his built-in hedge. Writing in her journal for Shelley's inquisitive eyes, Mary found Hogg's arguments "a sad bungle" and a "muddle." By early December, she liked him "better tonight than before" but still thought he was a lost child.

Illness now pervaded the household. Claire was bled by a doctor, Shelley experienced his "Slight spasm in the side,"[35] and Mary's miscarriage symptoms recurred. Also, Harriet was experiencing difficulties with Shelley's other unborn child. Shelley and Peacock went for Harriet's Dr. Sims, who later sent word that Harriet was not in great danger. Shelley, forbidden to see Harriet, wrote her asking for funds and wondered if she were "confined." He was realistically concerned that Eliza had left town just when Harriet was in a "terrible state of dejection."[36]

In November, ten days before giving birth, Harriet, lonely and embittered, contrasted her life with Shelley's in a letter to Mrs. Nugent. Shelley, "living with Godwin's two daughters," had "become profligate and sensual, owing entirely to Godwin's *Political Justice.* . . . The man I once loved is dead. This is a vampire." Eliza had taken Ianthe to Southampton and Harriet, alone, was expecting her baby the end of December.[37] On December 6, Mary was still "very unwell" and also alone, as Shelley and Claire were out. A letter from Hookham had news that, in Mary's words, "Harriet has been brought to bed of a son and heir." That same day, Harriet wrote Shelley confirming his son's birth a week earlier on November 30.

Harriet's letter, styled by Mary as from a "deserted housewife," reflected the disturbed parental scene into which this vulnerable eight-month child was born. Named Charles Bysshe, he was the heir to the title and estates of his three living Shelley sires. A more crucial inheritance was the liability of an absent father and a depressed, abandoned mother living in the home of her parents, whom she despised.

Shelley wrote to his family and others announcing Charles's birth but Mary, sardonic about her own unmarried pregnant state, noted the birth should be celebrated "with the ringing of bells &c. for it is the son of his wife." Shelley quickly saw his lawyers and Harriet,[38] who reported a "good" labor. The baby, healthy considering his early arrival, looked "very like his unfortunate father." Harriet did not expect that Charles's arrival would effect a reconciliation with Shelley, who "said he was glad it was a boy, because he would make money cheaper."[39] This hope, that having a son would facilitate procuring loans, goaded Shelley to spend much of December seeking loans for Godwin.

If Harriet initially questioned her baby's paternity,[40] she was convinced Shelley was the father when she wrote Mrs. Nugent December 11. Shelley's later actions were always consistent with the belief that the child was his. Harriet, in 1816, wrote to Shelley of "your beautiful boy" and Timothy Shelley, years later, raised young Charles as a member of the Shelley family.

Early in the New Year, the newspapers announced that Shelley's grandfather had died January 6.[41] Shelley's first caller was Hookham, who realized that Sir Bysshe's death had major financial implications for Shelley. By this time, they needed new lodgings to avoid Harriet's creditors. With Hogg's help, they soon moved to 41 Hans Place, a more fashionable area between Chelsea and Kensington. Hogg was increasingly attentive to Mary, now five months pregnant and still feeling unwell. She stayed home when Shelley and Claire went to Field Place for the reading of Sir Bysshe's will on January 12. Shelley ignored Whitton's appeal that he not go because his presence would "be most painful" to his mother.[42] Leaving Claire at nearby Slinfold, Shelley arrived at

Field Place to be refused entrance by his father, now Sir Timothy. While the will was being read inside, Shelley sat on the doorstep reading Mary's copy of Milton's *Comus* until a Dr. Blocksome came outside. Seeing Mary's name in the book, he told Shelley his father was "very angry with him." Shelley's sympathetic half-uncle, John Shelley-Sidney of Penshurst, then came out to tell his nephew it was "a most extraordinary will."[43]

Shelley, apparently seeing none of his family, spent the night with Claire at Kingston. Shortly after, Shelley saw Whitton and learned he would have an income of £100,000 when his father died if Shelley entailed the estate. When Sir Bysshe was buried at Horsham Church on January 18, Shelley kept his pledge made to Elizabeth Hitchener exactly three years earlier that he would neither grieve the "hardhearted apostate" nor attend his funeral.

It was reported that banknotes worth £12,816 were found sewn in Sir Bysshe's dressing gown, hidden in the sofa, and between leaves of his few books.[44] His fortune had two major pieces, about £80,000 in real estate he had inherited or acquired by marriage, and about £140,000 representing his personal fortune.[45] Sir Bysshe controlled the £140,000, but not the £80,000, which would ultimately pass to Shelley when his father died. To prevent Shelley from writing more *post obit* bonds on his estate, Sir Bysshe proposed in his will that only if Shelley relinquished absolute right to the £80,000 could he get the interest from the £140,000. In essence, Sir Bysshe put the two pieces together, a total of over £220,000, and prevented the selling of either. Aiming all this at Shelley, Sir Bysshe hoped to lure his errant grandson into an anticipated income of between £12,000 and £14,000 when Timothy died, perhaps twice as much as he would otherwise receive. Shelley, knowledgeable about financial and legal matters, detailed his situation to Godwin and concluded negatively that he was not entitled "to any *immediate* advantage."[46]

Shelley received a copy of his grandfather's will with Whitton's note saying "Sir Timothy was ready to concur" with the conditions spelled out in the will's five codicils. Shelley, despite having one year to accept these conditions, immediately decided to reject his grandfather's terms. By refusing the £140,000 bait, Shelley perhaps hoped that his access to his £80,000 portion would provide a bargaining tool with his father for immediate relief, rather than having to wait for his father to expire. If Timothy lived as long as Sir Bysshe, Shelley would have to wait another twenty-two years.

Shelley then heard that his father hoped he would reject the terms of the will so that the estate's larger portion might be inherited by his youngest son, John. Shelley decided to wait and keep his decision secret. However, Godwin's financial nose already had detected this latest scent of Shelley money and he urged Shelley not to reject the terms. Undeterred, Shelley signed a Deed of Disclaimer March 1, rejecting the conditions of his grandfather's will.[47] However, a promising third piece of Sir Bysshe's estate had come to light.

Sir Bysshe had omitted from his will £18,000 inherited from his brother John, a sum Shelley jointly controlled with his father. In a few months, money from this last portion afforded Shelley the immediate relief he sought. After Sir Bysshe's death, Timothy's financial negotiations with Shelley were more conciliatory and lenient, underscoring the control old Bysshe exercised and Timothy's subservience to his father. In agreements with his father, Shelley relinquished his rights over this £18,000 in return for a £1000 annuity as long as he and his father lived, plus £7400 for paying his debts.[48] To establish this arrangement's legality, a friendly Chancery suit brought by Shelley was finalized in March 1816. However, in May 1815, Shelley and his father settled on the payment of £7400. After paying previous and recent debts, Shelley had £4500 left.[49] He gave Harriet £200 for her debts and arranged a £200 annual income for her be paid from his £1000 annuity. With her father's allowance, Harriet's annual income was now £400. From his remaining £800 annual income, Shelley began giving £120 annually to Peacock, undoubtedly without Godwin's awareness.[50]

When Shelley only paid a part of his Tremadoc debts, Nanney accused him of having lied in a statement about the furniture he had hired for him at Tanyrallt.[51] Debts still unpaid at Shelley's death included the £532 bill from Charters, who had Shelley arrested in November 1816, and sued him unsuccessfully for a £1000 debt.[52] From his dwindling purse, Shelley gave £1000 to angry Godwin, who expected £1200. Godwin accepted the £1000 despite the rumors he had sold his two daughters to Shelley, his benefactor he still refused to see.

Love was vying with money. Hogg, professing his love for Mary on New Year's Day, sent a present and note to "Maie." Mary also was called "Pecksie" or "Dormouse," Hogg became "Alexy," and Shelley occasionally called himself "The Elfin Knight." Some details of the affair between Mary and Hogg are found in Mary's eleven letters to Hogg between January 1 and April 26. Significant information gaps include Mary's frequent torn out or skipped journal entries and Claire's missing journal. Hogg's biography of Shelley stopped just as the events of 1815 began.

Mary discussed Hogg's letter with Shelley on New Year's Day morning. Despite her "great pain" the previous night, she immediately wrote Hogg that despite his profession of love for her it would take time for her to feel love for him. However, she would "use every effort to promote your happiness."[53] That night, Shelley retired early, leaving Hogg and Mary alone. Some later censor of Mary's journal obliterated a record of where he slept.[54] Hogg's frequent visits pleased Mary, whose feelings for him ripened quickly. She enticed him to visit, saying Shelley and Claire would not return "till very late." He could "console a solitary lady. . . . I love you more and more." She ended "with one kiss." Shelley, apparently hearing by January 4 of his grandfather's imminent death, originally planned to go alone to Sussex.[55] That Claire accompanied Shelley suggests Mary's desire to be alone with Hogg and Shelley's possible intimacy with Claire at this time. Such sexual arrangements between couples genuinely in love, irrespective of marital status, reflect Shelley's views in his review of Hogg's novel.[56]

Throughout January and February, Hogg visited most every day, often staying overnight. When he asked for a lock of her hair in early January she sent it to him asking for more time for her affection to increase so that he could have what would "add to your happiness." There were also "phisical causes"—her pregnancy—that Hogg and "Shelley will be subject to." For now, "we need not be prudent."[57]

Peacock was off on his own fling, having left Marianne for a "rich heiress" in Liverpool who was in love with him. This mysterious affair ended when she proved moneyless and Peacock went to debtor's jail. While Shelley and Claire were in Sussex, Mary received a letter from "the foolish man" about his £40 debt. She sent him two pounds.

Another early January letter was from the mysterious Ryan, possibly an emissary from Harriet, who reportedly was threatening "to take all possible legal advantage of Shelley." Shelley waited at home to see Ryan, but he did not appear until the next day when Mary, alone with Hogg, refused to see him.[58]

Another caller later in January was George Cannon, whose multifarious careers included lawyer, preacher, philosopher, writer, and pornographer. Having some connection to Oxford, in 1813 a letter—probably his—appeared in *Cobbett's Political Register* detailing Shelley's religious views and personal history.[59] Using the pseudonym "Erasmus Perkins," in early 1815 he was about to launch and edit a radical periodical, the *Theological Inquirer; or Polemical Magazine*, a publication with which Shelley became involved.[60] Shelley and the devious Cannon perhaps became acquainted through Godwin, who was visited twice by Cannon earlier in January.[61]

Cannon was the most intriguing tie Shelley had with the radical, and often unsavory, underground press. A religious freethinker, Cannon was a friend of Daniel Isaac Eaton, the publisher of Holbach's *Ecco Homo*, an attack on Jesus that Shelley mentioned in *Queen Mab*.[62] Shelley evaded Cannon when he first called, and he left with Hogg and Mary "papers" for them to read. Cannon's call nine days later elicited Shelley's comment in Greek, "He shattered a most blissful sleep." Cannon, who stayed the evening, Shelley considered "the most miserable wretch alive . . . [a] vulgar brute." Shelley possibly was obfuscating. Several days later he wrote in the journal, "after a conversation of uncommon wit & genius Erasmus exclaimed aut Morus aut diabolus [either More or the devil]."[63] Was Shelley the devil to Cannon's Erasmus? Advancing this possibility, St Clair translated literally Shelley's Greek journal entry as "he throws down the sleep blessed by the daimon." Shelley possibly was referring to Cannon's refusal to publish the first part of *Queen Mab*, a section Shelley soon revised and published as *The Daemon of the World*.[64]

Cannon soon began printing extensive excerpts of *Queen Mab* and part of *A Refutation of Deism* in the first issue of his *Theological Inquirer*. The real reader interest was in the *Queen Mab* excerpts, with laudatory commentary and a poem, "Ode to the author of *Queen Mab*."[65] Cannon, like some other radical publishers of the time, would switch to publishing pornography and was sentenced to prison for obscene libel in 1830.[66]

As January ended, Shelley wrote in Greek in the journal that for the past month "Maia's child begins to live and is stirring."[67] Mary, in a letter to "dearest Alexey," wrote her most effusive expression of love for Shelley during his lifetime. Her "soul is entirely wrapt up in him . . . to see his love his tenderness . . . draw tears more delicious than the smiles of love from your eyes."[68]

This domestic mood changed drastically when, on February 8, after less than a month at 42 Hans Place, they moved to 1 Hans Place. Mary's journal entry the next day, "a mess," was followed by four days of torn-out entries. By February 14, Shelley was "feverish & fatigued" and Mary was "unwell in the evening" when Hogg came to "put us to bed." Too ill to visit the moneylenders, Shelley read Byron's *Lara* to Mary. Suddenly, on February 22, Shelley recorded Mary had given birth to a premature female infant "not quite 7 months." Dr. Clarke, arriving five minutes after the birth, said the child was not expected to live. Hogg stayed the night.[69]

The next day, Mary was well but the baby's condition was still dire. Hogg visited and Fanny, spending the night, brought linen from Mrs. Godwin. A stubborn Godwin still refused to see Mary, despite her baby's precarious state. On February 24, the infant seemed better and a hopeful Mary began nursing her child. When Dr. Clarke called he supported their hopes. Mary began reading Madame de Staël's *Corinne*, the novel she would reread under conditions of stress.

Shelley now became ill, a recurrent event after the birth of each of his subsequent children. Three days after giving birth, Mary considered herself and the baby "very well" but Shelley was still "very unwell." Mary, out of bed the next day, sent Shelley out to buy a cradle, despite his spasm.

Hogg recalled that Shelley "coughed at times violently" and had occasional pain in his side and chest, which Shelley called "spasms." He was skeptical that Shelley's lung complaint was consumption,[70] but Shelley's spasms may have been due partially to kidney stones. It is possible a brief episode of tuberculosis created a kidney stone that caused some of his spasms.[71] Years later, Mary recalled that in the spring of 1815 Shelley saw an "eminent physician"—probably William Lawrence—who "pronounced that he was dying rapidly of consumption, abscesses were formed on his lungs, and he suffered acute spasms." Mary noted a sudden "complete change took place . . . every symptom of pulmonary disease vanished." She noted that his "nerves," always extremely "sensitive," were made "more susceptible by the state of his health."[72] Continuing consultations with Lawrence in the spring and summer, Shelley believed his health was "considerably improved."[73] As the stress during the first half of 1815 subsided, Shelley's symp-

toms ceased, probably not as suddenly as Mary recalled. Shelley
in 1815 also twice consulted Dr. Christopher Pemberton, the leading liver specialist who was a doctor to the despised Prince Regent.

Despite the health problems of baby and father, Mary notified
Hogg they were moving that day, March 2, to 13 Arabella Road in
Pimlico because of the danger of being fleeced by the landlady.[74]
Mary went to the new home with her eight-day-old premature in-
fant at three in the afternoon, joined at six by Shelley and Claire.
Four days later, Mary wrote, "find my baby dead." She immediately
sent a poignant appeal to Hogg: "My dearest Hogg my baby is
dead—will you come to me as soon as you can—I wish to see you."
Mary thought it had died of convulsions.[75] Hogg spent the night
and the next day.

There is no record of the unnamed baby's burial. After Hogg left,
there was a "fuss"—Mary's word when she quarreled with Shelley—and it was three before they got to bed. Perhaps this was the
night Claire recalled years later to Edward Silsbee. Mary came
into her room and "putting her head on her pillow & crying bitterly
saying Shelley wants her to sleep with Hogg—that he said Beau-
mont & Fletcher had one mistress." Later in her life, Claire wrote
disapprovingly of Shelley's ideas of love, but to Silsbee she defended his "Greek ideas . . . [he] considered it right to have all in
common even wives—not that he was lacking delicacy in the matter—he treated the matter as a prejudice."[76]

Being ignored by Godwin and his family intensified Mary's feelings of loss and hurt. Godwin's embargo on contact was now simply cruel. In her anguish, Mary wrote in her journal, "still think
about my baby—'tis hard indeed for a mother to loose a child."
Hogg moved in on March 10 to stay for the next five weeks.

The death of Mary's baby effectively ended the emotional viabil-
ity of her relationship with Hogg, even as it lingered for several
more weeks. Mary's deep wish to replace her infant, to rekindle a
life—as would Victor Frankenstein—soon appeared in her journal:
"Dream that my little baby came to life again—that it had only been
cold & that we rubbed it by the fire & it lived."

Mary's loss brought her emotionally and sexually closer to Shelley and inevitably decreased her desire for Hogg. Her monoga-
mous feelings probably were reinforced by her anger toward
Claire and Shelley. Confined, ill, and in pain throughout the difficult
pregnancy, she had to resent their close relationship during the
early months of 1815. Claire later told Byron that Shelley was her

lover this spring. However, Mary turned to Shelley to father another child and renewed her efforts to get Claire out of the household. Before mid-March, Mary had talked to Shelley "about Clary's going" but it seemed "hopeless." She was happy the next day when Claire did not get up until four.

A new development blocked any idea that Claire would return to Skinner Street. It was planned that Fanny, almost twenty-one, would live with her mother's two sisters in Dublin to assist teaching in their school. However, Everina Wollstonecraft and Eliza Bishop, incensed by Godwin's publication of his scandalous relationship with their sister in his *Memoirs* of Wollstonecraft, refused to have Claire at Godwin's home, lest she taint innocent Fanny. After Mrs. Godwin sent this letter about Fanny and Claire to Shelley, he responded to this "prejudice" by saying he would take care of Claire financially in his will.[77] In a fruitless stratagem, Shelley, Mary, and Claire apparently placed a disguised ad in the paper for a teaching position. To keep the Godwins in the dark, the "English young lady" was "now in France."[78]

Peacock was a frequent visitor in March, but Mary found him annoying. Mary read Ovid and played chess with Hogg, who received the purse she had netted for him. Shelley finished Livy and played chess with Claire, who gave him a volume of Seneca. When the four were spotted by Godwin on one of their excursions about town, Godwin remarked to Charles Clairmont that Shelley "was so beautiful it was a pity he was so wicked." That night, after Godwin fought with his wife, she left the house in a "pet" and stayed out all night.

Shelley, walking occasionally to the Serpentine to sail paper boats, called on Harriet in early April to find her in a surprisingly good mood. After Chancery ruled favorably on Shelley's suit concerning financial terms with his father, he saw Harriet to arrange for their son's required appearance in court. However, on his last recorded visit with Harriet, April 22, she apparently balked at letting Shelley take the infant to court, perhaps fearing he might try to keep their son. It is not known if Shelley took baby Charles when he appeared in court two days later. A year later, a court-appointed guardian stood in for Charles.[79]

Mary's journal is uninformative about her resumed physical relationship with Hogg. Late March entries were deleted from her journal and those for sixteen days during April were destroyed. What lovemaking she allowed Hogg probably was short of consummation.[80] With the new law term, Hogg returned to his lodgings April 17 but still visited when he was free. Despite the favorable Chancery suit, Shelley was short of money and his father's first payment was not until late June.

Precipitously on April 24, the day Shelley was to be in court, he and Mary escaped to Salt Hill, near Eton. Shelley left a brief note telling Hogg they would be gone only a day and night, but they stayed longer. Mary wrote Hogg denying she was "hardhearted" as they left for fear of bailiffs. If Hogg were free, she and Shelley would be very glad to see him.[81]

The two days and three nights Shelley and Mary spent at the Windmill Inn in Salt Hill produced significant changes among the now dissolved ménage. Mary had reasserted her sexual position with Shelley twenty miles away from Hogg and a sulky Claire. The major outcome was Mary's becoming pregnant at the Windmill Inn. Testing Hogg's romantic resolve in four letters to him from Salt Hill, she teased him to join them. Knowing his sense of duty to the law courts, she chided him as "Prince Prudent" for refusing to join them, calling herself "a dormouse who had escaped her London Cage." She enclosed Shelley's lines that the Dormouse was "In a wild & mingled mood / Of Maiëishness & Pecksietude."[82]

Mary, alone when writing Hogg, enjoyed the view from the inn of nearby Chalvey Brook and the windmill. Shelley, on a day trip to London to see his lawyer, Longdill, returned immediately to this favored spot he had known at Eton. The old Salt Hill windmill from Shelley's Eton days became an important image in his dreams and poetry. Sometime in 1815, after visiting Salt Hill with Mary, he wrote in his dream journal of revisiting a scene connected with an early dream containing a windmill, a "common scene . . . little calculated to kindle lawless thought." This dream later led to an eerie experience at Oxford where, walking with Hogg, he came upon a scene with a windmill that was the same as in his dream long before. Recalling this incident in his journal, he wrote, "Here I was obliged to leave off, overcome by a thrilling horror." Mary later appended a note recalling how "pale and agitated" he was after writing about this experience as he sought "refuge in conversation from the fearful emotions it excited."[83]

Shelley's phrase, "lawless thought"—a reference to prostitution in *Zastrozzi*—appears to have a sexual connotation in his dream recollection.[84] Hogg's tongue-in-cheek ten-page narrative of this walk is a sexual allegory, a real or imagined joint excursion to visit prostitutes in the "magic circle" of a secret garden, substituted for the windmill. Shelley, overcoming his "modest confusion," precipitously fled "from the garnished retirement he had unwittingly penetrated." Hogg demurred from examining whether Shelley's "conduct, at certain periods, was altogether such as ought to be proposed for imitation."[85]

At Salt Hill, Shelley wrote Hogg explicitly about the threesome's sexual arrangements, saying he would be happy "to give you your share of our common treasure of which you have been cheated for several days." Further, "the Maie knows how highly you prize this exquisite possession. . . . Do not fear. . . . A few months We will not again be deprived of this participated pleasure."[86] The implication that Mary and Hogg were involved sexually has a fair amount of Shelleyan indirection. The canceled "few months" suggests when the "participated pleasure" could begin in earnest. What sexual relationship, if any, began or resumed between Mary and Hogg when she and Shelley soon returned to London is unclear. However, Shelley's letter makes clear he approved of his friend's intimacy with Mary.

Mary's comments in her last Salt Hill letters to Hogg add further doubt as to how far she wished the affair to go. She anticipated Claire's departure and moving out of London. She taunted Hogg to come to Salt Hill "incontinently" or his "love is all a farce" and asked him to send money.[87] Within two weeks, Shelley signed the agreement with his father establishing his £1000 annuity. The £200 annual income for Harriet ended her threat to prosecute Shelley "for atheism" if she did not receive "a handsome settlement."[88]

Claire rejoined Shelley and Mary in London and they soon moved to 26 Marchmont Street, near Russell Square.[89] Hogg visited regularly while Shelley and Claire resumed their time and talks together. After torn-out pages, Mary's journal entry May 8 was, "Jefferson—scolds." Mary tried unsuccessfully to place Claire with Godwin's old landlady but Shelley planned and financed—without the Godwins' knowledge—Claire's removal to Lynmouth. The day before Claire left, she went out with Shelley to have what Mary called "a last conversation." When Claire left the next day, Shelley advised her not to eat meat.[90]

At Lynmouth, Claire wrote to lonely Fanny that she was pleased to hear that "Papa" had received his £1000 from Shelley. Telling Fanny not to be "melancholy," she was enjoying "constant tranquility" after "so much discontent, such violent scenes, such a turmoil of passion and hatred." About to turn seventeen, Claire vainly instructed Fanny that "solitude" teaches "the soul . . . the calm determined path of Virtue & Wisdom."[91]

Mary, writing in mid-May that she was happy with Claire's absence and Shelley's completed financial arrangements with his father, drew a line across the page and wrote, "I begin a new journal with our regeneration," not realizing it included her unborn child.[92] Her feelings for Hogg waning, she and Shelley made plans for a June trip to Devon to seek a house of their own.

Before they left, news came of Napoleon's defeat at Waterloo. Byron and Hazlitt wore black crepe on hearing of Waterloo, but Shelley believed Napoleon had perverted the French Revolution. In his Napoleon sonnet, Shelley loathed this "minister" of "Treason and Slavery, Rapine, Fear, and Lust" but saw a greater "eternal foe" in the political and religious values supporting both the Hanover kings at home and the restored Bourbons in France.[93]

18

The Mirror of Self-Analysis

HEALTH DICTATED THE DESTINATIONS SHELLEY AND MARY CHOSE IN the West Country. Suspecting her pregnancy by mid-June, Mary wanted a rural home. They first stayed at Britain's warmest spot, the seashore resort of Torquay. William Lawrence, advocate of open air cures, possibly prescribed this climate for Shelley's presumed lung problem, which disappeared during the summer. If Lawrence prescribed mercury for Shelley, used commonly to treat tuberculosis and syphilis, Mary discretely avoided mentioning it by saying his lung problem was cured spontaneously.[1] They both wrote lighthearted prescriptions in her journal, Mary's "a small quantity of spermaceti;" "the Elfin Knight" wanted "human blood ... gunpowder ... putrified brain 13 mashed grave worms."[2]

From Torquay, Shelley wrote John Williams in Tremadoc indicating an interest in renting a "remote or solitary" house. Expecting added financial relief from his father in the fall, he could repay his £100 debt to Williams and also consider buying a house. Still in Torquay at the end of June, he again wrote Williams, deferring his plans to go to Wales. Peacock apparently had found a furnished house near Windsor, and Shelley indicated he would leave July 1 to look at it.[3]

Shelley and Mary went north to Clifton, a Bristol suburb well known for its medicinal springs. Leaving Mary in Clifton, Shelley departed in search of their new home and probably consulted Lawrence in London. This three-week separation marked a critical period in their troubled relationship. Shelley possibly sent his "sweetest Pecksie" a draft for £300 with instructions that if she should ever need it—that is, should he die—she should "go without a day's delay to London with it herself; or it may be of no use."[4]

Mary, lonely and vexed, wrote Shelley from Clifton to return immediately or she would come after him: "We ought not to be absent any longer indeed we ought not—I am not happy at it." She had "heaps of things <u>very particular</u> to say." Once again pregnant and wary of what Shelley was up to, she suspected he and Claire were together again: "it would not in the least surprise me if you have written to her from London & let her know that you are there without me that she would have taken some such freak." Mary was upset that she and Shelley would not be together "tomorrow," the anniversary of their elopement, and entreated him to join her for an excursion to nearby Tintern Abbey before his birthday.[5] Years later, in her roman à clef novel *Lodore,* Mary wrote, with some denial, that during this "first" three-week marital separation the wife "did not for an instant suspect his faith."

Mary's letter brought quick results. Either Shelley came for her or she went after him. On August 3, the day before his twenty-third birthday, they moved into a two-story cottage in Bishopsgate on the eastern edge of Windsor Great Park. The cottage grounds merged with the lovely huge trees of the King's park. They resided nine months at Bishopsgate, the longest period they would live together à *deux.* The secluded Bishopsgate cottage is close to the Thames, Virginia Water, and Runnymede. Peacock lived with his mother some miles west at Marlow. The cottage's owner, Lady Sophia Lumley, was Shelley's distant relative whom he may have contacted when in London.[6]

Shelley, a frail reed when they settled into Bishopsgate, possibly was losing weight from his mercury treatment and his vegetable diet. His physician in neighboring Egham, Dr. George Furnivall, observed that Shelley needed "a good slice of mutton" but would only take "a dish of milk and a piece of bread." Furnivall, also Mary's doctor, was struck by her control over Shelley. Her later view was that she "interfered in the legislative" aspects of their relationship, deferring to Shelley on the "executive part of our little government."[7] Furnivall's physician son reported that Shelley "would come in and swing his legs, and talk away until he quite captivated the worthy old doctor with his manner." Furnivall soon learned "that Shelley was not master in his own house," Mary treating him like "an inspired boy."[8] Shelley found a replacement for Dr. Lind when he befriended the "worthy old" Quaker, Dr. Pope, who encouraged him to speak his thoughts on theology: "I like to hear thee talk, friend Shelley; I see thou art deep."[9]

An early guest at Bishopsgate was Charles Clairmont, still searching for a career. After Shelley refused to finance his trips to the West Indies and America, Charles's latest scheme was a business possibility in Ireland. While Mary was in Clifton, Charles approached a hesitant Shelley in London about providing money for Claire to accompany her brother. When Claire joined Charles in October for the trip, Shelley sent her ten pounds.[10] Charles, returning with a plan for a distillery business, got the abstemious Shelley to promise him a loan at prevailing interest rates. Charles next sought money from Godwin's backer, Francis Place, who disliked Shelley. Charles's long letter to Place was a defense of Shelley's character and his separation from Harriet. The distillery scheme evaporated when Place promptly refused to be a part of "any transaction between you and Shelley."[11]

Writing Hogg in late August, Shelley said his health was "considerably improved" under Lawrence's care but he struck a somber chord central to the gestating *Alastor:* "Yet who is there that will not pursue phantoms, spend his choicest hours in hunting after dreams, and wake only to perceive his error and regret that death is so near? One man there is . . . a cold and calculating man . . . who alas! cannot enjoy [life]." That "calculating" man probably was Peacock, whom Harriet Boinville called "cold scholar." However, Shelley, chaser of phantoms, was alluding to disillusionments in love, including Mary.

Shelley told Hogg in this letter that current political issues were submerged under the weight of his deeply introspective mood. Establishing the mood of *Alastor,* he observed: "Those leaves have lost their summer glossiness which, when I see you again, will be fluttering in the wind of autumn. Such is mortal life."[12] Peacock, often staying several days at the Shelleys' cottage, joined Charles Clairmont in late-August excursions exploring the countryside. The two hatched a plan to alleviate Shelley's gloomy mood and health preoccupations. Shelley and Mary would join them on a boat trip up the Thames to its source.

Setting off upriver the end of August in their skiff, the men took turns at the oars. The trip possibly started August 30, Mary's eighteenth birthday, and lasted about ten days. Shelley's physical symptoms had shown some improvement in the warm, dry season, and Mary, beginning her fourth month, was healthier than in her first pregnancy. Leaving Old Windsor, they followed the Thames as it snaked its way through Henley, Marlow, and Reading. Seeing the spires of Oxford, Shelley, according to Peacock, "was so much out of order that he feared being obliged to return."[13] Peacock, unimpressed by Shelley's physicians, said he "had been living chiefly on tea and bread and butter, drinking occasionally some spurious lemonade, made of some powder in a box." This drink was possibly an antidote for the mercury treatment Shelley may have been taking for his tubercular cough.[14] Peacock, echoing Dr. Furnivall, prescribed for Shelley "three mutton chops well peppered." This new diet had "obvious and immediate" success and Shelley, "for the rest of our expedition, rowed vigorously, was cheerful, merry, overflowing with animal spirits, and had certainly one week of thorough enjoyment of life."[15] Charles Clairmont commented on Shelley's "quite remarkable change," including a ruddy complexion and being "twice as fat as he used to be."[16] Shelley wrote Hogg of the expedition's favorable effect on his health, saying his "habitual dejection & irritability have almost deserted me, & I can devote 6 hours in the day to study without difficulty."[17]

Spending the night at Oxford,[18] they paid their shillings to visit the Bodleian Library and Picture Gallery, saw the adjacent Clarendon Press, and toured the quadrangles of the colleges, including the rooms of Shelley and Hogg.[19] Unknown to the four, Bodleian records indicate that perhaps on the very day Shelley's party was there, the Duke and Duchess of Orléans visited the Library. The Duchess's journal confirms the visit. The Duke's younger brother, Louis Philippe, Duc de Montpensier, was the probable painter of Shelley's portrait while a student at Syon House Academy.[20]

Reaching Lechlade, the voyagers tried to find the Thames's source, near Cricklade. Charles Clairmont wrote that at Lechlade Shelley proposed "in his wildness" they should go even further. His "airy scheme" was to proceed by canals and rivers to North Wales, Durham, the Lakes, on to the Tweed, the Forth, and the Falls of the Clyde in Scotland. Charles reckoned they would have gone two thousand miles by the time they returned. However, they lacked the £20 needed to enter the Severn Canal. Three miles beyond Lechlade, at Inglesham, thick weeds forced them to turn back amid cows standing in the shallow river.

One or two nights were spent at an inn in Lechlade where, at twilight, Shelley visited the churchyard with its somber gravestones and composed a lyric with new depths of poetic maturity. The serene mood of "A Summer Evening Churchyard, Lechlade, Gloucestershire" covers a deeper sense of loss: "The winds are still, or the dry church-tower grass / Knows not their gentle motions as they pass." This "awful hush is felt inaudibly" and leads to

a final meditation that he could "hope, like some inquiring child /
Sporting on graves" that beside death's "breathless sleep / . . .
loveliest dreams of perpetual watch did keep."

Back at Bishopsgate, a revitalized Shelley ordered books to re-
plenish his library.[21] He wrote Hogg he had begun "several literary plans, which if my present temper of mind endures I shall probably complete in the winter." These plans included *Alastor* and
revisions of *Queen Mab*. He reported Mary's progress studying
Latin and they would "welcome you again to our fireside."[22] When
Hogg visited that fall, Shelley and Peacock were immersed in their
classical studies. Finding Mary in advanced pregnancy, Hogg had
to be satisfied with a winter of "mere classicism."[23]

During the fall, Shelley refused Harriet's request to increase the
allowance for their two children and offered to support his daughter if Ianthe lived with him. He apparently pressured Harriet by
stating that if she did not comply he would withdraw her allowance.
The Westbrooks then considered legal action against Shelley in
Chancery for maintenance of the children, threatening to use his
religious principles against him. Through Whitton, Mr. Westbrook
broached the possibility of supporting one of the children if Sir
Timothy agreed to support the other. This legal shadowboxing
was an ominous precursor of the coming Chancery suit over Shelley's children. Whitton told Sir Timothy he had heard and believed
that Shelley, under the name of Cooks, was acting in a Shakespeare
play being staged in Windsor. Neither Peacock nor Hogg mentioned this acting episode; however, Shelley possibly concealed his
acting. Overseeing the printing of *Alastor* in nearby Weybridge, he
had time for the stage that November. Mary's journal for this
period is missing and Claire was in Ireland. Whitton, careful about
his facts, had theater contacts and was certain enough to discuss
the matter with Shelley's lawyer.[24]

Composing *Alastor*, Shelley shifted from his "optimistic utopi-
anism"[25] and his more rational Godwinian position of *Queen Mab*
to a deeper, darker, and introspective skepticism. The fruit of his
intervening self-questioning concerning his failures in love was his
greater candor in *Alastor* compared to *Queen Mab*. The Pyg-
malion-like theme of the earlier poem, Ianthe's transformation
under Mab's influence, was replaced by the more direct self-con-
frontation Shelley achieved in the Narcissus-like character of the
Poet in *Alastor*. Shelley's myth in *Alastor*, the tale of the early death
of the introspective Poet, incorporated the warning of Tiresias to

Narcissus's mother—a river naiad—that her son would only live to an old age if he never came to know himself.

In the poem's Preface, Shelley discussed how love becomes the search for an idealized conception in the form of an actual person on whom the image is projected. Both Shelley's summary of *Alastor* and his self-analysis stress the self-destructive failure of narcissistic love:

> The poem entitled "Alastor," may be considered as allegorical of one of the most interesting situations of the human mind . . . a youth of uncorrupted feelings and adventurous genius led forth by an imagination inflamed . . . drinks deep of the fountains of knowledge, and is still insatiate. . . . His mind is at length suddenly awakened and thirsts for intercourse with an intelligence similar to itself. He images to himself the Being whom he loves . . . the vision in which he embodies his own imaginations unites all of wonderful, or wise, or beautiful, which the poet, the philosopher, or the lover could depicture. . . . The Poet . . . uniting these requisitions [attaches] them to a single image. He seeks in vain for a prototype of his conception. Blasted by disappointment, he descends to an untimely grave.[26]

First enunciated in *Alastor*—and later in *Athanase* and *Epipsychidion*—Shelley's formulation of love as the projection of an internalized, idealized image or "soul within our soul" upon an external object or "antitype," was restated in his later essay, *On Love:*

> We are born into the world, and there is something within us, which from the instant that we live, more and more thirsts after its likeness. It is probably in correspondence with this law that the infant drains milk from the bosom of its Mother. . . . We dimly see within our intellectual nature, a miniature as it were of our entire self, yet deprived of all that we condemn or despise, the ideal prototype of every thing excellent or lovely that we are capable of conceiving as belonging to the nature of man . . . an assemblage of the minutest particles of which our nature is composed; a mirror whose surface reflects only the forms of purity and brightness; a soul within our soul that describes a circle around its proper Paradise which pain and sorrow and evil dare not overleap. To this we eagerly refer all sensations, thirsting that they should resemble or correspond with it. The discovery of its antitype: the meeting with an understanding capable of clearly estimating the deductions of our own.[27]

The guiding myth of Narcissus and Echo underlying *Alastor* would prompt Freud's concept of narcissism: the boy, identifying with his mother, "remains unconsciously fixated to the mnemic image of his mother."[28] Peacock claimed he suggested the term *alastor* as "an evil genius," saying the "poem treated the spirit of solitude as a spirit of evil." However, Shelley's full title—*Alastor; or, The Spirit of Solitude*—could refer to the poem's wandering Poet who "seems to be a spirit to those he meets."[29]

After stating in the Preface that the *Alastor* Poet's flaw was turning his desire toward a doomed, narcissistically inspired search for love, Shelley then defended and identified with the "speedy ruin" of his Poet who, in his "self-centered seclusion was avenged by the furies of an irresistible passion pursuing him." Shelley condemned those "meaner spirits" who "loving nothing on this earth . . . are morally dead. . . . Those who love not their fellow-beings live unfruitful lives, and prepare for their old age a miserable grave."[30] This attack on the older Wordsworth (and perhaps Coleridge)[31] reflected the *Alastor* Poet's dilemma between continued erotic renewal, "to aspire grandly even at . . . the risk of crushing disappointment," Shelley's position, versus Wordsworth's position, to sublimate love and "conserve his energies in cold self-restraint."[32] Shelley's oedipal battle with his poetic father Wordsworth hovers over *Alastor.* Ending his Preface, Shelley quoted Wordsworth's *The Excursion,* attacking the older poet's love-starved conservatism: "The good die first, And those whose hearts are dry as summer dust, Burn to the socket!" Next, in his epigraph, Shelley championed enduring love in his favorite quote from St. Augustine's *Confessions.*

Shelley's use of the mirror as the governing metaphor for narcissistic love anticipated psychoanalysis.[33] He later stated in *Athanase:*

> How many a one though none be near to love,
> Loves then the shade of his own soul, half seen
> In any mirror[34]

(251–53)

Alastor's mirroring includes the doubling of the wandering Poet and the poem's narrator, who tells the Poet's life story. These two personae are essentially one, Shelley narrating the story of himself as Poet.[35] The Poet's life begins as a single-minded thirst for knowledge which proves unsatisfying and culminates in his erotic dream of a veiled maiden. At this turning point, a quest for this internalized image will end in the Poet's death.

The Poet's infancy and childhood is a story of alienation from family:

> When early youth had passed he left
> His cold fireside and alienated home
> To seek strange truths in undiscovered lands.
>
> (75–77)

On his lonely quest, the Poet encounters a nurturing "Arab maiden" who fed him daily from the food of "her father's tent." Her reticent passion having failed to arouse his dormant sexuality, she returned "to her cold home." This frustrating encounter leads to the poem's core event, the Poet's fantasized sexual experience with the maiden.

This erotic dream, depicted by Shelley as a nocturnal emission, occurs after the solitary Poet leaves the Arab maiden to wander east to the Vale of Cashmire. This locale's sexual significance began as early as 1811, when Shelley wrote passionately of the heroine in Sydney Owenson's *The Missionary,* the "divine angel" Luxima who lived in Cashmire. Cashmire also was the locale of "Zeinab and Kathema," Shelley's 1811–1812 poem of loss, search, and resulting suicide.

The *Alastor* Poet's dream of the dark-haired maiden—also a poet—is Shelley's first explicit poetic formulation of the Doppelgänger motif of the self and its feminine counterpart that would become a hallmark of his poetry:

> He dreamed a veiled maid
> Sate near him, talking in low solemn tones.
> Her voice was like the voice of his own soul
> Heard in the calm of thought
>
> Knowledge and truth and virtue were her theme,
> And lofty hopes of divine liberty,
> Thoughts the most dear to him, and poesy,
> Herself a poet.
>
> (151–61)

The sexual dream continues to its climax as the Poet sees:

> Her glowing limbs beneath the sinuous veil
> Of woven wind, her outspread arms now bare,
> Her dark locks floating in the breath of night,
> Her beamy bending eyes, her parted lips

Outstretched, and pale, and quivering eagerly.
His strong heart sunk and sickened with excess
Of love. He reared his shuddering limbs and quelled
His gasping breath, and spread his arms to meet
Her panting bosom: . . . she drew back awhile,
Then, yielding to the irresistible joy,
With frantic gesture and short breathless cry
Folded his frame in her dissolving arms.

(176–87)

If the adolescent Poet was experiencing his first wet dream at about the age when Shelley began to express his poetic creativity, this passage suggests Shelley's awareness of his dependence upon fantasy in lieu of real loving relationships.[36]

Left with a "vacant brain" after the "shock" and sexual release of his dream, the fearful Poet begins his search for his dream love "Through the tangled swamps." A deathly process of premature aging begins, his visage a "cheek of death" with hair "Sered by the autumn of strange suffering." Seeking out simple "cottagers," the "youthful maidens" who try to nurture him misinterpret his capacity to love and tearfully watch "his departure from their father's door."

The Poet pauses at a "lone Chorasmian shore" whose "wide and melancholy waste" mirrors his feeling of emptiness. Startling a swan among the reeds, he enviously watches its homeward flight to its mate as he begins his final turbulent voyage. The Poet merges with his boat and his experience with the dream maiden is allegorized as "the boat becomes ummistakably orgasmic."[37]

The "frail" boat is swept on by a "whirlwind" and its "whirlpool driven" seas as he is sucked up an ascending river within a yawning cavern. Upon reaching the eye of a "whirlpool" formed by a tremendous waterfall, he finds "A pool of treacherous and tremendous calm." At this climactic moment, the boat "paused shuddering," recapitulating the "shuddering limbs" of the Poet's sexual climax in his earlier dream encounter.

The expression of Shelley's deep-seated psychic conflict in this section of *Alastor* is suggested by his pervasive *whirl* imagery. Within the space of sixty lines (ll. 320–83), Shelley repeated the whirling language of inner turmoil beyond control, including "whirlwind," "whirlpool," "eddying," and "circling." Whirling imagery has been found to be characteristic of males who have died young by suicide or other causes.[38]

The Poet is saved when a gust of west wind blows his flimsy craft into a safe cove. The poem's Narcissus theme becomes explicit with the mirror imagery of yellow narcissi that "ever gaze on their own drooping eyes, / Reflected in the crystal calm." The Poet, at the "liquid mirror" of a well, peers into the water at the "treacherous likeness" of his own reflected eyes and hair. As if evoking the source of this reflected image, "A Spirit seemed / To stand beside" the Poet who hallucinates "Two starry eyes, hung in the gloom of thought" that "beckon him" by a "rivulet." In a final premonition of his extinction, the Poet and the "stream" become one:

> Thou imagest my life. Thy darksome stillness,
> Thy dazzling waves, thy loud and hollow gulfs,
> Thy searchless fountain and invisible course
> Have each their type in me:
>
> (505–8)

Turning from the hallucinated eyes, the Poet reverses direction downstream towards his final dissolution.[39] The prematurely aged and white-haired Poet finds his final resting place by a solitary pine. Sinking to the ground like dead leaves borne by the "autumnal whirlwind," he sees the "dim and hornèd moon hung low." The dying Poet's "last sight" is the projected eyes, now "two lessening points of light," the two tips of the crescent moon. After the moon-eyes are "quenched" and the heaven is "Utterly black," the Poet dies, "An image, silent, cold, and motionless."

With this devastating conclusion, Shelley's narrator's hopeful ambivalence toward the powerful "great Mother" with which he began *Alastor* has turned to a despairing impasse. The poem's initial image, of the narrator awaiting "thy breath, Great Parent" to stir from "the deep heart of man" the strings of his poetic lyre, has come full circle to his final after-death appeal for "Medea's wondrous alchymy," the magic potion that restores youth.[40]

Alastor was the product of an emotionally bleak 1815. One scholar observed, "It is impossible to conceive of a happy man writing such a poem."[41] However much his relationship with Mary had its compensating satisfactions, Shelley's grim self-recognition in *Alastor* never left his future life and poetry. Perhaps the darkest issue Shelley posed in *Alastor* is the incompatibility of love and creativity, the possibility that the narcissistic basis of the Poet's creativity precludes anything but a destructive outcome to loving relationships.

Shelley broke new creative ground in *Alastor.* Aside from its daring explicit sexual fantasy, his psychological doubling motif would influence Byron's *Manfred* and Mary's *Frankenstein.*[42] Shelley reached a level of disquieting self-recognition in *Alastor* perhaps not surpassed until *Julian and Maddalo* and *The Triumph of Life.* Part of this recognition, largely unconscious, was that his failed love for Harriet would likely be repeated with Mary.

The autobiographical import of *Alastor* was recognized by Shelley's intimates. His father delivered *Alastor's* first critical review in a perceptive commentary to Whitton on reading the poem: "P. B. has published a Poem with some fragments, somewhat in his usual style, not altogether free from former sentiments, and wants to find out one person on earth the Prototype of himself."[43] However, no one was more threatened by *Alastor* than Mary. After Shelley's death, she asserted, "None of Shelley's poems is more characteristic" than *Alastor,* "the outpouring of his own emotions." Not wishing to dwell on the "misfortunes that chequered his life," she stressed that the theme of *Alastor* reflected his "recent anticipation of death" in the spring of 1815.[44] Later, she wrote that after recovering "from a severe pulmonary attack," he spent much time outdoors that summer on his physician's advice as he meditated on *Alastor* under the trees of Windsor Great Park: "He never spent a season more tranquilly than the summer of 1815."[45]

Mary's lack of awareness, or defensiveness, also was evident in her later comment on another poem included in the volume with *Alastor,* "O there are spirits of the air," with its allusions to Shelley's affair with Cornelia Turner. Titling it "To ———", Mary said the poem "was addressed" to Coleridge. Wordsworth and Coleridge may have helped stimulate the figure of the Poet in *Alastor,* but the poem "To ———" and another poem published with *Alastor* that echoes the lost Cornelia Turner and Harriet, "Stanzas.—1814," indicate Shelley is speaking less to Coleridge than to himself.[46]

Carefully constructing the *Alastor* volume of twelve poems, Shelley dropped his earlier anonymity and openly presented himself for the first time to the world as the author of poetry. The *Alastor* theme of loss is continued in "Mutability," with its lovely initial lines, "We are as clouds that veil the midnight moon; / How restlessly they speed, and gleam, and quiver." Juxtaposing two sonnets, "To Wordsworth" and "Feelings of a Republican on the Fall of Bonaparte," Shelley pitted himself as Wordsworth's poetic heir against the militaristic dictator. Shelley also included in the volume his most powerful atheistic passages from *Queen Mab*, titled "Superstition." Sensitive to charges of blasphemy, he changed "God!" to "Intelligence, and unity, and power."

Also included were two sonnets that are among his most beautiful creations—one a translation from the Italian of Dante, the other perhaps from the Greek of Moschus—that reveal his gift for translation. "Dante Alighieri to Guido Cavalcanti" is a Shelleyan flight in a magic air ship "with charmed sails" and a crew of loved ones to establish, "where'er our thoughts might wend," the ideal community, his guiding restoration fantasy until he died.

Shelley concluded the *Alastor* volume with *The Daemon of the World*, his extensive revision of the first two cantos of *Queen Mab*. The ruins of the past ages in *Queen Mab* become in *The Daemon* a vivid Gothic scene with destructive imagery "Of murder, human bones, barbaric gold, / Skins torn from living men, and towers of skulls," culminating in a "thronèd king" who "did gnaw / By fits, with secret smiles, a human heart." As he composed these lines, Shelley drew four faces of these "fiendly shapes" on the pages of *Queen Mab* he was revising, initially, as "The Queen of the Universe." After drawing the faces, he crossed out "None dare relate what fearful mysteries / The Spirit saw," then composed thirty-four lines of these "fearful mysteries," a remarkable example of Shelley's creative process at work.[47]

Shelley was expecting to complete the settlement with his father in November but qualms about its legality surfaced and it was postponed. Despite this, to shield Godwin from a lawsuit, Shelley began arranging to pay Godwin's £200 debt.[48] Godwin finally ended his months-long silence, writing Shelley in November the first of a barrage of thirty-three letters over the next five months. Still the master injustice collector, Godwin was cold, moralistic, and more than a little insolent, refusing to begin his letters with a greeting and leaving them unsigned.[49]

With the advent of 1816, Shelley tried to work out an arrangement with Godwin. Explaining in detail the legal issues delaying his settlement with his father, Shelley proposed that Godwin obtain a loan on his security.[50] However, an exchange of angry letters ensued, leading Shelley to pointedly tell Godwin he was "unconscious" of his own anger.[51] Shelley next raised Godwin's anxiety level with the news that a friendly lawsuit with his father on the legality of his settlement, potentially damaging to Shelley, was to be decided in Chancery Court.[52]

Shelley declined writing to Godwin on January 24, the day Mary gave birth to a son. He was named William, a paternal obeisance to Godwin denied Timothy in the naming of Shelley's three sons. Little blue-eyed blond William became the most dear to Shelley of his children. Resuming correspondence with Godwin on the 25th, Shelley did not mention the baby's birth until the end of his letter. Without mentioning Godwin, Shelley said "Fanny & Mrs. Godwin will probably be glad to hear" the news.[53] Godwin duly noted his grandson in his diary in Latin, perhaps trying to reduce the sting of his illegitimate birth.

The *Alastor* volume appeared shortly after William's birth. The printer, Samuel Hamilton of Weybridge, near Bishopsgate, would wait five years before Shelley paid his bill.[54] Shelley wanted the same publisher as Byron but John Murray rejected *Alastor*,[55] leading Shelley to arrange joint publication by Baldwin and Carpenter, upon whom Shelley urged the "utmost exertions for its success."[56]

His hopes were dampened by dismissive conservative reviewers who, grudgingly recognizing his genius, generally derogated *Alastor* as incomprehensible. One commented on the "sublime obscurity" amidst "some beautiful imagery," and another granted him "the madness of a poetic mind," adding "it is for the genius of Mr. Shelley to make streams run up hill." Shelley sent copies of *Alastor* to Byron, Southey, and an appreciative Leigh Hunt, who unfortunately delayed acknowledging it in his *Examiner* until year's end.[57]

Shelley, ready to locate as far from Godwin as possible, had two trunks made for his carriage and informed Godwin in February he would "certainly" leave London and "possibly even execute my design of settling in Italy."[58] Deciding against Italy, he soon wrote Godwin that he planned to settle in "Cumberland or Scotland." For the first time, Shelley stated that "one of the chief motives" behind his strong desire to "desert my native country" was "the perpetual experience of neglect or enmity from almost every one but those who are supported by my resources." In stating he felt the need to insulate himself, Mary, and his children from the ostracism, prejudice, and "contempt which we so unjustly endure," he was indicting Godwin as well as the broader society. Separated from his first two children and concerned about the vulnerability of his subsequent children to the "evils" of the social stigma associated with his unwed union, Shelley saw "exile as the only resource to them."[59]

Shelley's frequent and increasingly bitter letters to Godwin included one prompted by a visit from Cornelia Turner's inept lawyer husband Tom on Godwin's behalf.[60] In early March Shelley was attacking Godwin for his "harshness and cruelty." He told Godwin not to "talk of *forgiveness* again to me, for my blood boils in my veins . . . when I think of what I . . . have endured of enmity and contempt from you and from all mankind." Again, Shelley continued trying to bail out Godwin and circumvent his father's ban on *post obit* bonds. Feeling guilty after leaving London in early May without seeing Godwin, he wrote, "I have been unjust to you.—forgive me.—burn those letters which contain the records of my violence . . . I shall always feel towards you as the most affectionate of friends."[61]

It was during this stressful period that Shelley experienced at Bishopsgate what Peacock called one of his "semi-delusions." Shelley told Peacock that Williams of Tremadoc had just visited telling him "of a plot laid by my father and uncle, to entrap me and lock me up."[62] Shelley repeatedly tried to convince Peacock of the reality of Williams's visit, claiming Williams had sent him a diamond necklace. Supporting Peacock's view of this episode are the similarities to Tremadoc, where Shelley was also under financial pressure in relation to his father, now compounded by Godwin's demands. As in Wales, his relationship with the woman with whom he was living was under strain. A new child now added to his family responsibilities and he had completed a major poetical work dealing with his disturbing feelings. A further similarity to Tremadoc was his plan to flee the country. Shelley, using his agitation to evade "active exertion" on Godwin's demands, had "symptoms of irritable fever" that required "rest to prevent serious effects."[63] Godwin had hopes, soon dashed, that John Murray, at Byron's suggestion, would give him £600 of a larger amount Byron had declined.[64]

Adding to Shelley's agitation had been Claire's December return from Ireland with her brother Charles, who began cashing checks from Shelley totaling £77 for his hopeless distillery scheme.[65] Having attended William's birth, Claire returned to London and began hatching the most fateful scheme of her life. Her plan, she later said, provided her with "ten minutes" of "happy passion" that "discomposed the rest of my life."[66]

She possibly lived at some of Shelley's varied addresses and saw him in February on his frequent London visits negotiating with lawyers and moneylenders. In March, he had two addresses near the Strand on Norfolk Street before returning to his earlier Marchmont Street lodgings. Shelley, supporting Claire, gave her £41 in March, possibly allowing her to establish lodgings for effecting her Byronic scheme.[67]

Years later, Claire said that she "ran off," presumably from Godwin's house, causing much alarm. Peacock tracked her down at Shelley's former Arabella Row lodgings in Pimlico. When Shelley sent her a check for £20 on March 11, she also used an address on Foley Road in Marylebone.[68] From this address, Claire, not yet eighteen, embarked on her disastrously successful campaign to form a liaison with Byron. There is no evidence that Shelley was aware of Claire's intentions, but his financial support played into her plans. Claire's affair with Byron was, in part, her attempt to deal with her unstable relationship with Shelley by reaching out to the sexually notorious Byron. Just back from being exiled by Shelley and Mary, long ago abandoned by her father and feeling rejected by her stepfather, Claire turned to Byron. He was a good candidate if she were seeking further rejection from a man. The popularly acclaimed Byron was a stellar poet stand-in for the relatively unknown Shelley. Byron's greater prominence gratified Claire's anger toward Shelley and jealousy toward Mary, whom she would use to advance her cause with Byron.

In old age, Claire told Edward Silsbee that she met Byron through his housekeeper, a friend of her landlady.[69] From "21, Foley Place, Mary le Bonne," she first wrote Byron at his nearby residence, 13 Piccadilly Terrace. Introducing herself as "An utter stranger," Claire offered herself to Byron as a woman whose "reputation has yet remained unstained." Being "without either guardian or husband," should she "throw herself upon your mercy . . . [and] confess the love she has borne you many years . . . could you betray her, or would you be silent as the grave?"[70] Hoping to impress the Lord, she signed herself "E. Trefusis," the name of her putative aunt. Byron recognized that Trefusis was the name of an acquaintance, Lord Clinton, whose poet sister Ella was receiving romantic notoriety at the time.[71]

Byron often received overtures from young ladies but Claire's note caught the twenty-eight-year-old Lord at a critical point in his stormy, rapidly dissolving year-old marriage to Annabella Milbanke. Annabella had borne Byron's daughter Augusta Ada in December 1815. By mid-January she had left their Piccadilly apartment, scene of marital fights exacerbated by money problems and such provocations as the presence, until March 16, of Byron's beloved pregnant half-sister Augusta Leigh. He was continuing an affair with a minor actress at Drury Lane Theatre, on whose governing board he was serving. On March 17, about the time of Claire's first letter, Byron signed a preliminary separation agreement and began making plans to leave for the Continent. He wished to escape the bailiffs and the increasingly public feud with Lady Byron, not to mention the scandal of his complicated sexual life, including rumors of incest with his half-sister, homosexuality, and infidelity. After signing the final separation papers April 21, Byron left for Europe two days later.[72] This March to April period was the duration of Claire's London affair with Byron.

Byron apparently failed to respond to her first letter, but Claire persisted. Signing her second note "G. C. B.," she "requested" he tell her if "seven o'clock this Evening will be convenient to him to receive a lady [who] desires to be admitted alone and with the utmost privacy." Byron replied he would be home.[73] This first meeting did not arouse the distracted Byron, whose servants told Claire on her next two visits he was out of town. Claire persevered, writing Byron for help in pursuing a theatrical career. Turning romantically poetic, she hoped "It is not the sparkling cup which should tempt you but the silent & capacious bowl." Worried that Byron thought her an "impostor," she said, "the romance of my story" was "not so improbable" and she had "confided to you the utmost secrets." Some of these secrets included Shelley and Mary, as she apparently brought a copy of *Alastor* to Byron to aid in her conquest. Using the name Shelley had first used for her a year earlier, she signed this letter, the third of her fifteen London letters Byron kept, "Clara Clairmont."[74]

She was pleased with Byron's "approbation" of Shelley's poetry, but she believed Shelley's strength was in translation. After Byron suggested she contact his close friend on the Drury Lane Theatre management committee, Douglas Kinnaird, Claire shifted her artistic grounds. She admitted to an interest in being a writer and wanted Byron's candid opinion of her "half a novel," perhaps the *Ideot*. Shelley has "a good opinion of my literary talents, but his affection might blind him." Writing in Italian, she included Dante's sonnet that Shelley had translated and presented herself as a foe of marriage. Her outline of her novel's heroine probably amused Byron for its self-portraiture as a young woman "committing every violence against received opinion." Guided only by her impulses, any errors in her actions were due to "the unfortunate circumstances which first attended her entrance into the world."[75] If Claire pressed her suit by displaying her lovely singing voice, Byron possibly remembered in lines dated March 28, beginning, "There be none of Beauty's daughters."

Byron, despite some show of bemused toleration, found her an intriguing young woman. Medwin's later description of Claire suggests why both Shelley and Byron found her a lively, attractive companion: "She was a brunette, with very dark hair, and eyes that flashed with the fire of intelligence, and might have been taken for an Italian. Her history was a profound secret ... she possessed considerable talents. . . . Though not strictly handsome, she was animated and attractive, and possessed an *esprit de société* rare among our countrywomen."[76]

By late March, Mary and William had joined Shelley on Marchmont Street. Claire increasingly brought Shelley and Mary into her designs. Byron offered his box at the theater for her and Shelley but she refused because Shelley "would not endure it." In April, Claire began seeing Byron in the evening to avoid his many callers, including Coleridge, whom Byron was urging to publish *Christabel.* Leigh Hunt, waiting in an adjoining room, heard Coleridge recite "Kubla Khan." Claire boldly sent Byron some of Shelley's letters to her so Byron would remove her "from the list of those whom you suspect." Mary promised to accompany Claire to meet her friend, unaware he was Byron and that they were having an affair. Byron was confiding to Claire some of his marital animosities, including his hatred for a maid of his wife with the similar last name, Clermont.[77] By mid-April, Claire was delighted when Byron "betrayed passions I had believed no longer alive in your bosom." Awaiting his reply confirming her plan for an overnight tryst out of town, she perhaps read an attack on Byron in the London *Morning Post* for his bitter poems about his "angelic" wife. When Byron offered an alternative to Claire's plan, she replied, "I never was so happy."[78]

They arranged to meet, for what may or may not have been their first sexual union, on Saturday evening, April 20.[79] Because Byron was leaving imminently for Europe, Claire entreated him to meet her someplace other than his busy house. Believing Byron viewed her as "vicious and depraved," she may have been teasing him about her sexual prowess rather than her lapsed virginity when she wrote, "On Saturday a few moments may tell you more than you yet know."[80]

Claire wrote to Byron on April 21, the day his deed of separation was granted, saying she would bring Mary to see him that night. Claire had just told Mary of Byron but "She has not the slightest suspicion of our connection." Byron was to "breathe not a word." After the visit, Claire wrote Byron the same night, "Mary is delighted with you . . . she entreats me in private to obtain your address abroad that we may if possible have again the pleasure of seeing you. . . . She perpetually exclaims 'How mild he is! how gentle! So different from what I expected.'" After Byron told Claire she was not to come alone to Geneva to be with him, she assured him, "I shall find protection." Eager to see him before he left, Claire wrote, "But tomorrow Shelley's chancery suit will be decided & so much of my fate depends on the decision; besides tomorrow will inform me whether I should be able to offer you <u>that</u> which it has long been the passionate wish of my heart to offer you." Claire's offer of "that" has been construed to mean her virginity, but she was past that point in their relationship. Her words suggest Claire was anticipating the start of her menstrual period the next day and if it failed to occur she could be pregnant and thus "offer" Byron their child. They may have been having sexual relations for several weeks and Byron was without his usual supply of condoms. Claire carefully recorded her periods and possibly was aware by late April of being pregnant, whether or not she told Byron.[81] Assuming an average gestation period of thirty-nine weeks, Claire would have become pregnant about mid-April.

Byron later entertained suspicions that Shelley might have been the father.[82] However, Byron wrote to Kinnaird just after Claire had her baby saying he had "a good deal" of sex in London and Switzerland with "that odd-headed girl" and had "reason" to think "the brat mine" as "she had not lived with S[helley] during the time of our acquaintance." He had not "pretended to love her," but "This comes of 'putting it about' . . . and thus people come into the world."[83]

Immediately after Byron signed his deed of separation, Claire requested a half-hour visit before he left. Receiving no answer, she wrote again the same day looking forward to seeing him in Switzerland, "the land of my ancestors" and asked where in Geneva she might find him.[84] She learned of his Geneva hotel, but he did not return her letters as she had requested earlier so "they may be committed to the flames." In his extravagantly outfitted £500 carriage—modeled after Napoleon's with a bed, library, plate-chest, and dining facilities—Byron and his entourage slipped out of his rented Piccadilly mansion for Dover on the morning of April 23, only minutes before bailiffs occupied the place.

That same day, Shelley attended Chancery to hear Lord Eldon's unfavorable decision on the friendly suit involving Timothy, Shelley, and Shelley's son Charles. Harriet resisted having seventeen-month-old son Charles appear in court and a court-appointed guardian stood in for him.[85] Shelley apparently did not see Harriet during the spring before leaving for Europe. The Chancellor decided that the £60,000 from timber on the family estates had to be invested, Timothy receiving only the interest during his lifetime. Whitton, immediately writing Timothy about these severe restrictions, said Shelley was "greatly disappointed" because "he has some very pressing occasions for money."[86] Shelley effectively faced limited access to his estate until his father died. Timothy, not ungenerously, agreed to continue Shelley's allowance and indicated that in the next several months he would make available £2000 to pay off his debts.

Armed with this unpleasant Chancery news, which threw his ongoing financial maneuvers in limbo, and now fully aware that Claire's liaison with Byron promised a Geneva meeting with his fellow poet, Shelley acquiesced to her "pressing solicitations" to go to Switzerland.[87] He made plans to leave England secretly before Godwin returned May 3 from a month's trip to Edinburgh. The unfavorable first review of *Alastor* did nothing to increase his desire to stay. Shelley did not notify Harriet of his departure, heightening her sense of abandonment within the unpleasant confines of her father's house. On May 2, the day Shelley left London, he wrote of his imminent departure to the Sussex lawyer Bryant, with whom he was negotiating. Saying he would be gone a week or two, he failed to mention he was leaving the country.[88] Having just seen the unsuspecting Hogg the previous night, Shelley wrote him that because of his false shame ("mauvaise honte"), he had not told him of his plans. For his summer vacation, Hogg had been expecting to accompany Shelley to the Continent. Now, Shelley asked him to mail the enclosed letter to his lawyer, Longdill. Once more left out of Shelley's plans, Hogg probably doubted Shelley's statement that he would be back "soon."[89]

Having obtained his coach from Charters, Shelley packed Mary, three-month-old William, and Claire into the cab and set off for

Dover May 2, the day before Godwin arrived home. Shelley delayed writing Godwin of his departure until waiting for the Dover packet to leave on May 3. Without mentioning Claire, he said he and Mary intended to settle in Geneva and reiterated his feeling of social ostracism, heightened now by the birth of his illegitimate child. Smarting from Godwin's stubborn refusal to reconcile with him, Shelley exaggerated the negative Chancery result to provoke Godwin's anger: "I shall receive nothing from my father except in the way of charity." More accurately, he said he would return in several months to sign the agreement papers with his father for the money to pay his debts. In addition to two increasingly doubtful pending negotiations, Shelley offered a possible bone of £300 for Godwin that might be gleaned from his father's loan. After saying he might be leaving England "forever," he expressed his intellectual debt to the "philosopher who first awakened, & who still as a philosopher to a very great degree regulate my understanding." He asked Godwin to burn his "unjust" angry letters,[90] but Godwin would be as unforgiving a father as Timothy.

19

The Creative Swiss Summer

THE SECOND CROSSING OF THE CHANNEL IN TWO YEARS WAS AUGmented by baby William. This time, Claire, not Mary, was pregnant. From their Paris lodgings on the rue Richelieu, Claire wrote Byron that they were "the whole tribe of Otaheite philosophers," Tahitians with guiltless sexuality. Mentioning Mary's "admiration" for Byron, Claire supposed he would "fall in love with her; she is very handsome & very amiable." As for herself, Byron should address her as "Madame Clairville" because "Madame's have their full liberty abroad." Aware of Byron's lack of feeling or "even interest for me," she would "ten times rather be your male friend than your mistress."[1]

Two days later the travelers set off in their carriage along the same route they had taken on foot in 1814. From Troyes, they took the road for Geneva through Dijon, ascending the Jura Mountains in a violent rainstorm that later became heavy snow in the unusually late cold spring. Having bribed the authorities to avoid the more dangerous road to Gex, they hired ten men and four horses to get through the snow-clogged roads. Shelley wrote Peacock of the "awfully desolate . . . uninhabited desart" snowscape whose "natural silence" was punctuated by the loud patois of the men struggling to keep the chaise from careening over precipices.[2]

Dropping to the sunlit shores on Lake Geneva, they passed through Coppet, Madame de Staël's home, arriving May 13 at Geneva's Hôtel de Sécheron, also known as Dejean's Hôtel d'Angleterre. Popular with English visitors, its lakeside garden provided a view of majestic Mont Blanc. Avoiding social contact, they sailed each evening from six to ten o'clock in Shelley's rented boat. They knew Byron had not arrived when Claire spotted her letter to him languishing in the post office.

Accompanying Byron on his leisurely tour of Belgium, the Waterloo battlefield, and the Rhine was the twenty-year-old physician, John William Polidori. Having obtained his Edinburgh medical degree when nineteen, Polidori had literary aspirations and—with publisher John Murray's financial backing—was keeping a daily journal of their trip. Adept at irritating Byron, Polidori asked him what he could do better besides writing poetry. Byron, after mentioning his pistol-shooting and swimming skills, snapped back, "and thirdly, I can give you a d——d good thrashing."[3]

When Byron signed the register at the Hôtel de Sécheron the evening of May 25, he gave his age as one hundred. Discovering his entry, Claire wrote him a note saying she supposed his "venerable age" had slowed his travel and requested he respond through Shelley.[4] Not rushing to respond, Byron spent the next day inspecting Villa Diodati across the lake in Cologny.

Frustrated at Byron's avoidance, Claire wrote him of his "unkind, so cruel . . . marked indifference" after her two weeks' hotel wait. It was Polidori who recorded that Byron, stepping ashore after another visit to Villa Diodati, "met M Wollstonecraft Godwin, her sister, and Percy Shelley." Polidori, adding three years to Shelley's age, wrote succinctly that he was "bashful, shy, consumptive . . . separated from his wife; keeps the two daughters of Godwin, who practise his theories; one L B's."[5]

Shelley, eager to leave the expensive hotel with its prying English guests, rented Maison Chappuis in Montalègre just across the lake and they settled in as June began.[6] Maison Chappuis was a two-story, fair-sized stone house secluded by trees and ideally situated near the lakeshore with a harbor for mooring their boat. A short walk through an adjacent vineyard led up a narrow path on the Cologny hill to the more sumptuous Villa Diodati, which Byron negotiated to rent until November.

Before moving to Diodati, Byron came over daily with Polidori for evening sails with the Shelleys. The weather turned wet and windy, and once the stormy water almost drove them onto some pilings as Byron sang an Albanian song with a "wild howl."[7]

Polidori soon recorded Shelley's personal history, including Dr. Lind's intervention: "Shelley is another instance of wealth inducing relations to confine for madness, and was only saved by his physician being honest." After recording that Harriet Grove broke their engagement "because he was an atheist," Polidori mentioned Shelley's reasons for marrying Harriet Westbrook. Shelley "paid Godwin's debts, and seduced his daughter; then wondered that he would not see him." The entire Montalègre group was "All clever, and no meretricious appearances."[8]

Polidori, after writing of Shelley's first marriage, said that "he tried all he could to induce" Mary "to love" Hogg. In a fusion of the "attacks" at Keswick and Tanyrallt, Polidori wrote that Shelley, "having hired a house, a man wanted him to pay more, and came trying to bully him, and at last challenged him. Shelley refused, and was knocked down; cooly said that would not gain him his object, and was knocked down again."[9]

Polidori and Mary spent time together rowing at night, having tea, and reading Tasso. After taking little William to be vaccinated, Polidori received a gold chain from the appreciative Shelleys. Claire, usually unmentioned by Polidori, found him "very handsome."[10] Noting the philosophical discussions of Shelley and Byron, Polidori said they "talked, till the ladies brains whizzed with giddiness about idealism."[11]

Byron and Shelley cemented their friendship by jointly purchasing for 25 louis the only keeled sailboat on the lake. Presumably fitted out to withstand the area's frequent squalls, Medwin later found it drew too much water and was "narrow and crank."[12] The boat was moored near the Maison Chappuis and Byron recalled "Shelley was on the Lake much oftener than I, at all hours of the night and day: he almost lived on it; his great rage is a boat."[13] Soon, the two poets made plans to circumnavigate Lake Geneva.

The increasingly inclement weather forced the colony to spend more time indoors at Villa Diodati. Byron and Claire renewed their sexual intimacy but she complained to him that Polidori might be "suspicious."[14] Two months pregnant, she probably had not yet informed Byron, Shelley, or Mary. Rationalizing his renewed affair, Byron assured his half-sister Augusta that Claire was "a foolish girl . . . but I could not exactly play the Stoic with a woman—who had scrambled eight hundred miles to unphilosophize me."[15]

Byron told Augusta of the voyeuristic gossip mushrooming among the Genevese and the hordes of English tourists. Using spyglasses from boats on the lake, tourists were sure that sheets drying at Diodati were ladies' undergarments. One later tourist the two poets believed spread vicious accusations was Southey, provoking an irate Byron to write: "The Son of a Bitch . . . said that Shelley and I 'had formed a League of Incest' . . . he lied like a rascal . . . there was no promiscuous intercourse—my commerce being limited to the carnal knowledge of Miss C[lairmont]."[16]

The stormy weather began having its literary effect. Descriptions of thunderstorms would appear in the early pages of *Frankenstein* and the third canto of *Childe Harold*. The extraordinarily stormy, wet, and cold weather of that spring and summer was caused by atmospheric volcanic ash from the 1815 Indonesian eruption.[17]

Polidori's anger also erupted when, after apparently losing a sailing race with Shelley, he challenged him to a duel. Shelley laughed at the idea but Byron, not having Shelley's "scruples about duelling," told Polidori he would duel for Shelley. When Polidori sprained his ankle trying to help Mary over a wall, Byron's expression of concern elicited Polidori's, "I did not believe you had so much feeling."[18]

The night of the sprained ankle, June 15, the group assembled by the fireplace in the Diodati's grand salon. Polidori reported that he and Shelley, talking "about principles," discussed "whether man was to be thought merely an instrument." This may have been the impetus to the ghost story competition and *Frankenstein*.[19] Mary recalled being a "devout but nearly silent listener" for several nights as Shelley talked with Byron. One night the talk was about "various philosophical doctrines" including "the nature of the principle of life" and "the experiments of Dr. [Erasmus] Darwin . . . who preserved a piece of vermicelli in a glass case, till by some extraordinary means it began to move. . . . Perhaps a corpse would be re-animated; galvanism had given token of such things: perhaps the component parts of a creature might be manufactured, brought together, and endued with vital warmth."[20] The precocious Polidori, who wrote his medical thesis on somnambulism, perhaps helped stimulate Mary's fancy.[21]

The emotional intensity increased the night of June 16, probably the wet evening when they read German ghost stories translated into French.[22] Mary recalled Byron proposed each of the five should write a ghost story, telling her, "You and I will publish ours together."[23] The heavy rain that night forced the Montalègre contingent to sleep at Diodati; on the 17th Polidori noted, "The ghost-stories are begun by all but me."[24] Mary reported that Shelley's now-lost ghost story was "founded on the experiences of his early life."[25]

The stimulus for the ghost story Mary began on June 17 was her nightmarish waking dream: "I saw the pale student of unhallowed arts kneeling beside the thing he had put together . . . the hideous phantasm of a man stretched out, and then, on the working of some powerful engine, show signs of life, and stir with an uneasy, half vital motion."[26] Mary recalled her eyes opened "in terror . . . a thrill of fear ran through me . . . I could not so easily get rid of my hideous phantom." She announced the next day that she had thought of a story.

Mary planned to write only a few pages until Shelley urged her "to develope the idea at greater length." She added: "I certainly did not owe the suggestion of one incident, nor scarcely of one train of feeling, to my husband, and yet but for his incitement, it would never have taken the form in which it was presented to the world." Mary referred to *Frankenstein* as "my hideous progeny . . . the off-spring of happier days."[27]

The night of June 18, Polidori began his ghost story, not *The Vampyre*, which possibly derived from Byron's "sketch" of his own first ghost story effort.[28] By midnight, Polidori said the group "really began to talk ghostly." When Byron repeated the lines from Coleridge's *Christabel* of Geraldine exposing her deformed breast and her snake-like scaly torso, "a silence ensued and Shelley, suddenly shrieking and putting his hands to his head, ran out of the room with a candle."[29] Polidori "Threw water in his face and gave him ether." Shelley, who was looking at Mary when Byron spoke the lines, "suddenly thought of a woman he had heard of who had eyes instead of nipples, which, taking hold of his mind, horrified him." Later, Polidori wrote that Shelley's "wild imagination . . . pictured . . . the bosom of one of the ladies with eyes (which was reported of a lady in the neighbourhood where he lived)."[30]

Byron thought the actual events related in Polidori's 1819 version of "Shelley's agitation" and "fit of phantasy" over *Christabel* were "*not exactly*" as Polidori described. Byron was at a loss to explain what "seized" Shelley as he certainly did not "want courage."[31] Before Byron read from *Christabel* that night, he may have loaned Shelley the poem's manuscript he had received from Coleridge the previous October. On August 26, Shelley first read *Christabel* from the just-published copy.[32]

Shelley's Diodati anxiety attack had similarities to his panic reactions at Keswick and Tanyrallt, including loss of consciousness and leaving the scene, this time, to join Byron sailing around Lake Geneva. Shelley apparently believed, as he later told Tom Medwin, that the mysterious lady who had visited him first in 1814 before he left England was now ensconced in Hôtel de Sécheron.[33] Financial concerns, important in the previous episodes, also occupied Shelley in Geneva. Several days after his attack, Shelley wrote his London banker for a statement of his present accounts, requesting Peacock be sent £5 as part of Shelley's support of his friend.[34] By June 18 he probably had received Godwin's May 29 letter decrying Shelley's "unfortunate absence" and detailing urgent financial machinations for money Godwin hoped to procure from Shelley family properties. In reply, Shelley arranged a £10 payment to Godwin.[35] Included with Godwin's letter was one from Fanny, who said she understood from "Mamma" that she was ridiculed by, and the "laughing stock" of, Shelley and Mary.[36]

Shelley apparently recovered quickly from his attack as Polidori's diary mentions no further distress. However, a disconsolate Polidori soon anticipated his own mode of suicide five years later. Learning he was to be excluded from the poets' lake trip, he prepared to take some poison only to be interrupted by a consoling Byron.[37]

Leaving Polidori behind, Byron and Shelley began their nine-day sailing trip June 22 with two boatmen, a servant, and a copy of *Julie, ou La Nouvelle Héloïse.* Byron knew Rousseau's story thoroughly but it was Shelley's first close reading of the illicit love between Saint Preux and his pupil Julie. Byron probably did not know what Shelley learned before departing, that Claire was pregnant. His ankle better, Polidori became the full-time consort of Mary and Claire. He even took the two to Mass, but the service having begun, they left.

Shelley's efforts to imbue Byron with Wordsworth's sublime poetic ethos influenced some of the finest passages in the third canto of *Childe Harold.* Recognizing that Shelley had temporarily "dosed" him with Wordsworth, Byron wrote notes about the scenery during their trip. Byron had read *Alastor* and probably discussed it with Shelley. The poem's psychological doubling soon influenced Byron's *Manfred.*

Stopping at Nernier the first day, Shelley was captivated by one boy without the bodily deformities of the other children, a "child . . . far more beautiful than I had ever seen . . . a model of grace."[38] Arriving at Evian in rain, lightning, and thunder, Byron, writing to invite his friend John Cam Hobhouse to Villa Diodati, ridiculed Polidori as the "Childish Dr. Pollydolly."[39]

The next morning, deploying only one of their four sails, a "violent" wind carried their two-masted boat toward the east "with inconcievable speed." Writing later to Peacock, Shelley typically understated the physical danger, saying, "The boat was heavily laden, the sea very high, & there appeared to be some danger of swamping." Hugging the rocky coast, they arrived at Meillerie where Shelley savored the local honey. Shelley later lamented not having read enough of *Julie* to appreciate Meillerie, the scene of "St Preux's visionary exile." He read the novel avidly the next several days. Deceived by improved weather, the five left Meillerie in their "heavily laden" boat only to be overtaken by "a tremendous storm [with] waves at least 15 feet high. We all prepared for a swamp as it was impossible to keep the smallest sail and the water began to break over the head."[40] Shelley later related that one of the boatmen, "a dreadfully stupid fellow," mishandled the sail and a broken rudder made steering difficult as the boat took on water. Byron recounted that because "the boat was filling fast" and knowing Shelley couldn't swim, he took off his coat and made Shelley do the same and "take hold of an oar." He told Shelley that "being myself an expert swimmer," he could "save him if he would not struggle when I took hold of him—unless we got smashed against the rocks which were high & sharp with an awkward Surf on them at the minute; we were then about a hundred yards from shore—and the boat in peril.—He answered me with the greatest coolness—'that he had no notion of being saved—& that I would have enough to do to save myself and begged me not to trouble me.'"[41]

As both sat with arms crossed, Shelley later said he "felt in this near prospect of death a mixture of sensations, among which terror entered, though but subordinately. My feelings would have been less painful had I been alone; but I know that my companion would have attempted to save me, and I was overcome with humiliation, when I thought his life might have been risked to preserve mine."[42] Mary later wrote that "Shelley positively refused" Byron's help "and seating himself quietly upon a locker, and grasping the rings at each end firmly in his hands, declared his determination to go down in that position, without a struggle."[43] Shelley's courage and selflessness made a lasting impression upon Byron.

Shelley wrote of his near-disaster, "Contrary to all chances we arrived safe" at St. Gingolph, whose inhabitants "were watching on the shore to see who had ventured in so perilous a sea."[44] Hiring a carriage, the two explored the mouths of the Rhône before sunset. Byron reminded Shelley that the spot where they were almost swamped was the same place "where Julie and her lover were nearly overset," St. Preux being "tempted to plunge with her into the lake."[45]

Immediately after his brush with death, Shelley drafted a will to provide for those dependent upon him, enclosing it in a letter to his solicitor Hayward.[46] He implored Hayward to keep it secret and draw up the will immediately so that a friend (Hogg) could bring it when he came to visit at the end of July.

This will, signed by Shelley in its final form in September, reveals the priority of his commitments to his extensive and complicated personal relationships as he approached his twenty-fourth year.[47] First, "Mary Wollstonecraft Godwin" received his "whole estates" except for some legacies to "be paid within four years from the time of her obtaining posession of the estate." The first legacy was to "Harriet Shelley my wife" who would receive the interest from £6000 during her life, "with reversion after her death to Charles Bysshe Shelley, my son by her." Charles was also to receive an additional £5000, as was Ianthe. Next came the complicated situation of "Mary Jane Clairmont (the sister in law of Miss Godwin)." Shelley divided his generous £12,000 bequest to her into two parts, providing £6000 for Claire and £6000 for her unborn child. It is possible Shelley had discussed Claire's pregnancy with Byron and that his liberal settlement partly reflected Byron's lack of interest in supporting Claire and his feeling some responsibility for her affair with Byron.[48] In London, Claire had written to Byron that Shelley was "the man whom I have loved, and for whom I have suffered much."[49] Shelley would write in *Epipsychidion* that Claire's conflicted feelings toward him propelled her into Byron's bed.[50]

Drafting his will on the trip, Shelley kept Claire's legacy from the disapproving eyes of Mary, who later resented it.[51] Shelley left £2000 each to Hogg and Byron, and £500 to Peacock, who also was to receive a £2000 annuity. Shelley apparently did not share information about the will with Byron, who was named executor, as was Peacock.

The morning after drafting his will, Shelley awoke before Byron and gathered "a nosegay" of flowers not seen in England. The two then sailed through the turbulent confluence of the Rhône to the Castle of Chillon, its prison chambers lapped by the deep water. Byron began considering a poem but Shelley found Chillon an interruption from reading Rousseau's *Julie*, "an overflowing of sublimest genius."[52] Observing Chillon's dungeons and cells where prisoners were hung, Shelley had never seen "a monument more terrible of that cold and inhuman tyranny."

They continued against a strong wind to Clarens where they strode the terraces that Rousseau's Julie and St. Preux had walked. For Shelley, "the spirit of old times had deserted" the place and they sailed north to Vevey. It had associations from Rousseau's *The Confessions* and *Julie*, and Shelley thought it "a town more beautiful in its simplicity than any I have ever seen." They were detained in Ouchy for two days and three nights by a "violent wind and rain." In Lausanne, their next stop, Byron gathered acacia leaves at Gibbon's home to commemorate the historian. Shelley, believing Gibbon had a "cold and unimpassioned spirit," refrained from gathering leaves, "fearing to outrage the more sacred name of Rousseau."[53]

Fair weather and a lake-spanning rainbow brought them to Montalègre two days later, the end of June. Shelley was pleased with Mary's initial progress on *Frankenstein* during his absence and she accepted his suggestion to expand her dream-narrative into a more ambitious novel.

Shelley possibly began drafting *Hymn to Intellectual Beauty* on the trip as he wrote several months later it "was composed under the influence of feelings which agitated me even to tears."[54] *Julie's* important influence on *Hymn to Intellectual Beauty* was evident when Shelley wrote Peacock shortly after the excursion that the novel had "excited" his "creed" of "immaterialism," a creed of "intellectual beauty," the power and attraction of the psychological beauty of the feminine mind.[55] Both Shelley and Peacock esteemed the beauty of a woman's mind. At least as early as 1811, Shelley had read of "intellectual beauty" in Amelia Opie's *Adeline Mowbray*, a novel influenced by Wollstonecraft's *A Vindication of the Rights of Woman*. In 1813, he read in Wieland's *Agathon* of "the intellectual Beauty of the soul." A similar idealization of the beauty of a woman's personality was Constantia Dudley in Charles Brockden Brown's *Ormond*.[56]

The *Hymn* is a testament to the profoundly personal origins of Shelley's poetic mission. Believing poets were the precursors of religious divines, Shelley invoked the Spirit of Beauty as a *psychological*, not religious, experience. The *Hymn* is a humanistic, secular manifesto. Shelley rejected finding any transcendent values in Christianity, with its negation of this world's primacy and its need to invoke the "false names" of "Ghosts & God & Heaven."

Leigh Hunt, perhaps concerned about blasphemy when he printed the *Hymn*, substituted "Demon" for "God" and "poisonous" for "false." Shelley restored the original words in his personal copy.[57] Asserting, "No voice from some sublime world hath ever / To sage or poet these responses given," Shelley based his credo on the human values of "Love, Hope, and Self-Esteem." Love included the erotic "sympathies, / That wax and wane in lovers' eyes."

Shelley's Spirit of Beauty is inscribed in the first line as "The awful shadow of some unseen Power," an unconscious presence that, as the "Dear . . . mystery," can be expressed only through analogies and similes. This seemingly feminine presence "floats though unseen amongst us"; in the first draft she more humanly "walks." Her fleeting, "inconstant glance" is mirrored in shadowy nocturnal images and the sounds of her voice are "harmonies of evening," "Like memory of music fled." This sense of loss continues in the second stanza:

> where art thou gone?
> Why dost thou pass away and leave our state,
> This dim vast vale of tears, vacant and desolate?
>
> (15–17)

Only "Thy light alone," not a "voice from some sublimer world" of religion, "Gives grace and truth to life's unquiet dream." Wishing that the Spirit of Beauty would stay, Shelley composed one of his most striking similes: "Thou, that to human thought art nourishment, / Like darkness to a dying flame!"

With his fondness for seeking childhood roots, Shelley experienced the Spirit of Beauty, "While yet a boy." In an early adolescent sexual awakening with its "News of buds and blossoming," "Sudden, thy shadow fell on me: / I shrieked, and clasped my hands in extacy!" Having "vowed that I would dedicate my powers / To thee and thine," "With beating heart and streaming eyes, even now" he called her "O awful Loveliness":

> They know that never joy illumined my brow
> Unlinked with hope that thou wouldst free
> This world from its dark slavery
>
> (68–70)

The beautiful, autumnal final stanza ends as an invocation for the Spirit's continuing influence:

Thus let thy power, which like the truth
Of nature on my passive youth
Descended, to my onward life supply
Its calm, to one who worships thee,
Whom, SPIRIT fair, thy spells did bind
To fear himself, and love all human kind.

(78–84)

Meanwhile, any idea Claire had of obtaining Byron's love was fleeting at best. Her "pretext" to see an increasingly a reticent Byron was to copy his poems. Shelley delivered her entreating letters to Byron: "If you want me, or anything of, or belonging to me I am sure Shelley would come and fetch me if you ask him."[58] When she defended Shelley, Byron said, "good God . . . you are in love with him."[59] Byron declined Shelley's invitation to accompany the Montalègre group's planned trip to Chamonix and Mont Blanc.

Byron found acceptance in Genevan society with Madame de Staël and her entourage at Coppet. Shelley declined joining Byron and Polidori at Coppet, having "no great curiosity" to see de Staël and her "literary people . . . unwilling as I am to pay the invidious price . . . to range oneself according to peculiar parties."[60]

Shelley communicated his private misgivings about Byron to Peacock, in part, to reduce Peacock's jealousy:

Lord Byron is an exceedingly interesting person, & as such is it not to be regretted that he is a slave to the vilest & most vulgar prejudices, & as mad as the winds? I do not mean to say that he is a Christian, or that his ordinary conduct is devoid of prudence. But in the course of an intimacy of two months, & an observation the most minute I see reason to regret the union of great genius, & things which make great genius useless. For a short time I shall see no more of Lord Byron, a circumstance I cannot avoid regretting as he has shewn me great kindness, & as I had some hope that an intercourse with me would operate to weaken those superstitions of rank & wealth & revenge & servility to opinion with which he, in common with other men, is so poisonously imbued.[61]

Shelley asked Peacock to locate a house with a garden near Bishopsgate with a lease "for 14 or 21 years" as his "present intention is to return to England & to make that most excellent of nations my perpetual resting place." Uncertain when they might return, their latest idea was to descend the Danube by boat to visit "Constantinople & Athens, then Rome & the Tuscan cities & returning by the South of France; always following great rivers" because "They imitate mind which wanders at will over the pathless deserts & flows thro natures loneliest recesses which are inaccessible to any thing besides." He was similarly vague with Hogg, saying "Circumstances" now nullified plans for Hogg to join them in Europe. Shelley gave Avignon as his next address.[62] Their tentative plan, soon canceled, was to remain on the Continent until Claire's baby was born. Shelley was still hoping to arrange his financial affairs without returning to England.[63]

Soon after arriving in Geneva, Shelley and Mary had hired a Swiss nursemaid for William, twenty-one-year-old Louise Duvillard, called Elise. Blond and blue-eyed, she was considered "pretty" by Claire. Skilled as a seamstress, unmarried Elise had cared for younger stepsiblings.[64]

Leaving six-month-old William with Elise, Shelley, Mary, and Claire set off July 21 for Chamonix at the base of Mont Blanc, a popular English tourist excursion. Following the valley of the Arve River, swollen from the incessant rains, Shelley recorded his observations in Mary's new journal.[65] Leaving Bonneville for Cluse, the inspirational effect of the Alps' awesome grandeur—including waterfalls "imitating a veil of the most exquisite woof"—began stimulating Shelley's composition of *Mont Blanc*.[66]

In the registry books of numerous hostels where they stopped, Shelley identified himself as "atheos," his Greek for atheist easily translated by other English travelers. One, a Lutheran minister, soon met Shelley's distant relatives Sir John and Lady Shelley. They did not want "to be confounded with a Mr. Percy Bysshe Shelley, of Sussex, & his lady; whose names we had seen in every Inn's Register since we left Cluse, with the horrid avowal of atheism industriously subjoined."[67] Shelley made at least four such registry inscriptions, including two hotels in Chamonix, an inn perhaps at Sallanches, and the mountain hut on the Montenvers. These scandalous inscriptions were Greek verse footnotes to the atheistic message of *Mont Blanc*. In one register, Shelley wrote their destination was "L'Enfer," proclaiming in Greek hexameter, "I am a lover of mankind, democrat, and atheist." His Greek inscriptions elicited written Greek rejoinders from subsequent travelers, one attacking him as a "fool."[68]

Byron, encountering one of Shelley's inscriptions in late August, tried to do him "a service" by scratching it out.[69] Southey, visiting Chamonix a year later, spotted an inscription of Shelley, Mary, and

Claire as "atheists one and all."[70] Southey undoubtedly passed this information on to Shelley's Eton classmate, John Taylor Coleridge, who attacked Shelley for the inscription in his review of Hunt's volume, *Foliage,* without using Shelley's name. This attack, in the January 1818 *Quarterly Review,* soon ricocheted through other periodicals. Shelley and Byron suspected Southey was the original author of the attack; Byron's excited "choler" would evoke another attack on his old enemy Southey and his "bag of venom."[71]

At St. Martin, Shelley's party, hiring a guide, switched to mules for the long day's journey to Chamonix. At Servoz they crossed a wooden bridge over the Arve, the Pont Pellissier. Mary wrote that Shelley experienced "one of the loveliest scenes in the world" with the "view of that mountain and its surrounding peaks and valleys, as he lingered on the Bridge of Arve on his way through the Valley of Chamouni."[72] This scene inspired *Mont Blanc* and led Shelley to write Byron that at Servoz, "Mont Blanc and its connected mountains . . . exceeds and renders insignificant all that I had before seen, or imagined."[73] Shelley wrote to Peacock, "Mont Blanc was . . . covered with cloud; its base, furrowed with dreadful gaps . . . The immensity of these aerial summits excited, when they suddenly burst upon the sight, a sentiment of extatic wonder, not unallied to madness." The scene, "the ravine, clothed with gigantic pines, and black with its depth below, so deep that the very roaring of the untameable Arve, which rolled through it, could not be heard above," became part of the poem's message: "all was as much our own, as if we had been the creators of such impressions in the minds of others as now occupied our own. Nature was the poet, whose harmony held our spirits more breathless than that of the divinest."[74]

Entering the valley of Chamonix, they heard a "burst of smothered thunder rolling above" as their guide Ducrée pointed to an avalanche's smoky path on the opposite mountain. Their road having washed away, they crossed with difficulty, Claire on a mule, Mary carried by the guide, and Shelley walking.[75] That evening, Shelley registered with his usual inscription at the Hôtel de Londres in Chamonix.

They set off early in the morning on mules to see the source of the Arvéron. Shelley, describing to Peacock the glaciers as ravaging destroyers and nourishing givers of water, was taken with Buffon's idea of a glacial apocalypse. Shelley and Ducrée, "the only tolerable person I have seen in this country," soon visited the Glacier des Bossons. This elicited a glacier–volcano contrast[76] appearing in *Mont Blanc*, which he probably began composing that night, July 23, the date placed at the end of the poem.

He had time the next day to work on the heavily revised draft of his poem when rain and mishaps forced the drenched Shelley and Mary to cut short their excursion to Montenvers and the Mer de Glace. Shelley wrote Peacock that when his mule stumbled he "narrowly escaped being precipitated down the mountain." Mary added that Shelley received a "blow" on their ascent; on the descent, he tripped and fell, causing him to faint and be "for some minutes incapacitated."[77]

The following day, joined by Claire, they successfully reached the Mer de Glace and its bordering Montenvers hut, where Shelley inscribed in the visitors' book, "atheists one and all." As if anticipating Southey's Chamonix visit a year later, Shelley told Peacock of his disgust at the "melancholy exhibitions of tourism" by "some English people here" which "make this place another Keswick."

The glaciers, then much larger and more ominous than today, became the core imagery of *Mont Blanc*. Walking some distance across the jagged surface of the Mer de Glace with its waves of ice fifteen feet high, it was "as if frost had suddenly bound up the waves & whirlpools of a mighty torrent." They peered down ice chasms of "unfathomable depth" amid the echoing sound of falling rocks, ice, and snow from the surrounding mountains. Shelley wrote, "One would think that Mont Blanc was a living being & that the frozen blood forever circulated slowly thro' his stony veins."[78] Shelley's icy language in *Mont Blanc* reveals a scientific understanding of the glaciers' powerful destructive movement as they "creep / Like snakes that watch their prey," producing "A city of Death," "a flood of ruin," leaving "vast pines . . . in the mangled soil" that are "Branchless and shattered" alongside "rocks, drawn down / From yon remotest waste."[79]

Shelley leaves no settled emotional or philosophical posture in this, one of his most complex poems. Unlike the unseen but rapturous "awful Loveliness" of Intellectual Beauty, the veiled, cloud-covered, remote, and inaccessible mountain yields a sense of emptiness, loss, vacancy, and solitude, "a desart" surrounded by a "wilderness" whose "mysterious tongue / . . . teaches awful doubt." The doubt, skepticism, and ambivalence permeating the poem yields from this "mysterious tongue" not only "awful doubt" but "faith so mild / . . . that man may be / . . . with nature reconciled."

Shelley's skeptical "may" hovers over his prophetic utterance of potential human understanding of the mountain's silent voice:

> Thou hast a voice, great Mountain, to repeal
> Large codes of fraud and woe; not understood
> By all, but which the wise, and great, and good
> Interpret, or make felt or deeply feel.
>
> (80–83)

As if backing away from such prophetic utterance, Shelley returned with a more questioning voice in his final lines about the mountain's silent potential:

> The secret strength of things
> Which governs thought, and to the infinite dome
> Of heaven is as a law, inhabits thee!
> And what were thou, and earth, and stars, and sea,
> If to the human mind's imaginings
> Silence and solitude were vacancy?
>
> (139–44)

Perhaps, as a critic has it, "What is meaningless emptiness in a supposedly external world is an absolute plenitude to the Imagination."[80] Shelley's sense of "vacancy" experiencing Mont Blanc gives impetus to "the human mind's imaginings," the "secret springs . . . The source of human thought." Vacancy produces neither prophecy nor a dogmatic message but "my own my separate fantasy," a creatively retrieved presence "In the still cave of the witch Poesy," that is like "some faint image; till the breast / From which they fled recalls them, thou art here!"

Looking forward, Shelley retrieved from the mountain before heading home "a large collection of the seeds of rare Alpine plants" that he would "colonize in my garden in England."[81] Arriving at Diodati the evening of July 27, the three talked to Byron for three hours before retiring at midnight.

As the final month of the Montalègre–Diodati colony began, Claire was obviously pregnant and arrangements were necessary for her child. Byron planned to move to Italy and Polidori was increasingly troublesome for Byron and Shelley. Mary recorded that July 28 was the second anniversary of her elopement with Shelley, who "talks with Clare," no doubt about her increasingly strained situation with Byron. For Shelley's approaching twenty-fourth birthday, Mary made him a fire balloon and bought him a telescope.

Byron's final reckoning with Claire began August 2. Pointedly excluding a puzzled Mary, he summoned Shelley and Claire up to Diodati, probably to discuss future arrangements for Claire's child, due in January. Claire's parting from Byron was sealed when Shelley learned he had to return to England to negotiate the £2000 loan from his father and presumably to collect his next quarterly allowance, due the end of September. Put in "very bad spirits" by this news, Shelley obtained £125 through Byron's banker to cover local expenses and finance the return trip to England.[82]

It is unclear what was agreed in the final conferences Claire and Shelley had with Byron. If Byron offered financial aid, it was refused. Shelley's insistence that Claire return with him and Mary to England for the birth of her child meant he would incur not only her living expenses but the inevitable social opprobrium of being assumed to be the illegitimate child's father.

Mary's cryptic mid-August journal entry—"war"—hinted of conflict following a meeting she, Claire, and Shelley had with Byron. Polidori's impulsive anger was erupting, having been served a writ of arrest after an altercation with an apothecary. Sometime in August, after challenging Shelley to a duel, Polidori "threatened to shoot S[helley]."[83]

As Mary continued with *Frankenstein,* another writer of Gothic tales arrived at Diodati in mid-August, Matthew Gregory "Monk" Lewis. One evening as the men discussed ghosts, Shelley became enthralled by the five "grim" ghost stories Lewis recounted and Mary carefully wrote them out in her journal.[84] Monk Lewis—who died two years later—had Shelley, Byron, and Polidori witness a codicil to his will which provided for the welfare of slaves he owned in the West Indies and prohibited their sale.[85] In a few years, Shelley wrote that slavery was "the deepest stain upon civilized man," praising the "necessarily cautious" freeing of the slaves in the West Indies.[86]

In a disturbing letter, Fanny Godwin wrote of the "plagues" in her life, including her "dreadful state of mind," a depression "which I in vain endeavour to get rid of." Saying Shelley was deceived about Godwin's dire economic situation, she reminded him that the £200 he promised Godwin had not arrived. Fanny, twenty-two, accurately described herself as "dependent in every sense of

the word . . . [without] a sous of my own." Soon her unpleasant Aunt
Everina would visit from Ireland and "my future fate will be de-
cided."[87] A concerned Mary responded immediately and went with
Shelley to Geneva to buy Fanny a gold watch. One who escaped
Skinner Street, Charles Clairmont, wrote from France seeking
money from Shelley.[88]

Shelley made solitary trips in August to Geneva, visiting a book
dealer who commissioned him to translate *Political Justice,* a
project never completed.[89] It is not known if Shelley contacted the
mysterious lady, who may have been in Geneva.

Three days before Shelley and his party left, Byron's next guests
arrived, John Cam Hobhouse and the Regency dandy, Scrope
Berdmore Davies. Davies, a gambling devotee, had just visited his
friend Beau Brummell, hiding on the Continent from his £50,000
gambling debts in England. Shelley's final days in Geneva became
linked with Davies when—in a startling 1976 literary find—a trunk
belonging to Davies was discovered in the Pall Mall Barclays Bank
where he had left it before fleeing England to escape his gambling
debts. In addition to betting slips, the trunk contained a fair copy
of the third canto of *Childe Harold* in Byron's hand and Mary's
transcript of *The Prisoner of Chillon.* A small notebook of Shelley's
contained a copy of *Mont Blanc* in his hand, a copy of *Hymn to Intellectual Beauty* in Mary's hand, and two previously unknown
sonnets in her hand that Shelley wrote while in Switzerland, "Upon
the wandering winds" and "To Laughter." Both texts of the longer
poems have important differences from previously known drafts
and published versions.[90]

The imagery of "Upon the wandering winds" is suggestive of the
Hymn, as the "inconstant motion" of evening air "sends its spirit
into all." The sonnet ends with Shelley in "the divinest thrall / Of
some sweet lady's voice," perhaps that of Claire.

"To Laughter," with its first line, "Thy friends were never mine
thou heartless fiend [?friend]," may be a veiled attack on Byron,
with its allusions to his "hollow heart" in rejecting Claire and her
unborn child. His condemnation of Byron seemingly continued
with " . . . thou fearest / A fair child clothed in smiles," ending
with "I, now alone, weep without shame to see / How many broken
hearts lie bare to thee."

Leigh Hunt later wrote that "Lord Byron never talked with any
man to so much purpose" as he did with Shelley and that Byron
"probably was never less under the influence of affectation" than

with Shelley.[91] Byron, who said, "I never open a Greek book," composed his "Prometheus" ode that summer after Shelley orally translated for him Aeschylus's *Prometheus Bound*.[92] Sensing Byron was frustrated because his poetic talents were not developing, Shelley wrote him soon after leaving Geneva saying "your powers are astonishingly great" and urging Byron to "immediately apply yourself to the composition of an Epic Poem."[93] Shelley suggested Byron's theme should be the French Revolution.

Byron gave Shelley Claire's transcription of the third canto of *Childe Harold* for delivery to John Murray for publication. Shelley was also to contact Byron's friend Douglas Kinnaird about the sale of *Childe Harold*. A week after Shelley left, Davies returned to England with the other fair copy of the third canto destined for Barclays Bank.

Claire's final days in Switzerland had to be difficult. She accompanied Shelley to Diodati for the last time on August 25; the evening of the 28th Polidori walked down to Montalègre to say goodbye. Shelley, aware that Byron was thinking of discharging the disturbed young doctor, later wrote Byron not to have "scruples" about dismissing Polidori. Before leaving Geneva, Shelley heard an anecdote about Polidori that "made my blood run cold."[94]

Later that evening Byron arrived at Maison Chappuis for what would be his last meeting with Claire. She then sent a note to Byron revealing her confused vulnerability: "I feel as if we parted ill friends. . . . There is nothing in the world I love or care about except yourself." She did not mention their unborn child.[95] Shelley, on August 29, departed with three young women—Mary, Claire, and Elise—and his son; that same day Byron headed for Chamonix with Hobhouse and Davies.

Shelley wrote most of the journal entries about their eleven-day return to England. Finding Fontainebleau less impressive than Versailles, he wished a Greek architect had been turned loose on the latter's "effeminate & royal" apartments whose "vacant rooms . . . imaged well the hollow shew of monarchy."[96]

The creative energy flowing through this gifted group in the summer of 1816 found expression in Mary's *Frankenstein*, Polidori's *The Vampyre*, Byron's third canto and *The Prisoner of Chillon*, and Shelley's *Hymn* and *Mont Blanc*. The deep sense of personal separateness and alienation reflected in much of their writing was quickened into creative expression by the unique set of relationships provided by this Swiss interlude. Sadly, the group's productive energy did not reach Claire, the person responsible for bringing this group together.

A boatman on the lake recalled both poets years later after Shelley's death. The boatman shared his memories with Lady Blessington, who believed he admired Byron and loved Shelley, "a different sort of man [from Byron], so gentle, so affectionate, so generous. . . . He would not hurt a fly—nay, he would save everything that had life, so tender and merciful was his nature." Thinking Shelley "was too good for this world," the boatman had rowed Englishmen who "tried to make me think ill of him, but . . . we plain people judge by what we *see,* and not by what we *hear.*"[97]

Notes

1. THE POLITICS OF PATERNITY

1. Birth certificates list BS's name as Piercey Bysshe Shelley and Piercey Bish Shelley. Baptized by this name, the 1742 extract of his baptismal certificate has Piercey crossed out, indicating that by age eleven BS had dropped his first name. MS. Shelley adds. c. 9, Bodleian; *SG*, 4.

2. James Bieri, "Shelley's Older Brother," *KSJ* 39(1990): 29–33. See also, *GY*, 571 n. 38. Horace Smith's 17 April 1821 letter to PBS (*SM*, 612) referred to the pending marriage of TS's natural son, "Captain Shelley," to the daughter of William Whitton. This paragraph was omitted from Lady Shelley's 1859 *Shelley Memorials* and her four volume edition of *SM*. Another reference to this illegitimate son is in Miss Rickman's letter to Lady Shelley: "an illegitimate older son of Sir Timothy [who] was thought by the young folks to be the greater favorite with the father, and not the friend of the intellectual and imaginative Percy." Richard Garnett, Misc. mss., "Notes, memoirs, and transcripts of letters to Shelley. nd. A, T, and Tcc ms.", HRC. Garnett and Lady Shelley suppressed the information of this illegitimate child, as did PBS's authorized biographer, Edward Dowden.

3. BS to Robert Hurst, 1791–1793. Hurst MSS, West Sussex Record Office.

4. MS. Shelley adds. c. 12, Bodleian; *SG*, 9.

5. Field Place, in the Shelley family until 1929, was restored architecturally to its 1788 configuration by its present owner, K. V. Prichard Jones. See Ken Prichard Jones, "The Influence of Field Place and Its Surroundings upon Percy Bysshe Shelley," *KSR* 8 (1993–1994): 132–50; DK (1999), 3–6; Ingpen, 7–8.

6. William Albery, *Parliamentary History of the Ancient Borough of Horsham* (London: Longmans, 1927), 123–91.

7. Thompson, 107–8.

8. DK (1999), 8.

9. Sally N. Hand, "Timothy Shelley, Merchant of Newark: The Search for Shelley's American Ancestor," *KSJ* 29 (1980): 31–42; John Malone, "A Search for Shelley's American Ancestor," *Century Magazine* 23 (August 1892): 634–36.

10. Medwin, 8. See also, Hand, "A Search," 37–38.

11. Evidence in Newark of a possible earlier child of Timothy and Joanna suggests Timothy came to America in 1727. See Hand, "The Search," 32–33.

12. John Baker, 15 March 1774, *Diary of John Baker*, ed. P. C. Yorke (London, 1931).

13. Hand, "A Search," 38–39; White, 1:7–8; *SG*, 4.

14. MS. Shelley adds. c. 9, Bodleian; *SG*, 4. The May 1742 document signed by the Reverend Aaron Burr and Jonathan Evans is an extract of the baptismal certificates

of Piercey Bysshe and John Shelley. The Reverend Aaron Burr, father of the future Vice President, was a Presbyterian minister in Newark.

15. John Shelley (d. 1772), "The Lunatic" in the family papers, was diagnosed "imbecility of mind" in a day when mental retardation was often equated with insanity. He outlived his brothers Bysshe (d. 1733), Timothy (d. 1770), and Percy (d. 1771).

16. Ingpen, 5–6.

17. BS to Robert Hurst, 26 June 1792, Hurst MSS (Accession 4539), West Sussex Record Office.

18. BS to Robert Hurst, c. January 1793, Hurst MSS (Accession 4539), West Sussex Record Office. See also, DK (1999), 49–73.

19. Ingpen, 8.

20. Archives, HM.

21. Medwin, 8; Lady Irwin's Hills Place servant to her Ladyship at Windsor Castle, 16 October 1752, Archives, HM.

22. Ingpen, 7 n. 1.

23. Shelley-Ingpen Papers, Series 1, Box 2, Bancroft.

24. John Shelley (1784–1858) has a curiously shifting name in the published Army lists, coinciding with the fate of BS, probably his father. Beginning as James Shelley, assistant surgeon (1805) 35th Sussex Foot Regiment, he became surgeon (1811), Greek Light Infantry. By 1817 he began listing himself as James N Shelley, then James Nichols Shelley. In 1821 he became John Nichols Shelley. From 1847, he is listed as John Nicholas Shelley.

25. *SC*, 3:443–45.

26. DK (1999), 69 n. 182.

27. TS, Bixby Shelley Family Notebook, Huntington.

28. F. M. L. Thompson, *English Landed Society in the Nineteenth Century* (London: Routledge and Kegan Paul, 1963), 47–48.

29. Dawson, 18–24.

30. 18 M 51.116–43, Hampshire Record Office.

31. DK (1999), 81.

32. Medwin, 11.

33. [Joseph Gibbons Merle], "A Newspaper Editor's Reminiscences", *Fraser's Magazine* 23 (June 1841): 699–710.

34. Hogg, 2:38, 42.

35. Ingpen, 351. Mrs. Clarke, the Duke of York's mistress, was accused of accepting bribes to persuade the Duke to appoint officers.

36. Medwin, 102.

37. Hogg, 1:138–39.

38. Medwin, 12.

39. Blunden, 15.

40. TS to Thomas Medwin, 15 December 1778, Ms. No.543, HM.

41. TS to Thomas Medwin, 8 October 1780, Ms. No.2985.1, HM.

42. Information courtesy Bruce Barker-Benfield, Bodleian and Maggie MacDonald, Oxford University Archives.

43. *SG*, 5.

44. For TS's letters from Field Place, 1778–1780, 1788–1790, see DK (1999), 15–16, 26–33. For architectural evidence suggesting TS's bachelor quarters, see Prichard Jones, "Influence of Field Place," 142.

45. White, 1:11.

46. Medwin, 10.

47. Gelpi, 89.

48. TS to Thomas Medwin, 14, 17, 18 April 1790; TS to Rev. George Marshall, n.d., DK (1999), 32–33, 75–76.

49. Dawson, 20.

50. White, 1:10.

51. Hogg, 1:206–7.

52. Mrs. Mathilda C. Houstoun, *A Woman's Memories of World-Known Men*, 3rd. ed. (London, 1883), 68; White, 1:11–12.

53. Houstoun, *Woman's Memories*, 68; White, 1:13, 563.

54. Medwin, 105; Maud Rolleston, *Talks with Lady Shelley* (London: G.G. Harrop, 1925), 95, 138.

55. Medwin, 13.

2. "An Infancy Outlasting Manhood"

1. YS, 4. See also Barbara A. Schapiro, *The Romantic Mother: Narcissistic Patterns in Romantic Poetry* (Baltimore: Johns Hopkins University Press, 1983); Christine Gallant, *Shelley's Ambivalence* (London: Macmillan, 1989); Gelpi.

2. Sarah Hurst, *Diary of Sarah Hurst, Horsham*, extracts 4–5 February, 5–6 April 1759, HM.

3. Elizabeth Pilfold, b. n.d., bpt. 24 February 1763.

4. Elizabeth Pilfold's siblings were: Charlotte, b. 1764, d. 1828; Charles, b. 1765, d. unmarried in India; John, b. 1768, d. 1834; James, b. 1771, d. n.d; Bathia, b. 1773, d. 1847; Ferdinand, b. 1775, d. after 1788. The mother, Bethia White Pilfold, d. 1779; the father, Charles Pilfold, d. 1790.

5. A "Miss Pilford" [*sic*] staying at the Pooles July 1776 attended the "great ball at Brighton." W. S. Blunt, "Extracts from Mr. John Baker's Diary," *Sussex Archaeological Collections* 52 (1909): 78.

6. Medwin, 13.

7. *Diary of John Baker*, ed. P.C. Yorke (London, 1931), 29 July 1771.

8. Judith Brent, "The Pooles of Chailey and Lewes: The Establishment and Influence of a Gentry Family, 1732–1739," *Sussex Archaeological Collections* 114 (1976): 69–80.

9. Ingpen, 19–21. Ingpen stated that TS, after completing Oxford, made a Grand Tour on the continent, having first become engaged to Elizabeth Pilfold. This could place the engagement as early as 1778. Ingpen had access to TS papers subsequently sold and dispersed.

10. *The Journal of Harriet Grove*, ed. Roger Ingpen (London: Privately Printed, 1932).

11. *Grove Diaries*, 2.

12. The settlement BS drew up in 1782 for the Sussex Michell estates from his first wife assured they went to TS. Another settlement, August 1791, of the estates of Edward Shelley, was drawn up by BS and TS specifying they be passed on to TS's male heir. Thomas Medwin Sr. wrote PBS 18 June 1813 about this 1791 settlement, "you were then Unborn, tho' not unthought of."

13. TS to Thomas Medwin, 20 October 1791, MSS Cat. no. 2985.14, HM.

14. Kim Leslie, *Shelley's Sussex,* West Sussex County Council, 1992.

15. Mary Pilfold, daughter of Charles Pilfold's brother John, in 1778 married Thomas Charles Medwin, Horsham solicitor. Their son, Thomas Medwin, was born in 1788.

16. Medwin, 104.

17. Alice F. Kennedy to Roger Ingpen, Shelley–Ingpen papers, box 12, Bancroft.

18. MS Bundle 543, HM. Despite the pencil date "Dec.1781?" written on the letter, its contents indicate a later date. "Kitty" was "Miss Kate" to young PBS.

19. TS to T. C. Medwin, 4, 28 March 1789, MSS Cat. nos. 2985.2, 2985.3, HM.

20. Elizabeth Shelley to Thomas C. Medwin, MSS Cat. no. 2985.33, HM.

21. Elizabeth Shelley to "D. Stedman Esqr. Solr. Horsham," 25 July [1844], MSS Cat. no. 557.1, HM. After Thomas Charles Medwin died in 1829, his youngest son, Pilfold Medwin, assumed his father's law practice. For two letters (1826 and 1846) from Elizabeth Shelley to Pilfold Medwin, see MSS Cat. nos. 112.18, 557.12, HM.

22. To CC, 27 October 1844, *LMWS,* 3:157.

23. SH 31, Huntington. TS's note states that PBS, born at ten o'clock, was baptized by Reverend Woodward at eleven and publicly baptized Friday September 7 by Reverend Tom Thuckford of Warnham.

24. "A Shelley Letter: Communicated by F. Bentham Stevens, F.S.A.," *Sussex Notes and Queries,* vol. 9, No.4 (November 1942): 73–77. I am indebted to C. R. Davey, East Sussex County Archivist, for bringing this letter to my attention.

25. Elizabeth Shelley's third child, Hellen, died May 1796, age four months.

26. Hellen Shelley, born 1799, was "very like the poet, her tall slender figure her thick wavy fair hair, her shrewd critical, observant, yet kindly eyes—her rather sharp tongue—& love of a good story or joke." Grace Heathcote to Roger Ingpen, 25 July 1931, Shelley–Ingpen Papers, series 1, box 12, Bancroft.

27. "Ann," probably Ann Wood, born 1750, was the unmarried daughter of Elizabeth Shelley's deceased aunt Mary Pilfold Wood.

28. Dowden, 1:5.

29. To Felicia Browne, ?13 March 1811, MS. Don. c. 180, fols. 13–16, Bodleian.

30. Miss Rickman to Lady Shelley, 10 September 1860, Richard Garnett, Misc. mss. Shelley, HRC. Miss Rickman is reporting the reminiscences of her friend, Mrs. Fields (Matilda Evans), the Shelley sisters' schoolmate at boarding school in Clapham.

31. Dowden, 1:78; *Reminiscences of Horsham,* ed. William Albery (Folcroft, Pa.: Folcroft Library, 1975), 70, 79.

32. Dowden, 1:7.

33. Hellen Shelley to JW, c. 1856, Hogg, 1:28–29, 32. Hellen's memories probably are best construed as idealized family mythology.

34. One child miniature portrait shows brown eyes with dark pupils. Written on the back are "Lord Byron" and "Leigh Hunt" and a note signed by LH: "Genoa, October 17, 1822. This miniature was given to me by my poor dear friend Shelley in the presence of Lord Byron. Leigh Hunt." The adult portrait, a watercolor attributed to his friend Edward Elleker Williams, was completed near the end of PBS's life. In Williams's portrait, the eyes are blue with dark pupils.

35. G. R. Taylor, *The Angel Makers* (London: Secker & Warburg, 1958), 330.

36. Gelpi, 90.

37. Hogg, 1:20.

38. Margaret Mahler, Fred Pine, and Anita Bergman, *The Psychological Birth of the Human Infant* (New York: Basic Books, 1975).
39. Brown, 33–34.
40. *Letter to Maria Gisborne,* lines 73–74.
41. Richard S. Caldwell, "'The Sensitive Plant' as Original Fantasy," *Studies in Romanticism* 15 (1976): 212–52; Barbara C. Gelpi, "The Nursery Cave: Shelley and the Maternal," in *The New Shelley: Later Twentieth-Century Views,* ed. G. Kim Blank (New York: St. Martin's Press, 1991), 42–63; Gelpi, chap. 1. For symbiosis in infant development, see Margaret Mahler, *On Human Symbiosis and the Vicissitudes of Individuation* (New York: International Universities Press, 1968).
42. Sperry, 170, 221 n. 16.
43. Jacques Lacan, "The mirror stage as formative of the function of the I," chap. 1 in *Ecrits,* trans. Alan Sheridan (New York: Norton, 1977); Heinz Lichtenstein, *The Dilemma of Human Identity* (New York: Aronson, 1977).
44. Donald W. Winnicott, *Playing and Reality* (New York: Basic Books, 1971), 112.
45. Glenn O'Malley, *Shelley and Synesthesia* (Evanston: Northwestern University Press, 1964).
46. R. C. Bak, "Being in love and object loss," *International Journal of Psychoanalysis* 54 (1973): 1–8.

3. THE YOUNG PROMETHEUS

1. White, 1:18.
2. *SE,* 18:120–21.
3. Hogg, 2:547.
4. *CPPBS,* 1:157; *SC,* 2:628.
5. See chap. 1 n. 2.
6. [Joseph Gibbons Merle], "A Newspaper Editor's Reminiscences," *Fraser's Magazine* 23 (June 1841): 699–710. See also, *CW,* 8:xxiii–xxv; Dowden, 1:52; Ingpen, 340–41; White, 1:48–50, 574–75 n. 64; *SC,* 2:623; *SC,* 9:118–23.
7. Dowden, 1:13.
8. To James T. T. Tisdall, 10 January 1808, *L,* 1:2; Medwin, 68.
9. T. P. Hudson, *A History of Horsham* (Chichester: West Sussex County Council, 1988), 132–33.
10. D. H. Reiman, *Intervals of Inspiration* (Greenwood, Fla.: Penkevill, 1988), 396 n. 34.
11. Hogg, 1:7.
12. *SE,* 9:152.
13. *SC,* 2:712; Hogg, 1:21.
14. Hogg, 1:19.
15. Ibid.
16. Ibid., 1:13.
17. Ibid., 1:15.
18. Ibid., 1:20.
19. Ibid., 1:51–54.
20. Ibid., 1:8–10.
21. Medwin, 72.

4. Exiled to Education

1. Medwin, 14.
2. Ingpen, 242.
3. Peacock, 41.
4. To EH, ?10 December 1811, *L*, 1:200.
5. Peacock, 41–42.
6. DK (1999), 5–6.
7. Medwin senior, not mentioning Syon House, spent £600 on Tom's "School Education and Maintenance." PBS called Tom his "schoolfellow."
8. Sir John Rennie, *Autobiography* (London, 1875 [written 1867]), 1–2. Rennie was architect and engineer of the Waterloo Bridge.
9. W. C. Gellibrand's recollections of PBS are in Augustine Birrell, *Athenaeum*, May 3, 1884.
10. Medwin entered Trinity College, Oxford, fall 1805 and left the next March to become his father's Horsham law clerk. After qualifying in London (1811) as a solicitor and being arrested for debt (1812), his father bought him a commission in the army. See DK (1995), 11–18; Lovell, chap. 1.
11. Medwin, 27.
12. Ibid., 27–28. Sleep-walking and nightmares, often present in the same person, may occur when stress evokes a level of brain activation common to somnambulism and nightmares, a neurological–emotional pattern possibly related to the seizure-like states Medwin described.
13. Medwin, 447.
14. Ibid., 15–19.
15. Ibid.
16. *CPPBS*, 1:135–36, 296–98; Nora Crook, "Shelley's Earliest Poem?" *MLA Notes* (December 1987): 486–90; *SC*, 4:815–16.
17. *SC*, 4:813–14.
18. *SC*, 4:819; Peck, 1:8.
19. Thompson, 198.
20. The average age of heirs of squires at their father's death was about 30; TS was about 57. See Lawrence Stone, *Family, Sex and Marriage in England 1500–1800* (London: Oxford, 1977), 53.
21. "Written in very early youth," dated "likely" 1809 (*Esdaile*, 275), "possibly" 1808 (*PS*,1:4).
22. *CPPBS*, 1:435–37; Medwin, 35–37.
23. Hogg, 1:23–24. For late 1818 or early 1819 date of the essay, see Brown, 267 n. 82.
24. Rennie mentioned a Syon House contemporary from Sussex named Tredcroft who died young, "another peculiar character [who] also had considerable poetic talent." Robert Tredcroft was one year older than PBS. See White, 1:566–67.
25. *EL*, 1:249.
26. *Prose*, 347.
27. For PBS's "Resolutions" occurring 1809–10 at Eton, see *SC*, 9:77, 81–86. For this as a composite of several events, see White, 1:28–29, 567 n. 32, Holmes, 16.
28. *BSM*, 13:xvi–xvii.
29. To WG, 10 January 1812, *L*, 1:227.
30. Medwin, 22–24.

31. Medwin suggested PBS cribbed these lines. See Medwin, 21; Peacock, 20–21.

32. Peacock, 22.

33. F. Turner, "Percy Bysshe Shelley at Syon House Academy," Extracts, *Middle-sex & Hertfordshire Notes and Queries,* January–April 1896.

34. Medwin, 24; Ingpen, 46.

35. Medwin, 24; White, 1:29.

36. Hogg, 1:16.

37. Brown, 51.

38. Medwin, 24–26.

39. Hogg, 1:8–9.

40. Medwin, 41.

41. White, 1:23.

42. Nora Crook, "Shelley and the Solar Microscope," *KSR* 1 (1986): 49–60; Nora Crook, "Letter to the Editor," *KSR* 4 (1989): 112–13.

43. *JCC,* 47.

44. Carl Grabo, *The Magic Plant: The Growth of Shelley's Thought* (Chapel Hill: University of North Carolina Press, 1936); Hugh Roberts, *Shelley and the Chaos of History: A New Politics of Poetry* (University Park: Pennsylvania State University Press, 1997).

45. Medwin, 38–39; *GY,* 394, 635 n. 6.

46. Richmond's Theatre Royal's playbill, 3 August 1801. Rodney Bennett kindly supplied the theater information.

5. "Untaught Foresters"

1. For Shelley's identification with Christ, see Teddi Chichester Bonca, *Shelley's Mirrors of Love: Narcissism, Sacrifice, and Sorority* (Albany: State University of New York Press, 1999).

2. Brown, 141.

3. Crompton, 79–81.

4. Brown, 141–42.

5. Crompton, 358–59.

6. Ibid. 81.

7. Leslie Marchand, review of Crompton, *KSJ* 35 (1986): 191.

8. W. T. Stead, quoted in Brown, 141.

9. John Chandos, *Boys Together: English Public Schools 1800–1864* (New Haven: Yale University Press, 1984), 87.

10. Jonathan Gathorne-Hardy, *The Old School Tie: The Phenomenon of the English Public School* (New York: Viking, 1978), 167.

11. Leonard Woolf, *Sowing: An Autobiography of the Year 1880 to 1904* (New York: Harcourt Brace Janovich, 1960), 65–66, 87–90.

12. H. C. Maxwell Lyte, *A History of Eton College,* 4th ed., (London, 1911), 426.

13. Chandos, *Boys Together,* 63; Gathorne-Hardy, *School Tie,* 167.

14. Lyte, *History of Eton,* 426.

15. Gathorne-Hardy, *School Tie,* 40–41.

16. Brown, 284.

17. Hogg, 1:40.

18. Peacock, 24–25.

19. Notes by MWS, c. 1823–1824, for a PBS biography she never wrote, printed by Hogg with his biased changes in his PBS biography. See Hogg, 1:27–28; Elizabeth Nitchie, "Shelley at Eton: Mary Shelley vs. Jefferson Hogg," *KSMB* 11 (1960): 48–54. In MWS's novel *Lodore*, "Derham" (PBS) at Eton "would not fag."

20. Nitchie, "Shelley at Eton," 53.

21. Lyte, *History of Eton*, 425–26; White, 1:37, 571.

22. F. St. John Thackeray, *Memoir of Edward Craven Hawtrey* (London, 1896). Cited in White, 1:569.

23. Thackeray, *Memoir;* White, 1:37.

24. *Athenaeum*, 4 March 1848; reprinted, White, 2:489–92. W. H. Merle is not PBS's later friend, Joseph Gibbons Merle.

25. *Athenaeum*, 15 April 1848; reprinted, White, 2:494–96.

26. Lyte, *History of Eton*, 426.

27. Ibid.; J. T. Coleridge review of LH's *Foliage* in *Quarterly Review*, January 1818.

28. Medwin, 70.

29. *Shelley Memorials*, 13.

30. Peacock, 24.

31. To WG, 18 January 1812, *L*, 1:228.

32. *AM*, 192.

33. To LH, 8 April 1825, *LMWS*, 1: 475.

34. *YS*, 9.

35. White, 1:38; *Selections from the Reminiscences of Captain Gronow*, ed. Nicolas Bentley (London: Folio Society, 1977), 118–19. The incident of spouting lines from Homer was attributed to a fight prior to Shelley's. See White, 1:570.

36. Michael Meredith, letter to author, 30 October 1986.

37. Hogg, 1:31.

38. Dowden, 1:25.

39. *Byron*, 3:951.

40. *Shelley Memorials*, 14; *SC*, 9:87 n. 48.

41. Dowden, 1:26; *SC*, 9:82 n. 34.

42. Hogg, 1:43–44.

43. Brown, 142.

44. Bentley, *Captain Gronow*, 118.

45. Brown, 210–11.

46. *AM*, 193–94.

47. *AM*, 200.

48. Ibid., 126.

49. *GY*, 56–57; CG, 15.

50. CG, 137.

51. CG, chap. 9.

52. Ibid., 126.

53. Brown, 210.

54. Richard Garnett, *Relics of Shelley* (London, 1862), 67–73.

55. *Prose*, 223.

56. Hunt, 213.

57. CG, 35.

58. Hunt, 183.
59. CG, 153, 249 n. 40. In MWS's novel, *The Last Man,* the well was a favorite place of Adrian (PBS).
60. Hogg, 1:11.
61. CG, 30, 248 n. 26.
62. "A Shelley Letter," *Sussex Notes and Queries* 9, No.4 (November 1942): 77.
63. CG, 22.
64. S. C. Woolsey, ed., *Diary and Letters of Frances Burney, Madame D'Arblay* (Boston, 1890), 1:200. See also, *DNB,*11:1151–52.
65. *Diary and Letters,* 185. Burney reported Lind told her he unsuccessfully excavated an "Elephanta" statue in the East Indies.
66. Christopher Goulding, "The real Doctor Frankenstein?" *Journal of the Royal Society* 95 (2002): 257–59; CG 21–31; J. H. Gosset [Lind's grandson] to Edward Dowden, MS 3152/853, Trinity College Library Dublin.
67. An 1813 edition of Lucretius, apparently printed at the personal expense of Keate for his students, was acquired by HM. Jeremy Knight, letter to author, 26 February 1998.
68. Medwin, 37.
69. Hogg, 1:31–32.
70. Lind's youngest daughter, widow of the Vicar of Windsor, made Hogg apologize for his charge about her father ever making an oath. Hogg apparently intended a retraction in his lost vol. III of his PBS biography. See Dowden, 1:32–33.
71. Hogg, 1:32.
72. To WG, 10 January 1812, *L,* 1:228; William Michael Rossetti, *The Complete Poetical Works of Percy Bysshe Shelley and a Memoir* (London, 1881), 1:9–10.
73. To James Tisdall, 7 April 1809, *L,* 1:4; *Shelley Memorials,* 20.
74. *SC,* 7:110–32.
75. MS. Shelley e. 4 (fol. 72r), Bodleian; *BSM,* 3.
76. *Records,* 51.
77. Hogg, 1:chap.3.
78. CG, 30.
79. Ibid., 48–49; Medwin, 69–70.

6. Gothic "Wild Boy" and Harriet Grove

1. Cat. no. 1215/837,838,877, Huntington.
2. Dawson, 17–18.
3. Carl Grabo, *The Magic Plant: The Growth of Shelley's Thought* (Chapel Hill: The University of North Carolina Press, 1936), 2–3.
4. Hogg, 1:10–11.
5. Dawson, 33.
6. Hogg, 1:207.
7. Ibid., 1:15–16.
8. *First Love,* chap. 12; *Esdaile,* 305–9.
9. Medwin, 47.
10. "Fiordispina," *PW,* 631.

11. Hogg, 2:550. This incident was previously dated 1804, but Charles Grove (b. 1794, d. 14 July 1878) was age nine Easter 1803.

12. "To St Irvyne," written winter 1809–1810 with date, "Febry 28th 1805." See *Esdaile*, 171–72, 305–9; *PS*,1:84–85.

13. *Grove Diaries*, 43; *SC*, 2:509.

14. White, 1:67.

15. *First Love*, 41–42.

16. *Grove Diaries*, 112.

17. Ibid., 49.

18. Ibid., 53.

19. Ibid., 49.

20. To Tisdall, 10 January 1809, *L*, 1:2. See *SC*, 9:143 n. 9.

21. To Tisdall, 1 January 1809, *L*, 1:3.

22. To Tisdall, 26 March 1809, *L*, 1:3.

23. To Longman & Company, 7 May 1809, *L*, 1:4–5.

24. To WG, 10 January 1812, *L*, 1:227.

25. To WG, March 8, 1812, *L*, 1:266.

26. To Tisdall, 7 April 1809, *L*,1:4.

27. Hogg, 1:18.

28. PBS began *The Wandering Jew* by the winter of 1809–1810. See *CPPBS*, 1:41, 202; White, 1:580 n. 17; *Esdaile*, 274.

29. *First Love*, 23–24.

30. *Grove Diaries*, 67.

31. *SC*, 9:72–73, 102. For PBS's 1810 diary, see *SC*, 9:91–114; *First Love*, App. 2. Entries from 1 January to 4 June 1810.

32. *First Love*, 140; *CPPBS*, 1:189, 214. The week of 26 February–1 March, under "wandering Jew", PBS recorded passages from Revelation (6:8, 12), the former verse footnoted in *The Wandering Jew* (Canto 1; *CPPBS*, 1:50). Medwin, who claimed to coauthor this work, lived in Horsham at this time.

33. *Esdaile*, 131–43, 266.

34. The parcel probably contained early sections of *The Wandering Jew*. See *CPPBS*, 1:189.

35. *Grove Diaries*, 74–75.

36. *First Love*, 33–34.

37. Hogg, 2:555–56.

38. To Graham, 22 April 1810, *L*, 1:7–8. William Michael Rossetti titled this poem "St. Irvyne's Tower."

39. Harriet possibly thanked PBS for books sent through Graham (*L*, 1:13), with whom she had several singing lessons in London.

40. The Grove family, after leaving Field Place April 18, visited Sergison in Cuckfield while staying with Captain Pilfold.

41. *Esdaile*, 171–72, 305–9.

42. *YS*, 326 n. 156; Hogg, 1:136–38; Timothy Webb, "'The Avalanche of Ages': Shelley's Defence of Atheism and Prometheus Unbound," *KSMB* 35 (1984): 1 n. 1.

43. Medwin, 37. PBS's 1810 diary (*First Love*, 138–39) records payment of £2.15 to "Graham for Pliny."

44. *First Love*, 61, 140.

45. PBS wrote Graham August 1810 of a tragedy he would offer Covent Garden, adding, "my friend is composing" a farce. The tragedy was "not yet finished" in Sep-

tember but he intended sending the farce, not mentioning its author. See *L,* 1:14. No trace exists of either work.

46. To Graham, 23 April 1810, *L,* 1:9. PBS's journal entry, 4 June 1810: "to go to W. Wickham with Dashwood & Leslie. Resolution made." *First Love,* 37, 141; *SC,* 9:77–83.

47. To Graham, 29 May 1810, *L,* 1:12.

48. To Graham, ? August 1810, *L,* 1:14.

49. CG, 33.

50. To Graham, 20, 29 May 1810, *L,* 1:11–12.

51. [Joseph Gibbons Merle], "A Newspaper Editor's Reminiscences," *Fraser's Magazine* 23 (June 1841): 701–2. See also, White, 1:48–50, 574–75 n. 64; *SC,* 2:624–25. Merle later edited a Tory periodical.

52. To Graham, 11 August 1810, *L,* 1:13.

53. To Graham, 14 September 1810, *L,* 1:16.

54. Brown, 52.

55. Peter Finch, "Monstrous Inheritance: The Sexual Politics of Genre in Shelley's *St. Irvyne,*" *KSJ* 48 (1999): 35–68.

56. Brown, 206.

57. Curran, 276–77.

58. Holmes, 32–33.

59. To Graham, 23 April 1810, *L,* 1:10.

60. *Zastrozzi's* title page has "P. B. S." as author.

61. To J. J. Stockdale, 19 November 1810, *L,* 1:21.

62. MWS (*PW,* 536) wrote that PBS read "the *Nouvelle Héloïse* for the first time" in 1816. However, he knew its radical sexual message by 1810. See Finch, "Monstrous Inheritance," 47–48.

63. To Stockdale, 19 November 1810, *L,* 1:21. For the subtitle as an afterthought, gleaned from Barruel's *Memoirs,* see Hogle, 87.

64. *Z&SI,* 180–81.

65. *Hymn to Intellectual Beauty; Dedication to Laon and Cythna; Julian and Maddalo.* A poem, "I will kneel at thine altar," titled "1809," suggests a similar, possibly earlier experience. See *Esdaile,* 250–54; *PS,* 1:150.

7. A RADICAL POETIC IDENTITY

1. *Esdaile,* 3–4; "The Esdaile Notebook," ed. Donald H. Reiman, *MYR,* 1:xiii–xxvi.

2. Medwin, 102.

3. To LH, 2 March 1811, *L,* 1:55.

4. Dawson, 46–47.

5. Kenneth Keniston, *Young Radicals: Notes on Committed Youth* (New York: Harcourt, Brace and World, 1968), chap. 4.

6. *Esdaile,* 266; *PS,* 1:13.

7. *YS,* 49–51; Mac-Carthy, 77–103.

8. *YS,* 46.

9. James Phillips did surveying, printing, and other work for Thomas Medwin, senior. He wrote the elder Medwin, 10 December 1810, asking him "to lend me a pound note to send to London until the 15th of this month as I shall then have the 75£ to take of P.B. Shelley Esq. for printing done for him." No. 437, HM. *The Necessity of Atheism*

also bore the C. and W. Phillips imprint. If James Phillips did print both of Shelley's early works, it possibly was part of Shelley's effort to hide his authorship.

10. To Stockdale, 6 September 1810, *L*, 1:15.

11. *First Love*, 135–36.

12. Wrongly attributed to Monk Lewis, from whom PBS likely thought he was stealing it. See C. R. Zimansky, *KSJ* 30 (1981):15; *CPPBS*, 1:157. For other plagiarisms in *Original Poetry*, see *YS*, 305–6; *CPPBS*, 1:154–59.

13. Peck, 1:30; Medwin, 44–45; *Esdaile*, 273–74.

14. *Stockdale's Budget*, 13 December 1826; quoted in *YS*, 305.

15. *YS*, 305–6.

16. White, 1:58–59.

17. *CPPBS*, 1:157; *YS*, 34, 305–6; *Esdaile*, 258–60; *SC*, 2:628–31.

18. PBS obfuscated in dating the poems in *Original Poetry*. Only the offending Charlotte–Sergison poem has a full date, April 30, 1810, indicating it was shared with Harriet in London on that date. PBS dated "Cold, cold is the blast" July, 1810; the 1808 version in *Esdaile*, 259, ("Cold are the blasts"), could be his earliest published poem.

19. *CPPBS*, 1:183; *YS*, 310.

20. To Graham, [? August 1810], *L*, 1:14; Holmes, 35.

21. Medwin, 39–41; *CPPBS*, 1:197.

22. PBS, *The Wandering Jew*, ed. Bertram Dobell (London: The Shelley Society, 1887).

23. *CPPBS*, 1:196–204.

24. *CPPBS*, 1:200–4; *SC*, 2:649–59; *PS*, 1:40; *YS*, 310–13; G. K. Anderson, *The Legend of the Wandering Jew* (Providence: Rhode Island University Press, 1965); CG, 29–30; Bruce Barker-Benfield, "Shelley's Bodleian Visits," *The Bodleian Library Record* 12, no.5 (October 1987): 381–99.

25. To Graham, 1 April 1810, *L*, 1:5–6.

26. Ballantyne & Co. to PBS, 24 September 1810, *L*, 1:17.

27. *CPPBS*, 1:189–96.

28. Dobell, *Wandering Jew*, xxxii.

29. CG, 49, 62, 148.

30. CG, 163; Holmes, 638.

31. PBS presumably had one of two Leicester appointments to University College controlled by his father's half-brother, Sir John Shelley-Sidney. PBS's entry in the Matriculation Register reads, "Coll. Univ. [Aprilis 10mo] Percy Bysshe Shelley 17. Timothei de Warnham in Com. Sussex.- Armi(igeri) fil(ius)." It was customary for fathers to join their sons at matriculation. See Barker-Benfield, *Bodleian Visits*, 387.

32. Ibid., 383.

33. *Shelley Memorials*, 14.

34. *UH*, 33–39; White, 1:56–57.

35. Charles Henry Grove to Lady Shelley, 24 February 1860, in William R. Thurman, Jr., "Letters about Shelley from the Richard Garnett Papers" (Ph.D. diss., The University of Texas at Austin, 1972), 54–56.

36. Polidori, 12–13.

37. Hogg, 1:18.

38. Medwin, 13.

39. *CPPBS*, 1:237–38; White, 1:76. Henry Slatter to Robert Montgomery, 18 December 1833, in Robert Montgomery, *Oxford: a Poem*, 3d ed. (London, 1833). See also, *SG*, 25.

40. Ingpen, 629; *SC*, 2:726–30.

41. The firm became "Munday and Slatter," January 1811. See Ingpen, 101. For PBS's possible involvement in Munday's *Oxford Herald*, see Mac-Carthy, 56.

42. Mac-Carthy, 24–25.

43. Ibid., 19–25; *YS*, 47.

44. Hogg, 1:317; *SC*, 2:726, 850; *L*, 1:53, 129; White, 1:109. Hogg reported PBS received a long letter from the helpful vicar, including sketches. The poem was not completed.

45. Unknown writer to Lady Shelley, 10 May 1867, reporting recollections of "Prof. Covington—an ex-fellow of University [College]." See Thurman, "Letters about Shelley," 481.

46. Thomas Jefferson Hogg, *Shelley at Oxford*, ed. R. A. Streatfeild (London: Methuen, 1904), 6–12; from articles Hogg first published in *The New Monthly Magazine*, 1832–1833. See also Hogg, 1:chaps. 3–8.

47. Medwin, 67. De Quincey's account is in *Tait's Magazine*, January, 1846.

48. Peacock, 27.

49. Hogg, 1:69–79.

50. Ibid., 1:138–39.

51. Ibid., 1:319.

52. Scott, chap. 1.

53. *SC*, 3:1–2.

54. Terrot and Wordsworth were close friends at Cambridge. See *SC*, 3:197–200.

55. *SC*, 1:34–38; *CPPBS*, 1:239–40.

56. To Graham, 21, 30 November 1810, *L*, 1:22–23.

57. Hogg, *Shelley at Oxford*, 201.

58. Montgomery's *Oxford: a Poem*, quoted in *YS*, 318 n. 75. PBS's quick composition at times perhaps resulted from memorizing lines before committing them to paper. See *CPPBS*, 1:238.

59. To Graham, 30 November 1810, *L*, 1:23.

60. *YS*, 54–55.

61. Charles Kirkpatrick Sharpe to Lady Charlotte Campbell, 15 March 1811, *Letters to and from Charles Kirkpatrick Sharpe*, ed. Alexander Allardyce, 2 vols. (Edinburgh and London, 1888)1:442. See also, CG, 41–43; Peck, 1:105–6, 110; Peck, 2:446; White, 1:94–97, 595–96; *YS*, 21–23, 318–19 n. 75.

62. CG, 41.

63. Ibid., 42.

64. *CPPBS*, 1:253.

65. To Graham, 21, 30 November 1810, *L*, 1:22–23. No known copies have deleted lines.

66. Hogg, 1:262–66.

67. A. M. D. Hughes, *The Nascent Mind of Shelley* (Oxford: Clarendon Press, 1947), 52; Peck, 1:83; White, 1:93–94.

68. *GY*, 223, 610; Holmes, 49.

69. Brown, 248 n. 28.

70. CG, 42–43.

71. *CPPBS*, 1:254.

72. Hogg, 1:263.

73. CG, 40.

74. Ibid., 41; White, 1:596.

75. Elijah Barwell Impey to Charles Kirkpatrick Sharpe, 18 March 1811, Allardyce, *Letters to and from Sharpe*, 1:445. Miss Burton was a joked-about much older "Oxford belle" spinster.

76. CG, 42.

77. *YS*, 21–22; White, 1:597. Both Slatter and Sharpe stated PBS gave proceeds from *Posthumous Fragments* to Finnerty. The editor of the *Dublin Weekly Messenger* said PBS gave £100 (an unlikely amount) to Finnerty from profits from an unidentified "very beautiful poem," possibly the unlocated "*Poetical Essay*."

78. Elizabeth Grant Smith, *Memoirs of a Highland Lady*, ed. Lady Strachey (London, 1899), 124–25.

79. Hogg Oxford Exercise Book, Hg 114, Pforzheimer Collection, The New York Public Library.

80. Hogg, 1:119.

81. Allardyce, *Letters to and from Sharpe*, 1:442, 2:204. For PBS's possible self-medication to treat venereal disease, see CG, chaps. 2, 3.

82. CG, 45–47.

83. Ibid., 20.

84. Hogg, 1:75.

85. Ibid., 1:132.

86. CG, 52.

87. Ibid., 237 n. 34.

88. Hogg, 1:71.

89. PBS did not read the major French materialist philosopher d'Holbach until 1812. See *L*, 1:303.

90. Hogg, 1:239–40.

91. To James Roe, 1810–1811, *L*, 1:19.

92. To Stockdale, 18 December 1810, *L*, 1:24.

93. Blunden, 10.

94. To Stockdale, 19 November 1810, *L*, 1:21.

95. To Hogg, 20 December 1810, *L*, 1:28.

8. ICARUS AT OXFORD

1. To Hogg, 16 January 1811, *L*, 1:47.

2. To WG, 10 January 1812, *L*, 1:227–28.

3. To Graham, 21 November 1810, *L*, 1:22.

4. Hogg, 1:220–21.

5. *SC*, 2:729; Dowden, 1:108.

6. Hogg, 1:79–81.

7. Ibid., 1:134–35, 217–21.

8. Ibid., 1:235.

9. MS. Don. c. 180, Bodleian.

10. *Esdaile*, 115–22; *CPPBS*, 1:307–8.

11. To Hogg, 3 January, 8 May 1811, *L*, 1:36, 77.

12. To Hogg, 14 May 1811, to Stockdale, 18 December 1810, to Hogg, 20 December 1810, *L*, 1:84, 25, 27.

13. *First Love*, 62.

14. To Hogg, 20 December 1810, *L,* 1:26.
15. Ingpen, 160–62, 135–37.
16. *SC,* 2:668–71.
17. *YS,* 125–26, 298 n. 77; Scrivener, 43, 327 n. 17.
18. To Stockdale, 11 November 1810, *L,* 1:18–19.
19. PBS was at Field Place December 10, the date on the copy of *St.Irvyne* he sent to his uncle, Robert Parker. See *SC,* 2:674.
20. To Stockdale, 18 December 1810, *L,* 1:24–25.
21. To Hogg, 20 December 1810, *L,* 1:27–29.
22. To Hogg, 23 December 1810, *L,* 1:29–30.
23. To Hogg, 3 January 1811, *L,* 1:36.
24. *SC,* 2:659–67.
25. To Hogg, 3 January 1811, *L,* 1:36.
26. To Hogg, 26 December 1810, *L,* 1:31–32. For Hogg's alteration of this letter, see *L,* 1:31 n. 1; *SC,* 2:675.
27. To Hogg, 26, 28 December 1810, *L,* 1:31–33.
28. CG, 65.
29. After voting with the opposition majority on the Regency question January 1, 1811, TS "disappeared from view" in Parliamentary activity until his vote against Catholic relief, June 22, 1812. See R. G. Thorne, *The History of Parliament: The House of Commons,* vol. 5 (London: Secker and Warburg, 1986).
30. To Hogg, 1, 6 January 1811, *L,* 1:33–34, 37.
31. Hogg, 2:552; *First Love,* 66–70.
32. *First Love,* 74; *Grove Diaries,* 110.
33. *Grove Diaries,* 93; *First Love,* 67.
34. *Grove Diaries,* 99. PBS wrote Stockdale December 18 to send *St. Irvyne* to Miss Marshall and others, plus "6 copies to myself." He did not request one be sent to Harriet Grove. See *L,* 1:26–27.
35. *First Love,* 70.
36. For the December 30 to January 2 period as PBS's first visit with Harriet Westbrook, see *YS,* 334–35 n. 19.
37. *YS,* 16.
38. Hogg, 1:18.
39. To Hogg, 3 January 1811, *L,* 1:36.
40. Hogg, 2:332; CG, 46.
41. To Hogg, 20 December 1810, *L,* 1:27–29.
42. To Hogg, 3 January 1811, *L,* 1:35.
43. *SC,* 2:685.
44. *Esdaile,* 128, 257–58.
45. To Stockdale, 11 January 1811, *L,* 1:40.
46. *Grove Diaries,* 64.
47. To Hogg, 11 January 1811, *L,* 1:41–43.
48. *Grove Diaries,* 18.
49. Alice F. Kennedy to Roger Ingpen, Shelley-Ingpen papers, 73/237, Bancroft.
50. Ibid.
51. Ibid.
52. To Hogg, 11 January 1811, *L,* 1:42.
53. *SC,* 2:696–99.
54. To Hogg, 12 January, 16 January 1811, *L,* 1:43–45, 46–47.

55. Murray, 1:319; YS, 330–31; SC, 2:711–12.
56. To Hogg, 12 January 1811, L, 1:43–45.
57. To Hogg, 20 December 1810, 3 January 1811, L, 1:28, 36.
58. MS. Don. c. 180, fols. 7–12, Bodleian; SG, 23.
59. To Hogg, 14 January 1811, L, 1:46.
60. To Hogg, 17 January 1811, L, 1:47.
61. To Hogg, c. 20 January 1811, L, 1:48.
62. Hogg, 2:552.
63. YS, 76–78, 328–31; Murray, 1:319–27. Murray notes that PBS's later use of its arguments in his *Queen Mab* Note, "There is no God," indicated PBS accepted "complete responsibility" for *Necessity*.
64. PBS, reportedly friendly with the young woman, would "spend hours" learning to set type. See Ingpen 188–89; YS, 330; Samuel J. Looker, *Shelley Trelawny and Henley* (Worthing: Aldrich, 1950), 24–27.
65. Hogg, 1:272.
66. YS, 76. For PBS's atheism, not the agnosticism some ascribe to him, see Murray, 1:323–25.
67. To EH, 26 January 1812, L, 1:239.
68. To Hogg, 28 April 1811, L, 1:72.
69. Medwin, 13.
70. To Hogg, 17 May 1811, L, 1:90.
71. To TS, 6 February 1811, L, 1:50–51.
72. Mac-Carthy, 108.
73. To Graham, 14, 17 February 1811, L, 1:51–53.
74. To TS, 17 February 1811, L, 1:53. PBS's 12 January 1811 letter to Hogg suggests he may have read in Nicholson's *Encyclopedia* the erroneous statement that Spinoza had been burned to death for atheism. See SC, 2:709.
75. Dowden, 1:108.
76. Ingpen, 281–83; White, 1:95–96, 591 n. 63.
77. Medwin, 58–60; SG, 26.
78. MS. Don. c. 180, fols. 13–16, Bodleian; SG, 26.
79. SG, 26.
80. Hogg, 1:15.
81. Mrs. Hemans to ——, 15 November 1822, Shelley-Ingpen Mss., series 1, box 2, Bancroft.
82. The letter's sale catalogue offered a probably less accurate, but more amusing rendering: "the hen thrives on many a dunghill, but its lays are so pure, so celestial that they were never contaminated by it."
83. SC, 2:727–30; Dowden, 1:107–8; Ingpen 147, 630–32; White, 1:96, 591 n. 64.
84. To LH, 2 March 1811, L, 1:54–55. Since 1808, LH edited, and his older brother John published, the liberal *Examiner*. Prosecution for libel was first instituted against both brothers in 1809. In 1812, both were accused, severely fined, and imprisoned for two years when a fourth charge of seditious libel was successful. See White, 1:272.
85. Mac-Carthy, 57–61; CPPBS, 1:App.D.
86. YS, 50; Mac-Carthy, 100; Dowden, 1:108; CPPBS, 1:444–48.
87. PBS's expulsion notice in the Bodleian records includes a list of four of his publications, the last being "A Poetical Essay on the existing State of Things," published in quarto at "Oxford 1811." The other publications listed were "*St. Irvyne*, a romance; *Fragments of Margaret Nicholson* (quarto); & The Necessity of Atheism." See SG, 31;

White, 1:599–600 n. 149. *The Necessity of Atheism* was integrated into the notes of *Queen Mab*. White, among others, cites Dowden's idea that some of "A Poetical Essay" may have been reworked and incorporated into *Queen Mab*, supporting Medwin's contention that *Queen Mab* was begun at Oxford. See Dowden, 1:110–11.

88. To EH, 11 June 1811, *L*,1:101. PBS, ordering *The Curse* from Stockdale early December 1810, probably read it that month. See *PS*, 1:148; *YS*, 50.

89. Mac-Carthy, 100; *YS*, 51.

90. Allardyce, *Letters to and from Sharpe*, 1:442.

91. To Hogg, 12 January 1811, *L*, 1:45. For Faber, see *SC*, 2:749.

92. MS. Don. c. 180, fols. 25–47, Bodleian; *SG*, 33.

93. G. S. Faber to Hogg, 23 April 1811, MS. Don. c. 180, fols. 41–45, Bodleian.

94. Murray, 1:2.

95. *SC*, 2:723.

96. Hogg, 1:273.

97. To Hogg, c. 20 January 1811, *L*, 1:48.

98. John Freeman, "Shelley's early letters," in Everest, 118.

99. Ingpen, 147.

100. Ibid., 186–87. Forman reported "on good authority" *The Necessity* was on sale for twenty minutes. See Dowden, 1:118.

101. White, 1:112; Dowden, 1:118–19.

102. Slatter's recollections, in Montgomery's *Oxford*, 3rd ed., 1833. See Dowden, 1:119 n.; Ingpen, 195 n.

103. Ingpen, 193–94.

104. White, 1:113, 598 n. 142.

105. M. E. Sadler, Master of University College, wrote (*TLS*, 4 December 1927) of no proof of intervention by Copleston, who was very strict and known as "smooth-tongued, imperious Copleston," ablest resident of his day, and one who would have overwhelmed Griffith. Shelley-Ingpen Papers, 72/2372, Bancroft.

106. To WG, 10 January 1812, *L*, 1:228.

107. White, 1:598–99, n. 146, 618–20 n. 88.

108. Hogg, 1:278–86.

109. For the College expulsion record, see Dowden, 1:124.

110. Hogg, 1:44.

111. White, 1:117–18.

112. Hogg, 1:287–96.

113. Dowden, 1:122–24.

114. Ingpen, 192, 196. For Sharpe's October 1811 observations, see Lady Charlotte Bury, *Diary Illustrative of the Reign of George the Fourth* (London, 1838)1:88.

115. *Antijacobin Review* 41 (February 1812): 221. See White, 1:116.

116. Stuart Peterfreund, "An Early Response to Shelley's *The Necessity of Atheism*," *KSJ* 36 (1987): 26–31; Louise S. Boas, "'Erasmus Perkins' and Shelley," *Modern Language Notes* 70 (1955): 412.

9. DOUBLING AFTER THE FALL

1. *SC*, 2:726–28. PBS apparently never repaid this loan. See Ingpen, 206 n. 1; to John Slatter, 16 April 1811, *L*, 1:61.

2. Medwin, 87–88; DK (1995), 15, 59–63.

3. *SG,* 29.

4. To TS, 29 March 1811, *L,* 1:55–56.

5. *SC,* 2:738.

6. Robert Clarke to John Hogg, 8 April 1811, MS. Don. c. 180, fols. 32–33, Bodleian.

7. TS to John Hogg, 5, 6 April 1811, *SC,* 2:732–35.

8. MS. Don. c. 180, fols. 21–24, 32–33, 50–52, 66–70, Bodleian.

9. Robert Clarke to John Hogg, 5 April 1811, MS. Don. c. 180, fols. 23–24, Bodleian. The last execution for blasphemy was in 1697 but the law prescribing the death penalty for blasphemy was not repealed until 1813.

10. *SC,* 2:736–37.

11. Hogg, 1:304–11; Ingpen, 222.

12. Murray, 1:364–67.

13. Ingpen, 226; *SC,* 1:741; Charles Withal to Roger Ingpen, 31 December 1915, Shelley-Ingpen Papers, 72/2372, Bancroft.

14. TS to PBS, 9 April 1811, *SC,* 2:739–41.

15. To TS, 9 April 1811, *L,* 1:56–57.

16. TS to Whitton, 8 (?9) April 1811, Ingpen, 226.

17. Robert Clarke to John Hogg, 8 April 1811, MS. Don c. 180, fols. 32–33, Bodleian.

18. To TS, [10 April 1811], Ingpen, 227–28; Dawson, 33.

19. TS to Whitton, 11 April 1811, Ingpen, 228.

20. Ingpen, 226–27.

21. TS to Whitton, 11 April 1811, Ingpen, 228.

22. Mrs. Faber to Mrs. John Hogg, nd. [?18 Apr. 1811], MS. Don. c. 180, fol. 40, Bodleian.

23. Rev. Faber to John Hogg, 7 April 1811, MS. Don. c. 180, fols. 27–29, Bodleian.

24. PBS to Rev. Faber, n.d. [early April 1811], MS. Don. c. 180, fol. 30, Bodleian.

25. PBS to John Hogg, ?12 April 1811, *SC,* 2:743–44. Hogg, 1:330–32.

26. John Grove to TS, 11 April 1811, Ingpen, 230–31.

27. Whitton to Messers. C. & W. Phillips, 13 April 1811, Ingpen, 194.

28. Robert Parker to TS, 12 April 1811, Ingpen, 229–30.

29. To Stockdale, 11 April 1811, *L,* 1:59.

30. To John Hogg, ?12 April 1811, *SC,* 2:743–44.

31. To TS, ?13 April 1811, Ingpen, 232–33, *L,*1:60; MS. Don. c. 180, fol. 35, Bodleian.

32. BS to Whitton, 14 April 1811, Ingpen, 237–38.

33. TS to Robert Clarke, 14 April 1811, *SC,* 2:747–48.

34. TS to Whitton, 14 April 1811, Ingpen, 235–37.

35. Robert Clarke to TS, 15 April 1811, Ingpen, 239–40.

36. TS to Whitton, 16 April 1811; Whitton to TS, 16 April 1811, Ingpen, 240–41.

37. TS to Whitton, 18 April 1811, Ingpen, 241–44.

38. Hogg to Faber, 18 April 1811, Faber to Hogg, 23 April 1811, MS. Don. c. 180, fols. 38–39, 41–45, Bodleian. No copy exists of PBS's letter of apology to Faber.

39. Hogg, 1:339–41.

40. Ibid., 1:298–304; Medwin, 90–91; Ingpen, 213.

41. HM has the two volumes of Cowper's poems Hellen Shelley received, signed by the schoolmistress "A. Hawks" 2 December 1812. On the flyleaf, PBS's sister Mary signed her name after inscribing, "Absent or dead still let my name be dear / A sigh the absent claim, the dead a tear."

42. *Shelley Memorials,* 28–29.

43. Lovell, 22; Brown, 51.

44. Medwin, 88–90.

45. *Esdaile,* 81, 157.

46. Hogg, 1:332–33.

47. Ibid., 1:205–6; Ibid., 2:553; Ingpen, 257.

48. Dowden, 1:133–34.

49. Charles Grove to Hellen Shelley, 25 February 1857, Hogg, 2:556–57. See *CPPBS,* 1:448–51; Cameron *YS,* 114–15; Dowden, 1:135–36.

50. To Graham, c. 19 June 1811, *L,* 1:105–6.

51. To EH, 20 June 1811, *L,* 1:110.

52. To EH, 8 October 1811, *L,* 1:144.

53. CG, 231 n. 2.

54. Hogg, 2:552–53.

55. CG, 15, 70.

56. Medwin, 136. Medwin misdated PBS's medical interest.

57. CG, 97.

58. *Esdaile,* 156.

59. To John Slatter, 16 April 1811, *L,* 1:61.

60. *SC,* 2:752.

61. White, 1:394–99. Under the will of his great-uncle, John Shelley, PBS was tenant-in-tail after BS and TS.

62. Whitton to PBS, 17, 18, 19 April 1811, Ingpen, 151–52, 244, 249; to Whitton, 18 April 1811, *L,* 1:65.

63. TS to Whitton, 22 April 1811, Ingpen, 253–55.

64. To Hogg, 18 April 1811, *L,* 1:64.

65. *YS,* 89.

66. Westbrook's other tavern was in Cheapside, a rough neighborhood. At his death in 1835, John Westbrook's estate, left to his daughter Eliza, was between £60,000 and £70,000 after "heavy outgoings." See *SC,* 2:866–67; Edmund Blunden, Letter to the Editor, *TLS,* July 13, 1946; Norman, 38.

67. Hogg, 1:466–67.

68. Ibid., 1:474. Most citations give 1751 as John Westbrook's birth year, 1757 as Ann Westbrook's birth year. See Shelley adds. c. 9, Bodleian.

69. John Westbrook married Ann Elliott July 15, 1780, in St. George's Church, Hanover Square, where their children were baptized. Shelley-Ingpen Papers, Bancroft; Louise Schutz Boas, *Harriet Shelley: Five Long Years* (Oxford: Oxford University Press, 1961), 4, 219 n. 2. For the baptism dates of four daughters and one son, see, Blunden, *TLS.* PBS's counsel in the 1817–1818 Chancery case gave thirty as Eliza's age in 1811 (Dowden, 1:141; White, 1:134), perhaps PBS's recall error. See Shelley adds. c. 9, Bodleian.

70. HS to EH, 29 January 1812, *L,* 1:247.

71. Hogg, 1:474.

72. *YS,* 100.

73. Hogg, 1:459.

74. Ibid., 1:455–56; *YS,* 342.

75. Boas, 7; Scott, 49–51; Brown, 54–55.

76. Hogg, 1:440, 458; Hogg, 2:5.

77. Hogg, 2:6–8.
78. Mrs. Fields (Matilda Evans) to Miss Rickman, 7 September 1860, Garnett Misc. Mss., HRC; Medwin, 108.
79. Hogg, 1:25–26.
80. *SC*, 2:754.
81. To Hogg, 24 April 1811, *L*, 1:66–68.
82. To Hogg, 20 April 1811, *L*, 1:71. For "Emily" in PBS's 1810 Pocket Book, see *SC*, 9:71.
83. Mrs. Fields to Miss Rickman, HRC.
84. Hogg, 1:17.
85. Mrs. Fields to Miss Rickman, HRC.
86. To Hogg, ?25 April, 8 May 1811, *L*, 1:76–77.
87. Dowden, 1:142.
88. To Hogg, 12 May 1811, *L*, 1:83.
89. To Hogg, ?25 April 1811, *L*, 1:76.
90. HS to EH, 14 March 1812, *L*, 1:273–74.
91. To Hogg, 24, 29 April 1811, *L*, 1:67, 74.
92. Alice Kennedy to Roger Ingpen, 1 May 1930, Shelley-Ingpen papers, Bancroft. His money exhausted, Captain Pilfold returned to a lowly naval command before dying of a stroke. See Desmond Hawkins, *The Life and Times of Captain John Pilfold* (Horsham: Horsham Museum Society, 1998).
93. *ALH*, 2:21; to Graham, [? 15–19 May] 1811, *SC*, 9:140.
94. To Hogg, 26 April, 8 May 1811, *L*, 1:69, 77. See *CPPBS*, 1:195.
95. To Hogg, 8 May 1811, *L*, 1:77–78.
96. Ibid., 78.
97. To Hogg, 17 May 1811, *L*, 1:90.
98. To Hogg, 29 April 1811, *L*, 1:75.
99. To Hogg, 9 May 1811, *L*, 1:81.
100. To Hogg, 26, 29 April 1811, *L*, 1:70, 74.
101. To Hogg, 8, 9 May 1811, *L*,1:78–82. See also, *L*, 2:364; John Freeman, "Shelley's early letters," chap. 6 in Everest, 123.
102. To Hogg, 8 May 1811, *L*, 1:76–77.
103. To Hogg, 12 May 1811, *L*, 1:82–83.
104. To Hogg, 14 May 1811, *L*, 1:83–85.
105. To Graham, [? 14 May 1811], *L*, 1:85.
106. Ibid., 86–87. This verse letter is in the Berg Collection, The New York Public Library.
107. Neville Rogers, "An unpublished Shelley Letter," *KSMB* 24 (1973): 20–24; SC, 9:146–68; Gelpi, 116–23. The handwriting in the note matches that in a letter written by PBS's mother.
108. To Graham, [? June 1811], *L*, 1:112–13.
109. Edward Graham, b. 1784/85, d. 8 June 1854 in London. See *SC*, 9:118.
110. [Merle], "Editor's Reminiscences," 706–7.
111. To Hogg, 18–19 June 1811, *L*, 1:107–8. For the poems, see *CPPBS*, 1:322–23; *Esdaile*, 238–40.
112. To Hogg, 17, 21 May 1811, *L*, 1:90–93.
113. Eliza Westbrook to PBS, 11 June 1811, *L*, 1:104.
114. To Hogg, 16 June 1811, *L*, 1:103–5.

115. To Hogg, 18–19 June 1811, *L*, 1:106.
116. To Janetta Philipps, 16 May, [? May 1811], *L*, 1:88–89.
117. Ingpen, 281–82.
118. EH to PBS, 23 October 1811, *L*, 1:159–61.
119. EH to PBS, 15 November 1811, *L*, 1:187–88.
120. To Hogg, 2 June 1811, *L*, 1:95.
121. Virginia Woolf, "Shelley and Elizabeth Hitchener," in *The Essays of Virginia Woolf,* ed. Andrew McNeillie (New York: Harcourt Brace Janovich, 1986), 1:174.
122. To EH, 5 June 1811, *L*, 1:97–98.
123. George Ensor, *On National Education* (London, 1811), 263, 283. See White, 1:624–26.
124. EH to PBS, [7–10] June 1811, *L*, 1:98–99.
125. To EH, 11 June 1811, *L*, 1:101.
126. EH to PBS, 14 June 1811, *L*, 1:102–3.
127. To Hogg, [23 June 1811], L, 1:113.
128. Hogg to Mrs. Timothy Shelley, [? 6–18 July] 1811, *SC*, 2:820–23. Extensively revising this draft letter, Hogg carefully presented his case to Mrs. Shelley. See F. L. Jones, "Hogg's Peep at Elizabeth Shelley," *Philological Quarterly* 29 (October 1950): 424.
129. Hogg to Mrs. Timothy Shelley, 22 August 1811, *SC*, 2:873–76.
130. To EH, 25 June 1811, *L*, 1:117.
131. Charles Grove to Hellen Shelley, 16 February 1857, Hogg, 2:554. See *L*, 1:103 n. 1; *SC*, 2:818–19.

10. Elopement and Betrayal

1. To EH, [? 13 July 1811], *L*, 1:119.
2. To Hogg, 6–8 July 1811, *L*, 1:117.
3. To Hogg, [? 18 July 1811], *L*, 1:118. See *SC*, 2:830–38 for exact dates.
4. To EH, 20 June 1811, *L*, 1:109.
5. Following old Bysshe's 1784 example, both Thomas Groveses became sheriffs of Radnorshire. See Desmond Hawkins, "The Groves of Cwm Elan," *The Radnorshire Society Transactions* (1985): 45–49.
6. To Hogg, [? 18 July 1811], *L*, 1:118.
7. To EH, 26 July, [? 13 June] 1811, *L*, 1:127–28, 119–20.
8. William Lisle Bowles's 1798 poem "Coombe-Ellen" possibly influenced PBS. See *PS*, 1:179–84; Hawkins, *Groves of Cwm Elan*, 46–47.
9. *Esdaile*, 81–82.
10. *PS*, 1:182 n.
11. *Esdaile*, 148–54, 275–80.
12. "To Harriet * * * * * * * * *" ("Oh Harriet, love like mine that glows"), *Esdaile*, 168–69.
13. Ibid., 77–78.
14. CG, 75.
15. *Esdaile*, 155–60.
16. Ibid., 212–13.

17. "To Harriet" ("It is not blasphemy") lines 13–17. *Esdaile*, 85–87.

18. To Graham, [? 15–19 May 1811], *SC*, 9:140.

19. To Hogg, ?21 July 1811, *L*, 1:129. See also CG, 74.

20. To Hogg, [? 22 July 1811], *L*, 1:123.

21. To EH, [25 July], [? 13 July], 26 July 1811, *L*, 1:126, 119–20, 126–28.

22. To Hogg, [? 21 July 1811], *L*, 1:129.

23. StC, 164.

24. Ibid., 322.

25. To Hogg, [? 27–29 July 1811], *L*, 1:122–23.

26. *YS*, 341 n. 72.

27. To Hogg, 3 August 1811, *SC*, 2:856.

28. Charles Grove to Lady Shelley, 24 February 1860, Garnett Misc. mss., HRC.

29. Charles Clairmont to Francis Place, 12 January 1816, *CC*, 1:18.

30. Henry W. Reveley, "Notes and observations to the 'Shelley Memorials,'" *SC*, 10:1134.

31. Polidori, 107.

32. *PW*, 837.

33. To WG, 3 June 1812, *L*, 1:302–3.

34. To EH, 28 October 1811, *L*, 1:162.

35. To Hogg, [? 8–9 August 1811], *L*, 1:133.

36. To EH, 28 October 1811, *L*, 1:162.

37. To Hogg, 15 August 1811, *L*, 1:133–35.

38. EH to PBS, 11 October 1811, *L*, 1:145.

39. To EH, 19 August 1811, *L*, 1: 135–36.

40. Charles Grove to Lady Shelley, 24 February 1860, Garnett Misc. mss., HRC. See also, Charles Grove to Hellen Shelley, 16 February 1857, Dowden, 1:173; Hogg, 2:554.

41. Ingpen, 301–2.

42. Charles Grove gave two different names for this inn; for a third, see Dowden, 1:173. PBS perhaps intended, before Harriet's lateness, to take the 11 A.M. coach to Edinburgh. See *YS*, 339 n. 55.

43. Ingpen, 307.

44. To TS, 25 August 1811, *L*, 1:137; Ingpen, 306. See also, *SG*, 39.

45. Ingpen, 307.

46. White, 1:155. There is no mention of any decision by Mr. Westbrook in Ingpen, 307–8.

47. TS to John Hogg, 8 September 1811, *L*, 1:138.

48. To Hogg, 26 August 1811, *L*, 1:139. PBS's £25 loan from Mr. Medwin possibly advanced his elopement timetable.

49. Hogg to Mrs. Timothy Shelley, 22 August 1811, *SC*, 2:873–75. It is not known if this letter was sent.

50. Hogg, 1:452.

51. *Chamber's Journal*, 31 March 1900. See also *Letters of Percy Bysshe Shelley*, ed. Roger Ingpen (London: Pitman, 1909), 1:137–38. Cumming was PBS's landlord.

52. Dowden, 1:176.

53. Ingpen, 309–10. Ingpen gave no source for this "certificate of marriage."

54. In 1814 PBS stated that Robertson married them August 29. For documents and details of PBS's marriage, see Ingpen, 308–10, 422; Ingpen, *Letters of Shelley*, 1:136–38; Peck, 1:170–74. The article in *Chamber's Journal*, 31 March 1900, present-

ing the certificate of banns, notes that there is no record in Edinburgh papers of Shelley's marriage on August 28, the date another marriage was recorded.

55. To Thomas C. Medwin, 21 October 1811, *L*, 1:154.

56. John Pilfold to Thomas Charles Medwin, 31 January 1813, MS. 552, HM. Desmond Hawkins detected this sentence written as a postscript above Medwin's address, followed by the initials "JP."

57. Peacock, 34.

58. Hogg, 1:437.

59. To TS, 30 August 1811, *L*, 1:139–40.

60. Ibid., 1:139. See also, Peck, 1:170; White, 1:159–60, 610–11 n. 149, 612 n. 9. This dance possibly occurred on PBS' second Edinburgh visit, late 1813. Sharpe's Edinburgh friend, Lady Charlotte Campbell, was lady-in-waiting until 1814.

61. Hogg, 1:465, 467.

62. Ingpen, 317.

63. To TS, 16 September 1811, *L*, 1:140–41.

64. To TS, 27 September 1811, *L*, 1:141–43.

65. Hogg, 1:466.

66. To EH, 16 October 1811, *L*, 1:150–51.

67. Hogg, 1:469–70.

68. To TS, 3 October 1811, *L*, 1:143.

69. To TS, 12 October 1811, *L*, 1:146–47.

70. To BS, 12 October 1811, *L*, 1:147. For BS's codicil of 26 October 1811, see *SC*, 4:605–7.

71. To EH, 16 October 1811, *L*, 1:151.

72. To TS, 15 October 1811, *L*, 1:148–49.

73. To EH, 16 October 1811, L, 1:149–52.

74. TS to Whitton, 25 October 1811, *L*, 1:165–66.

75. To Thomas C. Medwin, 21 October 1811, *L*, 1:154.

76. TS to Captain Pilfold, 21 October 1811, Ingpen, 337.

77. Captain John Pilfold to T. C. Medwin, 6 October 1811, MS 255, HM; DK (1995), 16.

78. John Hogg to TS, 21 October 1811, *L*, 1:148.

79. TS to Whitton, 27 October 1811, Ingpen, 349.

80. To TS, 22 October 1811, *L*, 1:154.

81. To Mrs. Timothy Shelley, 22 October 1811, *L*, 1:155. PBS added a postscript: "You had better acquaint my Father with the debt with Mrs. Bowley—*he* is the proper person to do away with the obligation." The mysterious debt perhaps involved Mrs. Bowley as intermediary between Mrs. Shelley and Graham.

82. To Elizabeth Shelley, 22 October 1811, *L*, 1:156.

83. To Charles Grove, 29 October 1811, *L*, 1:164.

84. To EH, 28 October 1811, *L*, 1:163.

85. Medwin, 111.

86. To Whitton, 22 October 1811, Whitton to PBS, 22, 23 October 1811, *L*, 1:156–57.

87. Whitton to PBS, 24 October 1811, *L*, 1:165.

88. To Whitton, 30 October 1811, *L*, 1:165.

89. Ingpen, 346.

90. To Thomas C. Medwin, 26 November 1811, *L*, 1:197.

91. Hogg, 1:475.

92. Ibid., 1:476; Ibid., 2:1–4.
93. To TS, 26 October 1811, *L*, 1:157. See also, Ingpen, 350–53.
94. TS to Whitton, 27 October 1811, Ingpen, 348.
95. To EH, 28 October 1811, *L*, 1:163.
96. To Charles Grove, 29 October 1811, *L*, 1:164; to The Duke of Norfolk, 28 October 1811, *L*, 1:158–59; Norfolk to PBS, *L*, 1:159 n. 5.
97. To EH, 14 November 1811, *L*, 1:182.
98. To EH, [? 8 November 1811], *L*, 1:168.

11. SEEKING NEW FATHERS

1. To EH, ? 8 November 1811, *L*, 1:169.
2. To Hogg, 6 November 1811, *L*, 166–68.
3. Since PBS's stay, a second story was added to Chestnut Hill Cottage.
4. White, 1:174, 615 n. 54.
5. To EH, 26 November 1811, *L*, 1:194.
6. B. J. Capella, "Shelley's Keswick Years: Some New Information," *KSJ* 34 (1985): 20–21.
7. To Hogg, 7–8 November 1811, *SC*, 3:41–42.
8. To Hogg, 17–18 November 1811, *L*, 1:184.
9. CG, 75–76.
10. To Hogg, 13, 14 November 1811, *SC*, 3:46–47, 50.
11. To Hogg, 17–18 November 1811, *SC*, 3:57.
12. To EH, 14 November 1811, *L*, 1:182.
13. To Hogg, 12 November 1811, *L*, 1:176.
14. To Hogg, 7–8, c. 12 November 1811, *SC*, 3:41–42, 45.
15. To Hogg, 17–18 November 1811, *SC*, 3:57–58.
16. To Hogg, 13, 14, 17–18 November, *SC*, 3:48, 54, 58.
17. *Esdaile*, 41, 181; CG, 75–76.
18. To Hogg, 14 November 1811, *SC*, 3:50–54.
19. Ibid.
20. To Hogg, to EH, 14 November 1811, *L*, 1:179, 181.
21. Hogg, 2:488–97; *SC*, 3:55–56.
22. To EH, 15 December 1811, *L*, 1:207–8.
23. To Hogg, 9–10 December 1811, *SC*, 3:67–68.
24. To EH, 16–17, 29 January 1812, *L*, 1:232, 246.
25. *SC*, 3:70; *L*, 1:197 n. 3.
26. To Thomas C. Medwin, 26, 30 November 1811, *L*, 1:196–98.
27. *SC*, 3:70; Mac-Carthy, 119–20.
28. LB to John Murray, 25 October 1822, *BLJ*, 10:69.
29. To EH, 29 January 1812, *L*, 1:246.
30. To EH, ? 9 December 1811, *L*, 1:199.
31. To EH, ? 10 December 1811, *L*, 1:200–201.
32. To TS, 13 December 1811, *L*, 1: 203–4.
33. TS to PBS, 19 December 1811, *L*, 1:209.
34. To TS, 23 December 1811, *L*, 1:209–10.
35. Dowden, 1:207–8.

36. To EH, 15 December 1811, *L,* 1:207. The quote, *Hamlet,* I.v.55–57, should read "radiant angel."

37. To EH, 26 December 1811, EH to PBS, 19 December 1811, *L,* 1:210–14.

38. EH to HS, 17 December 1811, *L,* 1:210.

39. To Allen Etheridge and Hellen Shelley, ? 13 December 1811, *L,* 1: 205–6.

40. To EH, ? 11 November, 14 November 1811, *L,* 1:174, 183. See Sunstein, 51; StC, 338–39.

41. To EH, 15 December 1811, *L,* 1:208–9.

42. *Cornhill Magazine* 14 (May 1890): 507. See White, 1:182, 617.

43. To EH, 26 December 1811, *L,* 1:210–12.

44. HS to EH, 26 January 1812, *L,* 1:241. De Quincey later regretted PBS had to rely on Southey's "Spanish library" rather than his own collection of the German philosophers.

45. To EH, 2 January 1812, *L,* 1:218–19.

46. Southey to Grosvenor Bedford, 4 January 1812, *L,* 1:219.

47. Southey to John Rickman, 6 January 1812, White, 1:619–20.

48. Southey to Charles Danvers, 13 January 1812, *NLRS,* 2:19–22.

49. Holmes, 101–2, 362; *Henry Crabb Robinson on Books and Their Writers,* ed. E. J. Morley (London: Dent, 1938), 1:212.

50. To LH, 27 September 1819, *L,* 2:122. LH wrote PBS in August 1819 stating that Lloyd was "a great admirer" of PBS. See *SM,* 397. Lloyd never met PBS, who sent him a presentation copy of *Rosalind and Helen.*

51. Hoagwood, 16–21; C. E. Pulos, *The Deep Truth: A Study of Shelley's Scepticism* (Lincoln: University of Nebraska Press, 1962), chap. 2.

52. Southey to John Rickman, 6 January 1812, White, 1:618–20.

53. *Esdaile,* 178, 180.

54. To EH, 7 January 1812, *L,* 1:221–26. See also *Esdaile,* 62–66.

55. To EH, 7 January 1812, *L,* 1:223.

56. To EH, 2 January 1812, *L,* 1:214–19.

57. To EH, 2, 7 January 1812, *L,* 1:218, 223.

58. To EH, 2 January 1812, *L,* 1:218.

59. To WG, 3 January 1812, *L,* 1:219–21. The sign over WG's residence read "M. J. Godwin," the initials of his wife, who operated the Juvenile Library.

60. StC, 316.

61. White, 1:189; Locke, 244.

62. To WG, 10 January 1812, *L,* 1:227.

63. After PBS's Eton "perusal" of *Political Justice,* at Oxford he ordered a copy, November 1810. His two novels reveal little influence of the book. See White, 1:577.

64. Locke, 12; StC, 6–11.

65. Dawson, chap. 3.

66. To WG, 16 January 1812, *L,* 1:230–31.

67. To WG, 10 January 1812, *L,* 1:228.

68. StC, 312.

69. To WG, 16 January 1812, *L,* 1:230.

70. To WG, ? 26 January 1812, *L,* 1:243.

71. To William Sandham, ? 26 November 1811–26 January 1812, *SC,* 3:63–67. Sandham rented property from TS and BS. See *The Horsham Companion,* ed. Susan C. Djabri (Horsham: Horsham Museum Society, 1995), 48.

72. To WG, 16 January 1812, *L,* 1:231.

73. To WG, ? 26 January 1812, *L*, 1:242–43.

74. Reiman, xv–xvi.

75. Peter H. Marshall, *William Godwin* (New Haven: Yale University Press, 1984), 124.

76. To EH, ? 16 January 1812, to WG, ? 26 January 1812, *L*, 1:233–34, 243. Most of the *Address* was drafted December 1811–January 1812. See Murray, 1:328.

77. To WG, 24 February 1812, *L*, 1:258–60.

78. *Cumberland Pacquet*, 28 January 1812.

79. White, 1:622 n. 110.

80. Southey to James Burney, 19 January 1812, *NLRS*, 23.

81. Dowden, 1:227; White, 1:622 n. 110.

82. PBS and HS to EH, 26 January 1812, *L*, 1:237–40.

83. To EH, 7 January 1812, *L*, 1:221–22.

84. F. J. Carruthers, "Shelley: Keswick's Undesirable Visitor," *The Cumberland News*, 27 September 1974, 10. See Capella, "Shelley's Keswick Years," 21.

85. Thompson, 564.

86. To EH, 16–17 January 1812, *L*, 1:232–37.

87. *Esdaile*, 43, 182.

88. To EH, 26 January 1812, *L*, 1:240.

89. To EH, ? 16 January 1812, *L*, 1:235–37. See also *PS*, 1:230–31; "The Devil's Walk," eds. Donald H. Reiman and Neil Fraistat, *RC*.

90. Hogg, 2:276; Dawson, 39.

91. To EH, 29 January 1812, *L*, 1:244–46.

92. PBS and HS to EH, 26 January 1812, *L*, 1:240–41.

93. To EH, 14 February 1812, *L*, 1:252.

94. To EH, 26 January 1812, *L*, 1: 237–41.

95. To EH, c. 16 November 1811, *L*, 1:183.

96. HS to EH, 29 January 1812, *L*, 1:247.

97. To EH, 3 February 1812, *L*, 1:249.

98. To EH, 26 January 1812, *L*, 1:239.

99. To EH, 2 January 1812, *L*, 1:214–15.

100. To EH, 23 November 1811, *L*, 1:189.

101. To EH, 3 February 1812, *L*, 1:248–49.

102. To WG, ? 26 January 1812, *L*, 1:243.

103. To EH, 26 January 1812, *L*, 1:239.

104. TS might have voted for Catholic emancipation had he been a member from Horsham, a more pro-emancipation borough. See Dawson, 34–35.

105. To EH, ? 16 January 1812, *L*, 1:233–34. WG earlier was a Socinian; see StC, 15–16, 35.

106. To EH, 14 February 1812, *L*, 1:255.

107. HS to EH, 29 January 1812, *L*, 1:247–48.

108. To EH, 3 February 1812, *L*, 1:249.

12. The Irish Expedition

1. HS to EH, 29 January 1812, PBS to EH, 13 February 1812, PBS to WG, 24 February 1812, *L*, 1:248, 250, 258; Dowden, 1:234–35.

2. To EH, 13 February 1812, *L*, 1:250.
3. *YS*, chap. 4; Dawson, 24–40, chap. 4.
4. Paul Foot, *Red Shelley* (London: Sidgwick and Jackson, 1980), 23–25.
5. "On Robert Emmet's Tomb," *Esdaile*, 60–61.
6. "To The Republicans of North America," *Esdaile*, 71–72.
7. To EH, 14, ? 24 February 1812, *L*, 1:250–58. See also *SC*, 10:1062 n. 1.
8. To EH, 18 February 1812, *L*, 1:256.
9. Murray, 1:328.
10. Mac-Carthy, 166; to Hamilton Rowan, 25 February 1812, *L*, 1:262.
11. To EH, 27 February 1812, L, 1:263.
12. HS to EH, 18 March 1812, *L*, 1:280.
13. Healey possibly took the name Hill later in Devon with PBS to hide his identity from the authorities. See Dowden, 1:295.
14. *L*, 1:262 n. 8; StC, 329; to EH, 10 March 1812, *L*, 1:271.
15. PBS and HS to EH, 27 February 1812, *L*, 1:263–65.
16. To EH, 10 March 1812, *L*, 1:270.
17. To EH, 27 February 1812, *L*, 1:264–65.
18. Murray, 1:462.
19. To EH, 27 February 1812, *L*, 1:263.
20. Dawson, 154–56.
21. Ibid., 43–45.
22. *CW*, 5:237–39; Dawson, 152–53.
23. *CW*, 5:233–34.
24. Dowden, 1:239–40; Murray, 1:292.
25. Mac-Carthy, xiii–xiv; Dawson, 140.
26. *YS*, 145–46; Dawson, 139.
27. To EH, 14 March 1812, *L*, 1:275.
28. *YS*, 355. Contrary to Holmes, 120, there is no evidence PBS was invited to speak. See Dawson, 136.
29. Dowden, 1:251–53; Mac-Carthy, 223–47; *YS*, 145–47; Murray, 1:291–93.
30. Ingpen, 382–83; Dawson, 139 n. 2.
31. To EH, 14 March 1812, *L*, 1:275. It is unlikely PBS spoke for an hour. See *YS*, 355–56.
32. Hogg, 2:112; Murray, 1:291; Dawson, 156–57.
33. To WG, 8 March 1812, *L*, 1:268–69.
34. *UH*, 105.
35. Murray, 1: 293–301; *CW*, 7:317–35; Mac-Carthy, 239–43.
36. To EH, 10 March 1812, *L*, 1:271. See also, *YS*, 356 n. 80.
37. Mac-Carthy, 238–41.
38. Murray, 1:338; *YS*, 356 n. 82.
39. Murray, 1:43.
40. To EH, 27 February 1812, *L*, 1:263–64. See also Dawson, 158–62; Murray, 1:339; *L*, 1:264 n. 4.
41. Murray, 1:53.
42. WG to PBS, 4 March 1812, *L*, 1:260–62. See also StC, 324–25, 548 n. 11.
43. To WG, 8 March 1812, *L*, 1:267–68.
44. To EH, 10 March 1812, *L*, 1:271.
45. WG to PBS, 14 March 1812, *L*, 1:269–70; Hogg, 2:95–100.
46. WG to PBS, 30 March 1812, PBS to WG, 18 March 1812, *L*, 1:278, 276–78.

47. To WG, 18 March 1812, *L*, 1:276–78.

48. *CW*, 7:65. See Dawson, 78, 108–9; Deane, 97–99.

49. *CW*, 6:255; Dawson, 89.

50. To WG, 8 March 1812, *L*, 1:267–68.

51. To WG, 25 April 1812, *L*, 1:287.

52. To EH, 10 March 1812, *L*, 1:270–71.

53. Mac-Carthy, pp. 400–407.

54. To EH, 10, 14 March 1812, *L*, 1:271–72, 275. See also P. M. S. Dawson, "Shelley and the Irish Catholics," *KSMB* 29 (1978):29.

55. To Thomas C. Medwin, 20 March 1812, *L*, 1:280.

56. To EH, 10 March 1812, *L*, 1:271–72.

57. Murray, 1:293, 341–42; Ingpen, 383–84; Dawson, 141 n. 5.

58. Mac-Carthy, 304–6. Earlier reports about PBS went to the previous Home Secretary, Richard Ryder. Mac-Carthy questioned Conway's veracity. See *YS*, 354–55 n. 68; Dawson, 141.

59. Ingpen, 379–84.

60. Alfred Webb, "Harriet Shelley and Catherine Nugent," *The Nation* 48 (1889): 464–67, 484–86; *YS*, 144–45, 355 n. 70. No letters survive from Catherine Nugent to HS. For Catherine Nugent, see Dowden,1:257–58; White, 1:224, 632 nn. 52, 53; *CW*, 8:298 n. 1.

61. *YS*, 144, 355 n. 70; HS to EH, 18 March 1812, *L*, 1:279–80.

62. *North British Review* 8 (November 1847):237.

63. Ibid.

64. HS to EH, 14 March 1812, *L*, 1:274–75.

65. HS to Catherine Nugent, March 1812, *L*, 1:283.

66. Murray, 1:56–60, 348–52; *YS*, 152; Dawson, 55–64.

67. Murray, 1:60.

68. HS to EH, 18 March 1812, *L*, 1:279–80. See also, Mac-Carthy, 308–20.

69. Murray, 1:292.

70. Mac-Carthy, 306–22.

71. Medwin, 115.

72. *YS*, 156–59, 357–58 n. 116.

73. To EH, ? 10 December 1811, *L*, 1:202, 202 n. 7. John Stockdale, Abbey Street, Dublin, is not the John Joseph Stockdale, London. The Dublin printer of PBS's *Proposals* was "I. Eton, Winetavern-Street," perhaps a Shelleyan pseudonym to protect Stockdale. See Reiman, xxiv n. 22; *Esdaile,* 17–18. The Irish Stockdale died January 11, 1813. See Mac-Carthy, 260–61.

74. To WG, 18 March 1812, 24 February 1812, *L*, 1:277–78, 260.

75. Dawson, 35.

76. To EH, ? 16 April 1812, *L*, 1:282.

13. WANDERING REFORMER

1. HS to Catherine Nugent, 16 April 1812, *L*, 1:283–84.

2. To WG, 25 April 1812, *L*, 1:287.

3. To EH, ? 16 August 1812, *L*, 1:281. TLP said a farmer occupying Nantgwillt "let some of the best rooms" to PBS. See Mac-Carthy, 340.

4. HS to Catherine Nugent, 16 April 1812, *L*, 1:284.

5. To WG, 25 April 1812, *L*, 1:287. See also, P. P. St. George, "Cwm Elan and Nant-gwillt: Two Vanished Sites," *KSJ* 17 (1968): 7–9.

6. To EH, 25 April 1812, to TS, 24 April 1812, *L*, 1:288, 285.

7. To EH, 1 May 1812, *L*, 1:291.

8. To EH, 7 May 1812, *L*, 1:295.

9. To EH, 25 April 1812, *L*, 1:288.

10. To Thomas Hitchener, 14 May, 30 April 1812, *L*, 1: 298, 290–91.

11. To EH, 7 May 1812, *L*, 1:293–96.

12. Holmes, 142.

13. To TS, 24 April 1812, *L*, 1:284–85; Ingpen, 390.

14. To Thomas C. Medwin, 25 April 1812, Thomas C. Medwin to PBS, 6 May 1812, Thomas C. Medwin to PBS, 24 May 1812, *L*, 1:285–86, 299.

15. To James Davies, 30 May 1812, to BS, 2 June 1812, *L*, 1:299–301.

16. To EH, 2 June, 1812, *L*, 1:301–2.

17. To WG, 3 June 1812, *L*, 1:302–3.

18. HS to Catherine Nugent, 7 June 1812, PBS to EH, 6 June, *L*, 1:304–5.

19. F. S. Schwarzback, "'Harriet 1812': Harriet Shelley's Commonplace Book," *The Huntington Library Quarterly* 56 (1993):41–66.

20. *PS*, 1:226.

21. To EH, 11 June 1812, *L*, 1:306.

22. To EH, 18 June 1812, *L*, 1:308–9.

23. To EH, 18 June 1812, to WG, 11 June 1812, *L*, 1:306–9. See Murray, 1:61–73, 353–55; *YS*, 179–86.

24. To EH, ? 16 Apr. 1812, *L*, 1:282.

25. Thompson, 570, chap. 14; *YS*, 161; Dawson, chap. 5.

26. To EH, 7 May, to Catherine Nugent, 7 May 1812, *L*, 1:294, 297. See also, *YS*, 163–65.

27. Dawson, 169–71.

28. To EH, ? 16 April 1812, *L*, 1:282. See also Thompson, 608–10.

29. *YS*, 163.

30. HS to Catherine Nugent, 30 June 1812, *L*, 1:309–10.

31. To WG, 5 July 1812, *L*, 1:310–12.

32. Hogg, 2:133.

33. To WG, 5 July 1812, *L*, 1:310–12.

34. WG to PBS, c. 4 July 1812, *L*, 1:313. See also StC, 331.

35. To WG, 7 July 1812, *L*, 1:312–15.

36. HS to Catherine Nugent, 4, 11 August 1812, *L*, 1:320–22.

37. To Thomas Hookham, 29 July, 18 August 1812, *L*, 1:319, 324.

38. Medwin, 50; CG, 27–29.

39. Hogg, 2:155–56; White, 1:243–44.

40. *YS*, 179–86; Murray, 1:61–73, 353–56.

41. Murray, 1:73; *YS*, 362 n. 91.

42. *YS*, 186.

43. *PS*, 1:230; White, 1:633 n. 63; "Devil's Walk," *RC*; Mac-Carthy, 345–48; *YS*, 172–77, 361 n. 58.

44. Mrs. Blackmore to Mathilde Blind (1871), Section 7, Garnett's notebook, HRC. See also Dowden, 1:292–300; White, 1:248–51; Home Office, H.O. 42/126,127.

45. *SPP*, 5–6.

46. Peck, 1:270–73.
47. Mrs. Blackmore to Mathilde Blind, HRC.
48. HS to Catherine Nugent, 4 August 1812, *L*, 1:320.
49. *YS*, 174–77.
50. *YS*, 172–73.
51. To Thomas Hookham, 18 August 1812, *L*, 1:324–25.
52. To James Henry Lawrence, 18 August 1812, *L*, 1:322–23. Lawrence printed PBS's letter with "Love: An Allegory" in his 1828 volume, *The Etonian Out of Bounds.*
53. To Thomas Hookham, 18 August 1812, *L*, 1:324–25. It is unlikely PBS met TLP earlier in Wales. See White, 1:242, 637 n. 47.
54. *Esdaile*, 85–107, 217–35.
55. *PS*, 1:247–48.
56. StC, 191, 208, 260–61, 543 n. 12.
57. StC, 332–35.
58. WG to Mrs. Godwin, 19 September 1812, *L*, 1:326.
59. HS to Catherine Nugent, 11 August 1812, *L*, 1:327.
60. "On Waiting," *Esdaile*, 91.
61. *Selections from The Reminiscences of Captain Gronow*, ed. Nicolas Bentley (London: Folio Society, 1977), 118.
62. HS to Mrs. Nugent, October 1812, *L*, 1:326–27.
63. Schwarzback, "Commonplace Book," 53–54.
64. *YS*, 187–91; White, 1:254–58; Holmes, 165–67.
65. StC, 345; Hogg, 2:173.
66. P. G. Davies, "The Attack on Shelley at Tanyrallt: A Suggestion," *KSMB* 23 (1972): 40–43.
67. The late Captain "Sandy" Livingstone-Learmouth, whose family owned Tanyrallt since 1840, graciously showed the author through Tanyrallt before it became a private school.
68. S. Girdlestone to John Williams, 17, 28 September 1812, National Library of Wales, Aberystwyth, quoted in White, 2:496–98, 499–500.
69. To Hogg, 7 February 1813, *L*, 1:351.
70. *North Wales Gazette*, October 1, 1812. See also *CW*, 7:326–29.
71. PBS probably promised to pay his £100 pledge on becoming twenty-one. See White, 1:643 n. 7.
72. Medwin, 119.
73. Mrs. A. Williams to Mrs. Sandback, 28 March 1860, Garnett Misc. mss., HRC.
74. White, 1:255–56, 643–64 n. 10; Ingpen, 633–34; *SC*, 3:118–20; *SC*, 9:188–92.
75. StC, Chap. 18; *JCC*, 13–20; *CC*, 1:xvii; Robert Gittings and Jo Manton, *Claire Clairmont and the Shelleys* (Oxford: Oxford University Press, 1992), 3–4, 8–9. WG married his second wife twice on 21 December 1801. She gave her name as Mary Clairmont at the first ceremony, changing it to her actual family name, Mary Vial, at the second. See also, Herbert Huscher, "The Clairmont Enigma," *KSMB* (1960) 21: 13–20.
76. HS to Catherine Nugent, October 1812, *L*, 1:327.
77. Grylls, 24; Dowden, 1:304–5; White, 1:260; StC, 336–38.
78. StC, 241, 243; Locke, 206.
79. HS to Catherine Nugent, 16 January 1813, *L*, 1:349–50. Amelia Curran was visiting England from Rome, where she lived. See Sunstein, 58.

80. To Thomas Hookham, 17 December 1812, 7 February 1813, *L*, 1:341, 353.

81. To FG, 10 December 1812, *L*, 1:337.

82. Dowden, 1:306–7; White, 1:261, 645 n. 22.

83. CG, 77–78.

84. Hogg, 2:166–73.

85. Peacock, 37.

86. To Thomas Hookham, 3 December 1812, *L*, 1:334.

87. *SC*, 3:193–94; White, 1:256.

88. To John Williams, 7 November 1812, *L*, 1:329–30.

89. Dowden, 1:312.

90. Hogg, 2:365–70.

91. White, 1:645–46 n. 33; *YS*, 366 n. 61.

92. To Hogg, 3 December 1812, *L*, 1:335–36.

93. HS to Catherine Nugent, 14 November 1812, *L*, 1:331–32.

94. Medwin, 118.

95. [Merle], "Editor's Reminiscences," 709–10.

96. To John Williams, 30 March 1813, *L*, 1: 362–63.

97. White, 1:645 n. 33; *CW*, 8:xxviii–xxix. See also Donald H. Reiman, ed., *Romantic Context: Poetry; David Booth and Elizabeth Hitchener* (New York: Garland, 1978), i–iv.

98. EH published (1818) *The Fireside Bagatelle* and a volume of verse, *The Weald of Sussex* (1822), from which these lines are taken. See Reiman, *Romantic Context*, i–iv; Dowden, 1:314–15; *CW*, 8:xxviii–xxix; Medwin, 118; *YS*, 366–67 n. 66.

99. To Mrs. Timothy Shelley, 6 November 1812, *L*, 1:328. The loan from this benefactor, probably John Bedwell (see *L*, 1:361–62), yielded £20 of the £30 PBS owed Mrs. Hooper. See, to Mrs. Hooper, ? 10 November 1812, *L*, 1:331.

100. To John Williams, 7 November 1812, *L*, 1:329–30.

101. *L*, 1:329 n. 4. If PBS contacted his uncle in late 1812, it possibly prompted John Pilfold's 31 January 1813 letter to Medwin senior about the validity of PBS's marriage. See chap. 10.

102. To John Williams, 7 November 1812, *L*, 1:329.

103. StC, 348–49.

104. HS to Catherine Nugent, 14 November 1812, *L*, 1:331–32.

105. To FG, 10 December 1812, *L*, 1:338.

106. *Esdaile*, 53–55, 190–93.

14. PHANTASMAGORIA AT TANYRALLT

1. *PW*, 832 n. 1.

2. Dowden, 1:319–20. These are Mrs. Williams's recollections of what Williams told her; they married in 1820. See White, 1:646 n. 42.

3. To John Evans, 3, ? 11 December 1812, *L*, 1:332–33, 339.

4. Leeson to PBS, 5 March 1813, *L*, 1:357–58. PBS confirmed Leeson's obtaining the pamphlet from Williams in his 6 March 1813 letter to Williams. Williams's wife, perhaps protecting her husband, later asserted Leeson privately admitted EH had been the source. See *SC*, 3:120–25; *L*, 1:357–58; *CW*, 9:51; Dowden, 1:356; HS to Thomas Hookham, 12 March 1813, *L*, 1:355–56 n. 2.

5. Murray, 1:14–17.

6. To Hogg, 27 December 1812, *L*, 1:347.

7. To Thomas Hookham, ? November 1812, *L*, 1:332.

8. To Thomas Hookham, 3 December 1812, *L*, 1:334.

9. To Hogg, 3 December 1812, *L*, 1:335–36.

10. To John Williams, 4 December 1812, *L*, 1:336.

11. TS to PBS, January 1813, *L*, 1:346–47.

12. WG to PBS, 10 December 1812, *L*, 1:340–41.

13. To Thomas Hookham, 2, 26 January 1813, *L*, 1:348, 350. PBS apparently neglected this Latin translation of Kant. Hogg believed PBS never studied Kant. See Hogg, 2:311. MWS believed had her husband lived, Kant would have had a major impact. See *CW*, 5:xi.

14. PBS cited Cabanis in *Queen Mab*. For Cabanis's influence on PBS, see Deane, chap. 6.

15. CG, 77.

16. To Thomas Hookham, 26 January 1813, *L*, 1:350.

17. For the possible contents of the lost *Biblical Extracts*, see *YS*, 382 n. 2. PBS probably obtained his manuscripts from the Stockdale firm March 1813. See *YS*, 381; *Esdaile*, 17–30; *SC*, 4:911–12.

18. To Thomas Hookham, 26 January 1813, *L*, 1:350.

19. HS to Catherine Nugent, 16 January 1813, *L*, 1:349–50.

20. Undated note, E. G. Bayle-Bernard, Garnett Mss., HRC. Unaware of this note, White found "no basis" for the sunken ship story reported by Garnett. See White, 1:267, 646 n. 38.

21. To Hogg, 7 February 1813, *L*, 1:351–53.

22. To Thomas Hookham, ? 15 February 1813, *L*, 1:354.

23. *YS*, 240–42.

24. *PS*, 1:375–81.

25. *YS*, 243–44, 320–21 n. 98; Deane, 98.

26. *On the Vegetable System of Diet*, probably written late 1813. See Murray, 1:392–94.

27. Sperry, 14.

28. Ibid., 13; Holmes, 202.

29. *YS*, 270.

30. Sperry, 16.

31. Ibid., 17, considered this scene (7:176–92) "the most powerful and revealing" in *Queen Mab*.

32. *YS*, 202–3; White, 1:272.

33. HS to Thomas Hookham, 31 January 1813, *L*, 1:351.

34. To Hogg, 27 December 1812, *L*, 1:346.

35. To Thomas Hookham, ? 15 February 1813, *L*, 1:353–54.

36. To Thomas Hookham, 27 February 1813, *L*, 1:355–56.

37. To John Williams, 27 or 28 February 1813, *L*, 1:357.

38. To Thomas Hookham, 6 March 1813, *L*, 1:358–59.

39. Hogg, 2:211–12. Writing forty-five years later, Hogg believed HS's account sent to Hookham was "precisely similar" to his lost letter from her. Hogg was told HS sent "descriptive circulars" of her narrative of the night's events "to other persons." Hogg stated PBS never mentioned the attack to him. Holmes does not believe Hogg received a letter such as the one to Hookham, but it seems reasonable that HS wrote to

him, as they expected Hogg's March visit to Tanyrallt. See PBS to Hogg, 7 February 1813 [misdated "1812"], *L*, 1:351.

40. HS to Thomas Hookham, 12 March 1813, *L*, 1:355–56.

41. Mrs. A. Williams to Mrs. Sandback, 28 March 1860, Garnett Mss., HRC. The account in Dowden, 1:354–55 is incomplete. Another visitor clearly remembered being shown the screen in 1848 by Mrs. Williams. The devil drawing on the large folding screen was outlined in thick ink strokes. E. D. Copleston to Edward Dowden, 16 December 1886 (written after Dowden's biography was published), MS 3152/832, Trinity College Library Dublin.

42. Undated note, E. G. Bayle-Bernard, Garnett Mss., HRC. This note makes clear that Miss Fanny Holland, friend of Bayle-Bernard, "made the exact copy" of the sketch PBS made on the fire screen of the devil.

43. Ingpen, 635; *YS*, 381. Owen Williams's widow was attempting to collect on this debt thirty-one years later.

44. *L*, 1:354–55 n. 5.

45. *Shelley Papers*, 18–20, but first published in "Memoirs of Shelley," *The Athenaeum*, 1832. For substantially the same account in Medwin's later biography of PBS, see Medwin, 116–17, where the intruder is referred to as "stout" as well as short and powerful. Tanyrallt's owner, Captain "Sandy" Livingstone-Learmouth, told the author he believed the "intruder" was the "poltergeist" man of the neighborhood who went around in a long black cloak. He also said no bullet holes were ever found; what others thought were bullet holes were knot holes. Mrs. Williams stated Madocks was never in Tremadoc while Shelley lived there. See *YS*, 367 n. 83.

46. H. M. Dowling, "The Attack at Tanyrallt," *KSMB* 12 (1961), 51. Holmes, 196, corrects "parties" to "hoxters." Dowling found this letter in the Carnarvonshire County archives. Other letters in the County Record Office are cited in Holmes, chap. 8.

47. *YS*, 213.

48. Ibid., 212, 369 n. 101.

49. *Z&SI*, chaps. 1–3.

50. *SG*, 46.

51. HS to Catherine Nugent, 22 June 1813, 11 October 1813, *L*, 1:372, 378.

52. *YS*, 209–14. Cameron's detailed analysis of the Tanyrallt events is the most compelling among previous PBS biographers. My analysis gives more weight to unconscious forces in PBS's behavior.

53. Hogg, 2:212–14. Hogg reported never hearing PBS, HS, or Eliza refer to the attack. Hogg emphasized PBS's tendency to fabricate events as part of presenting him as an etherialized buffoon. TLP's coolly circumspect views of PBS covered a profound ambivalence.

54. Peacock, 36–37. TLP never stated directly that he visited Tanyrallt.

55. Dowden, 1:354–55. In 1885, Richard Garnett, writing Dowden, had "little doubt that [the Tanyrallt attack] was a delusion." In 1890, Dowden was still attempting to locate the fire screen on which PBS had drawn the apparition. See *LAS*, pp. 131–32, 175. The 1905 story that PBS was attacked by a resentful sheepherder is rebutted in White, 1:282.

56. White, 1:280–85. White noted PBS's autobiographical madman in *Julian and Maddalo* asserts he "could see / The absent with the glance of phantasy" (445–46).

57. *YS*, 205–14.

58. S. Girdlestone to John Williams, 28 September 1813; White, 2:499–500. See also *YS*, 215–16.

59. Holmes, 187–97. Dowling, "The Attack," disbelieved Leeson was the intruder but thought one of his "henchmen" could have been.

60. Kenneth N. Cameron, review of *Shelley: The Pursuit,* by Richard Holmes, *KSJ* 25 (1976): 165.

61. The copy of PBS's drawing made by Miss Fanny Holland on a visit to Tanyrallt, and the sheepherder as attacker story, appeared in the *Century Magazine* 48 (October 1905): 905–9.

62. MS. Shelley adds. e. 9, Bodleian. Rogers, 68, 90, noting this iconic similarity of "the monsters of his thought" in PBS's drawings, disdains the "astonishing credulity" of those believing the attack actually happened. For another analysis of PBS's drawing of the Tanyrallt assailant, see W. H. McCulloch, "The Last Night at Tan-yr-allt February 26, 1813," *KSMB* 8 (1957): 20–32.

63. MS. Shelley adds. e. 20 p.34 rev., Bodleian. The rounded thighs and calves are evident in the Tanyrallt drawing. In MS. Shelley adds. c. 4, Bodleian, PBS drew a figure in this characteristic running posture with a bat's head and two horn-like ears.

64. Freud discussed the devil with breasts and horns in his "A Seventeenth-Century Demonological Neurosis," *SE,* 19:89–91. PBS (Ms. adds. e. 9, Bodleian) drew his pursued hermaphrodite next to a drawing of a devil's head. The hermaphrodite, with penis, breasts, and long hair, is pursued by an ambiguously sexed figure with short hair and no genitals. The claw-like right hand of this figure grasps the hermaphrodite's hair and the left hand holds a dagger aimed into the back of the hermaphrodite. These two figures are running over cliff-like mountains, reminiscent of those at Tanyrallt, replete with a crescent moon half-hidden by clouds, which would have appeared about 5 am that night. See White, 1:282, 650 n. 93.

65. *YS,* 211.

66. White, 1:283; *YS,* 210, 213–14; Holmes, 113.

67. Peacock, 61–63.

68. Henry W. Reveley, "Notes and observations to the 'Shelley Memorials,'" *SC,* 10:1133. Dowden had access to this ms. but did not refer to this quote. See Dowden, 2:206; *LAS,* 92–93.

69. White, 1:283.

70. P. G. Davies, "The Attack on Shelley at Tanyrallt: A Suggestion," *KSMB* 23 (1972): 40–43.

71. John Cam Hobhouse to TLP, 2 May 1860, quoted in Butler, 241.

72. White, 1:320, 348–49, 357, 609–610; *SC,* 3:364–65.

73. *YS,* 213–14, 369 n. 103; Sperry, 170–71, 183–84, 221 n. 16; White, 1:316–17. For a discussion of the "overall pattern" linking Shelley's attacks, including his "morbid trains of fantasy, suspicions and fears," see Holmes, 113–14.

74. To John Williams, 6 March 1813, *L,* 1:358.

75. HS to Thomas Hookham, 12 March 1813, *L,* 1:356.

76. To Thomas Hookham, 6 March 1813, *L,* 1:358–59.

15. MARITAL DISENGAGEMENT

1. HS to Thomas Hookham, 12 March 1813, *L,* 1:355.

2. To Thomas Hookham, March 1813, *L,* 1:361.

3. To John Williams, ? 9 March 1813, *L,* 1:360.

4. To John Williams, 21 March 1813, *SC*, 9:186–87.

5. Eliza Westbrook to John Williams, ? 21 March 1813, *SC*, 3:128 n. 5. See also *SC*, 9:205–7. Lady Shelley apparently heard from HS's daughter Ianthe that Eliza "often in after years related the [Tanyrallt] circumstance as a frightful fact." See *Shelley Memorials*, 66; Dowden, 1:356; *YS*, 367–68 n. 86.

6. Hogg, 2:263.

7. To John Williams, 31 March 1813, *L*, 1:362–63. Misdated 30 March.

8. Hogg, 2:264–65.

9. Ibid., 2:389–90.

10. Ibid., 2:270.

11. Hookham's nephew stated *Queen Mab* caused PBS's quarrel with Hookham, who destroyed all but one copy of the *Letter to Lord Ellenborough*. See *CW*, 8:xxxiii; *YS*, 387 n. 23.

12. HS to Catherine Nugent, 21 May 1813, *L*, 1:367–68.

13. HS copied the dedicatory verses in the *Esdaile* notebook, which was found in Ianthe Eliza Shelley's coat pocket when she died (*Esdaile*, 287). The Grove family later claimed the dedication was to Harriet Grove. PBS possibly intended some confusion. See *PS*, 1:270.

14. White, 1:653 n. 10–11; StC, App. 3; *UH*, 95–98, 370; H. B. Forman, "The Vicissitudes of Queen Mab," *Shelley Society Papers* 1 (1887): 19–35.

15. White, 2:304.

16. George Bernard Shaw, *Pen Portraits and Reviews* (London: Constable, 1892), 236–46.

17. Norman, 149–53; White, 2:304.

18. *SC*, 3:153–75.

19. Ibid., 3:154–57.

20. HS to Catherine Nugent, 21 May 1813, *L*, 1:367.

21. To TS, 18 May 1813, *L*, 1:366–67.

22. TS to PBS, 26 May 1813, *L*, 1:368.

23. To The Duke of Norfolk, 28 May 1813, *L*, 1:368–69.

24. Hogg, 2:271.

25. Hogg to HS; HS to Hogg, 9 May 1813, *SC*, 3:141–42.

26. To Hogg, [early] June 1813, *SC*, 4:822–23. Hogg altered this letter. See *SC*, 4:833–34.

27. *Esdaile*, 165–66, 293–99; *PS*, 1:429.

28. StC, 351; *L*, 1:372 n. 1.

29. To Thomas C. Medwin, ? 16 June 1813, *L*, 1:371.

30. Cat. No. 473.10, 437.2, 437.3, HM. See also, DK (1999), 83–85.

31. To Thomas C. Medwin, 16, 21, and 28 June 1813, 6 July 1813, *L*, 1:370–74.

32. The newspaper obituary gave her name as Eliza Ianthe. See Louise Schutz Boas, *Harriet Shelley: Five Long Years* (Oxford: Oxford University Press, 1961), 129, 176; *Esdaile*, 287–89; Norman, 240.

33. Dowden, 1:372–73.

34. *YS*, 224–30, 377 n. 180; Murray, 1:361.

35. *YS*, 223–28.

36. CG, 81–82.

37. *SC*, 3:256–57.

38. StC, 300–1.

39. Dowden, 1:378–83; Blunden, 105–6; *SC*, 3:275–78.

40. HS to Catherine Nugent, 11 October 1813, *L,* 1:378.
41. Peacock, 38–40.
42. *SC,* 3:234–36.
43. Peacock, 37.
44. *Esdaile,* 163–64, 290–92.
45. *YS,* 216, 370 n. 124.
46. HS to Catherine Nugent, 8 August, 10 September, to John Williams, 12 August 1813, *L,* 1:376–77.
47. *SC,* 3:244–47; StC, 351–52; *JMS,* 1:41–42 n. 1.
48. To Thomas Hookham, 4 October 1813, *L,*1:377. See also *SC,* 3:246. For Francis Place's papers and Godwin, see Ford K. Brown, *The Life of William Godwin* (London: Dent, 1926); Peck, 2:412–20. TS settled this first *post obit* bond in 1815 for £833. See White, 1:398.
49. HS to Catherine Nugent, 11 October 1813, *L,* 1:378.
50. HS to Catherine Nugent, 20 October 1813, *L,* 1:378–79.
51. To J. B. Pereira, 16 September 1815, *L,* 1:431; Peacock, 52.
52. Hogg, 2:374.
53. *YS,* 377 n. 174; *SC,* 3:259.
54. To Hogg, 22–23 November 1813, *L,* 1:379–80.
55. Ibid. Postmarks indicate someone carried the letter to London, where it was mailed. See *SC,* 3:267.
56. Hogg, 2:483.
57. Peacock, 53.
58. *SC,* 3:262–67; Peacock, 42–43.
59. White, 1:321; Ingpen, 636–37.
60. To ? Thomas Hookham, 28 November 1813, *SC,* 3:267–70.
61. Dowden, 1:395; StC, 352.
62. StC, 353.
63. Peacock, 40–41.
64. Dowden, 1:373.
65. CG, chap. 6.
66. Hogg, 2:334–37.
67. CG, 88.
68. Hogg Oxford Exercise Book, Hg 114, Pforzheimer Collection, The New York Public Library..
69. Hogg, 2:337.
70. Grylls, 269–70 n.; CG, 89; *SC,* 3:262–65.
71. CG, 89–95.
72. Ibid., chap. 6.
73. Ibid., 94, 243 n. 22.
74. To Hogg, 16 March 1814, *L,*1:383.
75. White, 1:326, 666 n. 143.
76. Ibid., 1:665 n. 127.
77. Hogg, 2:508–9.
78. Murray, 1:364–66.
79. C. E. Pulos, *The Deep Truth: A Study of Shelley's Scepticism* (Lincoln: University of Nebraska Press, 1962), chap. 3; Wasserman, chap. 1; Hoagwood, chap. 1.
80. Cicero's *De natura deorum,* Hume's *Dialogues Concerning Natural Religion,* and Drummond's *Academical Questions.*

81. To Janetta Philipps, ? May 1811, *L*, 1:89.
82. *YS*, 223, 276–77, 285–86, 373 n. 154; Deane, 119.
83. Peck, 2:410.
84. Harriet Boinville to Hogg, 11 March 1814, *SC*, 3:273–75.
85. *CPPBS*, 1:145, 328–29.
86. To Hogg, 16 March 1814, *L*, 1:383–85.
87. StC, 353–54.
88. To TS, 13 March 1814, *L*, 1:382.
89. Ingpen, 411–12.
90. To TS, 23 March 1814, *L*, 1:385.
91. Hogg, 2:518, 531–33.
92. Ibid., 2:524–30.
93. Harriet Boinville to Hogg, 18 April 1814, *L*, 1:386 n. 1; Hogg, 2:533.
94. "Abandon all hope, ye who enter here." *Inferno*, canto 3; to Hogg, 4 October 1814, *L*, 1:401–3.
95. Dowden papers #478, Trinity College Library Dublin.

16. Mary Wollstonecraft Godwin

1. Dowden, 2:543, 549; *CC*, 2:659 n. 19.
2. MS Ashley 394, fols. 105r rev-103v rev, BL; *JCC*, 61 n. 80; *PS*, 1:439–40.
3. Dowden, 1:373.
4. *SC*, 8:994.
5. Dowden, 2:543; Sunstein, 70; *GY*, 8; *L*, 1:388 n. 2.
6. *SC*, 3:332–39.
7. Dowden, 2:542–43.
8. StC, 250.
9. *JCC*, 431.
10. *Recollections*, 20.
11. To Richard Teasdale, 6 May 1814, *L*, 1:386–87.
12. Charles E. Robinson, "Shelley to Byron in 1814: A New Letter," *KSJ* 35 (1986): 104–10.
13. Hogg, 2:537–38.
14. To Hogg, 4 October 1814, *L*, 1:402.
15. John Kennedy, "Reminiscences of Percy Bysshe Shelley," April 29, 1857, *SC*, 9:168–85.
16. To James Davies, 12 June 1814, *L*, 1:387–88.
17. Dowden, 1:436–38.
18. Mary Wollstonecraft had visited Count Schlabrendorf in a French prison after receiving a note declaring his love for her. See StC, 359; Dowden, 1:415.
19. Dowden, 1:416; Ingpen, 520.
20. To Hogg, 4 October 1814, *L*, 1:402–3.
21. To MWG, 28 October 1814, *L*, 1:414.
22. Emily W. Sunstein, "A William Godwin Letter, and Young Mary Godwin's Part in *Mounseer Nongtongpaw*," *KSJ* 45 (1996): 19–22.
23. StC, chap. 21; *SC*, 2:544–55; Sunstein, chaps. 1–3; Mellor, chap. 1.
24. *SC*, 2:598–601.

25. StC, 293.

26. Mrs. Julian Marshall, *The Life and Letters of Mary Wollstonecraft Shelley*, 2 vols. (London, 1889), 1:22–24; Sunstein, 55–56; *JCC*, 18–19.

27. *Mary Shelley: Collected Tales and Stories*, ed. Charles E. Robinson (Baltimore: Johns Hopkins University Press, 1976), 244; Sunstein, 27–34.

28. StC, 180, 537 n. 6.

29. Mellor, 13; Grylls, 10–11.

30. Sunstein, 54–55; Mellor, 12–14.

31. Sunstein, 53; StC, 182–84, 550 n. 2.

32. To Hogg, 4 October 1814, *L*, 1:403.

33. Hogg, 1:32.

34. *JMS*, 1:9; *Esdaile*, 295–96.

35. WG to John Taylor, 27 August 1814, *L*, 1:390–91.

36. StC, 358–59; White, 1:338–39.

37. Dowden, 2:543.

38. HS to Thomas Hookham, postmark 7 July 1814, *L*, 1:389.

39. StC, 355, 360.

40. WG to John Taylor, 27 August 1814, *L*, 1:390–91. See also StC, 367.

41. Dowden, 2:545.

42. To HS, ? 14 July 1814, *L*, 1:389–90.

43. HS to Catherine Nugent, 20 November 1814, *L*, 1:421.

44. Dowden, 2:App. B; StC, 360–61.

45. CC stated she accompanied MWG to Chapel Street the "end of June" and witnessed MWG's "whole interview" with HS. See CC to EJT, ? April 1871, *CC*, 2:615.

46. StC, 360–61, 550 n. 6.

47. Dowden, 2:544; White, 1:673 n. 14.

48. *CC*, 2:616, App. C.

49. EJT reportedly told William Michael Rossetti that PBS mentioned two suicide attempts at this time. See *LAS*, 51.

50. CC to EJT, ? April 1871, *CC*, 2:615.

51. That period's annual norm for divorces was four.

52. *GY*, 16–17.

53. Peacock, 54–55.

54. Dowden, 1:424–25.

55. William Michael Rossetti to Richard Garnett, 9 July 1869, *LAS*, 28.

56. CC to EJT, August 30–September 21, 1875, *CC*, 2:631.

57. To HS, ? 14 July, 13 August 1814, *L*, 1:390, 393. Hookham probably was directly receiving PBS's quarterly allowance.

58. WG to PBS, 25 July 1814, quoted in StC, 361–62, from 1923 sales catalogue (StC, 550, n. 6).

59. Medwin, 204–10. For the 1816 date, see White, 1:710 and *GY*, 72. Medwin's statement that the lady followed PBS to Geneva does not make clear this was after their first meeting. See *BSM*, 9:lvii–lix; xcviii n. 79. 1814 seems the correct date.

60. *JMS*, 1:6.

61. CC to EJT, ? April 1871, *CC*, 2:615. See also Dowden, 1:440; CC, 2:616 n. 7; *L*, 1:403.

62. *JCC*, 442.

63. *JMS*, 1:6–24.

64. Dowden, 2:545; White, 1:683 n. 57.

65. StC, 362–63.

66. *JMS*, 1:10.

67. To HS, 13 August 1814, *L*, 1:391–93.

68. HS to Catherine Nugent, 25 August 1814, *L*, 1:393.

69. *SC*, 3:342.

70. Ibid., 3:350.

71. Ibid., 3:350–51, 355.

72. *JMS*, 1:18; *JCC*, 29.

73. *JMS*, 1:17–18; *JCC*, 29. See also Dawson, 158–62.

74. *SC*, 3:365–70; *JMS*, 1:19 n. 1.

75. Murray, 1:384–87; E. B. Murray, "The Dating and Composition of Shelley's *The Assassins*," *KSJ* 34 (1985):14–17.

76. *JCC*, 30; *JMS*, 1:19–25; *CW*, 6:104; *SG*, 47.

77. *EL*, 1:x–xi; Murray, 126.

78. Murray, 1:132; *SG*, 56; Ya-Feng Wu, "'The Assassins': Shelley's Appropriation of History," *KSR* 9 (1995): 51–62; Cian Duffy, "Revolution or Reaction? Shelley's *Assassins* and the Politics of Necessity," *KSJ* 52 (2003): 77–93.

79. MS. Shelley adds. c. 5. f 42v, Bodleian; Murray, 1:133–34; Murray, "Dating and Composition," 15.

80. Rieger, chap. 5.

81. *JMS*, 1:20; *JCC*, 31.

82. *H6WT*, 33–34.

83. *JMS*, 1:21–22.

84. CC to LB, [? March or April 1816], *CC*, 1:33.

17. Births and Deaths

1. To HS, [14] September 1814, *L*, 1:394.

2. *JMS*, 1:25–26.

3. Dowden, 2:546; StC, 368.

4. To HS, [17] September 1814, *L*, 1:395.

5. To HS, 26, 27 September 1814, *L*, 1:396–99.

6. *SC*, 3:377–84; StC, 369–70; *JMS*, 1:41 n. 3.

7. To HS, ? 3 October 1814, *L*, 1:399–400.

8. To HS, 5 October 1814, *L*, 1:404–5.

9. Peacock, 57–58.

10. *JMS*, 1:30; *JCC*, 46–48.

11. *JMS*, 1:32–33; *JCC*, 48–49.

12. To HS, ? 25 October 1814, *L*, 1:410.

13. *JCC*, 50 n. 87; to HS, ? 25 October 1814, *L*, 1:410.

14. *JMS*, 1:35; *JCC*, 50.

15. *JMS*, 1:35–36.

16. To MWG, 24 October 1814, *L*, 1:407.

17. Ibd., *L*, 1:408–9.

18. Nora Crook, "Shelley and the Solar Microscope," *KSR* 1 (1986): 49–59.

19. To MWG, 27 and 28 October 1814, *L*, 1:412–14.

20. To PBS, 3 November 1814, *LMWS*, 1:5.

21. To MWG, 4 November 1814, *L*, 1:419.

22. *JMS*, 1:40, 48.

23. StC, 381; *JMS*, 1:41–42 n. 3, 43 n. 2; *JCC*, 59.

24. To G. B. Ballachey, ? 5 November 1814, *L*, 1:419–20. See also *SC*, 3:164–68; *SC*, 4:3–5.

25. Ingpen, 448.

26. To MWG, ? 7 November, 8 November 1814, *L*, 1:420.

27. To MWG, 8 November 1814, *L*, 1:421; *JMS*, 1:43; *JCC*, 59.

28. *LMWS*, 1:4–5 n. 2; *JMS*, 1:42 n. 1.

29. *JMS*, 1:45.

30. Peacock, 42–43.

31. *CC*, 2:597–98.

32. Dowden, 2:547.

33. *Critical Review,* December 1814.

34. Murray, 1:142.

35. *JMS*, 1:47–49.

36. To HS, 12 October 1814, *L*, 1:406.

37. HS to Catherine Nugent, 20 November 1814, *L*, 1:421.

38. *JMS*, 1:50.

39. HS to Catherine Nugent, 11 Dec. 1814, *L*, 1:422.

40. Sunstein, 93.

41. Ingpen, 449; Dowden, 1:507.

42. Ingpen, 449.

43. *JMS,* 1:60. Sir John Shelley-Sidney, when his son Philip became of age, reportedly offered PBS £3000 to renounce his contingency to the Shelley-Sidney estate. PBS refused. Philip Sidney, married to a natural daughter of William IV, Lady Sophia Fitz-Clarence, became Baron de L'Isle and Dudley as well as second baronet. See Medwin, 10.

44. Ingpen, 18.

45. *SC,* 4:605–8; Dowden, 1:508–11; Ingpen, 451–54; White, 1:395–99.

46. To WG, 26 February 1816, *L*, 1:454–55.

47. *SC,* 4:608–9.

48. Ingpen, 644–46; *SC*, 3:442.

49. White, 1:398.

50. *SC,* 4:591.

51. White, 2:500–502.

52. *SC,* 3:165–70.

53. To Hogg, 1 January 1815, *LMWS,* 1:6.

54. *JMS,* 1:56–57.

55. *SC,* 3:437; *LMWS,* 1:7–8.

56. N. I. White, F. L. Jones, and K. N. Cameron, *An Examination of the Shelley Legend* (Philadelphia: University of Pennsylvania, 1951), 107–9.

57. To Hogg, 7 January 1815, *LWMS,* 1:8.

58. *JMS,* 1:58–60; White, 2:504.

59. Iain McCalman, *Radical Underworld: Prophets, Revolutionaries, and Pornographers in London, 1795–1840* (1988; repr., Oxford: Clarendon, 1993), chaps. 4 and 10. See also StC, 513, 558 n. 3.

60. *RR,* 2:849; Stephen C. Behrendt, *Shelley and His Audiences* (Lincoln: University of Nebraska Press, 1989) 51, 89, 92, 272 n. 8.

61. StC, 394, 470–71, 512–17. For Erasmus Perkins's influence promoting *Queen Mab,* see StC, 514–18. Richard Carlile, who pirated *Queen Mab,* called Cannon "a notoriously bad character."

62. *GY,* 258–59; Murray, 1:397.

63. *JMS,* 1:62–64, 62 n. 2.

64. StC, 512–13.

65. McCalman, *Radical Underworld,* 73, 81, 257–58 n. 50; StC, 514.

66. McCalman, *Radical Underworld,* chap. 10. McCalman, 211, comments that prosecution for pirating editions of *Queen Mab* was for its presumed sexual immorality as well as its irreligious ideas.

67. *JMS,* 1:61 n. 1.

68. To Hogg, 24 January 1815, *LMWS,* 1:9.

69. *JMS,* 1:64–65.

70. Hogg, 2:332; *JMS,* 1:67, 69. See also, CG, 102–7; *GY,* 54–57.

71. *GY,* 56.

72. *PW,* 30. MWS's note on *Alastor.*

73. To Hogg, 26 August 1815, *L,* 1:428.

74. To Hogg, 2 March 1815, *LMWS,* 1:10.

75. To Hogg, 6 March 1815, *LMWS,* 1:10–11.

76. Box 7, file 2, Silsbee; *CC,* 1:11 n. 3. Silsbee recorded CC said MWG's crying episode was "4 mos after the elopement Hogg was the only one who came there."

77. Dowden, 2:549; StC, 398–99.

78. White, 1:694 n. 116; *JMS,* 1:71 n. 1.

79. *SC,* 4:680; *JMS,* 1:76.

80. Sunstein, 98.

81. PBS and MWG to Hogg, 24 April 1815, *LMWS,* 1:11.

82. To Hogg, 25 April 1815, *LMWS,* 1:12.

83. *Prose,* 193–94. See also, CG, chap. 4.

84. CG, 57–60; Medwin, 80; Holmes, 296.

85. Hogg, 1:110–19.

86. To Hogg, 26 April 1815, *SC,* 3:470–71.

87. To Hogg, 25a, 25b, and 26 April 1815, *LMWS,* 1:12–14.

88. To Hogg, 25 April 1815, *LMWS,* 1:13.

89. PBS possibly had lodgings simultaneously on Arabella Road and on Marchmont Street to avoid the bailiffs. See *SC,* 4:748–50.

90. *JMS,* 1:78; StC, 400.

91. CC to FG, 28 May 1815, *CC,* 1:9–10. This letter refutes Mrs. Godwin's claim to have arranged CC's trip to Lynmouth. See *CC,* 1:11. Mrs. Godwin apparently had a sister living in Lynmouth in 1816. See also, Herbert Huscher, "The Clairmont Enigma," 11 *KSMB* (1960), 15–16; R. G. Grylls, *Claire Clairmont* (London: Oxford University Press, 1939), 279.

92. *JMS,* 1:78–79.

93. *PW,* 526–27.

18. The Mirror of Self-Analysis

1. CG, 104–6. These authors suggest PBS was taking mercury about this time; tuberculosis and syphilis were occasionally linked as "venereal consumption."

2. *JMS,* 1:80.

3. To John Williams, 22, 30 June 1815, *L,* 1:428–29.

4. To MWG, after 13 May 1815, *L,* 1:426–27.

5. To PBS, 27 July 1815, *LMWS*, 1:15–16.

6. *SC*, 4:572–76.

7. To Hogg, 28 February 1823, *LMWS*, 1:316.

8. Ingpen papers, series 4, box 1, Bancroft.

9. Peacock, 60.

10. To Brookes & Company, 9 October 1815, *L*, 1:434.

11. Charles Clairmont to Francis Place, 12 January 1816; Draft of Place's reply, n.d., *CC*, 1:17–21. See also *CC*, 1:13; White, 1:416–17.

12. To Hogg, 26 August 1815, *L*, 1:429–30.

13. Peacock, 59–60.

14. CG, 105.

15. Peacock, 60.

16. Charles Clairmont to CC, 13–20 September 1815, *CC*, 1:13–16.

17. To Hogg, 22 September 1815, *L*, 1:432.

18. Charles Clairmont to CC, 13–20 September 1815, *CC*, 1:13–16.

19. Bruce Barker-Benfield, "Shelley's Bodleian Visits," *The Bodleian Library Record* 12 no.5 (October 1987): 381–99.

20. The Duc resided at Twickenham, near Syon House. See Barker-Benfield, "Shelley's Bodleian Visits," 393, 399 n. 64.

21. To Lackington, Allen & Co., 10 September 1815, *L*, 1:430–31.

22. To Hogg, 22 September 1815, *L*, 1:432.

23. Peacock, 60.

24. Whitton to TS, 30 November 1815, Ingpen, 457–60.

25. Wasserman, 5.

26. *SPP*, 73.

27. Ibid., 504. Probable date, July 1818. See *SC*, 6:639.

28. *SE*, 11:100.

29. Michael Ferber, *Alastor*, in *SPP*, 655.

30. *SPP*, 73.

31. Joseph Raben, "Coleridge as the Prototype of the Poet in Shelley's *Alastor*," *Review of English Studies* 17 (1966): 278–92; *SC*, 7:11–12; Hogle, 46.

32. Sperry, 27.

33. Jacques Lacan, "The mirror stage as formative of the function of the I as revealed in psychoanalytic experience," in *Ecrits* (New York: Norton, 1977); Heinz Lichtenstein, "The role of narcissism in the emergence and maintenance of a primary identity," *International Journal of Psychoanalysis* 45 (1964): 49–65; D. W. Winnicott, "Mirror-role of Mother and Family in Child Development," in *Playing and Reality* (New York: Basic Books, 1971); Heinz Kohut, *The Restoration of the Self* (New York: International Universities Press, 1977).

34. *PW*, 165.

35. William Keach, *Shelley's Style* (New York: Methuen, 1984), 81–97; Neil Fraistat, "Poetic Quests and Questioning in Shelley's *Alastor* Collection," *KSJ* 33 (1984): 261–81.

36. *SC*, 6:644; Brown, 129–31, 263 n. 33.

37. J. C. Bean, "The Poet Borne Darkly: The Dream-Voyage Allegory in Shelley's *Alastor*," *KSJ* 23 (1974): 67–68.

38. C. B. Thomas and K. R. Duszynski, "Words of the Rorschach, Disease, and Death," *Psychosomatic Medicine* 47 (No. 2, March/April 1985): 201–11. I am indebted to Dr. Mary Sue Moore for this reference.

39. Reiman, 24–25; Sperry, 36; Ferber, *SPP,* 654–63.
40. Ovid, *Metamorphosis,* VII.
41. *GY,* 232–33.
42. *Shelley and Byron,* 45.
43. TS to Whitton, 27 February 1816, Ingpen, 463.
44. *PW,* 30.
45. Ibid., 528.
46. *PS,* 1:447–48; White,1:329–30; Dowden, 1:472; *GY,* 611 n. 23.
47. *SC,* 4:505–6. For these faces, see Fig. 12.
48. To R. Hayward, 19 October 1815, *L,* 1:435.
49. StC, 384; *L,* 1:435 n. 1.
50. To WG, 7 January 1816, *L,* 1:439–40.
51. To WG, 18, 21 January 1816, *L,* 1:442, 444.
52. To WG, 28 January, 18 February 1816, *L,* 1:447, 451–52; Ingpen, 460–62; *SC,* 4:680–82.
53. To WG, 25 January 1816, *L,* 1:447.
54. *SC,* 4:594–99.
55. To John Murray, 6 January 1816, *L,* 1:438.
56. To Carpenter & Son, 6 February 1816, *L,* 1:449; *SPP,* 71–72.
57. *RR,* 2:425–27; White, 1:422–23.
58. To WG, 16 February 1816, *L,* 1:450.
59. To WG, 21 February 1816, *L,* 1:452–54.
60. Ibid.
61. To WG, 3 May 1816, *L,* 1:473.
62. Peacock, 61–63.
63. To WG, 26 February 1816, *L,* 1:457.
64. *BLJ,* 5:13, 16; StC, 401–2.
65. Peck, 2:436–37.
66. CC to JW, December 1826, *CC,* 1:241.
67. Peck, 2:436. See also PBS to Brookes & Dixon, 11 March 1816, *L,* 1:463; *SC,* 4:634.
68. *CC,* 1:25 n. 1.; box 7, file 3, Silsbee.
69. *CC,* 1:25 n. 1.
70. CC to LB, ? March or April 1816, *CC,* 1:24–25.
71. StC, 401; *CC,* 1:26 n. 4; *SC,* 1:296–97. Most of CC's London letters to LB have PBS's Pimlico address, 13 Arabella Row.
72. *Byron,* 2:chap.XV; *SC,* 4:638–53.
73. *CC,* 1:26; *Byron,* 2:591–92.
74. *CC,* 1:27–28.
75. Ibid., 1:33–34, 31 n. 4.
76. Thomas Medwin, *The Angler in Wales* (London, 1834) 2:187.
77. CC to LB, ? 9 April, ? 11 April 1816, *CC,* 1:35–36, 35 n. 1.
78. CC to LB, ? 16 April 1816, *CC,* 1:36–37, 37 n. 1.
79. *CC,* 1:39 n. 2.
80. Stocking believes CC possibly was implying she was a virgin. See *CC,* 1:39 n. 4.
81. *JCC,* 7; *CC,* 1:40, 41 n. 4; *BLJ,* 5:71.
82. *GY,* 30, 573 n. 95; PBS to CC, ? February 1822, *L,* 1:391–92.
83. LB to Douglas Kinnaird, 20 January 1817, *BLJ,* 5:162.
84. CC to LB, 22 April 1816, *CC,* 1:41–42. For CC's ancestry, see StC, 247–52; *CC,* 1:42–43 n. 2.

85. *SC*, 4:678–81.
86. Ingpen, 460–62; *JMS*, 1:105–6.
87. CC to LB, 6 May 1816, *CC*, 1:43–44.
88. To William Bryant, 2 May 1816, *L*, 1:470.
89. To Hogg, 2 May 1816, *L*, 1:470.
90. To WG, 3 May 1816, *L*, 1:471–73.

19. The Creative Swiss Summer

1. CC to LB, 6 May 1816, *CC*, 1:43–44.
2. To TLP, 15 May 1816, *L*, 1:475–76.
3. *GWJL*, 122.
4. CC to LB, 25 May 1816, *CC*, 1:46.
5. Polidori, 101.
6. Ibid., 110–13; Medwin, 145; H. W. Häusermann, *The Genevese Background* (London: Folcroft, 1952), 2–6; *LMWS*, 2:20; *Byron*, 2:623–25.
7. *BLLJ*, 316–18.
8. Polidori, 107–12.
9. Ibid., 128.
10. Box 7, file 2, Silsbee.
11. Polidori, 113.
12. Medwin, 145; *BLLJ*, 319.
13. *Conversations*, 15.
14. CC to LB, [June–July 1816], *CC*, 1:51.
15. LB to Augusta Leigh, 8 September 1816, *BLJ*, 5:92.
16. LB to John Cam Hobhouse, 11 November 1818, *BLJ*, 6:76.
17. *SC*, 7:43 n. 17.
18. *BLLJ*, 318.
19. Polidori, 123; Robinson, 1:lxxvii–lxxviii.
20. Mary Shelley, introduction to *Frankenstein*, 3d ed., (London, 1831).
21. D. L. Macdonald, *Poor Polidori* (Toronto: University of Toronto Press, 1991), chap. 4.
22. Sunstein, 121; Robinson, 1:lxxvii, cvi.
23. Mary Shelley, introduction to *Frankenstein*.
24. Polidori, 125.
25. Mary Shelley, introduction to *Frankenstein*.
26. Ibid; Robinson, 1:lxxviii.
27. Mary Shelley, introduction to *Frankenstein*.
28. Jonathan Wordsworth, introduction to *The Vampyre: 1819*, by John Polidori, ed. Jonathan Wordsworth (Oxford: Woodstock Books, 1990); *SC*, 6:778 n. 10; *SG*, 65.
29. Polidori, 127–28.
30. From Polidori's 1819 *The Vampyre* as printed in *SG*, 65.
31. LB to John Murray, 15 May 1819, *BLJ*, 6:125–26.
32. *JMS*, 1:131; *CC*, 1:56.
33. Medwin, 207.
34. To TLP, 16 May 1816, *L*, 1:474–76; to Brookes, Dixon & Son, 21 June 1816, *L*, 1:477.
35. WG and FG to MWG and PBS, 29 May 1816, *CC*, 1:47–49; *L*, 1:473.

36. *CC*, 1:48–49.
37. *BLLJ*, 318.
38. To TLP, 17 July 1816, *SC*, 7:29.
39. LB to Hobhouse, 23 June 1816, *BLJ*, 5:80–81.
40. To TLP, 17 July 1816, *SC*, 7:25–35.
41. LB to John Murray, 15 May 1819, *BLJ*, 6:126.
42. *H6WT*, 122.
43. *BLLJ*, 320.
44. To TLP, 17 July 1816, *SC*, 7:32.
45. *H6WT*, 133.
46. *SC*, 4:702–9.
47. Ingpen, 470–73; *SC*, 4:715–16.
48. *SC*, 4:714.
49. CC to LB, 18 April 1816, *CC*, 1:38, 39 n. 1.
50. White, 2:266–67; *GY*, 287; *SC*, 4:714.
51. *SC*, 4:712–13; *LMWS*, 3:124 n. 2.
52. To TLP, 17 July 1816, *SC*, 7:33.
53. *H6WT*, 134–39; *JMS*, 1:110–11; *SC*, 7:33–35.
54. To LH, 8 December 1816, *L*, 1:517.
55. To TLP, 17 July 1816, *SC*, 7:33; *GY*, 238.
56. Nathaniel Brown, "The 'Brightest Colours of Intellectual Beauty': Feminism in Peacock's Novels," *KSR* 2 (1987): 91–104.
57. MS Shelley adds. e. 16, Bodleian; Chernaik, chap. 2, App. B.; *SPP*, 92–93.
58. CC to Byron, [July 1816], *CC*, 1:51–52.
59. Box 7, file 3, Silsbee.
60. To Hogg, 18 July 1816, *L*, 1:493.
61. To TLP, 17 July 1816, *SC*, 7:27–28.
62. To Hogg, 18 July 1816, *L*, 1:493–94.
63. To WG, 17 July 1816, *L*, 1:491–92.
64. Emily W. Sunstein, "Louise Duvillard of Geneva, the Shelleys' Nursemaid," *KSJ* 29 (1980): 27–30; box 7, file 2, Silsbee.
65. *JMS*, 1:112–14.
66. *H6WT*, 145.
67. John Pye Smith, *Journal of a Tour in France, Switzerland, and Italy, in the months of July, August, & September, 1816,* (MS. Eng. Misc. e. 1375–1376, Bodleian), quoted in *CC*, 1:53 n. 2.
68. Gavin de Beer, "An 'Atheist' in the Alps," *KSMB* 9 (1958): 1–15; Timothy Webb, "'The Avalanche of Ages': Shelley's Defence of Atheism and *Prometheus Unbound*," *KSMB* 35 (1984):1–39.
69. de Beer, "An 'Atheist'," 3–4, 11.
70. Robert Southey to Mrs. Robert Southey, 2 July 1817, *NLRS*, 2:164–65.
71. de Beer, "An 'Atheist'," 5–6, 7–8; *UH*, 124–25, 157 n. 3; Webb, "Avalanche of Ages," 18–19, 21–22.
72. *JMS*, 1:114–15; *PW*, 536.
73. To LB, 22 July 1816, *L*, 1:494.
74. To TLP 22 July 1816, *L*, 1:495–502; *H6WT*, 151–52.
75. *L*, 1:497; *JMS*, 1:115.
76. To TLP, 24 July 1816, *L*, 1:499.
77. *JMS*, 1:118.

78. To TLP, 25 July 1816, *L*, 1:500–502.

79. Joe Francis, "Doubting the Mountain: An Approach to *Mont Blanc*," *KSR* 16 (2002): 14–21.

80. Wasserman, 229.

81. To TLP, 27 July 1816, *L*, 1:501.

82. *JMS*, 1:122; Ingpen, 467–68; *SC*, 7:62–66.

83. Polidori, 135–36; *JMS*, 1:124–25.

84. *JMS*, 1:126–29.

85. Dowden, 2:38.

86. *Prose*, 239; Dawson, 17–18.

87. FG to MWG, 29 July–1 August 1816, *CC*, 1:54–59.

88. *JMS*, 1:124; *SM*, 114–27.

89. To J. J. Paschoud, 9 November 1816, *L*, 1:512. MWG recorded PBS's solo trips to Geneva on August 12, 19, and 24.

90. Judith Chernaik and Timothy Burnett, "The Byron and Shelley Notebooks in the Scrope Davies Find," *Review of English Studies* 29 (February 1978): 36–49. See also *SPP*, 92–93, 616–20.

91. Hunt, 90–91.

92. Medwin, 161; *Conversations*, 223.

93. To LB, 29 September 1816, *L*, 1:507.

94. To LB, 8 September 1816, *L*, 1:504.

95. CC to LB, ? 29 August 1816, *CC*, 1:69–70.

96. *JMS*, 1:132–34.

97. *Journal of Lady Blessington*, 22 October 1822, from the *Observer* and *Times of London*, 9 July 1922, quoted in White, 1:464.

Index

Page numbers in italics refer to illustrations.

258–59, 265, 266, 268–69, 307, 309, 325, 366, 422 n. 75; anti-matrimonialism of, 190, 221, 223, 319; and Cannon, 347; censure of PBS by, 239, 272; and Coleridge, 218, 222; as critic of *Queen Mab,* 302; and disapproval of relationship between PBS and Mary, 318–24, 337, 339, 341, 348–50, 365, 373; early correspondence between PBS and, 221–26; and financial concerns, 222–24, 234–35, 252, 258–59, 268, 282, 295, 298, 300, 302, 306, 312, 319, 320, 336–37, 340, 343, 345, 352–53, 365, 367, 373, 375, 379, 389, 428 n. 48; intellectual and political influence on PBS of, 145, 169, 190, 209, 222–25, 231, 236, 253, 271–72, 358, 373; and Ireland, 225, 230; Juvenile Library of Jane and, 221, 262, 268, 300, 316, 417 n. 59; meeting of PBS and, 262–63; rationality and coldness of, 225, 312, 317, 340, 349, 365, 367, 373; as surrogate father to PBS, 76, 132, 224, 252, 302, 322, 373; and Thomas Turner, 297–98; upbringing of, 223. Works: *Caleb Williams,* 210, 272, 342; *Enquirer,* 272; *Enquiry Concerning Political Justice,* 30, 55, 76, 132, 136, 140, 145, 190, 214, 221–25, 240–41, 243, 252, 319, 342, 390, 417 n. 63; *Fleetwood,* 190, 222, 248, 272, 300, 325, 329; *Memoirs,* 318, 350; *Mounseer Nongtongpaw,* 316; *Pantheon or Ancient History of the Gods of Greece and Rome,* 316; *St. Leon,* 95, 113, 210, 225, 272; "To the People of Ireland," 225

Godwin, William (son of author), 253, 262, 316, 325

Goethe, Johann Wolfgang von, 117, 215, 314; *The Sorrows of Young Werther,* 215

Goodall, Joseph, 84, 93

Gothic novels, 77–78, 92, 100, 103, 109, 111–13, 282, 389

Gothic style, 110, 173, 330, 365

Grafton, third Duke of (Augustus Henry Fitzroy), 45

Graham, Dr. James, 36

Graham, Edward Fergus, 57, 117, 125, 127, 154, 160, 162, 176, 187, 189, 196, 199, 402 n. 43, 402–3 n. 45; and advertising/distribution of PBS's writings, 148, 154; relationship with Mrs. Shelley of, 57, 110–11, 178–80, 205–8, 287, 415 n. 81; and plan to set PBS's poems to music, 108, 111; as accomplice in PBS's pseudonymous letter writing, 136

Grant, Elizabeth, 129

Grasmere, 212

Gray, Thomas: *Elegy Written in a Country Churchyard,* 74, 89; "Ode on the Death of a Young Cat," 59

Greenlaw, Rev. Alexander (Headmaster, Syon House Academy), 68, 69, 71, 76, 101

Grenville, Lord, 121

Greta Hall, 212, 218, 219

Greystoke Castle, 212, 215, 216, 218, 233

Griffith, Rev. James (Master, University College), 121, 155–57, 409 n. 105

Gronow, Capt. Howell, 259

Grove, Charles, 101, 102, 107, 120, 138, 142, 146, 160, 167, 168, 170, 187, 206–7, 210, 402 n. 11; as accomplice in PBS's elopement, 191–96, 199, 414 n. 42

Grove, Charlotte (cousin of PBS), 102, 103, 106, 108, 142, 144, 404 n. 18

Grove, Charlotte Pilfold (aunt of PBS), 44, 45, 46, 50

Grove, Emma, 102

Grove, George, 102

Grove, Harriet, 45, 101–11, 114–20, *134,* 137, 138, 141–45, 167, 173, 183, 188, 194, 407 n. 34, 427 n. 13; beauty of, 101, 105; beginning of PBS's interest in, 93, 101; breaking of engagement to PBS by, 97, 114, 120, 144, 189, 375; correspondence with PBS of, 102–3, 105, 106, 108, 117, 402 n. 39; diary of, 102, 105, 107, 108, 142, 143; engagement of PBS and, 107, 114; and *Laon and Cythna,* 315; London